1 MONTH OF
FREE
READING

at

www.ForgottenBooks.com

By purchasing this book you are eligible for one month membership to ForgottenBooks.com, giving you unlimited access to our entire collection of over 1,000,000 titles via our web site and mobile apps.

To claim your free month visit:
www.forgottenbooks.com/free953469

ISBN 978-0-260-51854-5
PIBN 10953469

No. 7849

United States
Circuit Court of Appeals
For the Ninth Circuit

ARTHUR LETTS, JR.,

          Petitioner,

      vs.

COMMISSIONER OF INTERNAL REVENUE,

          Respondent.

Transcript of Record

Upon Petition to Review an Order of the United States
Board of Tax Appeals

FILED

MAY 29 1935

PAUL P. O'BRIEN,

PERNAU-WALSH PRINTING CO., 755 MARKET ST., SAN FRANCISCO

No. 7849

United States
Circuit Court of Appeals
For the Ninth Circuit

ARTHUR LETTS, JR.,

Petitioner,

vs.

COMMISSIONER OF INTERNAL REVENUE,

Respondent.

Transcript of Record

**Upon Petition to Review an Order of the United States
Board of Tax Appeals**

INDEX

[Clerk's Note: When deemed likely to be of an important nature, errors or doubtful matters appearing in the original certified record are printed literally in italic; and, likewise, cancelled matter appearing in the original certified record is printed and cancèlled herein accordingly. When possible, an omission from the text is indicated by printing in italic the two words between which the omission seems to occur.]

APPEARANCES.

THOMAS R. DEMPSEY, Esq.,

A. CALDER MACKAY, Esq.,

For Taxpayer.

ELDEN McFARLAND, Esq.,

WALTER W. KERR, Esq.,

For Commissioner.

DOCKET ENTRIES.

1932

Feb. 22—Petition received and filed. Taxpayer notified. (Fee paid.)

" 23—Copy of petition served on General Counsel.

Apr. 22—Answer filed by General Counsel.

May 4—Copy of answer served on taxpayer. Assigned to Circuit Calendar.

1933

Aug. 3—Hearing set in Long Beach, Calif. beginning Sept. 25, 1933.

Oct. 2—Hearing had before Mr. Van Fossan, Div. 9. (Leech) Submitted on the merits. Stipulation of facts filed at hearing. Briefs due December 1, 1933—no exchange.

" 2—Answer to amended petition filed at hearing.

" 16—Transcript of hearing of Oct. 2, 1933, filed.

Nov. 23—Motion for extension of time to Jan. 30, 1934, to file brief, filed by taxpayer.

1933

Nov. 27—Motion for extension of time to Jan. 30, 1934, to file brief granted to both parties.

" 29—Motion for extension of time to Jan. 2, 1934, to file brief, filed by General Counsel. 12/2/33 granted both parties to 1/30/34.

1934

Jan. 19—Brief filed by General Counsel.

" 26—Brief filed by taxpayer.

May 25—Opinion rendered, J. Russell Leech, Div. 6. Judgment will be entered under Rule 50.

Jun. 11—Motion to amend findings of fact and opinion, memorandum in support thereof filed by taxpayer.

" 21—Brief in opposition to motion to reconsider opinion filed by General Counsel.

" 21—Motion to amend findings of fact and opinion denied.

" 27—Notice of settlement filed by General Counsel.

" 28—Hearing set July 18, 1934, on settlement.

Jul. 16—Notice of settlement filed by taxpayer. 7/16/34 copy served.

" 18—Hearing had before Mr. Leech on contested settlement under Rule 50.

" 19—Transcript of hearing of July 18, 1934, filed.

" 31—Decision entered, J. Russell Leech, Div. 6.

Oct. 27—Petition for review by U. S. Circuit of Appeals (9) with assignments of error filed by taxpayer.

1934

Oct. 27—Proof of service filed.

Dec. 18—Motion for 30 days extension to file statement of evidence filed by taxpayer.

" 18—Order enlarging time to Jan. 25ʼ 1935, for preparation of evidence and delivery of record entered. [1]*

1935

Jan. 21—Motion for 60 days extension to file statement of evidence filed by taxpayer.

" 21—Order enlarging time to March 27, 1935, for preparation of evidence and delivery of record entered.

Mar. 12—Statement of evidence lodged.

" 12—Notice of lodgment of statement and of hearing on March 27, 1935, to approve statement filed by taxpayer.

" 22—Praecipe with proof of service thereon filed by taxpayer.

" 27—Hearing had before Mr. McMahon on approval of statement of evidence. Respondent agrees to statement—Mr. Leech for approval.

" ⸳27—Statement of evidence approved and ordered filed.

" 27—Order enlarging time to May 15, 1935, for transmission and delivery of record entered. [2]

---

*Page numbering appearing at the foot of page of original certified Transcript of Record.

United States Board of Tax Appeals.

Docket No. 62,106.

ARTHUR LETTS, JR.,

Petitioner.

vs.

COMMISSIONER OF INTERNAL REVENUE,

Respondent.

PETITION.

The above named petitioner hereby appeals from the determination of the respondent set forth in his deficiency letter dated December 24, 1931 (IT:AR:E -2 HEH-60D) and as the basis of this proceeding alleges as follows:

I.

Petitioner during the year 1927 was a resident of the City of Los Angeles, State of California.

II.

The notice of deficiency, copy of which is attached hereto, marked Exhibit "A", was mailed to petitioner on or about December 24, 1931.

III.

The taxes in controversy are income taxes for the calendar year 1927 and amount to the sum of $92,-721.18.

IV.

The determination of the taxes set forth in said deficiency letter is based upon the following errors:

(a) The respondent erred in including in petitioner's income subject to capital net gain the sum of $442,425.95.

(b) The respondent erred in applying ordinary, normal and surtax rates to $355,528.17 of petitioner's income after determining that such amount constituted an amount "distributed in complete liquidation of a corporation", the [3] capital stock of which had been owned more than two years.

(c) The respondent determined that certain dividends, paid by Holmby Corporation during the year 1927, applied against and reduced the basis in the hands of its stockholder, yet respondent erroneously applied ordinary, normal and surtax rates to said dividends when the stock had been held more than two years.

V.

The facts upon which the petitioner relies as the basis of this proceeding are as follows:

(1) Petitioner during the year 1927 was a resident of the City of Los Angeles, State of California, and is now a resident of Calneva, Nevada.

(2) On April 28, 1923, petitioner acquired by gift from his father 100 shares of the capital stock of Holmby Corporation, a California corporation, and upon information and belief petitioner alleges that these shares had a cost basis in the hands of the donor of $5000.00. Petitioner also owned one director's qualifying share of said Holmby Corporation stock.

(3)   During the period from May 18, 1923, to December 31, 1926, the Holmby Corporation paid to petitioner dividends of $2408.85 on said stock which dividends the respondent has determined constituted "amounts distributed in complete liquidation" of Holmby Corporation and applied against and reduced the base of said stock in petitioner's hands.

(4)   During the year 1927 petitioner received dividends in the amount of $1736.43 upon the said stock which were reported by petitioner on his income tax return for said year as dividends, but which dividends the respondent has determined to have been "amounts distributed in complete liquidation" of Holmby Corporation. During the said year 1927 the said Holmby Corporation redeemed and cancelled 83 of the said 101 shares and paid to petitioner in such [4] redemption and cancellation the sum of $8300.00.

(5)   Petitioner's father, Arthur Letts, Sr., died a resident of Los Angeles, California, on May 18, 1923, leaving a last will and testament, copy of which is attached hereto, marked Exhibit "B" and by reference made a part hereof. Said decedent, under the terms of said last will and testament, gave, bequeathed and devised all the residue of his estate to Arthur Letts, Jr., petitioner herein, Malcolm McNaghten, Harold Janss, J. G. Bullock and Harry G. R. Philp as trustees to be held in trust for certain enumerated purposes. Said trustees were given power to manage and control all the residue of said

property so acquired by them and were required under the terms of said testamentary trust to hold said property during the lives of petitioner, Florence Edna Letts McNaghten and Gladys Letts Janss, or the survivor of them, but in no event beyond the term of ten years from the date of the death of the decedent; said trustees were further empowered and directed to collect and receive all rents, interest, dividends and income from said trust properties and to distribute the net income from said trust properties to the following named persons in the following proportions:

30% to Arthur Letts, Jr., petitioner herein,
30% to Florence Edna Letts McNaghten,
30% to Gladys Letts Janss,
10% to Letts Foundation.

(6) Said trustees under and pursuant to said testimentary trust received among other properties 69,168 shares of the capital stock of Holmby Corporation which stock had a value at the date of the death of Arthur Letts, Sr., as determined by the respondent, of $104.32 per share.

(7) That during the period from May 18, 1923, the date of decedent's death, to and including December 31, 1926, there was paid in the form of ordinary dividends by the said Holmby Corporation the sum of $1,649,656.80 [5] or $23.85 per share on the capital stock referred to in paragraph (6) above, which dividends the respondent has determined constituted amounts distributed in complete liquidation of Holmby Corporation and which applied against

and reduced the basis of Holmby Corporation stock in the hands of the holders thereof.

(8)   During the year 1927 said Holmby Corporation paid into said trust and said trustees received further dividends in the sum of $1,185,094.74 which the respondent has determined also constituted amounts distributed in complete liquidation of Holmby Corporation and of which the trustees distributed to petitioner as a beneficiary of said trust the sum of $353,791.74 which he reported on his income tax return for said year as dividends.

(9)   That on May 17, 1927, said trustees received in redemption and in cancellation of 19,207 shares of the said capital stock of Holmby Corporation the total sum of $1,920,700.00 and on October 11, 1927, said trustees received in redemption and cancellation of 38,931 shares of the capital stock of said Holmby Corporation property of the value of $3,893,100.00, and notwithstanding the fact that the amounts so received constituted capital to the trust, and no part thereof was distributable under the terms of the testamentary trust, and no part thereof was ever distributed to petitioner, the respondent has nevertheless included in petitioner's income for the year 1927 a portion of these amounts, to-wit, the sum of $442,425.95.

(10)   In addition to including the aforesaid sum, which was capital of the trust, in petitioner's income for said year as capital net gain the respondent has failed and neglected to reduce petitioner's ordinary net income subject to normal and surtax rates by

the aforesaid amount of $353,791.74 which the respondent has determined to be a liquidating dividend and applied against and reduced the cost of said shares.

Wherefore, petitioner prays that the Board hear and determine this [6] appeal and render judgment in accordance with the foregoing. Petitioner prays for such other and further relief as may be deemed meet and proper in the premises.

THOMAS R. DEMPSEY,
A. CALDER MACKAY,
Attorneys for Petitioner,
1104 Pacific Mutual Building,
Los Angeles, California. [7]

STATE OF CALIFORNIA,
COUNTY OF LOS ANGELES.—ss.

ARTHUR LETTS, JR., being first duly sworn, deposes and says: That he is the petitioner above named; that he has read the foregoing petition and knows the contents thereof and that the same is true of his own knowledge, except the matters which are therein stated to be upon information and belief and that as to those matters he believes it to be true.

(Signed) ARTHUR LETTS, JR.

Subscribed and sworn to before me this 16th day of February, 1932.

[Seal]   (Signed) WM. J. WALTERS,
Notary Public in and for said County and State. [8]

EXHIBIT "A"

Treasury Department

Washington

Office of

Commissioner of Internal Revenue

Address Reply to

Commissioner of Internal Revenue

and refer to

Dec 24 1931

Mr. Arthur Letts, Jr.,

301-303 Subway Terminal Building,

Los Angeles, California.

Sir:

You are advised that the determination of your tax liability for the year 1927 discloses a deficiency of $92,721.18, as shown in the statement attached.

In accordance with Section 274 of the Revenue Act of 1926, notice is hereby given of the deficiency mentioned. Within sixty days (not counting Sunday as the sixtieth day) from the date of the mailing of this letter, you may petition the United States Board of Tax Appeals for a redetermination of your tax liability.

HOWEVER, IF YOU DO NOT DESIRE TO PETITION, you are requested to execute the enclosed form and forward it to the Commissioner of Internal Revenue, Washington, D. C., for the attention of IT:C:P-7. The signing of this form will expedite the closing of your return(s) by permitting an early assessment of any deficiency and preventing the accumulation of interest charges, since the interest period terminates thirty days after filing the form, or on the date assessment is made, whichever is earlier; WHEREAS IF THIS FORM IS NOT FILED, interest will accumulate to the date of assessment of the deficiency.

Respectfully,

DAVID BURNET,

Commissioner.

By J. C. Wilmer (Signed)

Enclosures: Deputy Commissioner.

Statement

Form 882

Form 870 [9]

STATEMENT

IT:AR:E-2

HFH-60D

In re: Mr. Arthur Letts, Jr.,

301-303 Subway Terminal Building,

Los Angeles, California.

Tax Liability

Year	Tax Liability	Tax Assessed	Deficiency
1927	$169,239.19	$76,518.01	$92,721.18

The reports of the internal revenue agent in charge at Los Angeles, California covering an examination of your books and records for the year 1927 have been reviewed by this office in connection with your protest submitted under date of May 6, 1930.

Careful consideration has been accorded your protest in connection with the agent's findings and the reports on the conferences held with your representatives on May 31, 1930 in the office of the agent in charge and on February 10, 1931 and October 14, 1931 in this office. The adjustments recommended by the agent have been approved as submitted with the exception indicated hereinafter.

Your return has been adjusted as follows:

Ordinary net income reported on return		$413,1
Capital net gain reported on return		7,9
Total net income reported on return		$421,1
Plus:		
Additional income and unallowable deductions:		
Capital net gain reported on return	$7,975.15	
(a) Capital net loss disallowed $75,346.85		
(b) Adjusted income from Holmby Corporation	442,425.95	
Total increase in capital net gain	517,772.80	
Correct capital net gain		$525,7
Ordinary net income reported on return	$413,174.40	
(c) Increased by profit from Janss Investment Company	36,794.39	
Correct ordinary net income		449,9
Total net income adjusted		$975,7

Mr. Arthur Letts, Jr.   State

Computation of Tax

Net income adjusted		$975,
Less:		
Capital net gain		525,
Net income subject to surtax		$449,
Less:		
Personal exemption	$3,500.00	
Credit for dependents	800.00	4,
Balance subject to normal tax		$445,
Normal tax at 1½% on $4,000.00		$
Normal tax at 3% on 4,000.00		
Normal tax at 5% on 437,668.79		21,
Surtax on 449,968.79		81,
Tax at 12½%—capital net gain $525,745.95		65,
Total tax		$169,
Less: Earned income credit		
Tax liability		$169,
Tax previously assessed		76,
Deficiency .		$ 92,

Explanation of Changes

(a) (b) Capital net gain has been increased from $7,973.15 to $525,745.95 due to the fact that a profit of $442,425.95 is disclosed on the liquidation of the Holmby Corporation instead of a loss of $75,-346.85 as originally reported. The profit of $442,-

425.95 is the difference between $2,109,801.78, the liquidating dividends received in 1927, and $1,667,-375.83, representing the remainder of the cost of the stock as reduced by liquidating dividends received from the Holmby Corporation in prior years.

(c)   In accordance with the recommendation of the examining officer the profit derived from the Janss Investment Company which was previously omitted by you, has been included as income.

Due to the fact that the statute of limitations will presently bar any assessment of additional tax against you for the year 1927, the Income Tax Unit will be unable to afford you an opportunity to discuss your case before mailing formal notice of its determination as provided by section 274(a) of the Revenue Act of 1926. It is, therefore, necessary at this time to issue this formal notice of deficiency.

Consent which will expire December 31, 1931 except as extended by the provisions of section 277(b) of the Revenue Act of 1926 is on file for the year 1927. [11]

EXHIBIT "B"
WILL

I, ARTHUR LETTS, of Los Angeles, California, being of the age of the age of sixty years, do make, publish and declare this my last Will and Testament, hereby revoking all former Wills by me at any time made.

FIRST: I hereby certify and declare that all property of every kind and nature whatsoever now owned by me is the community property of my wife, Florence M. Letts, and me, having been acquired by me since my marriage to my said wife, and none of said property has been acquired by me by gift, bequest, devise or descent; and I am advised and understand that under the laws of the State of California, upon my death, one-half of all of our community property will go to my said wife if she survives me, regardless of this Will.

If at the time of my death I should own any separate property and my said wife, Florence M. Letts, should survive me, I give, bequeath and devise to my said wife, Florence M. Letts, an undivided one-half interest in all such separate property.

In order that there may be no misunderstanding concerning the present status of my property, I further certify and declare that on or about April 20th, 1916, a property settlement agreement was entered into between my said wife and me, and in order to better carry out the provisions of said property settlement agreement a certain written indenture was executed by my said wife and me under date of April 20th, 1916, and recorded in Book 6366, of Deeds, at page 81, in the Records of Los Angeles County, California, wherein we both certified and declared that at that time we had no community property, etc., but thereafter it was agreed between my said wife and me that said property settlement agreement and said written indenture so filed of record be, and the same were, canceled and annulled, and that all property then standing in my name or owned or held by me should again become the community property of my said wife and me. Wherefore all [12] property of every kind and nature whatsoever now standing in my name or owned or held by me is the community property of my said wife, Florence M. Letts, and me.

SECOND: I give, bequeath and devise to my said wife, Florence M. Letts, all of my right, title and interest in and to our home place, being the property described as follows:

All of the real property situated in Lots Eleven (11) and Twelve (12) of the west portion of the Lick Tract, in the County of Los Angeles, State of California, according to map recorded in Book 7, page 92, of Miscellaneous Records of said County; excepting such portions of said lots as are contained in Tract No. 4502, according to map of said Tract recorded in Book 49, pages 44 and 45, of Maps, in the Records of said County:

Also all buildings and improvements located on said property, and all appurtenances to said property, and all household furniture, furnishings and equipment located in the dwelling house and other buildings on said property, and all garden tools and implements located on said property, and all automobiles used by me for my personal accommodation: Also all personal wearing apparel and jewelry owned by me at the time of my death.

Having in mind the fact that on said home place are gardens of considerable extent and beauty which are planted with many varieties of trees, shrubs and plants brought from all parts of the world and which are of unusual interest and of much scientific value, and that for many years I have opened said gardens to the public for study, inspection and enjoyment, and earnestly desire that the said gardens shall continue to be open at reasonable times for the inspection and enjoyment of the public but that the same shall be done only under the supervision and watchful care of a member of my family who will take a pride and interest in the collections made by me and in the proper facilities to permit the public to enjoy them; and also having in mind the fact that under a trust created by a Declaration of Trust dated December 22nd, 1920, made by Los Angeles Trust and Savings Bank, as trustee, and by me, as trustor, provision is [13] made for the reasonable cost of the maintenance and care of said gardens to the extent of Fifteen Thousand Dollars ($15,000.00) per year so long as the residence situated in said gardens is owned or occupied by my said wife, Florence M. Letts, or by one or more of my children or grandchildren; and without any intention of incumbering or limiting in any manner the title or ownership of the property constituting the said home place, I earnestly request that so long as my said wife shall live she will not dispose of said property, and that she will so arrange her affairs that at her death said property shall go to our children or grandchildren in order that my wishes above expressed concerning said property shall be carried out.

THIRD: I give and bequeath the following described legacies to the following described persons
and institutions, to-wit:

(a)   To my son-in-law, Malcolm McNaghten,
Forty-one Hundred and Sixty-six (4166) shares of
the capital stock of Bullock's, a corporation:

(b)   To my son-in-law, Harold Janss, Forty-one
Hundred and Sixty-six (4166) shares of the capital
stock of Bullock's, a corporation:

(c)   To my sister, Ada Letts, the sum of Five
Thousand Dollars ($5000.00):

(d)   To my sister, Mabel G. Letts Aldritt, the
sum of Five Thousand Dollars ($5000.00):

(e)   To my sister, Flora Edith Letts Weaver, the
sum of Five Thousand Dollars ($5000.00):

(f)   To my sister, Annie Letts Kilner, the sum
of Five Thousand Dollars ($5000.00):

(g)   To my brother, Richard Letts, whose present address is Holmby Tommys Creek, Cloncurry,
North Queensland, Australia, the sum of Ten Thousand Dollars ($10,000.00):

(h)   To my brother, Francis C. Letts, whose
present address is 11 Corborne [14] Street, Toronto,
Canada, the sum of Ten Thousand Dollars ($10,-
000.00):

(i)   To my brother, George F. Letts, whose present address is Somer Lodge, Hadleigh, Suffolk,
England, the sum of Ten Thousand Dollars ($10,-
000.00):

(j)   To my brother, Louis Letts, whose present address is Strathroy, Canada, the sum of Ten Thousand Dollars ($10,000.00):

(k)   To my brother, Ernest A. Letts, whose present address is R. R. No. 1, Everitt, Ontario, Canada, the sum of Ten Thousand Dollars ($10,000.00):

(l)   To the Los Angeles Council of the Boy Scouts of America the sum of Five Thousand Dollars ($5000.00):

(m)   To the National Council of the Boy Scouts of America the sum of Five Thousand Dollars ($5000.00):

(n)   To the Young Men's Christian Association, of Los Angeles, California, the sum of Ten Thousand Dollars ($10,000.00):

(o)   To the Young Women's Christian Association, of Los Angeles, California, the sum of Five Thousand Dollars ($5000.00):

(p)   To the Los Angeles Branch of the Salvation Army, Inc., the sum of Ten Thousand Dollars ($10,000.00).

FOURTH: I give, bequeath and devise all of the rest, residue and remainder of my property of every kind and nature whatsoever and wheresoever situated to my son, Arthur Letts, Jr., my son-in-law, Malcolm McNaghten, my son-in-law, Harold Janss, J. G. Bullock and Harry G. R. Philp, or to the survivors of them, as trustees, to be held IN TRUST for the following uses and purposes, to-wit:

(a)   Said trustees, or the survivors of them, shall hold, control, manage, sell, convey, mortgage, pledge, loan, lease, rent, assign, transfer, invest and reinvest the said trust property, or any part thereof, or any substitute therefor, as to them, or the survivors of them, may seem best, to the end that [15] said trust estate may produce the maximum income therefrom consistent with a due regard for the safety, development and preservation of the trust estate.

(b)   Said trustees, or the survivors of them, shall collect and receive all of the rents, interest, dividends and income from said trust property; and from the gross income derived from said trust property, said trustees, or the survivors of them, shall pay and discharge all taxes, assessments, costs, charges and expenses incurred in the care, administration and protection of the trust property and in the maintenance and protection of this trust and in its defense against legal or equitable attack by any person; and said trustees, or the survivors of them, shall pay and distribute the net income from said trust to the following named persons in the following proportions, to-wit: One-third of said net income to my son, Arthur Letts, Jr., or to his heirs, legatees or devisees; another one-third of said net income to my daughter, Florence Edna Letts Mc-Naghten, or to her heirs, legatees or devisees; and the remaining one-third of said net income to my daughter, Gladys Letts Janss, or to her heirs, legatees or devisees. The distribution of said net income shall be made at least semi-annually and more frequently if the same can be done, in the judgment of my trustees, without inconvenience to the proper and reasonable management of the trust estate.

(c) I expressly authorize my said trustees to include in the expenses of the administration of this trust and to. pay to themselves a reasonable compensation for their services as such trustees.

(d) It is my desire that my said trustees, when acting as such trustees or when acting as executors of this Will, shall make every reasonable effort to cooperate with each other in order that all acts performed by said persons, either as trustees or executors, shall be according to the unanimous judgment of the persons so acting; but should any difference of opinion arise pertaining to any matters which said persons shall be obliged to act upon, the judgment of a [16] majority of said trustees or executors shall be binding upon all such trustees or executors.

(e) Each and every beneficiary under this trust is hereby restrained therefrom, and shall be without right, power or authority to sell, transfer, pledge, mortgage, hypothecate, alienate, anticipate or in any other manner affect or impair his beneficial or legal rights, titles, interest, claims or estates in or to the income or principal of this trust during the entire term hereof; and the rights, titles, interest or estates of any beneficiary hereunder shall not be subject to the rights or claims of creditors of any beneficiary, or subject or liable to any process of law or Court; and all of the net income and principal under this trust shall be transferable, payable and deliverable only, solely, exclusively and personally to the above designated beneficiaries hereunder at the time entitled to take the same under the terms of this trust: PROVIDED, HOWEVER, that nothing herein contained is intended to prevent the transfer of the interest of any beneficiary under this trust to his or her heirs, legatees or devisees in the event of his or her death, either by Will or under the laws of succession.

(f) The trust hereby created shall exist and continue during the lives of my said son, Arthur Letts, Jr., my said daughter, Florence Edna Letts McNaghten, and my said daughter, Gladys Letts Janss, or the survivor of them; but in no event shall this trust continue beyond the term of ten (10) years from the date of my death. Should all of my said children die within the period of ten (10) years after the date of my death, upon the death of the last survivor of my said children, or in any event upon the expiration of the term of ten (10) years after the date of my death, this trust shall cease and terminate and all of the principal or corpus of said trust estate then remaining subject to this trust and all undisturbed net income therefrom shall be and become the absolute property [17] of my said children, Arthur Letts, Jr., Florence Edna Letts McNaghten and Gladys Letts Janss, share and share alike if they be alive; but in the event of the death of any of my said children prior to the termination of this trust, upon the termination of this trust the share of such deceased child in said trust estate shall be and become the absolute property of the heirs, legatees or devisees of such deceased child.

(g) Without any intention of limiting the general powers hereinbefore granted to my said trustees, but for the purpose of specifically authorizing my said trustees to do anything necessary or convenient to carry out my wishes and desires as hereinafter expressed, I call the attention of my trustees to the fact that I have heretofore caused to be incorporated under the laws of California a corporation known as "Holmby Corporation", which corporation up to the present time has organized by the adoption of By-Laws and the election of the following named persons as directors, to-wit, Arthur Letts, Arthur Letts, Jr., Malcolm McNaghten, J. G. Bullock and Harry G. R. Philp; and it is my wish and desire, provided the permit of the Corporation Commissioner so to do can be procured, to have said corporation acquire about One Hundred Sixty Thousand (160,000) shares of the capital stock of Bullock's, a corporation, about Thirty Thousand (30,-000) shares of the capital stock of The Broadway Department Store, a corporation, all of my interest and the interest of my wife, Florence M. Letts, in the property generally known as the "Wolfskill Ranch" which is situated in Los Angeles County, California, and is now held in trust by the Los Angeles Trust and Savings Bank, of Los Angeles, California, and such other property as it may be deemed best to transfer to said corporation, at the price of the fair market value thereof, payable in shares of the capital stock of said Holmby Corporation at par. Should I die before a transfer of said properties to said Holmby Corporation has been accomplished, it is my earnest wish and desire that my said wife, [18] Florence M. Letts, shall cooperate with the persons herein appointed as executors and trustees, to accomplish the transfer of said properties to said Holmby Corporation, in order that said properties may be managed and controlled by said Holmby Corporation. It is also my earnest wish and desire that, upon the transfer of said properties to said Holmby Corporation having been accomplished, my wife, Florence M. Letts, will voluntarily transfer and assign to the same persons as are herein appointed trustees of the trust herein created, all shares of stock of said Holmby Corporation to which she may become entitled by reason of the transfer of any of said properties to said Holmby Corporation, and will authorize and empower said persons, as such trustees, to manage and control her interest in said stock of said Holmby Corporation, in the same manner and to the same extent as they will be authorized hereunder to manage and control the trust estate herein created, for the full term of the trust herein created; with the understanding, of course, that all net income accruing from such proposed trust estate to be created by my said wife, Florence M. Letts, shall be paid to her, and upon the termination of the trust all of the principal of said trust property shall again become her absolute property.

I further desire to call the attention of my said trustees to the fact that, in my judgment, it will be for the best interest of the trust estate if the business now owned and conducted by Bullock's, a corporation, be continued during the term of this trust under the management of substantially the same persons who are now managing the said business, and according to the plans and policies now being followed in the conduct of said business: and also to the further fact that, in my judgment, it will be for the best interest of the trust estate if the business now owned and conducted by The Broadway Department Store, a corporation, be continued during the term of this trust under the management of substantially the same persons who are now managing the said business, and according to the [19] plans and policies now being followed in the conduct of said business. Referring to the property generally known as the Wolfskill Ranch, at this time I have no well defined plan for conducting or developing said ranch or for selling and realizing upon the same, but I desire my trustees to follow their best judgment with regard to this property.

(h) It is my wish and desire that the persons herein appointed as trustees of the trust herein created shall be elected as directors of said Holmby Corporation, and shall continue to act as directors of said Holmby Corporation during the term of said trust; but should any of my said trustees, for any reason whatsoever, be unable to act as one of the directors of said Holmby Corporation, it is my wish and desire that any vacancy created in said Board of Directors of said Holmby Corporation by reason of the inability of such person to act as a director shall be filled by the election of some other person as director, by the other directors in office, and such other person shall have all of the authority usually vested in a director of a corporation, but shall not thereby become a trustee of the trust herein created.

(i) It is also my wish and desire that my said trustees, or the survivors of them, with reasonable diligence, shall create or organize a charitable trust or corporation which shall be known as the "Letts Foundation", and which shall have for its purposes the right to acquire and dispose of one-tenth of the net income derived from the trust created in this Will, and one-tenth of the principal or corpus of the trust estate created in this Will upon any termination of said trust, for charitable purposes for the benefit of needy and/or deserving persons who are or shall be or at any time have been employed by The Broadway Department Store, a corporation, or by Bullock's, a corporation; such charitable trust or corporation to continue in effect so long as any property remains in said charitable trust or corporation. The persons herein named as trustees of [20] the trust created in this Will are generally familiar with my ideas with reference to said proposed Letts Foundation; and having full confidence in their integrity and in their ability to carry out my wishes, it is my intention that they shall have such broad and general powers as it is possible for me to give them under the law in order to carry out my wishes with reference to said proposed Letts Foundation. Therefore, notwithstanding the fact that I have hereinbefore otherwise directed the disposition of all net income and of the principal or corpus of the trust created in this Will upon its termination, should it be legally possible for my trustees to carry out the provisions of this subparagraph "i" of this Will, I authorize and direct my said trustees to create or organize a trust or corporation, to be known as the Letts Foundation, for the purposes above described, and to pay and distribute one-tenth part of the net income derived from the trust created in this Will to such proposed Letts Foundation; and also, upon any termination of the trust created in this Will, to assign, transfer and deliver to said proposed Letts Foundation one-tenth part of the principal or corpus of the trust estate created by this Will. It is also my earnest wish and desire that my wife, Florence M. Letts, will voluntarily so arrange her affairs that the said proposed Letts Foundation shall receive one-tenth of the net income derived from, and one-tenth of the principal or corpus of, her share of our community property other than the home place and personal property described in the "SECOND" subdivision of this Will.

My said trustees shall have full authority so to do, and shall arrange a reasonable and comprehensive plan for the appointment of a trustee or trustees or

directors of said proposed Letts Foundation; and
the trustee or trustees or directors of said Letts
Foundation shall have full power to determine when
and under what circumstances a person may be in
need and/or deserving of assistance from said proposed Letts Foundation. [21]

In the event that, at any time in the future, all
of the property held by the said proposed Letts
Foundation be not required for the reasonable ac-
complishment and continuation of the purposes
above provided, any excess funds or property held
by said proposed Letts Foundation may be used and
applied for general charitable purposes for the
benefit of needy and deserving persons residing in
the City of Los Angeles, California.

FIFTH: I direct that all taxes, including inheritance taxes and federal estate taxes, which may
be charged against my estate or against any of the
gifts, bequests or devises made under this Will, shall
be paid out of the general assets of my estate, as a
claim against my estate.

SIXTH: I hereby nominate and appoint my
said son, Arthur Letts, Jr., my said son-in-law, Malcolm McNaghten, my said son-in-law, Harold Janss,
J. G. Bullock and Harry G. R. Philp, or the survivors of them, executors of this my Will; and it is
my desire that my said executors shall not be required to give bond of any kind as such executors,
nor shall said persons be required to give any bond
as trustees hereunder.

SEVENTH: Without any intention of limiting the powers of the executors or trustees appointed in this Will, but having in mind the fact that S. F. Macfarlane has acted as my personal attorney for several years and is more or less familiar with my ideas for the management and conduct of my estate, I recommend that if, in the opinion of my said executors and trustees, they deem it at that time advisable, that they employ S. F. Macfarlane as their attorney to advise and counsel with them in the management of my estate and in the carrying out of the trust herein created.

IN WITNESS WHEREOF, I have hereunto signed my name and affixed my seal at Los Angeles, California, on the 27th day of June, 1922.

[Seal]   Arthur Letts   [22]

The foregoing instrument, consisting of thirteen (13) typewritten pages including this page, was, at the date herein, by the said ARTHUR LETTS, signed, sealed and published as, and declared to be, his last will and testament, in the presence of us, who, at his request and in his presence and in the presence of each other, have subscribed our names as witnesses hereto.

Helen M. Coll, residing at Los Angeles, California.

Wm. J. Walters, residing at Los Angeles, California.

S. F. Macfarlane, residing at Los Angeles, California.

[Endorsed]: Filed Feb. 22, 1932.   [23]

[Title of Court and Cause.]
ANSWER.

Comes now the Commissioner of Internal Revenue, by his attorney, C. M. Charest, General Counsel for the Bureau of Internal Revenue, and for answer to the petition of the above-named taxpayer, admits and denies as follows, to-wit:

I, II, III. Admits the allegations contained in paragraphs I, II, and III of the petition.

IV (a), (b), (c). Denies that the respondent erred as alleged in subparagraphs (a), (b), and (c) of paragraph IV of the petition.

V (1). Admits the allegations contained in subparagraph (1) of paragraph V of the petition.

(2), (3), (4), (5), (6), (7), (8), (9), (10). Denies the allegations contained in subparagraphs (2), (3), (4), (5), (6), (7), (8), (9) and (10) of paragraph V of the petition.

Denies generally and specifically each and every allegation set forth in the petition not hereinbefore admitted, qualified or denied.

WHEREFORE, it is prayed that the appeal of the taxpayer be denied.

(Signed)   C. M. CHAREST,
General Counsel,
Bureau of Internal Revenue.

ALLIN H. PIERCE,
IRVING M. TULLAR,
   Special Attorneys,
     Bureau of Internal Revenue,
      Of Counsel.

[Endorsed]:   Filed Apr. 22, 1932.   [24]

[Title of Court and Cause.]

AMENDED PETITION.

By leave of the Board first had and obtained, the above named petitioner hereby files his first amendment to his petition appealing from the determination set forth in respondent's deficiency letter dated December 24, 1931 (IT:AR:E-2 HFH-60D) and as the basis of this proceeding alleges as follows:

I.

Petitioner during the year 1927 was a resident of the City of Los Angeles, State of California.

II.

The notice of deficiency, copy of which is attached to the original petition, was mailed to the petitioner on or about December 24, 1931.

III.

The taxes in controversy are income taxes for the calendar year 1927 and amount to the sum of $92,721.18.

IV.

The determination of the taxes set forth in said deficiency letter is based upon the following errors:

(a)   Respondent erred in increasing petitioner's capital net gain to the sum of $525,745.95 or to any sum in excess of $104,302.58.

(b)   The respondent erroneously determined that petitioner derived [25] a capital gain of $10,036.43 by reason of distributions in liquidation of Holmby

Corporation, whereas petitioner's capital gain from that source did not exceed the sum of $7,445.28.

(c) The respondent, notwithstanding the fact that he had determined that the distributions in liquidation of Holmby Corporation resulted in capital gain to petitioner, and were taxable as such, nevertheless, also erroneously included a portion thereof to-wit, $1,736.43, in petitioner's ordinary net income subject to both normal and surtax.

(d) The respondent determined that the trustees under the will of Arthur Letts, deceased, derived a capital gain by reason of distributions in liquidation of Holmby Corporation. Notwithstanding the fact that only $21,508.50 of the capital gain so derived was distributable or distributed to petitioner as a beneficiary of the trust, the respondent, nevertheless, erroneously included in petitioner's capital net gain the sum of $432,389.52.

(e) The respondent, after determining the capital gain as stated in (d) above and erroneously including $432,389.52 thereof in petitioner's capital net gain, also erroneously included $353,791.74 thereof in petitioner's ordinary net income subject to both normal and surtaxes.

(f) Respondent erred in failing and neglecting to deduct from petitioner's total net income before computing normal tax as provided in Section 216 (a)(1) of the Revenue Act of 1926 the sum of $20,-491.47, being dividends received by petitioner during the year 1927 from stocks owned by him other than Holmby Corporation stock.

(g) Respondent erred in determining that the total distributions in the sum of $10,036.43 received by petitioner from Holmby Corporation during the year 1927 on the stock owned outright by him represented capital gain in its entirety when in fact petitioner's unrecovered cost or basis for said shares [26] on January 1, 1927 was at least $2,591.15.

V.

The facts upon which the petitioner relies as the basis of this proceeding are as follows:

(1) Petitioner during the year 1927 was a resident of the City of Los Angeles, State of California, and is now a resident of Calneva, Nevada.

(2) On April 28, 1923, petitioner acquired by gift from his father 100 shares of the capital stock of Holmby Corporation, a California corporation, and upon information and belief petitioner alleges that these shares had a cost basis in the hands of the donor of $5,000.00. Petitioner also owned one director's qualifying share of said Holmby Corporation stock.

(3) During the period from May 18, 1923 to December 31, 1926 the Holmby Corporation made distributions from its earnings and profits to petitioner amounting to $2,408.85 on said stock which distributions the respondent has determined constituted amounts distributed in complete liquidation of Holmby Corporation and applied against and reduced the base of said stock in petitioner's hands.

(4) During the year 1927 petitioner received further distributions from said source amounting to $1,736.43 upon the said stock which were reported by petitioner on his income tax return for said year as dividends, but which the respondent has determined to have been amounts distributed in complete liquidation of Holmby Corporation. During the said year 1927 the said Holmby Corporation redeemed and cancelled 83 shares of the said 101 shares owned outright by petitioner and paid to petitioner in such redemption and cancellation the sum of $8,300.00. Although petitioner's remaining unrecovered cost or base for said shares on January 1, 1927 was not less than $2,591.15 the respondent has, nevertheless, included the total amount received by [27] petitioner, namely, $10,036.43, in petitioner's capital net gain for the year 1927.

(5) Petitioner's father, Arthur Letts, Sr., died testate, a resident of Los Angeles, California, on May 18, 1923. Said decedent, under the terms of his last will and testament, gave, bequeathed and devised the residue of his estate to Arthur Letts, Jr., petitioner herein, Malcolm McNaghten, Harold Janss, J. G. Bullock and Harry G. R. Philp as trustees to be held in trust for certain enumerated purposes. Said trustees duly and regularly qualified as such and acted in that capacity until May 18, 1933. Said trustees were given power to manage and control all of said property so acquired by them and were required under the terms of said will to hold said property during the lives of petitioner, Florence

Edna Letts McNaghten and Gladys Letts Janss, or the survivor of them, but in no event beyond the term of ten years from the date of the death of the decedent; said trustees were further empowered and directed to collect and receive all rents, interest, dividends and income from said trust properties and to distribute the net income from said trust properties to the following named persons in the following proportions:

30% to Arthur Letts, Jr., petitioner herein,
30% to Florence Edna Letts McNaghten,
30% to Gladys Letts Janss,
10% to Letts Foundation.

(6) Said trustees under and pursuant to said testamentary trust received among other properties 69,168 shares of the capital stock of Holmby Corporation which stock had a value at the date of the death of Arthur Letts, Sr., as determined by the respondent, of $7,215,605.76.

(7) That during the period from May 18, 1923, to and including December 31, 1926 the said Holmby Corporation made distributions from its [28] earnings and profits amounting to $1,649,656.80 to the said trustees on said stock. The respondent has determined that the said distributions constituted amounts distributed in complete liquidation of Holmby Corporation and were to be applied against and reduced the basis of the stock.

(8) During the year 1927 said Holmby Corporation made further distributions from the same source to the trustees amounting to $1,185,088.24

(of which $71,695.00 was distributed on December
1, 1927). The respondent has also determined that
these distributions constituted amounts distributed
in complete liquidation of Holmby Corporation. The
trustees distributed $353,791.74 of said amount to
petitioner as a beneficiary of said trust, which
sum he reported on his income tax return for said
year as dividends.

(9) That on May 17, 1927 said trustees received
in redemption and in cancellation of 19,207 shares
of the said capital stock of Holmby Corporation the
total sum of $1,920,700.00 and on October 11, 1927
said trustees received in redemption and cancellation of 38,931 shares of the capital stock of said
Holmby Corporation property of the value of
$3,893,100.00. No part of said amounts was dis-
tributable under the terms of the will nor was any
thereof distributed to petitioner. The respondent
has, nevertheless, included a portion of these
amounts in petitioner's income for the year 1927.

(10) The respondent has erroneously failed and
neglected to deduct the amount of dividends received
by petitioner from corporations other than Holmby
Corporation amounting to $20,491.47 from the total
net income before computing the normal tax thereon
as provided in Section 216 (a)(1) of the Revenue
Act of 1926.

WHEREFORE, petitioner prays that the Board
hear and determine this amended petition and render judgment in accordance with the foregoing.
Petitioner prays for such other and further relief

as may be deemed meet and proper [29] in the premises.

T. R. DEMPSEY,
A. CALDER MACKAY,
1104 Pacific Mutual Building,
Los Angeles, California,
Attorneys for Petitioner.

STATE OF CALIFORNIA,
COUNTY OF LOS ANGELES.—ss.

ARTHUR LETTS, JR., being first duly sworn, deposes and says: That he is the petitioner above named; that he has read the foregoing amended petition and knows the contents thereof and that the same is true of his own knowledge except the matters which are therein stated to be upon information and belief and that as to those matters he believes it to be true.

ARTHUR LETTS, JR.

Subscribed and sworn to before me this 22nd day of September, 1933.

[Seal]   (Signed)   WM. J. WALTERS,
Notary Public in and for said County and State.

[Endorsed]: Filed at Hearing Sep. 25, 1933.

[30]

[Title of Court and Cause.]

ANSWER TO AMENDED PETITION.

Comes now the Commissioner of Internal Revenue, by his attorney, E. Barrett Prettyman, General Counsel, Bureau of Internal Revenue and for answer to the amended petition filed by the above-named taxpayer admits and denies as follows, to-wit:

I, II, III. Admits the allegations contained in paragraphs I, II, and III of the amended petition.

IV. Denies the allegations of error contained in paragraphs IV(a) to (g), inclusive, of the amended petition.

V. Denies the allegations contained in paragraphs V(1) to (10), inclusive, of the amended petition.

Denies generally and specifically each and every allegation set forth in the amended petition not hereinbefore admitted, qualified, or denied.

WHEREFORE, it is prayed that the appeal be denied.

E. BARRETT PRETTYMAN,
General Counsel,
Bureau of Internal Revenue.

ELDON McFARLAND,
Special Attorney,
Bureau of Internal Revenue,
Of Counsel.

tco
9-27-33

[Endorsed]: Filed at Hearing, Oct. 2, 1933. [31]

United States Board of Tax Appeals
Docket No. 62106.

ARTHUR LETTS, Jr.,

Petitioner,

vs.

COMMISSIONER OF INTERNAL REVENUE,
Respondent.

Promulgated May 25, 1934.

1. INCOME — LIQUIDATING DISTRIBU-
TIONS.—Under section 201 (c), Revenue Act of
1926, distributions in liquidation by a corporation,
whether made as from surplus or capital, held,
chargeable against the cost basis of the stock in the
hands of the recipient. Holmby Corp., 28 B.T.A.
1092, followed.

2. Id.—Liquidating distributions to a trustee and
representing in his hands capital net gain under sections 208 (a) and (b) and 219 (a) of the Revenue Act of 1926, held, subject to the same provisions in the hands of the beneficiary when distributed to him, although distributable only as dividends on the trust corpus under the terms of the
trust and the law of the state controlling its administration, under section 208 (e) of the same act.

THOMAS R. DEMPSEY, ESQ., and
A. CALDER MACKAY, ESQ.,

For the Petitioner.

ELDEN McFARLAND, ESQ.,

For the Respondent.

OPINION.

LEECH: This proceeding seeks redetermination of a deficiency of $92,721.18 in income tax determined by respondent for the calendar year 1927.

The respondent confesses error under the following assignments of petitioner: (a) The inclusion of $353,791.74 in ordinary income of petitioner after having included this same amount in computing capital net gain, (b) including in ordinary income $1,756.43 as dividends received and including the same item in computing capital gain, and (c) including $20,491.47 in income subject to normal tax where such income was reported as dividends received. Effect will be given to these admissions of error by respondent in the recomputation of the pending deficiency under Rule 50.

There remain for consideration two issues—(d) the taxability of certain distributions received by petitioner in the taxable year as liquidating dividends upon stock owned by him, and (e) peti- [32] tioner's taxability upon certain amounts distributed to him as beneficiary of a trust, representing liquidating distributions made in the taxable year to the trustees by a corporation upon stock belonging to the trust.

The facts are stipulated. Briefly stated, in respect to issue (d) they are that petitioner was in the taxable year owner of 101 shares of stock of the Holmby Corporation, having a cost basis in his hands of $5,000. This corporation had been in liquidation since May 18, 1923. All distributions by it to stockholders since that date were made in process of its liquidation. Prior to the calendar year 1927, this corporation had distributed liquidating dividends in the amount of $2,408.85 to petitioner, and, during the year 1927, distributed to petitioner $10,036.43. Of this latter sum, $1,736.43 was distributed as from corporate earnings and profits, and $8,300 in redemption of 83 shares of petitioner's stock. Petitioner included in his return for that year only the sum of $1,736.43 as ordinary dividends.

Respondent, in determining the deficiency, included the total distribution of $10,036.43 in income, but now admits that this is in error and that the taxable gain to petitioner is the excess of the total distributions of $10,036.43 and $2,408.85 over $5,000, petitioner's cost basis for the stock. This excess is $7,445.28.

Upon this issue we sustain the present position of the respondent. The distributions in liquidation by the Holmby Corporation, whether made as from surplus or capital, are all chargeable against the cost basis of the stock in the hands of the recipient. Holmby Corp., 28 B.T.A. 1092; Garrett v. Commissioner, 59 Fed. (2d) 315; Canal-Commercial Trust & Savings Bank v. Commissioner, 63 Fed. (2d) 619. Petitioner had recovered, prior to the taxable year, $2,408.85 of his capital cost, and the distributions made to him in the taxable year exceeded the unrecovered cost of such stock by $7,445.28. As petitioner had acquired this stock in 1923, this gain is subject to the capital gain provisions of the applicable taxing act. Sec. 208 (a) and (b), Revenue Act of 1926.

In reference to the remaining issue the facts are
that petitioner's father died May 18, 1923, leaving
a will in which a trust was created with respect to
certain of his property, for a period of 10 years, the
income of the trust estate during that time to be
paid in certain proportions to the beneficiaries of
the trust. Petitioner's interest as a beneficiary was
30 percent of the income payments and corpus upon
distribution. Included in the assets of this trust
estate were 69,168 shares of the capital stock of
Holmby Corporation, the fair market value of
which, at the time of the decease of petitioner's
father, was $7,215,605.76. [33]

During the period from May 18, 1923, to December 31, 1926, the Holmby Corporation, in the process
of complete liquidation, distributed to the trustees
$1,649,656.80. All of this sum was distributed as
from earnings and profits of the corporation. During the year 1927, the Holmby Corporation, continuing the process of complete liquidation, made additional distributions of $6,995,885.24. Of this sum
$1,185,088.24 was distributed as from earnings and
profits and the balance, $5,813,800, was paid as in
redemption of 58,138 shares of the total of 69,168
shares of stock belonging to the trust.

Included in the $1,185,088.24 received by the trus-
tees in 1927 as distributed from earnings and profits
was the sum of $353,791.74, which was distributed
by the trustees to petitioner during that year as his
beneficial share of the distributable trust income for
that year. This latter amount was reported by peti-

tioner on his return for such year as ordinary dividends.

In determining the present deficiency, respondent treated the liquidating distributions received by petitioner from the Holmby Corporation and his proportionate share of the distributions to the trustees, in the following manner:

Per Return:

Distributions from earnings and profits on own stock reported as "dividends"	$ 1,736.43
Distributions by Holmby Corporation from earnings and profits to Trustees and in turn distributed to petitioner, reported as "dividends"	353,791.74
Total reported on return	355,528.17

Added in Deficiency Letter:

Distributions on own stock above reported as dividends	1,736.43
Amount distributed from capital	8,500.00
Distribution from trust as above	353,791.74
Additional gain on liquidating distributions to trustees	78,397.78
Total addition to income in deficiency letter on account of Holmby Corporation distributions	442,425.95
Total amount of income included in "net income" in deficiency letter on account of above items	797,954.12

The sum, $355,528.17, included in the above total, was treated by the respondent as ordinary income subject to both normal and surtax and the remainder was treated as capital gain by the respondent.

The determination of petitioner's tax liability in reference to distributions received by the trustees, requires a determination of the grass taxable income received by the trustees included in such distributions, and the total credit against such income to which the trustees are entitled under section 219 (b) (2) of the Revenue Act [34] 1926,[1] as that portion distributable to petitioner upon which he is

---

[1] Sec. 219. (b) Except as otherwise provided in subdivisions (g) and (h), the tax shall be computed upon the net income of the estate or trust, and shall be paid by the fiduciary. The net income of the estate or trust shall be computed in the same manner and on the same basis as provided in section 212, except that—

*   *   *   ᴨ   ᴨ   ᴦ   ᴨ   ᴨ

(2) There shall be allowed as an additional deduction in computing the net income of the estate or trust the amount of the income of the estate or trust for its taxable year which is to be distributed currently by the fiduciary to the beneficiaries, and the amount of the income collected by a guardian of an infant which is to be held or distributed as the court may direct, but the amount so allowed as a deduction shall be included in computing the net income of the beneficiaries whether distributed to them or not. * * *

liable for the tax. The first factor, the taxable income received by the trustees, is ascertained by application of the same rule by which the preceding issue was concluded. The Holmby Corporation was in process of complete liquidation from May 18, 1923. All distributions subsequent to that date, whether made as from accumulated earnings or capital, are, for purposes of the taxing act, considered as received by the stockholder in exchange for his stock under the provisions of section 201 (c) of the Revenue Act of 1926.[2] Holmby Corp., supra;

---

[2] Sec. 201. (c) Amounts distributed in complete liquidation of a corporation shall be treated as in full payment in exchange for the stock, and amounts distributed in partial liquidation of a corporation, shall be treated as in part or full payment in exchange for the stock. The gain or loss to the distributee resulting from such exchange shall be determined under section 202, but shall be recognized only to the extent provided in section 203. In the case of amounts distributed in partial liquidation (other than a distribution within the provisions of subdivision (g) of section 203 of stock or securities in connection with a reorganization) the part of such distribution which is properly chargeable to capital account shall not be considered a distribution of earnings or profits within the meaning of subdivision (b) of this section for the purpose of determining the taxability of subsequent distributions by the corporation. [35]

Garrett v. Commissioner, supra; Canal-Commercial Trust & Savings Bank v. Commissioner, supra.

Applying this rule, we find that the cost basis of 69,168 shares of stock, stipulated to be $7,215,605.76, had been recovered to the extent of $1,649,656.80 by liquidating distributions received by the trustees prior to the taxable year, leaving an unrecovered cost of $5,565,948.96, against which must be applied the liquidating distributions of $6,998,888.24 received in 1927. It follows that the excess of these latter distributions over the unrecovered cost, or $1,432,939.28, is the gain, subject to Federal income tax, received by the trustees in 1927.

Having determined the net taxable gain received, there remains to be determined the proportion of such gain taxable to this petitioner. Under section 219 (b) (2), above cited, such gain is that portion of the income in question which was, under the terms of the trust, distributable to petitioner. In determining this gain, we must look to the law of the State of California, which controls the administration of the trust. The determination of that state's courts as to the distributable or nondistributable character of the gain realized by the trustees, is binding upon us. Freuler v. Helvering, 291 U. S. 35.

There is included in the formal stipulation filed, the decree of the Superior Court of California approving the distribution to the beneficiaries as current income, those amounts distributed in liquidation by the Holmby Corporation from accumulated earnings and profits of the corporation, and likewise approving the retention by the trustees as corpus, the total amounts distributed to them in redemption of stock. We accept this decree as final in determining that the only amount distributable, and therefore taxable, to petitioner, was the sum of $353,791.94 actually distributed to him by authority of that court. From the tabulation heretofore set out, it is noted that respondent, in determining the deficiency, included in petitioner's income as distributable to him, $78,397.78, representing the proportionate interest in the gain realized by the trustees in liquidating distributions made to them in redemption of stock, which was retained by them, with approval of the court, as nondistributable increase in the corpus. The trustees, in computing the trust income subject to Federal income tax, are permitted to take credit for distributions of such income, only, as is held to be distributable by the state court controlling the same. The item of $78,397.78 was not within that category and, therefore, upon this sum, they, and not petitioner, are liable for the tax. Canal Bank & Trust Co., 30 B.T.A.—(No. 57, Apr. 17, 1934).

Although the law of California, which controls the administration of this trust, concludes us as to the amount of the trust income distributable to this petitioner, Freuler v. Helvering, supra, its character for Federal income tax purposes and the resulting tax thereon, in the absence here of other intention expressed therein, is controlled by the Federal revenue act basing the present disputed tax. Bur-

net v. Harmel, 287 U. S. 103; Forrest Anderson, 30
B.T.A.—(No. 92, May 1, 1934).

Under the provisions of section 201 (c) of the
Revenue Act of 1926, the total gain included in the
distributions made by the Holmby Corporation to
the trustees in the year 1927, must be treated as
having been received in exchange for stock. And,
pursuant to sections 208 (a) (8) and (b) and 219
(a) of the same revenue act, the gain resulting from
such distributions was capital gain since the stock
exchanged had been held by the trust for more than
two years. That portion of such gain distributable
to petitioner and consequently taxable to him, as
determined by us, does not lose its character of
capital gain, we think, upon distribution to him.

Section 208 (e) of the Revenue Act of 1926 provides:

In the case of * * * the beneficiary of an estate or
trust, the proper part of each share of the net income which consists, respectively, of ordinary net
income, capital net gain, or capital net loss, shall
be determined under rules [36] and regulations to
be prescribed by the Commissioner with the approval of the Secretary and shall be separately
shown in the return of the * * * estate or trust and
shall be taxed to the * * * beneficiary or to the estate
or trust as provided in sections 218 and 219, but
at the rates and in the manner provided in subdivision (b) or (c) of this section.

It necessarily follows that the portion of the capital gain realized by the trust which was distributable to petitioner and consequently taxable to him

is, in computing his tax thereon, subject to the capital gain provisions of the statute.

Judgment will be entered under Rule 50. [37]

[Title of Court and Cause.]

MOTION TO AMEND FINDINGS OF FACT AND OPINION.

Comes now the petitioner in the above entitled case by his counsel and moves this honorable Board to amend its findings of fact contained in its opinion in the above entitled case promulgated on May 25, 1934, by the addition thereto of findings of fact to the effect that—

During the year 1927 the Holmby Corporation, `continuing in the process of complete liquidation, made additional distributions to the trustees in redemption of capital stock and from earnings on the dates and in the amounts as follows:

| Date | By Stock Redemptions | | From Earnings and Profits |
	Shares	Amount	Amount
February 8, 1927			$ 899,184.00
March 19, 1927			64,326.24
May 17, 1927	19,207	$1,920,700.00	
June 8, 1927			74,941.50
September 2, 1927			74,941.50
October 11, 1927	38,931	3,893,100.00	
December 1, 1927			71,695.00
	58,138	$5,813,800.00	$1,185,088.24

The above amounts received as distributions from earnings and profits were immediately distributable and were distributed to the beneficiaries within a short time after receipt. (Stipulation Exhibit B.)

Petitioner further respectfully moves that this honorable Board [38] reconsider that portion of its opinion in the above entitled matter in which it was held (page 5) that the $353,791.94 distributable during the year 1927 by the trustees was taxable to the petitioner and hold that only so much of the amount distributable as was distributed after October 11, 1927, the date on which the trustees recovered their entire cost, was taxable to the petitioner.

Dated, June 6, 1934.

THOMAS R. DEMPSEY,
A. CALDER MACKAY,
Counsel for Petitioner.

[Endorsed]: Filed Jun 11, 1934.

Denied Jun 21, 1934. (Signed) J. Russell Leech, Member U. S. Board of Tax Appeals. [39]

[Title of Court and Cause.]

MEMORANDUM OF ARGUMENT IN SUPPORT OF ATTACHED MOTION.

On page 3 of the Opinion the Board has found as a fact that "During the year 1927, the Holmby Corporation, continuing the process of complete liquidation, made additional distributions of $6,995,885.24. Of this sum, $1,185,088.24 was distributed as from earnings and profits and the balance, $5,813,800.00, was paid as in redemption of 58,138 shares of the total of 69,168 shares of stock belonging to the trust."

Petitioner respectfully moves this Honorable Board to further find, as stipulated by the parties, the date and amount of each of the Holmby Corporation distributions making up the above total. Petitioner also requests a further finding to the effect that these distributions were in turn immediately distributed to the petitioner. (Stipulation Exhibit B.)

Petitioner agrees with the Honorable Board in its conclusions of law except as to the one expressed in the sentence on page 5 of the Opinion, which reads as follows:

"We accept this decree as final in determining that the only amount distributable, and therefore taxable, to Petitioner, was the sum of $353,791.94 actually distributed to him by authority of the court."

The portion of the above sentence which the petitioner respectfully urges this [40] Honorable Board to reconsider is the statement to the effect that the full sum of $353,791.94 actually distributed to the petitioner was taxable. Petitioner submits that the provisions of Section 219 (b) quoted in the margin of the opinion permit of an additional deduction in computing net income of the trust only the amount of the income of the trust for its taxable year which is distributable. Admittedly the full $353,791.94 was distributable but the petitioner submits not all of that amount constituted income or gain to the trust

52 *Arthur Letts, Jr., vs.*

estate. The Board has found that the trustees had an unrecovered cost of $5,565,948.96 against which must be applied the liquidating distributions of $6,-998,888.24 received in 1927. These distributions were made on the dates in the amounts as follows (Stipulation p. 2):

Date	By Stock Redemptions Shares	By Stock Redemptions Amount	From Earnings and Profits Amount
February 8, 1927			$ 899,184.00
March 19, 1927			64,326.24
May 17, 1927	19,207	$1,920,700.00	
June 8, 1927			74,941.50
September 2, 1927			74,941.50
October 11, 1927	38,931	3,893,100.00	
December 1, 1927			71,695.00
	58,138	$5,813,800.00	$1,185,088.24

The $353,791.74 distributed to petitioner represented 30% of the above $1,185,088.24, less certain trust expenses (Stipulation Exhibit B). The said $353,791.74 was, therefore, received in installments on February 8, 1927, March 19, 1927, June 8, 1927, September 2, 1927 and December 1, 1927 (Stipulation Exhibit B). It is quite obvious that the trusttees did not recover the unrecovered cost at January 1, 1927, amounting to $5,565,948.96 until October 11, 1927. It therefore follows that the amounts distributed to petitioner between January 1, 1927 and October 11, 1927, constituted returns of capital from a federal income tax viewpoint. Section 219 (b) supra as above pointed out, permits the deduction only of amounts of income dis- [41] tributed.

Congress, in using the word "income" evidently intended it to have its well established meaning, viz., "the gain derived from capital * * * provided it be understood to include profit gained through a sale or conversion of capital assets". Applying this rule to the Holmby Corporation distribution on February 8, 1927 to the Trustees, we find no "gain" or profit from the sale of capital assets because, as the Board has held, the amount applied against the cost of the stock. The same conclusion must be reached with respect to each of the subsequent distributions until the one on October 11, 1927, which completed the return of cost and resulted in a gain,—a profit through a sale of capital assets and therefore income. This income, however, was not distributable since it was received by the trustees in redemption of stock and the Board has already found that amounts received in redemption of stock were not distributable under the court decree.

It is quite true, as the Board has held, that the trust derived a gain and, therefore, income, during the year from liquidating distributions on Holmby Corporation stock amounting to $1,432,939.28. Petitioner agrees that such portion of the trust income which was distributable was deductible in determining taxable net income, but submits that the only "income" of the trust which was so deductible was that received in the December 11, 1927 distribution.

Petitioner, therefore, respectfully prays that this Honorable Board amend its opinion in the above en-

titled case to hold that only such part of the aforesaid $353,791.94 distributed to him by authority of
the court represents income in the form of capital
gain as was received by the trustees and distributed
to him after they had recovered their cost of
Holmby Corporation stock.

> THOMAS R. DEMPSEY,
> A. CALDER MACKAY.

[Endorsed]: Filed Jun 11, 1934. [42]

United States Board of Tax Appeals

Docket No. 62,106

ARTHUR LETTS, JR.,

Petitioner,

vs.

COMMISSIONER OF INTERNAL REVENUE,

Respondent.

DECISION.

Pursuant to the Opinion of the Board promulgated May 25, 1934, the respondent herein on June
27, 1934, filed a notice of settlement and proposed
computation, and the petitioner on July 16, 1934,
filed counter proposal. It is

ORDERED AND DECIDED that there is an
overpayment in income tax of $7278.45 for the
year 1927.

ENTER:

(Signed)   J. RUSSELL LEECH,

Member.

Entered Jul 31 1934. [43]

[Title of Court and Cause.]

PETITION FOR REVIEW OF DECISION OF THE UNITED STATES BOARD OF TAX APPEALS.

To the Honorable Judges of the United States Circuit Court of Appeals for the Ninth Circuit:

Arthur Letts, Jr., in support of this, his petition, filed in pursuance of the provisions of Section 1001 of the Act of Congress approved February 26, 1926, entitled "The Revenue Act of 1926", as amended by Section 603 of the Act of Congress approved May 29, 1928, as further amended by Section 1101 of the Act of Congress approved June 6, 1932, entitled "The Revenue Act of 1932", and as further amended by the Revenue Act of 1934, for the review of the decision of the United States Board of Tax Appeals promulgated May 25, 1934, a final order of determination having been entered on the 31st day of July, 1934, respectfully shows to this Honorable Court as follows:

I.

STATEMENT OF THE NATURE OF THE CONTROVERSY.

Brief Statement of Facts.

The question presented in this appeal is whether the amounts distributed to petitioner as beneficiary by the trustees of the trust estate of Arthur Letts, Sr., out of the corpus of the trust estate constitute taxable income. [44]

Petitioner's father, Arthur Letts, Sr., died testate, a resident of Los Angeles, California, on May 18, 1923. Under the terms of his last will and testament decedent gave, bequeathed and devised the residue of his estate to petitioner, Malcolm McNaghten, Harold Janss, J. G. Bullock and Harry G. R. Philp, as trustees, to be held in trust for certain enumerated purposes. The trustees duly and regularly qualified as such and acted in that capacity until May 18, 1933. The trustees were given power to manage and control all of the property so acquired by them and were required under said will and trust to hold said property during the lives of petitioner, Gladys Janss and Edna L. McNaghten, or the survivor of them, but in no event beyond ten years from the date of the death of decedent; said trustees were further empowered and directed to collect and receive all rents, interest, dividends and income from said trust properties and to distribute the net income from said trust properties to the following named persons in the following proportions:

30,% to Arthur Letts, Jr. (Petitioner),
30% to Florence Edna Letts McNaghten,
30,% to Gladys Letts Janss,
10% to Letts Foundation.

Said trustees under and pursuant to said testamentary trust received on August 20, 1925, among other properties, 69,168 shares of the capital stock of Holmby Corporation, which stock had a fair market value of $7,215,605.76 at the date of the decedent's death.

During the period from May 18, 1923, to December 31, 1926, the Holmby Corporation, in process of complete liquidation which began May 18, 1923, distributed to the trustees the sum of $1,649,656.80. All of this sum was distributed from earnings and profits of the corporation. During the year 1927 said corporation made further distributions in liquidation from the same source to the trustees in the sum of $1,185,088.24, which sum was distributed by said [45] corporation and received by the trustees in the following amounts and on the following dates:

Date	Amount
February 8, 1927	$899,184.00
March 19, 1927	64,326.24
June 8, 1927	74,941.50
September 2, 1927	74,941.50
December 1, 1927	71,695.00

The trustees during the year 1927 distributed to said beneficiaries under said trust the total sum of $1,179,305.79, petitioner receiving as his share thereof, as one of the beneficiaries of said trust, the sum of $353,791.74, which was inadvertently and erroneously reported by petitioner in his income tax return for said year as ordinary dividends.

On May 17, 1927, said trustees received in redemption and cancellation of 19,207 shares of the capital stock of Holmby Corporation the total sum of $1,920,700.00, and on October 11, 1927, said trustees received in redemption and cancellation of 38,931 shares of the capital stock of said Holmby Corporation property of the value of $3,893,100.00.

In determining the deficiency the respondent treated the sum of $353,791.94 as ordinary income and also added to petitioner's net taxable income the sum of $78,397.78 which the respondent contended represented "additional gain and liquidation distributions to trustees". Petitioner contended before the Board, and now contends, that the amounts totaling $353,791.94 (except the amount of $21,-580.50) received by him from the trust estate were not distributions of income, but constituted distributions of a part of the corpus of the trust estate, the trustees not having recovered their base for said stock prior to October 11, 1927, and that no part thereof constituted taxable income to petitioner. [46]

II.

STATEMENT OF PROCEEDING HERETOFORE HELD.

The Commissioner of Internal Revenue, respondent herein, on the 24th day of December, 1931, mailed to petitioner what is termed a deficiency letter, wherein respondent proposed a deficiency of additional tax for the year 1927 in the sum of $92,721.18. In due course of time and within the sixty-day period petitioner filed his appeal before the United States Board of Tax Appeals wherein he alleged, among other things, that the action of respondent in including the sum of $353,791.94 as ordinary income was erroneous; that the action of the respondent in adding the sum of $78,397.78 to petitioner's net taxable income was erroneous.

Petitioner further alleged that no part of these sums constituted taxable income either as dividends, capital gain or ordinary income; that the sum of $78,397.78 was not received by petitioner, and therefore did not constitute taxable income; that the amounts totaling $353,791.94 (except $21,580.50) represented distributions of the corpus of the estate, no parts of which were taxable, and that petitioner's action in including the sum of $353,791.94 as dividends in his income tax return for the year 1927 was erroneous, and therefore petitioner was entitled to a refund. The issues were joined and the case was submitted upon a stipulation of facts signed by both parties litigant.

The Board of Tax Appeals held, among other things, that the Holmby Corporation was in process of complete liquidation from May 18, 1923 and that all distributions to that date whether made from accumulated earnings or capital were, for the purpose of the taxing act, considered as received by the stockholder in exchange for his stock under the provisions of Section 201 (c) of the Revenue Act of 1926. The Board found that the cost basis of the 69,168 shares of the stock of Holmby Corporation, stipulated to be $7,215,605.76, had been recovered [42] by the trustees to the extent of $1,649,656.80 by liquidating distributions received by the trustees prior to the taxable year, leaving an unrecoverable cost of $5,565,948.96, against which must be applied the liquidating distributions of $6,998,888.24 received in 1927. The Board held that these latter distributions over the unrecovered cost were $1,432,-

939.28 and constituted the taxable gain received by the trustees in 1927.

The Board of Tax Appeals held that petitioner was not liable for tax on the $78,397.78, but that the sum of $353,791.94 represented a capital gain to petitioner subject to the capital gain provisions of the Revenue Act of 1926.

Petitioner, on or about June 11, 1934, filed a motion to amend findings of fact and opinion, which motion was denied by the Board on June 21, 1934.

III.

DESIGNATION OF COURT OF REVIEW.

Petitioner, being aggrieved by the said findings of fact, opinion and order, and being a resident of Los Angeles, California, desires a review thereof, in accordance with the provisions of the Revenue Act of 1926, as amended by the Revenue Act of 1928, and as further amended by the Revenue Acts of 1932 and 1934, by the United States Circuit Court of Appeals for the Ninth Circuit, within which circuit is located the office of the Collector of Internal Revenue to which petitioner made his income tax return for the year 1927.

IV.

ASSIGNMENTS OF ERROR.

The petitioner, as a basis of review, makes the following assignments of error:

1. The Board of Tax Appeals erred in holding that the sum of $332,211.44 constituted taxable income to petitioner.

2. The Board of Tax Appeals erred in holding that the sum of $353,791.94 constituted a taxable gain realized by petitioner in 1927. [47]

3. The Board of Tax Appeals erred in failing to hold that the sum of $332,211.44 constituted a distribution · made by the trust estate out of its corpus, no part of which is taxable to petitioner.

4. The Board of Tax Appeals erred in holding that the statutory capital gain derived by the trustees of said trust estate was distributable under the terms of the trust to petitioner.

5. The Board of Tax Appeals erred in failing to hold that the statutory capital gain realized by the trustees of said trust became part of the corpus, which, under the terms of the trust instrument, was not distributable to petitioner.

6. The Board of Tax Appeals erred in failing to find as a fact as supported by the stipulation that the distributions made by Holmby Corporation to the trustees during the year 1927 were made on the dates and in the amounts as follows:

| Date | By Stock Redemptions | | From Earnings and Profits |
	Shares	Amount	Amount
February 8, 1927			$ 899,184.00
March 19,1927			64,326.24
May 17, 1927	19,207	$1,920,700.00	
June 8, 1927			74,941.50
September 2, 1927			74,941.50
October 11, 1927	38,931	3,893,100.00	
December 1, 1927			71,695.00
	58,138	$5,813,800.00	$1,185,088.24

7. The Board of Tax Appeals erred in failing to find as a fact as supported by the stipulation that the trustees immediately after receiving each of the amounts shown as earnings and profits of the Holmby Corporation, as shown in Paragraph 6, distributed the same to the beneficiaries of said trust estate. [48]

8. The Board of Tax Appeals erred in failing to determine that petitioner was entitled to a refund of tax overpaid by him for the year 1927 in at least the sum of $48,813.86, together with interest thereon as provided by law.

WHEREFORE, your petitioner prays that this Honorable Court may review the said findings, opinion, decision and order of the United States Board of Tax Appeals and reverse and set aside the same; and that this Honorable Court direct the entry of a decision by the said Board in favor of petitioner determining that there is a refund due petitioner of at least the sum of $48,813.86.

Petitioner prays for such other and further relief as may seem meet and proper in the premises.

.   THOMAS R. DEMPSEY,

A. CALDER MACKAY,

Attorneys for Petitioner,

1104 Pacific Mutual Building,

Los Angeles, California. [49]

STATE OF CALIFORNIA,
COUNTY OF LOS ANGELES.—ss.

A. CALDER MACKAY, being duly sworn, says that he is one of the attorneys for the petitioner above named and that as such is duly authorized to verify the attached petition for review by the United States Circuit Court of Appeals for the Ninth Circuit of the decision of the Board rendered therein; that he has read the said petition and is familiar with the statement herein contained, and that the facts set forth therein are true to the best of his knowledge and belief and that the said petition is filed in good faith.

(Sgd)   A. CALDER MACKAY.

Subscribed and sworn to before me this 23d day of October, 1934.

[Seal]   ALICE FAHION (Sgd)

Notary Public in and for said County and State.

[Endorsed]: Filed October 27, 1934. [50]

[Title of Court and Cause.]

NOTICE.

To Robert A. Jackson, Esq., Bureau of Internal Revenue, Washington, D. C., Attorney for the Respondent:

Sir: PLEASE TAKE NOTICE that on the 27th day of October, 1934, the undersigned presented to this Board and filed with the clerk thereof the petition of Arthur Letts, Jr., a copy of which is annexed hereto, for review by the United States Circuit Court of Appeals for the Ninth Circuit, of the final order and decision of the Board in the above entitled proceeding entered upon the records of said Board on July 31, 1934.

Dated at Washington, D. C., October 27th, 1934.
THOMAS R. DEMPSEY,
A. CALDER MACKAY,
1104 Pacific Mutual Building,
Los Angeles, California,
CHARLES D. HAMEL,
Shoreham Building,
Washington, D. C.,
Attorneys for Petitioner.

Service of a copy of the foregoing is hereby acknowledged this 27th day of October, 1934.
ROBERT H. JACKSON,
Asst. General Counsel, Bureau of Internal Revenue,
Attorney for Respondent.

[Endorsed]: Filed October 27, 1934. [51]

[Title of Court and Cause.]

STATEMENT OF EVIDENCE.

The above named case was submitted to the United States Board of Tax Appeals, Honorable James Russell Leech presiding, on a stipulation of facts, there being no oral testimony offered or received by either party. The stipulation so offered and received is hereinafter set out in full:

"United States Board of Tax Appeals.

Docket No. 62,106

ARTHUR LETTS, JR.,

Petitioner,

vs.

COMMISSIONER OF INTERNAL REVENUE,

Respondent.

STIPULATION OF FACT.

IT IS HEREBY STIPULATED AND AGREED by and between the parties hereto by their respective counsel, that:

(1) ʻPetitioner during the year 1927 was a resident of the City of Los Angeles, State of California.

(2) On April 28, 1923, petitioner acquired by gift from his father 100 shares of the capital stock of Holmby Corporation, a California corporation, which stock had a cost basis in the hands of the donor of $50.00 per share or $5000.00.

(3) On January 1, 1927, petitioner owned outright 101 shares of said Holmby Corporation stock,

being 100 shares acquired by gift on April 28, 1923, and 1 Director's qualifying share. [52]

(4)   During the period from May 18, 1923, to December 31, 1926, Holmby Corporation in the process of complete liquidation, distributed to petitioner on his 101 shares the sum of $2408.85 out of its earnings and profits.

(5)   During the year 1927 Holmby Corporation continuing the process of complete liquidation, made certain other distributions to petitioner both out of its earnings and profits and still other distributions out of its capital stock account in complete cancellation and redemption of certain shares of its capital stock.   The proceeds of these distributions received by petitioner on his 101 shares were as follows:

	Distributions		From
	By Stock Redemption		Earnings
	No of		and Profits
Date	Shares	Amount	Amount
February 8, 1927			$1,313.00
March 19, 1927			93.93
May 17, 1927	28	$2,800.00	
June 8, 1927			109.44
September 2, 1927			109.44
October 11, 1927	55	5,500.00	
December 1, 1927			110.62
	83	$8,300.00	$1,736.43

The sum of $1,736.43 received by petitioner as distributions from earnings and profits of Holmby Corporation was reported by petitioner on his income tax return for the year 1927 as ordinary dividends.

(6) On May 18, 1923, petitioner's father, Arthur Letts, Sr., died testate. Pursuant to the terms of said decedent's last will and testament (the material portions of which are included in the decree of distribution which is attached hereto, marked Exhibit 'A' and made a part hereof), certain named persons, to wit, Arthur Letts, Jr. (petitioner), Malcolm McNaghten, Harold Janss, J. G. Bullock and Harry G. R. Philp, were named trustees of the trust created under the terms of said will, each of whom duly and regularly qualified as such and acted in that capacity until May 18, 1933.

(7) On or about August 20, 1925, the Estate of Arthur Letts, Deceased, was distributed and the said trustees then received 69,168 shares of Holmby Corporation stock to be held in trust. This stock had a fair market value of $7,215,605.76 on May 18, 1923, the date of Arthur Letts' decease. [53]

(8) During the period from May 18, 1923, to December 31, 1926, the Holmby Corporation in the process of complete liquidation distributed out of its earnings and profits to the trustees above named the sum of $1,649,656.80 on the said 69,168 shares.

(9) During the year 1927 the Holmby Corporation, continuing the process of complete liquidation, made certain other distributions to said trus-

tees out of its earnings and profits and still other
distributions out of its capital stock account in complete cancellation and redemption of certain shares
of its capital stock. These distributions received
by said trustees on their 69,168 shares were made as
follows:

			Distributions From Earnings and Profits
	By Stock Redemption		
Date	Shares	Amount	Amount
February 8, 1927			$ 899,184.00
March 19, 1927			64,326.24
May 17, 1927	19,207	$1,920,700.00	
June 8, 1927			74,941.50
September 2, 1927			74,941.50
October 11, 1927	38,931	3,893,100.00	
December 1, 1927			71,695.00
	58,138	$5,813,800.00	$1,185,088.24

(10)   Of the $1,185,088.24 received by the trus-
tees from the distribution out of earnings and profits
of the corporation the sum of $353,791.74 was dis-
tributed by the trustees to petitioner during the
year 1927 as his beneficial share of said trust income
and reported by petitioner on his income tax return for said year as ordinary dividends.

(11)   Respondent has erroneously overstated
petitioner's ordinary gross income in his deficiency
letter for the year 1927 by the sum of $355,528.17

by reason of his inclusion of that amount in computing capital net gain and again including it in petitioner's ordinary gross income.

(12)   In his deficiency letter for the year 1927 respondent has, also, overstated petitioner's net income subject·to normal tax by $20,491.47, representing dividends received, through his failure to allow said sum as a credit in computing the normal tax as is provided in Section 216 (a) (1) of the Revenue Act of 1926.

(13)   The said several amounts received by petitioner from Holmby Corporation and the trustees in the year 1927 have received the following treatment on petitioner's income tax return for the year 1927 and in the deficiency letter for that year, viz.:
[54]

Per return
Distributions from earnings and profits
on own stock reported as "dividends"
(par. 5) $ 1,736.43
Distributions by Holmby Corporation
from earnings and profits to trustees
and in turn distributed to petitioner,
reported as "dividends"   353,791.74

    Total reported on return $355,528.17

Added in Deficiency Letter
Distributions on own stock above re-
ported as dividends (par. 5)   1,736.43
Amount distributed from Capital (par. 5) 8,500.00
Distribution from trust as above   353,791.74
Additional gain on liquidating distribu-
tions to trustees   78,397.78

    Total addition to income in deficiency
      letter on account of Holmby Cor-
      poration distributions $442,425.95

    Total amount of income included in
      "net income" in deficiency letter
      on account of above items $797,954.12

Of the above total $355,528.17 was treated by the
respondent as ordinary income subject to both
normal and surtax and the remainder was treated
as capital gain by the respondent.

(14) Attached hereto and made a part hereof is a copy of the "First Account Current and Report of" the trustees, which is marked Exhibit "B". Also attached hereto and made a part hereof and marked Exhibit "C" is a copy of the order of the Superior Court approving said "First Account Current and Report of" the trustees. No appeal was taken from said order.

THOMAS R. DEMPSEY,
A. CALDER MACKAY,
Counsel for Petitioner.
E. BARRETT PRETTEYMAN,
Counsel for Respondent."
[55]

EXHIBIT "A"

In the Superior Court of the State of California, in and for the County of Los Angeles.
No. 62,249

In the Matter of the Estate
of
ARTHUR LETTS, Deceased.

ORDER SETTLING FINAL ACCOUNT AND FOR DISTRIBUTION UNDER WILL.

The final account and petition for distribution herein of Arthur Letts, Jr., Malcolm McNaghten, Harold Janss, J. G. Bullock and Harry G. R. Philp, Executors of the Will of Arthur Letts, Deceased, by S. F. Macfarlane, their attorney, coming on regularly this 19th day of August, 1925, for settlement and hearing by the Court, notice of settlement and hearing having been duly given as required by law, and no person appearing to except to or contest said account or petition; the Court, after hearing the evidence settles said account and orders distribution of said estate as follows:

IT IS ORDERED, ADJUDGED AND DECREED that due notice to creditors of said deceased has been given; that said account be allowed and settled; that the payment of attorney's fees and executors' commissions as described in said account be approved; that said executors have in their possession belonging to said estate, after deducting the credits to which they are entitled, a balance of $14,789,118.35, consisting of $337,680.32 in cash and the other property hereinafter described, at the value of the appraisement; that all of said property was the separate property of said deceased; and that in pursuance of and according to the provisions of the Will of said deceased (the specific money legacies provided for in subsections "(c)" to "(p)" both inclusive, [56] of subdivision "THIRD" of said Will having been paid), all of the residue of the property of said estate hereinafter described, and all other property of said estate whether described herein or not, be distributed as follows:

To FLORENCE M. QUINN, formerly known as Florence M. Letts:

All of the right, title and interest of said deceased in and to the following described property:

All of the real property situated in Lots Eleven (11) and Twelve (12) of the west portion of the Lick Tract, in the County of Los Angeles, State of California, according to map recorded in Book 7, page 92, of Miscellaneous Records of said County; excepting such portions of said lots as are contained in Tract No. 4502, according to map of said Tract recorded in Book 49, pages 44 and 45, of Maps, in the Records of said County;

Also all buildings and improvements located on said property, and all appurtenances to said property, and all household furniture, furnishings and equipment located in the dwelling house and other buildings on said property, and all garden tools and implements located on said property, and all automobiles used by the said deceased for his personal accommodation, and all personal wearing apparel and jewelry owned by the deceased at the time of his death, all of which said personal property is particularly described in the inventory heretofore filed in Court;

To MALCOLM McNAGHTEN, Forty-one Hundred and Sixty-six (4166) shares of the capital stock of Bullock's, a corporation;

To HAROLD JANSS, Forty-one Hundred and Sixty-six (4166) shares of the capital stock of Bullock's, a corporation; [57]

To FLORENCE M. QUINN, formerly known as Florence M. Letts, the sum of $317,607.84 in cash, to offset the $105,000.00 of principal and $1225.00

interest paid out on account of the specific money legacies provided for in Subdivision "THIRD" of the Will of said deceased, and $211,382.84, being the appraised value of the 4166 shares of the stock of Bullock's, a corporation, distributed, to Malcolm McNaghten, and the 4166 shares of the stock of Bullock's, a corporation, distributed to Harold Janss;

To FLORENCE M. QUINN, formerly known as Florence M. Letts, an undivided one-half interest in and to all of the property hereinafter described, and in and to all other property of said estate whether described herein or not; and to MALCOLM McNAGHTEN, ARTHUR LETTS, JR., HAROLD JANSS, J. G. BULLOCK and HARRY G. R. PHILP, or to the survivors of them, as trustees, the other undivided one-half interest in and to all of the said property hereinafter described, and in and to all other property of said estate whether described herein or not, to be held in trust for the uses and purposes provided in the Will of said deceased, which are as follows:

"(a) Said trustees, or the survivors of them, shall hold, control, manage, sell, convey, mortgage, pledge, loan, lease, rent, assigns, transfer, invest and reinvest the said trust property or any part thereof, or any substitute therefor, as to them, or the survivors of them, may seem best, to the end that said trust estate may produce the maximum income therefrom consistent with a due regard for the safety, development and preservation of the trust estate."

"(b) Said trustees, or the survivors of them, shall collect [58] and receive all of the rents, interest, dividends and income from said trust property; and from the gross income derived from said trust property; said trustees, or the survivors of them, shall pay and discharge all taxes, assessments, costs, charges and expenses incurred in the care, administration and protection of the trust property and in the maintenance and protection of this trust and in its defense against legal or equitable attack by any person; and said trustees, or the survivors of them, shall pay and distribute the net income from said trust to the following named persons in the following proportions, to-wit: One-third of said net income to my son, Arthur Letts, Jr., or to his heirs, legatees or devisees; another one-third of said net income to my daughter, Florence Edna Letts McNaghten, or to her heirs, legatees or devisees; and the remaining one-third of said net income to my daughter, Gladys Letts Janss, or to her heirs, legatees or devisees. The distribution of said net income shall be made at least semi-annually and more frequently if the same can be done, in the judgment of my trustees, without inconvenience to the proper and reasonable management of the trust estate.

"(c) I expressly authorize my said trustee to include in the expenses of the administration of this trust and to pay to themselves a reasonable compensation for their services as such trustee.

"(d)   It is my desire that my said trustees, when acting as such trustees or when acting as executors of this Will, shall make every reasonable effort to cooperate with each other in order that all acts performed by said persons, either as trustees or executors, shall be according to the unanimous judgment of the persons so [59] acting; but should any difference of opinion arise pertaining to any matters which said persons shall be obliged to act upon, the judgment of a majority of said trustees or executors shall be binding upon all such trustees or executors.

"(e)   Each and every beneficiary under this trust is hereby restrained therefrom, and shall be without right, power or authority to sell, transfer, pledge, mortgage, hypothecate, alienate, anticipate or in any other manner affect or impair his beneficial or legal rights, titles, interest, claims or estate in or to the income or principal of this trust during the entire term hereof; and the rights, titles, interest or estate of any beneficiary hereunder shall not be subject to the rights or claims of creditors of any beneficiary, or subject or liable to any process of law or Court; and all of the net income and principal under this trust shall be transferable, payable and deliverable only, solely, exclusively and personally to the above designated beneficiaries hereunder at the time entitled to take the same under the terms of this trust; PROVIDED, HOWEVER, that nothing herein contained is intended to prevent the transfer of the interest of any beneficiary under this trust to his or her heirs, legatees or devisees in the event of his or her death, either by Will or under the laws of succession.

"(f) The trust hereby created shall exist and continue during the lives of my said son, Arthur Letts, Jr., my said daughter, Florence Edna Letts McNaghten, and my said daughter, Gladys Letts Janss, or the survivor of them; but in no event shall this trust continue beyond the term of ten (10) years from the date of my death. Should all of my said children die within the period of [60] ten (10) years after the date of my death, upon the death of the last survivor of my said children, or in any event upon the expiration of the term of ten (10) years after the date of my death, this trust shall cease and terminate and all of the principal or corpus of said trust estate then remaining subject to this trust and all undistributed net income therefrom shall be and become the absolute property of my said children, Arthur Letts, Jr., Florence Edna Letts McNaghten and Gladys Letts Janss, share and share alike if they be alive; but in the event of the death of any of my said children prior to the termination of this trust, upon the termination of this trust the share of such deceased child in said trust estate shall be and become the absolute property of the heirs, legatees or devisees of such deceased child.

"(g) Without any intention of limiting the general powers hereinbefore granted to my said trustees, but for the purpose of specifically authorizing my said trustees to do anything necessary or convenient to carry out my wishes and desires as here-

inafter expressed, I call the attention of my trustees
to the fact that I have heretofore caused to be
incorporated under the laws of California a corporation known as 'Holmby Corporation' which corporation up to the present time has organized by the
adoption of By-Laws and the election of the following named persons as directors, to-wit, Arthur Letts,
Arthur Letts, Jr., Malcolm McNaghten, J. G. Bullock and Harry G. R. Philp; and it is my wish and
desire, provided the permit of the Corporation Commissioner so to do can be procured, to have said
corporation acquire about One Hundred Sixty
Thousand (160,000) shares of the capital stock of
Bullock's, a corporation, [61] about Thirty Thousand (30,000) shares of the capital stock of The
Broadway Department Store, a corporation, all of
my interest and the interest of my wife, Florence
M. Letts, in the property generally known as the
'Wolfskill Ranch' which is situated in Los Angeles
County, California, and is now held in trust by the
Los Angeles Trust and Savings Bank, of Los Angeles, California, and such other property as it may
be deemed best to transfer to said corporation, at
the price of the fair market value thereof, payable
in shares of the capital stock of said Holmby Corporation at par. Should I die before a transfer of
said properties to said Holmby Corporation has
been accomplished, it is my earnest wish and desire
that my said wife, Florence M. Letts, shall cooperate
with the persons herein appointed as executors and
trustees, to accomplish the transfer of said properties to said Holmby Corporation, in order that

said properties may be managed and controlled by said Holmby Corporation. It is also my earnest wish and desire that, upon the transfer of said properties to said Holmby Corporation having been accomplished, my wife, Florence M. Letts, will voluntarily transfer and assign to the same persons as are herein appointed trustees of the trust herein created, all shares of stock of said Holmby Corporation to which she may become entitled by reason of the transfer of any of said properties to said Holmby Corporation, and will authorize and empower said persons, as such trustees, to manage and control her interest in said stock of said Holmby Corporation, in the same manner and to the same extent as they will be authorized hereunder to manage and control the trust estate herein created, for the full term of the trust herein [62] created; with the understanding, of course, that all net income accruing from such proposed trust estate to be created by my said wife, Florence M. Letts, shall be paid to her, and upon the termination of the trust all of the principal of said trust property shall again become her absolute property.

"I further desire to call the attention of my said trustees to the fact that, in my judgment, it will be for the best interest of the trust estate if the business now owned and conducted by Bullock's, a corporation, be continued during the term of this trust under the management of substantially the same persons who are now managing the said business, and according to the plans and policies now being followed in the conduct of said business; and also to the further fact that, in my judgment, it will be for the best interest of the trust estate if the business now owned and conducted by The Broadway Department Store, a corporation, be continued during the term of this trust under the management of substantially the same persons who are now managing the said business, and according to the plans and policies now being followed in the conduct of said business. Referring to the property generally known as the Wolfskill Ranch, at this time I have no well defined plan for conducting or developing said ranch or for selling and realizing upon the same, but I desire my trustes to follow their best judgment with regard to this property.

"(h) It is my wish and desire that the persons herein appointed as trustees of the trust herein created shall be elected as directors of said Holmby Corporation, and shall continue to act as directors of said Holmby Corporation during the term of said trust; [63] but should any of my said trustees, for any reason whatsoever, be unable to act as one of the directors of said Holmby Corporation, it is my wish and desire that any vacancy created in said Board of Directors of said Holmby Corporation by reason of the inability of such person to act as a director shall be filled by the election of some other person as director, by the other directors in office, and such other person shall have all of the authority usually vested in a director of a corporation, but shall not thereby become a trustee of the trust herein created.

"(i) It is also my wish and desire that my said trustees, or the survivors of them, with reasonable diligence, shall create or organize a charitable trust or corporation which shall be known as the 'Letts Foundation', and which shall have for its purposes the right to acquire and dispose of one-tenth of the net income derived from the trust created in this Will, and one-tenth of the principal or corpus of the trust estate created in this Will upon any termination of said trust, for charitable purposes for the benefit of needy and/or deserving persons who are or shall be or at any time have been employed by The Broadway Department Store, a corporation, or by Bullock's, a corporation; such charitable trust or corporation to continue in effect so long as any property remains in said charitable trust or corporation. The persons herein named as trustees of the trust created in this Will are generally familiar with my ideas with reference to said proposed Letts Foundation; and having full confidence in their integrity and in their ability to carry out my wishes, it is my intention that they shall have such broad and general powers as it is possible for me [64] to give them under the law in order to carry out my wishes with reference to said proposed Letts Foundation. Therefore, notwithstanding the fact that I have hereinbefore otherwise directed the disposition of all net income and of the principal or corpus of the trust created in this Will upon its termination, should it be legally possible for my trustees to carry out the provisions of this subparagraph 'i' of this Will, I authorize and direct

my said trustees to create or organize a trust or
corporation, to be known as the Letts Foundation,
for the purposes above described, and to pay and
distribute one-tenth part of the net income derived
from the trust created in this Will to such proposed Letts Foundation; and also, upon any termination of the trust created in this Will, to assign, transfer and deliver to said proposed Letts
Foundation one-tenth part of the principal or
corpus of the trust estate created by this Will. It
is also my earnest wish and desire that my wife,
Florence M. Letts, will voluntarily so arrange her
affairs that the said proposed Letts Foundation
shall receive one-tenth of the net income derived
from, and one-tenth of the principal or corpus of,
her share of our community property other than
the home place and personal property described in
the 'SECOND' subdivision of this Will.

"My said trustees shall have full authority so to
do, and shall arrange a reasonable and comprehensive plan for the appointment of a trustee or
trustees or directors of said proposed Letts Foundation; and the trustee or trustees or directors of
said Letts Foundation shall have full power to determine when and under what circumstances a person may be in need and/or deserving of assistance
[65] from said proposed Letts Foundation.

"In the event that, at any time in the future,
all of the property held by the said proposed Letts
Foundation be not required for the reasonable ac-
complishment and continuation of the purposes

above provided, any excess funds or property held by said proposed Letts Foundation may be used and applied for general charitable purposes for the benefit of needy and deserving persons residing in the City of Los Angeles, California.''

Description of Property.

CASH: $20,072.48, less so much thereof as may be required to pay the excess, if any, of the reasonable expenses incurred by the Executors to close the administration of said estate and to make distribution thereof, over any income received by the Executors in the meantime.

CORPORATION STOCKS: 138,336 shares of Holmby Corporation, 1099 shares of Sinaloa Realty Company, 56 shares Sinaloa Land and Water Company, 20 shares 7% Preferred Stock of Al Maliakah Auditorium Company, 50 shares California Savings Bank of Los Angeles, California.

BONDS: 8—$1000.00 bonds, Delta Farms Reclamation District Number 2028, California, being bonds numbered 261 to 264, both inclusive, and 311 to 314, both inclusive.

MORTGAGES AND NOTES: 2 Promissory Notes of Roy R. Musser, one dated June 1, 1925, for $13,150.00 and the other dated April 24, 1924, for $500.00, secured by 100 shares common stock and 500 shares of preferred stock of Eno Rubber Corporation, of Los Angeles, California;

Promissory note of W. H. Steele, dated February 20, 1918 for [66] $4000.00, secured by first mortgage on SE¼ of Sec. 26, Twp 6, N. R. 8, W. S. B. M., situated in Los Angeles County, California, recorded in Book 4982, page 206, Official Records of said County, and Renewal Agreement dated February 18, 1925, recorded in Book 4867, page 395, Official Records of said County;

Total beneficial interest in Trust No. 3413 of Pacific-Southwest Trust and Savings Bank, formerly Los Angeles Trust and Savings Bank of Los Angeles, California.

Claim against Mrs. F. H. Shatto of $1121.50, dated June 19, 1922, secured by deposit of one diamond ring containing two diamonds;

One-tenth beneficial interest in Trust No. P-5460, of Title Insurance and Trust Co., pertaining to models of work of David Edstrom;

Two forty-thirds (2/43) interest in Trust No. 308, of Los Angeles Trust and Savings Bank, now known as Pacific-Southwest Trust and Savings Bank, of Los Angeles, California, under declaration of trust dated July 1, 1915, pertaining to real property situated in the Rancho Sausal Redondo, Los Angeles County, California;

Beneficial interest in Trust No. S-2799, of Title Insurance and Trust Co., standing in name of Malcolm McNaghten as agent for deceased, pertaining to certain lots in Midway Park Tract, Los Angeles County, California.

UNSECURED NOTES: W. H. Moore for $6580.00, dated December 14, 1922; Community Development Association for $500.00, dated June 1,

1925; K. William Curtis for $100.00, dated November 16, 1921; H. Cecil Ecclestone for $500.00, dated February 24, 1922; F. O. Conners for $125.00, dated March 29, 1922; Richard E. Letts for [67] $125.00, dated November 16, 1921; Burwell Syndicate for $6000.00, dated September 14, 1920; Bohemian Club, San Francisco, for $100.00, dated May 1, 1922.

MISCELLANEOUS   PERSONAL   PROPERTY: Certificate No. 413, Tournament of Roses Association of Pasadena; Certificate No. A-2152 for 60 shares of stock of California Delta Farms, Inc., Transferable life membership Los Angeles Athletic Club; Regular membership Eagle Waters Golf Club, Eagle River, Wisconsin; Membership in Bohemian Club, of San Francisco, California; Special membership Flintridge Country Club.

REAL PROPERTY:

Parcel 1.   That portion of Lot 2 of the Holland Tract, in the City of Los Angeles, County of Los Angeles, State of California, as per map recorded in Book 2, page 34, of Maps, in the office of the County Recorder of said County, described as follows: Beginning at the intersection of the south line of said Lot 2, with the West line of Mariposa Avenue, (formerly Fairmount Avenue), as conveyed to the City of Los Angeles, by deed recorded in Book 4562, Page 244, of Deeds, Records of said County; thence Westerly along the South line of said Lot 2, 140 feet; thence Northerly parallel with said West line of Mariposa Avenue, 50 feet; thence Easterly parallel with the South line of said Lot 140 feet to a point in the Northerly prolongation of said West line of Mariposa Avenue; thence Southerly 50 feet to the point of beginning.

Parcel 2.   That portion of Lot 25 of the West portion of the Lick Tract in the City of Los Angeles, County of Los Angeles, State of California, as per map recorded in Book 7, Page 92, of Miscella- [68] neous Records of said County, described as follows: Beginning at a point in the Northerly prolongation of the East line of Mariposa Avenue, (formerly Fairmount Avenue), as conveyed to the City of Los Angeles, by deed recorded in Book 4676, Page 215, of Deeds, Records of said County, distant Southerly 140 feet from the intersection of said prolonged line with the South line of Franklin Avenue; thence Easterly parallel with said South line of Franklin Avenue, 138 feet; thence Southerly parallel with said East line of Mariposa Avenue, 40 feet; thence Westerly parallel with said South line of Franklin Avenue, 138 feet; thence Northerly 40 feet to the point of beginning.

Parcel 3.   The North 45 feet of Lots 62 and 63 of Cumberland Tract, in the City of Los Angeles, County of Los Angeles, State of California, as per map thereof recorded in Book 19, Page 29, Miscellaneous Records of Los Angeles County.

Parcel 4.   Lots 383, 384, 389, 390, 391, 392 and 393, Hollywood Cemetery, Los Angeles County, State of California.

Dated August 20, 1925.

FRANK R. WILLIS,

Judge.

[Endorsed]: No. 62,249.

ORDER SETTLING FINAL ACCOUNT AND FOR DISTRIBUTION UNDER WILL.

Filed Aug. 20, 1925,

L. E. LAMPTON, County Clerk,

By J. N. CARSON, Deputy.

Entered August 25th, 1925, by Fawn Howell, Deputy. Book 318, page 381. [69]

Exhibit "A" (Concluded)

THE FOREGOING INSTRUMENT IS A COR-RECT COPY OF THE ORIGINAL AS THE SAME APPEARS OF RECORD.

Attest August 30, 1933.

[Seal]   L. E. LAMPTON,

County Clerk and Clerk of the Superior Court in and for the County of Los Angeles, State of California.

R. ZUKERMAN, Deputy. [70]

EXHIBIT "B"

In the Superior Court of the State of California
in and for the County of *Los* Angeles.

No. 62,249

In the Matter of the Estate of
ARTHUR LETTS,
Deceased.

FIRST ACCOUNT CURRENT AND REPORT
OF ARTHUR LETTS, JR., MALCOLM Mc-
NAGHTEN, HAROLD JANSS, J. G. BUL-
LOCK and HARRY G. R. PHILP, AS TRUS-
TEES UNDER THE WILL OF ARTHUR
LETTS, DECEASED.

TO THE SUPERIOR COURT OF THE COUNTY
OF LOS ANGELES, STATE OF CALIFOR-
NIA

ARTHUR LETTS, JR., MALCOLM Mc-
NAGHTEN, HAROLD JANSS, J. G. BULLOCK
and HARRY G. R. PHILP, as Trustees Under the
Will of ARTHUR LETTS, Deceased, render to the
Court their first account current and report for the
period from August 20th, 1925, to and including
May 1, 1928.

Said Trustees are chargeable with:

(1)   Property received under Decree
of Distribution in above entitled estate,
as stated in "Exhibit A", hereto attached, amounting to $6,799,814.32

(2) Increase in corpus account principal transactions, as stated in "Exhibit B", hereto attached, amounting to   152,804.10

(3) Income receipts, as stated in "Exhibit C", hereto attached, amounting to   ·   1,824,630.00

TOTAL CHARGES $8,777,248.42

And said Trustees ask to be allowed credit for:

(1) Decrease of corpus account principal transactions, as stated in "Exhibit D" hereto attached amounting to   463.28

[71]

Brought forward   463.28

(2) Income Disbursements and charges, as stated in "Exhibit E", amounting to $1,823,694.47

TOTAL CREDITS   1,824,157.75

TOTAL CHARGES $8,777,248.42
TOTAL CREDITS   1,824,157.75

BALANCE chargeable to next account current and described in "Exhibit G", hereto attached $6,953,090.67

In pursuance of the terms of said trust as set forth in the Will of Arthur Letts, deceased, said trustees did, on or about the 7th day of January,

1925, organize a charitable corporation under the
laws of the State of California, which is known as
"Letts Foundation", which has for its purposes the
right to acquire and dispose of one-tenth of the net
income derived from said trust, and one-tenth of the
principal or corpus of this trust upon any termination of this trust, for charitable purposes, for the
benefit of needy and/or deserving persons who are
or shall be, or at any time have been employed by
The Broadway Department Store, a corporation, or
by Bullock's, a corporation; and said charitable corporation, Letts Foundation, ever since said date has
been and is now a duly organized and existing charitable corporation in accordance with the terms of the
trust created by said Will.

Distribution of the net income from said trust has
been made, one-tenth thereof to said Letts Foundation, and one-third of the remainder thereof to each
of the following named persons: Arthur Letts, Jr.,
Florence Edna Letts McNaghten and Gladys Letts
Janss, as beneficiaries of said trust, as more fully
appears by said "Exhibit E", and attached hereto
[72] marked "Exhibit J" is a written statement
signed by all of said beneficiaries acknowledging receipt of the sums shown by said "Exhibit E", as
having been distributed to said beneficiaries, and approving the acts of the trustees as shown in this
account and report.

The names and post office addresses of the cestui
que trust are as follows:

Letts Foundation, a corporation, Room 301-303
Subway Terminal Building, Los Angeles, California;

Arthur Letts, Jr., Room 301-303 Subway Terminal Building, Los Angeles, California;

Florence Edna Letts McNaghten, 2 Oak Knoll Terrace, Pasadena, California;

Gladys Letts Janss, 375 Carolwood Drive, Beverly Hills, California.

It has been necessary to employ an attorney for the preparation and hearing of this Account and Report, and your petitioners ask that a reasonable attorney's fee be allowed S. F. Macfarlane for his services as such attorney herein.

Your petitioners make no charge or claim for compensation for their services to date as trustees of said trust, but hereby waive all claim for compensation for their services to date.

WHEREFORE, petitioners pray that their First Account Current and Report as Trustees be approved, allowed and settled, and that a reasonable attorney's fee be allowed S. F. Macfarlane, the attorney herein, and for such other and further relief as may be proper in the premises.

Dated, July 31st, 1928. [73]

> ARTHUR LETTS, JR.,
> MALCOLM McNAGHTEN,
> HAROLD JANSS,
> JOHN G. BULLOCK,
> HARRY G. R. PHILP,
>> Trustees Under the Will of
>> Arthur Letts, Deceased.

S. F. MACFARLANE,
Attorney for Trustees and Petitioners. [74]

STATE OF CALIFORNIA,
COUNTY OF LOS ANGELES.—ss.

ARTHUR LETTS, JR., MALCOLM Mc-
NAGHTEN, HAROLD JANSS, J. G. BULLOCK
and HARRY G. R. PHILP, each being first duly
sworn, says:

That he is one of the Trustees making the foregoing Account and Report; that he has read said
Account and Report and knows the contents thereof; that all statements therein made are true of
his own knowledge; that each item of expenditure
therein set forth was actually paid out at the time
and place and to the person as therein specifically
stated, and that the same contains a full and true
statement of all charges against said Trustees and
all of the credits to which they are entitled on
account of said trust.

> ARTHUR LETTS, Jr.
> MALCOLM McNAGHTEN,
> HAROLD JANSS,
> JOHN G. BULLOCK,
> HARRY G. R. PHILP.

Subscribed and sworn to before me this 4th day
of October, 1928.

(SEAL)   WM. J. WALTERS,
            Notary Public in and for the County of
            Los Angeles, State of California.

[75]

EXHIBIT A

PROPERTY ACQUIRED BY TRUSTEES UNDER DECREE OF DISTRIBUTION.

Description	Appraised Value
Holmby Corporation stock, 69,168 shares @ 97.46	$6,741,113.28
One-half interest in assets as follows:	
Al Maliakah Auditorium Co. stock, 20 sh. @ 27.00	270.00
California Savings Bank stock, (50 sh. @ 10.00—$250.00) Liq. No Value in Final Account of Est.	
Sinaloa Realty Co. stock, 1099 shares	5.00
Sinaloa Land & Water Co. stock, 56 shares	5.00
Delta Farms Reclamation Dist. #2028 bonds, $8000 par. V	4,060.00
Note of Bohemian Club, S. F. for $100.00	50.00
Note of Burwell Syndicate for $2500.00	1,250.00
Note of Community Dev. Assn. for $500 and int. of $87.50	293.75
Note of Richard E. Letts for $125 and int. of $11.25	68.12
Note of Roy R. Musser for $13,150 and $500	1,000.00
Note of W. H. Steele for $3500.00	1,750.00

Description	Appraised Value
Account against Mrs. F. H. Shatto for $1100.00	550.00
Beneficial Int. in Trust #308, Pac. S. W. Tr. & Sav. B.	27,553.23
Beneficial Int. in Trust #3413, Pac. S. W. Tr. & Sav. B.	4,250.00
Beneficial Interest in Trust #S-2799, Title Ins. & Trust Company	1,171.04
Tournament of Roses Assn. Certificate	50.00
Eagle Waters Golf Club Membership	250.00
Flintridge Country Club Membership	775.00
Los Angeles Athletic Club Membership	350.00
Portion of Lot 2, Holland Tract	2,750.00
Portion of Lot 25, W. portion of Lick Tract	1,500.00
Parts of Lots 62 and 63, Cumberland Tract	1,500.00
Lots 383, 384, 389, 390, 391, 392, 393, Hollywood Cemetery	No Value
Beneficial Interest in Trust #P-5460, Edstrom	No Value
Note of W. H. Moore for $6580.00	No Value
Note of K. William Curtis for $100.00	No Value

Description	Appraised Value
Note of H. Cecil Ecclestone for $500.00	No Value
Note of F. O. Conners for $125.00	No Value
California Delta Farms Inc. Int. in Stock Syndicate, 60 shares	No Value
No appraised value—Value in Final Accounting of Estate	390.00
	$6,790,954.42
Cash subsequently received from Estate	8,859.90
	$6,799,814.32

[76]

EXHIBIT B

PRINCIPAL TRANSACTIONS

Increase of Corpus	Appraised Value	Amount Received	

1925

Sept. 26,

  Flintridge Country
Club, One-half in-
terest in a member-
ship sold $ 775.00 $ 800.00 $

1927

May 17,

  Holmby Corporation
Capital Distribu-
tion, 19,207 Shares
Cancelled, Appraised
@ 97.46 per sh.   1,871,914.22
Taken up @ 100.00
per sh.   1,920,700.00

Oct. 11,

  Holmby Corporation
Capital Distribu-
tion, 38,931 shares
Cancelled. Ap-
praised @ 97.46
per sh.   3,794,215.26
Taken up @ 100.00
per sh.   3,893,100.00

Increase of Corpus	Appraised Value	Amount Received	I
1926			
June 3,			
Cash received from Income Tax Refund Under Arthur Letts Returns for 1921-1922		5,089.87	
1927			
Nov. 16,			
City and County of San Francisco Water Bonds Purchased at	15,836.00		
Amortization taken prior to sale	18.71		
	15,817.29	15,836.00	
			$15

reas·

25/

EXHIBIT C.
INCOME RECEIPTS.

1925

Sept. 8,	Dividend—Holmby Corporation—69,168 sh. @ 37½	$ 25,938.00
Dec. 1,	Dividend—Holmby Corporation—69,168 sh. @ 37½	25,938.00

1926

Feb. 4,	Interest 9/17/25-2/1/26 $57,000 Sanitary Dist. of Chicago bonds 4%—6 mos.	842.02
Mar. 2,	Dividend—Holmby Corporation—69,168 sh. @ .75	51,876.00
June 1,	Dividend—Holmby Corporation—69,168 sh. @ 2.25	155,628.00
3,	Interest—Cert. of Deposit—$735.56—6 mos. 4%	14.71
Aug. 3,	Interest to 8/1/26—$57,000 Sanitary Dist. of Chicago bonds, 6 mos. 4%	1,140.00
8,	Interest, Cert. of Deposit—$297.98, 6 mos. 4%	5.95
Sept. 1,	Dividend—Holmby Corporation, 69,168 sh. @ 1.50	103,752.00
Dec. 1,	Dividend—Holmby Corporation, 69,168 sh. @ 1.50	103,752.00
11,	Interest 6/14-12/1/26 $5000 Sanitary Dist. of Chicago bonds—4½%, 6 mos.	104.37
21,	Interest, Cert. of Deposit, $712.43—6 mos. 4%	14.25

1927

Feb. 7,	Interest, Cert. of Deposit, $297.98—6 mos. 4%	5.95

1927

8,	Dividend—Holmby Corporation, 69,168 sh. @ $13.00	
	U. S. Treasury Certificates $881,372.80	
·	Accrued Interest 16,860.80	
	Cash 950.40	899,184.00
9,	Interest to 2/1—$57,000 Sanitary Dist. of Chicago bonds, 4%	1,140.00
Mar. 15,	Interest to 3/15/27—$880,-000 U. S. Treasury Certificates, 4¾%	4,039.20
19,	Dividend—Holmby Corporation—69,168 sh. @ .93	64,326.24
June 2,	Interest—5/24-6/1/27—$40,-000 City of San Diego Sutherland Dam Bonds 4½%	35.00
	Interest—5/24-6/3/27—$50,-000. Fresno School Dist. Bonds, 5%	62.50
4,	Interest to 6/1/27—$5000. Sanitary Dist of Chicago Bonds—4½%—6 mos.	112.50
8,	Dividend—Holmby Corporation, 49,961 sh. @ 1.50	74,941.50
16,	Interest—Cert. of Deposit —$712.43—6 mos. 4%	14.25
July 1,	Interest—5/23-7/1/27—$15,-000 City and Co. San Francisco Water Bonds —4½%	71.25

1927

July   1,   Interest—5/23-7/1/27—$25,-
000. Oakland High School
Bonds, 5%   131.94

Interest—5/23-7/1/27—$40,-
000. San Luis Obispo Co.
Highway bonds—5%   211.11

Interest—5/24-7/1/27—$80,-
000. East Bay Mun. Util-
ity Water bonds—5%   411.11

Interest—5/24-7/1/27—$100,-
000 Federal Land Bank
bonds—4¼%   436.81

Interest—5/17-7/1/27—$375,-
000. Federal Land Bank
bonds—4¼%   7,968.75

Interest to 7/1—6 mos. $6,-
000. L. A. Co. Flood Con-
trol Bonds—5%   150.00

Interest to 7/1—6 mos. $13,-
000. L. A. Co. Hall of Jus-
tice bonds—5%   325.00

Interest to 7/1—6 mos. $7,-
000. L. A. Hall of Justice
bonds—5%   175.00

Interest 6/2-7/1—$25,000.)
City   of   Sacramento)
bonds—4%   )

Interest 6/6-7/1—$60,000.)   278.12
City   of   Sacramento)
bonds—4%   )

[78]

1927

July 1,	Interest to 7/2—6 mos. $11,-000. L. A. County Flood Control Bonds—5%	$275.00
	Interest to 7/2—6 mos. $8,-000. L. A. County Flood Control Bonds—5%	200.00
Aug. 1,	Interest to 8/1—6 mos. $57,-000. Sanitary Dist. of Chicago bonds—4%	1,140.00
	Interest 5/24 — 8/1/27 $400,000. State of Calif. Veterans Welfare bonds —4½%	3,350.00
	Interest to 8/1—6 mos. $6,-000. City of L. A. Electric Plant Bonds—5%	150.00
	Interest to 8/1—6 mos. $5,-000. City of Pasadena Civic Center bonds—5%	125.00
	Interest to 8/1—6 mos. $25,-000. L. A. High School bonds, 5%	625.00
	Interest to 8/1—6 mos. $24,-000. L. A. City School bonds, 5%	600.00
	Interest to 8/1—6 mos. $17,-000. L. A. City School bonds, 5%	425.00

1927

Aug. 2,	Interest—Cert. of Deposit— $297.98—6 mos. 4%	5.96
Sept. 1,	Interest 5/24—9/1/27— $100,000—City & Co. of San Francisco School bonds—5%	1,347.22
	Interest to 9/1—6 mos. $5,-000. L. A. High School bonds, 4¾%	118.75
	Interest to 9/1—6 mos. $31,-000. L. A. City School bonds, 4¾%	736.25
	Interest to 9/1—6 mos. $17,-000. L. A. City School bonds, 4¾%	403.75
Sept. 2,	Dividend—Holmby Corporation — 49,961 sh. @ $1.50	74,941.50
17,	Interest to 9/15—6 mos. $600. U. S. A. Third Liberty Loan—4¼%	12.78
Oct. 31,	Interest to 10/15—6 mos. $300. U. S. A. Fourth Liberty Loan—4¼%	6.37
Nov. 1,	Interest 5/23 — 11/1/27— $50,000. Alameda County Hospital bonds—5%	1,097.22
	Interest 5/23 — 11/1/27—) $25,000. Federal Land) Bank Bonds—4¼%)	

1927

Nov. 1,	Interest 5/24—11/1/27—) $200,000. Federal Land) Bank bonds—4¼%) Interest 5/27 — 11/1/27—) · $50,000. Federal Land) Bank bonds—4¼%)	5,082.29
16,	Interest 7/1-11/16/27—$15,- 000. City & Co. San Francisco Water Bonds— 4½%	251.25
	Interest to 11/15—6 mos. $100. U. S. A. Second Liberty Loan, 4¼%	2.12
29,	Interest 7/1-11/29/27—$6,- 000. L. A. Co. Flood Control Bonds—5%	123.33
	Interest 7/1-11/29/27—$20,- 000. L. A. Co. Hall of Justice bonds—5%	411.11
	Interest 8/1-11/29/27—$25,- 000. L. A. High School bonds—5%	409.72
	Interest 9/1-11/29/27—$5,- 000. L. A. High School bonds—4¾%	58.06
	Interest 8/1-11/29/27—$5,- 000. City of Pasadena bonds—5%	81.94

1927

Nov. 29, Interest 9/1-11/29/27—$48,-
000. L. A. City School
bonds—4¾%   557.33

[79]

Interest 8/1-11/29/27—$6,-
000. L. A. Electric Plant
bonds, 5%   98.33

Interest 7/2-11/29/27—$19,-
000. L. A. Co. Flood Con-
trol bonds—5%   387.92

Interest 8/1-11/29/27—$41,-
000. L. A. City School
bonds—5%   671.94

Dec. 1,   Dividend—Holmby Corporation—11,030 sh. @ $6.50   71,695.00

Interest to 12/1—6 mos. $5,-
000. Sanitary Dist. of
Chicago bonds—4½%   112.50

Interest to 12/1—6 mos.
$40,000. City of San Di-
ego S. Dam bonds—4½%   900.00

Interest to 12/3—6 mos.
$50,000. Fresno School
Dist. bonds—5%   1,250.00

Interest 11/14—12/1/27—
$100,000. State of Mis-
souri Road bonds—4¼%   200.69

Interest 11/22-12/1/27—
$100,000. Cook Co. Ills.
Rd. & Br. bonds—4%   100.00

1927

Dec. 1,   Interest   11/28-12/1/27—
           $100,000. Cook Co. Ills.
           Rd. & Br. bonds—4%   33.33
           Interest   11/28-12/1/27—
           · $10,000. City of San Di-
           ego water bonds—4½%   3.75

1928

Jan. 1,   Interest   7/21-12/15/27—
           $10,000. City & Co. of
           Honolulu bonds—5%   200.00
           Interest to 1/1—6 mos.—
           $25,000. Oakland High
           School bonds—5%   625.00
           Interest to 1/1—6 mos.—
           $40,000.00 San Luis
           Obispo Co. Highway
           bonds—5%   1,000.00
           Interest to 1/1—6 mos.—
           $80,000. East Bay Mun.
           Utility Dist. bonds—5%   2,000.00
           Interest to 1/1—6 mos.—
           $475,000. Federal Land
           Bank bonds—4¼%   10,093.75
           Interest to 1/1/28—6 mos.)
           —$85,000. City of Sac-)
           ramento bonds—4½%   )
           Interest—11/7/27-1/1/28—)   2,351.25
           $65,000. City of Sacra-)
           mento bonds—4½%   )

1927

Jan. 1,   Interest   11/8/27-1/1/28—
           $50,000. Oakland School
           Dist. bonds—5%   368.05
           Interest   11/8/27-1/1/28—
           $25,000.   Oakland   High
           School bonds—5%   184.03
           Interest 11/10/27 to 1/2/28
           —$100,000. L. -A. Flood
           Control bonds—5%
           Interest 11/15/27 to 1/2/28
           —$100,000. L. A. Flood
           Control bonds—5%   1,375.00
           Interest   11/10/27-1/1/28—
           $100,000.   Kansas   City,
           Mo., School bonds—4½%   637.49
           Interest   11/10/27-1/1/28—
           $100,000.   City of New
           York bonds—4¼%   602.08
           Interest   11/14/27-1/1/28—
           $70,000. East Bay Mun.
           Utility bonds—5%   456.95
           Interest   11/28/27-1/1/28—
           $100,000.   Oakland High
           School bonds—5%   458.33
           Interest   11/28/27-1/1/28—
           $10,000. San Luis Obispo
           Co. Highway bonds—5%   45.83

1927

Jan. 1,	Interest 11/14/27-1/1/28—) $20,000. East Bay Mun.) Utility bonds—5%)	
	Interest 11/28/27-1/1/28—) $30,000. East Bay Mun.) Utility bonds—5%)	236.11 [80]
	Interest on Term Accounts to 12/31/27, Security Trust & Savings Bank	170.59
	Interest 11/15/27-1/1/28— $100,000. City of Phila- delphia bonds, 4¼%	543.22
Jan. 13,	Interest 11/8/27-1/15/28— $40,000. Multnomah Co., Ore. bonds—4½%	335.00
Febr. 1,	Interest to 2/1—6 Mos. $57,- 000. Sanitary Dist. of Chicago bonds—4%	1,140.00
	Interest 11/7/27-2/1/28— $100,000. City of Long Beach Harbor bonds—5%	1,166.67
	Interest 11/7/27-2/1/28— $100,000. City of Pasa- dena bonds—4½%	1,050.00
	Interest to 2/1—6 mos. $400,000. State of Calif. Veterans Welfare bonds —4½%	9,000.00
	Interest 11/10/27—2/1/28 —$50,000. State of Calif.	

1927

	Veterans Welfare bonds —4½%	506.25
Febr. 1,	Interest 11/10/27-2/1/28— $50,000. State of Calif. Veterans Welfare bonds —4¼%	478.12
	Interest 11/14/27-2/1/28— $200,000. State of Calif. Veterans Welfare bonds —4%	1,711.11
	Interest 11/8/27-2/1/28— $100,000. City of Portland, Ore. bonds—4%	922.22
	Interest 11/7/27-2/1/28— $300,000. State of Calif. Veterans Welfare bonds —4¼%	2,975.01
Mar. 1,	Interest to 3/1—6 mos. $100,000 City & Co. San Francisco School bonds —5%	2,500.00
	Interest 11/8/27-3/1/28— $60,000. Multnomah Co. Ore. Br. bonds—4½%	847.50
	Interest 11/10/27-3/1/28— $50,000. City & Co. San Francisco School bonds— 5%	770.83
	Interest 11/23/27-3/1/28— $100,000 City of Pittsburgh bonds—4¼%	1,156.94

1927

Mar. 1,   Interest   11/28/27-3/1/28—
            $100,000 City of Omaha
            bonds—5%   1,291.67
            Interest   11/28/27-3/1/28—
            · $100,000 City of Newark,
            N. J. bonds—4¼%   1,097.92
            Dividend—Holmby Corpo-
            ration, 11,030 sh. @ 6.50   71,695.00

Mar. 15,   Interest 11/10/27-3/15/28—
            $100,000. City of Detroit
            bonds—4¼%   1,475.70
            Interest to 3/15—6 mos.
            $600. U. S. A. Third
            Liberty Loan Bonds—
            4¼%   12.72

Apr. 1,   Interest   11/10/27-4/1/28—
            $50,000 State of Oregon
            Highway bonds—4¼%   832.29
            Interest   11/10/27-4/1/28—
            $25,000 State of Oregon
            Highway bonds—4½%   440.62
            Interest   11/14/27-4/1/28—
            $38,000 Sanitary Dist. of
            Chicago bonds—4¼%   614.60
            Interest   11/10/27-4/1/28—
            $25,000 State of Oregon
            Veterans Aid bonds—
            4¼%   416.14
            Interest   11/28/27-4/1/28—
            $100,000 City of St. Louis,
            Mo. bonds—4%   1,366.67

1927
Apr. 15,   Interest   12/2/27-4/15/28—
             $50,000 City of Beverly
             Hills bonds—4¼%   785.07
             Interest to 4/15—6 mos.
             $300. U. S. A. Fourth
             Liberty Loan bonds—
             4¼%   6.36
                                                      [81]
1928
May 1,   Interest to 5/1—6 mos.—
             $50,000 Alameda County
             Hospital bonds—5%   1,250.00
             Interest to 5/1—6 mos.
             $275,000 Federal Land
             Bank bonds—4¼%   5,843.75
             Interest   11/8/27-5/1/28—
             $200,000 City of L. A.
             Electric Plant bonds—
             4½%   4,325.00
             Interest 11/10/27-5/1/28—
             $200,000 State of Illinois
             Highway bonds—4%   3,799.34
                                                  _____

                                                 $1,832,176.12
             Less Amortization of Pre-
             mium on Bonds   7,546.12
                                                  _____

             Total Income Receipts $1,824,630.00
                                                 ============

                                                      [82]

EXHIBIT D
Principal Transactions

se of Corpus	Appraised Value	Amount Received	Decrease
L. A. Athletic Club one-half interest in a membership sold	$ 350.00	$ 300.00	$ 50.00

Bonds received from Holmby Corporation as Capital Distribution sold Nov. 29, 1927 at less than value at which received.—

Bonds	Value at Which Received	
City of Los Angeles Electric Plant, 5%	6,126.60	6,031.86
Los Angeles County Hall of Justice, 5%	20,477.00	20,215.44
Los Angeles County Flood Control, 5%	25,603.40	25,276.71
Los Angeles City School Dist., 4¾%	48,738.70	48,337.70
Los Angeles City School Dist. 5%	41,914.60	41,383.80
Los Angeles High School Dist. 4¾%	5,075.00	5,024.75
Los Angeles High School Dist. 5%	25,562.50	25,377.00
Pasadena City Civic Center 5%	5,105.50	5,026.55
	$178,603.30	$176,673.81
Amortization previously taken		1,516.21
		$178,190.02	413.28

$463.28

EXHIBIT E.

INCOME DISBURSEMENTS.

1925

Sept. 8,	Distribution to Beneficiary, Arthur Letts, Jr..............	$ 7,781.40
	" " " Edna L. McNaghten..............	7,781.40
	" " " Gladys Janss	7,781.40
	" " " Letts Foundation	2,593.80
Oct. 22,	Rent of Safety Deposit Box..............	6.00
Dec. 1,	Distribution to Beneficiary, Arthur Letts, Jr.............	7,614.75
	" " " Edna L. McNaghten..............	7,614.75
	" " " Gladys Janss	7,614.75
	" " " Letts Foundation	2,593.80
	7, Minute Book..............	5.40
	Letterheads, envelopes and checks..............	12.30
	10, L. A. Athletic Club, Christmas fund..............	2.50

1926

Jan. 8,	Excise Tax—Flintridge Country Club Membership....	7.50
	18, Ledger and Journal binders..............	33.98

Feb. 4,	Collection and safekeeping charge on bonds at bank			14.25
Mar. 2,	Distribution to Beneficiary, Arthur Letts, Jr.			15,750.00
	"	"	Edna L. McNaghten	15,750.00
	"	"	Gladys Janss	15,750.00
	"	"	Letts Foundation	5,187.60
	"	"	Letts Foundation	64.69
Apr. 16,	Excise Tax, L. A. Athletic Club Membership			4.20
June 1,	Distribution to Beneficiary, Arthur Letts, Jr.			46,688.40
	"	"	Edna L. McNaghten	46,688.40
	"	"	Gladys Janss	46,688.40
	"	"	Letts Foundation	15, 380
Aug. 3,	Collection and safekeeping charge on bonds at bank			14.25
	Eagle Waters Golf Club, dues 1926			19.25
Sept. 1,	Distribution to Beneficiary, Arthur Letts, Jr.			31,467.74
	"	"	Edna L. McNaghten	31,467.74
	"	"	Gladys Janss	31,467.74
	"	"	Letts Foundation	10, 424

EXHIBIT E (continued).

1926		
Dec. 1,	Distribution to Beneficiary, Arthur Letts, Jr.	31,125.60
"	" " Edna L. McNaghten	31,125.60
"	" " Gladys Janss	31,125.60
"	" " Letts Foundation	10,375.20
7,	Flintridge Country Club, Christmas Fund	2.50
	Telegram	.72
	Los Angeles Athletic Club, Christmas Fund	2.50
	Collection and safekeeping charge on bonds at bank	1.25
1927		
Jan. 10,	Excise Tax—Flintridge Country Club membership	7.50
Feb. 9,	Collection and safekeeping charge on bonds at bank	14.25
Mar. 15,	Distribution to Beneficiary, Arthur Letts, Jr.	270,892.85
"	" " Edna L. McNaghten	270,892.85
"	" " Gladys Janss	270,892.85
"	" " Letts Foundation	90,297.60

19,	Distribution to Beneficiary, Arthur Letts, Jr.			19,297.87
"	"	"	Edna L. McNaghten	19,297.87
"	"	"	Gladys Janss	19,297.87
"	"	"	Letts Foundation	6,432.62
Apr. 14,	Excise Tax, L. A. Athletic Club membership			4.20
May 25,	Rent of Safe Deposit box			61.00
				[84]
June 3,	Personal Property Tax, 1927			170.13
4,	Collection and safekeeping charge on bonds at bank			1.25
6,	Rent of Safe Deposit box, additional			40.00
8,	Distributions to Beneficiary, Arthur Letts, Jr.			22,482.45
"	"	"	Edna L. McNaghten	22,482.45
"	"	"	Gladys Janss	22,482.45
"	"	"	Letts Foundation	7,494.15
July 1,	Rule & Sons, Inc., Premium on All Risk Insurance on bonds:			
	$635,000.00 1 year		$806.79	
	140,000.00 1 year		185.68	
				992.47

EXHIBIT E (continued).

1927

Holmby Corp., Premium on All Risk Insurance on bonds:		
$1,200,000.00 July 1, 1927-Feb. 7, 1928..............	1,000.00
Office Services, Wm. J. Walters, June..............	25.00
Ledger and Journal sheets..............	44.00
Stationery	8.25
Distribution to Beneficiary, Arthur Letts, Jr..........	2,550.00
" " " Edna L. McNaghten..........	2,550.00
" " " Gladys Janss	2,550.00
" " " Letts Foundation	850.00
July 13, Eagle Waters Golf Club, Dues..............	25.00
Aug. 1, Distribution to Beneficiary, Arthur Letts, Jr..........	1,233.55
" " " Edna L. McNaghten..........	1,233.55
" " " Gladys Janss	1,233.55
" " " Letts Foundation	411.18
Office Services, Wm. J. Walters, July..........	25.00

31,	Office Services, Wm. J. Walters, Aug.	25.00
Sept. 2,	Distribution to Beneficiary, Arthur Letts, Jr.	23,120.46
"	" Edna L. McNaghten	23,120.46
"	" Gladys Janss	23,120.46
"	" Letts Foundation	7,706.92
16,	Excise Tax, Eagle Waters Golf Club membership	2.50
30,	Office Services, Wm. J. Walters, Sept.	25.00
Oct. 21,	Tax of Insurance premiums on ⎰ his, pd. 7/1/27	476
31,	Office Services, Wm. J. Walters, Oct.	25.00
Nov. 1,	Distribution to Beneficiary, Athur Letts, Jr.	1,784.62
"	" Edna L. McN ght ʀ	1,784.62
"	" ʀs Janss	1,784.62
"	" Letts Foundation	536.98
28,	Rent of Safe Deposit Box	100.00
Dec. 1,	Distribution to Beneficiary, Arthur Letts, Jr.	22,171.70
"	" Edna L. McNaghten	22,171.70
"	" Gladys Janss	22,171.70
"	" Letts Foundation	7,390.55
	Office Services, Wm. J. Walters, Nov.	25.00

EXHIBIT E (continued).

1928
Jan. 1, Distribution to Beneficiary, Arthur Letts, Jr............. 5,500.00
　　　" 　" 　" 　Edna L. McNaghten............. 5,500.00
　　　" 　" 　" 　Gladys Janss 5,500.00
　　　" 　" 　" 　Letts Foundation 1,830.00
　　Office Services, Wm. J. Walters, Dec............. 25.00
　　Los Angeles Athletic Club, Contribution............. 1.00
　　Office Supplies............. 2.10

[85]

Jan. 26, Telegram 1.22
Aronson Gale Ins. Agency, Premium on All Risk Insurance on bonds:
　　$1,065,000.00 1 year............. 1,318.73
Rule & Sons, Inc., Premium on All Risk insurance on bonds:
　　$2,575,000.00 1 year............. 2,889.29
Feb. 1, Distribution to Beneficiary, Arthur Letts, Jr............. 3,600.00
　　　" 　" 　Edna L. McNaghten............. 3,600.00

	"	"	Gladys Janss	3,600.00
	"	"	Letts Foundation	1,200.00
	Office Services, Wm. J. Walters, January	25.00
	Office Supplies	1.95
	Bond files	68.40
	Johnson & Higgins, Premium on All Risk Insurance on bonds: $500,000.00 one year	625.00
Feb. 8,	Telegram	.77
	Eagle Waters Golf Club Assessment	50.00
29,	Office Services, Wm. J. Walters, February	25.00
	Johnson & Higgins, Premium on All Risk insurance on bonds: $1,200.00 one year	1,500.00
Mar. 1,	Distribution to Beneficiary, Arthur Letts, Jr.	23,890.26
	"	"	Edna L. McNaghten	23,890.26
	"	"	Gladys Janss	23,890.26
	"	"	Letts Foundation	7,963.43
Apr. 1,	Distribution to Beneficiary, Arthur Letts, Jr.	1,454.83
	"	"	Edna L. McNaghten	1,454.83
	"	"	Gladys Janss	1,454.83
	"	"	Letts Foundation	484.93

EXHIBIT E (continued).

1928				
	ffice Services, Wm. J. Walters, March..........			25.00
6,	Seyler Day Co., Premium on All Risk Insurance on bonds:			
	$500,000.00 one year.................			643.75
May 1,	ffice Services, Wm. J. Walters, April.......			25.00
	Distribution to Beneficiary, Arthur Letts, Jr....			5,268.40
	" " " Edna L. McNaghten.			3.40
	" " " Gladys Janss			5,268.40
	" " " Letts Foundation			1,714.42
	TOTAL INCOME DISBURSEMENTS......			$1,822,321.67
	INCOME CHARGE			
1927				
Mar. 15,	Loss on U. S. Treasury Certificates received as a			
	dividend from Holmby Corporation, Feb. 8, 1927,			
	at a value of	$881,272.80		
	Matured at par of.................	880,000.00		1,372.80
				$1,823,694.47

INCOME ACCOUNT

Income Receipts:
Dividends:
  Holmby Corporation $1,723,667.24
Interest:
  Bonds $108,277.22
  Less Amortization of Premium   7,546.12
                                        _____
                                        100,731.10
  Bank Accounts, Certificates of Deposits   231.66   100,962.76
                                                        _____
Total Income Receipts $1,824,630.00
                                                        =============

Income Disbursements:
Operating Expenses:
  Office Expense, Rent of Safety Deposit
    Boxes, etc.   917.09
  Insurance on bonds   8,969.24
  Taxes   230.79 $ 10,117.12
                                                       _____

EXHIBIT F (continued).

Loss on U. S. Treasury Certificates received
as a dividend from Holmby Corporation

at a value of	881,372.80	
Matured at par value of	880,000.00	
		1,372.80

Distributions to Beneficiaries:

Arthur Letts, Jr.	543,674.88	
Edna I. McNaghten (Florence Edna Letts McNaghten)	543,674.88	
Gladys Janss (Gladys Letts Janss)	543,674.88	
Letts Foundation	181,179.91	
		1,812,204.55

Total Income Disbursements and Charges	$1,823,694.47
Undistributed Income	935.53
	$1,824,630.00

[87]

EXHIBIT G

PROPERTY HELD BY TRUSTEES AS OF MAY 1, 1928

Assets		Appraised Value	Cost
STOCKS:			
Holmby Corporation 11,030 shares @ $97.46		$1,074,983.80	
BONDS:			
As per schedule attached	$5,837,493.98		
Less amortization of premium	6,011.20		$5,831,482.78
Prepaid Accrued Interest			2,779.16
CASH:			
Citizens National Tr. & Savings Bank, Commercial Account	160.93		
Security Trust & Sav. Bank, Term Account	43,381.50		43,542.43

EXHIBIT G (continued).

ACCOUNTS RECEIVABLE:
Mrs. Florence M. Quinn   2.50

MISCELLANEOUS:
One-half interest in Lots 383, 384, 389, 390, 391, 392, 393, Hollywood Cemetery,   No Value
Tournament of Roses Cert. No. 413   50.00
Eagle Waters Golf Club Membership   250.00

    $1,075,283.80 $5,877,806.87

Balance chargeable to next Account Current $6,953,090.67

[88]

EXHIBIT H.

SCHEDULE OF BONDS HELD BY TRUSTEES AS OF MAY 1, 1928

Description Rate Basis Maturity Par Value Cost
(Details Omitted)

	Par Value	Cost
Total	$5,510,900.00	$5,837,493.98

[89]

EXHIBIT I.

CHANGES A/C CONVERSION OF CORPUS

	Appraised Value	Amount Received
1925		
Aug. 20, Sale to Holmby Corporation for cash		
One-half interest in assets as follows:		
Al Mal cah Aditorium Co. stock............$	270.00	$ 270.00
Sinaloa Realty Co. s tok...................	5.00	5.00
Sinaloa Land & Water Co. stock..........	5.00	5.00
Delta Farms Recl. Dist. #2028, bonds....	4,060.00	4,060.00
Note of Bohemian 16b, S. F.............	50.00	50.00
Note of Burwell Syndicate...............	1,250.00	1,250.00
Note of Community Dev. Assn...........	2375	293.75
Note of Richard E. Letts...............	68.12	68.12
Notes of Roy R. Musser................	1,000.00	1,000.00
Notes of W. H. Steele.................	1,750.00	1,750.00
dunt against Mrs. F. H. Shatto.........	550.00	550.00
Beneficial Interest in Tr. 308, Pac.		
S. W. Tr. & Sav. Bank............	27,553.23	27,553.23

Beneficial Interest in Tr. 3413,		
Pac. S. W. Tr. & Sav. Bank............	4,250.00	4,250.00
Beneficial Interest in Tr. S-2799,		
Title Insurance & Trust Co..........	1,171.04	1,171.04
Portion Lot 2, Holland Tract........	2,750.00	2,750.00
Portion Lot 25, Lick Tract..........	1,500.00	1,500.00
Portion Lots 62 and 63, Cumberland Tr......	1,500.00	1,500.00
	$ 48,026.14	$ 48,026.14
California Delta Farms, Inc. stock		
60 shares, No appraised value,		
Value Final Accounting of Estate...	390.00	390.00
	$ 48,416.14	$ 48,416.14

1927
May 17, Holmby Corporation Capital Distribution

Cash and Securities received in lieu of 19,207 shares of stock turned in and cancelled @ $100.00 per share........................ ...$1,920,700.00

EXHIBIT I (continued).

Cash

	$1,362,358.40
City of Los Angeles Elec. Plant 5% Bonds.....	6,126.60
Los Angeles Co. Hall of Justice 5% Bonds.....	20,477.00
Los Angeles Co. Flood Control 5% Bonds.....	25,603.40
Los Angeles City School 4¾% Bonds.........	48,738.70
Los Angeles City School 5% Bonds.........	41,941.60
Los Angeles High School 4¾% Bonds.........	5,075.00
Los Angeles High School 5% Bonds.........	25,562.50
Pasadena City Civic Center 5% Bonds.........	5,105.50
U. S. A. Liberty Loan 4¼% Bonds.........	1,006.20
Federal Land Bank 4½% Bonds.........	378,750.00
	$1,920,717.90

Refund in cash of excess of value of securities and cash received over par value of Holmby Corporation stock cancelled.................   17.90

$1,920,700.00

shares of stock of Bullock's at a value of $50.00 per share or $3,893,100.00, received in exchange for 38,931 sh. of Holmby Corporation turned in and cancelled at par, or $100.00, ... $3,893,100.00

Nov. 4, Cash reed from sale of 77,862 sh. of Bullock's stock at $50.00 per share 3,893,100.00

Cash received invested in bonds as per "Exhibit H".

Cash received from Estate of Arthur Letts, Dec.	$	8,859.90
" " " Holmby Corporation.......		48, 4614
" " " "		1,362,358.40
" " " sale of Bullock's stock.....		3,893,100.00
" " " sale of bonds		176,673.81
		$5,489,408.25

(NOTE: The total of bonds as stated in "Exhibit H," is $5,837,493.98
Of this amount there was received from Holmby Corporation as stated above............. 378,750.00

$5,458,743.98
...... 30,664.27

Balance in cash in bank....

EXHIBIT J.

We, ARTHUR LETTS, JR., FLORENCE EDNA LETTS McNAGHTEN, GLADYS LETTS JANSS, and LETTS FOUNDATION, a charitable corporation, hereby acknowledge that we have read the First Account Current and Report of Arthur Letts, Jr., Malcolm McNaghten, Harold Janss, J. G. Bullock and Harry G. R. Philp, as Trustees under the Will of Arthur Letts, Deceased, to which this statement is attached, and as beneficiaries under said trust we acknowledge receipt of the sums shown by said account as having been distributed to us, respectively, and we hereby approve of all the acts of the Trustees as shown by the said account and Report.

EXECUTED at Los Angeles, California, on the 31st day of July, 1928.

Arthur Letts, Jr.,
Florence Edna Letts McNaghten,
Gladys Letts Janss,
LETTS FOUNDATION,
By Arthur Letts, Jr.,
President.
Malcolm McNaghten,
Secretary.

(Seal)   [92]

(ENDORSED) No. 62,249.

FIRST ACCOUNT CURRENT AND REPORT OF ARTHUR LETTS, JR., MALCOLM Mc-NAGHTEN, HAROLD JANSS, J. G. BULLOCK· and HARRY G. R. PHILP, as Trustees Under the Will of ARTHUR LETTS, Deceased.

FILED OCT. 9, 1928.

> L. E. LAMPTON, County Clerk,
> By C. E. Clough.

Los Angeles, Cal., OCT. 9, 1928.

The hearing of the within petition for SETTLEMENT OF ACCOUNT CURRENT is hereby set for the 5 day of NOV., 1928, at 2 o'clock P. M., in Dep't. 1 of the Superior Court of Los Angeles County, California.

> L. E. LAMPTON, County Clerk,
> By N. P. Grant, Deputy Clerk.
> (SEAL)

[93]

(Probate Form 48)

No. 62,249

STATE OF CALIFORNIA,
COUNTY OF LOS ANGELES.—ss.

I, L. E. LAMPTON, County Clerk and ex-officio clerk of the Superior Court within and for the county and state aforesaid, do hereby certify the foregoing to be a full, true and correct copy of the original First Account Current and Report of Arthur Letts, Jr., Malcolm McNaghten, Harold Janss, J. G. Bullock and Harry G. R. Philp, as trustees under the will of Arthur Letts, deceased, with Exhibits "A", "B", "C", "D", "E", "F", "G", "H", "I", and "J", in the Matter of the Estate of ARTHUR LETTS, deceased, as the same appear of record, and that I have carefully compared the same with the original.

IN WITNESS WHEREOF, I have hereunto set my hand and affixed the seal of the Superior Court, this 30th day of August, 1933.

(SEAL)   L. E. LAMPTON, County Clerk,
              by R. ZUCKERMAN (Sgd)
                                    Deputy.
                                    [94]

EXHIBIT "C".

On November 5, 1928, in department one of the Superior Court of the State of California in and for the County of Los Angeles, Hon. Walter J. Desmond, Judge, presiding, the following proceedings were had, to-wit:

IN THE MATTER OF THE ESTATE
OF ARTHUR LETTS, Deceased.

No. 62,249

ORDER SETTLING FIRST ACCOUNT CURRENT OF TRUSTEES.

The first account current and report herein of Arthur Letts, Jr., Malcolm McNaghten, Harold

Janss, J. G. Bullock and Harry G. R. Philp, as trustees under the will of Arthur Letts, deceased, by S. F. MacFarlane, their attorney, coming on regularly this 5th day of November, 1928, for hearing and settlement by the Court, showing after deducting the credits to which said trustees are entitled, a balance of $6,953,090.67 belonging to said estate, and no person appearing to except to or contest said account and report, and the evidence having been heard, it is ordered, adjudged and decreed by the Court that said account and report be in all respects approved, allowed and settled as rendered; and that the sum of $1000.00 be allowed said attorney for services rendered said estate.

The foregoing instrument is a correct copy of the original as the same appears of record attest September 22, 1933.

> L. E. LAMPTON, County Clerk
> and Clerk of the Superior Court
> in and for the County of Los
> Angeles, State of California.
> By (Signed) L. J. MILLER,
> Deputy.

(SEAL)

[95]

Petitioner, Arthur Letts, Jr., tenders and presents the foregoing as a statement of evidence in this case and prays that the same be approved by

the United States Board of Tax Appeals and made
a part of the record in this case.

THOMAS R. DEMPSEY,
A. CALDER MACKAY,
Attorneys for Petitioner.
1104 Pacific Mutual Building,
Los Angeles, California.

The foregoing evidence is all of the evidence
adduced at the hearing before the United States
Board of Tax Appeals and the same is approved
by Robert H. Jackson, Assistant General Counsel
for the Bureau of Internal Revenue, as attorney
for the Commissioner of Internal Revenue.

Dated   , 1935.

ROBERT H. JACKSON,
Assistant General Counsel,
Bureau of Internal Revenue.

This statement of evidence is duly approved and
settled, this 27th day of March, 1935.

(Sgd) J. RUSSELL LEECH,
Member, United States Board of
Tax Appeals,

(Endorsed): Lodged March 12, 1935.
Filed March 27, 1935.

[96]

[Title of Court and Cause.]

PRAECIPE FOR TRANSCRIPT OF RECORD.

To the Clerk of the United States Board of Tax Appeals:

You will please prepare and certify to the clerk of the United States Circuit Court of Appeals for the Ninth Circuit within the time provided by the rules of that court in this respect, as extended, a transcript of record for review herein consisting of the following documents:

1. The docket entries of the proceedings before the United States Board of Tax Appeals.

2. All pleadings and exhibits attached thereto before the United States Board of Tax Appeals in this case.

3. Findings of fact, opinion and decision of the Board.

4. Motion to amend findings of fact and opinion.

5. Petition for review and notice of filing, with acknowledgment of service.

6. Statement of evidence, as settled and allowed.

7. Order enlarging time for the preparation of the evidence and for the transmission and delivery of the record.

8. This praecipe.

THOMAS R. DEMPSEY,
A. CALDER MACKAY,
Attorneys for Petitioner,
1104 Pacific Mutual Building,
Los Angeles, California.

Receipt of a copy of the foregoing is hereby acknowledged this 22nd day of March, 1935.

ROBERT H. JACKSON,
Assistant General Counsel for
the Bureau of Internal Revenue,
Attorney for Respondent.

(Endorsed): Filed Mar. 22, 1935.

[97]

[Title of Court and Cause.]

CERTIFICATE.

I, B. D. Gamble, clerk of the U. S. Board of Tax Appeals, do hereby certify that the foregoing pages, 1 to 97, inclusive, contain and are a true copy of the transcript of record, papers, and proceedings on file and of record in my office as called for by the Praecipe in the appeal (or appeals) as above numbered and entitled.

In testimony whereof, I hereunto set my hand and affix the seal of the United States Board of Tax Appeals, at Washington, in the District of Columbia, this 12th day of April, 1935.

(Seal)   B. D. GAMBLE, Clerk,
United States Board of Tax
Appeals.

[Endorsed]: No. 7849. United States Circuit Court of Appeals for the Ninth Circuit. Arthur Letts, Jr., Petitioner vs. Commissioner of Internal Revenue, Respondent. Transcript of the Record. Upon Petition to Review an Order of the United States Board of Tax Appeals.

Filed April 29, 1935.

PAUL P. O'BRIEN,

Clerk of the United States Circuit Court of Appeals for the Ninth Circuit.

TOPICAL INDEX.

TABLE OF AUTHORITIES CITED.

INDEX TO APPENDIX.

No. 7849.

In the United States
Circuit Court of Appeals
For the Ninth Circuit.

Arthur Letts, Jr.,

Petitioner,

vs.

Commissioner of Internal Revenue,

Respondent.

BRIEF OF PETITIONER.

HISTORY AND PREVIOUS OPINION.

The Commissioner of Internal Revenue on December 24, 1931, determined a deficiency in tax against petitioner for the year 1927 in the total sum of $92,721.18 from which petitioner appealed to the United States Board of Tax Appeals. The case was submitted on a stipulation of facts and documentary evidence.

Petitioner was the beneficiary of a testamentary trust created by his father, and as such beneficiary received from the trust during the year 1927 the sum of $353,-791.74, which petitioner erroneously reported in his income tax return as dividends. The respondent conceded this error but added the sum to petitioner's ordinary income and also to petitioner's capital gain. Among the proceeds received by the trust estate were 69,168 shares of stock of Holmby Corporation which at decedent's death had a fair market value of $7,215,605.76. The Commissioner of Internal Revenue determined that the Holmby Corporation, immediately after the date of death of Mr. Letts, Sr. and on May 18, 1923, began a process of complete liquidation. From this last mentioned date and until January 1, 1927, the trustees received from Holmby Corporation the total sum of $1,649,656.80 and during the year 1927 the trustees also received in further liquidation of the Holmby stock the total sum of $1,185,-088.24. The sum of $353,791.74 received by petitioner during the year 1927 was part of this last mentioned sum.

In addition to receiving the sum of $1,185,088.24 (which was designated as having been paid by Holmby Corporation out of its earnings and profits) the trustees received during the year 1927 in redemption of a certain number of its shares of stock of the Holmby Corporation the total sum of $5,813,800.00, no part of which was distributable to petitioner. Despite the fact that the $1,185,088.24 (out of which the $353,791.74 was distributed to petitioner) constituted a return of capital to the trust estate the Board of Tax Appeals held that the amount so received by petitioner constituted taxable income in the nature of a capital gain. Whereupon petitioner filed a motion for reconsideration and a motion to amend its findings of fact.

JURISDICTION.

Arthur Letts, Jr. was and is a resident of the County of Los Angeles, State of California, and as such filed his income tax return with the Collector of Internal Revenue for the Sixth Collection District of the State of California. [R. p. 65.]

The opinion of the United States Board of Tax Appeals was promulgated on May 25, 1934 [R. pp. 39-49], and the final order of redetermination was entered on July 31, 1934. [R. p. 54.]

Petitioner filed his petition for review by this Honorable Court with the Clerk of the United States Board of Tax Appeals on October 27, 1934. [R. p. 63.] This appeal was taken pursuant to the provisions of Sections 1001, 1002 and 1003 of the Act of Congress approved February 26, 1926, entitled "The Revenue Act of 1926" (44 Stat. 1, 109, 110; U. S. C. A., Sections 1224, 1225, 1226), as amended by Section 603 of the Act of Congress approved May 29, 1928, entitled "The Revenue Act of 1928" (45 Stat. 873), and as further amended by Section 1101 of the Act of Congress approved June 6, 1932, entitled "The Revenue Act of 1932" (47 Stat. 286), and as further amended by Section 519 of the Act of Congress, approved May 10, 1934, entitled "The Revenue Act of 1934" (48 Stat. 760, 26 U. S. C. A., Section 1225).

QUESTIONS INVOLVED.

I.

DOES THE SUM OF $353,791.74 RECEIVED BY PETITIONER OUT OF THE CORPUS OF THE TRUST ESTATE OF ARTHUR LETTS, SR. CONSTITUTE TAXABLE INCOME?

II.

DID THE BOARD OF TAX APPEALS ERR IN FAILING TO ADOPT AS ITS FINDINGS OF FACT THE FACTS STIPULATED BY PETITIONER AND RESPONDENT?

STATUTES INVOLVED.

See Appendix pages 1 to 4.

STATEMENT OF FACTS.

Petitioner's father died testate on May 18, 1923, and in his will created a trust in which petitioner was given a 30% beneficial interest. Under the terms of this will the trustees were to collect all income from the trust estate and, after deducting therefrom all proper charges and expenses of the trust, were to distribute the remainder—the "net income"—to the beneficiaries. [R. p. 42.]

On or about August 20, 1925, the decedent's estate was distributed and the trustees received, among other properties, 69,168 shares of the capital stock of the Holmby Corporation as part of the trust estate. This stock had a fair market value at the date of Mr. Letts' death of $7,215,605.76, or $104.32 per share. [R. p. 42.]

The Holmby Corporation has been in the process of complete liquidation at all times since May 18, 1923. [R. p. 42.] .

Between May 18, 1923, and December 31, 1926, the Holmby Corporation in its process of complete liquidation distributed to the trustees the sum of $1,649,656.80, all from earnings and profits accumulated since February 28, 1913, and during the year 1927 it made further distributions to the trustees from earnings and profits in the total sum of $1,185,088.24, such distributions having been made on the dates and in the amounts as follows:

February 8, 1927	$ 899,184.00
March 19, 1927	64,326.24
June 8, 1927	74,941.50
September 2, 1927	74,941.50
December 1, 1927	71,695.00
Total	$1,185,088.24

Although the foregoing payments were stipulated the Board failed to find as a fact that the above payments were made on the dates set opposite them. This, we urge, is error on the part of the Board.

Immediately after the receipt of each of these amounts from the corporation the trustees distributed them to the beneficiaries, petitioner receiving $353,791.74 thereof as his distributive share, and in his income tax return for the calendar year 1927 petitioner erroneously included as taxable dividends the said item of $353,791.74. [R. p. 42.]

On May 17, 1927, the Holmby Corporation made a distribution of $1,920,700.00 in cash and bonds, and on October 11, 1927, it made a distribution of property of the value of $3,893,100.00 to the trustees who, at the time of the said distributions, surrendered certificates representing 19,207 shares and 38,931 shares of stock of the said corporation, respectively. The Holmby Corporation charged these distributions to its capital stock account. No part of either of said amounts was distributed by the trustees to petitioner, the trustees having retained the full amount thereof as part of the *corpus* of said trust estate. [R. p. 68.] The Superior Court of the State of California approved the action of the trustees in retaining the entire amount received by them upon these redemptions. [R. p. 132.]

The Board recognized that the sum of $353,791.74 received by petitioner was part of the sum of $1,185,088.24 which represented part of the corpus of the trust estate, being a return of capital to the trustees, but, nevertheless, held that the sum so received by petitioner constituted taxable income. Petitioner contends that the character of moneys received is to be determined from the facts known at the date of receipt, and that such character does not change by the happening of subsequent events.

ASSIGNMENTS OF ERROR RELIED UPON.

Petitioner relies upon all the assignments of error which are as follows:

1. The Board of Tax Appeals erred in holding that the sum of $332,211.44 constituted taxable income to petitioner.

2. The Board of Tax Appeals erred in holding that the sum of $353,791.74 constituted a taxable gain realized by petitioner in 1927.

3. The Board of Tax Appeals erred in failing to hold that the sum of $332,211.44 constituted a distribution made by the trust estate out of its corpus, no part of which is taxable to petitioner.

4. The Board of Tax Appeals erred in holding that the statutory capital gain derived by the trustees of said trust estate was distributable under the terms of the trust to petitioner.

5. The Board of Tax Appeals erred in failing to hold that the statutory capital gain realized by the trustees of said trust became part of the corpus, which, under the terms of the trust instrument, was not distributable to petitioner.

6. The Board of Tax Appeals erred in failing to find as a fact as supported by the stipulation that the distributions made by Holmby Corporation to the trustees during the year 1927 were made on the dates and in the amount as follows:

Date	By Stock Redemptions		From Earnings and Profits
	Shares	Amount	Amount
February 8, 1927			$ 899,184.00
March 19, 1927			64,326.24
May 17, 1927	19,207	$1,920,700.00	
June 8, 1927			74,941.50
September 2, 1927			74,941.50
October 11, 1927	38,931	3,893,100.00	
December 1, 1927			71,695.00
	58,138	$5,813,800.00	$1,185,088.24

7. The Board of Tax Appeals erred in failing to find as a fact as supported by the stipulation that the trustees immediately after receiving each of the amounts shown as earnings and profits of the Holmby Corporation, as shown in paragraph 6, distributed the same to the beneficiaries of said trust estate.

8. The Board of Tax Appeals erred in failing to determine that petitioner was entitled to a refund of tax overpaid by him for the year 1927 in at least the sum of $48,813.86, together with interest thereon as provided by law.

LAW AND ARGUMENT.

The Sum of $353,791.74 Received by Petitioner From the Arthur Letts, Sr., Trust Did Not Constitute Taxable Income to Him Under the Provisions of the Revenue Act of 1926.

The question presented in this case is whether the sum of $353,791.74 received by petitioner as a beneficiary of the trust of Arthur Letts, Sr. constituted taxable income to him. Inasmuch as this amount was received by petitioner as a beneficiary of the trust, we must necessarily examine the provisions of the Revenue Act relating to trusts and distributions. Section 219 (b) (2) provides that the *net income* of the trust estate which is distributable to the beneficiaries thereof is taxable to them, whereas such portion of the net income of the estate which is not distributable to the beneficiaries is not taxable to them. From this section it is apparent that the mere distributability of the *receipts* of a trust to the beneficiaries thereof is not sufficient to make the said beneficiaries taxable with respect to such receipts. On the contrary, the fact of distributability *must* be combined with the fact that such receipts constituted "income" to the trust. In the instant case the petitioner concedes that the $353,791.74 was distributable to him, hence the true issue is whether such amounts constituted "income" to the trust within the meaning of the 16th Amendment of the Constitution and section 219 (b) (2) of the Revenue Act of 1926.

To determine the amount of distributable income received by the fiduciary reference must be had to the terms of the will or trust, and a decree of a court of competent jurisdiction which determines this is conclusive and binding on the federal courts. *Freuler v. Helvering,* 291 U. S. 35-41. However, that which may be income under the will, and therefore distributable, may not be such under the general provisions of the Revenue Act of 1926. Likewise, that which may be capital under the will may be income under that Act. The instant case furnishes examples of these two seeming contradictions, and in such contradictions we find the cause of the apparent confusion arising in the mind of the Board.

To illustrate the above point, we may assume the dividend paid by the corporation in the process of complete liquidation, out of its earnings and profits since the incidence of the trust belongs to the life beneficiaries—that is to say, it is income and therefore distributable. (Restatement of the Law of Trusts, §236(b); *Estate of Gartenlaub,* 185 Cal. 375.) For income tax purposes, the same dividend must be applied against the statutory base of the stock, and if less than such base it does not contain any element of income under the Act. (Section 202 of the Revenue Act of 1926.) We may further assume, to continue the illustration, that after such corporation has exhausted its surplus it proceeds to redeem its stock, which results in gain—income—under the Act. Notwithstanding the fact that such a transaction would simply amount to a conversion of the *corpus,* not income, under the will, and not distributable; it is, nevertheless, taxable income to the trustees under the Revenue Act of 1926.

That there can be such difference between the conception of the two terms—income and capital—under the law applying to the trust and the income tax law is not surprising. Were it possible for a testator to define income for tax purposes as well as for distribution purposes, the tax law could be defeated.

> *Merchants Loan & Trust Co. v. Smietanka,* 255 U. S. 509.

The Revenue Act of 1926, as well as the other federal income tax acts, levies taxes on income, *i. e.,* "the gain derived from capital, from labor, or from both combined, provided it be understood to include profit gained through a sale or conversion of capital assets." (*Eisner v. MacComber,* 252 U. S. 189.)

As we have seen, it levies a tax on the income of trusts as well as the income of individuals. It levies a tax on the trust income against the taxable entity who has the benefit of it; that is, it levies a tax on the trustee and, therefore, on the persons ultimately entitled to it if it is not currently distributable, or on the beneficiary if he is entitled to receive it.

However, the Act does not levy taxes on a return of capital regardless of whether it be distributed or not. Therefore, the distribution of a portion or all of the *corpus,* as distinguished from income (*i. e.,* income within the meaning of the Revenue Act), of a trust does not result in income tax. We believe the above are statements of principles so well established as not to be open to contradiction. We proceed to their application to the facts of this case.

The trustees under the last will and testament of Arthur Letts, Sr., had distributed to them from the estate of the said Letts, 69,168 shares of the capital stock of Holmby Corporation which, of course, constituted a part of the *corpus* of the trust estate. This stock had a fair market value at the date of Arthur Letts' death of $7,215,605.76 or $104.32 per share which constituted the base of the stock in the hands of the trustees. [R. p. 67.] Holmby Corporation began its process of complete liquidation on May 18, 1923, and from that date until December 31, 1926, distributed to the trustees from its earnings and profits the sum of $1,649,656.80. [R. p. 67.] During the year 1927 the trustees received from Holmby Corporation the further sum of $1,185,088.24, which was designated as having been paid from its earnings and profits and was received by the trustees on the dates and in the amounts as follows:

February 8, 1927	$ 899,184.00
March 19, 1927	64,326.24
June 8, 1927	74,941.50
September 2, 1927	74,941.50
December 1, 1927	71,695.00
	$1,185,088.24

If these had been the only distributions by Holmby Corporation in 1927 the case would be entirely without complication and the answer clear. We would simply add the amounts received in prior years to the 1927 receipts and see that the total received amounted to $2,834,745.04, whereas the base was $7,215,605.76, thereby leaving an unrecovered base of $4,380,860.72 and as long as the base was not recovered, no taxable gain arose.

Under such circumstances, the trustees would have had no taxable income, hence no part of their distributions to the beneficiaries could have been taxable. This would have been true because the distributions would have been of capital, and not income distributions which alone are taxable under the Revenue Act of 1926. However, these were not the only distributions made by Holmby Corporation during the year, there being certain other distributions made in redemption of stock, but we shall attempt to show that the latter distributions did not change the taxable status of the distributions made from earnings and profits prior to the recovery of the base.

Here is a practical situation in which the court which had jurisdiction over the trustees held that the Holmby Corporation dividends received in and prior to 1927 constituted income under the will. Yet they were obviously not income under the Revenue Act of 1926 because they were paid by a corporation in the process of complete liquidation, and the base for the stock on which paid had not been recovered at the time they were paid. Not being income for tax purposes they can not be taxed as such.

Of the $1,185,088.24 received by the trustees the total sum of $353,791.74 was distributed by them to the petitioner on the dates and in the amounts as follows:

March	15, 1927	$269,755.20
March	19, 1927	19,297.87
June	8, 1927	22,482.45
September	2, 1927	20,747.72
December	1, 1927	21,508.50
		$353,791.74

In addition to the $1,185,088.24 distributed by Holmby Corporation from its earnings and profits it also distributed to the trustees the sum of $5,813,800.00 in redemption of 58,138 shares of its capital stock. Said amount was received on the dates and in the amounts as follows:

Date	Shares Redeemed	Amount
May 17, 1927	19,207	$1,920,700.00
October 11, 1927	38,931	3,893,100.00
	58,138	$5,813,800.00

The redemption of October 11, 1927, resulted in the trustees' recovery of the remaining base and a gain of $1,361,244.28. The question here presented is: Was that gain or any part thereof distributable and, therefore, taxable to the beneficiaries of the trust? We think not.

As above stated, the Superior Court, which had jurisdiction over the trustees, decreed that the receipt of the $5,813,800.00 was a principal transaction and that the money was not distributable. Since no part of the total amount was distributable, we submit that no part of the gain included therein could have been distributable either. Here, then, is a situation in which the receipt included income for tax purposes, yet was wholly *corpus* or capital under the will, and we see no reason why this should not be true. For tax purposes, all distributions out of the corporation's surplus were liquidating dividends and were applicable to the reduction of the cost or base of the stock. To the extent that the cost had been so recovered, the gain or loss on the redemption should be respectively increased or decreased. Under the will, however, the dividends were considered income and in no sense reduced the *corpus,* hence the $100.00 per share in cash paid on the redemption substantially represented the original *corpus.* In other words, it was a mere conversion of *corpus* from one form to another to which the remaindermen were entitled in full.

The following table shows the trustees' receipts from Holmby Corporation, both from earnings and profits and in redemption of stock, in chronological order and also the gain derived by the trustees:

TABLE I.

Date	Nature of Distribution	Unrecovered Base at Time of Distribution	Amount of Distribution	Unrecovered Base *After* Distribution	Gain to Trustees
Date acquired by Trustee Distributed prior to Jan. 1, 1927		$7,215,605.76	$1,649,656.80	$5,656,948.96	—0—
Feb. 8, 1927	Earnings & Profits	5,565,948.96	899,184.00	4,666,764.96	—0—
Mar. 19, 1927	" "	4,666,764.96	64,326.24	4,602,438.72	—0—
May 17, 1927	Redemption	4,602,438.72	1,920,700.0	2,681,738.72	—0—
June 8, 1927	Earnings & Profits	2,681,738.72	74,941.50	2,606,797.22	—0—
Sept. 2, 1927	"	2,606,797.22	74,941.50	2,531,855.72	—0—
Oct. 11, 1927	Redemption	2,531,855.72	3,893,100.0	—0—	1,361,244.28
Dec. 1, 1927	Earnings & Pfts		71,695.0	—0—	71,695.00

Total Gain Realized by Trustees $1,432,939.28

The Board, in referring to the decree of the Superior Court holding that the amounts received in redemption of stock were not distributable, while $1,185,088.24 distributed by Holmby Corporation out of its earnings and profits was distributable, stated in its opinion [R. p. 47]:

"* * * We accept this decree as final in determining that the only amount distributable, and therefore taxable, to petitioner, was the sum of $353,-791.94 actually distributed to him by authority of that court. * * *"

We respectfully submit that this is the main point at which the Board fell into error. As we have already seen, (and as the Board recognized in other parts of its Opinion) the $353,791.74 was distributed by the trustees from the $1,185,088.24. All of the latter sum except $71,695.00 was received and distributed by the trustees before October 11, 1927, the date on which they recovered their base for the Holmby stock. It is true that the $1,185,088.24 was distributed from the Holmby Corporation's surplus, and that its distribution was, therefore, income under the terms of the will. That is to say, it was income within the conception of the testator. But that did not make it income under the Revenue Act of 1926, since the Act specifically required that the amount should be applied in reduction of the base of the stock. After October 11, 1927, all subsequent distributions by Holmby Corporation out of its earnings and profits continued to be income under the will and therefore distributable, and, because the base was recovered on that date, they were likewise income under the Revenue Act of 1926. So it is that the distribution of December 1, 1927, of $71,695.00 was a distribution of income and, therefore, taxable to the beneficiaries under section 219(b)(2), but that was the *only* amount taxable to them for the year 1927. Of that amount this petitioner received $22,171.70 and we submit that this is the maximum amount of taxable income with which this petitioner can be charged as having received from the trust during the year 1927.

An analysis of Table I confirms the above conclusions. The distribution of February 8, 1927, in the amount of $899,184.00, being a distribution in liquidation, applied against and reduced the basis of the stock in the hands of the trustees, and after its receipt the unrecovered base amounted to $4,666,764.96. This conclusively establishes the fact that such distribution was a return of capital in its entirety. The same conclusion must be reached as to each of the distributions from earnings and profits made on March 19, 1927, June 8, 1927, and September 2, 1927, for the same reason. From these distributions the petitioner received $331,620.04, all of which constituted a return of capital to him in the same manner as it constituted a return of capital to the trustees. It was a return of capital at the dates when received by the trustees and we submit that its character could not be changed by the happening of subsequent events. It is a fundamental rule of income tax law that the nature and character of the receipt, *i. e.*, whether it is taxable or nontaxable, must be determined in the light of the facts existing at the date when received.

We, of course, recognize that taxable net income is a yearly matter, but we believe that this does not conflict with the principles stated. The yearly income is simply a merger of all items of income, deductions, and losses received or suffered during the taxable year.

As an example of this proposition we may use the case of a gain arising from the sale of property in the early part of a taxable year, but offset by losses from similar sales later in the year. Assume for instance that on May 1st a particular piece of property is sold at a profit of $100,000.00; assume further that on September 1st another parcel is sold at a loss of $75,000.00 and that on December 1st still another parcel is sold at a loss of $50,000.00. If this gain and these losses constituted the taxpayer's only income and deductions for the particular year, then it is obvious that he would have no taxable income to report at the end of the year, but this would not alter in the slightest degree the immutable fact that on May 1st of the year he had actually received a taxable gain of $100,000.00.

As another example, and one which is perhaps more closely related to the case at bar, we may use the case of dividends declared by a corporation. Let us assume that on February 1, 1927, a corporation had a surplus of $150,000.00. $100,000.00 of which had been earned prior to March 1, 1913 and $50,000.00 of which had been earned subsequently to that date. If the corporation were to declare the entire $150,000.00 as a dividend, only $50,000.00 thereof would be taxable to the recipient. (Art. 1543, Regulations 69.) Let us assume further, however, that after the declaration of this dividend, but prior to the end of the year 1927 the corporation accumulated a new earned surplus of $100,000.00, none of which it declared as a dividend during that year. Would this change the character of the $100,000.00 which it distributed in February out of the surplus earned prior to March 1, 1913? The answer is obviously "no" and the reason is clear, namely, that what occurred subsequently to February 1, 1927, could not possibly affect the fact that on that date the $100,000.00 declared out of the surplus earned prior to March 1, 1913, constituted a nontaxable receipt which applied against and reduced the basis of the stock in the hands of the recipient. The character of a receipt does not change.

Section 219 (b)(2) of the Revenue Act of 1926, as heretofore stated, requires the beneficiaries of the trust to return that portion of *the income* of the trust which is distributable to him. The Board fell into error by reason of the fact that it did not distinguish the difference between income under the will and income for tax purposes. Section 219 cannot be construed as taxing income as defined by will when it is not in fact such under the Revenue Act.

The Commissioner of Internal Revenue in determining the deficiency here involved, and the Board in determining the profit, both used what we might term a "lump sum" method of computing the gain derived by the trustees in 1927 from the liquidation of Holmby Corporation. We are inclined to the belief that such a method was erroneous and that a "per share" method was the proper one to use in computing the gain. An illustration of the latter method may, in any event, serve as a test of the correctness of the petitioner's contentions.

The base per share for Holmby Corporation stock in the hands of the trustees was $104.32 ($7,215,605.76 divided by 69,168 shares). The "lump sum" method ignores the essential difference between the distributions of earnings and profits and those made in actual redemption of stock. The distributions from surplus were made *generally* on all the shares of stock held by the trustees when made, whereas those made in actual redemption of stock applied solely to the shares redeemed. Petitioner thoroughly agrees with the Board that the difference in the sources of these distributions, that is, capital or surplus, is immaterial in so far as their treatment is concerned, since they were all made in the process of complete liquidation, but he does believe that a very real and important difference exists in the fact that the actual redemptions were accompanied by a surrender by the trustees of the stock redeemed.

Section 202 of the Revenue Act of 1926 prescribes the method for determining gain or loss from the sale or other disposition of property. The gain on the surrender of the stock by the trustees in the instant case is, by section 201 (c) of the Revenue Act of 1926, required to be computed as prescribed by section 202; therefore, such gain must be computed in the same manner as the gain resulting from an ordinary sale of stock. It follows, therefore, that if the method adopted by the Board in this case were correct under section 202 and that if the amount received by the trustees in actual redemption of certain shares simply applied to reduce the basis of all the shares, then it would appear that if a taxpayer should sell a portion of a block of stock he would not have to report any profit thereon at the time of the sale, but might simply apply the amount received in the sale of the portion of the stock to the cost of the entire block. It requires no argument to illustrate the fallacy of this statement.

It would appear, therefore, that the Board erred in failing to find that the trustees realized a gain as the result of and at the time of *each* of the redemptions.

From May 18, 1923, and continuing through the year 1927 the Holmby Corporation was in the process of complete liquidation, and as one of the steps in this process it made several distributions of earnings and profits to its stockholders. The total of all the distributions so made to the trustees prior to January 1, 1927, amounted to $1,649,656.80, and from January 1, 1927, to and including March 19, 1927, additional distributions of the same nature were made to them amounting to $963,510.24.

As stated above, all of these distributions were made as steps in the process of complete liquidation, hence they constituted liquidating dividends and as such constituted part payment in exchange for the stock upon which made and served to reduce the basis thereof in the hands of the trustees. (Revenue Act of 1926, Sec. 201 (c).) Until the time such basis had been fully recovered the distributions did not constitute income to the trustees. (*Milton J. Tootle, et al.*, 20 B. T. A. 892, affirmed 58 Fed. (2d) 576.)

The distributions made on and before March 19, 1927, were made generally on all (69,168) shares in the hands of the trustees and served to reduce the basis of each of such shares in an equal amount, namely, $\dfrac{\$2,613,167.04,}{69,168}$ or $37.38 per share, thus leaving a remaining unrecovered base of $66.54 per share after the distribution of March 19, 1927.

On May 17, 1927, the Holmby Corporation distributed $1,920,700.00 in cash and bonds to the trustees who surrendered therefor 19,207 shares of the corporation's stock. The amount so received by the trustees represented a further and final payment in exchange for the stock surrendered.

Section 201 (c) of the Revenue Act provides:

"Amounts distributed * * * in partial liquidation of a corporation shall be treated as in part or full payment in exchange for the stock. The gain or loss to the distributee resulting from such exchange shall be determined under section 202 * * *"

Section 201 (h) defines a partial liquidation as follows:

"As used in this section the term 'amounts distributed in partial liquidation' means a distribution by a corporation *in complete cancellation or redemption of a part of its stock,* or one of a series of distributions in complete cancellation or redemption of all or a portion of its stock." (Emphasis supplied.)

The redemption of May 17th was clearly a distribution in partial liquidation within section 201 (h) above cited since it was distribution in complete cancellation or redemption of a part of the corporation's stock. Since the amount received in redemption constituted a full and final payment in exchange for the stock surrendered, gain or loss on the exchange must be computed under section 202 of the Revenue Act of 1926. (See Regulations 69, Article 1545, Example 2.)

The basis upon which such gain or loss must be computed is the original cost or other basis of the stock in the hands of the trustees, reduced, however, by the amounts theretofore distributed on the shares redeemed. As heretofore stated, the original basis of all shares in the hands of the trustees was $104.32 per share and distributions had been made prior to the redemption amounting to $37.38 per share. Therefore, the basis upon which gain or loss on this redemption must be computed was $66.54 per share. The redemption price of each of the shares redeemed was $100.00, hence the gain realized by the trustees amounted to $33.46 per share on each of the 19,207 shares redeemed, or a total of $642,666.22.

The May 17th redemption, since it applied only to certain specific shares, i. e., those actually surrendered by the trustees, did not affect the basis of the 49,961 shares unredeemed. These latter shares, therefore, still retained the basis of $66.54 each. On June 8th and September 2, 1927 the Holmby Corporation made two further distributions from earnings and profits totaling $149,883.00, thereby reducing the basis of the remaining 49,961 shares to $63.54 each.

On October 11, 1927, the Holmby Corporation canceled and redeemed an additional 38,931 shares from the trustees at $100.00 per share, the trustees receiving in exchange therefor property of the value of $3,893,100.00. As a result of this redemption, as was the case in the one which occurred in May, the trustees realized a gain to the extent of the difference between the redemption price of $100.00 per share and the then remaining base of $63.54. The profit thus realized on this redemption was, therefore, $36.46 per share, or a total of $1,419,424.26 on the 38,931 shares so. redeemed.

The October 11th redemption likewise applied only to those shares actually surrendered by the trustees and did not affect the basis of the remaining 11,030 shares unredeemed. The latter shares, therefore, retained the basis of $63.54 each. This base, however, was reduced to $57.54 on December 1, 1927, by a further distribution from earnings and profits of $71,695.00.

Tables II and III on the opposite page are illustrative of the above statements.

From these tables it seems apparent that there were two items of gains realized by the trustees during the year 1927 from the distributions made by the Holmby Corporation: a gain of $642,666.22 from the redemption of the 19,207 shares on May 17, 1927, and a gain of $1,419,424.26 from the redemption of the 38,931 shares on October 11, 1927. It likewise seems apparent that all of the distributions from earnings and profits made by the Holmby Corporation to the trustees were returns of capital, and not income, since under section 201 (c) of the Revenue Act of 1926 they applied against and reduced the basis of the stock upon which received—a basis which had not been recovered on any of the shares redeemed prior to their actual redemption, and a basis with respect to the shares unredeemed which had not been recovered by the end of the year 1927.

TABLE II.
DISTRIBUTIONS FROM EARNINGS AND PROFITS

Date	Shs. Held at Time of Distribution	Basis at Time of Distribution Per Sh.	Total	Amount Distributed Per Sh.	Total	Basis After Distribution Per Sh.	Total
Date used by Trustees	9,668	$104.32	$7,215,605.76	$	$	$	$
Prior to Jan. 1, 1927	69,168	104.32	7,215,605.76	23.85	1,649,656.80	80.47	5,565,948.96
Jan. 1, 1927 and Mar. 19, 1927	69,168	80.47	5,565,948.96	13.93	963,510.24	66.54	4,602,438.72
June 8, 1927 and Sept. 2, 1927	*49,961	66.54	3,324,404.94	3.00	149,883.00	63.54	3,174,521.94
Dec. 1, 1927	**11,030	63.54	700,846.20	6.50	71,695.00	57.04	629,151.20

*Shares remaining after redemption of May 17, 1927.
**Shares remaining after redemption of October 11, 1927.

TABLE III.
DISTRIBUTIONS IN REDEMPTION OF STOCK

Date	1 No. Shs. Redeemed	2 Basis of Stk. Redeemed in $ per Sh.	3 Redemption Price in $ per Sh.	4 Gain on Redemption in $ per Sh.	5 Gain to Trustees
May 17, 1927	19,207	66.54	$100.00	$33.46	$ 642,666.22
October 11, 1927	38,931	** 63.54	100.00	36.46	1,419,424.26
					$2,062,090.48

*Basis remaining after surplus distribution of March 19, 1927.
**Basis remaining after surplus distribution of September 2, 1927.

The "per share" method of computing gain clearly shows that the only gain—income—derived by the trustees during the year 1927 was that arising from the redemption of stock on May 17, 1927, and October 11, 1927. The decree of the Superior Court is clear that no part of such gain was distributable. Also, under this method it would appear that no part of even the December 1, 1927 distribution was taxable to the beneficiaries. This statement is supported by the provisions of section 219 (b) (2) of the Revenue Act of 1926 which provides in part as follows:

> "There shall be allowed as an additional deduction in computing the net income of the estate or trust the amount of the income of the estate or trust for its taxable year *which is to be distributed currently by the fiduciary to the beneficiaries,* and the amount of the income collected by a guardian of an infant which is to be held or distributed as the court may direct, but the amount so allowed as a deduction shall be included in computing the net income of the beneficiaries whether distributed to them or not. Any amount allowed as a deduction under this paragraph shall not be allowed as a deduction under paragraph (3) in the same or any succeeding taxable year;" (Italics ours.)

In *Freuler v. Helvering, supra,* the Supreme Court, referring to a similar section of the Revenue Act of 1921, stated as follows:

> "Plainly the section contemplates the taxation of the entire net income of the trust. Plainly, also, the fiduciary, in computing net income, is authorized to make whatever appropriate deductions other taxpayers are allowed by law. *The net income* ascer-

tained by this operation *and that only* is the taxable income. *This* the fiduciary may be required to accumulate, or, on the other hand he may be under a duty currently to distribute it. If the latter, then the scheme of the act is to treat the amount so distributable, not as the trust's income, but as the beneficiary's." (Italics ours.)

In view of the foregoing, it is respectfully submitted that the $1,185,088.24 (except the December 1, 1927 receipt of $71,695.00) was, under the Board's method of computing the gain to the trustees on the liquidation of the corporation, a pure return of capital, and was not income to the trustees under the Revenue Act and, therefore, not income to the beneficiaries when distributed to them. If, however, the Board's method of computing gain by the "lump sum" basis was incorrect and the "per share" method was the proper one to use, then it is apparent that no part of the $1,185,088.24, and hence no part of the $353,791.74 constituted income to the beneficiaries of the trust.

Respectfully submitted,

THOMAS R. DEMPSEY,

A. CALDER MACKAY,

Attorneys for Petitioner.

APPENDIX.

Revenue Act of 1926, Section 201 (c):

"Amounts distributed in complete liquidation of a corporation shall be treated as in full payment in exchange for the stock, and amounts distributed in partial liquidation of a corporation shall be treated as in part or full payment in exchange for the stock The gain or loss to the distributee resulting from such exchange shall be determined under section 202, but shall be recognized only to the extent provided in section 203. In the case of amounts distributed in partial liquidation (other than a distribution within the provisions of subdivision (g) of section 203 of stock or securities in connection with a reorganization) the part of such distribution which is properly chargeable to capital account shall not be considered a distribution of earnings or profits within the meaning of subdivision (b) of this section for the purpose of determining the taxability of subsequent distribution by the corporation."

Revenue Act of 1926, Section 201 (h):

"As used in this section the term 'amounts distributed in partial liquidation' means a distribution by a corporation in complete cancellation or redemption of a part of its stock, or one of a series of distributions in complete cancellation or redemption of all or a portion of its stock."

Revenue Act of 1926, Section 202 (a):

"Except as hereinafter provided in this section, the gain from the sale or other disposition of property shall be the excess of the amount realized there-

from over the basis provided in subdivision (a) or
(b) of section 204, and the loss shall be the excess of
such basis over the amount realized."

Revenue Act of 1926, Section 204 (5):

"If the property was acquired by bequests, devise,
or inheritance, the basis shall be the fair market value
of such property at the time of such acquisition.
The provisions of this paragraph shall apply to the
acquisition of such property interests as are specified
in subdivision (c) or (e) of section 402 of the
Revenue Act of 1921, or in subdivision (c) or (f) of
section 302 of the Revenue Act of 1924, or in subdivision (c) or (f) of section 302 of this Act."

Revenue Act of 1926, Section 219 (b)(2):

"(b) Except as otherwise provided in subdivisions (g) and (h), the tax shall be computed upon
the net income of the estate or trust, and shall be
paid by the fiduciary. The net income of the estate
or trust shall be computed in the same manner and
on the same basis as provided in section 212, except
that—

(2) There shall be allowed as an additional deduction in computing the net income of the estate or
trust the amount of the income of the estate or trust
for its taxable year which is to be distributed currently by the fiduciary to the beneficiaries, and the
amount of the income collected by a guardian of an
infant which is to be held or distributed as the court
may direct, but the amount so allowed as a deduction
shall be included in computing the net income of the
beneficiaries whether distributed to them or not.
Any amount allowed as a deduction under this para-

graph shall not be allowed as a deduction under paragraph (3) in the same or any succeeding taxable year;" * * *

Regulations 69, Article 1543:

"A tax-free distribution made by a corporation out of earnings or profits accumulated or increase in value of property accrued prior to March 1, 1913, shall be applied against the basis of the stock for the purpose of determining gain or loss from its subsequent sale. The fact that such distribution is in excess of the cost of other basis (provided in section 204 and articles 1591-1603) of the stock on which declared does not render it subject to tax. The provisions of this paragraph are also applicable to a distribution by a "receiving" corporation made under the conditions set forth in the first paragraph of this article, and to the distributees in determining gain or loss from the subsequent sale or other disposition of stock in the "receiving" corporation.

"Example.—A purchased certain shares of stock subsequent to February 28, 1913, for $10,000. He received in 1925 a distribution of $2,000 paid out of earnings and profits of the corporation accumulated prior to March 1, 1913. This distribution is not subject to tax if the earnings and profits of the corporation accumulated after February 28, 1913, have been distributed. If A subsequently sells the stock for $6,000, a deductible loss of $2,000 is sustained. If he sells the stock for $9,000, he realizes a taxable gain of $1,000."

Regulations 69, Article 1545, Example 2:

"A owns 10 shares of preferred stock and 10 shares of common stock in the M corporation which he purchased in 1915 for $1,100.00 and $1,000.00 respectively. In 1925 the M corporation has on hand $225,000.00 of capital, earnings and profits of $25,-000.00 accumulated prior to March 1, 1913, and earnings and profits of $125,000.00 accumulated after February 28, 1913. If the preferred stock is retired at $125.00 per share, $125,000.00 being used by the corporation for this purpose, A will receive $1,250.00 in exchange for his 10 shares of preferred stock and is therefore subject to the normal tax and the surtax on $150.00, or at his option, in lieu of such taxes, to the tax upon capital net gain. If the M corporation then distributes a cash dividend of $25,000.00 on the common stock, it would be subject to the surtax. If, without any further accumulation of earnings and profits, the M corporation thereafter liquidates completely, A, who will receive $2,250.00 in exchange for his 10 shares of common stock, will be subject to the normal tax and the surtax on $1,250.00 or at his option, in lieu of such taxes, to the tax upon capital net gain."

INDEX

(I)

In the United States Circuit Court of Appeals for the Ninth Circuit

No. 7849

ARTHUR LETTS, JR., PETITIONER

v.

COMMISSIONER OF INTERNAL REVENUE, RESPONDENT

ON PETITION FOR REVIEW OF DECISION OF THE UNITED STATES BOARD OF TAX APPEALS

BRIEF FOR THE RESPONDENT

OPINION BELOW

The only previous opinion in this case is that of the Board of Tax Appeals (R. 39–49), which is reported in 30 B. T. A. 800.

JURISDICTION

This appeal involves income taxes from the year 1927 in the amount of $41,535.41, and is taken from a decision of the Board of Tax Appeals entered July 31, 1934 (R. 54). The case is brought to this Court by petition for review filed October 27, 1934 (R. 63), pursuant to the provisions of Sections 1001–1003 of the Revenue Act of 1926, c. 27, 44 Stat. 9, as amended by Section 1101 of the Revenue Act of 1932, c. 209, 47 Stat. 169.

2

Whether the petitioner is taxable upon the sum of $353,791.74 which was received by him as his distributive share of the income of a trust estate.

STATUTE AND REGULATIONS INVOLVED

The applicable statute and Regulations involved herein will be found in the Appendix, *infra,* pp. 11–14.

STATEMENT

The facts may be summarized as follows (R. 40–49, 65–134):

Petitioner's father died testate on May 18, 1923, leaving a will in which a trust was created with respect to certain of his property (R. 42, 67). Under the terms of such trust the petitioner was to receive currently 30% of the income, and that same percentage of the corpus upon its termination (R. 42). Included in the assets of this trust estate were 69,168 shares of the capital stock of Holmby Corporation, the fair market value of which, at the time of decease of petitioner's father, was $7,215,605.76 (R. 42, 67).

During the period from May 18, 1923, to December 31, 1926, the Holmby Corporation, in the process of complete liquidation, distributed to the trustees, out of earnings and profits, the sum of $1,649,-656.80 (R. 42, 67). During the year 1927 the Holmby Corporation, continuing the process of complete liquidation, made additional distributions of $6,995,885.24. Of this sum $1,185,088.24 was distributed as from earnings and profits, and the balance, $5,813,800, was paid as in redemption of 58,138 shares of the total of 69,168 shares of stock belonging to the trust (R. 42, 67–68).

Included in the $1,185,088.24 received by the trustee in ·1927 as distributed from earnings and profits, was the sum of $353,791.74, which was distributed by the trustees to petitioner during that year as his beneficial share of the distributable trust income for that year. This latter amount was reported by petitioner on his income-tax return for such year as ordinary dividends (R. 42–43, 68).

The Board of Tax Appeals held that the said sum of $353,791.74 was taxable income to the petitioner and subjected it to tax under the capital net gain provisions of the Revenue Act of 1926.

SUMMARY OF ARGUMENT

A trust estate and the beneficiaries are separate taxable entities, and the distributable income of a trust is taxable to the beneficiaries, even though the trust may have a net loss for the year. Nor is the aggregate distributable income upon which the beneficiaries are taxable necessarily the same as the net income of the trust. In the instant case the trust had income which was taxable under the income-tax laws and also income which was distributable under the terms of the trust instrument. Being distributable, it was taxable to the beneficiaries.

Petitioner's error lies in the assumption that the distributable income of a trust is to be computed under the Federal income-tax laws rather than under the terms of the trust instrument and the laws of the State where it is being administered. Petitioner admits that the sum of $353,791.74 was properly distributable to him, and he is accordingly taxable upon such income.

. The sole question presented in this case is whether the sum of $353,791.74, received by the petitioner as a beneficiary of the trust estate created by the will of his father, constitutes taxable income to him in the year 1927.

Section 219 (b) of the Revenue Act of 1926, *infra,* provides that the net income of a trust estate shall be computed in the same manner and on the same basis as the net income of an individual, except that there shall be allowed as an additional deduction, in computing the net income of the trust, the amount of income which is to be distributed currently by the fiduciary to the beneficiaries. During the year 1927, the trustees, one of whom was the petitioner, distributed to the petitioner as a beneficiary of the trust, the sum of $353,791.74. The petitioner concedes that under the provisions of the trust such sum was distributable to him during the year, but contends that it does not constitute taxable income. In order to determine whether the said sum of $353,791.74 represents taxable income to the petitioner, it is necessary to determine whether, in the year 1927, the trust was in receipt of income which, under the terms of the trust, was distributable to the beneficiaries.

The trust was the owner of 69,168 shares of stock of the Holmby Corporation, which corporation had been, since May 18, 1923, in process of complete liquidation. Such stock had a cost base in the hands of the trustees of $7,215,605.76. During the period from May 18, 1923, to December 31, 1926, the corporation had distributed to the trustees the sum of $1,649,656.80, all of such sum being distributed as from earnings and profits of the corporation. During the year 1927 there was a further distribution to the trustees of $6,995,885.24. Of this sum $1,185,088.24 was distributed as from earnings and profits, and the balance of $5,813,800 was designated as in redemption of 58,138 shares of the total of 69,168 shares of stock belonging to the trust. To summarize, the trustees received from the corporation during the period from May 18, 1923, to the end of the year 1927 distributions in liquidation as follows:

May 18, 1923, to December 31, 1926, out of earnings and profits	$1,649,656.80
During 1927, out of earnings and profits	1,185,088.24
During 1927, in redemption of 58,138 shares of stock	5,813,800.00
Total	8,648,545.04

Under Section 201 (c) of the Revenue Act of 1926 all amounts received in complete or partial liquidation of a corporation are treated as in part or full payment of the stock. We thus have the

situation of where liquidating distributions totaling $8,648,545.04 were received by the trustees, in
liquidation of stock which had a cost base in their
hands of $7,215,605.76. Clearly the difference be-
tween the cost base of the stock in the hands of
the trustees and the amount received in liquidation
of the corporation, namely, $1,432,939.28, is recog-
nizable gain and taxable to the trustees. However,
under the provisions of Section 219 (b), *infra,*
amounts which are distributable currently are de-
ductible by the trust in computing its taxable income, but such amounts are taxable to the beneficiaries. Petitioner admits that under the provisions of the trust instrument the sum of $1,185,-
088.24 was distributable, and that his distributive
share of such sum was $353,791.74. Clearly the dis-
tribution meets all the requirements of the statute,
and the sum is properly taxable to the petitioner.

Petitioner contends that since the profit on the
liquidation represents appreciation in the value of
the trust property and is therefore not distributable, and since under the provisions of the trust
instrument he was entitled to receive only his portion of the distributable income, the sum of $353,-
791.74 does not represent taxable income. He apparently loses sight of the fact that during the
year 1927 the trustees did receive income which
was distributable, and which was actually distributed to him.

Petitioner's whole case is based upon the erro-
neons theory that before a beneficiary is taxable

upon his distributive share of the income of a trust, it must appear (1) that the trust has a net taxable income for the year, and (2) that the particular taxable income upon which the trust is taxed is distributable to the beneficiaries. But the authorities are all to the contrary. It is well settled that beneficiaries are taxable upon their distributive income, even though the trust or estate may have a net loss for the year. *Baltzell* v. *Mitchell,* 3 F. (2d) 428 (C. C. A. 1st), certiorari denied, 268 U. S. 690; *Abell* v. *Tait,* 30 F. (2d) 54 (C. C. A. 4th). Nor is the aggregate distributable income upon which the beneficiaries of a trust are taxed necessarily the same as the net income of the trust. *Burnet* v. *Whitcomb,* 65 F. (2d) 803 (App. D. C.); *Kaufmann* v. *Commissioner,* 44 F. (2d) 144 (C. C. A. 3d); *Hubbell* v. *Burnet,* 46 F. (2d) 446 (C. C. A. 8th).

A trust estate and its beneficiaries are separate taxable entities. *Merchants' L. & T. Co.* v. *Smietanka,* 255 U. S. 509.

In *Baltzell* v. *Mitchell, supra,* the trust estate had received the sum of $133,000, which was distributable and actually was distributed to the beneficiaries, but during the same year the trustees had sold securities belonging to the trust and suffered a loss thereon of $147,000, so that the trust estate, instead of having a net income, had a loss for the year. Nevertheless the court held that the beneficiaries were taxable upon their entire distributive share of the income, saying (pp. 430–431):

The beneficiary clearly has no distributive
share in the net income of the estate or
trust; but he has a distributive share of
income to be paid him under and in accordance with the terms of the trust, and resort
must be had to them to ascertain his proportion of the income or his distributive
share. The beneficiary is not interested in
the capital of the trust, but only in the income. If there are accretions to the capital,
these are not distributable as income, so that
the beneficiary may receive any part of
them; and if there are capital losses they
cannot be made good out of the income.

*   *   *   *.   *

It cannot be supposed that Congress intended that the taxes under sections 210 and
211 should be paid by an individual who was
engaged in some business or gainful occupation which yielded an income upon which
such tax could be levied and collected, and
also provided that the beneficiary of a trust,
although paid a large amount in accordance
with the terms of such trust, should escape
all taxation upon the amount so paid, because
the trust, as such, through losses of capital,
did not show a net income.

Thus it will be seen that a trust estate may have
a net loss for the year, and yet at the same time
have distributable income which is taxable to the
beneficiaries, whether distributed or not. In the
instant case the trust estate had taxable income and
also income which was distributable to the beneficiaries. Being distributable, it meets the sole test

laid down by the decided cases, and petitioner is therefore taxable upon his distributive share.

A number of cases have held that there is no relationship between the net income of a trust and its distributable income. In *Codman* v. *Miles,* 28 F. (2d) 823 (C. C. A. 4th), the court declined to allow a deduction from the amount actually distributed to the beneficiary on account of exhaustion of the corpus. A deduction for depreciation of buildings was denied the life tenants in *Kaufmann* v. *Commissioner, supra.* In *Hubbell* v. *Burnet, supra,* the amounts were actually set aside for depreciation by the trustees, but the court ruled that their retention was unauthorized, and being distributable, they were subject to the tax.

The facts in the instant case will serve as an apt illustration of a case where income is distributable and therefore taxable to the beneficiary, yet the trust estate may not have any taxable income for the year. Suppose that the liquidating dividend of $1,185,088.24, which was paid out of earnings and profits, was the only distribution received by the trustees during the year. As such sum was paid in process of complete liquidation, under Section 201 (c) no part of the amount would represent taxable income to the trust, but would apply against and thus reduce the cost base of the stock in the hands of the trustees. Yet the sum would in fact be distributable income in the hands of the trustees and therefore would be taxable income to the beneficiaries.

Petitioner devotes a large portion of his brief to a computation which shows a gain of $2,062,090.48 ($642,666.22 plus $1,419,424.26; Br. 27) to the trustees in 1927 from the liquidation of the Holmby Corporation, and argues that since such profit represents an accretion to the capital of the trust, it is therefore not distributable to the beneficiaries. His error lies in the assumption that the distributable income of a trust is to be computed under the Federal income-tax laws rather than under the laws of the State where the trust is being administered. See *Freuler* v. *Helvering*, 291 U. S. 45. What we are here concerned with is the amount of the distributable income received by the trustees during the year, not the method of computing gain from distributions received in liquidation of a corporation. Since petitioner admits that the sum of $353,791.74 was properly distributable to him, he is accordingly taxable upon such income.

CONCLUSION

It follows that the decision of the Board of Tax Appeals is correct, is in accordance with law, and should be affirmed.

Respectfully submitted.

FRANK J. WIDEMAN,
Assistant Attorney General.
SEWALL KEY,
ELLIS N. SLACK,
Special Assistants to the Attorney General.

NOVEMBER 1935.

APPENDIX

Revenue Act of 1926, c. 27, 44 Stat. 9:

SEC. 201. (c) Amounts distributed in complete liquidation of a corporation shall be treated as in full payment in exchange for the stock, and amounts distributed in partial liquidation of a corporation shall be treated as in part or full payment in exchange for the stock. The gain or loss to the distributee resulting from such exchange shall be determined under section 202, but shall be recognized only to the extent provided in section 203. In the case of amounts distributed in partial liquidation (other than a distribution within the provisions of subdivision (g) of section 203 of stock or securities in connection with a reorganization) the part of such distribution which is properly chargeable to capital account shall not be considered a distribution of earnings or profits within the meaning of subdivision (b) of this section for the purpose of determining the taxability of subsequent distributions by the corporation.

* * * * *

(h) As used in this section the term "amounts distributed in partial liquidation" means a distribution by a corporation in complete cancellation or redemption of a part of its stock, or one of a series of distributions in complete cancellation or redemption of all or a portion of its stock.

ESTATES AND TRUSTS

SEC. 219. (b) Except as otherwise provided in subdivisions (g) and (h), the tax shall be computed upon the net income of the estate or trust, and shall be paid by the fiduciary. The net income of the estate or trust shall be computed in the same manner and on the same basis as provided in section 212, except that—

* * * * *

(2) There shall be allowed as an additional deduction in computing the net income of the estate or trust the amount of the income of the estate or trust for its taxable year which is to be distributed currently by the fiduciary to the beneficiaries, and the amount of the income collected by a guardian of an infant which is to be held or distributed as the court may direct, but the amount so allowed as a deduction shall be included in computing the net income of the beneficiaries whether distributed to them or not. Any amount allowed as a deduction under this paragraph shall not be allowed as a deduction under paragraph (3) in the same or any succeeding taxable year;

* * * * *

Treasury Regulations 69, promulgated under the Revenue Act of 1926:

ART. 342. *Method of computation of net income and tax.—*

* * * * *

(2) The amount of the income of the estate or trust for its taxable year which is to be distributed currently by the fiduciary to the beneficiaries, and the amount of the income collected by a guardian of an infant which is to be held or distributed as the court may direct, shall be allowed as an ad-

ditional deduction in computing the net income of the estate or trust. The amount so allowed as a deduction must be included by a beneficiary in computing his net income, whether distributed to him or not. If the taxable year of the beneficiary differs from that of the estate or trust, the amount which he is required to include in computing his net income shall be based upon the income of the estate or trust for its taxable year ending within his taxable year. The amounts which are allowed as a deduction under this paragraph shall not be allowed as a deduction under paragraph (3) of this article in any taxable year.

*　　　*　　　*　　　*　　　*

ART. 1545. *Distributions in liquidation.*— Amounts distributed in complete liquidation of a corporation are to be treated as in full payment in exchange for the stock, and amounts distributed in partial liquidation are to be treated as in part or full payment in exchange for the stock so canceled or redeemed. The phrase "amounts distributed in partial liquidation" means a distribution by a corporation in complete cancellation or redemption of a part of its stock, or one of a series of distributions in complete cancellation or redemption of all or a portion of its stock. A complete cancellation or redemption of a part of the corporate stock may be accomplished, for example, by the complete retirement of all shares of a particular preference or series, or by taking up all the old shares of a particular preference or series and issuing new shares to replace a portion thereof.

The gain or loss to a shareholder from a distribution in liquidation is to be determined, as provided in section 202 and article 1561, by comparing the amount of the distribution with the cost or other basis of the stock provided in section 204 and articles 1591–1603; but the gain or loss will be recognized only to the extent provided in section 203 and articles 1571–1580. Any gain to the shareholder may, at his option, be taxed as a capital net gain in the manner and subject to the conditions prescribed in section 208 and articles 1651–1654. In the case of amounts distributed in partial liquidation, other than a distribution in pursuance of a plan of reorganization as described in section 203 (g), the part of such distribution which is properly chargeable to capital account shall not be considered a distribution of earnings or profits within the meaning of section 201 (b) for the purpose of determining the taxability of subsequent distributions by the corporation.

*   *

U S. GOVERNMENT PRINTING OFFICE: 1935

No. 7849.

In the United States
Circuit Court of Appeals
For the Ninth Circuit.

Arthur Letts, Jr.,

Petitioner,

vs.

Commissioner of Internal Revenue,

Respondent.

REPLY BRIEF FOR PETITIONER.

Thomas R. Dempsey,
A. Calder Mackay,
1104 Pacific Mutual Building,
Los Angeles, California.
Attorneys for Petitioner.

Parker, Stone & Baird Co , Law Printers, Los Angeles.

No. 7849.

In the United States
Circuit Court of Appeals
For the Ninth Circuit.

Arthur Letts, Jr.,

 Petitioner,

vs.

Commissioner of Internal Revenue,

 Respondent.

REPLY BRIEF FOR PETITIONER.

ARGUMENT.

In Order for an Amount Distributed to the Beneficiary of a Trust to Be Taxable to Such Beneficiary, the Amount So Distributed Must Have Constituted Income to the Trust Within the Meaning of the Revenue Act Levying Such Tax.

It is respectfully submitted that the respondent's entire argument, as set forth in his brief, is in error because he ignores the principle of law stated in the above heading. That the respondent has ignored this principle is clearly shown by the following statement appearing in his "Summary of Argument":

"In the instant case the trust had income which was taxable under the income-tax laws and also income which was distributable under the terms of the trust instrument. Being distributable, it was taxable to the beneficiaries."

From this statement it is apparent that respondent recognizes the fact that the trust received two different types of income during the year 1927, *only one of which was taxable under the income tax laws,* but, despite his recognition of this fact, he immediately thereafter ignores it by arguing that the other income of the trust which was *not* taxable under the income tax laws should, nevertheless, be taxed to the beneficiaries simply because it was distributable to them. We submit that such an argument involves a patent and irreconcilable conflict of law and logic.

The only amounts taxable to any taxpayer under the Federal income tax law are those which constitute "income" to him under the Revenue Act covering the year in question, and whether any particular amount does constitute "income" under any Revenue Act must be determined in the light of the definition of "income" as laid down by the Supreme Court in *Eisner v. Macomber,* 252 U. S. 189, namely:

"* * *. the gain derived from capital, from labor, or from both combined, provided it be understood to include profit gained through a sale or conversion of capital assets."

In the instant case the liquidating dividends received by the trustees during the year 1927, with the exception of the one received on December 1, were less than the base of the stock upon which received, hence they represented pure capital returns and *not* income within the above definition.

Section 219 (b) (2) of the Revenue Act of 1926 and the corresponding provisions of the other Acts does not purport to alter the general rules of income tax law so as to permit or require the taxation of receipts which are not in fact "income" within the meaning of *Eisner v. Macomber, supra.* The sole purpose of the section is to provide that the tax on the amounts received by a trust, which in fact constitute "income" within the settled meaning of the word for income tax purposes, shall be paid by the persons who receive, or who are entitled to receive, such income. The truth of this statement is not open to argument, it having been definitely settled by the Supreme Court in the case of *Freuler v. Helvering,* 291 U. S. 35, wherein the court, at page 41, states as follows:

> "Plainly the section contemplates the taxation of the entire net income of the trust. Plainly, also the fiduciary in computing net income, is authorized to make whatever appropriate deductions other taxpayers are allowed by law. *The net income ascertained by this operation, and that only, is the taxable income. This* the fiduciary may be required to accumulate, or, on the other hand, he may be under a duty currently to distribute it. If the latter, then the scheme of the Act is to treat the amount so distributable, not as the trust's income, but as the beneficiary's. * * *"

Petitioner does not believe that any one will seriously contend that the Supreme Court employed the word "income" in the above statement in such a loose manner as to include receipts of a trust which do not fall within the meaning of its definition in *Eisner v. Macomber, supra.*

Respondent argues that since the amounts here in question were income to the trust *under the terms of the will* and likewise distributable to the beneficiaries all of the requirements of the statute providing for the taxation thereof to the beneficiaries were met. This is but another example of the result of ignoring the basic principle heretofore stated. There are many classes of receipts of a trust which are very definitely income to the trust within the meaning of the trust instrument, but which are never taxed to the beneficiaries even though actually distributed to them. An example of this may be found in the instant case quite aside from the point in dispute. During the year 1927 the trustees received substantial amounts as interest from state and municipal bonds, all of which was income under the will and all of which was properly distributed to the beneficiaries. The respondent does not contend that these amounts are taxable to the beneficiaries, nor, to our knowledge, has he ever so maintained in any other case. Why is this true?

The answer is clear, namely, that such income, being exempt from taxation to the trust, is likewise exempt from taxation to the beneficiaries; and we see no possible grounds for a distinction between income which is exempt from taxation by statute and that which is exempt from taxation under the Sixteenth Amendment to the Constitution.

We submit, then, that the distributions here in question, not having been "income" to the trust within the meaning of the Constitution and the Revenue Act of 1926, do *not* fulfill the requirements of the statute and that there is no authority for taxing them to the petitioner.

Respondent states that petitioner's whole case is based upon the "theory that before a beneficiary is taxable upon his distibutive share of the trust, it must appear (1) that the trust has a net taxable income for the year, and (2) that the particular income upon which the trust is taxed is distributable to the beneficiaries."

This statement bears no resemblance whatever to petitioner's true theory. Petitioner contends only this: That the only part of the distributive receipts of the trust which may be taxed to him are those receipts which constituted taxable income to the trust under the Revenue Act of 1926. We have already pointed out the fact that the correctness of this theory is definitely settled by the case of *Freuler v. Helvering, supra.*

None of the cases cited by the respondent conflict in any way with this theory for the reason that the only point therein decided is that if any part of the *gross income* (as defined by the Revenue Acts) of a trust is distributable to the beneficiaries, then such part of *such income* is taxable to the beneficiaries despite the fact that the amount so taxed to them is greater than the net taxable income of the trust. In view of the quoted statement of the Supreme Court in the *Freuler* case to the effect that section 219 contemplates only the taxation of the entire *net* income of the trust one may pause to question the correctness of the earlier cases cited by the respondent; however, even assuming that such cases are correct, they have no bearing on the instant case for the reason that the point which they decide is not here involved.

In conclusion, we would request this Honorable Court to consider the effect of the method of taxation advocated by the respondent. He would apply the liquidating dividends in question to the reduction of the base of the stock in the hands of the trustees, thereby increasing the ultimate profit to be realized and taxed to them, and at the same time he would have the beneficiaries pay a tax on the same liquidating dividends when received. In other words, and this conclusion is inescapable, he advocates double taxation upon the same receipts—an object which was never intended by the statute.

Respectfully submitted,

THOMAS R. DEMPSEY,

A. CALDER MACKAY,

Attorneys for Petitioner.

1104 Pacific Mutual Building,
Los Angeles, California.

No....... 7783

IN THE

United States
Circuit Court of Appeals

FOR THE NINTH CIRCUIT.

UNITED STATES OF AMERICA,
Appellant,

vs.

THE L O S A N G E L E S SOAP COM-
 ˋPANY, a Corporation, and W E S T-
CHESTER FIRE INSURANCE COM-
PANY,

Appellees.

. Apostles on Appeal

Appeal From the District Court of. the United States,
Southern District of California,
 Central Division

Independent-Review, Law Printers, 222 So. Spring St., Los Angeles. TU 1377

No..

IN THE

United States
Circuit Court of Appeals

FOR THE NINTH CIRCUIT

UNITED STATES OF AMERICA,

Appellant,

vs.

THE LOS ANGELES SOAP COM-
PANY, a Corporation, and WEST-
CHESTER FIRE INSURANCE COM-
PANY,

Appellees.

Apostles on Appeal

Appeal From the District Court of the United States,
Southern District of California,
Central Division

INDEX

(Clerk's Note: When deemed likely to be of important nature, errors or doubtful matters appearing in the original record are printed literally in italic; and, likewise, cancelled matter appearing in the original record is printed and cancelled herein accordingly. When possible, an omission from the text is indicated by printing in italics the two words between which the omission seems to occur.)

INDEX—*Continued*

NAMES AND ADDRESSES OF ATTORNEYS

For Appellant:

PEIRSON M. HALL,
United States Attorney,

LEO V. SILVERSTEIN,
JACK L. POWELL,
Assistants United States Attorney,

Federal Building,
Los Angeles, California.

For Appellees:

OVERTON, LYMAN & PLUMB,
L. K. VERMILLE,
Roosevelt Building,
Los Angeles, California.

DERBY, SHARP, QUINBY & TWEEDT,
S. HASKET DERBY,
Merchants Exchange Building,
San Francisco, California.

SINGLE & TYLER,
116 John Street,
New York, New York.

IN THE DISTRICT COURT OF THE UNITED
STATES FOR THE SOUTHERN DISTRICT OF
CALIFORNIA CENTRAL DIVISION.

THE LOS ANGELES SOAP COMPANY, a corporation,

Libellant,

Vs.

THE UNITED STATES SHIPPING MERCHANT
FLEET CORPORATION,

Respondent.

No. 3327 C Adm.

RECORD OF ENROLLMENT.

On the 21st day of November, 1928, a libel was filed
herein;

On the 3rd day of December, 1928 Affidavit of Service
was filed herein;

On the 8th day of February, 1929, Exceptions to Libel
were filed herein;

On the 8th day of July, 1929, Amended Exceptions to
Libel were filed herein;

On the 27th day of January, 1930, the Court made and
entered an order herein, sustaining exceptions to articles
six and nine, and denying as to all other exceptions, and
thirty days allowed respondent to amend, etc.;

On the 28th day of March, 1930, Amendment to Libel
was filed herein;

On the 1st day of May, 1930, Answer to Amended
Libel was filed herein;

On the 9th day of May, 1930, Stipulation that testimony
taken by depositions in any of the consolidated causes may

be used in evidence in all of the consolidated causes, and Order therefor, was filed herein;

On the 22nd day of August, 1930, Notice of motion for leave to amend libel and amendment to libel was filed herein, substituting the United States of America as respondent instead of the United States Shipping Board Merchant Fleet Corporation;

On the 22nd day of September, 1930, the Court made and entered an order herein, granting Motion for leave to amend libel without prejudice, etc., substituting the United States of America as party respondent;

On the 10th day of October, 1930, Exceptions to second amended libel were filed herein;

On the 14th day of October, 1930, Answer to second amended libel and to amended amendment to libel, etc., was filed herein;

On the 5th day of March, 1931, Notice of motion for leave to consolidate this cause, and causes Nos. 3663-C and 3691-C for trial was filed herein;

On the 10th day of May, 1932, an Order transferring cause to the Calendar of Judge McCormick for further proceedings was filed herein;

On the 3rd day of May, 1933, on Stipulation, an Order was entered consolidating cases 3327, 3663, 3691 for trial, and Order transferring these causes to Judge Cosgrave's Calendar for further proceedings; thereupon further proceedings were had before Judge Cosgrave in the consolidated causes;

On the 4th day of May, 1933, on further proceedings of consolidated cause before Judge Cosgrave, the Court made and entered an order herein, that Motions for judgment and for reference, in consolidated cause, stand submitted;

On the 16th day of September, 1933, Stipulation of facts was filed herein;

On the 21st day of August, 1934, the Court made and entered an Order herein, finding in favor of The Los Angeles Soap Co., and that counsel prepare Findings, and Decree, in accordance with Memorandum of Decision, which was also filed this day;

On the 12th day of September, 1934, the Court made and entered an Order herein, for the filing and entering of Findings, etc., and Interlocutory Decree; thereupon Findings, etc., and Interlocutory Decree were signed, filed, entered and recorded.

32/346

IN THE DISTRICT COURT OF THE UNITED STATES FOR THE SOUTHERN DISTRICT OF CALIFORNIA CENTRAL DIVISION.

THE UNITED STATES OF AMERICA,

Libelant,

vs.

THE LOS ANGELES SOAP COMPANY, a corporation,

Respondent.

No. 3663-C-Adm.

RECORD OF ENROLLMENT.

On the 15th day of August, 1929, a Libel was filed herein, and Citation issued thereon, which was returned, and filed herein August 30, 1929;

On the 4th day of September, 1929, Alias citation issued, which was returned, and filed herein September 6, 1929;

On the 29th day of April, 1930, Answer was filed herein;

On the 29th day of April, 1930, Cross-libel of The Los Angeles Soap Co., a corp., was filed herein;

On the 9th day of May, 1930, Stipulation that testimony taken by depositions in any of the consolidated causes may be used in evidence in all of the consolidated causes, and Order therefor, was filed herein;

On the 22nd day of May, 1930, Exceptions to cross-libel were filed herein;

On the 1st day of July, 1930, Amendment to cross-libel of The Los Angeles Soap Co., a corp., was filed herein;

On the 23rd day of July, 1930, Exceptions to amended cross-libel were filed herein;

On the 8th day of December, 1930, Amendment to Exceptions to amended cross-libel were filed herein;

On the 8th day of December, 1930, the Court made and entered an Order herein, on hearing on exceptions of the libellant to amended cross-libel of The Los Angeles Soap Co., a corp., and that briefs be filed on behalf of both sides, and that the same stand submitted on said briefs, etc.;

On the 14th day of March, 1932, an order overruling Exceptions of libellant to amended cross-libel was entered;

On the 5th day of May, 1932, Answer to amended cross-libel was filed herein;

On the 10th day of May, 1932, an Order transferring this cause to Judge McCormick's Calendar; and a minute order to the same effect was made and entered;

On the 3rd day of May, 1933, on Stipulation, an Order was entered consolidating cases 3327, 3663, 3691 for trial, and Order transferring these causes to Judge Cosgrave's Calendar for further proceedings; thereupon further proceedings were had before Judge Cosgrave in the consolidated cause;

On the 4th day of May, 1933, on further proceedings of consolidated cause before Judge Cosgrave, the Court made and entered an order herein, that Motions for judgment and for reference, in consolidated cause, stand submitted:

On the 16th day of September, 1933, Stipulation as to certain facts was filed in case No. 3327-C;

On the 21st day of August, 1934, an order was made and entered, on the filing of Memorandum of Decision in case No. 3327-C, in consolidated cause, that counsel prepare Findings, etc., and Decree, in accordance with said memorandum decision;

On the 12th day of September, 1934, the Court made and entered an Order herein, for the filing and entering of Findings, etc., and Interlocutory Decree; thereupon, in consolidated cause No. 3327-C, said Findings, etc., and Interlocutory Decree, were filed.

Calendar for further proceedings; thereupon further proceedings were had before Judge Cosgrave in the consolidated cause:

On the 4th day of May, 1933, on further proceedings of consolidated cause before Judge Cosgrave, the Court made and entered an order herein, that Motions for judgment and for reference, in consolidated cause, stand submitted:

On the 21st day of August, 1934, an Order was made and entered, on the filing of Memorandum of Decision in case No. 3327-C, consolidated cause, that counsel prepare Findings, etc., and Decree, in accordance with memorandum decision;

On the 12th day of September, 1934, the Court made and entered an Order herein, for the filing and entering of Findings, etc., and Interlocutory Decree; thereupon, in consolidated cause No. 3327-C, said Findings, etc., and Interlocutory Decree, were filed.

[TITLE OF COURT AND CAUSE]

IN ADMIRALTY—3327-C
LIBEL

TO THE HONORABLE, THE JUDGES OF THE UNITED STATES DISTRICT COURT, IN AND FOR THE SOUTHERN DISTRICT OF CALIFORNIA.

The libel of the Los Angeles Soap Company, a corporation, against The United States Shipping Board Merchant Fleet Corporation, a corporation, in a cause of contract, cargo damage and General Average, civil and maritime, alleges and respectfully shows to this Court, as follows:

First: That the Los Angeles Soap Company, a corporation, libellant herein, was, at and during all the times hereinafter mentioned, and now is a corporation duly organized and existing under and by virtue of the laws of the State of California and was at all times with its office and principal place of business in the City of Los Angeles, County of Los Angeles, State of California.

Second: At and during all the times hereinafter mentioned the respondent was and still is a domestic corporation organized, created and existing under and by virtue of an Act of Congress of the United States of America and the laws of the District of Columbia, and was and still is engaged in the business of owning, and/or operating, managing and controlling steamers as a common carrier of merchandise by water for hire, between among others, ports of the United States and the Philippine Islands, with its office and principal place of business in the City of Washington in the District of Columbia, United States, and also that with an office and doing business at No. 122 East Seventh Street in the City and County of Los Angeles in the State of California, and within the jurisdiction of this honorable court.

Third: At and during all the times hereinafter mentioned, the Steamship "WEST CAJOOT" was owned and/or operated, managed and controlled by the respondent as a common carrier of merchandise by water for hire.

Fourth: Heretofore and on or about and between the 15th and 23rd days of September 1927, one Jao Cui Pien delivered to the respondent at Manila, P. I. 663,523 lbs. of cocoanut oil all in good order and condition, to be carried, in consideration of an agreed freight, to the Port of Los Angeles, California, and there to be delivered in like good order and condition as when received by the respondent, to the order of the Los Angeles Soap Company.

FIFTH: Thereupon this respondent received and accepted the said cocoanut oil in said good order and condition, and agreed in consideration of the payment of a certain freight, and in accordance with the valid terms of a certain bill of lading then and there signed and delivered to the shipper by the duly authorized representative of the respondent, to safely carry and deliver the same in like good order and condition to said port of Los Angeles in accordance with aforesaid agreement for the carriage thereof.

SIXTH: Thereafter the said Steamship, "WEST CAJOOT" sailed from the Port of Manila, having on board the above mentioned cocoanut oil and subsequently but not in due course arrived at the port of Los Angeles, but has failed to deliver the said shipment of cocoanut oil to the respondent herein in like good order and condition as when received on board, but on the contrary short and slack and seriously damaged and contaminated by contact with fuel oil.

SEVENTH: Prior to the arrival of the said Steamship "WEST CAJOOT" at said port of Los Angeles, the Los Angeles Soap Company became the owner for value of the aforesaid shipment of cocoanut oil and entitled to the delivery thereof and in accordance with the aforesaid agreement for the carriage thereof.

"WEST CAJOOT" to be drydocked at Kobe, Japan, with said cargo stowed within said ship.

FOURTEENTH: The aforesaid loss, damage and contamination of said cocoanut oil was due to and caused by the drydocking of the said Steamship with cargo within her, and was a breach of aforesaid agreement and contract of carriage.

FIFTEENTH: Said breach of aforesaid agreement and contract of carriage constituted and was an unjustifiable, material and unreasonable deviation and rendered the respondent liable as an insurer of the libellants' shipment of cocoanut oil.

FOR A THIRD CAUSE OF ACTION

SIXTEENTH: Your libellant here repeats and realleges each and every allegation contained in Articles "FIRST" to "ELEVENTH", both inclusive of this libel, as fully and with the same force and effect as if the same were here repeated, realleged and set forth at length.

SEVENTEENTH: That after the said Steamship "WEST CAJOOT" sailed from Manila with the said cargo laden on board consisting of 663,523 pounds of cocoanut oil, and while proceeding from Manila and bound for Los Angeles, by way of Hongkong, said steamship stranded in the Vandieman Straits. Later she was floated and her master then directed his course for Kobe, Japan, where respondent caused, ordered or procured said vessel to be drydocked for inspection and repairs. Respondent failed to discharge libellants' aforementioned cargo of cocoanut oil prior to and before said steamship was drydocked at Kobe, and as a result thereof said ship and her tanks were strained and impaired with the resulting damage as aforesaid.

EIGHTEENTH: That the freight upon the said cargo amounts to the sum of $3,823.70.

NINETEENTH: That the value of the damaged, and lost and/or contaminated cocoanut oil is estimated at $40,000, and the value of that brought forward about $20,000.

TWENTIETH: That the contributory value of respondent's said Steamship is estimated at about the sum of $300,000.

TWENTY-FIRST: That libellant is entitled to general average contribution for such damage, and the amount of the contribution in General Average which respondent's said Steamship and freight should pay is estimated at the sum of $20,000

WHEREFORE, libellant prays that process in due form of law according to the course and practice of this Honorable Court in a cause of Admiralty and Maritime jurisdiction may issue against the said respondent, citing it to appear and answer under oath all and singular the matters aforesaid, and the interrogatories hereto attached, and that this Honorable Court may be pleased to decree to the libellants their damages with interest and costs and that the libellants may have such other and further relief as in law and justice they may be entitled to receive.

OVERTON, LYMAN & PLUMB,
Proctors for Libellant,
Office and P.O. Address:
621 South Hope Street,
City of Los Angeles,
State of California.

(Verified.)

INTERROGATORIES PROPOUNDED TO RESPONDENT TO BE ANSWERED UNDER OATH

As to the S.S. "WEST CAJOOT" when she sailed from Manila, P.I., for San Francisco, September 23, 1927.

I. Were you not the operator?
   (a) If the answer is no, who was the operator?
   (b) What was your relation to the S.S. "WEST CAJOOT"?

II. Was not the American Australia Orient. Line your Agent at Manila?
   (a) If your answer is no, who was your agent?
   (b) Was not the American Australia Orient Line party to a managing operating. agreement to which you were one of. the parties?
      1. If yes, please attach copy.

III. Did not your Operating Department have general direction and control as to:
   (a) Sailing.
   (b) Time of sailing.
   (c) Repairs.
   (d) Extent of repairs.
   (e) Inspections.
   (f) Allocations of cargo.
      1. If your answer to any of the above is no, please state. who did have such general direction and control.

IV. State where, with reference to the section of the ship, the. libellants' cargo of cocoanut oil was stowed?

(a) Identify the tank by number in which it was stowed.

(b) Was said tank above or below any fuel oil tank or tanks.

(c) State when and where said tank in which the cocoanut oil was inspected prior to the stowage of said cargo at Manila.

(d) By whom was it inspected?

(e) State where and when and by whom the fuel oil tanks of the "WEST CAJOOT" were inspected?

(f) Who supervised the loading and stowage of said cocoanut oil on board the "WEST CAJOOT"?

(g) State the name and address of such party or parties.

V. State the time when and where the ship stranded.

VI. State how she was floated.

(a) Whether by her own power, or

(b) Salvage vessels.

VII. Prior to the loading of said cargo were the fuel oil tanks tested, and if so, how?

(a) What were the results of said tests?

VIII. Prior to the loading of said cargo were the tanks containing the cocoanut oil tested?

(a) What was the result of said tests?

IX. After the stranding and after the ship was floated and before she was drydocked were the cocoanut oil tanks tested?

X. After the stranding and after the ship was floated and before she was drydocked were the fuel oil tanks tested?

XI. If there was a fuel oil tank below the cocoanut oil did such tank contain fuel oil when the ship left Manila?

    (a) If there was fuel oil in the tank or tanks below the cocoanut oil tank, was said fuel oil used on the voyage from Manila to the point where she stranded?

XII. Were any of the fuel oil tanks pierced or damaged due to the stranding?

    (a) If so, state how and give the location of the damaged tank with reference to the tank in which the cocoanut oil was stowed

XIII. Who was the person that instructed or ordered the ship to be drydocked with her cargo aboard?

XIV. State the name of the drydock or company where the "WEST CAJOOT" was drydocked.

XV. State what measures and tests were made of the cocoanut oil tank and the fuel oil tanks while the ship was on drydock.

XVI. State what tests or examinations were made of the fuel oil tanks or cocoanut oil tank after the vessel was again floated.

OVERTON, LYMAN & PLUMB,
Proctors for Libellant.

(Endorsed):   Filed Nov 21-1928.

AMENDED EXCEPTIONS TO LIBEL 3327-C

(Original exceptions filed 2/8/29)

To the Honorable, the Judges of the United States District Court in and for the Southern District of ICalifornia, Central Division:

Comes now the United States Shipping Board Merchant Fleet Corporation by its proctors, Samuel W. McNabb, United States Attorney, and Ignatius F. Parker, Assistant United States Attorney, for the Southern District of California, and excepts to the Libel of the Los Angeles Soap Company herein in a cause of contract, cargo damage and general average, civil and maritime, upon the following grounds and for the following reasons:

First: That the Ninth Article of said Libel is vague, general, indefinite and insufficient in law.

Second: That the Sixth, Thirteenth and Fifteenth Articles of the Libel are vague, general, indefinite and insufficient in law.

Third: That the said Sixth, Ninth, Thirteenth and Fifteenth Articles of the Libel do not conform to the Twenty-second Rule of practice for the Courts of the United States in admiralty and maritime jurisdiction.

Fourth: That it is impossible to determine from the allegations of the Libel herein, and particularly Articles Sixth, Thirteenth and Fifteenth thereof, what Libellant intends to allege as constituting a deviation of the voyage in question.

Fifth: That for the reasons stated herein and upon the grounds alleged the Libel herein does not state facts sufficient to constitute a cause of action.

It is therefore respectfully submited that the Amended Exceptions should be sustained and that the Respondent should have such other and further relief as may be just.

(Endorsed) : Filed Jul 8, 1929.

AMENDED EXCEPTIONS TO INTERROGA-
TORIES NOS. 4 and 6-16 INCLUSIVE
PROPOUNDED TO RESPONDENT
BY LIBELANT—3327-C.
(Original exceptions filed 2/8/29)

To the Honorable the Judges of the U. S. District Court, In and for the Southern District of California, Southern Division :

Comes now the United States Shipping Board Merchant Fleet Corporation by its proctors, Samuel W. McNabb, United States Attorney, and Ignatius F. Parker, Assistant United States Attorney, for the Southern District of California, and excepts to Interrogatories Nos. 4 and 6 to 16 inclusive, addressed by the Libelant, The Los Angeles Soap Company, to the said Respondent and assigns the following reasons for said exception:

First: That the aforesaid interrogatories are not in compliance with Rule 31 of the Admiralty rules of the United States Supreme Court.

Second: That the matters propounded in the said interrogatories are not a proper subject for interrogatories.

Third: That there is nothing in the libel supporting said interrogatories.

Fourth: That said interrogatories do not purport to develop any evidence which is in Respondent's possession and the burden of proof of which rests on the libelant.

rived at the Port of Los Angeles, but has failed to
deliver the said shipment of cocoanut oil to the libelant
herein in like good order and condition as when received
on board, but on the contrary short and slack and
seriously damaged and contaminated by contact with
fuel oil.

III

Libelant amends Article Ninth of its said original libel
as follows:

NINTH: The aforesaid shortage, damage and contamination to the said cocoanut oil was not due to or
contributed to by any fault or neglect of the libelant, the
shipper or consignees of said cocoanut oil or their
servants, agents or employees.

IV

Libelant amends Article Thirteenth of its said original
libel as follows:

SIXTEENTH: Contrary to and in breach of the
provisions of said agreement and contract of carriage,
the respondent did not prosecute the voyage with
dispatch, but caused, ordered and procured the said
Steamship "West Cajoot" to be drydocked at Kobe,
Japan, and at San Francisco, California, with said cargo
stowed within said ship.

V

Libelant adds to its said original libel the following
acticle:

SEVENTEENTH-a: That upon the arrival of said vessel at San Francisco, California, respondent again
caused, ordered or procured said vessel to be drydocked
for inspection and repairs. Respondent failed to dis-

charge libelant's aforementioned cargo of cocoanut oil prior to and before the vessel was drydocked at San Francisco and as a result thereof said vessel and her tanks were again strained and impaired with the resulting damage as aforesaid.

VI

Libelant adds to its said original libel the following ause of action.

FOR A FOURTH CAUSE OF ACTION

TWENTY-SECOND: Your libelant here repeats and re-alleges each and every allegation contained in Articles First to Eleventh, both inclusive, of its said original libel as fully and with the same force and effect as if the same were here repeated, re-alleged and set forth at length.

TWENTY-THIRD: Contrary to and in breach of the provisions of said agreement and contract of carriage the respondent did not prosecute the voyage with dispatch but caused ordered and procured said vessel with libelant's cargo within her to proceed from Manila to Hong Kong, China, thence to Kobe, Japan, thence to Yokohama, Japan, thence to San Francisco, California, thence to Oakland, California, thence to San Francisco, California, and thence to San Pedro, California, where libelant's said cargo of cocoanut oil was finally discharged.

TWENTY-FOURTH: That the aforesaid loss, damage and contamination of said cocoanut oil was due to and caused by deviation of said vessel upon her voyage from Manila to San Pedro as aforesaid and was a breach of said agreement and contract of carriage.

TWENTY-FIFTH: Said breach of aforesaid agreement and contract of carriage constituted and was an unjustifiable, material and unreasonable deviation and rendered the respondent liable as an insurer of the libelant's shipment of cocoanut oil.

WHEREFORE, libelant prays that a decree be entered herein as prayed for in the original libel filed herein on the 21st day of November, 1928, and for such other and further relief as in law and justice it may be entitled to receive.

OVERTON, LYMAN & PLUMB,

Proctors for libelant.

(Verified)

(Endorsed): Filed Mar 28-1930.

No. 3327-C

ANSWER TO AMENDED LIBEL.

TO THE HONORABLE, THE JUDGES OF THE UNITED STATES DISTRICT COURT, IN AND FOR THE SOUTHERN DISTRICT OF CALIFORNIA.

The answer of the United States Shipping Board Merchant Fleet Corporation by its proctor, Samuel W. McNabb, United States Attorney for the Southern District of California, to the amended libel of the Los Angeles Soap Company in an alleged cause of contract, cargo damage and general average, civil and maritime, upon information and belief alleges as follows:

FIRST: For answer to the allegations of Article First of said amended libel, respondent, for lack of knowledge and information sufficient to form a belief, denies these allegations and puts libelant to its full proof thereof.

SECOND: This respondent denies the allegations of Article Second of the amended libel.

THIRD: This respondent denies the allegations of Article Third of the amended libel.

FOURTH: This respondent denies the allegations of Article Fourth of the amended libel.

FIFTH: This respondent denies the allegations of Article Fifth of the amended libel.

SIXTH: This respondent admits that "the said Steamship 'WEST CAJOOT' sailed from the Port of Manila, having on board the above mentioned coconut oil". and subsequently arrived at the Port of Los Angeles but denies all and singular the remaining allegations of Article Sixth of the amended libel.

SEVENTH: For answer to the allegations of Article Seventh of said amended libel, this respondent, for lack of knowledge or information sufficient to form a belief, denies these allegations and puts libelant to its full proof thereof.

EIGHTH: This respondent denies the allegations of Article Eighth of the amended libel.

NINTH: This respondent denies the allegations of Article Ninth of the amended libel.

TENTH: This respondent denies the allegations of Article Tenth of the amended libel.

ELEVENTH: This respondent admits the admiralty and maritime jurisdiction of the United States and of this Honorable Court but denies that all and singular the premises are true.

AND FOR ANSWER TO THE SECOND
CAUSE OF ACTION.

TWELFTH: This respondent repeats and realleges Article First to Eleventh, both inclusive, of this answer as fully and with the same force and effect as if the same were here repeated, re-alleged and set forth at length.

THIRTEENTH: This respondent denies the allegations of Article Thirteenth of the amended libel.

FOURTEENTH: This respondent denies the allegations of Article Fourteenth of the amended libel.

FIFTEENTH: This respondent denies the allegations of Article Fifteenth of the amended libel.

AND FOR ANSWER TO THE THIRD
CAUSE OF ACTION

SIXTEENTH: This respondent repeats and realleges Article First to Eleventh, both inclusive, of this answer, as fully and with the same force and effect as if the same were here repeated, realleged and set forth at length.

SEVENTEENTH: This respondent admits that after the said Steamship WEST CAJOOT sailed from Manila with the said cargo laden on board, consisting of coconut oil, and while proceeding from Manila and bound for Los Angeles, said steamship stranded in the Van Dieman Straits. Later she was floated and her master directed her course for Kobe, Japan and that the WEST CAJOOT was there drydocked but this respondent denies all and singular the remaining allegations of Article Seventeenth of the amended libel.

SEVENTEENTH-A: This respondent admits that the WEST CAJOOT was drydocked at San Francisco but denies all and singular the remaining allegations of Article Seventeenth-A of the amended libel.

EIGHTEENTH: This respondent admits the allegations of Article Eighteenth of the amended libel.

NINETEENTH: For answer to the allegations of Article Nineteenth of said amended libel, this respondent, for lack of knowledge and information sufficient to form a belief, denies these allegations and puts libelant to its full proof thereof.

TWENTIETH: This respondent denies the allegations of Article Twentieth of the amended libel.

TWENTY-FIRST: This respondent denies the allegations of Article Twenty-first of the amended libel.

AND FOR ANSWER TO THE FOURTH CAUSE OF ACTION

TWENTY-SECOND: This respondent repeats and realleges Articles First to Eleventh, both inclusive, of this answer, as fully and with the same force and effect as if the same were here repeated, realleged and set forth at length.

TWENTY-THIRD: This respondent denies the allegations of Article Twenty-third of the amended libel.

TWENTY-FOURTH: This respondent denies the allegations of Article Twenty-fourth of the amended libel.

TWENTY-FIFTH: This respondent denies the allegations of Article Twenty-fifth of the amended libel.

FURTHER ANSWERING THE SAID AMENDED
LIBEL AND BY WAY OF SEPARATE DE-
FENSE THERETO, THE UNITED STATES
SHIPPING BOARD MERCHANT FLEET COR-
PORATION BY ITS PROCTOR SAMUEL W.
McNABB, UNITED STATES ATTORNEY FOR
THE SOUTHERN DISTRICT OF CALIFORNIA,
ALLEGES UPON INFORMATION AND BELIEF,
AS FOLLOWS:

TWENTY-SIXTH: That in September, 1927 there was
shipped on the SS. WEST CAJOOT at Manila certain merchandise purporting to consist of 546.24241 long tons or
1,223,583 pounds of coconut oil. Said coconut oil was
shipped under a Bill of Lading dated at Manila, September 21st, 1927, duly issued for the master of the
Steamship WEST CAJOOT by Swayne & Hoyt, Inc., Managing Agents for the United States Shipping Board.
A copy of said Bill of Lading is attached hereto, incorporated into and made a part of this answer and marked
"Exhibit A." Said cocoanut oil was loaded into the deep
tanks of the Steamship WEST CAJOOT but prior to such
loading the deep tanks were examined, tested, inspected,
cleaned, made tight and in every way rendered fit and
proper receptacles for the carriage of said coconut oil.
Said Bill of Lading, marked "Exhibit A", contains
among others the following clause:

> "And it is further expressly agreed that the re-
> port of Morton & Ericksen, Inc., the surveyors at
> the port of loading, that the vessel is in all respects
> seaworthy for the carriage of said oil and fit to
> receive and transport said oil and that the loading

and stowage of said oil is proper shall be and be held to be conclusive proof as to shipper, consignee and/or owner or interested party that at the time of shipment and commencement of the voyage, ship-owners had exercised due diligence to make the vessel seaworthy in all respects for the carriage of said oil and fit to receive and transport same, and that the loading and stowage of said oil was proper."

Morton & Ericksen, Inc., the surveyors at the port of loading, Manila, duly issued a report dated September 20, 1927, that "both sections of the deep tank SS. WEST CAJOOT are now in fit condition to receive and carry coconut oil in bulk as well as cargo on the voyage intended." Respondent claims the benefit of this clause.

FURTHER ANSWERING THE SAID AMENDED LIBEL AND BY WAY OF SECOND DEFENSE THERETO, THE UNITED STATES SHIPPING BOARD MERCHANT FLEET CORPORATION BY ITS PROCTOR SAMUEL W. McNABB, UNITED STATES ATTORNEY FOR THE SOUTHERN DISTRICT OF CALIFORNIA, ALLEGES UPON INFORMATION AND BELIEF, AS FOLLOWS:

TWENTY-SEVENTH: That while on the voyage aforesaid and while passing through Van Dieman Strait, at 12:54 A. M. October 2nd, 1927, the Steamship WEST CAJOOT struck a submerged rock or reef, severely injuring the vessel's bottom and causing the flooding of No. 1 Hold. For the safety of the vessel and cargo the master of the Steamship WEST CAJOOT altered the course of the WEST CAJOOT to Kobe, Japan where the vessel was drydocked and the injury to the WEST CAJOOT and her cargo was repaired so that the vessel was enabled to continue her voyage and the cargo of coconut oil was discharged at Los Angeles. That, if as alleged in said libel, the coconut oil was found to be contaminated by fuel oil on its discharge at Los Angeles, this contamination was caused by the striking of the submerged rock or reef by the WEST CAJOOT, as aforesaid, and the consequent tearing and straining of the structure of the ship, which caused a leaking of the tanks of the ship.

The said Bill of Lading marked "Exhibit A" contains among others the following clause:

"Neither the vessel, her owner, nor agent, shall be liable for loss or damage resulting from: Act of God, perils, dangers and accidents of the sea or other navigable waters:"

Respondent claims the benefit of this clause.

That prior to said stranding, due diligence had been exercised to make said steamship "WEST CAJOOT" in all respects seaworthy and properly manned, equipped and supplied, and said steamship was at all of said times, in fact, in all respects seaworthy and properly manned, equipped and supplied.

That any damage to, or loss or cargo was caused by one or more, and/or a combination of two or more risks and/or perils excepted in said bill of lading, and/or by the provisions of the Act of Congress of the United States approvel February 13, 1893, commonly known as the Harter Act.

FURTHER ANSWERING THE SAID AMENDED
LIBEL AND BY WAY OF THIRD ADDITIONAL
DEFENSE THERETO, THE UNITED STATES
SHIPPING BOARD MERCHANT FLEET COR-
PORATION BY ITS PROCTOR SAMUEL W.
McNABB, UNITED STATES ATTORNEY FOR
THE SOUTHERN DISTRICT OF CALIFORNIA,
ALLEGES UPON INFORMATION AND BELIEF,
AS FOLLOWS:

TWENTY-EIGHTH: That said Bill of Lading, marked
"Exhibit A", under which the said coconut oil was shipped, contained among others the following clause:

> "Notice of loss, damage, or delay must be given
> in writing to the vessel's agent within thirty (30)
> days after the removal of the goods from the cus-
> tody of the vessel, or in case of failure to make
> delivery within thirty (30) days after the goods
> should have been delivered; Provided, that notice of
> apparent loss or damage must be given before the
> goods are removed from the custody of the vessel,
> and proper notation made on the receipt given to
> the vessel for the goods, shall constitute the notice
> herein required. Written claim for loss, damage or
> delay must be filed with the vessel's agent within
> six (6) months after giving such written notice.
> Unless notice is given and claim filed as above pro-
> vided, neither the vessel, her owner or agent shall
> be liable. No suit to recover for loss, damage, delay
> or failure to make delivery shall be maintained un-
> less instituted within one year after the giving of
> written notice as provided herein."

That no notice of loss, damage or delay was given in writing to the vessel's agent within the time limited in Clause 11 of this Bill of Lading, nor was notice of apparent loss or damage given within the time limited in Clause 11, nor was written claim for loss, damage, or delay filed with the vessel's agent within the time limited in Clause 11 of the Bill of Lading.

FURTHER ANSWERING THE SAID AMENDED LIBEL AND BY WAY OF A FOURTH ADDITIONAL DEFENSE THERETO, THE UNITED STATES SHIPPING BOARD MERCHANT FLEET CORPORATION BY ITS PROCTOR SAMUEL W. McNABB, UNITED STATES ATTORNEY FOR THE SOUTHERN DISTRICT OF CALIFORNIA, ALLEGES UPON INFORMATION AND BELIEF, AS FOLLOWS:

The said Bill of Lading, marked "Exhibit A" under which the said coconut oil was shipped contained among others the following clause:

"The value of each package shipped hereunder does not exceed two hundred and fifty dollars ($250.00), unless otherwise stated herein, on which basis the freight is adjusted, and the vessel's liability shall in no case exceed that sum or the invoice value (including freight charges, if paid, and including duty, if paid, and not returnable), whichever shall be the less, unless a value in excess thereof be specially declared, and stated herein, and extra freight as may be agreed upon, paid. Any partial loss or damage for which the carrier may be liable shall be adjusted pro rata on the above basis."

That no value greater than two hundred and fifty dollars ($250.00) was stated by the shipper nor was there any agreement stating any greater value nor any extra freight paid thereon.

FURTHERING ANSWERING THE SAID AMEND-
ED LIBEL AND BY WAY OF A FIFTH ADDI-
TIONAL DEFENSE THERETO, THE UNITED
STATES SHIPPING BOARD MERCHANT
FLEET CORPORATION BY ITS PROCTOR
SAMUEL W. McNABB, UNITED STATES AT-
TORNEY FOR THE SOUTHERN DISTRICT OF
CALIFORNIA, ALLEGES UPON INFORMA-
TION AND BELIEF, AS FOLLOWS:

Whatever the respondent did in or about the operation of the said steamship WEST CAJOOT at any time mentioned in the amended libel, and in and about the carriage and delivery of the shipment described in the amended libel, was done solely for the United States of America; and the respondent at no time had, and has not any interest in the said vessel, or the operation of the said vessel, or the carriage or delivery of the said shipment, or in the freight for the carriage and delivery of the same.

WHEREFORE, the respondent, the United States Shipping Board Merchant Fleet Corporation, by its proctor Samuel W. McNabb, United States Attorney for the Southern District of California, prays that the amended libel may be dismissed with costs, and that it may have

such other and further relief as may be just and the
Court competent to give in the premises.

> UNITED STATES SHIPPING BOARD
> MERCHANT FLEET CORPORATION,
>> By: Samuel W. McNabb,
>> SAMUEL W. MCNABB,
>> *United States Attorney for the*
>> *Southern District of California.*

(verified)

(Endorsed): Filed May 1, 1930

R. S. ZIMMERMAN, Clerk U. S. District Court,
    Southern District of California

By Edmund L. Smith, Deputy

    (SEAL)

EXHIBIT A

AMERICAN AUSTRALIA ORIENT LINE
Port of
. Destination Los Angeles
Operated for United States Shipping Board
by SWAYNE & HOYT, INC. Managing Operators

B/L No. 5

San Francisco, Los Angeles, Yokohama, Kobe,
Shanghai, Hongkong, Manila.

BILL OF LADING—PACIFIC FORM

SHIPPED in apparent good order and condition, by Jao
Cui Pien to be transported by the steamer "WEST
CAJOOT" from the port of Manila to the port of Dock
of the Vegetable Oil Products Co., Inc., Los Angeles
Harbor, Calif. thence to be transshipped,...........................
the following goods being marked and numbered as

and otherwise to the shipper. Neither the vessel, her
owner, nor agent shall be liable for loss or damage resulting from: Act of God, perils, dangers, and accidents of the sea or other navigable waters; fire, from
any cause or wheresoever occuring, barratry of master
or crew; enemies, pirates, or robbers; arrest or restraint
of princes, rulers, or people or seizure under legal process. fumigation under governmental orders; riots, strikes,
lockouts, or stoppage of labor; saving or attempting to
save life or property at sea, inherent vice, nature, defect,
or change of character of the goods; insufficiency or
absence of marks, numbers, address or description; explosion, bursting of boilers, breakage of shafts, or any
latent defects in hull, machinery, or appurtenances, or
unseaworthiness of the vessel, whether existing at time
of shipment or at the beginning of the voyage, provided
the owners shall have exercised due diligence to make
the vessel seaworthy, properly manned, equipped, and
supplied. Except when caused by negligence on the part
of the vessel, neither the vessel, her owner, nor agent,
shall be liable for loss or damage resulting from: heat,
frost, decay, putrefaction, rust, sweat, breakage, leakage, smell, taint, or evaporation from any other goods,
drainage, ullage, vermin, or by explosion of any of the
goods, whether shipped with or without disclosure of
their nature; and such goods may be thrown overboard
or destroyed at any time without compensation; nor for
risk of craft, hulk or transshipment; nor for any loss
or damage caused by the prolongation of the voyage.

General average shall be adjusted at San Francisco
and shall be payable according to York-Antwerp Rules.

plosives or dangerous articles shall have plainly marke(
thereon its contents, and whoever delivers to any com
mon Carrier any explosive or dangerous article unde1
false or deceptive marking, description, invoice, shippin₤
order, etc., is liable to a fine of not more than $2000, o1
imprisonment for not more than eighteen months, c:
both.

IN ACCEPTING THIS BILL OF LADING the shipper,
owner, and consignee of the goods and the holder of thₑ
bill of lading agree to be bound by all its stipulations
exceptions, and conditions, whether written, printed o:
stamped, on the front or the back hereof, as fully as, i
they were all signed by said shipper, owner, consignee
or holder, any local custom or privileges to the contrar〟
notwithstanding.

IN WITNESS WHEREOF, the Master, or Agent of saic
vessel has affirmed to Three bills of lading, all this teno:
and date, one of which being accomplished, the other t(
stand void.

Dated at Manila, P. I. this 21st day of September
1927.

For the Master

SWAYNE & HOYT, INC. MANAGING AGENTS FO1

UNITED STATES SHIPPING BOARD

By E. P. Bush

J. C. T.
    Shippers
"Exhibit A".

(Endorsed): Filed May 1, 1930.

certificates required to accompany the goods. If on a sale of the goods, the proceeds fail to cover all sums due the carrier in respect of said goods, the carrier shall be entitled to recover the difference from the shipper and/or consignee.

4. If the vessel be prevented from reaching her destination by quarantine, shallow water, blockade, conditions of weather surf, ice, war, or civil disturbances; or, if it becomes impracticable to discharge the goods at destination on account of congestion, strike, labor difficulties, or otherwise, occuring before or after receipt of the goods by the carrier, vessel shall have liberty, without proceeding to or near port of destination, to proceed to and discharge the goods at a nearby available strikefree, uncongested port. Notice of discharge of the goods shall be despatched to consignee, if named herein, otherwise, to the shipper, and such discharges shall be deemed a complete delivery under this contract and full freight shall be deemed earned. All expenses incurred on the goods shall be a lien thereon.

5. The vessel may commence discharging immediately on arrival and discharge continuously, any custom of the port to the contrary notwithstanding; the collector of the port being authorized to grant a general order for discharge immediately on arrival, and if the goods be not taken from alongside by the consignee directly they come to hand in discharging the vessel, the master or vessel's agent to be at liberty to enter and land the goods, or put them into craft, or store at the risk and expense of the owner of the goods, dispatching notice thereof to the consignee, if named herein (at destination named), and

(b) Damage to fragile goods or goods not properly packed;

(c) Discoloration, splits, shakes or breakage of woodenware, staves lumber or logs

(d) Broken bundles or number of pieces in bundles.

Unless required as a result of vessel's negligence, repacking, recoopering and reconditioning shall be done at the expense of the goods.

11. Notice of loss, damage, or delay must be given in writing to the vessel's agent within thirty (30) days after the removal of the goods from the custody of the vessel, or in case of failure to make delivery within thirty (30) days after the goods should have been delivered; Provided, that notice of apparent loss or damage must be given before the goods are removed from the custody of the vessel, and proper notation made on the receipt given to the vessel for the goods shall constitute the notice herein required. Written claim for loss, damage, or delay must be filed with the vessel's agent within six (6) months after giving such written notice. Unless notice is given and claim filed as above provided, neither the vessel, her owner or agent shall be liable. No suit to recover for loss, damage, delay or failure to make delivery shall be maintained unless instituted within one year after the giving of written notice as provided herein.

12. If within goods do not satisfy all requirements of any authorities for importation into the country of destination, shipper and/or consignee will indemnify the vessel, her owner, and/or agent, for any expense for detention of the vessel arising in consequence thereof.

If, goods are not permitted to be landed at destination, they may be carried to any other port or returned to the port of loading and there discharged at the risk and expense of the goods.

13. TRANSSHIPMENT CLAUSE. Transshipment of cargo for ports not included within the vessel's itinerary is subject to all conditions, stipulations, and exceptions in bill of lading or freight note in use by the carrier or carrier s completing the transit. Neither the vessel, her owner, nor agent shall be deemed to be the agent of such carrier or carriers. If, upon the arrival at the port of transshipment, there shall be no carrier ready to receive the goods, said goods may be discharged into lighters or stored under suitable, available protection, at the risk and expense of the goods. Neither the vessel, her owner, nor agent shall be liable for loss, damage, or delay occurring after the discharge of said goods.

14. TIENTSIN AND SHANGHAI cargo may be lightered from below the bar and Hongkong cargo from alongside the vessel at the vessel's option and expense but at the consignee's risk. In the event Taku Bar delivery is impossible account ice conditions, steamer has option to deliver freight at the nearest convenient open port, as if such port were named as port of discharge, and all charges beyond such port for the account of, and collectable from consignees.

15. PHILIPPINE CARGO. In accordance with regulations of Philippine Customs Service, cargo is to be conveyed by the vessel's agent at the risk and expense of the goods from vessel to the custom house wharf and there delivered into the custody of the United States Custom

House or other proper authority for account of the consignee; and such delivery shall constitute full discharge of the carrier's obligation under this bill of lading.

16. CONTRABAND. Authorities' permit to land shipments at Shanghai and/or other ports, for transshipment or discharge, of spelter, salt, saltpeter, chlorate of potash, gunpowder, cartridges, ammunition, guns, cannon, or other firearms, or any other goods designated as contraband, must be delivered to vessel's agent at port of loading at least five (5) days before vessel sails.

17. SWEEPING. If any bag or baled goods are landed slack or torn, the receiver and/or consignee shall accept such proportion of the sweepings as may be alloted by the vessel's agent, and the same shall be deemed full settlement of any claim for loss in weight. Vessel not responsible for loss of weight in bags or bales torn, mended or with sample holes.

18. TYPHOONS. In case of stress of weather at Manila during the typhoon season, vessel may discharge at Cavite cargo consigned to Manila, giving notice thereof to the consignee, if named herein (at destination named), and such discharge shall be regarded as a complete delivery under this bill of lading.

19. WEIGHTS CLAUSE. All weights and/or measurements are subject to correction, and where goods are weighed or measured by the carrier to ascertain freight, the expense of reweighing and/or remeasuring shall be paid by the party in error any custom of the port to the contrary notwithstanding; the consignee also to pay any excess of freight discovered and the carrier to have a lien on the goods for such charges.

20. Dangerous Goods. The shippers shall be liable for any loss or damage to steamer, goods lighter or wharf caused by inflammable, explosive, or dangerous goods, shipped without full disclosure of their nature, whether such shipper be Principal or Agent; and such goods may be thrown overboard or destroyed, at any time without compensation. Extra charges, if any, for discharging, lighterage or other expense on hazardous goods declared or considered as such by civil or military authorities, must be borne by shippers and/or consignees.

21. Live Stock Clauses. In addition to the foregoing clauses, the carrier shall have the benefit of the following additional clauses as to any live stock received by it for carriage:

That freight is payable as above on the number of animals embarked, ship lost or not lost, without regard to and irrespective of the number landed, and vessel or her cargo or freight are not to be responsible for any general or other average contribution based on the destruction of such live stock, by jettison or by any cause ordinarily giving rise to claim for average contribution, or for accident, injury or death arising from any cause whatsoever.

That the animals are to be received and taken delivery of immediately on the vessel being ready to discharge them; failing this the agents of the vessel are hereby authorized to land the animals and yard them at the expense and risk of the agents, owners or consignees of the animals, or of the holders of the Bill of Lading in the place provided for that purpose, or elsewhere, as the Collector of the Port shall direct, and when so placed to be subject to rent and charges. The Collector of the Port

such other value as may be stated herein and extra freight paid upon).

It is expressly agreed that if shipowners shall have exercised due diligence to make the vessel herein mentioned seaworthy and properly manned, equipped, and supplied, carrier shall not be or be held liable for any loss of or damage to coconut or other vegetable oil carried in bulk which shall be the result of contamination, discoloration, leakage, seepage, rust, effects due to carrying said oil in bulk, effects of steam coils and/or their connection, or the result of any other causes or circumstances of any nature, kind, or character unless it be first proven that such loss or damage was caused by or resulted from carriers neglect or fault or failure in proper loading, stowage, custody, care or proper delivery of said oil.

And it is further expressly agreed that the report of Morton & Ericksen Inc., the surveyors at the port of loading, that the vessel is in all respects seaworthy for the carriage of said oil and fit to receive and transport said oil and that the loading and stowage of said oil is proper shall be and be held to be conclusive proof as to shipper, consignee and/or owner or interested party that at the time of shipment and commencement of the voyage, shipowners had exercised due deligence to make the vessel seaworthy in all respects for the carriage of said oil and fit to receive and transport same, and that the loading and stowage of said oil was proper.

It is also further agreed that consignees are to take delivery upon notice of vessel's readiness to discharge, Sundays and Holidays included, subject to twelve (12) hours prior notice of steamer's expected arrival. (After steamer's actual arrival, two hours shall be allowed by carriers to consignees for the purpose of installing pumps and rigging gear for the discharge.) Discharge once commenced is to proceed continuously day and night at no expense to vessel for overtime at the rate of not less than one thousand (1000) manifest tons per twenty-four (24) hours, Sundays and Holidays included. Failure to discharge at the above specified rate owner and/or consignee of oil shall pay demurrage at the rate of 25 cents U. S. Currency per net registered ton of the steamer or pro-rata for part of a day.

It is further understood that we agree to liquify the oil before discharging and such liquification to be limited to the capacity of the coils already installed in the vessel. If any additional heating other than that furnished by the ship coils is required at the discharge port, all expenses covering such are to be borne by the shipper and/or consignee.

All appliances for taking the oil out of the Steamer's tanks to be provided by the owner and/or consignee of the oil at his expense, steamer furnishing steam for the heating and/or for discharge if required.

J. C. T.
Shipper

AMERICAN FAR EAST LINE
Operated For U. S. Shipping Board,
By Strutners & Barry, Managing Agents
By...

Ship Agent

For answer to interrogatory IV (a), respondent is not informed that such deep tanks have any designation other than the "port" and "starboard" deep tank.

For answer to interrogatory IV (b), respondent says that it is informed that the said deep tanks were above fuel oil tanks.

For answer to Interrogatory IV (c), respondent says that it is informed that the said deep tanks were inspected at Manila Harbor in September, 1927 prior to the loading of the coconut oil and that the said deep tanks were thus found tight and proper for the carriage of coconut oil.

For answer to interrogatory IV (d), respondent says that it is informed that the deep tanks were inspected by J. I. HARRIS, Surveyor to the American Bureau of Shipping on behalf of the vessel and by C. B. Nelson, Lloyds Surveyor at Manila on behalf of the shipper of the said coconut oil.

For answer to interrogatory IV (e), respondent says that it is informed that the fuel oil tanks were inspected at Manila Harbor in September, 1927, prior to the loading of the coconut oil, by J. I. Harris, Surveyor to the American Bureau of Shipping on behalf of the vessel and by C. B. Nelson, Lloyds Surveyor at Manila on behalf of the shipper of the said coconut oil.

For answer to interrogatory IV (f), respondent says that it is informed that the loading and stowage of the said cocoanut oil was supervised by the officers of the SS WEST CAJOOT but respondent is not at the present time informed as to which officers of the SS. WEST CAJOOT supervised the loading and stowage of the said coconut oil.

For answer to interrogatory IV (g) respondent refers to its answer to interrogatory IV (f).

FIVE: For answer to interrogatory V, respondent states that it is informed that the SS. WEST CAJOOT stranded at 12:54 A.M., October 2, 1927, in approximately, latitude 30 degrees, 42 minutes north, longitude 130 degrees, 25 minutes west.

SIX. For answer to interrogatory VI, respondent states that it is informed that the SS. WEST CAJOOT was floated by her own power.

SEVEN. For answer to Interrogatory VII and VII (a), respondent refers to the certificate of survey dated September 20, 1927 by J. I. Harris and incorporates this certificate as a part of its answer to this interrogatory.

EIGHT. For answer to interrogatory VIII and VIII (a), respondent refers to the certificate of survey dated September 20, 1927 by J. I. Harris and incorporates this certificate as a part of its answer to this interrogatory.

NINE. For answer to interrogatory IX, respondent states that it is informed that the deep tanks were tested.

TEN. For answer to interrogatory X, respondent states that it is not informed at the present time.

Eleven. For answer to interrogatory XI and XI (a), respondent states that it is not informed at the present time.

Twelve. For answer to interrogatory XII, respondent says "Yes".

For answer to interrogatory XII (a), respondent says that such fuel oil tanks were damaged by contact with the reef and that one damaged tank was below the port deep tank.

Thirteen. For answer to interrogatory XIII, respondent says that it is not in a position to answer this interrogatory at the present time.

Fourteen. For answer to interrogatory XIV, respondent states that it is informed that the SS. West Cajoot was drydocked at the Kobe works of Mitsubishi Josen Kaisha.

Fifteen. For answer to interrogatory XV, respondent says that it is informed that tests were made by the examination of samples of the coconut oil and the fuel oil and by soundings.

Sixteen. For answer to interrogatory XVI, respondent says that it is informed that tests were made by the examination of samples of the coconut oil and of the fuel oil and by soundings.

> United States Shipping Board
> Merchant Fleet Corporation
> By Samuel W. McNabb
> Samuel W. McNabb
> United States Attorney for the Southern
> District of California

This motion is based upon all the records on file in the case and upon the affidavit of Edward J. Keane attached hereto and upon the memorandum in support of the motion also attached hereto.

Dated: Los Angeles, California, August 22nd, 1930.

Single & Single

Overton, Lyman & Plumb

Proctors for Libelant.

(Endorsed): Filed Aug. 22, 1930.

At a stated term, to-wit: The September Term, A.D. 1930 of the District Court of the United States of America, within and for the Central Division of the Southern District of California, held at the Court Room thereof, in the City of Los Angeles on Monday, the 22nd day of September in the year of our Lord one thousand nine hundred and thirty.

Present:

The Honorable Paul J. McCormick, District Judge.

Los Angeles Soap Company, a Corporation,
Libellant,

vs.

U. S. Shipping Board Merchant Fleet Corporation,
Respondent.

No. 3327-C-Adm.

This cause coming before the Court for hearing on motion for leave to amend libel; L. K. Vermille, Esq., appearing as counsel for the libellant, argues to the Court

Section 5, 41 Stat. 525, 46 U.S.C., Sec. 741, commonly known as the SUITS IN ADMIRALTY ACT.

UNITED STATES OF AMERICA
By: SAMUEL W. MCNABB,
United States Attorney for the
Southern District of California.

(Endorsed): Filed Oct. 10, 1930.

ANSWER TO SECOND AMENDED LIBEL AND TO AMENDED AMENDMENT TO LIBEL

To THE HONORABLE, THE JUDGES OF THE UNITED STATES DISTRICT COURT, IN AND FOR THE SOUTHERN DISTRICT OF CALIFORNIA.

Now comes the UNITED STATES OF AMERICA by its proctor, Samuel W. McNabb, United States attorney for the Southern District of California, and Ignatius F. Parker, Asst. U. S. Attorney for said District, in conformity with the order of court entered herein on September 22nd, 1930, substituting it for the UNITED STATES SHIPPING BOARD MERCHANT FLEET CORPORATION, without waiving and still excepting to the jurisdiction of the court upon the grounds stated in the Memorandum filed herein September 22, 1930 in opposition to libelant's motion for leave to file an amendment to its Amended Libel, and also upon the grounds stated in its exceptions to Second Amended Libel, which exceptions were filed herein October 10, 1930 and for answer to the second amended libel of the Los Angeles Soap Company in an alleged cause of contract, cargo damage

TENTH: This respondent admits the admiralty and maritime jurisdiction of the United States and of this Honorable Court but denies that all and singular the premises are true.

AND FOR ANSWER TO THE SECOND CAUSE OF ACTION

ELEVENTH: This respondent repeats and realleges Articles First and Tenth, both inclusive, of this answer as fully and with the same force and effect as if the same were here repeated, realleged and set forth at length.

TWELFTH: This respondent denies the allegations of Article Thirteenth of the second amended libel.

THIRTEENTH: This respondent denies the allegations of Article Fourteenth of the second amended libel.

FOURTEENTH: This respondent denies the allegations of Article Fifteenth of the second amended libel.

AND FOR ANSWER TO THE THIRD CAUSE OF ACTION

FIFTEENTH: This respondent repeats and realleges Articles First to Tenth, both inclusive, of this answer, as fully and with the same force and effect as if the same were here repeated, realleged and set forth at length.

SIXTEENTH: This respondent admits that after the said Steamship WEST CAJOOT sailed from Manila with the said cargo laden on board, consisting of coconut oil, and while proceeding from Manila and bound for Los Angeles, said steamship stranded in the Van Dieman Straits. Later she was floated and her master directed

TWENTY-FOURTH: This respondent denies the allegations of Article Twenty-fourth of the second amended libel.

TWENTY-FIFTH: This respondent denies the allegations of Article Twenty-fifth of the second amended libel.

FURTHER ANSWERING THE SAID SECOND AMENDED LIBEL AND BY WAY OF SEPARATE DEFENSE THERETO, THE UNITED STATES OF AMERICA BY ITS PROCTOR SAMUEL W. McNABB, UNITED STATES ATTORNEY FOR THE SOUTHERN DISTRICT OF CALIFORNIA, ALLEGES UPON INFORMATION AND BELIEF, AS FOLLOWS:

TWENTY-SIXTH: That in September, 1927 there was shipped on the Steamship WEST CAJOOT at Manila certain merchandise purporting to consist of 546.24241 long tons or 1,223,385 pounds of cocoanut oil. Said cocoanut oil was shipped under a Bill of Lading dated at Manila, September 21st, 1927, duly issued for the master of the Steamship WEST CAJOOT by Swayne & Hoyt, Inc., Managing Agents for the United States Shipping Board. A copy of said Bill of Lading is attached hereto, incorporated into and made a part of this answer and marked "Exhibit A". Said coconut oil was loaded into the deep tanks of the Steamship WEST CAJOOT but prior to such loading the deep tanks were examined, tested, inspected, cleaned, made tight and in every way rendered fit and proper receptacles for the carriage of said coconut oil. Said Bill of Lading, marked "Exhibit A", contains among others the following clause:

CAJOOT struck a submerged rock or reef, severely injuring the vessel's bottom and causing the flooding of No. 1 Hold. For the safety of the vessel and cargo the master of the Steamship WEST CAJOOT altered the course of the Steamship WEST CAJOOT to Kobe, Japan, where the vessel was drydocked and the injury to the Steamship WEST CAJOOT and her cargo was repaired so that the vessel was enabled to continue her voyage and the cargo of coconut oil was discharged at Los Angeles. That, if as alleged in said libel, the coconut oil was found to be contaminated by fuel oil on its discharge at Los Angeles, this contamination was caused by the striking of the submerged rock or reef by the steamship WEST CAJOOT, as aforesaid, and the consequent tearing and straining of the structure of the ship, which caused a leaking of the tanks of the ship.

The said Bill of Lading marked "Exhibit A" contains among others the following clause:

> "Neither the vessel, her owner, nor agent, shall be liable for loss or damage resulting from: Act of God, perils, dangers and accidents of the sea or other navigable waters;"

Respondent claims the benefit of this clause.

That prior to said stranding, due diligence had been exercised to make said Steamship WEST CAJOOT in all respects seaworthy and properly manned, equipped and supplied, and said steamship was at all of said times, in fact, in all respects seaworthy and properly manned, equipped and supplied.

That any damage to, or loss of cargo was caused by one or more, and/or a combination of two or more risks

recover for loss, damage, delay or failure to make delivery shall be maintained unless instituted within one year after the giving of written notice as provided herein."

That no notice of loss, damage or delay was given in writing to the vessel's agent within the time limited in Clause 11 of this Bill of Lading, nor was notice of apparent loss or damage given within the time limited in Clause 11, nor was written claim for loss, damage, or delay filed with the vessel's agent within the time limited in Clause 11 of the Bill of Lading.

FURTHER ANSWERING THE SAID SECOND AMENDED LIBEL AND BY WAY OF A FOURTH ADDITIONAL D E F E N S E THERETO, THE UNITED STATES OF AMERICA BY ITS PROC-TOR SAMUEL W. McNABB, UNITED STATES ATTORNEY FOR THE SOUTHERN DISTRICT OF CALIFORNIA, ALLEGES UPON INFORMA-TION AND BELIEF, AS FOLLOWS:

The said Bill of Lading, marked "Exhibit A" under which the said coconut oil was shipped contained among others the following clause:

"The value of each package shipped hereunder does not exceed two hundred and fifty dollars ($250.00), unless otherwise stated herein, on which basis the freight is adjusted, and the vessel's liability shall in no case exceed that sum or the invoice value (including freight charges, if paid, and including duty, if paid, and not returnable), whichever shall be the less, unless a value in excess thereof be specially

IN THE DISTRICT COURT OF THE UNITED STATES FOR THE SOUTHERN DISTRICT OF CALIFORNIA.

THE LOS ANGELES SOAP COMPANY, a corporation,

Libelant,

vs.

THE UNITED STATES OF AMERICA,

Respondent.

IN ADMIRALTY

No. 3327-C

ANSWERS TO LIBELANT'S INTERROGATORIES.

ONE: For answer to interrogatory No. I, respondent says that the American Australia Orient Line, Swayne & Hoyt, Inc., were managing operators for the United States Shipping Board.

(b) The United States of America was the owner of the Steamship WEST CAJOOT.

TWO: For answer to interrogatory No. II, respondent says that the American Australia Orient Line, Swayne & Hoyt, Inc., was a party to a managing operating. agreement under which the steamship WEST CAJOOT was operated.

THREE: For answer to Interrogatory No. III, respondent says that the American Australia Orient Line, Swayne & Hoyt, Inc., managing operators for the United States Shipping Board, had such general direction and control, subject to the orders of the owner of the steamship West 'Cajoot, the United States of America.

Four: For answer to interrogatory IV, respondent says that the cargo of coconut oil was stowed in the port and starboard deep tanks of the steamship West Cajoot.

> For answer to interrogatory IV (a), respondent is not informed that such deep tanks have any designation other than the "port" and "starboard" deep tank.

> For answer to interrogatory IV (b), respondent says that the said deep tanks were above fuel oil tanks.

> For answer to interrogatory IV (c), respondent says that the said deep tanks were inspected at Manila Harbor in September, 1927, prior to the loading of the coconut oil and that the said deep tanks were thus found tight and proper for the carriage of coconut oil.

> For answer to interrogatory IV (d), respondent says that the deep tanks were inspected by J. I. Harris, Surveyor to the American Bureau of Shipping on behalf of the vessel and by C. B. Nelson, Lloyds Surveyor at Manila on behalf of the shipper of the said coconut oil.

> For answer to interrogatory IV (e), respondent says that the fuel oil tanks were inspected at Manila Harbor in September, 1927, prior to the loading of the coconut oil, by J. I. Harris, Surveyor to the American Bureau of Shipping on behalf of

the vessel and by C. B. Nelson, Lloyds Surveyor
at Manila on behalf of the shipper of the said
coconut oil.

For answer to interrogatory IV (f), respondent says
that the loading and stowage of the said coconut
oil was supervised by the officers of the steamship WEST CAJOOT but respondent is not at the
present time informed as to which officers of the
steamship WEST CAJOOT supervised the loading
and stowage of the said coconut oil.

For answer to interrogatory IV (g), respondent refers to its answer to interrogatory IV (f).

FIVE. For answer to interrogatory V, respondent states
that the steamship WEST CAJOOT stranded at 12:54
A.M., October 2, 1927, in approximately, latitude 30
degrees, 42 minutes north, longitude 130 degrees, 25
minutes west.

SIX. For answer to interrogatory VI, respondent states
that the steamship WEST CAJOOT was floated by her
own power.

SEVEN. For answer to interrogatory VII and VII (a),
marked Exhibit B
respondent refers to the certificate of survey/dated
September 20, 1927 by J. I. Harris and incorporates
this certificate as a part of its answer to this interrogatory.

EIGHT. For answer to interrogatory VIII and VIII (a),
respondent refers to the certificate of survey dated
September 20, 1927 by J. I. Harris and incorporates

this certificate as a part of its answer to this interrogatory.

NINE. For answer to interrogatory IX, respondent states that the deep tanks were tested and proven tight.

TEN. For answer to interrogatory X, respondent states that it is not informed at the present time.

ELEVEN. For answer to interrogatory XI and XI (a), respondent states that it *it* is not informed at the present time.

TWELVE. For answer to interrogatory XII, respondent says "Yes".

For answer to interrogatory XII (a), respondent says that such fuel oil tanks were damaged by contact with the reef and that one damaged tank was below the port deep tank.

THIRTEEN. For answer to interrogatory XIII, respondent says that it is not in a position to answer this interogatory at the present time.

FOURTEEN. For answer to interrogatory XIV, respondent states that it is informed that the steamship WEST CAJOOT was drydocked at the Kobe works of Mitsubishi Josen Kaisha.

FIFTEEN. For answer to interrogatory XV, respondent says that tests were made by the examination of samples of the coconut oil and the fuel oil and by soundings.

SIXTEEN. For answer to the interrogatory XVI, respondent says that tests were made by the examination of samples of the coconut oil and of the fuel oil and by soundings.

THE UNITED STATES OF AMERICA

By:...

SAMUEL W. MCNABB,
United States Attorney for the Southern
District of California.

IGNATIUS F. PARKER,
Assistant United States Attorney for said
District.

(Note: "Exhibit A" referred to in the answer herein is the same as "Exhibit A" in the answer (filed 5/1/30) of the United States to the amended libel of the Los Angeles Soap Company.)

1760

MORTON & ERICKSEN, INC.
Surveyors
American Bureau of Shipping
(American Lloyd's)

————

United States Salvage Association, Inc.

————

Derham Building

The British Corporation for the Survey
and Registry of Shipping

Port Area

————

Registro Italiano

————

Imperial Japanese Marine Corporation

Registered Marine & Cargo Surveyors
Cable Address: Morteric
P: O. Box 2103 Telephone 22516
Manila, P. I., September 20, 1927.

CERTIFICATE OF SURVEY
DEEP TANK S/S "WEST CAJOOT"

THIS IS TO CERTIFY that we, the undersigned Registered Marine and Cargo Surveyors, at the request of Messrs. Swayne & Hoyt, Local Agents, did attend on board the American S/S "WEST CAJOOT" of Los Angeles, 3339 tons net, Capt. Thorsen, on September 15, 1927, and subsequent days as she lay anchored in Manila Harbor, P. I., for the purpose of surveying and ascertaining the condition of vessel's deep tank and its fitness to receive and carry cocoanut oil in bulk as cargo to San Francisco and/or Los Angeles to be loaded by Jao Cui Peng, Manila, and have to report as follows:

The deep tank S/S "WEST CAJOOT" is situated in way of No. 2 cargo hold just forward of fireroom, is divided into port and starboard sections by a longitudinal bulkhead, and is fitted with bilges on the sides. A coffer-dam approximately 2 ft. wide has been built around settling tanks in the deep tank.

On vessel's arrival at this port, the deep tank was full of water and a head of approximately 8 ft. was put on same for the purpose of testing the tank top, bulkheads and ship's sides. On examination, a number of leaks were found in tank top and forward and after bulkheads. These leaks were all caulked and made tight with the tank full of water. After this test both sections were pumped out, washed down with chemical solutions, scraped, rubbed down with copra meal and coconut oil and thoroughly cleaned.

Ballast suctions were blanked off in the tank, bilge suctions were cleaned and blanked off in the fireroom, vent pipes were blanked off in the tween deck, sounding pipes and steam smothering lines were fitted with screw plugs in the tank.

A full head of fuel oil was put on bottom of deep tank by way of double bottoms for the purpose of testing the double bottom tank top. A head of fuel oil was put on double bottom tank forward of and adjacent to the deep tank. On examination, a few slight weeps were found which were caulked and made tight with the double bottoms under pressure. After this test and before loading oil, the pressure was taken off the double bottom tank tops.

Piping fitted to heat the oil was tested several times with steam and made tight, after which the piping was filled with fresh water thru riser pipes and at time of loading oil, all piping was sound and tight and full of fresh water.

In the opinion of the undersigned, both sections of deep tank S/S "WEST CAJOOT" are now in fit condition to receive and carry coconut oil in bulk as cargo on the voyage intended, provided no fuel oil pressure is put on bottom of deep tank while coconut oil is being carried in the deep tank.

The tank was also tested, inspected and accepted on behalf of the shipper by Mr. C. B. Nelson, Lloyd's Surveyor, Manila.   NORTON & ERICKSEN, INC.

Per J. I. Harris

Survey fee—$100.00

Exhibit "B"

IN THE UNITED STATES DISTRICT COURT FOR THE SOUTHERN DISTRICT OF CALIFORNIA. CENTRAL DIVISION.

THE LOS ANGELES SOAP COMPANY, a corporation,

Libelant,

versus

THE UNITED STATES OF AMERICA,

Respondent.

IN ADMIRALTY

No. 3327-C

INTERROGATORIES.

INTERROGATORIES PROPOUNDED TO THE LIBELANT BY THE RESPONDENT TO BE ANSWERED BY IT UNDER OATH.

1. Please state whether or not notice of loss, damage, or delay was given in writing to the vessel's agent.

2. If your answer to Interrogatory One is in the affirmative, please state to whom such notice was given.

3. If your answer to Interrogatory One is in the affirmative, please state when such notice was given.

4. If your answer to Interrogatory One is in the affirmative, please attach a true copy thereof to your answers to these interrogatories.

5. Please state whether or not written claim for loss, damage or delay was filed with the vessel's agent.

6. If your answer to Interrogatory Five is in the affirmative, please state with whom such notice was filed.

7. If your answer to Interrogatory Five is in the affirmative, please state when such notice was filed.

8. If your answer to Interrogatory Five is in the affirmative, please attach a true copy thereof to your answers to these interrogatories.

9. Please state whether or not notice of loss, damage or delay was given in writing to any person.

10. If your answer to Interrogatory Nine is in the affirmative, please state to whom such notice was given.

11. If your answer to Interrogatory Nine is in the affirmative, please state when such notice was given.

12. If your answer to Interrogatory Nine is in the affimative, please attach a true copy thereof to your answers to these interrogatories.

13. Please state whether or not written claim for loss, damage or delay was filed with any person.

14. If your answer to Interrogatory Thirteen is in the affirmative, please state with whom such notice was filed.

15. If your answer to Interrogatory Thirteen is in the affirmative, please state when such notice was filed.

16. If your answer to Interrogatory Thirteen is in the affirmative, please attach a true copy thereof to your answers to these interrogatories.

17. State whether or not "Exhibit A" attached to the answer is a true copy of the certain bill of lading referred to in article Fifth of said amended libel.

(Endorsed): Filed Oct. 14, 1930.

[TITLE OF COURT AND CAUSE]

IN ADMIRALTY

No. 3327-C

ANSWER OF LIBELANT TO THE INTERROGA-
TORIES ADDRESSED TO LIBELANT BY RE-
SPONDENT, UNITED STATES OF AMERICA.

FIRST INTERROGATORY: Yes

SECOND INTERROGATORY: To Messrs. Swayne & Hoyt, Inc., 240 Front Street, San Francisco, California, and 122 East 7th Street, Los Angeles, California.

THIRD INTERROGATORY: Notice was given to Messrs. Swayne & Hoyt, Inc., at San Francisco by Messrs. Curtis & Tompkins, chemists, on November 26, 1927. Notice was given again to Messrs. Swayne & Hoyt, Inc., at Los Angeles on December 2, 1927 by the Los Angeles Soap Company. A bill for the damage was sent to Messrs. Swayne & Hoyt, Inc. at Los Angeles by the Los Angeles Soap Company by letter of January 23, 1928.

FOURTH INTERROGATORY: Copies thereof are hereto attached.

FIFTH INTERROGATORY: Messrs. Swayne & Hoyt, Inc. were the vessel's agents.

SIXTH INTERROGATORY: Refer to answer to Interrogatory Number Two.

SEVENTH INTERROGATORY: Refer to answer to Interrogatory Number Three.

EIGHTH INTERROGATORY: Refer to answer to Interrogatory Number Four.

NINTH INTERROGATORY: Refer to answer to Interrogatory Number One.

TENTH INTERROGATORY: Refer to answer to Interrogatory Number Two.

ELEVENTH INTERROGATORY: Refer to answer to Interrogatory Number Three.

TWELFTH INTERROGATORY: Refer to answer to Interrogatory Number Four.

THIRTEENTH INTERROGATORY: Refer to answer to Interrogatory Number Two.

FOURTEENTH INTERROGATORY: Refer to answer to Interrogatory Number Two.

FIFTEENTH INTERROGATORY: Refer to answer to Interrogatory Number Three.

SIXTEENTH INTERROGATORY: Refer to answer to Interrogatory Number Four.

SEVENTEENTH INTERROGATORY: Yes.

OVERTON, LYMAN & PLUMB
Proctors for Libelant.

(Verified).

(Endorsed): Filed Nov. 20, 1930.

CURTIS & TOMPKINS, CHEMISTS.

November 26th, 1927.

Swayne & Hoyt, Inc.,
240 Front Street,
San Francisco, Calif.

Dear Sirs:—

COCOANUT OIL PER SS. WEST CAJOOT
a/c LOS ANGELES SOAP CO.

This is to confirm the verbal conversation between the writer and your Mr. Jergens today with reference to the discharge of port and starboard tanks of cocoanut oil on SS. WEST CAJOOT at Los Angeles.

Preliminary samples were drawn at this port. That from the port or contaminated tank was only drawn to a point about half way down, as beyond that point the oil was solid. The sample of liquid oil taken, showed it to be contaminated but not beyond use. The starboard tank of apparently good oil was drawn to within about 2′ of the bottom where hard oil was encountered, and it showed no signs of contamination.

It is assential to see that the equalizing valve is kept closed the entire time during transportation and discharge. To avoid the possibility of contaminating the good tank with contaminated oil, the damaged port tank should be pumped first, in case there might be a rupture in the center bulkhead which would permit the contam·inated oil to enter the good tank. Of course while both tanks are at about the same level, there would not be any circulating interchange to cause such contamination. However, the lowering of the level of one tank or the other would permit leakage and it is therefore necessary to remove the contaminated oil first.

We understand that the contamination took place through a rupture in the double bottom, due to the miss-hap, and it therefore seems logical that to minimize the contamination, the double bottoms should be kept slack and the oil not heated to a point where all the oil at the bottom is melted, but with the idea of allowing a foot or 6 inches of hard oil to remain at the bottom as an insulating medium.

We are instructing our representatives at Los Angeles, Mr. Beedle and Mr. Huffman of the Gooch Laboratories, that it is desirable to remove the oil from damaged tank, pumping from the top down and watching the oil continuously for any serious change in color, in order that all of the usable oil may be segregated from any very black oil at the bottom of the tank, which we believe will be confirmed to the mixture of hard oil in the last 6" or foot.

If the oil can be segregated in this manner, it will enable a much greater portion being recovered in a usable state, and while off color, not as badly contaminated as would be anticipated near the bottom.

We would therefore advise beginning to gradually heat this tank only about three days before the intended pumping and not having the temperature carried about 100°F maximum. When the best of the oil has been removed or when it is noted that a very much inferior grade is coming over, this could be placed in a separate tank or container, and any hard oil at the bottom that

LOS ANGELES SOAP CO.,
617 East First Street,
Los Angeles.

December 2, 1927.

Swayne & Hoyt, Inc.,
122 E. 7th St.,
Los Angeles, Calif.

Gentlemen:—

With reference to shipment of Cocoanut Oil shipped by Jao Cui Pien on September 21st on board SS. WEST CAJOOT for our account now being unloaded at the docks of the Vegetable Oil Products Company, Wilmington, Calif.

All of the oil loaded in the port tank of the ship is so badly contaminated with fuel oil that it is of no value to us, therefore we must refuse delivery. We are so advising Mr. Ralph S. Cochrane, 310 Sansome St., San Francisco, agent for the Westchester Fire Insurance, Company of New York, who wrote the insurance on this cargo.

Yours very truly,

LOS ANGELES SOAP COMPANY

J. A. WOOD Auditor

JAW:DM　　　　　　　By..

(Copy)

[TITLE OF COURT AND CAUSE]

IN ADMIRALTY.

No. 3663-C

LIBEL

TO THE HONORABLE, THE JUDGES OF THE UNITED STATES DISTRICT COURT, IN AND FOR THE SOUTHERN DISTRICT OF CALIFORNIA:

The libel of the United States of America, a sovereign, as owner of the Steamship WEST CAJOOT, by its proctor, Samuel W. McNabb, United States Attorney for the Southern District of California, on behalf of itself and all other parties in interest, against the Los Angeles Soap Company, in a cause of contract and of general average, civil and maritime, upon information and belief alleges as follows:

FIRST: That at all the times hereinafter mentioned, the United States of America was and is a corporation sovereign.

SECOND: That at all the times hereinafter mentioned, the United States of America was the owner of the Steamship WEST CAJOOT.

THIRD: That the respondent herein, the Los Angeles Soap Company, is a corporation duly organized and existing under and by virtue of the laws of the State of California, with its office and principal place of business in the City of Los Angeles, County of Los Angeles, State of California, and that said respondent has goods, chattels and credits within the jurisdiction of this Honorable Court.

the Master or vessel's agents, before delivery of the goods. If the owner shall have exercised due diligence to make the vessel in all respects seaworthy and properly manned, equipped and supplied, it is hereby agreed that in case of danger, damage, or disaster resulting from faults or errors in navigation, or in the management of the vessel, or from any latent or other defects in the vessel, her machinery or appurtenances or from unseaworthiness, whether existing at the time of shipment, or at the beginning of the voyage (provided the latent or other defect or the unseaworthiness was not discoverable by the exercise of due diligence), the shippers, consignees, and/or owners of the cargo shall nevertheless pay a salvage and any special charges incurred in respect of the cargo, and shall contribute with the shipowners in general average to the payment of any sacrifices, losses, or expense of a general average nature that may be made or incurred for the common benefit or to relieve the adventure from any common peril."

SIXTH: That the United States of America, the owner of the Steamship WEST CAJOOT, exercised due diligence to make said vessel in all respects seaworthy, properly manned, equipped and supplied, and that at the inception of the voyage hereinafter described, the Steamship WEST CAJOOT, was, in fact, tight, staunch, strong, properly manned, equipped and supplied, and in all respects seaworthy.

SEVENTH: That after receiving the aforesaid shipment of cocoanut oil at Manila, while on the voyage

ercising this lien, the Los Angeles Soap Company executed a general average bond dated November 27, 1927, in which the Los Angeles Soap Company agreed to pay the proportionate contribution to the general average expenses and sacrifices due from the aforesaid cargo, received by the Los Angeles Soap Company and more particularly described in the aforesaid Bill of Lading, "Exhibit A". A photostatic copy of said general average bond is attached hereto, marked "Exhibit B" incorporated into and made a part of this libel. In consideration of the execution and delivery of the aforesaid general average bond, libelant refrained from exercising this lien and the said shipment of cocoanut oil was delivered to and received by the respondent without the enforcement of a lien for the cargo's proportionate contribution to the general average expenditures and sacrifices. By virtue of these premises libelant became entitled to receive from the Los Angeles Soap Company, the cocoanut oil's proportionate contribution to the general average expenditures and sacrifices.

EIGHTH: In accordance with the provisions of the bill of lading, dated September 21, 1927, a general average statement was prepared at San Francisco according to York-Antwerp Rules, 1890, and as to matters not therein provided, according to the laws and customs of the Port of San Francisco, by Messrs. Marsh and McLennan, Average Adjusters, and a copy thereof, dated April 15, 1929, was duly presented to the Los Angeles Soap Company, respondent herein and/or its agent.

NINTH: As appears from the said general average statement, the contributory value of said shipment of

INTERROGATORIES PROPOUNDED TO THE RESPONDENT TO BE ANSWERED IN WRITING UNDER OATH.

FIRST INTERROGATORY: Have you received a copy of the general average statement, dated April 15, 1929, referred to in the libel?

SECOND INTERROGATORY: If your answer to the First Interrogatory is in the affirmative, state whether you admit that the said statement is made according to York-Antwerp Rules, 1890, and as to matters not therein provided, according to the laws and customs of the port of San Francisco.

THIRD INTERROGATORY: If your answer to the Second Interrogatory is in the negative, state, with particularity, wherein you claim the statement is erroneous.

FOURTH INTERROGATORY: If in your answer to the Third Interrogatory you have pointed out errors, state whether you claim that you had, prior to the commencement of this suit, pointed them out to libelant, or its agents.

FIFTH INTERROGATORY: If your answer to the Fourth Interrogatory is in the affirmative, state whether the communication was oral or in writing. If in writing, attach a true copy thereof to your answer. If oral, state the person from whom and the person to whom the communication was made, and the approximate date thereof.

SIXTH INTERROGATORY: If your answer to the First Interrogatory is in the affirmative, state whether you admit that the statement is correct as to charges and expenses, contributory value and amounts of contribution, assuming for the purpose of your answer that the statement has been made up according to the applicable law.

SEVENTH INTERROGATORY: If your answer to the Sixth Interrogatory is in the negative, state, with particularity, wherein you claim the statements is erroneous.

EIGHTH INTERROGATORY: If, in your answer to the Seventh Interrogatory, you have pointed out errors, state whether you claim that you had, prior to the commencement of this suit, pointed them out to libelant or its agents.

NINTH INTERROGATORY: If your answer to the Eighth Interrogatory is in the affirmative, state whether the communication was oral or in writing. If in writing, attach a true copy thereof to your answer. If oral, state the person from whom and the person to whom the communication was made, and the approximate date thereof.

(NOTE: "Exhibit A" referred to in the libel herein is the same as "Exhibit A" in the Answer (filed 5/1/30) of the United States to the amended libel of the Los Angeles Soap Company in case No. 3327.)

AVERAGE BOND

ORDER OF—The First National Bank of Los Angeles.

NOTIFY—Los Angeles Soap Company, 617 E. 1st St., L. A.

WHEREAS, the steamer "WEST CAJOOT" whereof Thorsen was master having on board a cargo of lumber, hemp, copra, rubber and general merchandise sailed from Brisbane, Australia on or about the second day of August............ 1927 bound for Pacific Coast ports, via ports and in the course of her said voyage, it is alleged that the vessel struck a reef, and put into Kobe as a port of refuge.

AND WHEREAS, by reason of the occurrences of the voyage, certain losses and expenses have been incurred, and other further losses and expenses may yet be incurred, which may be a charge by way of General Average or otherwise upon the vessel, her freight, her cargo, or either of them; or which may be charges upon specific interests.

Now, therefore, we the subscribers, owners, and/or charters of said vessel, owners of her freight, owners, shippers or consignees of her cargo, or agents of one or more of said parties having such interest as we have severally described and set opposite our respective signatures hereto, in consideration of the waiver of the rights of the owner and/or other party interested herein to take immediate action against hull and/or freight and/or cargo for the enforcement of liens and/or General Average claims and/or other claims arising from this disaster not giving rise to liens do hereby for ourselves personally, our respective successors, executors and administrators and for our principals, their successors, executors and administrators, severally but not jointly or one for the other covenant and agree to and with American Australia Orient Line and/or United States Shipping Board and MARSH & McLENNAN, who are hereby appointed trustees for all concerned, that all losses and expenses as aforesaid which shall be made to appear to be due from us or our principals or from any firm of which we are or were co-partners at the time any liability arose under the premises shall be paid unto the said American Australia Orient Line and/or United States Shipping Board and/or MARSH & McLENNAN as trustees for all concerned, provided that such losses and expenses shall be stated and apportioned by MARSH & McLENNAN, Average Adjusters, in accordance with the established usages and laws in similar cases; and that such payment shall be made upon the completion of the statement of such losses and expenses and after due notice has been given thereof.

And we do further agree to furnish promptly to said adjusters upon their request all such information and all such documents as they may require from us to make the said adjustment.

This bond may be executed in several parts of like tenor and date, the whole of which are to constitute but one bond with the same effect as if each of said parts were severally signed by us.

In the event of the compensation for any services which have been or may hereafter be rendered in whole or in part to the cargo, whether of the nature of salvage or otherwise, being fixed by agreement or arbitration, We hereby agree to pay our proportion of the sum thus fixed; and in the event of action being brought to recover for such services, We hereby agree to give bond for our proportion of the sum sued for, in the same manner as if the person or persons by whom suit is brought, be they salvors or otherwise, had required such bond direct from us, before surrendering the cargo; and We further agree to pay and fully satisfy any final decree that may be rendered, according to our proportion thereof.

IN WITNESS WHEREOF we have to these presents set our hands in the City of Los Angeles this seventeenth day of November in the year of our Lord one thousand nine hundred and twenty seven

SIGNATURES	MARKS AND NOS.	INTEREST	AMT. OF INVOICE	NAME OF UNDERWRITER
LOS ANGELES SOAP CO. J. A. WOOD, Auditor	B/L No. 5, IN BULK	Manila, P.I. to L.A.Harbor, Calif. 546.24241 L.Tons Cocoanut Oil Shipped by Jao Qui Pien		Westchester Fire Ed. A. Keler & Co., Ltd., Agents, Manila Policy No. 80251 $110 000.00

MARSH & McLENNAN
Average Adjusters
114 Sansome St, San Francisco

BOND MUST BE DATED WHEN SIGNED

"This bond must be signed by a member of the firm or an officer of the Company or some party having 'power of Attorney' and if signed by an officer or Attorney it must be so designated hereon."

Exhibit B   Ok 11-21-27

(Endorsed): Filed Aug. 15, 1929.

libel and accordingly demands strict proof thereof, if pertinent.

FIFTH: That respondent admits the allegations contained in the "Fifth" Article of the libel.

SIXTH: Answering unto Article "Sixth" of said libel, respondent alleges that it has no information or belief sufficient to enable it to answer the allegations, or any of them, contained therein, and therefore, denies said allegations and calls for strict proof thereof, if pertinent.

SEVENTH: Answering unto Article "Seventh" of said libel, respondent alleges that it has no information or belief sufficient to enable it to answer the allegations, or any of them, contained therein, and therefore, denies said allegations and calls for strict proof thereof, if pertinent; except that respondent denies that the alleged expenses, sacrifices and drydocking of the vessel with the cocoanut oil cargo aboard were necessary for the preservation of the cargo and the completion of the venture, and/or that libelant became entitled to a proportionate contribution from the shipment of cocoanut oil to the alleged general average expenditures and/or sacrifices.

EIGHTH: Answering unto the allegations contained in Article "Eighth" of said libel, respondent alleges that it has no information or belief sufficient to enable it to answer the allegations, or any of them, except that respondent admits that a copy of the alleged General Average Statement was presented to it.

NINTH: Answering unto the allegations of Article "Ninth" of said libel, respondent alleges that it has no information or belief sufficient to enable it to answer

information and belief, alleges and respectfully shows to this Honorable Court as follows:

FIRST: That The Los Angeles Soap Company, a corporation, cross-libelant herein, was, at and during all the times hereinafter mentioned, and now is a corporation duly organized and existing under and by virtue of the laws of the State of California and was at all times with its office and principal place of business in the City of Los Angeles, County of Los Angeles, State of California.

SECOND: At and during all the times hereinafter mentioned, the cross-respondent was and still is a corporation sovereign.

THIRD: At and during all the times hereinafter mentioned, the Steamship West Cajoot was owned and/or operated, managed and controlled by the cross-respondent as a common carrier of merchandise by water for hire.

FOURTH: Heretofore and on or about and between the 15th and 23rd days of September, 1927, one Jao Cui Pien delivered to the cross-respondent at Manila, P. I., 546.24241 long tons or 1,223,583 pounds of cocoanut oil all in good order and condition, to be carried in consideration of an agreed freight, to the port of Los Angeles, California, and there to be delivered in like good order and condition as when received by the cross-respondent, to the order of the Los Angeles Soap Company.

FIFTH: Thereupon this cross-respondent received and accepted the said cocoanut oil in said good order and condition, and agreed in consideration of the payment of

TENTH: By reason of the damage and loss aforesaid your cross-libelant has sustained damage in the sum of $40,000. as nearly as the same can now be estimated, no part of which has been paid although the same has been duly demanded.

ELEVENTH: All and singular the premises are true and within the admiralty jurisdiction of the United States and of this Honorable Court.

FOR A SECOND CAUSE OF ACTION

TWELFTH: Your cross-libelant here repeats and realleges each and every allegation contained in Articles "FIRST" to "ELEVENTH" both inclusive of this cross-libel, as fully and with the same force and effect as if the same were here repeated, realleged and set forth at length.

THIRTEENTH: Contrary to and in breach of the provisions of said agreement and contract of carriage, the cross-respondent did not prosecute the voyage with dispatch, but caused, ordered and procured the said Steamship West Cajoot to be drydocked at Kobe, Japan, and at San Francisco, California, with said cargo stowed within said ship.

FOURTEENTH: The aforesaid loss, damage and contamination of said cocoanut oil was due to and caused by the drydocking of the said Steamship at Kobe and at San Francisco with cargo within her, and was a breach of the aforesaid agreement and contract of carriage.

FIFTEENTH: Said breach of the aforesaid agreement and contract of carriage constituted and was an unjusti-

FOR A FOURTH CAUSE OF ACTION

TWENTIETH: Your cross-libelant here repeats and re-alleges each and every allegation contained in Articles "FIRST" to "ELEVENTH", both inclusive of this cross-libel, as fully and with the same force and effect as if the same were here repeated, realleged and set forth at length.

TWENTY-FIRST: That after the said Steamship West Cajoot sailed from Manila with the said cargo laden on board consisting of 546.24241 long tons or 1,223,583 pounds of cocoanut oil, and while proceeding from Manila and bound for Los Angeles, by way of Hong Kong, said Steamship stranded in the Vandieman Straits. Later she was floated and her master then directed his course for Kobe, Japan, where cross-respondent caused, ordered or procured said vessel to be drydocked for inspection and repairs. Cross-respondent failed to discharge cross-libelant's aforementioned cargo of cocoanut oil prior to and before said Steamship was drydocked at Kobe, and as a result thereof, said ship and her tanks were strained and impaired.

That on or about the 29th day of November, 1927, cross-respondent again caused, ordered and procured said vessel to be drydocked at San Francisco, California, for inspection and repairs, without discharging cross-libelant's aforementioned cargo of cocoanut oil, and as a result thereof, said vessel and her tanks were again strained and impaired. That the drydocking of said vessel at Kobe and at San Francisco with cross-libelant's said cargo stored within said ship resulted in the damage as aforesaid.

[TITLE OF COURT AND CAUSE]

No. 3663-C

EXCEPTIONS TO CROSS-LIBEL

To THE HONORABLE THE JUDGES OF THE UNITED STATES DISTRICT COURT, IN AND FOR THE SOUTHERN DISTRICT OF CALIFORNIA, CENTRAL DIVISION.

Now COMES the United States of America by its Proctor, Samuel W. McNabb, United States Attorney for the Southern District of California and excepts to the cross-libel filed in this cause, for the following reasons:

FIRST: That the First Cause of Action in the said cross-libel is vague, general, indefinite and insufficient in law.

SECOND: That the First Cause of Action in the said cross-libel does not conform to the Twenty-second Rule of Practice of the United States in matters of Admiralty and Maritime jurisdiction in the following respects:

(a) That the First Cause of Action in the said cross-libel fails to allege when the cargo of coconut oil was delivered by the Steamship WEST CAJOOT to the cross-libelant.

(b) That the First Cause of Action in the said cross-libel fails to disclose when cross-libelant's cause of action accrued to it.

THIRD: That the Second Cause of Action in the said cross-libel is vague, general, indefinite and insufficient in law.

FOURTH: That the Second Cause of Action in the said cross-libel does not conform to the Twenty-second

Rule. of Practice of the United States in. matters of Admiralty and Maritime jurisdiction: in the following respects:

(a) That the Second Cause of Action in the said cross-libel fails to allege .when the cargo of coconut oil was delivered by the Steamship WEST CAJOOT to the cross-libelant.

(b) That the Second Cause of Action in the said cross-libel fails to disclose when cross-libelant's cause of action accrued to it.

FIFTH: That the Third Cause of Action in the said cross-libel is vague, general, indefinite and. insufficient in law.

SIXTH: That the Third Cause of Action in the said cross-libel does not conform to the Twenty-second Rule of Practice of the United States in matters of Admiralty and Maritime jurisdiction in the following respects:

(a) That the Third Cause of Action in the said cross-libel fails to allege when the cargo of coconut oil was delivered by the Steamship WEST CAJOOT to the cross-libelant.

(b) That the Third Cause of Action in the said cross-libel fails to disclose when cross-libelant's cause of action accrued to it.

SEVENTH: That the Fourth Cause of Action in the said cross-libel is vague, general, indefinite and insufficient in law.

EIGHTH: That the Fourth Cause of Action in the said cross-libel does not conform to the Twenty-second

Rule of Practice of the United States in matters of Admiralty and Maritime jurisdiction in the following respects:

(a) That the Fourth Cause of Action in the said cross-libel fails to allege when the cargo of coconut oil was delivered by the Steamship WEST CAJOOT to the cross-libelant.

(b) That the Fourth Cause of Action in the said cross-libel fails to disclose when cross-libelant's cause of action accrued to it.

(c) That the Fourth Cause of Action of said cross-libel fails to allege when the cross-libelant became entitled to an allowance in general average.

> THE UNITED STATES OF AMERICA
> By: Samuel W. McNabb
> SAMUEL W. MCNABB,
>   United States Attorney for the
>   Southern District of California.
>
> IGNATIUS F. PARKER
> Ignatius F. Parker,
>   Assistant U. S. Attorney for said
>   District.

(Endorsed): Filed May 22, 1930

[TITLE OF COURT AND CAUSE]

No. 3663-C

AMENDMENT TO CROSS-LIBEL OF LOS ANGELES SOAP COMPANY.

TO THE HONORABLE THE JUDGES OF THE UNITED STATES DISTRICT COURT, IN AND FOR THE SOUTHERN DISTRICT OF CALIFORNIA:

The amendment to the cross-libel of the Los Angeles Soap Company, a corporation, as owner of a cargo of cocoanut oil, against the United States of America, owner of the S. S. "West Cajoot", in a cause of cargo damage, civil and maritime, upon information and belief alleges and respectfully shows to this Honorable Court as follows :

I.

Cross-libelant herein repeats and re-alleges each and every allegation contained in Article First to Fifth inclusive and Seventh to Twenty-fifth inclusive of its original cross-libel filed in this Court April 29, 1930, as fully and with the same force and effect as if the same were here repeated, re-alleged and set forth at length.

II.

Cross-libelant amends Article Sixth of its said original cross-libel as follows:

SIXTH: Thereafter the said Steamship West Cajoot sailed from the Port of Manila, having on board the above mentioned cocoanut oil and subsequently arrived at the port of Los Angeles, where the cross-respondent, on or about the 2nd day of December, 1927, made delivery of part of said shipment, but cross-respondent

of two years, as required by Section 5 of the Suits in Admiralty Act, 41 Stat. 525, U. S. C., Title 46, Section 741.

SECOND: That the second cause of action in the said amended cross-libel is insufficient in law in that the said amended cross-libel was not brought within the period of two years, as required by Section 5 of the Suits in Admiralty Act, 41 Stat. 525, U. S. C., Title 46, Section 741.

THIRD: That the third cause of action in the said amended cross-libel is insufficient in law in that the said amended cross-libel was not brought within the period of two years, as required by Section 5 of the Suits in Admiralty Act, 41 Stat. 525, U. S. C., Title 46, Section 741.

FOURTH: That the fourth cause of action in the said amended cross-libel is insufficient in law in that the said amended cross-libel was not brought within the period of two years as required by Section 5 of the Suits in Admiralty Act, 41 Stat. 525, U. S. C., Title 46, Section 741.

THE UNITED STATES OF AMERICA
By Samuel W. McNabb
Samuel W. McNabb,
United States Attorney for the Southern District of California.

I. F. Parker
I. F. PARKER
Assistant U. S. Attorney for said District.

(Endorsed): Filed Jul 23, 1930

[TITLE OF COURT AND CAUSE]

No. 3663-C

ANSWER TO AMENDED CROSS-LIBEL.

To THE HONORABLE THE JUDGES OF THE UNITED STATES DISTRICT COURT, IN AND FOR THE SOUTHERN DISTRICT OF CALIFORNIA, CENTRAL DIVISION.

The answer of the United States of America by its proctor, Frank M. Chichester, Assistant United States Attorney for the Southern District of California, to the amended cross-libel of the Los Angeles Soap Company in an alleged cause of contract, cargo damage and general average, civil and maritime, without waiving but still insisting upon the exceptions hithertofore filed to the said amended cross-libel, upon information and belief, alleges as follows:

FIRST: This cross-respondent denies the allegations of article FIRST of said amended cross-libel.

SECOND: This cross-respondent admits the allegations of article SECOND of said amended cross-libel.

THIRD: This cross-respondent admits the allegations of article THIRD of said amended cross-libel.

FOURTH: This cross-respondent denies the allegations of article FOURTH of said amended cross-libel.

FIFTH: This cross-respondent denies the allegations of article FIFTH of the amended cross-libel.

SIXTH: This cross-respondent admits that "the Steamship 'WEST CAJOOT' sailed from the Port of Manila, having on board a consignment of coconut oil" and subsequently arrived at the Port of Los Angeles but denies all and singular the remaining allegations of article SIXTH of the amended cross-libel.

SEVENTH: For answer to the allegations of article SEVENTH of said amended cross-libel, this cross-respondent, for lack of knowledge or information sufficient to form a belief, denies these allegations and puts cross-libelant to its full proof thereof.

EIGHTH: This cross-respondent denies the allegations of article EIGHTH of the amended cross-libel.

NINTH: This cross-respondent denies the allegations of article NINTH of the amended cross-libel.

TENTH: This cross-respondent denies the allegations of article TENTH of the amended cross-libel.

ELEVENTH: This cross-respondent admits the admiralty and maritime jurisdiction of the United States and of this Honorable Court but denies that all and singular the premises are true and within the jurisdiction of the United States and of this Honorable Court.

AND FOR ANSWER TO THE SECOND CAUSE OF ACTION.

TWELFTH: This cross-respondent repeats and realleges articles FIRST to ELEVENTH, both inclusive, of this answer as fully and with the same force and effect as if the same were here repeated, realleged and set forth at length.

THIRTEENTH: This cross-respondent denies the allegations of article THIRTEENTH of the amended cross-libel.

FOURTEENTH: This cross-respondent denies the allegations of article FOURTEENTH of the amended cross-libel.

FIFTEENTH: This cross-respondent denies the allegations of article FIFTEENTH of the amended cross-libel.

AND FOR ANSWER TO THE THIRD CAUSE OF ACTION

SIXTEENTH: This cross-respondent repeats and realleges articles FIRST to ELEVENTH, both inclusive, of this answer, as fully and with the same force and effect as if the same were here repeated, realleged and set forth at length.

SEVENTEENTH: This cross-respondent denies the allegations of article SEVENTEENTH of the amended cross-libel.

EIGHTEENTH: This cross-respondent denies the allegations of article EIGHTEENTH of the amended cross-libel.

NINETEENTH: This cross-respondent denies the allegations of article NINETEENTH of the amended cross-libel.

AND FOR ANSWER TO THE FOURTH CAUSE OF ACTION

TWENTIETH: This cross-respondent repeats and realleges articles FIRST to ELEVENTH, both inclusive, of this answer, as fully and with the same force and effect as if the same were here repeated, realleged and set forth at length.

TWENTY-FIRST: This cross-respondent admits that after the SS WEST CAJOOT sailed from Manila and while proceeding from Manila and bound for Los Angeles, said steamship stranded in the Van Dieman Straits. Later she was floated and her master directed her course for Kobe, Japan, and that the SS WEST CAJOOT was there drydocked. This cross-respondent admits that the SS WEST CAJOOT was drydocked at San

steamship WEST CAJOOT by Swayne & Hoyt, Inc., Managing Agents for the United States Shipping Board. A copy of said Bill of Lading is attached hereto, incorporated into and made a part of this answer and marked "Exhibit A". Said coconut oil was loaded into the deep tanks of the steamship WEST CAJOOT but prior to such loading the deep tanks were examined, tested, inspected, cleaned, made tight and in every way rendered fit and proper receptacles for the carriage of said coconut oil. Said Bill of Lading, marked "Exhibit A", contains among others the following clause:

> "And it is further expressly agreed that the report of Morton & Ericksen Inc., the surveyors at the port of loading, that the vessel is in all respects seaworthy for the carriage of said oil and fit to receive and transport said oil and that the loading and stowage of said oil is proper shall be and be held to the conclusive proof as to shipper, consignee and/or owner or interested party that at the time of shipment and commencement of the voayge, shipowners had exercised due diligence to make the vessel seaworthy in all respects for the carriage of said oil and fit to receive and transport same, and that the loading and stowage of said oil was proper."

Morton & Ericksen, Inc., the surveyors at the port of loading, Manila, duly issued a report dated September 20, 1927, that "both sections of the deep tank steamship WEST CAJOOT are now in fit condition to receive and carry coconut oil in bulk as well as cargo on the voyage intended." Cross-respondent claims the benefit of this clause and of all the other clauses of the bill of lading.

God, perils, dangers and accidents of the sea or other navigable waters;"

Cross-respondent claims the benefit of this clause.

That prior to said stranding, due diligence had been exercised to make said steamship "West Cajoot" in all respects seaworthy and properly manned, equipped and supplied, and said steamship was at all of said times, in fact, in all respects seaworthy and properly manned, equipped and supplied.

That any damage to, or loss of cargo was caused by one or more, and/or a combination of two or more risks and/or perils excepted in said bill of lading, and/or by the provisions of the Act of Congress of the United States approved February 13, 1893, commonly known as the Harter Act.

FURTHER ANSWERING THE SAID AMENDED CROSS-LIBEL AND BY WAY OF SEPARATE THIRD DEFENSE THERETO, THE UNITED STATES OF AMERICA, BY ITS PROCTOR, FRANK M. CHICHESTER, ASSISTANT UNITED STATES ATTORNEY FOR THE SOUTHERN DISTRICT OF CALIFORNIA, ALLEGES UPON INFORMATION AND BELIEF, AS FOLLOWS:

TWENTY-EIGHTH: That said Bill of Lading, marked "Exhibit A", under which the said coconut oil was shipped, contains among others the following clause:

"Notice of loss, damage, or delay must be given in writing to the vessel's agent within thirty (30) days after the removal of the goods from the custody of the vessel, or in case of failure to make delivery within thirty (30) days after the goods should have been delivered; Provided, that notice of apparent loss or damage must be given before the goods are removed from the custody of the vessel, and proper notation made on the receipt given to the vessel for the goods, shall constitute the notice herein required. Written claim for loss, damage or delay must be filed with the vessel's agent within six (6) months after giving such written notice. Unless notice is given and claim filed as above provided, neither the vessel, her owner or agent shall be liable. No suit to recover for loss, damage, delay or failure to make delivery shall be maintained unless instituted within one year after the giving of written notice as provided herein."

That no notice of loss, damage or delay was given in writing to the vessel's agent within the time limited in Clause 11 of this Bill of Lading, nor was notice of apparent loss or damage given within the time limited in Clause 11, nor was written claim for loss, damage, or delay filed with the vessel's agent within the time limited in Clause 11 of the Bill of Lading.

FURTHER ANSWERING THE SAID AMENDED
CROSS-LIBEL AND BY WAY OF SEPARATE
FOURTH DEFENSE THERETO, THE UNITED
STATES OF AMERICA, BY ITS PROCTOR,
FRANK M. CHICHESTER, ASSISTANT UNITED
STATES ATTORNEY FOR THE SOUTHERN
DISTRICT OF CALIFORNIA, ALLEGES UPON
INFORMATION AND BELIEF, AS FOLLOWS:

TWENTY-NINTH: The said Bill of Lading, marked
"Exhibit A", under which the said coconut oil was shipped contains among others the following clause:

> "The value of each package shipped hereunder
> does not exceed two hundred and fifty dollars
> ($250.00), unless otherwise stated herein, on which
> basis the freight is adjusted, and the vessel's liabil-
> ity shall in no case exceed that sum or the invoice
> value (including freight charges, if paid, and includ-
> ing duty, if paid, and not returnable), whichever
> shall be the less, unless a value in excess thereof be
> specially declared, and stated herein, and extra
> freight as may be agreed upon, paid. Any partial
> loss or damage for which the carrier may be liable
> shall be adjusted pro rata on the above basis."

That no value greater than two hundred and fifty dollars ($250.00) was stated by the shipper nor was there
any agreement stating any greater value nor any extra
freight paid thereon.

Suits in Admiralty Act, 41 Stat. 525, U. S. C., Title 46 Section 741.

WHEREFORE, the cross-respondent, the United State of America, by its proctor Frank M. Chichester, Assist ant United States Attorney for the Southern District o California, prays that the amended cross-libel may b dismissed with costs and that it may have such othe and further relief as may be just and the Court com petent to give in the premises.

UNITED STATES OF AMERICA

By: FRANK M. CHICHESTER,
Frank M. Chichester,
Assistant United States Attorney for th
Southern District of California.

(Verified)

(Note: "Exhibit A", referred to in the Amended An swer herein, is the same as "Exhibit A" in the Answe (filed May 1, 1930) of the United States to the amende Libel of the Los Angeles Soap Company v. Unite States in No. 3327-C and printed in the Record herei at pp. 32 et seq.)

(Endorsed): Filed May 5-1932.

certain general average statement, hereinafter referred to. Included in and forming a part of said cargo of the Steamship WEST CAJOOT was certain merchandise, purporting to consist of 546.24241 long tons or 1,223,585 pounds of coconut oil. Said coconut oil was shipped under a bill of lading, dated at Manila, September 21, 1927, duly issued for the Master of the Steamship WEST1 CAJOOT by Swayne & Hoyt, Inc., managing agents for the United States Shipping Board. In said bill of lading the shipper was stated to be Jao Cui Pien and the consignee was designated as

"Order of the First National Bank of Los Angeles, Notify Los Angeles Soap Company, Los Angeles."

A photostatic copy of said bill of lading is attached hereto, incorporated into, made a part of this libel and marked "Exhibit A".

The aforesaid shipment of coconut oil was delivered to and received by the Los Angeles Soap Company at Los Angeles, the port of destination.

FIFTH: That the said bill of lading, "Exhibit A", contained among others, the following clauses:

"General average shall be adjusted at San Francisco and shall be payable according to York-Antwerp Rules, 1890, and as to matters not therein provided, according to the laws and customs of the Port of San Francisco. Average bond must be furnished, with such security as may be required by the Master or vessel's agent, before delivery of the goods. If the owner shall have exercised due diligence to make the vessel in all respects seaworthy

CAJOOT struck a submerged rock or reef, severely injuring the vessel's bottom and causing the flooding of No. 1 hold. For the safety of the vessel and cargo, the master of the Steamship WEST CAJOOT altered the course of the WEST CAJOOT to Kobe, Japan, where the vessel was drydocked and the injury to the WEST CAJOOT and her cargo was repaired so that the vessel was enabled to continue her voyage and the cargo of coconut oil was discharged at Los Angeles.

That during the period of the alteration of the course of the WEST CAJOOT and the drydocking of the vessel, the Steamship WEST CAJOOT incurred certain expenses and the vessel and her cargo experienced certain expenditures and damages, more fully set forth in the general average statement, hereinafter referred to.

That the expenses, sacrifices and drydocking, previously referred to, were necessary for the safety and preservation of the ship and of the cargo and for the completion of the venture. That the expenses, sacrifices, and drydocking were of a general average nature amounting to Twenty-Four Thousand One Hundred and Eighteen Dollars and Fifty-One Cents ($24,118.51) and the libelant, United States of America, became entitled to a proportionate contribution from the shipment of coconut oil. The libelant became entitled to a lien upon said cargo for the cargo's proportionate contribution to the general average expenditures and sacrifices. In consideration of the release of the said cargo, which was insured by the respondent, from the said lien by libelant without the requirement of a general average deposit, respondent executed and delivered to libelant a certain

Eighty-one Dollars and Forty-Nine Cents ($70,581.49), and the amount of the proportionate contribution payable by said shipment is Two Thousand Five Hundred and Eighty-Eight Dollars and Ninety-Two Cents ($2,588.92), together with interest from April 15, 1929. This amount has been duly demanded from the Westchester Fire Insurance Company and payment thereof has been refused.

TENTH: That all and singular the premises are true and are within the admiralty and maritime jurisdiction of this Honorable Court.

WHEREFORE, the libelant prays that process in due form of law, according to the course of this Honorable Court in cases of admiralty and maritime jurisdiction, may issue against the said Westchester Fire Insurance Company and that it may be cited to appear and answer upon oath all and singular the matters aforesaid and the attached interrogatories; and that this Honorable Court may be pleased to decree payment to the libelant of the aforesaid amount of Two Thousand Five Hundred and Eighty-Eight Dollars and Ninety-Two Cents ($2,588.92), with interest thereupon from April 15, 1929, and the costs, and that the libelant may have such other and further relief in the premises as in law and justice it may be entitled to secure and the court competent to give.

SAMUEL W. McNABB,
United States Attorney.

IGNACIUS F. PARKER,
Ignacius F. Parker,
Assistant United States Attorney.

admit that the statement is correct as to the charges and expenses, contributory value and amounts of contribution, assuming for the purpose of your answer that the statement has been made up according to the applicable law.

SEVENTH INTERROGATORY: If your answer to the Sixth Interrogatory is in the negative, state, with particularity, wherein you claim the statement is erroneous.

EIGHTH INTERROGATORY: If, in your answer to the Seventh Interrogatory, you have pointed out errors, state whether you claim that you had, prior to the commencement of this suit, pointed them out to libelant or its agents,

NINTH INTERROGATORY: If your answer to the Eighth Interrogatory is in the affirmative, state whether the communication was oral or in writing. If in writing, attach a true copy thereof to your answer. If oral, state the person from whom and the person to whom the communication was made, and the approximate date thereof.

(Note: "Exhibit A", referred to in the Libel herein, is the same as "Exhibit A" in the Answer (filed May 1, 1930) of the United States to the Amended Libel of the Los Angeles Soap Company v. United States in No. 3327-C and printed in the Record herein at p. 32, et seq.)

America, in an alleged cause of action, civil and maritime, alleges and respectfully shows to this Honorable Court as follows:

FIRST: That respondent admits the allegations of Article "First" of the libel.

SECOND: That respondent admits the allegations of Article "Second" of the libel.

THIRD: That respondent admits the allegations of Article "Third" of the libel.

FOURTH: That respondent admits that the Steamship "West Cajoot" sailed from Manila, Philippine Islands, for Pacific Coast ports in September, 1927, and that a consignment of cocoanut oil was shipped aboard said vessel at Manila under a bill of lading issued by Swayne and Hoyt, Inc., and dated September 21, 1927, wherein Jao Cui Pien was named as shipper; the cocoanut oil in question being shipped to the order of the First National Bank of Los Angeles, Notify Los Angeles Soap Company, Los Angeles, but denies on information and belief all the other allegations of the "Fourth" Article of the libel and accordingly demands strict proof thereof, if pertinent.

FIFTH: That respondent admits the allegations contained in the "Fifth" Article of the libel.

SIXTH: Answering unto Article "Sixth" of said libel, respondent alleges that it has no information or belief sufficient to enable it to answer the allegations, or any of them, contained therein, and therefore, denies said allegations and calls for strict proof thereof, if pertinent.

SEVENTH: Answering unto Article "Seventh" of said libel, respondent alleges that it has no information or belief sufficient to enable it to answer the allegations, or any of them, contained therein, and therefore, denies said allegations and calls for strict proof thereof, if pertinent; except that respondent denies that the alleged expenses, sacrifices and drydocking of the vessel with the cocoanut oil cargo aboard were necessary for the preservation of the cargo and the completion of the venture, and/or that libelant became entitled to a proportionate contribution from the shipment of cocoanut oil to the alleged general average expenditures and/or sacrifices.

EIGHTH: Answering unto the allegations contained in Article "Eighth" of said libel, respondent alleges that it has no information or belief sufficient to enable it to answer the allegations, or any of them, except that respondent admits that a copy of the alleged General Average Statement was presented to it.

NINTH: Answering unto the allegations of Article "Ninth" of said libel, respondent alleges that it has no information or belief sufficient to enable it to answer the allegations, or any of them, except that respondent admits that a demand has been made for the sum of $2,588.92, but the same has not been paid.

TENTH: Answering unto the allegations of Article "Tenth" of the libel, respondent denies that all and/or singular the premises are true, but admits that they are within the admiralty and maritime jurisdiction of the United States and of this Honorable Court.

WHEREFORE, respondent prays that the libel herein may be dismissed and that respondent may have its costs of suit incurred herein and such other and further relief as in law and justice it may be entitled to receive.

> OVERTON, LYMAN & PLUMB,
> L. K. VERMILLE,
>   Proctors for Respondent.

(Verified)

(Endorsed): Filed Apr. 29, 1930.

[TITLE OF COURT AND CAUSE]

No. 3691-C

ANSWER OF RESPONDENT TO THE INTER-ROGATORIES ADDRESSED TO RESPONDENT BY LIBELANT.

FIRST: "YES".

SECOND: Respondent is unable to answer as respondent is not sufficiently acquainted with the York Antwerp Rules, 1890, or with the laws and customs of the Port of San Francisco.

THIRD: The General Average Statement is erroneous in that the damage which was sustained was not the result of a General Average Act, but rather was due to flagrant deviations from the contract of carriage. Respondent refutes the General Average Statement on the ground of deviation.

FOURTH: "None".

FIFTH: "None".

answer at the pres-
ore it and it has no

[Title of Court and Cause]

STIPULATION

The Los Angeles Soap Company,)
a corporation,

                         Libelant,   )

                              vs.   )   No. 3327-C

The United States Shipping
Board Merchant Fleet Corpora-)
tion,

                         Respondent.   )

. . . .

United States of America, owner)
of the Steamship "West Cajoot",)
                         Libelant,   )

                              vs.   )   No. 3663-C

The Los Angeles Soap Company,)
a corporation,

                         Respondent.   )

————————————————   )

The Los Angeles Soap Company,)
a corporation,

                    Cross-Libelant,   )

                         vs.

United States of America, owner)
of the Steamship "West Cajoot",)
                    Cross-Respondent.)

. . . .   )   No. 3691-C

United States of America, owner)
of the Steamship "West Cajoot",)
                         Libelant,   )

                         vs.

Westchester Fire Insurance
Company,

                         Respondent.   )

[TITLE OF COURT AND CAUSE]

No. 3327-C
No. 3363-C
No. 3391-C .

STIPULATION AS TO SAMPLES OF COCOANUT OIL.

IT IS HEREBY STIPULATED AND AGREED by and between counsel in this case, as follows:

That if Carl P. Kremer were called as a witness in this case, he would testify that in November 1927 he was Assistant to the President of the United States P. & I. Agency Inc., a corporation organized and existing under the laws of the State of New York. That with letter, dated November 9, 1927, from Mr. Juergens of Swayne & Hoyt, Inc., the United States P. & I. Agency Inc. received the two bottles of cocoanut oil referred to in the said letter. That receipt of the said bottles of cocoanut oil by the United States P. & I. Agency, Inc. was acknowledged by letter to Swayne & Hoyt, Inc., dated November 19, 1927. That, while in the possession of the United States P. & I. Agency, Inc., the said bottles of cocoanut oil were not opened and remained intact. That, by letter of January 12, 1929, in response to the request of Admiralty Counsel Boal of the United States Shipping Board, the United States P. & I. Agency Inc. mailed under separate cover, to the Admiralty Counsel of the United States Shipping Board, the two bottles of cocoanut oil received from Swayne & Hoyt, Inc., and that said bottles of cocoanut oil were then intact and in the same order and condition as when

"We have your letter of August 27th, 1930. We are enclosing a copy of a letter which we have written to the Bureau of Standards, transmitting the samples of coconut oil.

"These samples were received by us after being forwarded by Mr. Watson. The samples are in glass jars. The labels on the jars are as follows:

"SS 'WEST CAJOOT'-Voy. 2-64 This sample oil is taken from the deep tank, Port side.'

"SS 'WEST CAJOOT'-Voy. 2-64 This sample oil is taken from the deep tank, starboard side.'

"The jars were sealed with wax and the seals are unbroken as the bottles have not been opened by us and consequently they are in the same condition as when taken at Kobe."

That previously, Chauncey G. Parker, General Counsel, United States Shipping Board, had received from Messrs. Single & Single, a letter dated August 27, 1930, which reads in part:

"August 27, 1930.

"SS. WEST CAJOOT
OUR FILE No. 4223
****

"United States Shipping Board
    Merchant Fleet Corporation,
        Washington, D. C.
            Att. Chauncey G. Parker, Esq.,
                General Counsel.

"Gentlemen:

"We have your letter of August 29, 1930, suggesting that it would be a matter of mutual con-

[TITLE OF COURT AND CAUSE] .

No. 3327-C

No. 3663-C

No. 3691-C

STIPULATION AS TO CERTAIN FACTS

IT IS HEREBY STIPULATED AND AGREED by and between the respective parties in the above captioned cases, as follows:

1. That the translation into the English language (copy of which has been previously furnished proctors of the *Low* Angeles Soap Company) of the testimony of B. Nagamatsu and Samuel Reid, taken in the Japanese language on letters rogatory, may be received in evidence and that the said translation is admitted to be a true and correct translation of the testimony in the Japanese language.

2. That 2 survey reports, dated November 1, 1927 and marked "Respondent's Exhibit Reid No. 1" and "Respondent's Exhibit No. 2", referred to in the testimony of Samuel Reid (taken on letters rogatory in Japan) and forwarded to the State Department by the American Embassy in Japan by letter of June 10, 1932, may be received in evidence.

3. That the Los Angeles Soap Company is a California corporation and the owner of the cargo involved herein and the proper party libelant.

4. That the amount of cocoanut oil received for shipment at Manila in September, 1927 was as described in the bill of lading, namely 1,223,583 lbs. at a

9. That if J. G. Reckert were called as a witness in this case, he would testify that he is the Head of the Fuel and Purchase Division of the Shipping Board and that the records of the Shipping Board, under his supervision, show that the fuel oil delivered to the SS. WEST CAJOOT at Manila in September 1927 was delivered at a temperature of 85° Fah., Beaume 17°; of which, in accordance with Bureau of Standards Circular No. 154, the specific gravity of such oil, at 60° Fah., would be approximately .9609. That this stipulation, as to what the said Reckert would testify, may be received in evidence with the same effect as if the witness had testified by deposition subject to all objections as to materiality, relevancy, etc.

10. That in October 1927 the market price at Yokohama of fuel oil, such as the SS. WEST CAJOOT would require, was $2.58 per barrel; that by virtue of its bunker contract at Yokohama, the Shipping Board could obtain for its vessels such fuel oil at a cost of $1.65 per barrel.

11. That, by reason of putting in to Yokohoma for bunkers, the increase in nautical miles of the SS. WEST CAJOOT's voyage over the normal passage from Kobe to San Francisco is 85 miles.

12. That, if Paul F. Blinn were recalled as a witness in this case, he would testify that, at the time of the taking of his deposition at San Francisco on December 19, 1930, there was available only, for refreshing, his recollection, the smooth engine room log books of the SS. WEST CAJOOT (which were marked "Exhibits Blinn

such oil as was pumped into the settling tanks on the 12 to 4 P. M. watch on October 3rd.

That in filling the settling tanks from No. 3 double bottom tanks, Second Assistant Engineer Appel was acting in accordance with the regulations of the vessel and did not disobey any instructions of the Chief Engineer when he filled the settling tanks from No. 3 double bottom tank at any time prior to discovery of the leakage from the deep tanks into the double bottom tanks.

(In connection with the rough Engine Room Log Book of the SS. WEST CAJOOT, counsel for the United States state, in the way of explanation as to the reason for the non-availability of the log book at the deposition of Chief Engineer Blinn, that the log book was sent by the Shipping Board at Washington, D. C. to the United States Attorney at San Francisco, to be used in connection with the deposition of Chief Engineer Blinn. In some manner the log was mislaid and could not be located until a long time afterwards, when it was returned from San Francisco to the Shipping Board Log Library, together with a number of other log books. Counsel for the United States are at a loss to account for the miscarriage of the rough engine room log book.)

That on the vessel's arrival at San Francisco, in addition to Second Assistant Engineer Appel, the Acting First Assistant Engineer Mone and the Third Assistant Engineer Parker were relieved; and other engineers, having licenses for their respective positions, were employed on the SS. WEST CAJOOT.

That the log book, marked "Blinn, Exhibit 5", bearing the number 81375, is the rough engine room log of

(TESTIMONY OF CHARLES V. BACON)

[TITLE OF COURT AND CAUSE]

No. 3327-M

DEPOSITIONS OF CHARLES V. BACON and THOMAS LAURENCE STANLEY

New York, April 12, 1933

IT IS STIPULATED AND AGREED that the depositions of CHARLES V. BACON and THOMAS S. STANLEY witnesses on behalf of libellant, may be taken at the office of Single & Hill, No. 116 John Street, Borough of Manhattan, New York City, at ten o'clock A.M. April 22, 1933, and that the provisions as to notice are waived; that the reading over, signing, sealing and certification are likewise waived, and that all objections save as to the form of the question are reserved for the trial.

APPEARANCES:

SINGLE & HILL, ESQS. (By DOUGLAS D. CRYSTAL, ESQ.), for the Libellant,

Samuel V. McNab, ESQ. (By M. H. AVERY, ESQ.), United States Attorney, for the Respondent.

CHARLES V. BACON, a witness called on behalf of libellant, being first duly sworn, testified as follows:

DIRECT EXAMINATION BY MR. CRYSTAL:

Q. Where do you live, Mr. Bacon? A. I reside at Mahwah, New Jersey, and I am in business in New York, at No. 3 Park Row.

Q. What is your business? A. Consulting chemist, chemical engineer and surveyor of bulk oils.

(TESTIMONY OF CHARLES V. BACON)

Q. Mr. Bacon, assume that the West Cajoot, which is one of these west coast vessels, loads at Manilla approximately 520 tons of coconut oil in her deep tanks and that the deep tanks are divided with a center plate type of division, bulkhead, so there are approximately 260 tons in the port tank and 260 tons in the starboard tank; and assume further that fuel oil is loaded in the double bottom tanks just below the deep tanks; and assume further that the West Cajoot sailed from Manilla via Hongkong for the west coast of the United States and that while enroute from Hongkong to the west coast she stranded on the southern end of the Japanese Islands; and assume further that the vessel was damaged so it was necessary to put into the port of Kobi for repairs and that upon arrival at Kobi the coconut oil in the deep tanks was examined; and assume further that the coconut oil in the starboard tank was found to be pure and in good condition but that the examination of the oil in the port tank showed that the upper and middle levels were pure and uncontaminated but that a contamination with fuel oil was found in the lower level of the deep tank to an extent of some six inches from the bottom. In view of the facts above stated what should have been done, in your opinion, in regard to the oil in the port deep tank?

Mr. Avery: I object to the question on the score that the assumed question does not correctly state the testimony as to the condition of the port tank and there is no evidence that this witness has any familiarity with the conditions at Kobi.

(Testimony of Charles V. Bacon)

Q. If, before this heating process which you have mentioned is necessary, there is some contamination in the deep tank, will the heating have any effect as to further contamination or not? A. The heating in this specific instance, or in any instance, if there were heavy fuel oil in the bottom of the tank, and these boats as a rule all burn bunker C fuel oil which is very heavy and very viscous, and if this were heated it will have a tendency to reduce viscosity of the oil, which acts the same with coconut oil.

Mr. Avery: I object to the answer as an assumption by the witness.

Q. Assume that it is not bunker C fuel oil but another type of fuel oil, would that change your answer in any respect?

Mr. Avery: Objected to as leading.

A. From the conditions that existed at Kobi I should say that any heat would have a tendency to accelerate the mixing of the two oils.

Q. Assume that coconut oil in a deep tank congeals so it is no longer in a liquid condition, is there any way to discharge that coconut oil without heating?

A. No, there is not.

Q. In your èxperience in surveying oils in New York, have you had occasion to make any returns of any kind of oils which were loaded at Kobi? A. Yes, I have; thousands of tons.

Q. What kind of oil? A. Primarily perrila and fish oils.

Mr. Avery: What is perrila oil?

(TESTIMONY OF CHARLES V. BACON)

The Witness: It ·is an oil ·somewhat similar to linseed oil in a general way but possesses some properties that are not available in linseed oil.

Q. Can ·you state, based on your experience, whether you would call the amount of oil loaded ·at Kobi a substantial amount? A. Yes, quite a substantial amount.

Q. How long, to your knowledge, had ·they been loading these types of fish ·oil and perrila oil at Kobi?

A. I should ·say my ·knowledge of that particular oil dates back to around 1924 or 1925.

Q. You have surveyed those oils loaded at Kobi since that date? A. I have, loaded at Kobi and discharged ·here in New York.

Q. In your surveys, do you, in the regular course of business, receive documents regarding the loading of these oils at Kobi? A. It is customary and invariably the practice to receive a document or a set of documents showing that the deep tanks have been inspected and also the general information as to the ·loading and how the oil has been handled in loading and the method of arriving at the quantity of oil contained in the deep tank, commonly known as a loading survey report. Sometimes these are delivered by the consignee and at other times they are placed on the vessel for ·the consignee's surveyor.

Mr. Avery: If this ·line of questioning is intended to develop the witness's familarity with conditions ·at Kobi, it is objected ·to as patently hearsay ·and not ·within the witness's knowledge.

Q. Can you state from the knowledge acquired in

(TESTIMONY OF CHARLES V. BACON)

your regular business routine how fish oil or perrila oil is loaded on the vessel at Kobi?

Mr. Avery: I make the same objection.

Mr. Crystal: You can have an objection to this entire line of questioning.

Q.   The oil is transferred from tanks ashore into tank barges. These tank barges are brought alongside of the vessel and the contents of the barges are discharged into the deep tanks of the vessel.

Q.   This vessel, the West Cajoot, put into Kobi in October 1927; did you, at my request, search your records to see if you had surveyed oil loaded at Kobi at approximately that date?   A.   I did.

Q.   Did you find whether you had surveyed a shipment of oil loaded at Kobi at approximately that date?

Mr. Avery: Objected to unless the nature of the oil is specified.

A.   I did.

Q.   What kind of oil was that?   A.   Fish oil.

Q.   Do you remember how many tons were loaded on the vessel?   A.   I don't remember the exact vessels. I have a report which I am reading from; 394 tons of crude sardine oil.

Q.   On what vessel was that loaded?   A.   That was loaded on the steamship Taketoya Maru at Kobi, Japan, on or about September 24, 1927.

Q.   How was that particular shipment loaded on the vessel?   A.   The oil was loaded from a tank barge, the entire quantity being pumped into one deep tank on board the vessel.

(TESTIMONY OF CHARLES V. BACON)

Q. Will you just explain what is done, if anything, to prepare the barge for cocoanut oil? A. The barge is steamed, cleaned, washed out with hot water and sometimes it becomes necessary to wash with caustic soda to get it away from the floors and brackets and angles, such as is commonly in barges, many of them.

Q. What would you assume the cost of cleaning a tank barge or barges would be to accommodate say, approximately, 250 tons of cocoanut oil, assuming that the barges had previously carried fish oil?

Mr. Avery: Objected to as based on an assumption not a part of the record.

A. From my refinery experience in cleaning tanks and handling tanks, changing from one oil to another, I should say that the cost would not exceed at the very most $150.

Q. Assume that this barge or any other barge in Kobi had been carrying kerosene or coal oil, could such barges be used for the storage of coconut oil? A. Absolutely.

Q. Would there be any considerable difficulty in cleaning a barge in which kerosene or coal oil had been stored previously? A. No, very little difficulty cleaning them because those barges would just steam right out and your coal oil is much more pale in color than your cocoanut oil.

Q. The record in this case shows that on the voyage out to Manilla the deep tank of the West Cajoot carried fuel oil and then was thoroughly cleaned at Manila to

(TESTIMONY OF CHARLES V. BACON)

put the deep tank in proper shape to carry this coconut oil. Will you please compare the difficulty of cleaning a tank which carries fuel oil and a tank which carries fish oil or kerosene or coal oil; which is the most difficult to clean?

Mr. Avery: Objected to on the ground that the witness obviously knows nothing of the structure of the two tanks he is trying to compare. As matter of fact I do not know what type of tank he is trying to compare with the West Cajoot.

Mr. Crystal: I will reframe the question.

Q. Will you please state whether any tank which has contained fuel oil is more or less difficult to clean for the purpose of receiving coconut oil than a tank which has contained kerosene, coal oil or fish oil? A. The order of cleaning, that is the simplicity of cleaning, would be in the following order: coal or kerosene oil, fish oil, fuel oil.

Q. As I understand you, then, a tank that has contained fuel oil is more difficult to clean than either of the others, is that correct? A. It is, because fuel oil has a tendency to contaminate.

Q. There is testimony in this case on behalf of the government that there were certain storage tanks at the Rising Sun Oil Company plant at Manila where gasoline and coal oil are stored but that these tanks were not suitable for storing coconut oil because they are large and cannot be cleaned perfectly; is that your opinion?

(TESTIMONY OF CHARLES V. BACON·)

Mr. Avery: I object to that on the ground that this witness obviously does not know the nature of the storage tanks at Manila.

Q. Take any storage tank, then, which has contained coal oil and kerosene. Can it be cleaned perfectly for the reception of coconut oil? A. It certainly can.

Q. There is also testimony given on behalf of the government that there were certain lighters in Kobi and Osaka, which is near Kobi, but the statement is also made that these lighters were not suitable for the storage of coconut oil for the same reasons, that is, that they could not be cleaned perfectly; is that a fact?

Mr. Avery: I make the same objection, the witness obviously knows nothing about these lighters.

A. That is not a fact. Any tank, lighter or carrier of kerosene or gasoline can be quite readily cleaned.

Q. And does that apply to fish oil, also?

A. That applies to practically any oil in varying degrees of difficulty, depending upon the commodity.

CROSS EXAMINATION BY MR. AVERY:

Q. You never have surveyed here in New York any shipments of coconut oil loaded at Kobi, have you?

A. I know of no shipments of coconut oil loaded at Kobi.

Q. That would indicate to you, then, that there was no one in Kobi who was particularly experienced in loading coconut oil? A. No, not necessarily. It would indicate to me that Kobi was not a point of shipment of coconut oil.

(TESTIMONY OF CHARLES V. BACON)

most of them, in fact, it designates the concern, as a rule, and the name of the lighter.

Q. Were there many of those different concerns that sent these shipments to Kobi? A. I don't recall off-hand whether there are many concerns but I do recall that the name of the tank barges is not a constant; that is to say, we have different names from time to time.

Q. Nothing in these reports would indicate to you whether or not these tank barges were owned by the companies making the shipments or whether they were common carriers which can be hired? A. It is my understanding, that is through the shipper's agents here, that they do not belong to the shippers.

Q. Elaborate on that a bit. A. I would say that it was taken from such and such a mill, such and such a place, and transferred in such and such a barge, as an example, Mitche barge number blank blank; it is my understanding that they are entirely different outfits.

Q. Isn't that concern a shipper of fish oil?

A. I simply gave that as an example.; I don't recall ever having brought in fish oil. I surveyed hundreds of thousands of tons or fish oil but I never recall their having brought it in.

Q. The testimony here indicates that the barges in Kobi belonged either to the fuel oil companies or other companies engaged in business at Kobi. I understand you differ with that. You do not want to say as a fact that barges that were owned by common carriers who had them for rent at Kobi, that you do not know to

(TESTIMONY OF CHARLES V. BACON)

Q. You know that the double bottom tanks filled up from the coconut oil barges? A. It is quite fair to assume that your coconut oil in all probability on the bottom may have been fairly hard, with the result that if these double bottoms had a bunker C fuel oil, which I know as matter of fact is common usage in Shipping Board boats, because I had the contract for testing all the fuels that were used in these boats of the Shipping Board and they always used bunker C oil—that oil is very viscous and in a cold double bottom you could almost cut it.

Q. It has been testified here that at the time this contamination was discovered, number C double bottom was filled so that in the sounding pipes to the double bottom the level of the oil was the same level as the level in the sounding pipes in the coconut oil; that would mean that having that oil in the sounding pipes you had something ahead on the deep tank, would it? A. You would have a head on your double bottom if they were equalized.

Q. If you started pumping out that coconut oil from the deep tank, don't you think that that pressure coming on that head from the double bottom would tend to force more of that fuel oil up into the deep tanks and increase the contamination? A. No, I don't.

Q. Why? A. Because to start with, you would start pumping from the top and the volume that would be moved by that sounding pipe would be comparatively nil.

(Testimony of Charles V. Bacon)

a salvage job, you would take the oil off from the top and you will watch it and inspect it. It is quite likely that if a rupture was in that tank your diffusion or your mixture may have been in spots with that heavy viscous fuel oil and not throughout the tank. If your double bottom was full, quite naturally as you stated you would not have much leakage into it.

Q. I don't think I made my question sufficiently clear to you. What I am saying is, the coconut oil and the fuel oil having reached a common level; now in pumping out the coconut oil in the deep tanks you have decreased that pressure, why wouldn't the fuel oil then have a tendency to come up into the deep tank and increase the contamination when the amount of pressure has been removed? A. Because you have no appreciable head on your oil to speak of other than the small volume of oil that stands in your sounding pipe. As you gradually pump, that is going to diffuse into the bottom of that tank very slowly and in all probability will not contaminate your coconut oil other than in the bottom where it has already been contaminated.

Q. Then I understand you to say the taking of the coconut oil will have a tendency to force up some oil from the double bottoms up into the deep tank but you say you do not think it would be very much?

A. I say that the amount of oil that would return to the deep tank would be a volume of oil equivalent to that in the sounding pipe which is twenty-four feet high and which would be about eight gallons.

Q. You think the result of the manoeuvre would be

(TESTIMONY OF CHARLES V. BACON)

Q. I only want to ask you a question or two about these barges at Kobi. Those barges that were used in carrying fish oil, kerosene oil and coal oil should, of course, be very thoroughly cleaned before using coconut oil to prevent contamination from those materials, should they not? A. It is a very simple matter cleaning a barge carrying kerosene.

Q. It would require careful cleaning? A. Any cleaning whatsoever it may be has to be careful, irrespective of what the oil is so long as you change oils.

Q. Would you consider it proper to load coconut oil into those barges without testing those barges for tightness in view of the fact that deep tanks of the vessels are always tested for tightness before coconut oil is loaded? A. That would be relatively a simple matter. You would with kerosene or gasoline barges; in order to get out your odor, you would in all probability fill it with water, ordinary sea water, harbor water, because you have a certain amount of gas that is difficult to get out even with steam; you go ahead and fill it with water.

Q. Those barges which were used in carrying fish oil, and in my experience living on the Maine coast fish oil has a rather strong odor, I suppose in time some of that stuff might harden into the barge unless it were cleaned out each time? A. No. We carry fish oil right here in the Port of New York and we go right back and take a load of other oil right in the same barge after it has been steamed and cleaned. Of course we always inspect them.

(TESTIMONY OF CHARLES V. BACON)

Q. If this coconut oil was congealing at Kobi, as appears in the affidavits, and so arrived at Los Angeles, assuming that four feet were found to be absolutely hard, wouldn't it indicate to you there was no further contamination or increase in contamination on the voyage across?

A. It would indicate to me that there was no further contamination.

Q. No further contamination? A. No, that would not necessarily indicate that would be the case.

Q. What would be your opinion about that?

A. That would be pretty hard to state. You have to know a little bit more about your temperatures. It is quite fair to assume, though, they would test oil or liquid as it went aboard in Kobi if they were able to secure samples; and then this boat was subject to agitation, handling and shifting about, it is quite likely that that oil that was in the double bottom would become mixed and it would contaminate the entire contents of the tank, I should say.

Q. Perhaps you have forgotten, I have asked you to assume that, as appears from the testimony, the oil was congealing at Kobi and that this congealing increased until when you got to Los Angeles you had four feet of hard oil at the bottom; under such circumstances wouldn't you say that it was highly improbable that there was any increase in the contamination once the oil started to congeal in the bottom?

A. Let us figure that this way. We will assume—

Q. You do not think you can answer that yes or no?

(Testimony of Charles V. Bacon)

A. No, I would not want to answer it yes or no. If I have to answer it yes or no, I will have to decline to answer.

By Mr. Crystal: Q. On that same line, before anyone could answer the last question put by Mr. Avery, you would have to know, would you not, that the congealing extended as far as any contamination extended? A. In other words, you would have to know, I think, whether or not your bottom was congealed. Of course you can work on the assumption that if your entire bottom was congealed and then this contamination existed, say, to a point of six inches, then when that boat starts working or shifting it is quite fair to assume that in all probability that six inch layer, the entire layer, would not congeal. It would close up very much like chocolate around the Eskimo Pie and maintain that oil in there in a liquid state for a considerable length of time; so if it did that and subject to agitation within this seal and the fuel oil had gone into the liquid or mushy strata, it is quite likely that the entire tank would become contaminated if the ship were on the sea.

By Mr. Avery: Q. Of course it is true, Mr. Bacon, that there might be a contamination by fuel oil which would not be visible to the eye? A. That would not be apparent?

Q. That would not be apparent. The mere fact that it was not apparent to the eye if there was any discoloration in the upper part of the deep tank would not necessarily indicate that there was no contamination, would it? A. Well, I have never seen a contamination

(TESTIMONY OF CHARLES V. BACON)

yet that is not visible to the eye; and, after all, when we speak of contamination, we have to consider trade practice; it is a question of whether or not you can sell the goods and I have never seen a contamination yet from fuel oil that is not visible to the eye.

Q. You mean to say that— A. I mean to say that any contamination that you may have with fuel oil not visible to the eye would in all probability not affect the sale or the price of the oil.

Q. Don't you think that a contamination of fuel oil not visible to the eye might still exist and destroy the value of the coconut oil for sale? A. It would be apparent to the eye.

By Mr. Crystal: Q. Have you examined the document which I hand you which is marked Respondent's for Identification Bower No. 2 (handing paper to witness)? A. I have casually seen this before.

Q. Would you state whether the results as shown on that page in your opinion constitute a slight contamination of the oil or not? A. I should say from the color of the oil that it was a pretty good contamination. The oil is dark, very dark in color; I mean, if you can go on his report here, 44 red and 260 yellow, I certainly would say that that would not look like any of the coconut oil I have been in the habit of seeing that is imported.

(TESTIMONY OF LAURENCE STANLEY)

THOMAS LAURENCE STANLEY, a witness called on behalf of Libellant, being first duly sworn, testified as follows:

DIRECT EXAMINATION BY MR. CRYSTAL:

Q. Mr. Stanley, where do you live? A. Oak Lane, Essex Fells, New Jersey.

Q. What is your business? A. Consulting engineer and marine surveyor.

Q. In New York? A. Yes.

Q. And your office is where? A. 15 Moore Street.

Q. Will you just roughly sketch your experience and education—just your experience in connection with marine matters? A. After leaving school I served between six and seven years as apprentice with Blair & Company, England, after which I went to sea for approximately six years in various capacities, including chief engineer; after which I spent roughly about a year in Robins Drydock in Brooklyn; after which I was chief surveyor for the Naval Construction Department in Quebec, Canada for about a year; after which I was superintendent engineer with the Submarine Boat Corporation in Newark, New Jersey, for about four to four and a half years; after which I was superintendent engineer for the Transit Marine Lines for about the same period of time, and I started in business for myself a little over six years ago.

Q. In that time you have been surveying cargoes?

A. No cargoes except insofar as cargoes where there has been some damage, damaged cargo. I am not a cargo surveyor. I have had to survey cargoes but it was

(TESTIMONY OF LAURENCE STANLEY)

primarily for the purpose of finding what, if any, defects caused the damage to the cargo.

Q. Are you familiar with the steamer West Cajoot? A. Yes, that is, to some extent. I have seen the West Cajoot and I have had reason to more or less investigate her for one or two cases that I have been involved in where she has been.

Q. You are familiar in a general way with the construction of the vessel in regard to the double bottom tanks and deep tanks and her other tanks? A. Yes.

Q. Assume that the West Cajoot loads at Manila approximately 520 tons of coconut oil in her deep tanks and that these deep tanks have a center plate, division plate so in reality two tanks, so approximately 260 tons of coconut oil is in her port tank and 260 tons in her starboard tank; and assume further the vessel leaves Manila and is bound for the west coast via Hongkong and on the way strands on the southern part of the Japanese Islands and that after she has gone off the strand it is ascertained that she has some hull damage so it is necessary to take her into the port of Kobi for repairs, and that after the vessel arrives at Kobi and before she goes on drydock the coconut oil in the deep tank is inspected and that the tests taken show that the coconut oil in the starboard tank is pure and uncontaminated and that the coconut oil in the port tank is pure and uncontaminated in the upper and middle stratas, but that the bottom level of the deep tank shows contamination with fuel oil; and further that this contamination extends up to some six inches of the bottom

(TESTIMONY OF LAURENCE STANLEY)

level, but that the rest of the oil above that layer of
contamination is sound and uncontaminated. Now, in
view of the facts above stated, the vessel being in Kobi,
what in your opinion should have been done with the
coconut oil in the port tank?

Mr. Avery: Objected to on the ground the witness
is not a cargo surveyer and is *now* shown to have any
familiarity with the carriage of cargo oils or conditions
at Kobi.

A.   With any oil cargo, other than a fuel oil cargo,
and even with that, I would say that before a vessel of
the type of the West Cajoot should be allowed to go to
sea at all, that the oil should be removed for the purpose
of eliminating the damage that is evident between the
double bottom tank and the deep tank, for several reasons: one, is the protection of the cargo in that deep
tank, and secondly, any ship of that type is provided
with a double bottom, one of the reasons being that this
is a second measure of safety, and if you have a rupture
in that tank as indicated by the fuel oil that has gone
into the deep tank, it shows that you have an unknown
quantity of leakage in that tank top, and so the second
skin, as you may term it, of that vessel for her protection is not there. In my opinion, any ship in that condition is not fit to go to sea, and I venture to say that
no specification under ordinary circumstances would
allow a vessel with a known leaky tank top to go to sea
under those conditions.

Q.   Are you familiar with the associations such as
Lloyds, the American Bureau and the Bureau of Veri-

(TESTIMONY OF LAURENCE STANLEY)

tas? A. I have spent the last 27 or 28 years of my life in the building, repairs or operating of ships which keeps me in constant touch with various surveyors of these classification societies.

Q. Do Lloyds and the American Bureau and the Bureau of Veritas issue rules regarding the construction, maintenance and classification of vessels? A. They do issue rules which call for certain standards to be met and certain tests at periodical dates to be carried out to show that the vessel has not depreciated below a level at which their classification has been issued.

Q. What are their rules with regard to tank tops with particular reference to whether they must be water or oil tight? A. The rule calls for them to be tested' and kept absolutely tight up to a certain head on that tank or tank top I should say. In the event of that having been changed from the condition where they inspected it; under those circumstances it is supposed to be put back into that condition in order to maintain that class.

Q. Is there any difference in the rules of these various societies regarding these requirements? A. Regarding the tightness of tank tops?

Q. Yes. A. No difference in that any classification I ever heard of; certainly not in the Societies you have mentioned; and the same applies to my knowledge of the Italian Lloyds, the same way.

Q. Then assume that it is found that fuel oil is in the bottom of the deep tank, what does that indicate to you concerning the condition of the tank top which sep-

(TESTIMONY OF LAURENCE STANLEY)

arates the double bottom from the deep tank? A. It indicates to me that that tank top is leaking more or less and the extent to which it is leaking can only be found out by removing the oil from the deep tank and subjecting the double bottom tank to hydrostatic test to show leakage.

Q. The vessel sails from Kobi with this leak unrepaired, is that in conformity with the classification of Society rules?

Mr. Avery: I object to that question.

A. It is not.

Q. Apart from any rules, in your opinion is a vessel which sails from Kobi on a trans-Pacific voyage with an unknown leak in her tank top in a seaworthy condition?

Mr. Avery: I object to the question as not based on sufficient facts as to the nature of the defect complained of.

A. It is not.

Q. Apart from the question of seaworthiness of the vessel, Mr. Stanley, when it was found, in view of the facts heretofore stated, there was a contamination of six inches in the bottom of the deep tank and the coconut oil in the upper and middle levels uncontaminated, what in your opinion should have been done with this coconut oil?

Mr. Avery: Objected to. No attempts were made to qualify the witness and the witness is not competent to answer this question.

in the. normal course of removing: the· oil in· any place and pumping· it out into those tanks; through hoses.

Q. Would: there be· any difficulty in: pumping · oil to: lighters· or tank barges alongside?· A. None at all:

Q. It has been testified in this case that it·would'not' be practicable to bring another vessel—by another vessel I mean a freighter, not a tank barge—alongside to pump the oil from either the deep tank of the· West Cajoot· into deep tanks or other tanks of another vessel, do you agree with that?

Mr. Avery: Objected to; the witness has no knowledge of conditions· for transferring oil at Kobi.

A. Absolutely not.

Q. Would· there be any difficulty· about bringing a vessel alongside of this vessel and transferring the ·il from one vessel to another? A·. I have had plenty of experience, plenty, in the transferring of: oil from one ship to another. It is done every day all over the world. There is no reason why there should· be any difference· in one oil as against another. As matter of fact, a low grade of fuel· oil would probably· give more trouble in this respect than possibly any other kind of oil that could be mentioned, due to its density and difficulty in liquifying it. But as far as the transfer of any oil from one vessel to another is concerned, it is impossible to imagine how there can be any· difficulty; in that. Why should it be any different in one place than another?

Mr. Avery: The witness is not' called upon· to use his imagination, but to state facts, and I ask that the answer be stricken out.

(TESTIMONY OF LAURENCE. STANLEY)

the carrying of fish oil, kerosene oil and coal oil, and it has been testified on behalf of the Government that these tank barges were not suitable for the storing of coconut oil because they could not be properly cleaned, is that a fact?

Mr. Avery: Objected to as obviously this witness knows nothing about the boats in question, their condition or their structure.

A. This is not so. I have seen numerous tankers where we have used kerosene oil or any other of the lighter oils and certainly it is a very much easier matter to clean than, for instance, to clean out fuel oil, which had previously been carried, I understand, in this deep tank of the West Cajoot. In other words, I personally cannot understand any oil that is harder to clean out of a tank than fuel oil.

Q. It has also been testified that storage tanks on shore and tank cars were not suitable for the same reason, that is, they could not be cleaned properly; is that so?

A. In my opinion it is not so because I don't know of any oil that is harder to clean out of a tank than fuel oil.

Q. In transferring this cocoanut oil in the deep tank to the afterpeak tank or forepeak tank or to tank cars alongside or tank barges or to another vessel, would the cost of such transfer be great?

Mr. Avery: I object to that as beyond this witness's knowledge.

(TESTIMONY OF LAURENCE STANLEY)

Q. By "floors", for the benefit of the court will you explain what a floor is? A. The division, you may call it.

Q. In other words, a floor in a deep tank is not horizontal but it is vertical? A. It is a vertical stiffener which divides the double bottom into compartments, as it were. I mean by that, there are holes in these divisions through which the oil can flow to the full length of the tank, but just the same that makes just that much more to be cleaned.

CROSS EXAMINATION BY MR. AVERY:

Q. You said that you have seen the West Cajoot; for the record will you tell us how large a vessel she is, approximately? A. If I remember rightly, somewhere in the vicinity of 8000 tons dead weight.

Q. And her gross tons would be what? A. I don't know that offhand.

Q. Prior to comeing to this country, your experience as an engineer was in what—oil burners or coal burners?

A. It was entirely coal burners.

Q. Have you made any voyages in the Pacific? A. No.

Q. And that means, of course, you have not been at Kobi and know nothing of the facilities at Kobi with respect to coconut oil? A. No, not with respect to coconut oil. As superintendent of the Transit Marine Lines and the Submarine Boat Corporation, sometimes we actually had 150 oil burning vessels—

(TESTIMONY OF LAURENCE STANLEY)

Q.   You testified I think that in your opinion a vessel which had a rupture between the double bottoms and the deep tank was unseaworthy, am I correct on that?

A.   Yes; that is correct.

Q.   Will you describe the extent and size of this rupture that you have in mind?   A.   If there was any rupture which was shown to have damaged cargo to a point where, as it was described here, being six inches of oil in the deep tank which was damaged with fuel oil by leaking from the double bottom or from somewhere, it would indicate to me there was a rupture which was unknown and in my opinion nobody has a right to allow a vessel to go to sea with a rupture in the tank top of which they have no idea to what extent it has been developed.

Q.   It makes no difference to you what the size of the rupture is?   A.   It makes a lot of difference as to the severity of the case, but if you have a rupture I still insist that they should determine to what extent it has been developed.

Q.   Are you aware that in this case the American Bureau issued a certificate of seaworthiness for this vessel?

A.   That does not alter my opinion in the slightest.

Q.   Will you tell me whether you knew it or not?

A.   I don't know it actually, but I presume she had.

Q.   And of course, this man being present at Yokohama would, in your opinion, be in a better position to know whether the vessel was seaworthy?   A.   If he

(TESTIMONY OF LAURENCE STANLEY)

same discoloration and the same contamination, what would your answer have been in that case? A. I would still take it out to find out the cause of the contamination. If you have a condition that is contaminating your cargo, in my opinion you have no right to proceed without finding out and endeavoring to stop that contamination, whatever it may be.

Q. About the behavior of coconut oil, do you know whether or not it tends to congeal? A. That is my understanding, that it does if it is in cold water. You have to provide heat in the tank to liquify the oil in order to pump it out.

Q. Do you also understand that it is a cargo that has to be handled with a good deal of care lest it take a contamination from other substances? A. Yes.

Q. If it had been stated to you that this rupture was a rupture between the shell of the vessel and the margin binding the tank and was extremely small so it was difficult to see even with a flash light, and if it were further testified that the coconut oil was already congealing so it would form a hard coat and prevent further fuel oil contamination from below, under those circumstances what would you say as to the seaworthiness of the vessel?`

Mr. Crystal: I object to this question on the ground that Mr. Avery is now questioning as to what would happen to the coconut oil and is making the witness his own.

Mr. Avery: I think that Mr. Crystal has examined the witness at length as to the proper procedure to follow with respect to the cargo of coconut oil. If I, departed from that, I fail to see it.

A. As I understand the question, your leakage that you have described is between where the tank top and the shell of the vessel meet. In other words, that the leakage was actually coming from the double bottom tank into the deep tank and that the shell of the vessel was not concerned at all.

Q. Where the margin board touches the shell which under ordinary forces gives you a tight connection, has been broken or ruptured, not in the sense that there was a physical break, but simply that the connection has broken so it is possible for oil either to run up or down between the two, does the testimony as to the break in this case, as testified to by the chief engineer, change your opinion—that is the testimony given by the chief engineer?

A. I would still consider that that vessel does not have a tight tank top and consequently is not fit to go to sea until the extent of that has been determined and rectified.

Q. And the fact that this coconut oil congealed and made a tight, impervious barrier does not influence your opinion? A. It does not influence my opinion for the simple reason that this coconut oil by the fact that it would become solidified and block up this leaky seam, as it were, would not affect the thing one particle, in my opinion. The pressure which the vessel would acquire would dislodge that; if she had a ruptured bottom.

(TESTIMONY OF LAURENCE STANLEY)

her tank top would not be available as a second skin in which to keep the ship afloat.

Q. Afloat under what conditions? A. If you had your vessel at sea and she had a leaky tank top and you, for some reason, ran over, we will say, a submerged rock and tear the bottom out, then you would float in on your tank top; that is one of the reasons, so you would have a second line of defense; but certainly any blocking of this leakage that would be caused by congealed oil would not amount to shucks under those conditions, and those are conditions that the tight tank top is anticipating for the safety of the vessel.

Q. Under the circumstances like that, are you not assuming there was a very large rupture when I have already indicated to you that it was a very small break?

A. You can have a rupture that will put a ship in danger but not only can you not see it when you put it under a hydrostatic test but you can't feel it if you test it with a set of feelers. Pressure will send plenty of water through a very small hole. And certainly, apart from the safety of the vessel, you could get, under those conditions, quite a considerable amount, in this case it would be oily water from the double bottom forced into that deep tank which would eliminate any value that that cargo would have.

Q. How do you think you can get any force up through that coconut oil after it becomes hard? A. In the first place, I do not anticipate that this oil will become hard, as that word describes it.

Q. Just tell us what you think will happen to the

(TESTIMONY OF LAURENCE STANLEY)

coconut oil? A. It will never become actually a solid right through in that place because it can easily be forced out. It is only going to be a small amount. It is one thing to force something into a hardened mass but if you have only a small amount stuck in between that opening or break in that tank it is going to force its way in there and add to the damage that has been already caused.

Q. So, to get the record clear on this, it makes no difference to you the size of that rupture—any rupture whetsoever in your opinion would make the vessel unseaworthy? A. Yes; if you don't have an absolutely tight tank top and you are aware that you have not got a tight tank top; in the first place you should know the extent of that damage and no one has a right to let that ship go to sea because she is manifestly unseaworthy, in my opinion, and secondly, the extent of the opening will of course indicate the rate which water or oil or whatever it may be can go through that opening, but that in itself will also be affected by the condition of the ship's bottom. For instance, if you put your double bottom tank just merely full you are not going to have any pressure going up, but if you rip the bottom out of that ship and subject her to the pressure created by the weight of the water, you may get a considerable stream of water going through there. It is true, it will be greater or less according to the size of the tank. But if you don't know the size of the tank you have no business to gamble with the ship in those conditions as to the extent of the damage.

(TESTIMONY OF LAURENCE STANLEY)

Q. How full do you think those deep tanks were— does it make any difference whether they were full or not, this water you are talking about coming up? A. I don't know just what you mean by that.

Q. You are talking of the danger of water coming into the deep tanks through this rupture? A. Yes.

Q. Does it make any difference to you whether or not these tanks are full of coconut oil? A. Frankly, I don't think that anybody can determine what is going to be done there. If you subject a tank with a double bottom to a stream under pressure, the amount which that stream will mix with the oil that is already in the tank is something I don't think anybody can *deyermine*.

Q. I think you have expressed your opinion as to the possibility of storing this coconut oil in lighters which may have been used in carrying fuel oil and kerosene oil; will you tell us how you go about it to prepare those lighters for the carriage of coconut oil? A. They would have to be cleaned out. First of all, you have to take something to soften up the fuel oil in there and then removed and wiped down with kerosene and meal and thoroughly cleaned out, in the same way as this deep tank had to be done before you started to use it.

Q. It is a process that has to be done very carefully? A. Naturally.

Q. And you have to have experienced and capable men to prepare these tanks? A. In any place you have to have people to clean tanks the same as they had in this particular ship here. They had to have them before the men could go ahead and do the repairs in the double bottoms. They have to clean the oil so there would be no possibility of any gas being created that would probably cause an explosion.

Q. All these things you say might have been done depends in the last analysis as to whether or not you could obtain those lighters, whether or not you could obtain the use of the storage tank or whether there was a ship available into whose tanks the coconut oil could be pumped, and of course not having any knowledge of the conditions at Kobi you can express no opinion? A. Kobi is quite a port and you can obtain fuel oil in Kobi. Of course, as you say, if for some reason or other at that particular time there were no receptacles available, naturally you could not use them; but you can always use in a pinch your own forepeak and your own afterpeak because they were there all the time; they are receptacles which have been there for the use of ballast purposes, and certainly they would be very, very much easier to clean than any tanks that had ever used any kind of oil before, very much easier to clean.

Q. Now, if the examination at Kobi had disclosed a.l levels of this coconut oil was contaminated, what advantage do you see as far as the coconut oil is concerned in removing it from the deep tanks? A. The first advantage is that if there is a contamination going through the entire body of that oil, naturally the vessel has got to find out from a seaworthy standpoint what caused it; that is one thing that has to be done before that vessel is allowed to proceed, especially in view of the fact that at Kobi she had a drydock where such repairs could be

(TESTIMONY OF LAURENCE STANLEY)

effected. As to the question of what could be gained in the coconut oil, certainly if it had been contaminated all through I don't propose to offer any suggestions as to whether that could be damaged any more than it was then or not; I mean, it is purely and simply a degree of contamination of which I have no knowledge at all. However, if that condition existed, one of two things is going to happen; if they keep on pressing up the double bottom tank you are going to subject it to further contamination or you are going to create a condition where probably some of the oil may, in the event of the double bottom being empty, fall down into the double bottom tank.

Q. Of course, you understand that at the time this contamination was discovered the double bottoms had been completely filled from the coconut oil leaking down through and that the sounding pipes from the deep tanks and of the double bottom were on the same level? A. So you had the same level in the sounding pipes in the double bottom, in other words, you had reached a level where they were solid; in other words, there might have been no tank top there at all. If such is the case, I very much doubt that a condition such as you have just described could have been brought about with anything that might be described as an insignificant leakage; you have an instance where your oil is falling down into the deep tank and maintaining a level for the two of them.

Q. In your opinion, there must have been a very substantial break? A. Yes.

Q. I don't want to mislead you; the testimony is

(TESTIMONY OF LAURENCE STANLEY)

there was a very insignificant break and that the tanks had reached their own level; that is the situation when the damage is discovered and the problem with which you are dealing. If you assume there is a small contamination throughout the tank, wouldn't you, as a chief engineer, just leave that stuff in there, realizing that the congealing of the coconut oil and the fact that it is already contaminated is going to mean very little if any increased damage? A. If I were chief engineer and I venture to say anybody holding an American license would not dare proceed to sea and have to face the power of inspectors afterwards with a vessel that had equalized itself, and had dared to proceed to sea under those conditions.

Q. You say that knowing what happened? A. That does not mean a thing to me. Those people were gambling on the extent of that damage which they did not know anything about. They did know that they had a damage sufficient to cause enough leakage from the deep tank into the double bottom tank to make the level in the sounding pipes of the No. 3 and the deep tank level a question, and under those circumstances I haven't the slightest hesitation in saying that nobody had the right to let that ship go to sea when they knew of the damage without finding what caused that condition. I certainly would not do it and I have never yet met a classification surveyor that I would expect would do it.

Q. Leave out the condition of this tank top, would not you as a chief engineer have left that coconut oil in the deep tanks knowing that it was already contaminated

(TESTIMONY OF LAURENCE STANLEY)

and that you could have it refined anyway and that no further damage could result?

Mr. Crystal: I object to the question. The question is not based on testimony shown by the record.

A. I don't think, according to my experience, that as chief engineer of the shop as you have brought out that I would have ever been asked to pass on such a question; it would be in the hands of the captain and not the chief engineer. The chief engineer would handle that tank when it was being used for fuel oil but certainly he would not handle it except to possibly overlook the cleaning.

Mr. Crystal: I think Mr. Stanley's testimony is exactly in accord with the chief engineer that is, that he wss not consulted.

Q. You have testified a great deal as an expert, have you not? A. Yes.

Q. You usually testify on behalf of the cargo and against the ship?

Mr. Crystal: I object to that last question as incompetent, irrelevant and immaterial.

A. I have testified for owners as well as underwriters and am always available whoever cares to retain my services.

Q. You know your reputation is as a cargo man rather than as a ship owner's man?

Mr. Crystal: I object to this line of questioning.

A. I must refuse to answer that yes or no. Nobody has any right under any circumstances to ever label me

(TESTIMONY OF LAURENCE STANLEY)

as you have described. They have absolutely no ground whatever for that. I am perfectly willing to testify for anybody who cares to retain me, provided I can do that in line with my own honest opinions—including yourself, Mr. Avery.

By Mr. Crystal:

Q. Do you recall whether Mr. Avery has referred to —did you testify in the pinellas case? A. I did.

Q. Have you ever read the reported opinion in that case. A. Yes.

Q. Did the Judge have any comment to make on your ability in that case and integrity in the reported opinion?

Mr. Avery: Don't you recall that you were rather severely talked to as being an advocate rather than an expert?

The Witness: I do, and I also remember that the Judge sided with me on that subject.

(Endorsed): Filed May 27 1933 R. S. Zimmerman, Clerk. By Theodore Hocke, Deputy Clerk.

LIB. EXHIBIT I.

SURVEY

of

ABOUT 394 TONS

CRUDE SARDINE OIL

in bulk

ex

S/S "TAKETOYA MARU"

for

SWAN-FINCH OIL CORPORATION

522 Fifth Avenue

New York, N. Y.

by

CHARLES V. BACON, Ch.E.

Analytical & Consulting Chemist & Chemical Engineer
Investigations, Expert Testimony, Experimental &
Research Work

3 Park Row

New York

This survey, conducted without prejudice for the interest of all parties concerned, at the request of The Swan & Finch Oil Corporation, 522 Fifth Avenue, New York. N. Y., pertains to a bulk cargo of Crude Sardine Oil, said to amount to about 394 tons, contained on board the S/S "Taketoya Maru."

The S/S "Taketoya Maru", a twin screw, oil burning vessel, was loaded at Kobe, Japan, on or about September 24, 1927.

The oil was loaded from a tank barge, the entire quantity being pumped into one deep tank known as "A"

Deep Tank, located in the aft portion of No. 3 Hatch, which is foreward of the engine room, the engine room forming the aft bulkhead of this tank. The foreward bulkhead of Tank "A" forms the aft bulkhead of Tanks "B" and "C", which tanks also contain oil.

There is no divisional bulkhead in Tank "A"; there are, however, several swash plates, all of which permit free and clear drainage of the oil from Port to Starboard sections of the tank.

The S/S "Taketoya Maru" sailed from Kobe on or about September 25, 1927, and arrived in the Port of New York on November 7, 1927, and was berthed at Pier 16, NYK Line, Brooklyn, N. Y., about noon.

Arrangements were made to discharge this cargo of oil while the ship was berthed at the aforementioned pier on November 8, 1927.

Surveyor arrived on board at 7:00 A.M., and at this time no one connected with the discharge of the oil was present.

At 7:30 A.M. the pumping crew of The Niger Company, Inc., arrived on board the vessel and promptly proceeded to load on board the necessary gear for pumping this oil, which consisted of the requisite metallic hose for steam and oil and two duplex pumps, the latter being placed on the tween deck.

The rigging of all equipment and getting everything in readiness to pump was completed about 10:30; the Marine Lighterage Company Tank Barge No. 16, which was to convey this oil to its final destination—the plant of the Swan & Finch Company, located at Morses Creek (Bayway (N. J.)—was in the meantime placed alongside the ship.

During the aforementioned rigging the cover of the Starboard side of the deep tank was removed. This took place about 8:10 A.M., at which time the Surveyor obtained the necessary temperatures and ullages (from top of coaming to the oil), which were as follows:

ULLAGES
STARBOARD

| Fore Port | 10¼″ | Fore Starboard 10½″ |
| Aft Port | 8¾″ | Aft Starboard 9¾″ |

TEMPERATURES

Top	Middle	Bottom
82° F	83° F	80° F

Draft: Fore 19′3″   Aft 22′6″   Trim 1½° Port

An examination of the expansion tanks at this time disclosed that the starboard expansion tank was empty, while the port expansion tank showed an ullage of 34¼″, temperature 78 F.

There was no ullages obtained from the manhole or cover of the deep tank on the port side, due to the admonition of the Chief Officer, who was afraid that owing to the 1½ degree port list and the presence of oil in the expansion tank, there would be danger of an overflow.

At the time the cover was removed from the Starboard section of the deep tank, and after completing the measurements, samples were obtained from the top, middle and bottom by means of the "Bacon Bomb Sampler." Same are in the writer's possession, being held pending instructions regarding their disposition. There was also drawn a bleeder sample during the entire pumping, known as our No. 15476.

The Marine Lighterage Company Barge, previously mentioned, was placed alongside the vessel at 9:30 A.M.; all four tanks were inspected and found to be clean and in a suitable condition to receive the oil.

Pumping into the above mentioned barge was started at 10:50 A.M., from the starboard section of the deep tank, using one large pump. At 1:10 P.M. the second pump was placed in operation. Both pumps continued without interruption until 3:20 P.M., at which time the oil was quite low in the tank, and the large pump was shut down; the small pump, however, continued operating until 3:45 P.M.

During the process of pumping and after the oil had become somewhat reduced in the tank, the cover of the Port section was removed, at about 2:30 P.M. Pumping was not resumed until about 5:50 P.M., as it was necessary to drop a small pump into the oil, due to the oil being low in the tank. This operation was somewhat slow, as it was impossible to lower this pump with the ship's boom thereby necessitating a manual operation. Pumping continued until about 7:05 P.M., at which time all the oil was removed. Prior to finishing, the tank was squeeged to the Port side and both bilges were pumped dry.

An inspection conducted at about 7:15 P.M., after all of the lines were blown, showed that the oil had been discharged very satisfactorily; it was the surveyor's estimate that the quantity remaining would not exceed 15 or 20 gallons. An inspection of the expansion tanks showed them to be empty, also.

The Marine Lighterage Company Barge No. 16 was towed from the ship at 6:40 A.M. on the following morning, November 9th, to the Plant of the Swan & Finch Oil Corporation, at Bayway, N. J., at which place the oil was to be discharged into storage tank No. 7.

The Surveyor arrived at the plant at 8:00 A.M., but the Barge did not reach the plant until 2:35 P.M., due to the prevailing heavy fog and adverse tide. The temperature of the oil in the Barge was determined and found to be 74°, which was considered a trifle low. Surveyor made the necessary arrangements to heat the oil while connections were being made for the pumping, and during this time storage tank No. 7 was inspected, found to be empty, and all lines leading to the tank were checked to insure all valves being closed.

Pumping from the Barge was started at 4:05 P.M., through a four-inch line on shore which was connected to the barge pump. This line runs above and under the ground, finally entering the tank overground at about five foot level.

Pumping continued without interruption until 10:25 P.M., at which time inspection disclosed that all the oil contained in the tanks on the Barge had been removed.

The line was then blown with steam and the valves on the dock and at the tank were closed. It was the Surveyor's understanding at this time that the line would be blown again by the use of compressed air during the following morning.

After all pumping was completed the Surveyor obtained a wet oil gauge of the oil contained in storage tank No. 7 which showed 22' 4⅛", with a mean temperature of 97° F.

The above measurements could not be taken as a definite loading quantity, due to the fact that the oil immediately after pumping contained considerable air and would, therefore, have to be gauged at a later date.

On November 11th Surveyor attempted to gauge this oil and proceeded to the Plant, but on arriving there found same was not in operation; he returned the following morning and there, in the presence of Mr. Shotwell, gauged this tank No. 7 and found the same contained (after securing three wet measurements) 21' 10⅜" at a temperature of 110° F.

The quantity of oil was calculated from the aforementioned measurements and found to amount to 114096.2 gallons, or 883,675 pounds, which figures represent the quantity of Crude Sardine Oil delivered into your storage tank No. 7, ex S/S "Taketoya Maru."

Appended hereto and made a part of this report will be found a sheet giving full details of the gauging.

Respectfully submitted,

CVB/b   CHAS. V. BACON.

GAUGING OF SARDINE OIL EX S/S TAKETOYA MARU CONTAINED IN SWAN-FINCH OIL CORPORATION'S STORAGE TANK #7 AT MORSES CREEK (BAYWAY) N. J., NOVEMBER 12, 1927, BY CHARLES V. BACON

Mean wet oil gauge 3 measurements	21' 10⅜"
Temperature of oil, top, middle & Bottom	110° F
Gallons per inch #7 storage tank	443.11
Coefficient of Expansion	0.000367
Specific Gravity of Oil @ 60° F	0.92984
Pounds per gallon, of oil, @ 60° F	7.74523

21' 10⅜" oil in tank @ 110° F	116260.99 Gals.
Plus oil contained in manhole	18.00 "
Total oil in #7 tank @ 110° F	116278.99 "
Less volume occupied by Coils	50.00 '
Net oil in #7 tank @ 110° F	116228.99 "
Volume occupied due to 50° F above normal temperature 60° F	2132.80 "
Net oil in #7 tank @ 60° F	114096.19 "

Therefore 114096.2 Gallons times weight per gallon @ 60° F—7.745 equals 883675 pounds Crude Sardine Oil delivered to Swan-Finch Oil Corporation at Bayway, N. J.

> CHAS. V. BACON,
> Inspector, Weigher & Sampler
> New York Produce Exchange
> licensed Weighmaster,
> State of New Jersey
> Certificate #975

[TITLE OF COURT AND CAUSE]

> IN ADMIRALTY No. 3327-M
> IN ADMIRALTY No. 3663-H
> IN ADMIRALTY No. 3691-M

THURSDAY, APRIL 27, 1933.

Depositions of JOE JORY and W. E. HEPPELL, on behalf of The Los Angeles Soap Company.

BE IT REMEMBERED: That on Thursday, April 27, 1933, pursuant to Notice of Taking Depositions and stipulation of counsel hereunto annexed, at the office of Messrs. DERBY, SHARP, QUINBY & TWEEDT, in the Merchants Exchange Building, in the City and County of San Francisco, State of California, personally appeared before me, ERNEST E. WILLIAMS, a United States Commissioner for the Northern District of California, authorized to take acknowledgments of bail and affidavits, etc., JOE JORY and W. E. HEPPELL, witnesses called on behalf of The Los Angeles Soap Company.

S. H. DERBY, ESQ. appeared as proctor for The Los Angeles Soap Company and Westchester Fire Insurance Company, and Miss ESTHER B. PHILLIPS, Assistant U. S. Attorney, appeared as proctor for the United States of America, and the said witnesses, having been by me first duly cautioned and sworn to testify the truth, the whole truth, and nothing but the truth in the cause aforesaid, did thereupon depose and say as is hereinafter set forth.

(It is hereby stipulated and agreed by and between the proctors for the respective parties that the depositions of the above-named witnesses may be taken de bene esse on behalf of The Los Angeles Soap Company and Westchester Fire Insurance Company, at the offices of Messrs. DERBY, SHARP, QUINBY & TWEEDT, in the Merchants Exchange Building, in the City and County of San Francisco, State of California, on Thursday, April 27, 1933, before ERNEST E. WILLIAMS, a United States Commissioner for the Northern District of California, and in shorthand by CHARLES R. GAGAN.

(It is further stipulated that the depositions, when written up, may be read in evidence by either party on the trial of the cause; that all questions as to the notice of the time and place of taking the same are waived,

(TESTIMONY OF JOE JORY)

and that all objections as to the form of the questions are waived unless objected to at the time of taking said depositions, and that all objections as to materiality, relevancy, and competency of the testimony are reserved to all parties.

(It is further stipulated that the reading over of the testimony to the witnesses and the signing thereof are hereby expressly waived.)

Mr. Derby: These depositions were originally to be taken on notice. I produce the original notice. As I understand it, Miss Phillips, you are willing to enter into the usual admiralty stipulation for the taking of these depositions?

Miss Phillips: Yes, I am.

Mr. Derby: And that the usual reading over and signing by the witnesses will be waived?

Miss Phillips: Yes.

JOE JORY, called for The Los Angeles Soap Company; Sworn.

Mr. Derby: Q. Captain Jory, where do you reside? A. Do you mean my business address or my home address?

Q. What is your home address? A. Alameda, California.

Q. What is your position at the present time? A. Surveyor to the Board of Marine Underwriters of San Francisco.

Q. With offices in San Francisco? A. With offices in San Francisco.

(Testimony of Joe Jory)

Q. How long have you been surveyor to the Bcard of Marine Underwriters of San Francisco? A. Twelve years.

Q. What did you do before that? A. I was a seaman.

Q. Did you hold a license as master? A. Master, unlimited, sail and steam, any ocean.

Q. How long were you a master? A. Nine years a master; twenty-five years at sea.

Q. Were you on all kinds of vessels? A. Various kinds of vessels.

Q. Were you a mate before you were a master? A. Yes.

Q. Have you had experience either as master or as marine surveyor with cargoes of vegetable oil? A. As a marine surveyor I have.

Q. Would that include cocoanut oil? A. Yes.

Q. Are you, in a general way, familiar with the former Shipping Board vessel "West Cajhoot"? A. Yes, sir.

Q. Are you familiar with her structure in the way of deep tanks and double bottom tank and other tanks? A. Yes, sir.

Q. Do you know, in a general way, the capacity of those tanks?

A. In a general way, yes.

Q. And where they are located on the vessel? A. Yes.

Miss Phillips: Mr. Derby, if it will be of any convenience to you and to Captain Jory, I have with me a certi-

(TESTIMONY OF JOE JORY)

fied copy of a blueprint of the vessel. I just received it yesterday from the East. If it will be of assistance to you and to the captain I will produce it.

Mr. Derby: We will be very glad to use it if. we need it.

Q. Have you ever been in Kobe, Captain Jory.. A. I was in Kobe in 1902.

Q. Are you familiar with the port of Kobe by reputation? A. I am familiar with it by reputation at later dates.

Q. I understand you were a captain of steam vessels, as well as of sailing vessels. A. Yes, sir.

Q. Captain, I will ask you to assume that the steamer "West Cajhoot" on a voyage from Manila to Los Angeles, via Hongkong and San Francisco, was carrying fuel oil in her double bottom tanks, and was also carrying a cargo of 1,223,583 pounds of cocoanut oil in her No. 3 port and starboard deep tanks, about half in each tank, which deep tanks were located immediately above the No. 3 bottom tank. Assume also that on October 2nd, 1927, the vessel stranded while passing through Van Diemen Straits, in Japan, and that after she was floated from the strand it was decided to make for Kobe, Japan as a port of refuge. Assume further that after the stranding the No. 1 hold and the No. 1 double bottom tank were sounded and it was discovered that sea water had entered said hold and tank. Assume also that tests were made to determine whether there was any water in the No. 2 and No. 3 holds, and it was found that there was none, but that later, by subsequent sound-

(TESTIMONY OF JOE JORY)

ings, a leak was discovered in the No. 2 hold, but not in the No. 3, and that no soundings were made of the No. 3 double bottom tank. In view of the above facts, what is your opinion as to whether the No. 3 double bottom tank should have been sounded or not after the vessel had floated from the reef? A. The usual procedure on all vessels is that it is considered necessary to sound all double bottom tanks after a vessel has stranded.

Q. Why is that, Captain? A. To find out the extent of damage.

Q. Would that be true even though there was no leak discovered in the No. 3 hold? A. Yes, you sound all tanks and double bottoms after a vessel has been ashore.

Q. Do you consider that a necessary precaution, Captain?

A. A very necessary precaution.

Q. Now, Captain, assume the same facts stated in the last long question, and further assume that after the arrival of the vessel in Kobe, and on or about October 5, 1927, and before the vessel went into the dry dock, it was discovered that there was a leak between the No. 3 double bottom tank and the port deep tank; assume further that the vessel was put into the dry dock on October 8, 1927; assume further that either before or shortly after the vessel went into the dry dock the cocoanut oil in the deep tanks was examined by taking samples from the different levels in the tanks, and it was found that the oil in the starboard deep tank was uncontam-

(TESTIMONY OF JOE JORY)

inated, but that the oil in the port deep tank was contaminated by contact with fuel oil, this contamination, however, being confined to about the bottom six inches of said deep tank, and the upper layers of the tank being apparently clear and uncontaminated. In view of these facts, what should have been done, in your opinion, in regard to the oil in the port deep tank?

Miss Phillips: Just a moment. Before the witness answers the question may I interpose an objection on the ground that the question assumes some facts which have not been proved, notably that the upper layers of the cocoanut oil had not been contaminated. A. I would remove the oil from the deep tank.

Mr. Derby: Q. Assume, Captain, that the leak between the two tanks was discovered before dry docking the vessel, was it proper, in your opinion, to dry dock the vessel without making a complete examination of the cocoanut oil in the port deep tank? A. I would have made a thorough investigation of the condition of the cocoanut oil in the tank and if, as stated, there was some contamination found at that time, I would remove the oil.

Q. Assuming the leak was discovered before the vessel went into the dry dock, should there have been an examination of the oil before the vessel went into the dry dock? A. Yes.

Q. In your opinion was it proper, knowing that some of the oil in the bottom of the port deep tank was contaminated, to leave the oil in there when it was known

(TESTIMONY OF JOE JORY)

that the vessel had to go on dry dock, and then proceed on her voyage to the west coast of North America? A. No.

Q. Assume now, Captain, that instead of the bottom six inches of the port deep tank being found contaminated all of the oil in said tank was contaminated, would it still be your opinion that the oil should have been removed? A. I would remove the oil anyhow.

Q. Would the contamination be apt to be increased by continuing the voyage? A. The agitation of the vessel under way and the change of temperature of the water would certainly contaminate the oil to a much greater extent.

Q. In your opinion, Captain, was the "West Cajhoot," with the leak between the port deep tank and the No. 3 double bottom tank in a fit condition to go to sea from Kobe? A. In my opinion, if I made a survey of the vessel I would not have given her a seaworthy certificate in that condition.

Q. Are you familiar, Captain, with the rules laid down by associations such as Lloyd's, the American Bureau, and the Bureau Veritas, regarding the construction, maintenance and classification of vessels? A. They have certain rules that we are familiar with, and the Board of Underwriters also has certain rules.

Q. What are the rules with regard to tank tops of tanks carrying oil, with particular reference to whether they must be water and/or oil tight? A. All double bottom tanks, or any tanks in a vessel, must be tested by hydrostatic tests and proven free from leak.

(Testimony of Joe Jory)

Q. If a vessel sails from Kobe with a leak between her tanks unrepaired, is that in conformity with the rules? A. No.

Q. Apart from any rules, in your opinion, Captain, is a vessel which sails from Kobe on a trans-Pacific voyage, with a leak of unknown dimensions in one of her tank tops, in a seaworthy condition? A. In my opinion I would not consider the vessel seaworthy.

Q. How would cocoanut oil be ordinarily removed from a vessel? A. It is generally removed with a pump. The pump is generally put aboard the vessel and steam run from the vessel's steam lines to the pump. It is a portable pump, as a rule.

Q. Into what kind of receptacles could that oil be removed? A. In an open port like Kobe, it could be put into barges; it could be put into another vessel: it could be put into a shore tank, or tank cars.

Q. Would the cost of transferring it to any of these other receptacles be a material item?

Miss Phillips: I object to that on the ground that the witness has not shown himself to be qualified as to these conditions at the port of Kobe. He might be qualified here at San Francisco, but certainly he has not been shown to be qualified as to the cost or any of the conditions assumed in the question at the port of Kobe on the date indicated.

Mr. Derby: I will withdraw the question temporarily.

Q. Captain, is it reasonable to assume that none of these facilities which you have mentioned would have been available in a port like Kobe?

(TESTIMONY OF JOE JORY)

Miss Phillips: I object to that, again, upon the ground that the witness has not been qualified to answer; upon the further ground that the question calls upon the witness to speculate; it also asks him to draw a conclusion.

A. No.

Mr. Derby: Q. Captain, there has been testimony in this case that it would not have been practicable, from a business standpoint, to transfer the oil to another large vessel; would there have been any such impracticability?

Miss Phillips: Just a moment. That question, again, assumes several things, and the witness has not been shown to be qualified to answer the question.

A. No.

Mr. Derby: Q. How would the transfer have been made to another vessel? A. The vessel could have been brought alongside, and the oil pumped from the vessel in distress into the other vessel.

Q. Would there have been any difficulty in doing that? A. No; that is done quite often.

Q. Assuming the other vessel could have come alongside, Captain, would there have been any necessity of first pumping the oil into small craft before making the transfer? A. No, understanding, of course, that the vessel could come alongside.

Q. Would the cost of transferring the oil in that way to another vessel have been great? A. No.

Q. There also has been testimony in this case, Captain, that ordinary oil lighters would not have been suit-

(TESTIMONY OF JOE JORY)

able for discharging the cocoanut oil into. I will ask you, assuming that such lighters had carried oil before, whether there would have been any difficulty in cleaning out such lighters?

Miss Phillips: That is objected to again on the ground that the witness has not been shown to be qualified to answer the question.

A. Any barge can be cleaned out to carry cocoanut oil, especially a barge designed and built for that trade.

Mr. Derby: Q. Have you had personal experience with cleaning out barges, Captain?

Miss Phillips: Just a moment. The question relates to the witness' general experience in cleaning the barges here at San Francisco. Apparently he has not been shown to have had any experience at Kobe.

Mr. Derby: Q. Have you had any experience in cleaning out barges, Captain? A. In San Francisco, yes.

Q. Would there be any appreciable cost in cleaning out such a barge, Captain?

Miss Phillips: I renew the objection. The witness has not been shown to be qualified to answer the question relating to the port of Kobe.

A. No.

Mr. Derby: Q. Could you give an approximate idea as to how much it would cost?

Miss Phillips: I renew the objection. He has not been shown to be qualified to answer the question.

A. To clean an average tank in this port of fuel oil

(TESTIMONY OF JOE JORY)

to make ready for cocoanut oil would run between $150 and $200.

Mr. Derby: Q. Do you know, how prices for work of that kind in San Francisco compare with prices in Kobe?

Miss Phillips: Again I renew the objection. The witness is not shown to be qualified to compare prices as between San Francisco and Kobe in the cleaning of tank cars.

Mr. Derby: We have not got to the tank cars yet, Miss Phillips; we are dealing with lighters now.

Miss Phillips: I thought you referred to tank cars.

Mr. Derby: No, not yet.

Q. Captain, did you understand that in those questions I asked you I was referring to lighters? A. That you were still on lighters, yes.

Q. There has been testimony introduced in this case, Captain, that tank cars could not have been used for the transfer of this cocoanut oil because they were dirty and unfit; would there have been any difficulty in cleaning such tank cars or pumping the oil into them if they could have been brought alongside?

Miss Phillips: I renew the objection. The witness has not been shown to be qualified to answer the question.

A. There would have been no difficulty in cleaning the tank cars. Tank cars are so built and constructed to be cleaned to carry different types and kinds of oil.

Mr. Derby: Q. Would there have been any difficulty in transferring the oil to tank cars if they could have been brought alongside the ship? A. No.

(TESTIMONY OF JOE JORY)

Q. There is also some testimony in this case that there were some large tanks of the Rising Sun Petroleum Company near Kobe, which had been used for the purpose of storing gasoline and coal oil. The testimony is that these tanks could not have been cleaned perfectly so as to have enabled the ship to put the cocoanut oil in them. What have you to say about that? Would there be any difficulty in cleaning such large tanks?

Miss Phillips: The same objection as to the previous question, the witness has not been shown to be qualified to answer the question.

A. Tanks that carry light oil, such as gasoline and kerosene are much easier to clean than tanks that are carrying fuel oil.

Mr. Derby: Q. Would there have been any difficulty in cleaning those tanks? A. Not at all.

Q. Would the cost of cleaning them have been great? A. No.

Q. There also has been testimony in this case, Captain, that the best plan was to leave the oil where it was, because there would not be material further contamination on the remaining legs of the voyage; what is your opinion on that? A. I have already stated that I believe the vessel under way, that the movement encountered during the voyage from the Orient to Los Angeles, that the oil would be more agitated by that movement, and, being more agitated, would have more of a mixture.

A. Assuming, Captain, as I stated in a previous question, that only approximately the bottom six inches of the port deep tank were found to be contaminated; in your

(TESTIMONY OF JOE JORY)

opinion could the upper layers of oil have been removed from the tank without further material contamination? A. Yes, by carefully watching the suction of your pump as you removed the oil.

Q. Assume, Captain, that between October 6, 1927, before the vessel went on the dry dock, but after she arrived at Kobe, and October 12, after the vessel went on the dry dock, that the amount of oil in the port deep tank increased four inches, and that in the starboard tank decreased four and one-half inches, what would that indicate to you, Captain? A. That there was a leak in the center line bulkhead.

Q. Would that have any effect on the answers to my questions as to the desirability of removing the cocoanut oil from the port deep tank? A. I would more readily then have wanted to remove it.

Q. Why so, Captain? A. There must have been considerable more leak.

Q. Could you state approximately, Captain, about how much cocoanut oil there would be in the bottom six inches of the port deep tank? A. No, not unless I took a look at the blueprint.

Q. Will you just take a look at the blueprint, the No. 3 port deep tank. A. The capacity of the deep tanks is marked on this scale in feet. It will give the barrels on this side and the feet on this side.

Q. Can you state roughly or approximately how many tons that would be? A. I would say about ten tons.

Mr. Derby: May I ask you, Miss Phillips, if this plan of the ship will be available at the trial?

(TESTIMONY OF JOE JORY)

Miss Phillips: Yes. If you wish to have it attached to Captain Jory's deposition it is all right. I am quite positive that I have another one in the office. That came in only yesterday. I think it came in in duplicate. If I am correct in that you may have this attached to his deposition.

Mr. Derby: I just want to meet your convenience, Miss Phillips. I want the plan available at the trial.

Miss Phillips: Oh, yes, it will be there all right.

Mr. Derby: Assuming, Captain, that there were in fact no facilities in Kobe for the transfer of this cocoanut oil, could the peak tanks on the "West Cajhoot" have been used, if available? A. If the peak tanks were available they could have been used.

Q. Will you look at that plan and state what the capacity of the fore and after peak tanks was? A. The forepeak tank, 108.5 tons; the after peak tank 241.7 tons, or a total of 350.2 tons.

Q. Assume, Captain, that as a result of the stranding in this case there was damage to the forepeak tank in that there were three floor plates with their frame angles slightly buckled, and the tank was flooded, what would you say about the availability of the forepeak tank for the transfer of the cocoanut oil under those circumstances? A. It would be necessary to put the vessed on dry dock and repair the leaky plates or rivets.

Q. About how long would that have taken, Captain?

Miss Phillips: Just a moment. Again, I do not believe the witness has been shown to be qualified to answer this question.

(TESTIMONY OF JOE JORY)

Mr. Derby: Q. Have you had to do with ship repairs, Captain? A. I have.

Q. How extensive has been your experience?

Miss Phillips: I concede that he is qualified here in San Francisco. You are asking him to estimate time in a Kobe dry dock. My objection is he has not been shown to be qualified to testify to that.

Mr. Derby: Q. How long would that take in San Francisco, Captain? A. In San Francisco that could be done in a day.

Q. What effect would the heating of the cocoanut oil, in your opinion, Captain, have on the extent of the contamination? A. The heating of the oil would make it more liquid, and the fuel oil would mix more readily with it.

Q. Would the contamination be more, the more the oil was heated? A. I would not like to state that, because I am not a chemist. That is a question for a chemist.

Q. Assuming that the oil was liquid while the vessel was at Kobe, Captain, what effect would that have upon your opinion as to the advisability of removing the oil to prevent further contamination? A. I would remove the oil in Kobe after the damage to the vessel, if I found the deep tanks had been leaking, or the double bottom making water.

Q. That is not quite an answer to my question, Captain. I was trying to get at what effect the fact that the oil was in a liquid condition at Kobe would have on your opinion as to the desirability of removing it. A. I would remove it anyway.

(Testimony of Joe Jory)

Q. You would remove it anyway, whether it wàs liquid or not?   A.   Yes, whether it was liquid or not.

Q. Would its being liquid make it easier to remove? A.   It would make it easier to handle.

Mr. Derby: I think that is all.

Cross Examination

Miss Phillips: Q.   Captain Jory, I observed that you said that as a marine surveyor you had had experience with the carriage of vegetable oil and cocoanut oil. Have you had experience in the carriage of it as a captain? A.   No.

Q. In speaking about the sounding of the different holds and tanks to ascertain whether water was coming in, I observed that you said that you thought the No. 3 double bottom should have been sounded. What is the process of sounding the double bottom?   A.   All tanks are fitted with a sounding tube from the tank top to the deck, and fitted at the deck head with a screw cap, one on each side of the vessel. The sounding is located at the after end of each tank. You remove the cap and lower the sounding rod down there. A sounding rod is a piece of steel with graduated marks of inches on it, and with a line attached. It is lowered down to the double bottom, and the water registers its mark on the rod, and when it comes up you can see how much there is on it.

Q. If the tank has fuel oil in it how does the water register?   A.   If it was fuel oil and water you could not tell, because your oil would come to the top and the water would be underneath, and your mark then would be oil; it would be pretty hard to tell what is fuel oil and what is water.

Q. Supposing you pumped out some of the contents of the double tank, if you actually hosed out some of it to look at it, would it be possible to see whether it was a mixture of seawater and fuel oil? A. It would, yes.

Q. Then you would achieve the same purpose, practically, by pumping it out and examining the mixture, itself, as you would by sounding? A. By pumping the tank out you would probably pump through to the settling tanks, and you could very readily tell whether you had oil or water.

Q. Captain Jory, I must confess that I am not exactly sure in my own mind about your theory of how the mixture of cocoanut oil and fuel oil can occur between a double bottom containing fuel oil and the deep tank containing cocoanut oil. I mean I am not very sure in my own mind, so I want to ask you to explain in a little further detail about that. You said that you thought that the agitation of the vessel under way would have a good deal to do with the fusion or the contamination of the two. Now, I wonder if I follow you. We start out by assuming that there is a leak between the deep tank and a double bottom tank. I think that has been testified to. We do not need to assume that, that is an admitted fact in the case. It was a small leak, but there was a leak. Now, as I figure it, the first thing that happens is what? When the leak occurs, what is the first thing that happens? A. From the testimony, the fuel oil got into the tank.

(Testimony of Joe Jory)

Q.   Is it your idea that the fuel oil rises to the upper tank, or is it your idea that the cocoanut oil leaks down? A.   It could be two ways.   In looking the situation over, if the vessel was stranded and had oil or part oil in her No. 3 double bottom, and allowed water to come in that double bottom, which would then fill the No. 3 double bottom, or put a head pressure on the double bottom tank, that would then force itself from the double bottom tank to the deep tank.

Q.   Then in order for the fuel oil to rise from the double bottom tank into the deep tank, you have to start with a full double bottom; is that it?   A.   I should think so.

Q.   I am just trying to work it out now in my own mind.   I am trying to carry along the physical fact here. If, on the other hand, there was no water in the double bottom tank, and some fuel oil had been used from it, so that it was not full, in other words, that there was an empty space there, would the process then be that your cocoanut oil would leak into your fuel oil tank? A.   Yes, it would leak down into the fuel oil tank.   In other words, the tank that has the head would follow its own gravity.

Q.   Exactly.   That is what I thought, myself.   The principal of gravity and the idea that nature abhors a vacuum, those are the two principles that would be in operation there?   A.   Yes.

Q.   So the process then would be that the cocoanut oil would leak down into the fuel oil tank: Is that right? A.   Yes.

(TESTIMONY OF JOE JORY)

Q. When the fuel oil tank is full, when is the process of further contamination of the deep tank going to occur? A. If the fuel tank is full of fuel oil and there is a pressure—any tank is pumped up to pressure, you know—

Q. I don't want to interrupt you, Captain Jory, but I was trying to carry on what I think is going to be the fact proven, that the fuel oil tank was not full and did not have water in it. So the process would be for the cocoanut oil to leak down and fill up the fuel oil tank? A. Yes.

Q. We will not get the benefit of your experience unless you testify on what we believe the evidence is going to show. After the double bottom tank has this mixture of fuel oil and cocoanut oil, and is full, then you think the process will be that it is being pressed up, you might say, and going through to the upper tank? A. Yes; in other words, the double bottom tank must have a head on it to reach the deep tank.

Q. Do you know what the specific gravity of fuel oil is, Captain Jory, as compared with cocoanut oil? A. No.

Q. Now, in this I will have to own up that I am greatly out of my own depth. I think that Allen's Commercial Organic Analysis of Chemistry, Volume 2, I think it is the Fourth Edition, page 188, gives the specific gravity of cocoanut oil at .868 to .874—of course water being 1. I believe the testimony in this case shows that the fuel oil, in fact I think the stipulation is that it is somewhere about .95. I believe that has been stip-

(TESTIMONY OF JOE JORY)

ulated to. I am giving that figure, .95, from memory. As I say, I think it is covered in our stipulation—

Mr. Derby: Here it is, Miss Phillips; it is .9609.

Miss Phillips: Yes, thank you, .9609.

Q. (Continuing)—the fuel oil is slightly heavier than the cocoanut oil. When I use the word "slightly," I do not mean to say that I am the judge of what is or what is not slight. Apparently, however, you would say that the fuel oil would rise into the cocoanut oil tank? A. Yes.

Q. Is it at that point you think the agitation of the ship is important? A. I do.

Q. If the ship were stationary it would probably not rise; is not that so? A. It would not rise as readily. My contention is that the agitation of the ship in a seaway would work, and work, and work, and if you have a slack tank your oil works up against the ship's side. If you have a full tank you have no motion with it. If a double bottom tank would be slightly or partly filled, and the tank above it filled, it might have much more action than it would just lying alongside a wharf.

Q. I think the law of physics would establish that the cocoanut oil would leak from the upper tank into the lower tank until it was filled. A. Yes.

Q. On the other hand, the law of physics would also indicate that the fuel oil, being heavier, would not rise quickly; would you not agree with that? A. I agree to a certain extent as to pure fuel oil, but fuel oil contaminated with water would have a different gravity.

(TESTIMONY OF JOE JORY)

Q. I think, Captain, we are going to have to strike out water from the case, because all the evidence shows there was no leakage of water into the double bottom tank. I wish you would confine your testimony to fuel oil contaminated with cocoanut oil. Would that rise readily? A. It would not rise readily; if the tank were filled it would rise.

Q. Even though the fuel oil is, say, 10 per cent. heavier than the cocoanut oil. You are going to have the heavier oil rise and contaminate the lighter oil. Is that your idea, Captain? A. That is my idea.

Q. In giving that as your idea, you think that would happen with the ship at sea? A. At sea.

Q. With the tossing back and forth. A. With the tossing and the working, yes.

Q. However, if the ship were stationary, the process would be very much more retarded: Is not that the fact? A. Yes.

Q. Would this process that you have described continue when the cocoanut oil in the upper tank congeals? A. No.

Q. Would the process that you have described, of mingling cocoanut oil and fuel oil in the lower tank, would that process, of its rising into the upper tank, continue if the cocoanut oil were congealed in the upper tank? A. It would not continue at all with a vessel lying still, but when cocoanut oil congeals and makes a caky-like substance over it in the working of a vessel it might leave ruptures or fractures in it. I have seen cases of congealed cocoanut oil where it has been broken

(TESTIMONY OF JOE JORY)

into cracks and in these cracks there have been fuel oil stains.

Q. You would not have any question in your own mind that as the cocoanut oil in the deep bottom tank got cold and mushy and then almost became solid the process of contamination then would be greatly retarded, would it not? A. Yes, it would be greatly retarded.

Q. Now, I want you to assume that at the time of the discharge in Wilmington, at the close of November, that the cocoanut oil in the deep tank was sufficiently hard so that it had to be actually dug out by spades, when would you say that the process of the oil moving from the bottom to the upper tank had ceased, or had practically ceased? A. That is a hard question to answer—

Mr. Derby: Just a second. I think I must object to the question on the ground that it incorrectly assumes facts which are not in evidence. It was only at the very bottom of the tank that the oil had to be dug out.

Miss Phillips: I think I said the bottom of the tank.

Mr. Derby: I didn't so understand you. Let us have the question read.

(The record was here read by the reporter.)

Miss Phillips: I thank you for the correction, Mr. Derby. I think later witnesses will have to show how many feet or inches, or feet and inches, there was solid cocoanut oil.

Q. I think the evidence will show, Captain Jory, that there was a solid *matte,* you might say, and as to the thickness of it I *dont'* know, of cocoanut oil that had

(TESTIMONY OF JOE JORY)

to be dug out by spades; would that indicate to you that the process of the oil moving from the lower to the upper tank had practically stopped? A. Yes, it would.

Q. Can you give me an idea when that would have stopped? A. No.

Q. You cannot? A. No, I cannot, because I don't know the temperature when the oil was loaded.

Q. The same text-book that I referred to a few minutes ago, Allen's Commercial Organic Analysis, gives cocoanut oil at melting between 72 and 82 degrees Fahrenheit, and tending to solidify at 72 or lower. Is that somewhere near right, Captain Jory, or do you feel yourself qualified to say? A. No, I would not say.

Q. Then I won't bother you in asking you to testify to that. Supposing that at the time of discharge in Wilmington the double bottom tank beneath this deep tank to which we have been referring was found to be not quite full, let us say 7, or 7 or 8 inches, or a foot, or somewhere near there, of slack, how would you explain that circumstance? A. Do you mean slack cocoanut oil?

Q. No. Perhaps my question was not clear. Pardon me. Supposing at the time of discharge the double bottom tank beneath the cocoanut oil tank is found not to be full, but to have somewhere near one-half of a foot of empty space, how would you explain that circumstance, in view of your previous opinion as to the method of contamination, and as to the admitted fact of contamination? A. It would be pretty hard to explain that. The vessel being on a sea voyage, they might

(TESTIMONY OF JOE JORY)

have pumped some of the tank, that is, they might have removed part of the fuel for burning purposes, or for trimming the ship, for stability. There must be some record on the ship, however, showing how much they took out of a double bottom.

Q. Would it be your idea that this mixed content of the double bottom tank, the fuel oil and the cocoanut oil, that something must have been pumped out of that empty space and then cocoanut oil in the upper tank had congealed before the oil could leak down into the fuel tank? A. Before more oil could leak down, yes.

Q. You say before more oil could leak down? A. Yes.

Q. Now, let me see if we have that clear. If it turns out that the double bottom tank had, let us say, somewhere between six inches and a foot empty space or slack, that would indicate to you that fuel oil had been pumped out at some time, leaving an empty space there, would it not? A. Yes.

Q. Inasmuch as you said that in order to contaminate the upper tank you must have had a full bottom tank, that is true, is it not? A. Yes.

Q. Then would it not follow that when that oil was taken out of the lower tank, the double bottom tank, there should have been a further leakage from the upper tank into the lower tank? A. If the oil in the double bottom had not congealed and stopped it from coming through at that time.

Q. Now, let me see if I follow you. We said that there was a space of six inches to a foot in the double bottom; you understand that, do you? A. In the double bottom, yes.

Q. Now, my question is: When that space occurred, whenever it occurred, why did not the cocoanut oil from the upper tank leak down and fill that six or eight or ten inch space? A. It might have leaked before, but at this time it did not leak any further because the cocoanut oil congealed.

Q. Your idea is that the cocoanut oil in the upper tank must have been congealed at the time of the pumping from the lower tank? A. At the time the double bottom tank was pumped.

Q. In other words, if the cocoanut oil had not been congealed there would have been a further leakage? A. It would run up to the level of the double bottom tank; in other words, it would put a head on the double bottom tank again.

Q. Exactly. Can you think of any other explanation which would account for the fact that at Wilmington, at the time of the discharge, there was an empty space, that is, a slackness of six, eight, or ten inches, or whatever it was, in the double bottom tank? Can you think of any other explanation for that? A. No.

Q. Then it would follow, would it not, Captain, that the last time there was a pumping from the double bottom tank fixes the date of the end of the contamination? Doesn't that follow, Captain? A. It might follow to a certain extent, but I am not satisfied from all the records kept on the vessel with regard to pumping, in other words, they show exactly right when the vessel was

(TESTIMONY OF JOE JORY)

stranded and then they show no record of soundings on
the double bottom tanks.   It seems to me it is a matter
of a poorly run organization.

Q.   I am not asking you about that, Captain.   I am
just trying here to explain a physical fact.   That is all
I am trying to explain.   I think that to any one the
problem here of physics is an interesting one; that is,
you have a heavy oil beneath a light one.   Unquestionably some of the heavy oil moves into that top space.
We are trying to trace the process of that movement.
Now, Captain, if I add the further fact that at the end
of the voyage the tank containing the heavier oil is not
full, it does not put a head on it.   I am trying now to
explain the physical fact of why the oil did not leak
from the upper tank into the lower.   A.   Well, it must
have been solid.

Q.   It must have been solid?   A.   Yes.

Q.   When you suggested that possibly the forepeak
tank and the afterpeak tank could have been used for
storing the oil, you said, I believe, that the forepeak
tank would have had to be repaired before you could
pump oil into the forepeak tank: Is not that correct?
A.   Yes.

Q.   That is, you could not pump the cocoanut oil into
the forepeak tank and then repair it?   A.   No.

Q.   That would mean, would it not, that the cocoanut
oil could not have been pumped into the forepeak tank
until the ship was in dry dock: Is not that correct?   A.
That is correct.

Q.   That is necessarily so, is it not?   A.   Yes.

(TESTIMONY OF JOE JORY)

Q. You would say, then, that it is your opinion that if the after peak tank was available it would have been proper to pump the oil from the No. 3 deep tanks into the after peak tank as well? A. I said it could have been done.

Q. Was it your idea that that could have been done and then kept there for the voyage home, or was it in your mind that it would be just used to store it there and then it would have to be pumped back into the deep tank? A. It was in my mind for a storage proposition, only.

Q. As a matter of fact, it would not have been practicable, or it would not have been good stowage to have carried the cocoanut oil in the after peak tank on the way home? A. It could have been carried in the after peak tank. When I made the statement about passing the oil from the deep tank to the peak tank I was thinking of the matter of inspection and repairs to the deep tank. Vessels, as a rule, do not carry cocoanut oil in peak tanks.

Q. Is not that because the peak tank, particularly the after peak tank, being so near the propeller, it is subjected to a great deal of vibration and the danger of leaking rivets? A. Yes.

Q. You might be jumping from the frying pan into the fire if you began carrying cocoanut oil, even though damaged, in the after peak tank. A. And the statement that the oil was so solidified that it could not run through a leak in the double bottom tank, if it was in the after peak tank the only contamination of it you

(TESTIMONY OF JOE JORY)

would get would be sea water, and if it was solid inside it could not leak out.

Q. In order to pump the oil from the double bottom tank into the after peak tank you would first have to put the after peak tank in order for it, would you not? A. Certainly.

Q. And then you would have to heat the cocoanut oil to get it in? A. You would have to heat it to handle it, to get it in and get it out.

Q. That is what I thought, Captain. Not being an expert on these matters you understand that I have to ask you a good many questions that perhaps the answers to those questions are quite obvious to you. I can comfort myself in the thought that perhaps not even the Court is an expert in the carriage of cocoanut oil. You said you thought that six inches of oil at the bottom of the No. 3 port deep tank would come to about ten tons, did you not? A. That is only my estimate. That is something that could be worked out from the records.

Q. May I ask you for your method of working that out? A. The scale on the deep tank shows how many barrels it will hold. In other words, the deep tank is calibrated. You could sit down and work out very closely just what it was, assuming that the measurements on here are accurate.

Q. In other words, you take the dimensions, do you not, and you get the cubic contents? A. Yes, that is it.

Q. And then you turn the cubic contents into barrels? A. Yes.

Q. Before we leave this, Captain, there is a ques-

(TESTIMONY OF JOE JORY)

tion I want to ask you that I really don't know the answer to, myself, at all. I am referring now to the fuel oil, I am referring to the second column at the bottom of this blueprint. It gives capacity: Cubic feet, gallons, barrels, tons. Is that measurement tons, is it long tons, or is it short tons? A. In this particular case it is weight tons or short tons.

Q. Now, in the same way, Captain, I notice here in the capacities as to water ballast, in giving the capacity of the deep tank and the forepeak and the after peak, in the third tabulation, almost in the center of the blueprint, I notice that that gives cubic feet, gallons, tons. For instance, the forepeak is given as 108.5; is that measurement tons, or short tons, or long tons? A. That is short tons.

Q. Is that customary in blueprints, Captain? A. On an English plan it will be different from an American plan; as a rule, unless these blueprints are certified to and are gone over by somebody who has the authority and has a knowledge of the measurements of the tanks, I mean an accurate knowledge, it is just a matter of data to look at. I will say that they are not always accurate. I will say that I have figures from our survey reports that do not conform to these tonnages, at all.

Q. In other words, Captain, what you mean is there could be a variation? A. There could be a variation of a few tons more or less. In other words, Miss Phillips, I would not want to swear to the exact poundage on any blueprint.

Q. I simply wanted to get at the terminology. When

(Testimony of Joe Jory)

this refers to tons, is it long tons, short tons, or measurement tons? A. On the tanks it is short tons.

Q. Short tons, 2000 pounds? A. Yes. Just a moment, I see now that it is noted on here, this blueprint
is marked. This must be a Government blueprint, isn't
it, Miss Phillips?

Q. Yes, it is. A. It says here: "The weights and
volumes used, 1 ton is 2240 pounds." That is a long
ton. On our regular ones it is 2000 pounds. I see that
everything is marked here. It even shows the degrees
Baume as to oil. The gallons are in cubic inches. There
is no argument at all about this plan; in other words, we
can take this plan and swear to it, because it is certified.

Q. I said that it was a Government print. As a
matter of fact, it is a print from the Los Angeles Dry
Dock & Shipbuilding Company. A. But it was made
for the Government. Q. Yes, exactly. There is one
more question I want to ask you, Captain. The poundage of cocoanut oil has been referred to several times.
I believe it is 1,223,583 pounds, or thereabouts. I think
the exact amount is stipulated to. In the various depositions two terms have been used in referring to quantity. Sometimes we speak of tons of this, that, or the
other—fuel oil, or cocoanut oil, and sometimes we talk
about barrels. I believe even to-day you spoke about
barrels of cocoanut oil. Do you know how many pounds
in a barrel? A. We take 6.7 barrels to a ton.

Q. Is that for cocoanut oil? A. No, I am talking
about fuel oil. We talk about vegetable oil in pounds

(TESTIMONY OF JOE JORY)

because they buy it by the pound. They don't say whether it is a short ton, or a long ton, or anything else. In English ships fuel oil goes by tons; in American ships it goes by barrels.

Q. You don't know how many barrels of cocoanut oil to the ton? A. No. In order to keep it simplified for everybody it goes by pounds. Speaking of vegetable oil we speak of so many pounds. It is sold by weight or by volume.

Q. I suppose the relationship betwcen the weight of cocoanut oil and fuel oil and water is sufficiently fixed now to make the galculation if we need to. There are 8-1/2 pounds of water to the gallon. A. Yes.

Q. And 31 gallons to a barrel. A. 31 and something.

Miss Phillips: That is all.

REDIRECT EXAMINATION

Mr. Derby: Q. I think you said, Captain, that in order to transfer the cocoanut oil from the deep tank to the after peak tank it would have to be heated. Would that be true if the oil were still liquid? A. No.

Q. In your opinion, was there any excuse, in the absence of some compelling necessity, to send the "West Cajhoot" to sea from Kobe with an unrepaired leak between her No. 3 double bottom tank and her No. 3 port deep tank?

Miss Phillips: That is objected to as calling for the conclusion of the witness as to a matter upon which he

(TESTIMONY OF JOE JORY)

does not know all of the facts or the evidence in the case. He is not shown to have that knowledge. He is plainly not qualified to answer the question. Furthermore, it is asking him to place himself in the position of the Court. I object to the question on all of the grounds stated.

A. No.

Mr. Derby: Q. Now, I want to ask the witness one question which I forgot to ask on direct examination. I want to ask you, Captain, whether it is proper practice on shipboard, when fuel oil is pumped from various double bottom tanks, not to keep a record of the amount of fuel oil pumped from each tank, but only a record of the total oil pumped each day from all the double bottom tanks? A. In my opinion and in my experience all vessels carrying fuel oil in double bottom tanks sound and know each day what is in the particular tank. In vessels having lumber cargo, where stability is concerned, it is very necessary to know the amount of oil in each double bottom tank which can only be known by sounding.

Q. In your opinion is it proper practice on any ship not to keep a record of the amount of oil pumped each day from each tank? A. As I stated, it is my opinion that it is proper to sound your tanks each day when you are moving oil.

Q. You should sound them, each individual tank? A. Each individual tank and each side of the tank.

Mr. Derby: That is all.

(TESTIMONY OF JOE JORY)

RECROSS EXAMINATION

Miss Phillips: Q. You say it is proper practice to sound each tank each day? A. When you are moving oil.

Q. I am not sure that I get your answer on that correctly. I understood you to say that it is proper practice to sound each fuel oil tank each day to ascertain exactly the amount and to know the exact amount of oil in each tank every day. A. I said when they are moving oil.

Q. What do you mean by that? A. For instance, you are pumping oil to-day from No. 2 tank; that is the tank to be sounded. He will not sound the others, because he is not moving oil from the others. Then the next day he pumps from No. 3. Then that is the tank for him to sound. He puts it down on his record. For instance, his record will show No. 1 two feet; that is, it will show port side two feet, starboard side two feet six. No. 3, full, No. 2 full. If in the meantime he takes oil out of No. 2 and the trim of his vessel is changing, the master will say to him: "Don't take any more oil there forward, Chief." Then he stops pumping out of No. 2 and goes to No. 4 or to No. 5 for the trim of the vessel; then he must sound No. 2 to find out how much oil he has left in No. 2. He has to know that, because the master will say to him, "How much oil have you forward there, Chief, I am making the canal to-day, I have to hold her on an even keel." Then he tells the master how much he has. The master may say, "You had better

(TESTIMONY OF JOE JORY)

take it out of No. 5." Then he will pump No. 5. That is the usual procedure on a ship that is run right.

Q. That is the proper practice?   A. That is the proper practice.

Q. It is common, I would take it from what you say, that even if records are not kept of the exact quantity they see-saw around in the different tanks so as not to empty a particular tank before another one is empty: Is that right?   A. Yes.

Q. And that is good practice in order to keep the trim of the ship right?   A. Yes, that is good safe practice. On some ships there is an oil meter to tell how much oil they consume a day. In a good properly run ship you can look on the board and find out, or on the report sent to the master each day by the chief, just how the fuel stands.

Q. I take it from what you have said, then, that you would not have approved carrying on the trip home all the cocoanut oil which could be removed from the port tank to the after tank leaving the starboard tank full, would you?   A. No, I would not, but I would have filled that tank up with water to keep my trim.

Q. Even though you would have had to leave part of the cocoanut oil from the port tank in it, you would still have filled it up with water, would you?   A. That is a peculiar question, because I would not have considered coming home at all with the vessel until she was repaired.

Q. We are getting off into all kinds of hypotheses, here. Your discussion of the tonnage capacity of the

(TESTIMONY OF JOE JORY)

ship shows that the forepeak tank and the after peak tank could not have carried all the quantity of cocoanut oil in the port tank. That is my suggestion.

Mr. Derby: I don't think that is so.

Miss Phillips: Well, I think we will have to look at the figures more definitely, perhaps, on that. I don't want the captain to go too far afield on that. I think that is all I want to ask him. Have you any further questions?

Mr. Derby: No. That is all. I offer in evidence the blueprint produced by Miss Phillips, and ask that it be marked "The Los Angeles Soap Company Exhibit Jory No. 1."

(The blueprint was marked "The Los Angeles Soap Company Exhibit Jory No. 1.")

W. E. HEPPELL,

Called for The Los Angeles Soap Company; Sworn.

Mr. Derby: Q. Captain Heppell, where do you reside? A. San Francisco.

Q. What is your occupation? A. Marine surveyor.

Q. How long have you been a marine surveyor? A. In San Francisco since 1920.

Q. As a marine surveyor, do you represent any steamship companies? A. Yes, a majority of the steamship companies out of this port.

Q. Will you state the names of some of those companies? A. The North German Lloyd; the Hamburg-American Line; the Fred Olson Line; the Robert Dollar

(TESTIMONY OF W. E. HEPPELL)

Company; the Panama Pacific Line; the Blue Star Line; the Klavness Line; Sudden & Christenson.

Q. As a marine surveyor representing those different lines, have you had to do with all kinds of cargoes? A. Yes.

Q. Have you had to do with vegetable oil cargoes? A. I have.

Q. Have you had to do with cocoanut oil cargoes? A. Yes.

Q. Before you became a marine surveyor, what was your occupation? A. A ship master.

Q. How long had you been a ship master? A. Seventeen years.

Q. What license did you hold? A. Master, unlimited, any ocean.

Q. Will you state a few of the lines that you worked for as master? A. The Blue Funnel Line; the China Navigation Company; the United States Transport Service, during the war.

Q. Did you have any experience as master in the Orient? A. Yes, for seventeen years.

Q. Did you run on any special line in the Orient? A. Yes, the Blue Funnel.

Q. Are you familiar with the port of Kobe? A. Very

Q. Did your voyagings as master take you into Kobe, at all? A. Yes, I was three years on the Shanghai, Kobe and Yokohama run.

Q. How many times, approximately, would you say you have been in the port of Kobe? A. I would say about forty times.

(TESTIMONY OF W. E. HEPPELL)

Q. Are you familiar in a general way with the shipping facilities of that port? A. Up to the time that I left it, yes.

Q. Have you tried to keep in touch with those facilities since that time? A. I have, yes.

Q. Are you, in a general way, familiar with the steamer "West Cajhoot?" A. Yes.

Q. Are you familiar, in a general way, with her structure, in the way of deep tanks, double bottom tanks, and other tanks? A. Yes.

Q. I will ask you to assume, Captain, that the "West Cajhoot," on a voyage from Manila to Los Angeles, via Hongkong to San Francisco, was carrying fuel oil in her double bottom tanks, and was also carrying a cargo of 1,223,583 pounds of cocoanut oil in her No. 3 port and starboard deep tanks, about half in each, which deep tanks were located immediately above the No. 3 double bottom tank. Assume also that on October 2, 1927, the vessel stranded while passing through Van Diemen Straits, in Japan, and that after being floated it was decided to make for Kobe, Japan, as a port of refuge. Assume further that after the stranding the No. 1 hold and the No. 1 double bottom tanks were sounded, and it was discovered that sea water had entered said hold and tank. Assume also that tests were made to determine whether there was any water in the No. 2 and No. 3 holds, and it was found that there was none but that later, by subsequent soundings, a leak was discovered in the No. 2 hold, but not in the No. 3, and that no soundings were made of the No. 3 double bottom tank. In view of the above facts, what is your opinion as to whether the No. 3 double bottom tank should have been sounded after the vessel was floated from the reef? A. After an accident of any kind by stranding all tanks and bilges should be sounded at once and continued soundings every fifteen or thirty minutes up to the vessel's arrival in port.

Q. Would that be true, in your opinion, Captain, as to the No. 3 double bottom tank, even though there was apparently no water in the 'No. 3 hold? A. Yes.

Q. Why would you say that, Captain? A. In order to find out whether the water was gaining on it.

Q. Now, Captain, assume the same facts as those stated in the last long question, and assume also that after the arrival of the vessel in Kobe, and on or about October 5, 1927, and before the vessel went on the dry dock, it was discovered that there was a leak between the No. 3 double bottom tank and the port deep tank; assume further that the vessel was put in the dry dock on October 8, 1927; assume further that either before or shortly after the vessel went into the dry dock the cocoanut oil in the deep tanks was examined by taking samples from different levels in the tanks, and it was found that the oil in the starboard deep tank was uncontaminated, but that the oil in the port deep tank was contaminated by contact with fuel oil, this contamination, however, being confined to about the bottom six inches of said deep tank and the upper layers being apparently clear and uncontaminated; in view of those facts, Captain, what, in your opinion, should have been done in regard

(TESTIMONY OF W. E. HEPPELL)

to the cocoanut oil in the port deep tank? A. It should have been discharged.

Q. Assuming that the leak between the two tanks was discovered before dry docking the vessel, was it proper, in your opinion, to dry dock the vessel without making a complete examination of the cocoanut oil in the port deep tank? A. No.

Q. In your opinion was it proper that, knowing that some of the oil in the bottom of the port deep tank was contaminated, to leave the oil in there when it was known that the vessel had to go on the dry dock and then proceed on her voyage to the west coast of North America? A. No.

Q. Now, Captain, assuming that instead of the bottom six inches of the port tank being found contaminated all of the oil in said tank had been found contaminated, would it still be your opinion that the oil should have been removed? A. Yes.

Q. In your opinion was the "West Cajhoot," with a leak between the port deep tank and the double bottom tank, in a fit condition to go to sea from Kobe? A. She was not.

Q. Are you familiar with the rules laid down by associations such as Lloyd's, the American Bureau, and the Bureau Veritas, regarding the construction, maintenance and classification of vessels? A. In a general way, yes.

Q. What are those rules in regard to tank tops, with particular reference to whether they must be water- or oil-tight? A. The tanks should be subjected to a hydro-

(TESTIMONY OF W. E. HEPPELL)

static test with a head on it up to the level of the deck, that is, the upper deck, after which the tank tops and manholes should be examined to see if they are tight.

Q. In other words, is it the rule that they must be tight? A. They must be, yes.

Q. If a vessel sails from Kobe with a leak between her tanks unrepaired, is that in conformity with the rules? A. It is not.

Q. Apart from any rules, is a vessel which sails from Kobe on a trans-Pacific voyage, with a leak of unknown dimensions in one of her tank tops, in a seaworthy condition? A. She is not.

Q. Now, Captain, you say that the oil from the port deep tank should have been removed under the circumstances stated to you; why, in your opinion, should it have been removed? A. In order to save the oil, and also to determine the cause of the fuel oil getting into the deep tank.

Q. What facilities could have been used in Kobe, Captain, in your opinion, for the discharge of the oil?

Miss Phillips: I object to the question on the ground the witness is not shown to be qualified to answer the question. He has not stated any date as to his last personal knowledge of facilities at Kobe. He said he had been there several years ago. I do not believe even as to that the dates were given. He has been in San Francisco since 1920. You are asking the captain as an expert witness to state what facilities could have been used in Kobe for discharging the oil.

Mr. Derby: I am asking him not only as an expert

(TESTIMONY OF W. E. HEPPELL)

witness, but I am asking him to base his answer in part upon his personal knowledge of Kobe, and also, if he knows it by reputation, since he has become a marine surveyor.

Miss Phillips: My objection to that is two-fold. First, you cannot prove such a thing as that by reputation. The reputation of Kobe is not ground for this witness to base his testimony upon. Secondly, you have carefully refrained from having the witness date his personal knowledge of the port of Kobe.

Mr. Derby: Q. When were you last in Kobe, Captain? A. In 1917.

Q. Were you familiar at that time with the facilities which could have been used for the discharge of oil cargoes? A. Yes, sir.

Q. Do you know whether those facilities have remained the same since then, or whether they have increased?

Miss Phillips: That is objected to on the ground that it is hearsay. Plainly, that is hearsay. A. They have increased very much.

Miss Phillips: I move to strike the answer of the witness on the ground that it is based on hearsay, according to his own admissions.

Mr. Derby: Q. What facilities were there in Kobe, as you knew it, for discharging cocoanut oil? A. Oil barges, storage tanks, tank cars; also other facilities could be used to transfer the oil. At that time we also had oil barges in Shanghai and Yokohama which could have been brought over if necessary.

(TESTIMONY OF W. E. HEPPELL)

Q. Is it reasonable to suppose, Captain, that none of those facilities would have been available in a large port like Kobe?

Miss Phillips: That is objected to as asking the witness to speculate; also it is asking him to assume facts which have not been proved.

A. It is not.

Mr. Derby: Q. Captain, there has been testimony in this case that it would not have been practicable from a business standpoint to transfer the oil to another large vessel; would there have been any such impracticability? A. None, whatever.

Q. What would have been done in the process of transferring? A. Bring the other vessel alongside and pump direct from one into the other.

Q. Would there have been any difficulty in doing that? A. None, whatever.

Q. Would there have been any necessity of pumping the oil into small craft before making the transfer? A. No, sir.

Q. Would there have been any difficulty in securing a pump long enough for the purpose? A. There would have been none.

Q. Do many large boats pass through Kobe, Captain? A. Yes.

Q. Do those include boats with oil tanks? A. Yes.

Q. It also has been testified in this case that ordinary oil lighters would not be suitable for the transfer of this cocoanut oil, too, because of the difficulty in cleaning

(TESTIMONY OF W. E. HEPPELL)

them. Would there be any difficulty in cleaning an ordinary oil lighter? A. None, whatever.

Q. How is it done? A. By steaming out, after which the lighters are hosed down with either caustic or oakite.

Q. What would be the approximate cost in San Francisco of cleaning out a lighter like that? A. It depends on the size of it.

Q. About how many tons would the ordinary oil lighter carry? A. To clean out the lighter sufficiently to accommodate—that is, sufficient tanks in the lighter to accommodate the cocoanut oil in the port deep tank only, that is, about 250 tons or 260 tons, that would cost in San Francisco about $300.

Q. Would the cost be greater or less in Kobe? A. A great deal less. You can get cheap labor to do it.

Q. There also has been testimony in the case that tank cars could not have been used because they would be dirty and unfit. Would there be any difficulty in cleaning such tank cars? A. None, whatever.

Q. Would there be any difficulty in pumping the oil into them after they were cleaned? A. None.

Q. Would the cost of the cleaning and the pumping operation amount to much of anything? A. No, very little compared to the value of the oil.

Q. When you were in Kobe, Captain, did you know of any shore tanks that could be used for the storage of oil? A. Yes, the Rising Sun Petroleum Company have tanks of that kind.

Q. There has been testimony in the case that those tanks could not have been used because they could not

(TESTIMONY OF W. E. HEPPELL)

be cleaned perfectly. In your opinion is there anything in that excuse? A. Nothing whatever.

Q. It also has been testified that the cost of cleaning such tanks would exceed the price of the cocoanut oil; is there anything in that? A. Nothing, whatever.

Q. How much would it cost, in your opinion?

Miss Phillips: That is objected to because the witness is certainly not shown to have been qualified to answer that. He has never been shown to have used a storage tank at the port of Kobe for cocoanut oil, or for anything else, or that he ever examined into the cost of it.

Mr. Derby: Q. Would the cost of cleaning any large storage tank for oil be appreciable, Captain, as compared with the value of a cargo of approximately 250 tons of cocoanut oil? A. No.

Q. Suppose those tanks of the Rising Sun Petroleum Company had only contained previously gasoline and coal oil, what would you say about the difficulty of cleaning them under those circumstances? A. There would be no difficulty, at all; they are very easily cleaned.

Q. Are tanks containing gasoline and coal oil more easily cleaned than tanks containing fuel oil? A. Yes, very much more easily, on account of the color.

Q. It also has been testified that it was thought that the best plan was to leave the oil where it was, because there would be no further contamination while the vessel was on the dry dock and on the remaining legs of the journey. What is your opinion on that? A. There was

(TESTIMONY OF W. E. HEPPELL)

danger of further contamination so long as the oil was in a liquid condition.

Q. In your opinion was it, in fact, the best plan to leave the oil where it was? A. No, it was not.

Q. In your opinion, would the contamination be apt to be increased by dry docking and then pursuing the voyage? A. It would.

Q. Assuming, as I stated in the previous question, that only the bottom six inches of the port deep tank were contaminated, could the clear oil on top have been transferred so as to prevent materially further contamination in the process of transferring? A. It could.

Q. Captain, assume in this case that after the vessel arrived in Kobe, and between October 6, 1927, before the vessel went on the dry dock, and October 12, 1927, after she went on the dry dock, the amount of the oil in the port deep tank increased four inches, and that in the starboard deep tank decreased four and one-half inches, what would that indicate to you? A. It would indicate that there was a leak in the longitudinal bulkhead between the two tanks.

Q. What effect would that additional leak have on your opinion, Captain, as to the advisability of removing the cocoanut oil from the port deep tank? A. It would strengthen it.

Q. Why is that, Captain? A. Because I would be sure there was a leak then, and I would be more determined to get the oil out in order to find out the reason for the change in depth of oil in the tanks.

(TESTIMONY OF W. E. HEPPELL)

Q. In your opinion, Captain, would it be possible for the contamination in the port deep tank to extend to only the bottom six inches of the port deep tank without affecting all the cocoanut oil in the tank? A. Yes, providing that the oil solidified.

Q. I mean when they first examined it at Kobe, when the oil was still in a liquid condition, would it be possible for there to be only a contamination in the bottom six inches with the other layers uncontaminated? A. Yes.

Q. Could you tell me approximately, and you can refer to the blueprint if you like, how much oil would be contained in the bottom six inches of the port deep tank? Here is the capacity scale, Captain. A. Not more than eight tons.

Q. Captain, assuming there were no facilities whatever in Kobe for the discharge and the temporary storage of the cocoanut oil in the No. 3 port deep tank, could any other tanks on the "West Cajhoot," herself, have been used for the purpose of storing such cocoanut oil? A. Yes, the fore and after peaks could have been used.

Q. What is the approximate capacity of the fore and after peaks? A. The forepeak is 108 tons; the after peak is 241; that is, roughly, 350 tons.

Q. Captain, assume that as a result of this stranding there was some damage in the forepeak, consisting of three floor plates with their frame angles slightly buckled, and that the tank was flooded, what effect would that have, in your opinion, on the ability to use the forepeak tank? A. Put the ship on the dry dock and have it repaired.

(TESTIMONY OF W. E. HEPPELL)

Q. About how long would it take to make that repair? A. Not more than a couple of days.

Q. Would she have had to go on the dry dock to make that particular repair? A. She would.

Q. When oil is pumped out of a double bottom fuel tank when a ship is at sea, what is the proper practice as to keeping a record of the amount of oil pumped out? A. A daily record should be kept of all fuel oil that is pumped from each respective tank into the settling tanks.

Q. In your opinion would it be proper practice, Captain, only to keep the amount of the total oil pumped from all the tanks, without keeping a separate record as to what was pumped from each tank? A. No, sir.

Q. How would you characterize that procedure, Captain? A. Each tank should be kept separate, so that you know exactly how much oil you are using from every tank.

Q. How would you characterize the practice of only keeping a record of the pumping from all the tanks? A. I don't quite understand what you mean.

Q. As to whether it would be proper or improper?

Miss Phillips: That is objected to as leading. You should ask him the question first.

Mr. Derby: The witness has said he did not understand the question. A. It is proper to keep a careful check on all oil pumped from every tank so that you know exactly how much oil you have, and that you don't have any slack tanks.

Q. What would you say of the practice of a chief engineer who only kept a record of the total oil pumped

(TESTIMONY OF W. E. HEPPELL)

from all the tanks without keeping any separate record of the amount pumped from each particular tank? A. I should say that he was very slack in his method.

Q. Captain, is there any doubt whatever in your mind about the advisability of discharging the cocoanut oil from the port deep tank under the circumstances that I stated to you? A. None, whatever.

Q. Captain, what do you think of the practice, under any circumstances of carrying vegetable oil in deep tanks over fuel oil in the double bottom tanks below those deep tanks? A. The practice is dangerous of carrying vegetable oil over a double bottom tank with fuel oil in it. For a long time we insisted upon keeping the double bottom tanks filled with water, with fresh water, but that was never an established rule.

Q. What was the danger? A. The danger was of the double bottom tank top leaking during the voyage, due to heavy strains, and the fuel oil leaking into the deep tank and contaminating the vegetable oil.

Mr. Derby: That is all.

CROSS EXAMINATION

Miss Phillips: Q. Captain Heppell, you said that after a stranding such as has been described it is proper to sound all the tanks and holds. How would you go about sounding a double bottom tank in which there is fuel oil? A. Through the sounding pipe. Q. How is it done? A. By dropping the sounding rod with a line attached into the tank right from the upper deck.

Q. You know I have never been an engineer on a ship, or a captain, either. That does not tell me what

(TESTIMONY OF W. E. HEPPELL)

the exact process is. That is what I want to know from you. A. There is no other method, Miss Phillips, except by sounding pipes. That is why they are built into the ship when the ship is constructed; they are built into all tanks and bilges.

Q. You say you use a sounding pipe. What is it you are looking for then, whether there is sea water in the bottom tank? A. To see whether there is any water or oil.

Q. After a collision, if you want to sound a fuel oil tank in which you know there is some fuel oil, and you want to sound it to find out whether any water has gotten in, what is the thing that shows to you whether water is or is not in the tank? A. The sounding rod and the sounding line. It depends on how high the water would rise up on the sounding pipe. As a rule, if there is a leak the water will rise to the height of the water on the outside.

Q. What is the effect of the mixture of the oil and the water there; do they mix, or which comes up first? A. The oil would come up first.

Q. Would there be any particular difficulty in ascertaining when there is a mixture? A. I don't think so.

Q. You don't think there would be? A. No.

Q. Would you say there is any other way of ascertaining whether the water has gotten into the double bottom tank? A. Yes, there would be by attempting to pump whatever was in there out.

Q. That is, to actually pump some of the contents of that double bottom tank out and look at it? A. Yes.

(TESTIMONY OF W. E. HEPPELL)

Q. That is it, is it? A. Yes.

Q. And then a visual inspection would show you whether it is fuel oil or whether it is a mixture, is that right? A. You see it at once.

Q. You see it at once, do you? A. Yes. You know there is an old saying that oil and water never mix.

Q. So that when you begin pumping out, the stuff coming out, it will show up at once, will it? A. Yes, there will be an emulsion.

Q. I say it will show up at once? A. Yes.

Q. I should think it would. A. Yes, it will.

Q. Captain Heppell, I think you made a comparison in regard to the use of shore tanks; you said that in your opinion there were at Kobe tanks of the Rising Sun Petroleum Company which you thought might have been available. Are those the big tanks that are used for the storage of gasoline and oils of all kinds? A. Yes.

Q. Somewhat similar to the tank farm we are familiar with? A. Exactly the same.

Q. They have a very large cubic capacity? A. The tanks have, yes.

Q. Your suggestion then is that the master and the agents of the "West Cajhoot" might have arranged to go and lease one of these shore tanks, have it cleaned, and then pump the cocoanut oil in pending repairs: Is that it? A. Provided that they could not get oil lighters or tank cars. I would much prefer an oil lighter first.

Q. That is because to use a very large tank for the storage of a relatively small quantity of cocoanut oil would involve a good deal of expense policing it, would

(TESTIMONY OF W. E. HEPPELL)

it not? A. It is not so much the expense as the distance in the pipe line; you see there is a long pipe line that you have to pump your oil through to the farm.

Q. You mean that would be a deterrent to this method? A. It would not exactly be a deterrent, but it would not be as good as using lighters.

Q. Is it not also true that with a vessel in dry dock under repairs, the exact length of which could not possibly be known, the company having a large tank might be unwilling to rent a large tank for an indefinite period: Is not that true? A. In that case you would transfer it to the fore and after peaks of the vessel.

Q. I am taking these up, Captain, one at a time; I think it is better to take up each possibility at a time. I am just directing that to your attention now. To use a very large tank to hold a very small quantity of oil for an indefinite period might involve quite substantial expenditure by way of rent charges, would it not? A. No, they have a regular monthly rental; I don't know what it is.

Q. So that the expense of doing that you really cannot undertake to estimate, can you? A. No.

Q. In the same way, when you were talking about the use of lighters for storage, and of the expense of cleaning, which you said in San Francisco might be around $300, and probably less in Kobe for a lighter—

Mr. Derby: No, not for a lighter; he said for the total cargo in the No. 3 port tank, as I understood him.

Miss Phillips: Q. I don't want to misquote you, Captain. As I took my notes when you were testifying

(TESTIMONY OF W. E. HEPPELL)

they, of course, had to be taken in a very abbreviated form, and it is entirely possible that I am incorrect. Just what was your idea on that? A. My idea was that to clean out sufficient tanks in a lighter, in an oil barge, which is subdivided to accommodate the cocoanut oil in the port deep tank only—

Q. Pardon the interruption, Captain, you mean in the oil barge, do you? A. Yes; in San Francisco it would cost approximately $300.

Q. But in that you do not include the rental charge? A. No, just the cleaning.

Q. And there, again, the question of whether an oil barge would be available for a period necessarily uncertain is a thing that you could not undertake to express an opinion about? A. No, I could not.

Q. The same would be true as to the leasing of tank cars there, would it not? A. Yes.

Q. With reference to the use of the forepeak and the after peak tank, I understood you to say that you thought that the forepeak tank would have to be repaired in dry dock before the oil in the deep tank could be transferred to it; did I understand you correctly? A. That is providing that the defects that Mr. Derby mentioned were correct.

Q. Yes, I am assuming that. Is it assumed that the defects in the forepeak tank were such that it caused it to be flooded prior to arrival at Kobe? A. Yes.

Q. And you say that that defect would have to be repaired in dry dock? A. Yes.

(TESTIMONY OF W. E. HEPPELL)

Q. Just what is the process that you say would be the one to be used in the event the fore and after peak tanks were to be used for storing the cocoanut oil? A. That is providing the tanks are in shape to receive it.

Q. I want you to go ahead and explain what you think would have to be done. You must understand, Captain, that I have not had any experience in this thing, and I want you to tell me what you think would have to be done, and what should be done. A. The ship would have to be put in dry dock to repair the forepeak to make it oil-tight, after which the fore and after peak tanks would have to be cleaned out. The after peak, being used as a fresh water tank or a water ballast tank, would not require much cleaning out. The forepeak, which I understand in this ship is used as a fuel oil tank, would have to be steamed out and washed down with chemicals, either oakite or tri-sodium phosphate, and thoroughly hosed down afterwards and inspected. Even if a small amount of fuel oil did remain in some of the crevices, it would be lost in a large volume of cocoanut oil like that without doing material damage to it.

Q. Now, we have got to the point where both the forepeak and the after peak tanks are in fit condition, as far as tightness and cleanliness go, to receive the cocoanut oil; what is the next step? A. In the meantime, while we are doing that, we are preparing portable coils or portable grates—steam grates. I am assuming that the oil in the port tank is beginning to solidify —certainly some of it would; it may not be absolutely

(Testimony of W. E. Heppell)

solid, it may be in a' mushy state, but not sufficiently liquefied to pump. I would commence heating from the top, the same as I have done here in this port on two occasions—heating from the top and pumping from the top, lowering the grate and lowering the hose as the oil went down, at the same time taking samples every few inches with my oil thief and examining those samples carefully to see if I had reached the contaminated oil; the moment I reached the contaminated oil I would stop.

Q. I take it, then, you would have then removed the contaminated oil entirely? A. No, I have removed the good oil.

Q. Oh, yes, we have the good oil out now. A. Then I would remove the contaminated oil.

Q. That is what I mean. A. Yes.

Q. And dispose of it elsewhere. A. That would not have gone forward in the ship.

Q. That would require the engine-room equipment, would it not, Captain, to do that? A. No.

Q. I mean the pumping process. A. No, I would have gotten independent pumps from the Mitsubishi dock yard and I would have gotten independent pipe lines. I would not use any of the ship's equipment, on account of the danger of contamination with fuel oil.

Q. You seem to be quite positive in your own mind that by the time that ship got to dry dock the process of solidification had at least begun. A. Yes.

Q. Are you quite positive of that, Captain? A. Yes, in the month of October, in Kobe, it would begin to a certain extent. The oil would not be hard, but it would

(TESTIMONY OF W. E. HEPPELL)

begin to congeal, particularly out of the ship's side, where the cold air was striking the metal.

Q. Even as it was, with the oil left in the tanks, in your judgment would that process of solidification continue? A. As the weather got colder.

Q. And when the ship finally got to sea, what would be the process then? A. That depends on the temperature of the weather.

Q. I think the testimony is that the ship sailed from Kobe on the 1st or the 2nd of November. The weather would not normally be such as to melt the oil, would it? A. Cocoanut oil liquefies at about 75 degrees Fahrenheit.

Q. And below that? A. Below that it begins to solidify slowly.

Q. So you think, then, that the process of solidification had begun during the month of October in Kobe? A. Yes.

Q. Then in your judgment, during the month of November, coming homeward, don't you think that process of solidification had continued? A. It depends on the temperature of the water outside and also on the heat in the vessel. Both the port and starboard deep tanks on this vessel are forward of the settling tanks into which the fuel oil is pumped before going to the boilers. That tank is always warm, the temperature ranging from 90 to 105 degrees.

Q. I wonder if that shows on the blueprint. Will you look and see, Captain? A. Yes, here is the deep tank; here is the settling tank right across the ship.

(TESTIMONY OF W. E. HEPPELL)

Q. Yes, it shows quite plainly there on the blueprint.
I wish you would explain to me a little more, your theory
of why contamination would increase. I think you said
you thought that the oil, being left in the deep tanks,
the danger of contamination would increase, and that
is why you thought the other step should have been
taken at Kobe, provided it were possible. What is your
theory of the means of contamination in this case? A.
The fuel oil having entered the port deep tank from the
No. 3 double bottom—

Q. Just a moment, Captain. I think you are beginning in the middle of it, I want you to go right back to
the beginning.

Mr. Derby: I don't think the witness is beginning in
the middle of it, at all.

Miss Phillips: I think so. Perhaps it is because my
question is not clear. I would like to have the question
read. (Question read.) It is very plain to me that the
question is not clear, Captain, for which I apologize.
Let me put the question again.

Q. The best description of the leak that occurred
has been given this way, that the bounding bar on the
port side, three frames from the forward bulkhead, was
set up, and that this was the cause of the No. 3 double
bottom tank leaking. That description I have just read
from Mr. Derby's cross-examination of the chief engineer, Blinn. I thought at the time that that was Mr
Derby's understanding of the fact. However, that is
neither here nor there. Supposing we have that slight

setting up, what is the next thing that happens? A. Your fuel oil goes into the deep tank.

Q. You are assuming, then, that the fuel oil tank is absolutely full? A. I am, yes.

Q. Supposing it was not full, supposing some had been used out of it? A. You say all used out of it?

Q. No, supposing there is some fuel oil in it, that it is slack. A. The rolling of the ship and the swishing of the oil would be enough to cause the oil to go up that fracture.

Q. Assuming now we are talking of conditions that happened around the 1st or 2nd of October, the day of the stranding; with that slight leak are you assuming that the cocoanut oil does not go downward? A. Some cocoanut oil would go down, too.

Q. That is why I was asking you to trace the process. Do you think the principle of gravity comes in and that the cocoanut oil would actually go down to the leak in the double bottom tank until the double bottom tank is full? A. Yes.

Q. Is that it, Captain? A. Yes.

Q. Which is the heavier, fuel oil or cocoanut oil? A. Fuel oil.

Q. You have the fuel oil, then, mixed with the cocoanut oil in the double bottom tank? A. Yes.

Q. Then you think that the moving and the swishing of the vessel in the water back to Kobe would cause the contents of this mixture in the double bottom to come up: Is that right? A. Yes, you would have a mixture

(TESTIMONY OF W. E. HEPPELL)

there of fuel oil and cocoanut oil, and with a full tank you would have that oil returning into the deep tank.

Mr. Derby: I want to say at this point that I think you are cross-examining the witness on something he did not testify to on direct. The point in the questions I put to him was that the fuel oil in fact did go into the cocoanut oil. I did not ask the witness in any way why it got there. I have no objection, however, to your questions.

Miss Phillips: Let me justify myself. Perhaps it is just vanity on my part. I certainly understood that the reason for the captain undertaking all this was that he thought there would be an increase in the contamination. If he said that on direct examination I have the right to ask why he thinks so. That is what I am trying to do.

Mr. Derby: As I say, I have no objection. I just wanted to make the point that it is stated as a fact that the fuel oil did get up to the cocoanut oil. Why it got there I have not asked him.

Miss Phillips: You asked him if it would increase and he said it would. I am examining him about that.

Q. So the actual motion of the ship, itself, between the time of the stranding and up to the time it got to Kobe, would cause this swishing and movement of the oil and cause the cocoanut oil below to go up to the tank on top? A. Yes, provided the double bottom tank was full.

Q. Now, don't let me misunderstand you, Captain. Did you say that you thought that the cocoanut oil would leak down and fill the fuel oil tank if there was

(TESTIMONY OF W. E. HEPPELL)

a slackness in the tank? A. Yes, if there was a slackness. ·

Q. That is just our old principle of gravity, isn't it? A. Yes. I don't know how much fuel oil there was, though.

Q. Neither do I. When the ship arrived at Kobe and it was more or less stationary would you say that this mixing is going to continue to an equal degree? A. Not as long as the ship is quiet.

Q. I should think not. I just wanted to ask your opinion on that. Would this process of the cocoanut oil swishing up into mixed cocoanut oil and fuel oil, swishing up from the lower tank through this little place in the bounding bar up into the upper tank, will that continue after the cocoanut oil is solidified? A. No, not after the cocoanut oil is properly solidified.

Q. Suppose we assume that in fact, at the time of the ship's arrival in Wilmington, the bottom of the port deep tank had congealed cocoanut oil for quite some appreciable amount—I won't say how much, it might have been a foot or two, it might have been less or it might have been more, but it was solid enough so that it had to be removed with shovels, you would say that the contamination had stopped certainly by the time that solidified, would you not? A. I would say that the double bottom tank top had been hermetically sealed.

Q. I should think so, too. That is very interesting. A. But I would not say that the contamination had stopped.

(TESTIMONY OF W. E. HEPPELL)

Q. Just explain that, Captain. A. Because in the process of heating the oil in that tank preparatory to pumping it at Wilmington there- was bound to be a mixture between the contaminated oil and the good oil on top.

Q. Even though in discharging they were very careful to heat the top first and pour it off by degrees? A. If they heated it from the top and not from the bottom and pumped from the top, that would minimize the loss.

Q. I think that will be developed by some other witnesses, just what was done in that regard. A. In fact, that is the process that should have been followed.

Q. Yes, I am quite sure the witnesses will show that that was followed. Some other witness will testify as to that. Now, I would like to ask you this, Captain. Supposing at the time of discharge in Wilmington it was found that the fuel tank beneath the deep tank where the fuel oil was, the No. 3, that that was not full at that time, let us assume that it was perhaps six, or seven, or eight, or nine inches slack, I don't know just what it was, but somewhere near there; what would that indicate to you in our history of contamination? A. It would indicate to me that the oil in the No. 3 deep tank on the port side had solidified, otherwise it would be full of cocoanut oil.

Q. I think we started out about ten minutes ago, Captain, to show that the process must originally have been for the double bottom tank to have been filled up and to have actually pressed up against the upper tank,

(TESTIMONY OF W. E. HEPPELL)

in order for contamination to have occurred: Is not that right? A. Yes.

Q. Then how do you explain this slackness of several inches at Wilmington? A. The only way I can explain that is that some must have been pumped out.

Q. If the cocoanut oil was still liquefied at that time should it not have leaked down and filled up the double bottom tank? A. No. Your previous question was to the effect that the oil in the bottom of the port deep tank was solidified upon arrival at Wilmington; therefore, the double bottom tank top was hermetically sealed.

Q. Exactly. Suppose beneath that we found that the double bottom tank was in fact slack for about seven inches, I am asking you if you can explain that. A. The only way I can explain it is that some must have been pumped out.

Q. I should think so, too. Might it have been that the fuel oil in fact had been pumped out, leaving an empty space there, and that at that time the upper tank must have been congealed—the bottom of the upper tank must have been congealed. Do I make myself clear? A. Yes, quite clear. I cannot explain how you could have a space there. The chief engineer would be the best man to testify to that.

Q. I know you have had a great deal of experience, Captain, in these things in surveys, and I am trying to get a physical explanation of the fact. What I suggested to you was this, that at the start you have the aperture between the two tanks, and the cocoanut oil

(TESTIMONY OF W. E. HEPPELL)

leaking down into a partially filled fuel tank, until the fuel oil tank is absolutely full of a mixture of cocoanut oil and fuel oil; then the vessel is still on her way to Kobe, and this swishes around and you have the mixture rising up into the upper tank. At that time the lower tank is full. You agree with me that far, do you, Captain? A. Oh, yes.

Q. Now, I suggest that at some subsequent time, we will not undertake to say right now when that was, some fuel oil was in fact pumped out of the lower tank? A. Out of the No. 3 double bottom.

Q. Yes. If the upper tank at that time was liquefied, should it not have filled up that lower tank? If the cocoanut oil above was liquefied then should it not have leaked down and filled up the double bottom tank? A. Not necessarily. If the aperture was so small, if the fracture was so small, as you have stated, it is possible it might have choked up with solidified cocoanut oil.

Q. Then your explanation of this would be that at or about the time there was oil withdrawn from the double bottom tanks, at that time the aperture from the upper tank was probably choked? A. It may have been, yes.

Q. Then that would mean that the upper tank solidified? A. In the bottom, yes, the bottom section.

Q. The bottom part of the upper tank had solidified? A. Yes.

Q. Then you would have the situation that the cocoanut oil in the upper tank is, you might say, sealed off by this solid wall of congealed oil; is that right? A. Yes.

(TESTIMONY OF W. E. HEPPELL)

Q. Would that explain the situation, if it is found to exist at Wilmington, of the double bottom tank with a few inches of slack, that that never was filled up, oil having once been withdrawn—would that explain it? A. I don't think it would.

Q. Captain, what I am suggesting to you is this: I am suggesting to you—A. You see, I don't know how much oil there was in those double bottom tanks. If I did know I could answer you intelligently. I don't want to do any guessing.

Q. Let me suggest that this is the only possible explanation of these facts. Let us assume that on arrival at San Pedro the No. 3 double bottom tank had somewhere around seven to eight, to nine inches slack, that is to say, empty space; immediately above it there are several inches—perhaps it may run more than that, perhaps two or three feet, of solid cocoanut oil; isn't this possible, that sometime while at Kobe oil was pumped out of the No. 3 tank which would account for the seven inches of slack. Isn't that possible? A. It is possible, yes.

Q. And at that time the cocoanut oil above it was sufficiently solid to prevent further leakage from the upper tank into the lower? A You mean at Wilmington?

Q. At Kobe, I am talking about. A. No, I don't think so.

Q. Why not? A. Because the fact of them taking samples of that tank, of both tanks, in Kobe, tells me that the oil was not solid, that it was liquefied, that it was in a liquid state upon the vessel's arrival at Kobe.

(Testimony of W. E. Heppell)

There is no record of any steam having been applied to liquefy the oil.

Q. I think you are right about that, Captain. You have said that the aperture here was exceedingly small. A. I am taking that from what you said; you said it was very small.

Q. You didn't go on board the ship, did you? A. I did not examine the aperture; I have been on board the ship.

Q. But you didn't examine this particular aperture? A. No.

Q. I am still asking you, Captain, if it is not true that at the time seven inches of oil were pumped out of the double bottom tanks, that at that time—whenever it was—the oil in the deep tank must have been congealed or the aperture stopped up? A. Otherwise the cocoanut oil would have run down and filled it up.

Q. Yes. Wouldn't you say that is true? A. The lower section of the deep tank may have been congealed, but not the whole thing.

Q. I mean the bottom part. There must have been a lower section there that was congealed at the time that the double bottom tank had some oil pumped out of it? A. Yes.

Q. Otherwise it would have been filled up: Isn't that so? A. Yes. I understand that the fracture was close to the forward bulkhead which was farthest removed from the settling tanks, and also from the heat in the boiler-room; so that really where the fracture was was

(Testimony of W. E. Heppell)

about the coldest part of the tank, and the oil would congeal there quicker than it would on the after end.

Q. Can you think of any other explanation of why there should have been six, or seven, or eight inches of slack in the double bottom tank, other than the one that you have just given? A. No, I cannot.

Q. I wondered if there was any other explanation. If there is, Captain, we would like to have it. A. There is none.

Q. Now, there is another question I want to ask you, Captain, and I am almost through with my cross-examination, you will be glad to hear. A. Oh, no, we are enjoying this; I know I am.

Q. I think questions of physics are very interesting. A. When I say, Miss Phillips, that I am enjoying it, I mean that sincerely.

Q. So do I, Captain Heppell. It is very nice for me to have this opportunity for a visit with you, I have not had one in a good while. A. I can assure you that the pleasure is mutual.

Q. In suggesting the various steps that might have been taken at Kobe in removing the cocoanut oil from the ship, I think you said something about these expenses would not be large in comparison with the value of the cocoanut oil; you did say something of that sort, didn't you, Captain? A. Yes, I did.

Q. In making that comparison, you did not have in mind the possibility that the cocoanut oil was already seriously damaged at the time of discovery, did you? A. No, I was taking it at its sound value.

(TESTIMONY OF W. E. HEPPELL)

Q. Yes, I thought so. I just wanted to clear that up. Now, there is another thing I want to ask you about. In declaring outages of deep tanks, outage refers to empty space, doesn't it? A. Yes.

Q. You are measuring emptiness? A. Yes; sometimes they are called outages and sometimes they are called ullages. It represents the space between the top of the tank and the surface of the oil.

Q. In making measurements of that sort and in comparing them with measurements made by somebody else there is a good deal of possibility of error, is there not? A. There is.

Q. You have different men comparing? A. Yes.

Q. And, possibly, using different methods? A. Yes.

Q. And, possibly, measuring from different points? A. No, the same points.

Q. They usually use the same points? A. Yes. I look after all the bulk oil that comes in here from the Orient on the Robert Dollar ships. On the ship's arrival, we get a copy of the Hongkong surveyor's certificate, or the Manila surveyor's certificate, on which there is a sketch of the tank opening, and on which is marked where the ullage was taken from—the outage—and the quantity; also the temperature, the draft of the vessel, and also the list of the vessel.

Q. Even when all those things are done you still have to make allowance for a little error, do you not? A. At the very best they are only approximate; a degree or two in the temperature alone will affect the quantity of oil.

(TESTIMONY OF W. E. HEPPELL)

Q: Oil expands with heat and contracts with cold? A. Yes.

Q. On direct examination, I believe counsel suggested to you or asked you that supposing the records showed an increase of the oil in the port tank and a decrease in the starboard tank, and asked you what that would indicate, and I think you said that would indicate a leak between the longitudinal bulkhead. A. No, in the longitudinal bulkhead.

Q. Between the two tanks? A. Yes.

Q. Had the port tank, in fact, contained more oil than the starboard tank and there was such a leak, there would have been leakage from the port tank into the starboard tank, would there not? A. Oil, like water, will always find its level; the pressure is always from the highest side.

Q. Yes, that is what I thought. A. Whenever we carry valuable vegetable oil in one tank in a vessel and the other tank is available we put water ballast in there to trim the vessel, but we always keep the level of the water below the level of the oil in the other tank, so that the pressure is from that side. The same holds good when we have four tanks in a vessel, like on the Dollar ships, where we will carry two shipments of wood oil, one of Perilla, and one of cocoanut oil, we see that the wood oil, being the most dangerous, is kept at a lower level than either the cocoanut or the Perilla, so that the pressure is against the bulkhead.

Q. Yes, I thought that was the fact. Let us assume that at Wilmington, at the time of discharge, the star-

(TESTIMONY OF W. E. HEPPELL)

board tank showed a less quantity of oil than the port tank. Let us assume that to be the fact— A. But was that the fact?

Mr. Derby: Would you mind repeating that, Miss Phillips, my attention was diverted for the moment.

Miss Phillips: Q. Let us assume that at the time of discharge in Wilmington the port tank had actually at that time more oil in it than the starboard tank. I believe that to be the fact. Unfortunately, I have not the report here that I thought I had—

Mr. Derby: You can use mine, Miss Phillips. I think that is true.

Miss Phillips: That is the fact, that at the time of arrival in Wilmington the port tank had actually more oil in it than the starboard tank.

Q. Had there been a leak in the longitudinal bulkhead, Captain, then the starboard tank should have been contaminated, should it not? A. Not necessarily.

Q. Then we get back to our question of congealing again, do we? A. Yes. They would naturally pump out the starboard tank first.

Q. I am talking about the time of arrival before anything is done to them. The outages showed more oil in the port than in the starboard. Had there been a leak in the longitudinal bulkhead, what I was suggesting to you was that there would have been contamination of the starboard tank? A. No, not necessarily.

Q. Why not? A. Are you sure, Miss Phillips, that that was the condition?

(TESTIMONY OF W. E. HEPPELL)

Q. Yes. I have the report here; Mr. Derby just handed it to me. A. On what date was that? Was that in October?

Q. That was on arrival at Wilmington. A. What date was that?

Q. That was in December, 1927. I think it was early in December. I cannot give you the exact date. A. Can you give me the outages, roughly, in the port tank?

Q. I think the port tank is going to show at Wilmington at the time of discharge, and that is after heating had occurred for some twenty-four hours before arrival at Wilmington— A. Then they did heat the oil before arrival, did they?

Q. Yes. A. Then they must have used the heating coils; therefore, they heated the oil from the bottom instead of from the top.

Q. We are getting into something now, Captain, that I am not sure about. I will have to check that back. The outages taken on December 1, 1927, at Wilmington, showed on the port side 57-1/8. That is the upper left-hand corner. Upper right, 61-5/8. Lower left, 54-3/4; lower right, 59-1/8. That is taking a square and looking down at it. On the starboard, 64-1/2 upper left; 63-1/2 upper right; 62 lower left; 61-1/8 lower right. That means that there is actually more in the port tank than there was in the starboard, does it not? A. That shows a greater outage or ullage in the starboard tank than in the port.

Q. Yes, and therefore less oil. A. Less oil.

Q. That was my query to you. So that had there

(TESTIMONY OF W. E. HEPPELL)

been a leakage between the tanks it should have been
from the port tank to the starboard tank, should it not?
A. No.

Q. Why not? A. I can't understand how there should
be a greater outage in the starboard tank than in the
port upon the vessel's arrival at Wilmington.

Q. Captain, I am asking you to assume that to be the
fact. Why it was I cannot tell you. I am saying that
the witnesses down there will say that that is so. Upon
that basis had there been leaky rivets between the two
tanks do you say that the flow would have been from the
starboard to the port tank, or from the port to the starboard tank. A. It depends upon the height of the fracture in the longitudinal bulkhead. It may have been just
at a point where the level of the oil was in the starboard
tank.

Q. You understand, Captain, that this leak that we
have been talking about is purely theoretical; there has
been no testimony that there was any.

Mr. Derby: Miss Phillips, you mean in between the
two tanks?

Miss Phillips: Yes.

Mr. Derby: The first mate testified that there may
have been a leak between the two tanks.

Miss Phillips: And that is what I am trying to
develop right now, whether the physical facts show he
was right or wrong. He said at the start there was the
possibility of a great deal of error in measuring outages.
Now I am asking him to explain the physical facts at
Wilmington on which all of the witnesses will agree,

(TESTIMONY OF W. E. HEPPELL)

probably. I do not believe you and I are in controversy on some of the physical facts. I do not believe we are.

Q. I will state to you again, Captain, with the quantity of oil in the port tank substantially in excess of that in the starboard tank, had there been a leak between the two which way would the oil have flowed? A. The oil would have flowed from the high level to the low.

Q. You said in speaking about the practice of carrying cocoanut oil over fuel oil that you considered it a dangerous practice, but that it had never been an established practice to do it. Maybe I misunderstood you. A. We tried to get that practice in force with the steamship companies; they did it for a while, but due to the long voyages they had to make and the excessive cost of fuel oil in the Orient, we had to abandon it and allow them to use the No. 3 double bottom tank for fuel oil.

Q. Instead of water? A. Instead of fresh water; our idea was to protect the cargo.

Miss Phillips: That is all.

REDIRECT EXAMINATION

Mr. Derby: Q. Now, Captain, assuming that when these samples were taken in Kobe the damage was confined to the bottom six inches of the port deep tank, I will ask you whether, even if no more fuel oil had leaked out from the double bottom tank, it still would have been advisable to remove the oil from the port deep tank? A. It would.

Q. Would the fuel oil in the bottom six inches of the port deep tank have tended to contaminate the upper

(TESTIMONY OF W. E. HEPPELL)

layers later? A. Provided that the oil had not solidified during the voyage.

Q. As I remember the testimony in this case, Captain, it is that the oil was still liquid when the vessel was at Kobe, and before she went on the dry dock; under those circumstances, would it necessarily have to have been heated before it was taken out of the deep tank? A. It depends entirely on how liquefied the oil was. If you can give me the temperature of the oil from the Kobe report I can answer that.

Q. But you could not say on the data you have whether or not you would have had to heat it before pumping it out? A. No, I could not.

Q. I think you said on cross-examination that it would be unwise to use the large tanks of the Rising Sun Petroleum Company if you could have got lighters or tank cars. A. Yes, I said that.

Q. What would you have to say about getting other vessels rather than using those tanks? A. I would prefer other vessels to anything else.

Q. You think that would have been the best way? A. It would have been the most economical, because there would be no necessity of transferring the oil back again to the "West Cajhoot", as you would have to do in the case of lighters, and by doing that you would avoid the lighterage charges or the tank car charges.

Q. In testifying as to the cost of cleaning out an oil barge, you said you did not include the rental that would have to be paid for such a barge. Do you know anything

(TESTIMONY OF W. E. HEPPELL)

about what that rental would have been? A. Not at Kobe, no.

Q. What would it amount to in San Francisco? A. In San Francisco you can rent an oil barge—it depends on the size—at from $20 to $30 per day.

Q. What would be the cost of the rental of a tank car in San Francisco? A. About $5 a day.

Q. Would you expect the cost to be greater or less in the Orient? A. Less.

Q. Why would you expect it to be less?

Miss Phillips: Just a moment. The captain said he didn't know about those matters over there. You are really asking him now to speculate.

Mr. Derby: I don't think so. I think we all know that costs are much less in the Orient than they are here.

Miss Phillips: Not as to everything. You can't assume that everything in the Orient is cheaper than it is here. That is not the fact. There are some things in the Orient that cost more than they do here. I object to the question on the ground that it is asking the captain to speculate upon a matter he does not know about. A. I am basing it on the hire of labor in the Orient.

Mr. Derby: Q. Do you mean that the cost of labor is greater or less in the Orient than it is here? A. Much less.

Q. Do you know of your own knowledge, Captain, that that was true in 1927? A. I do.

Q. Some question was asked you on cross-examination, I forget exactly what it was, but it was about some testimony that you gave on direct examination, that the cost of cleaning out the large tanks of the Rising Sun Petroleum Company and putting this cocoanut oil into them, would not compare to the value of the cocoanut oil, and you said you referred to the value of the cocoanut oil in sound condition. In your opinion would the cost of cleaning out one of those large tanks and renting it be comparable in any way with the value of cocoanut oil, whether it was damaged or not? A. Not in the least.

Q. The chief engineer testified that when the first samples were taken of the cocoanut oil in the deep tank at Kobe there was no indication that the cocoanut oil had become solidified or hardened. Under those circumstances would you have had to heat the oil in order to take it out of the deep tank? A. I take it that you are referring to the port section of the deep tank?

Q. Yes. A. There is no information where the chief engineer took his samples, but I presume that he took them through the manhole in the tank top which covers a very small area of the tank, and is about the middle of the tank; the oil may have been in a liquid form there, but out in the wings at the ship's side, and on the bottom, the oil may not have been in a liquid state, but if it were in a liquid state there would be no need to heat it; I cannot possibly tell you whether I would have to use heat or not, unless you can give me the temperature of that oil.

Q. The chief engineer states that when the first samples were taken the oil had not begun to solidify, but when the second samples were taken it was beginning to congeal—

(TESTIMONY OF W. E. HEPPELL)

Miss Phillips: Suppose you just read the testimony to him, Mr. Derby suppose you just read to him what was said on that.

Mr. Derby: All right, I will read the testimony given by the chief engineer:

"Q. Now, on the occasion when you took samples from the deep tanks, do you recall whether there was any indication that the cocoanut oil had become solidified or hardened? A. When the first samples were taken they were not, but on taking the second samples I noticed that the cocoanut oil was beginning to congeal." What would you say, in view of that testimony, Captain, as to the advisability of removing the cocoanut oil from the deep tank as soon as it was discovered that it was contaminated by the fuel oil? A. The cocoanut oil from the deep tank should have been discharged in order to find the cause of the fuel oil entering the tank and contaminating the cocoanut oil.

Q. Would the discharge become more difficult the more the oil solidified? A. Yes, it would.

Q. I think you said on cross-examination, Captain, that when the ship was lying stationary at Kobe the mixing of the two oils would not continue; do you mean it would not continue at all? A. It would be reduced to a minimum.

Q. Captain, the evidence is that when samples were taken in San Francisco they were able to take them half way down the port deep tank without any heating of the oil in that tank; what would you say as to the condition

(TESTIMONY OF W. E. HEPPELL)

of the oil, in view of that testimony, at the time of arrival in San Francisco?

Miss Phillips: Did the chief engineer say that, or do you mean you are going to have testimony on that?

Mr. Derby: That is in the letter of Curtis & Tompkins, which was introduced without objection in the testimony of the chief engineer.

Miss Phillips: That is all right, pardon me for interrupting. A. I would say that the cocoanut oil had not properly solidified, that it was still in a mushy condition. It is not a difficult matter to take off samples under those conditions, because we weight the oil thief and drop it down; the weight takes the oil thief down.

Mr. Derby: That is all.

RECROSS EXAMINATION

Miss Phillips: Q. Captain, you said that you thought the difference between prices in the Orient and prices here was largely relative to labor, labor in the Orient being much cheaper. A. Yes.

Q. You said, however, you did not know the rentals of lighters and tank cars and barges, and all that kind of thing. A. No, I do not.

Q. You mean that equipment of that sort might or might not be cheaper there: Is that not true? A. Yes, might or might not.

Q. In the event it was imported from some different country it might even be more expensive, might it not? A. Yes.

Q. That is something you don't know? A. I don't

(TESTIMONY OF W. E. HEPPELL)

know. The only way we can base our opinion as to that is on the price of labor.

Q. It takes labor to fill a barge, and it takes labor to take care of a barge; if a man in the Orient is only getting 50 per cent. of what they get over here we naturally expect that we can hire them much cheaper. A. That always has been the case in the Orient.

Q. On the other hand, in the event there were fewer equipment of the kind, and that, therefore, they were more valuable there, you might expect to have to pay a higher rental from the point of view of the investment, would you not? A. No. The fact, if it be a fact, that they have less equipment would indicate there was less demand for it. The Japanese are very quick to take advantage of all new and improved equipment. The Rising Sun Petroleum Company's plant is one of the finest plants in the world, now, and one of the most elaborate.

Q. Captain, don't forget that we are talking about events that occurred just a year after the great earthquake in Japan. The extent to which a thing was in demand is something that is impossible for us to speculate on, is it not? A. Yes, that is true.

Q. You said that when the ship was stationary further contamination was reduced to a minimum. What did you mean by saying "reduced to a minimum"? A. Because there is not the vibration, and in addition to that the heat from the boiler-room and the settling tanks in this case was so much less on account of there being no steam put on the boilers and therefore the shipment of cocoanut oil in both tanks was gradually solidified

(TESTIMONY OF W. E. HEPPELL)

from the outside in, and the more it solidified the less opportunity there was for an increase in contamination.

Q. It also would be true, would it not, that you have in the lower tank, the double bottom, heavier oil, which would not so easily rise into a lighter oil when there was no motion: Is not that correct? A. Yes. There must be some motion or pressure to cause that.

Miss Phillips: That is all.

FURTHER REDIRECT EXAMINATION

Mr. Derby: Q. I would like to ask one more question. Captain, assuming you had to heat the oil in the port deep tank before removing it at Kobe, and assuming also that at that time the damage was confined to the bottom six inches of the port deep tank, do you think you could have got the clear oil on top out uncontaminated? A. Oh, yes.

Q. Even though you would have had to heat it? A. Yes. I would have heated it from the top and pumped it from the top, and as the oil level dropped in the tank I would have taken with my oil thief samples every few inches, and I would have had my chemist right alongside of me, testing, giving it the Lovibond color test, and the moment that I found an increase in the red or yellow in the cocoanut oil I would have stopped pumping immediately. That would be the indication that we were coming to a contamination by what is known as fluorescence.

Q. Assuming there was some contamination in all of the oil in the deep tank at Kobe, could that contamination have been lessened by the removal of the oil at

(TESTIMONY OF W. E. HEPPELL)

Kobe? A. I do not think it could. The increase of the contamination could have been stopped by removing the oil, but once the oil is contaminated then it has to be chemically treated to remove the contamination.

Q. Would that have lessened the contamination—by the removal of it? A. It would have, yes.

FURTHER CROSS EXAMINATION

Miss Phillips: Q. Captain, I don't understand your last statement. I think you said that once the whole volume of the oil is contaminated there is contamination right through it from top to bottom, perhaps in varying degrees, but if it is all contaminated removal would not help matters unless you refined it and got the contamination out: Is that correct? A. Yes, it would have to be refined.

Mr. Derby: Q. But the sooner you removed it the less it would be contaminated and the more commercially valuable it would be? A. That is right, because there is always danger of further contamination.

Miss Phillips: Q. The question Mr. Derby put to you was: Assuming that all the oil is contaminated. A. In the port deep tank.

Q. Yes, in the port deep tank. Do you say that even if it was all contaminated it should have been removed at Kobe and refined there? A. I don't know whether they have any refining stations in Kobe. It should have come out of the ship.

Q. Just confine yourself to the question I put to you, Captain. Assume that it is all contaminated, are you

Miss Phillips: That is all.

———

Mr. Derby: At this time I desire to offer in evidence the survey report of Curtis & Tompkins, Chemists and Industrial Engineers, dated December 13, 1927, regarding the outturn at Wilmington of the cargo or cocoanut oil involved in these cases. I want to state that this report was made up in San Francisco from data furnished in Los Angeles. It is offered in order to save time, expense, and trouble in proving the facts therein stated at the trial. It is offered with the understanding that either party may offer evidence to disprove any of the statements therein made, if they are found to be erroneous, and upon the further understanding that Mr. Beadle, who furnished or supervised furnishing the data on which the report was made will be called as a witness by The Los Angeles Soap Company at the trial. I also want to state that the original report cannot be found, and possibly was never in the possession of The Los Angeles Soap Company, but that this is an exact carbon copy of the original report.

Miss Phillips: I make no objection at all to the fact that it is a carbon copy. The only suggestion I would add to the stipulation is that the actual chemical report, copy of which was appended to the deposition of Mr. Bower, of the Bureau of Standards at Washington, be admitted in evidence and be deemed a part of this report, or supplemental to it.

Mr. Derby: You mean the report of Curtis & Tompkins, dated December 7, 1927?

Miss Phillips: Yes.

Mr. Derby: We agree to that. We will ask that this be marked "Curtis & Tompkins Exhibit No. 1" and be attached to the deposition.

(The document was here marked "Curtis & Tompkins Exhibit No. 1.")

UNITED STATES OF AMERICA,
STATE AND NORTHERN DISTRICT OF CALIFORNIA,
CITY AND COUNTY OF SAN FRANCISCO.

I certify that, in pursuance of Notice of Taking Depositions and of stipulation of counsel, on Thursday, April 27, 1933, before me, ERNEST E. WILLIAMS, a United States Commissioner for the Northern District of California, at San Francisco, at the offices of Messrs. DERBY, SHARP, QUINBY & TWEEDT, in the Merchants Exchange Building, in the City and County of San

Francisco, State of California, personally appeared Joe Jory and W. E. Heppell, witnesses called on behalf of The Los Angeles Soap Company in the cause entitled in the caption hereof, who reside at a greater distance from the place of trial than one hundred miles; and S. H. Derby, Esq. appeared as Proctor for The Los Angeles Soap Company and Westchester Fire Insurance Company, and Miss Esther B. Phillips, Assistant U. S. Attorney, appeared as proctor for the United States of America, and the said witnesses, having been by me first duly cautioned and sworn to testify the truth, the whole truth, and nothing but the truth in said cause, deposed and said as appears by their depositions hereto annexed.

I further certify that the depositions were then and there taken down in shorthand notes by Charles R. Gagan, and thereafter reduced to typewriting; and I further certify that by stipulation of the proctors for the respective parties, the reading over of the depositions to the witnesses and the signing thereof were expressly waived.

Accompanying said depositions and referred to and specified therein are The Los Angeles Soap Company Exhibit Jory #1 and Curtis & Tompkins Exhibit #1.

And I do further certify that I have retained the said depositions in my possession for the purpose of mailing the same with my own hands to the Clerk of the United States District Court for the Southern District of California, Central Division, the Court for which the same were taken.

And I do further certify that I am not of counsel, nor attorney for either of the parties in said depositions and caption named, nor in any way interested in the event of the cause named in the said caption.

IN WITNESS WHEREOF, I have hereunto set my hand in my office aforesaid this 28th day of April, 1933.

(Seal)   ERNEST E. WILLIAMS,
                          United States Commissioner,
                          Northern District of California,
                          at San Francisco.

(C O P Y)

Ap. 27, 1933

CURTIS & TOMPKINS EXHIBIT No. 1

ERNEST E. WILLIAMS,
U. S. Commissioner.

Surveying & Gauging

CURTIS & TOMPKINS

Analytical Industrial and Engineering

CHEMISTS

236 Front Street

San Francisco

Laboratory of	Cable Address
Chemical Technology	"Analyst"
Established 1878	Western Union Code

No. 92980   SURVEY REPORT   Date 12/13/27

1. a/c Mr. Joa Cui Pien, c/o Mr. R. Lopez Forment, 71 Twin Peaks Boulevard, San Francisco.

2. SHIPPER Joa Cui Pien.

3. CONSIGNEE Los Angeles Soap Co.

4. OUTAGES TAKEN (date) 12/1/27 (time) from port side at 10:20 a. m. from top of four corners of hatch coaming and from top of manhole as follows—

| x |

5. KIND OF OIL Cocoanut Oil.

6. LOADED AT Manila.

7. VESSEL West Cajoot.

8. TANK NO. Port and Starboard sections of deep tank.

9. VESSEL ARRIVED (port) Wilmington, Cal. (date; 12/1/27.

10. DISCHARGED AT Veg. Oil Prod. plant.
  OUTAGE on starboard side at 12:40 p. m. from top of four corners of hatch coaming only—

Forward

| x |

Equalizing Valve Closed

Port	Port side		Starobard Side	Starboard
57-1/8"	61-5/8"	64-1/2"		63-1/2"
	| 60-3/8" |			
	| 0 |			
54-3/4"	59-1/8"	62"		61-1/8"

Aft

		Port tank		Stb tank		xx tank	xx tank
Temperature	top	84	°F	96	°F	°F	°F
	middle	78	°F	86	°F	°F	°F
	bottom	hard oil	°F	hard oil	°F	°F	°F
	average		°F		°F	°F	°F

Trim of Vessel:

forward	11'03"	10'10"
aft	13'03"	13' 0"
draft	2'.00"	2'02" by the stern (both)

Indicated ship list ·4° port   none· apparent

Full depth of tank from top of hatch coaming
    (approx.)   20'6"
Height 'of. hatch .coaming ,from inside· top of ·tank "   2'5"
Depth of tank proper from· inside top of tank   " 18'1"
Length of ship overall..410'0"
(top of manhole is 2-1/2"·above top of hatch coaming)

11. SAMPLES were drawn (date) 12/1/27 (time)..........
as follows and will be held ·for 3 months subject to your
further instructions if any:

> Port side 10:40 a. m. core sample to depth of 13'
> beyond which was hard oil. · Top sample drawn
> same time. Bottom sample drawn 7:30 p. m.,
> representing 2nd pumping from port tank. Core
> sample of ·storage tank #3 ·taken shortly after
> pumping. Core sample of last tank scale drawn
> in tank scale pumped·to storage tank #4.

12. ANALYSIS
Starboard Side—top and ·part ·of ·core sample
drawn at 12:40 p. m. Bottom and remaining core
sample drawn 1:30 a. m.

13. PUMPING began   (date)   (time)
PUMPING finished (date)   (time)   '
Discharged into
Notes concerning discharge:

See following page

14.   CLEAN-UP finished at (date)   (time)
         Pump:
         Line:
         Deep tank: bbls. recovered.
      Inspection at (date)   (time)   showed

15.   OUTTURN DETERMINED BY tank scale weights, as
follows:

         Starboard Side (good oil including scrapings)
                      Gross 562,039
                      Tare   8,096
                      NET   553,943 lbs.
         Port Side (contaminated oil)
         Storage tank #1—Gross 354,070
                      Tare   55
                      NET   354,015 lbs.
         Storage tank #3—Gross 167,515
                      Tare   15
                      NET   167,500 lbs.
         Storage tank #4—Gross 53,155
                      Tare   none
                      NET   53,155 lbs.
                                         _____

Total Delivery   1,128,613 lbs.   503,845 long tons
Shipment accord-
ing to survey re-
port of C. B.
Nelson,   Manila
9/21/27   1,223,883 lbs.   546.242 long tons
                _____   _____
SHORTAGE
(7.76%) on
above basis   94,970 lbs.   42.397 long tons

PROCEDURE OF DISCHARGE: 12/1/27 Pumping began on the port tank at 11:06 a. m. and was delivered to storage tank #1 from the tank scale.

Pumping stopped at 12:33 p. m. at which time all the melted oil had been taken off; about 4'6" hard oil remained in the bottom, and tons of it, frozen to skin of ship and forward bulkhead.

Sounding showed fuel oil in double bottom of port tank to be 3'—depth of double bottom tank 3'9". At 12:45 p. m. level of fuel oil in double bottom tank gravitated to level of bottom of deep tank, and fuel oil level was immediately lowered 2", giving it a level of 3'7". The object of raising the level of the fuel oil in the double bottom was to prevent excessive leakage through the rupture after the hard oil in the bottom became liquid.

At 12:30 p. m. heat was applied to the coils in the port tank and following are temperatures taken at times indicated:

Date	Time	Port Tank		Starboard Tank	
		Top	Bottom	Top	Bottom
12/1/27	3:30 p. m.	102°	Hard	106°	Hard
	4:00 p. m.	106°	"	108°	"
	5:00 p. m.	108°	"	112°	"
	5:30 p. m.	112°	"	116°	Soft (steam
	6:30 p. m.	122°	(steam almost off)	114°	shut off) (Steam on light)
	7:00 p. m.	124°		110°	

	7:30 p. m.	126°	110°
	11:10 p. m.		130°
12/2/27	1:30 a. m.		130°
	3:00 a. m.		127°
	4:30 a. m.		125°
	8:00 a. m.		120°

STARBOARD TANK (Good Oil) 12/1/27 Sampled down 14'—hard oil below. Pumping began 1:25 p. m.; first oil used to clean the line and was placed in #1 Storage tank with the oil pumped from top of port tank.

Stopped pumping from starboard tank at 3:05 p. m. Pump drained and vacuum put on discharge line. Level of oil approximately same as that in port tank, with tons, frozen, adhering to skin of ship and forward bulkhead.

PORT TANK (Contaminated) 12/1/27 at 3:30 p. m. there still remained considerable hard oil in the bottom of this tank and no pumping was attempted until 8:00 p. m. Actual pumping began at 8:35 p. m. using a small flexible hose from the pump to warm and wash down the oil from sides of tank.

At 10:10 p. m. the pump was shut down to allow the men to dig and scrape the hard oil from the walls. Pumping and scraping were continued alternately until 2:00 a. m. the 2nd. All the oil pumped during this time, except the last tank scale, showed more contamination than the first pumping, so was placed in storage tank

#3. Upon getting into the bilge, the oil was found to contain still more contamination and pumping was ordered stopped and the oil in the last tank scale was run into storage tank #4. There remained in the bilge, very badly contaminated oil, estimated at around 3,150 lbs.

STARBOARD TANK (Good oil) 12/2/27 Pumping was resumed at 9:00 a. m. and 576 lbs. of oil were used to flush the line. Pumping stopped at 10:50 a. m. after which 233 lbs. net of scrapings were removed from the tank, leaving not more than the usual tare of from 500 to 700 lbs.

> Scrapings—Gross 294 lbs.
> Tare   61 lbs.
> NET   233 lbs.

16. INSPECTION FOR LEAKAGE (date) as follows:
Shell of ship—no evidence of leaks.

Forward bulkhead—12/4/27 inspected in #2 cargo hold. Indications of several weeping rivets on both tanks, but no evidence of any leakage reaching floor of hold.

Inboard bulkhead—divided tanks.

After bulkhead—No evidence of leakage in cofferdam, and no leakage in that portion of bulkhead visible in engine room.

Bottom of tank—Inspection of bottom of tank will be covered in supplementary report, after tank has been cleaned while vessel is in dry dock and a complete examination can be made.

17. LOADING DATA copied from survey report of C. B. Nelson at Manila dated 9/21/27;

> Outage: "taken immediately after pumping on board, from the edge of manhole to surface of oil"

Port Tank	Starboard Tank
45-1/8"	43"

Temperature—88°F   Temperature—88°F

Ship Trim: Draft—forward   List—1/2° to star-
                —aft   board
0'11" by the stern

18. COMMENTS:

> While it is obvious that there are leaks from deep tank into double bottoms, since fuel oil from the double bottoms was forced up into cocoanut oil and was the cause of contamination, it has not been possible up to the present time, to designate all leaking points. As stated above, this will be done when vessel is in dry dock and the tank has been cleaned. A pressure test was had on double bottoms with cold salt water, but this was not satisfactory since the congealed cocoanut oil interfered and all the leaks could not be identified.

A recapitulation of the shortage of 94,970 lbs. shown on page 2, follows:

1. Oil recovered from Starboard Tank
   good .... 553,943 lbs.

2. Oil recovered from Port Tank
   (contaminated) .... 574,670 lbs.

3. Total oil recovered from both tanks......1,128,613 lbs.

4. Oil too badly contaminated to be of any
   practical. value, left in bilge of Port
   Tank ESTIMATED .... 3,150 lbs.

5. Total normal tare of port and star-
   board tanks ESTIMATED.......................... 1,200 lbs.

6. Total oil accounted for ....1,132;963 lbs.

7. Shipping weight according to C. B.
   Nelson, Manila ....1,223,583 lbs.

8. DIFFERENCE equal to oil lost due
   to leakage in port tank..................................... 90,620 lbs.

TOTAL LOSS DUE TO ACCIDENT

Oil lost through leakage (#8 above)   90,620 lbs.
Badly contaminated oil left in bilge
of port tank (#4 above)............................ 3,150 lbs.

Total   93,770 lbs.

SUMMARY OF TOTAL SHORTAGE

Oil lost through leakage (#8 above)...... 90,620 lbs.
Badly contaminated oil left in bilge of
port tank (#4 above)................................ 3,150 lbs.

Normal tare for both tanks (#5 above)   1,200 lbs.

Total   94,970 lbs.

COMPARISON OF OUTAGES

The leakage indicated by comparison of outages was estimated as follows, but the figures are only crudely approximate, due to Manila outages being taken only from manhole in tank covers, which preclude accurate computations to correct for list and draft; also due to the fact that no average temperature of contents of either tank could be obtained at Los Angeles owing to the presence of hard and liquid oil at totally different temperatures.

Manila outage (average of both tanks taken from manhole) temperature 88°F ....44-1/16"

Los Angeles outage (average of both tanks taken from 4 corners of hatch coaming and corrected for list ....56-3/16"
Height of manhole above hatch coaming .... 2-1/2 "

Temperature 82°F ....58-11/16"
Contraction of oil from 88°F to 82°F ....- 0-1/2"

Average Los Angeles outage computed to 82°F and basis of measurement from manhole......58-3/16"

DIFFERENCE—More outage at Los Angeles 14-1/8 "
This difference of 14-1/8" more average outage at

Wilmington, is equal to about 85,600 lbs. of oil, which more than confirms the visual inspection that the above loss was due to leakage.

Respectfully submitted,

CURTIS & TOMPKINS,

Industrial & Engineering Chemists.

(Endorsed): Depositions Filed Apr. 29. 1933

[TITLE OF COURT AND CAUSE]

LOS ANGELES, CALIFORNIA, WEDNESDAY, MAY 3, 1933.

10 o'clock A. M.

The Court: Proceed with the case on trial.

Mr. Vermille: This is the case of the Los Angeles Soap Company versus the United States; United States versus The Los Angeles Soap Company; and United States versus the Westchester Fire Insurance Company. These cases, if your Honor please, have been consolidated.

The Clerk: Three cases.

Mr. Vermille: Three cases. All these cases involve, your Honor, a shipment of a cargo of cocoanut oil from Manilla shipped on board this vessel by the name of West Cajoot which is owned by the Shipping Board, and for that reason we had to sue the Government rather than the vessel under the Suits in Admiralty Act.

The Court: What was this substance, the cargo?

Mr. Vermille: Cocoanut oil.

The Court: What is that?

Mr. Vermille: They take cocoanuts, grind them up and make cocoanut oil in bulk.

The Court: Oh yes, very well.

Mr. Vermille: The cocoanut oil was shipped, according to the bill of lading, on September 21, 1927, on board this vessel. The vessel sailed from the Philippines, Manila, to Hongkong and from Hongkong she was bound to Los Angeles by way of San Francisco. In proceeding to the United States she ran on a reef in the Van Diemen Straits off the coast of Japan and from there it was decided to go to Kobe, Japan, as a port of refuge. The vessel arrived at Kobe. She ran on the reef on October 1st and arrived at Kobe on October 2nd. They made certain examinations of the vessel and decided to remain there to put the vessel on dry dock. She left dry dock on about October 28th and arrived here December 1st. What I mean by here is Wilmington. That is where the cargo of cocoanut oil was to be discharged for the Los Angeles Soap Company.

There have been certain stipulations entered into between counsel which we think makes out a prima facie case against the Government.

The Court: Which you think what?

Mr. Vermille: Which does make out a prima facie case against the Government. It is admitted "that the Los Angeles Soap Company is a California corporation and the owner of the cargo involved in these actions.

"That the amount of cocoanut oil received for shipment at Manila in September, 1927, was as described in the bill of lading, namely, 1,223,583 pounds at a temperature of 88 degrees Fahrenheit and that, upon loading, said cocoanut oil was in good order and condition.

"That upon the arrival of the S. S. West Cajoot at Los Angeles, the cocoanut oil in the port deep tank was contaminated by fuel oil and some of the cocoanut oil in the port deep tank was short.

"That the terms of the bill of lading, with respect to filing of notice of claim, were complied with by the libelant."

That is one of the defenses that was set up in their answer. I will read on further:

"That libelant will produce as soon as possible and at all events at the trial or the submission of the cause, all written notices which it received of the contamination of the cocoanut oil by fuel oil, and said notice or notices, if written, may be introduced in evidence by the respondent subject to any objection by the libelant as to materiality, relevancy and competency; and if said information as to the contamination of the cocoanut oil was received orally by the libelant (instead of in writing), libelant will in the same manner produce a statement as to when such information was received and from whom, and the said statement of the oral information may be introduced in evidence by the respondent subject to the same conditions as the written information.

"That the attached contract, marked Libelant's Exhibit No. 10, dated August 27, 1924, is the agreement between the United States of America and Swayne & Hoyt, Inc.. for the operation of the S. S. West Cajoot and was in full force and effect at the times referred to in the libel herein and that the same may be received in evidence."

The Court: Who are the parties to the agreement?

Mr. Vermille: The parties to the agreement are Swayne & Hoyt, agents for the United States, and who contracted for the operation of the vessel. Swayne & Hoyt were the agents operating the vessel.

"That if J. G. Reckert were called as a witness in this case, he would testify that he is the head of the Fuel and Purchase Division of the Shipping Board and that the records of the Shipping Board, under his supervision, show that the fuel oil delivered to the S. S. West Cajoot at Manila in September, 1927, was delivered at a temperature of 85 degrees Fahrenheit, Beaume 17 degrees; of which, in accordance with Bureau of Standards Circular No. 154, the specific gravity of such oil, at 60 degrees Fahrenheit would be approximately .9609. That this stipulation as to what the said Reckert would testify, may be received in evidence with the same effect as if the witness had testified by deposition subject to all objections as to materiality, relevancy, etc.

"That in October, 1927, the market price at Yokohama of fuel oil, such as the S. S. West Cajoot would require, was $2.58 per barrel; that by virtue of its bunker contract at Yokohama, the Shipping Board could obtain for its vessels such fuel oil at a cost of $1.65 per barrel."

I might call your Honor's attention right there, the reason that is in there, the vessel after she left dry dock at Kobe, which is one of the largest ports in Japan, instead of bunkering at Kobe, proceeded out of her course to Yokohama to get here.

The Court: Instead of doing what?

Mr. Vermille: Instead of fueling at Kobe, they proceeded from Kobe to Yokohama, which is not on the direct course to San Francisco, to obtain fuel oil, because under a contract the Government had they could obtain the oil cheaper. That is all. There was a deviation.

The Court: Yes, but was that before the accident?

Mr. Vermille: That was after the accident. After the vessel was repaired and proceeded on her voyage from Kobe, instead of going from Kobe to San Francisco after the vessel was repaired, she went to Yokohama.

The Court: The injury to the oil, the cocoanut oil, was not the result of this wreck?

Mr. Vermille: That is our contention that it was not.

The Court: That it was not?

Mr. Vermille: Part of it.

The Court: I gather from what you say, your contention, at least, is that some of the fuel oil got mixed with the cocoanut oil. Is that correct?

Mr. Vermille: That is correct. It is our contention after the discovery of the contamination, after the vessel was at Kobe, after a survey was made, it was ascertained that the oil was contaminated with fuel oil, the surveys informed us how much that contamination was at that time.

The Court: This was at Kobe?

Mr. Vermille: At Kobe.

The Court: It was discovered that it was contaminated at Kobe?

Mr. Vermille: With fuel oil, according to the survey. Now, at the time of discovery of this contamination by fuel oil at Kobe, it is our contention that they should have used proper care and custody in discharging it and saving what could be saved, which was not done. The fuel oil was not discharged from the vessel. The vessel was allowed to stay in Kobe for a period of approximately 23 or 24 days. The vessel went on dry dock, was thoroughly repaired, and the cocoanut oil remained in the vessel all that time in contact with fuel oil after they knew that there was a leak between the two tanks. That is our contention, improper care and custody of the cargo, for which they are liable.

The Court: Well, the United States is the plaintiff?

Mr. Vermille: The United States is the defendant in one suit and the United States then filed an action in general average against The Los Angeles Soap Company for their proportionate amount of damage after the repair of the vessel. The Los Angeles Soap Company in their general average action filed a cross libel and set up the amount of their damage in the cross libel. Then the United States filed an action against the Westchester Fire Insurance Company on their bond, which bond must of necessity be given before any cargo can be discharged from the vessel if it is subject to general average.

Continuing with the stipulation, your Honor, agreed to:

"That by reason of putting in to Yokohama for bunkers, the increase in nautical miles of the S. S. West Cajoot's voyage over the normal passage from Kobe to San Francisco is 85 miles.

"That if Paul F. Blinn were recalled as a witness in this case, he would testify that, at the time of the taking of his deposition at San Francisco on December 19, 1930, there was available only, for refreshing his recollection, the smooth engine room log books of the S. S. West Cajoot (which were marked Exhibits Blinn Nos. 4-A and 4-B). These smooth engine room log books do not contain notations which show from what double bottom tanks fuel oil had been used in filling the settling

tanks of the S. S. West Cajoot and which was burned on
the S. S. West Cajoot on the voyage from Manila to
Hongkong and thence to Kobe. That at the time of the
taking of his deposition, it was the recollection of the
witness (without being refreshed by any log books or
documents) that when the S. S. West Cajoot stranded
there was only about 3 inches of fuel oil in the 'No. 3
double bottom tanks. Subsequent to the taking of his
deposition, the rough engine room log of the S. S. West
Cajoot was produced by counsel for the United States
of America and exhibited to the said Blinn at Washington in April, 1933. That the said rough engine room
log book, numbered 81375, contains entries made by
Second Assistant Engineer M. P. Appel, which shows
the tanks from which the fuel oil was pumped to the
settling tanks. Said entries show that the first occasion
on which fuel oil was pumped from the No. 3 double
bottoms was on the 12 to 4 P.M. watch on October 3rd.,
(Log sheet October 4th) which contains the following
entry: 'Filled Settler from No. 2 P—No. 3 P—S'. That
the said Blinn's independent recollection at the time of
taking his deposition as to the amount of oil remaining
in No. 3 double bottoms was confused either with the
No. 1 or the No. 2 double bottom tanks, which had been
practically emptied by previous pumping, and that the
only fuel oil which had been pumped out of No. 3
double bottoms after leaving Manila and prior to the
arrival of the S. S. West Cajoot at Kobe, was such oil
as was pumped into the settling tanks on the 12 to
4 P.M. watch on October 3rd.

"That in filling the settling tanks from No. 3 double
bottom tanks, Second Assistant Engineer Appel was

acting in accordance with the regulations of the vessel and did not disobey any instructions of the Chief Engineer when he filled the settling tanks from No. 3 double bottom tank at any time prior to discovery of the leakage from the deep tanks into the double bottom tanks.

"(In connection with the rough Engine Room Log Book of the SS. West Cajoot, counsel for the United States state, in the way of explanation as to the reason for the non-availability of the log book at the deposition of Chief Engineer Blinn, that the log book was sent by the Shipping Board at Washington, D. C. to the United States attorney at San Francisco, to be used in connection with the deposition of Chief Engineer Blinn. In some manner the log was mislaid and could not be located until a long time afterwards, when it was returned from San Francisco to the Shipping Board Log Library, together with a number of other log books. Counsel for the United States are at a loss to account for the miscarriage of the rough engine room log book.)

"That on the vessel's arrival at San Francisco, in addition to Second Assistant Engineer Appel, the Acting First Assistant Engineer Mone and the Third Assistant Engineer Parker were relieved; and other engineers, having licenses for their respective positions, were employed on the SS. West Cajoot.

"That the log book, marked Blinn Exhibit 5, bearing the number 81375, is the rough engine room log of the SS. West Cajoot, covering the period of August 10, 1927, to December 8, 1927, and may be received in evidence, subject to any objections as to materiality, relevancy, etc."

This last stipulation that I just read from was to the effect that Mr. Blinn would so testify.

The Court: Was what?

Mr. Vermille: That he would testify to the remarks that I made. One other thing, your Honor, in connection with the depositions. It has also been stipulated "that the translation into the English language, copy of which has been previously furnished to proctors for The Los Angeles Soap Company of the testimony of B. Nagamatsu and Samuel Reid taken in the Japanese, may be received in evidence and that the said translation is admitted to be a true and correct translation of the testimony in the Japanese language. That two survey reports dated November 1, 1927, and marked "Respondent's Exhibit Reid No. 1," and "Respondent's Exhibit No. 2," referred to in the testimony of Samuel Reid, taken on letters rogatory in Japan and forwarded to the State Department by the American Embassy in Japan by letter of June 10, 1932, may be received in evidence." That is the substance of the stipulation, if your Honor please, and that makes out a prima facie case against the Government, for the reason that it shows delivery of the cocoanut oil to the vessel in good order and condition, and on arrival here of the vessel shows that the *vessel* was contaminated. That makes out our prima facie case. And the Government will have to rebut that and show some cause. I think I am correct in that statement.

The Court: Well, what is the nature of 3691, United States against—

Mr. Vermille: 3691, that is an action filed by the United States against the insurance company on the bond.

Miss Phillips: Would your Honor like me to state that? I think perhaps I might summarize the Government's position on this in both suits?

The Court: May I have your name?

Miss Phillips: My name is Esther B. Phillips, for the United States.

The Court: For whom?

Miss Phillips: For the United States.

The Court: Are you an Assistant United States Attorney?

Miss Phillips: Yes, from San Francisco.

The Court: Proceed.

Miss Phillips: I might state, your Honor, that the Port of San Francisco is the regular headquarters of the particular ship in question and as many of the witnesses were in and out of San Francisco, it would save a great deal of money for the Government to have an Assistant United States Attorney located in San Francisco take the depositions, and as I took the depositions up there, the Attorney General's Office asked me to be associated in the trial of the case here with the United States Attorney's Office here. As your Honor perceives, this is a case of a shipment of a large quantity of cocoanut oil from the Port of Manila in September, 1927, upon the Shipping Board Vessel West Cajoot, and the sequence of events ran like this: The cocoanut oil was shipped in what are called the deep tanks on board the West Cajoot. They are large tanks about the center of the vessel called the No. 3 deep tanks. The vessel left Manila the 24th or 25th of September. She went from there to Hongkong in her regular call, and from Hongkong she was making her way up towards what is called the Great Circle or the Great Circle Route from the Orient to the Pacific Coast, being the regular route and the frequented route in that part of the world. In passing through the straits called Van Diemen straits to get to the Great Circle, the vessel struck upon a reef, which happened at midnight the night of October 1st, or rather it was 12:54, just at the beginning of October 2nd. The master having had squally, rainy, misty weather for many hours previously, he either was off his course or he struck upon a submerged rock which was not charted —whatever it was the result was immediately seen by the officers on the vessel. On sounding No. 1 bilges and hold they found water beginning to come in. By 2 in the morning, 20 feet of water was in No. 1 hold and No. 2 hold was beginning to fill up; so much so that the chief night engineer testified that he knew the water was coming in so fast in No. 1 hold that he had—he knew he could not pump it dry, so he devoted his energy to keeping No. 2 dry and pumped No. 2 then day and night until they could get to a port of·refuge. They got into the port of Kobe about 7 in the evening of October 3rd, that being the nearest port in which they could hope to obtain relief, and as your Honor can perceive, with 20 feet of water in the first hold of the vessel and with water coming in the second, their lives were in danger did they not make for a port of refuge. They went into the port of refuge. The ship was surveyed by marine surveyors and the divers. They very soon located where the serious damage was and determination was made to make repairs. This work began the night of arrival, October 3rd. and proceeded through October 4th. Upon the morning of the 5th they discovered what they had not previously

known, which was that there was a leak between what is
called the deep tank, where the cocoanut oil was stored,
and the fuel tank immediately below it. I think, your
Honor, if I go into a little more detail on this, you will,
I think, follow the testimony of the witnesses perhaps
more easily. The cocoanut oil, there are two tanks, deep
tanks on the ship, the port tank and the port No. 3 deep
tank and the starboard No. 3 deep tank, both of them
being stored with this cocoanut oil. Immediately beneath
them are what are called the No. 3 fuel tanks. Now, that
morning, the morning of October 5th, or some time
about noon, October 5th, they discovered that there was
cocoanut oil in the port No. 3 fuel tank. Now, that could
only mean that cocoanut oil had leaked, that there was
a leak between the two tanks. They found no leak between the double bottom tank, the bottom of it, there was
no sea water in it—if you can imagine a can here and a
can here, the leak is in this level here, not on the bottom
level of the double bottom tank. They discovered, when
they made the test at that time, they found there was
a leak. They then tested the port deep tank and found
that fuel oil was in the port deep tank, thus confirming
their judgment that there was a leak between the two.
The testing on the bottom of the fuel tank showed there
was no leak there, though subsequently in dry dock they
found what had happened. The double bottom was
dented and the denting of the bottom striking on the reef
apparently had pushed up what is called the binding bar
in here,—that is all covered in the depositions,—and had
caused a little aperture or leak between the two tanks.
I direct your attention to this, your Honor, because upon
the finding of the contamination of the cocoanut oil with

the fuel oil, the question before those men, as it would naturally be before your Honor or before me, would be what to do. They had, of course, an option, a course of procedure that they had to consider was, should they discharge the cocoanut oil and repair that leak, or, on the other hand, should they leave the oil in it as it was. The determination they made was that they would leave the oil there where it was. The reasons for that determination will be shown very amply in the depositions. At the conclusion of the month of October all repairs were completed, the vessel was certified to be seaworthy by the various surveyors, and she sailed from the Port of Kobe to Yokohama where she took on fuel oil, and thence to San Francisco. Upon arrival at San Francisco she discharged—then from San Francisco to Wilmington, and discharged the cocoanut oil at Wilmington, the port to which it had been consigned. Now, then, I said I was going to explain the theory on which the United States sues the cocoanut oil owner. It is this: It sues upon the principle of what is called general average. Your Honor may not have had occasion to try a general average case. It is one of the most interesting branches of marine law and I may say that it goes back hundreds of years. I ran across a reference to general average in the Codes of Justinian. It is that old. The simplest illustration of the law of general average is, supposing a vessel is in a storm and she has a lot of deck cargo and the ship is on the point of sinking and the master says, "Let's throw the deck cargo overboard and that will save us," and they do so and the ship is saved. Very nice for the ship and the other cargo owners, but what about the poor deck cargo owner? Is he to loose all of his cargo? The

marine law says, "No, that is a sacrifice of one property to save everybody. Therefore everybody will contribute." That is called "general average." And everybody is called on to contribute to that loss of that deck
cargo owner and that is called a contribution in general
average. When the ship owner arrives at a port and
gets ready to deliver the other cargo to the other cargo
owners—which is safe and sound because the poor deck
cargo owner lost his cargo—he may say to each cargo
owner, "Now, you don't get your cargo until you give
me a bond that you will contribute to the loss of the
deck cargo man who lost his cargo, and everybody gives
what is called a general average bond. That is the
simplest illustration of the law of general average, but
there are many others. Take, for instance, the case of
the West Cajoot. She strikes upon a reef. Not only the
ship is in danger but every cargo owner on board the
ship is in imminent danger of losing his cargo. The ship
proceeds as fast as she can to the Port of Kobe. She
undertakes a great many expenses, all sorts of examinations and surveys, to discover the cause. She goes into dry
dock. She has to transship some of the cargo in order
to make repairs. Now, is the ship to bear all of that?
No, the principle of general average comes into play and
that principle, the marine law says—your ship owner
involved a great deal of expense. Had he let the ship go
down, none of this expense would have been covered.
He involved himself in all of it. Therefore, the other
interests contribute, make a contribution in general average, and that is what happened here. When the ship
arrived at Wilmington each cargo owner before he could
get his cargo, he gives a bond that he will contribute to

general average. Now, how does the thing work out in this case? The cocoanut oil was delivered to its owner. He gives a contribution, a bond that he will contribute in general average if it is found to be due. However, the cargo owners' cocoanut oil is found damaged. Here in the United States, all this is worked out, what the total cost of all these expenses at Kobe is worked out, the United States says to the soap company, "Now, your contribution to general average is so much. These reputable general average people have worked it out. Here is the working out. You pay me what that shows. I think that is a fair contribution."

The soap company says, "No, no, not I. You damaged my cargo and furthermore you damaged it by negligence. I won't pay you general contribution, the contribution in general average. You pay me for the damage to my cocoanut oil," and that is how the suit comes before your Honor, the soap company says, "Pay me the damage to my cocoanut oil," and the United States saying as an answer to that suit, "Why, I won't pay you that damage to the cocoanut oil; that came from a peril of the sea; the ship stranded there on that strait; it was a part of that; there was no negligence involved here." And then by a separate suit it sued the soap company upon its promise to pay a general average contribution, and then sues the Westchester Insurance Company because it was the giver of the bond in that. That is the relation of the three parties.

Have I made it clear to your Honor?

The Court: I think fairly so.

Miss Phillips: Now, the position of the United States—

The Court: Now, let me ask, who is the party at interest on this general average bond, the United States? What interest has it in the general average bond?

Miss Phillips: Because the United States, through its agent, the Shipping Board, paid out all these expenses at the Port of Kobe. It is the owner of the Shipping Board Vessel West Cajoot.

The Court: Well, it is not for damage or loss to any other cargo owner?

Miss Phillips: No, your Honor, it is not.

The Court: Merely for the expenses?

Miss Phillips: It is only suing the Westchester Insurance Company upon the bond that company gave that the Los Angeles Soap Company would pay its contribution in general average, if it is found to be due.

The Court: And the loss was the cost of the repairs and the proceedings taken to save the vessel?

Miss Phillips: Yes, your Honor. Yes, your Honor.

The Court: All right.   .

Miss Phillips: Now, our position in the defense of the case is, first, we say that the evidence clearly shows that that leak between the two tanks was the result of that stranding, could not be anything else, and that it was, that all the evidence shows it—

The Court: .Could not be anything but what?

Miss Phillips: But the result of that stranding, a peril of the sea. That the leak between the two tanks was caused by the stranding of this vessel there on this reef and in the Japanese seas in stormy weather, that that was the cause of the leak in the first place. In the second place, that upon arrival at Kobe they could not transfer the cocoanut oil out of the ship, that there were no facilities there for handing it, and that had they done so they would have involved the ship and the cargo owner in a great deal more expense than they did as it was.

That is, our position is, why, when the ship, the leakage was discovered and the contamination was discovered on the 5th of October, it had already occurred. Now, if the damage was done at that time, the contamination was there, we say, "Why take all the cocoanut oil out and put it all over the Port of Kobe, if it were possible"—it was not possible—"and then put it back in there when the damage was done?" In the same way we say they complain because the ship went from Kobe to Yokohama, 85 miles out of her way. We say that was not a deviation; the bill of lading permitted that; and we also say that that did not increase the damage. Similarly, we say—

The Court: What relation has that to the case, this alleged deviation?

Miss Phillips: We say none, because if there was damage it already had occurred before that deviation. We say that that deviation, if it was a deviation, has nothing to do with the case. And similarly, the fact that she put into the Port of San Francisco before arriving at Wilmington, we say that was permissible, that was in the ordinary route of trade; there is nothing wrong in that, and furthermore, it did not increase the damage even if it was not permissible; the damage was done. But our main point, the point which the testimony, I think, will bring out, which we hope will bring out very clearly to your Honor, is that at the time the damage was discovered in Kobe on October 5th, the leak between the two tanks was discovered, but at that time the cocoanut oil was already contaminated with fuel oil. And that even had it been possible to transfer that half million pounds of cocoanut oil out of that tank into other containers, what good would it have done, because the fuel oil was already in it.

With that statement, your Honor, then, we can proceed with the trial.

The Court: All right.

Miss Phillips: Unless your Honor has another question or two to ask.

The Court: Well, the Court will need considerable light on the physical position of these tanks.

Miss Phillips: I think, your Honor, we are prepared to show that.

The Court: Yes, that will be a matter of evidence, of course.

Miss Phillips: We have blueprints ready, and so on.

The Court: Very well. You may proceed with the evidence.

Mr. Vermille: Your Honor, I think maybe I can enlarge upon the facts a little bit. If the oil had been discharged at Kobe, that would have been all a part of the general average; the ship would not have been—

Miss Phillips: If it could have been; if it could have been; if it could have been.

Mr. Vermille: Yes. At the time of arrival at San Francisco, the vessel again went on dry dock,—we don't know why.

The Court: The vessel what?

Mr. Vermille: Again went on dry dock in San Francisco, and then after coming off of dry dock it proceeded to Wilmington and discharged its cargo.

The Court: It went on dry dock at Kobe?

Mr. Vermille: At Kobe and also at San Francisco. Now, it is our contention that according to their survey, the Government survey made at Kobe, shows the contamination of the oil at the time of the discovery of the contamination, only existed in the bottom six inches of that tank, which is only approximately about 8 tons of that total amount of that cargo. That if that cargo had been discharged at Kobe, all of the balance of that cargo in the port tank could have been saved, but by reason of leaving that cargo in the tank and going on dry dock and proceeding to Los Angeles, the vessel, by reason of the motion of the vessel, contaminated all the cargo; that they could have discharged that cargo at Kobe and saved it.

The Court: That is the negligence?

Mr. Vermille: That is the negligence.

Miss Phillips: I believe that we should emphasize to the Court that the cocoanut oil upon arrival at Wilmington was not a total loss, it was damaged but it did have a value and could have been purified, and so on. Are you resting?

Mr. Vermille: We have made out the prima facie case, I think counsel will agree, on the stipulation, and I think the Government now should proceed with their defense and then put the burden upon us to prove negligence.

Miss Phillips: Your Honor, I would like to direct attention to the stipulation agreed to by both parties filed

a day or so ago. The substance—I have not the date of
the stipulation—the substance was regarding the receipt
in New York of certain samples of cocoanut oil which
had been shipped there from San Francisco. It is merely
tracing the history of certain samples of cocoanut oil.

Mr. Vermille: That is correct.

Miss Phillips: That is on file.

Mr. Vermille: There was such a stipulation, but,
your Honor, I would like to advise counsel and your
Honor that last Thursday I had my brief case stolen
that had an original deposition in it and had all my
correspondence, all my depositions were stolen, both the
brief case and the depositions stolen out of a car that
was locked—they broke into the car and stole it—so I
had to do the best I could and get copies of the depositions. There was one original deposition in my brief
case and I think counsel has consented to allow me to
introduce a carbon copy of that.

Miss Phillips: Certainly. Now, the deposition to
which I refer—

Mr. Vermille: That stipulation which you refer to
was also in my brief case. I remember what the substance of it was.

Miss Phillips: I believe the stipulation in your brief
case was a copy and I saw it in the files yesterday afternoon.

Mr. Vermille: Yes.

Miss Phillips: We will give you two copies if you
need them.

Mr. Vermille: Well, I know the substance of it.

The Court: Let me ask at this stage: The United

States is the plaintiff in the action against the Los Angeles Soap Company?

Mr. Vermille: That is correct.

Miss Phillips: Yes, your Honor.

The Court: How does that come? What does the United States want of the Los Angeles Soap Company?

Miss Phillips: We are suing for a contribution in general average.

The Court: Suing both the defendants?

Miss Phillips: Yes, your Honor. You see, there are two parties there, one the party, the Los Angeles Soap Company, was the person who was originally liable, we say, for a contribution in general average, and the Westchester Insurance Company is indemnitor which gave a bond. The decree might be in the alternative.

The Court: Is it possible to join both defendants in the same suit?

Miss Phillips: I think it could have been. It could have been possible. It is possible to sue them separately. We would not get a judgment against both, your Honor. It would have to be a judgment against one in the first instance and then against the Westchester Company in the event of the failure of the Soap Company to pay.

The Court: And as against that claim, the Los Angeles Soap Company is proposing to recoup its damage, from the Government, because of negligence.

Mr. Vermille: That is it, your Honor.

Miss Phillips: That is correct.

The Court: The same defense is made on behalf of the fire insurance company?

Mr. Vermille: The same defense.

The Court: Proceed. So the cases are practically—they, of course, will be tried on the same evidence?

Mr. Vermille: Yes, your Honor.

The Court: In all essentials.

Miss Phillips: The evidence taken in any one will relate to the evidence in the others. Shall we stipulate as to that?

Mr. Vermille: They are all consolidated, your Honor. There is a stipulation on file. They are all consolidated.

Miss Phillips: Your Honor, at this time I wanted to offer in evidence depositions which have been filed by the United States. I think the depositions are all here together. I will offer in evidence the deposition of Mr. Archie C. Watson taken at San Francisco on April 8, 1930. In each case, your Honor, I will state very briefly the point for which the deposition is being offered and who the witness was. That will be a convenience, I think, to your Honor.

This witness was the shore agent of the firm of Swayne & Hoyt, which in the Port of Kobe was the managing agent of the West Cajoot. His testimony was taken and is offered to show the situation of the vessel upon her arrival at Kobe, what was done towards her repair, and when the damage to the cocoanut oil was discovered what facilities there were at Kobe for effecting a transfer, what inquiries he made and what effort he made to find whether it was possible to transfer the cocoanut oil from the port deep tanks to shore cars or lighters or storage tanks. It is offered upon that, for all of those, to show what was done in that regard.

The Court: The deposition was taken in San Francisco?

Miss Phillips: In San Francisco. The witness was a resident of Kobe and was in San Francisco temporarily, and his deposition was taken there.

I will also offer in evidence the deposition of Paul Frazier Blinn.

The Court: Well, probably we might dispose of one as we go along.

Miss Phillips: The depositions are quite lengthy. Does your Honor wish them to be read?

The Court: The only thing I have in mind, that when it comes to Mr. Blinn's deposition, I will have forgotten about who he is.

Miss Phillips: Well, I will state each time. The depositions are quite lengthy. I think counsel and I had in mind—

The Court: All right, proceed in your own way.

· Miss Phillips: Well, whatever suits your Honor, whatever your Honor will find most helpful. I think what we had in mind—I will speak for myself first, though,—that we would state the depositions of the witnesses in court before your Honor, but the depositions would not be read.

The Court: Oh, I see.

Miss Phillips: But that counsel and I would undertake to file quite full briefs.

The Court: Oh, I see.

Miss Phillips: And making in the briefs the various points, quoting from testimony as it was, so that your Honor would have the record that way.

The Court: Well, that is entirely agreeable. Would you have any witnesses, then?

Miss Phillips: Yes, your Honor, several witnesses in court.

Mr. Vermille: There are approximately 20 depositions, and I think it would take about a week or so to read them.

Miss Phillips: Well, it might take quite a little while but I am sure there is nothing—

The Court: Counsel says it would take about a week.

Mr. Vermille: I meant in court, if counsel objected to every question.

The Court: Well, they must be very long depositions.

Mr. Vermille: They are. Depositions taken all around the orient.

Miss Phillips: Whatever your Honor wishes.

Mr. Vermille: It is perfectly satisfactory to us.

Miss Phillips: We had in mind that the Court would prefer not to have them read because it would save time, but if your Honor prefers to have them read, we want to do whatever the Court prefers.

The Court: The Court prefers the method adopted by counsel.

Miss Phillips: Very well, your Honor.

The Court: So, go ahead.

Miss Phillips: Then the next deposition that I referred to is a deposition of Paul Frazier Blinn taken at San Francisco on December 19, 1930. This witness was the chief engineer of the vessel. He testifies in regard to the events immediately after the stranding, describing the situation the ship was then in, to the Port of Kobe, in general upon the nature of the repairs at Kobe, the discovery of the contamination of the oil, what measures were taken in Kobe in regard to preventing further usage of oil from the No. 3 tanks. He testifies as to the usage of oil by the ship and then in general—rather briefly,—to the homeward voyage, and upon arrival at Wilmington to the method of discharge followed by the ship owner.

The next deposition that I offer in evidence is the deposition taken upon written interrogatories of Goan Sue Chan that was taken March 18, 1931. I believe that was taken in Japan. It is descriptive of the repairs made at the Port of Kobe.

The Court: Who is the gentleman?

Miss Phillips: That is a Japanese at Kobe, having to do—

Mr. Vermille: If you will pardon us a minute. I am just trying to save time.

Miss Phillips: Well, I have misspelled the name there. Chan was the deposition of a shipper at the Port of Manila upon the condition of the cocianut oil. I made a mistake there in those foreign names. That was taken at Manila.

The Court: What did he have to do with the cocoanut oil?

Miss Phillips: He had to do with the shipping of the cocoanut oil upon board the vessel, that is, the loading at Manila.

The Court: Was it shipped for his account?

Miss Phillips: He was a shipper. The consignee,—I think that is in the stipulation,—was the Los Angeles Soap Company. He was the man who originally shipped the oil to the American consignee.

The Court: He was probably the original owner.

Miss Phillips: Yes.

Mr. Vermille: Well, he shipped it to the Los Angeles Soap Company. The Los Angeles Soap Company bought the oil from Chan in Manila.

The Court: F. o. b. Manila?

Mr. Vermille: F. o. b. Los Angeles. Well, I don't remember which. It does not make any difference. There is a stipulation on file that the Los Angeles Soap Company was the owner of it.

The Court: Mr. Chan is in no sense involved?

Mr. Vermille: He is not involved in view of the stipulation because the stipulation admits the shipment in good order and condition and admits the amount that was shipped.

Miss Phillips: Your Honor, just a moment. This Chan was the agent of the shippers at Manila. He testified upon the condition of the oil at the time of the shipment and also his knowledge of the route the vessel was in and her customary route in proceeding from Manila to Hongkong and home.

The Court: When you say agent of the shipper, you mean the Los Angeles Soap Company?

Miss Phillips: I mean the original shipper, your Honor; the man who put the oil on the ship at Manila. Now, that shipper might have sold it to New York or somebody else. It is the fellow that shipped it at Manila.

The Court: Yes, I see.

Miss Phillips: We don't know just when this oil was sold. It might have been during the voyage that it was sold to the Soap Company.

The Court: Yes.

Miss Phillips: Chan was the agent of the shipper at Manila. He testified as to the condition of the oil at the time of shipment and also as to the route of the vessel, or customary route in proceeding home. Your Honor will remember that there is a charge here of deviation. The testimony of this witness shows what was the known customary route of this vessel, the vessels of this line, of which the West Cajoot was a member. The next witness whose deposition I offer is G. P. Bradford, taken at Manila on April 8, 1931. The gentleman was the agent of the ship at Manila. He testifies upon the condition of the ship at Manila, her seaworthiness, etc., and also as to the customary route of this vessel and other vessels of its line from Manila to the Pacific Coast, answering the question, your Honor, the charge of deviation. That witness' testimony is of relevancy in that.

I also offer in evidence the testimony of J. I. Harris. The testimony of this witness was taken at Manila April 8, 1931. This witness was a marine surveyor at Manila. He, in conjunction with other surveyors, examined the deep tanks of the vessel before the cocoanut oil was loaded into them; examined them both as to their tightness, their seaworthiness, and their cleanliness, whether or not they were in fit condition to receive cocoanut oil.

The Court: Were there only two tanks of cocoanut oil?

Miss Phillips: Yes, your Honor. Yes, your Honor. That is correct. No. 3, the deep tanks they are called, the port and the starboard. I also offer in evidence the testimony of Ralph M. Johnson. The testimony of this witness was taken in Manila on April 8, 1931. So the testimony of this witness was taken at Manila at the time of the stranding or at the time of the repairs, rather, he was in fact, living in Kobe. This gentleman was the far eastern representative of the Shipping Board for the United States in the handling of Shipping Board vessels. He was an engineer by profession. The repairing of the vessel at Kobe was under his immediate charge in the sense that it was,—he was the one to help in the decision of what was necessary in having bids solicited, and getting in touch with ship owners, then in having the repairs made, and in paying for them. He was the engineer located at Kobe in charge of all that sort of work for the far east.

I also offer in evidence the deposition of C. B. Nelson. The deposition of that witness was taken at Manila in April, 1931. This gentleman was a marine surveyor. He was in the employ of the owner of the cocoanut oil at Manila. It was his duty as an agent of the owner to see to it that these deep tanks were in fit condition for the shipment of cocoanut oil. He, with the witness Harris, to whom I referred a moment or two ago, were actually on board the vessel, saw to it that the tanks were properly tested for leaks, that they were in tight, seaworthy condition, that the tank was properly cleansed and fit to receive cocoanut oil.

I also offer in evidence the testimony of Victoriano Pascual, also taken in Manila in April, 1931. This witness was the foreman in charge of the loading of the cocoanut oil upon the vessel. He, too, had a direct responsibility in the cleansing of that tank,—of both tanks, rather,—seeing that they were suitable to receive cocoanut oil and that they were tight, seaworthy, no leaks of any kind.

I also offer in evidence the testimony of S. Reid taken at Kobe, Japan, on September 16, 1931. The testimony of this witness was taken in the Japanese language before the Japanese court. A translation has been filed for the convenience of the Court and of counsel. This witness was a marine surveyor at the Port of Kobe. He, in conjunction with the witness Johnson, to whom I referred a moment ago, the engineer of the Shipping Board then living at Kobe, this witness, Mr. Reid, in conjunction with Mr. Johnson and the ship officers, had to do with the surveying of the ship and finding out of what the damage was and of what needed to be done and what kind of repairs had to be made. The ship went into dry dock. The witness at the conclusion of dry docking had the responsibility of determining whether the ship was then seaworthy and fit to go to sea. He was also a cargo surveyor at Kobe, was experienced in the surveying of cargo and he, in conjunction with other witnesses, actually surveyed, examined samples of the cocoanut oil, and assisted in coming to the decision as to what should be done with the oil. This witness was a resident in Kobe for a long time. He, too, testified what facilities at Kobe there were for the reception of cocoanut oil, that it is impossible to transfer it from the ship ashore.

I also offer in evidence the deposition of B. Nagamatsu, the testimony of a witness taken in the Japanese language in Kobe in 1931 relative to the repairs on the ship made at Kobe.

I also offer in evidence the deposition of Henry F. Gelhaus. The deposition taken at San Francisco September 16, 1931. This witness was port engineer at San Francisco for Swayne & Hoyt, who were the operating agents of the ship. He testified that the employment of engineers upon the ship was immediately within his line of duty, and he testifies upon competency and fitness. Your Honor understands that in any suit involving damage to cargo where it is charged that the ship was unseaworthy, the ship owner makes his case, he proves seaworthiness all along the line, not only of the ship, but also of the personnel. That is, the ship is seaworthy in having a competent personnel.

I also offer in evidence the testimony of James S. Gade taken in San Francisco November 23, 1931. This witness also was in the employ of Swayne & Hoyt, the operating agent at San Francisco. He had immediately within his duty the employment of the deck officers of the ship.

The Court: What was his title up there?

Miss Phillips: I would say port captain. It is a port job that has, as a part of his duties, the employment of personnnel of the vessel, various vessels. Let us call him port captain. I think that is the best name to give him.

I also offer in evidence the deposition of William Claus Juergens. This witness was claims agent of Swayne & Hoyt at San Francisco. His testimony is quite short. He testifies to receiving in San Francisco from Japan a letter from the ship's agent at Japan, Mr. Watson, certain samples of cocoanut oil, the situation being that Watson takes the samples and sends them to Juergens and testifies that he did so. Juergens at San Francisco testifies to receiving those samples and sending them on to New York. The stipulation to which I referred in the beginning of my statement relates that somebody in New York got those samples and took them to a chemist in the Bureau of Standards at Washington to have them analyzed.

I also offer in evidence the testimony of Otto E. Thorsen. He was the captain of the West Cajoot throughout the voyage from Manila to San Francisco. He testifies as to the circumstances of the stranding, their putting into the port of refuge at Kobe, and to the voyage home.

I also offer in evidence the testimony of one Sorenson. For the moment I haven't his first name. It slipped me. Soren Peter Sorenson. Mr. Sorenson was the chief officer of the ship. His testimony is quite brief. It relates to the stranding, to their putting into the port of refuge, and quite briefly to their voyage home.

I also offer in evidence the testimony of John H. Bower. The testimony of this witness was taken in Washington within the last two weeks. He was a chem-

ist in the Bureau of Standards. He testifies as to the
test he made upon the samples which he had received
from the Shipping Board office. The history of this
sample being traced, your Honor, by the depositions of
Watson, by Juergens and by the stipulation which I
referred to at the beginning of my statement.

I also offer in evidence the testimony of Joseph J.
Daly. The testimony of that witness is in the same
folder or the same binder, rather, as the testimony of
that witness.

The Court: How do you spell his name?

Miss Phillips: Joseph J. Daly. His testimony was
taken at Washington on April 20th, about 2 weeks ago.
His testimony relates for the most part to what were
the customary lines of voyage of vessels in the trade
of this particular vessel.

The Court: Who is he?

Miss Phillips: This witness was in the employ of
the Shipping Board. He was branch head of the records
in the operating division of the Shipping Board and
had been for quite a number of years. He testifies as
to the movement of vessels and their customary routes.
The testimony of that witness touches upon the deviation question.

At this time I wish to ask counsel if they propose to
offer in evidence the depositions of Captain William
Heppell and Captain Jory taken on Thursday of last
week at San Francisco.

Mr. Vermille: I do.

Miss Phillips: You do propose to. Because if they
do not, I was present at the cross examination, and I

(TESTIMONY OF WILLIAM HENRY CURTIS)

would wish to offer in evidence their testimony upon the cross examination.

Mr. Vermille: We will offer them.

Miss Phillips: They will be offered. Very well.

The Court: At this time we will take a short recess for a period of about 5 monutes.

(Short recess.)

(After recess.)

Miss Phillips: Mr. Curtis.

WILLIAM HENRY CURTIS,

called as a witness on behalf of the Government, being first duly sworn, testified as follows:

Q. By the Clerk: Your full name?

A. William H. Curtis.

DIRECT EXAMINATION

By Miss Phillips:

Q. Your full name is William H. Curtis?

A. William Henry Curtis.

Q. What is your business?

A. Marine surveyor.

Q. A marine surveyor. How long have you been in that business?

A. 10 years. 10 years in this position here, and I was about 4 months in San Francisco, 1919.

Q. Have you ever been a ship officer?

A. Yes, sir.

Q. Do you hold any papers?

A. I do, Master's for sail and steam.

(TESTIMONY OF WILLIAM HENRY CURTIS)

Q. When did you get your Master's papers, Captain Curtis?

A. 1902.

Q. How long have you been going to sea?

A. 39 years.

Q. You say you are a marine surveyor? Where is your office located?

A. Wilmington, California.

Q. Are you associated with any firm down there at Wilmington?

A. Not at Wilmington now. With Pilsbury & Curtis of San Francisco.

Q. With Pilsbury & Curtis of San Francisco. You are the Wilmington representative of that firm, are you?

A. Yes, sir.

Q. Captain Curtis, have you any experience in the carriage of cocoanut oil?

A. Not in bulk. I have carried it in barrels and in small quantities.

Q. Have you had any experience in surveying cocoanut oil?

A. Lots.

Q. Lots. Tell me, did you survey the cocoanut oil on the West Cajoot upon her arrival at Wilmington about the 1st of December, 1927?

A. I did.

Q. You did. By the way, did you take notes of that survey upon making the survey?

A. I took a few preliminary notes.

Q. And did you make a written report upon it?

(TESTIMONY OF WILLIAM HENRY CURTIS)

A. I made a written report.

Q. Have you your notes with you and your report?

A. I have the report and I have the notes.

Q. Captain, have you refreshed your recollection by referring to your report?

A. Just a little.

Q. Just a little?

A. Yes.

Q. Now, if there is any point in which your memory fails you, we are going to ask you to refresh it as you go along. However, we will ask you questions first, without referring to your notes. Do you remember what conditions you found in the starboard and port deep tanks?

A. Well, the samples taken of the starboard tank showed no indications of contaminated oil.

Q. That is the starboard deep tank?

A. The starboard deep tank, No. 3.

Q. Now, what conditions did you find in the port deep tank?

A. Samples taken from the port deep tank showed contamination.

Q. It showed contamination?

A. It showed contamination.

Q. What did you find as to the fluidity of the cocoanut oil?

A. Well, in the center under the hatch it was liquid and as it went down and at the sides it was solid, solidified, and very hard at the bottom.

(TESTIMONY OF WILLIAM HENRY CURTIS)

Q. Now, Captain, you will have to assume now—remember that I have never carried cocoanut oil in bulk, though I might have used some in the kitchen. Tell me, cocoanut oil solidifies as it gets cool, does it not?

A. It does.

Q. And becomes liquid when it passes a certain degree of warmth?

A. Yes.

The Court: One minute. What did you say?

Miss Phillips: Yes, your Honor.

The Court: Did you say that that was the port tank that showed the contamination?

A. The port tank.

The Court: Does it have a letter or something like the other. The other one you indicated was tank D-3.

Miss Phillips: These tanks are in the middle of the ship and they are called the No. 3 deep tanks, No. 3 port and No. 3 starboard. He said that he examined the No. 3 starboard tank and found the oil in good condition. On examining the No. 3 port tank he found it contaminated. I then asked him its condition as to fluidity or liquidity. He said it was liquid in the center, hard at the sides and hard at the bottom.

I have a blueprint here. There is one attached to the deposition which was taken in San Francisco. I have a copy of it here which I think might assist the Court as we go along. The original is attached to Captain Hepple and Captain Jory's deposition. A certified copy of it. This is a copy of the one that would be in evidence when you offer it.

(Testimony of William Henry Curtis)

Mr. Vermille: Are you going to offer it?

Miss Phillips: It is already offered.

Mr. Vermille: You mean it is attached to the deposition?

The Court: At this point, let us take a short adjournment sufficient to receive a report from the Grand Jury. We will interrupt proceedings and you will retire, Captain.

(Proceedings in case on trial were suspended for a few minutes.)

William Henry Curtis

resumed the stand for further direct examination, being previously duly sworn, testified as follows:

Direct Examination (Continued)

By Miss Phillips:

Q. Captain Curtis, you say you went down—you examined the deep tanks, their condition on board the ship—your Honor, I have here a blueprint showing the location of the various holds of the West Cajoot. A certified copy of this blueprint is attached to the deposition which counsel, opposing counsel, have not yet offered in evidence. I had expected it to be offered in evidence upon the opening of their case and to refer to it at that time. I am going to ask leave—

Mr. Vermille: I will offer it in evidence now if you want me to.

Miss Phillips: Well, my only object is, this is a copy of the same—I think it might help the Court if we referred

(TESTIMONY OF WILLIAM HENRY CURTIS)

to the blueprint and have him point out to the Court the location on this map of the deep tanks.

The Court: Well, you may use that one.

Miss Phillips: Yes, your Honor, and then I can offer this in evidence as well. I think I have an extra copy of that and that would be convenient to counsel to refer to it while we are talking.

Q. By Miss Phillips: Will you just point out to his Honor the No. 3 port and starboard deep tanks?

A. This is the profile here. This is the side of the ship. These are the deep tanks here as though we were looking down through. This one is the No. 3 hold in which the deep tanks are situated in this particular ship. This shows here the hatch looking down as though we were looking down through this one. And this is another top view of the hatch looking down into the hatch, down, and this also shows the deep tanks, the small hatches, which are the openings to the tanks.

Q. By the Court: You mean, taken at different levels?

A. Taken at different levels, yes, sir. This is taken as though it was a side view looking through the ship side. This is taken so you can see a profile of the tanks here. This is No. 3 hold. The deep tanks, they go down here to the frame or double bottom tanks.

Q. By Miss Phillips: Tanks?

A. Tanks, yes.

Q. Now, referring to this blueprint, the top sketch shows the ship in profile?

A. In profile.

(TESTIMONY OF WILLIAM HENRY CURTIS)

Q. And looking at it in profile, the No. 3 deep tanks appear here near the center of the ship?

A. Yes.

Q. That is just aft, is that, of the engine room?

A. That is forward of the engine room, forward of the boiler and engine room.

Q. Now, will you point out to his Honor the fuel oil tanks of the ship?

The Court: Before you leave that, the depth of the tank, is that drawn to proportion?

Miss Phillips: Drawn to scale, your Honor.

A. Drawn to scale.

Q. By the Court: The depth of the tank, of course, is not indicated below the water-line?

A. Oh yes.

Q. Is that the bottom of the ship?

A. That is the bottom of the ship.

Q. Oh yes.

A. These little lines down here represent the frame of the vessel. These are the frames, spaced proportionately.

Q. Very well.

A. And this part of the tank is down below the water line. The center of the water line would run along about here somewhere.

Q. By Miss Phillips: The witness indicating the approximate water line at a line about one-third down the depth of the deep tank. Is that a fair statement, approximately?

A. Just about, approximately, yes.

(TESTIMONY OF WILLIAM HENRY CURTIS)

Q.   We understand you are not giving exact figures here. Will you point out to his Honor where the fuel oil tanks on this ship are located?

A.   The fuel oil tanks are located in No. 1 double bottom and this is No. 1 running from the bulk head here between No. 2 and No. 3 bulk head. That is what they call No. 2 double bottom and No. 3 double bottom, which is involved at present. Then, No. 4 is the water tank. Then again at 5 and 6 double bottom for fuel oil. And also the after peak is used for fuel oil.

Mr. Vermille: Now, just a minute there.

Miss Phillips: Just a moment.

Mr. Vermille: I move to strike that answer out.

Q.   By Miss Phillips: Yes. The witness pointed out the double bottom tanks, No. 1—

A.   1, 2, 3, 5 and 6.

Q.   1, 2, 3, 5 and 6. No. 4 being for water. Now, will you point out what are called the fore peak tank and the after peak tank?

A.   This is the fore peak tank here. It runs from this deck. There is a false deck in here that runs below between decks. Below that are store-rooms for stores for the ship. Below that again is this deck which they call the fore peak. It runs from the stem back to the collision bulkhead. This is what we call the collision bulkhead. That comprises the fore peak tank.

Q.   By the Court: That is a fuel tank?

A.   No, this is for water. This is used for water in this ship.

(Testimony of William Henry Curtis)

Miss Phillips: Just a moment, your Honor. I think I will put a witness on the stand who will show how the fore peak and after peak tanks are used on the ship. I am just asking this witness to locate them on the map for your Honor.

The Court: Well, of course, he has done that, if that is all you want with him.

Miss Phillips: Yes.

The Court: I think that you had better get that blackboard and pin this on it and have it over there opposite the light.

Miss Phillips: Just wherever your Honor can see best. I supplied opposing counsel with a copy so that for their convenience it would not be necessary to put it on the blackboard.

Mr. Vermille: His Honor might desire to glance at it from time to time.

Miss Phillips: Yes. Very well.

The Court: You are through with this witness?

Miss Phillips: No, no, your Honor. I was just waiting for him to put that up.

The Court: Well, it will be some little time before they can get the blackboard in, so you can go on with your examination.

Q. By Miss Phillips: Yes. Captain Curtis, you say that you made an examination of this hold. Do you remember whether soundings of the No. 3 fuel tank, that is the fuel oil tank immediately below the cocoanut No. 3, that is, I am talking now about the port No. 3 fuel tank—

A. Yes.

(Testimony of William Henry Curtis)

Q. Were soundings taken of that tank upon the ship's arrival at Wilmington?

A. We took soundings.

Q. It was?

A. It was.

Q. By the Court: When you speak of soundings, what do you mean, just measuring the depth of it?

A. Yes, sir, your Honor, measuring the depth of the liquid that was in the tank.

Q. You do that accurately?

A. Do that accurately, yes. We measure that with sounding rods or tape used for that purpose.

Q. By Miss Phillips: Did you measure the fuel tank? The No. 3 port fuel tank?

A. We did.

Q. Who was with you?

A. Mr. Beedle, representing Curtis & Tompkins, the chemists.

Q. Mr. Beedle is—

A. Mr. Beedle, he is a surveyor, chemist surveyor.

Q. Whom were you representing?

A. I was representing the ship.

Q. Do you know who Mr. Beedle was representing?

A. Representing Curtis & Tompkins, the chemists, and I think the L. A. Soap Company.

Q. I see. Well now, what was the depth of the soundings, what did the soundings in No. 3 port fuel tank show?

A. It showed 36 inches, 3 feet.

(TESTIMONY OF WILLIAM HENRY CURTIS)

Q. 3 feet. And what is the depth, what is the total depth of that tank?

A. The total depth is 45 inches, 3 feet and 9 inches.

Q. Then that would show at that time 9 inches empty space?

A. Approximately 9 inches.

Q. Or slack, is that the term to use

A. Slack.

Q. You must remember now if I don't always use the mariner's term, I will trust to you to supply it. Captain, you say you have had experience in surveying damaged cocoanut oil?

A. Yes.

Q. And good cocoanut oil too, I suppose?

A. Yes, good.

Q. Both?

A. Good and bad.

Q. Do you know which is the heavier, cocoanut or fuel oil?

A. At 60 degrees temperature, fuel oil was the heaviest.

Q. Fuel oil was the heaviest?

A. Fuel oil.

Q. Now, I would like to ask you to assume one or two facts. I want you to assume that this ship you surveyed, the West Cajoot, sailed from Manila about the 24th or 25th of September, 1927, and that at 12:54 in the morning of October 2nd, that is, shortly after midnight October 1st, 12.54 in the morning, she stranded on a reef and succeeded in getting off on her own power

(TESTIMONY OF WILLIAM HENRY CURTIS)

in a short time. I want you also to assume that there was,—that at the time of her arrival in Kobe, or about the time of her arrival in Kobe, there was a leak between the fuel oil tank No. 3 and the No. 3 deep tank. I am going to show you a sketch, a copy of a sketch, which Chief Officer Blinn made at the time of his deposition. Can you find the original deposition? Will you find his original deposition and I will show it to the Court?

The Court: We will pause a moment here. I have forgotten where you located the No. 3 fuel tank?

A. Right in here, your Honor, between the forward housing and the engine room.

Q. By the Court: Is it directly beneath?

A. Directly beneath.

Q. No. 3 deep tank?

A. No. 3 deep tank, yes, sir.

Miss Phillips: Well, this is a photostatic copy of the exhibit attached to Mr. Blinn's deposition.

Q. By Miss Phillips: I want you to assume, Captain Curtis, that the Chief Engineer of the vessel testified that while the ship was in dry dock he went in and about that tank and he found that the bottom of the tank was—there was a little dent in it.

Mr. Vermille: When was that?

Q. By Miss Phillips: Right here in the bilge. At Kobe.

The Court: Referring to the fuel tank?

Miss Phillips: Yes, your Honor. You see, here is the side of the ship.

The Court: Yes.

(TESTIMONY OF WILLIAM HENRY CURTIS)

Q. By Miss Phillips: Chief Officer Blinn testified that at Kobe he examined the bottom there and he found a dent as though the ship had touched that reef without being hard enough to smash a hole in it, but to dent it up, and he testified that subsequently after the cocoanut oil had been discharged, going into that very tank he found this leak between the deep tank and the fuel tank. Do you see right there?

A. Yes, I see it.

Q. And that is the way he marked it out on this sketch. That is a photostat copy of his sketch, your Honor. The original is here right now.

Mr. Vermille: I did not receive a copy of that attached to my copy.

Q. By the Court: Is this a fuel tank?

A. This is the deep tank. You see, this line running along here, below that line are the deep tanks—are the fuel tanks.

Q. Well, this curve—

A. That is the bottom.

Q. That is the bottom of the deep tanks?

A. The bottom of the ship. This is the bottom of the ship.

Q. Oh, I see.

A. This line running up here, this small line, and this one across here and down here, that comprises the double bottom tanks, or fuel tanks. This is what they call a keystone tank, keystone tank bottom.

Miss Phillips: Your Honor, the original sketch made by Mr. Blinn shows it more clearly. Perhaps the witness can explain this a little better than I. Point out the deep tank on this sketch.

A.   These are the deep tanks. This one here, this is the port deep tank. This is a center view looking to the ship from aft forward. Now, this is the starboard deep tank. This is the port deep tank. These two tanks here are the fuel tanks or the double bottom tanks. There is a center line bulk head, longitudinal bulk head, runs fore and aft. That divides the two tanks. Also divides the two fuel tanks. Down here on the port side is where he marks there with the imprint, the indenture when she hit the reef, pressed it inward. And here he has marked it here, shows where it hit approximately on the binding bar or shore bar that runs fore and aft of this marginal plate that this is fastened to.

Q.   By the Court: Which is the marginal plate?

A.   This little plate that comes up here from the side of the shell up to the tank bottom, up to the double bottom tanks. That is what they call a marginal plate. There is an end line which runs fore and aft which this marginal plate is attached to, which has been termed here as a binding bar, which, as we express it, is considered shell bar.

Q.   By the Court: The marginal plate is the division between the two tanks?

A.   The side, yes. It comes up on the side. This in here, this portion of the hull, is what they call the bilge, is where all the fuel, or the surplus, runs to in case they want to pump out. The sediment, and so forth, runs in there. This indenture,—as it struck, it pressed this angle

(TESTIMONY OF WILLIAM HENRY CURTIS)

bar up, pushed this angle bar up, and probably opened up the marginal plate and the binding bar or shell bar and left an aperture in there where the oil has forced itself in down through into the double bottom on this side, the oil being at that time in the liquid form had forced itself down through.

Q. By the Court: Wait just a moment. You mean that the cocoanut oil forced itself down into the fuel oil?

A. Yes.

Miss Phillips: Your Honor, may I cover that in the course—I think we are anticipating a little bit. Just a moment now. Let the witness, if he has finished his explanation—all I am asking him was to point out to the Court—may I withdraw that? I am necessarily referring back to the testimony of the Chief Engineer as to the presence of this little aperture in order to ask the witness my next question. I have had him explain this map to the Court in order to understand what the Chief Engineer has already testified to as to this little aperture. That is only by way of a preliminary to my next question.

A. All right. Then I have explained the situation of the tanks.

Q. By Miss Phillips: Yes. Now, Captain Curtis, I went ahead and asked you, if you will remember, to assume a stranding about midnight, October 1st, or rather 12 minutes,—or 54 minutes past 12, October 2nd. And I also asked you to assume on arrival at Kobe the Chief Engineer found this denting of the bottom of the ship right at No. 3 fuel tanks and I also asked you to assume

(TESTIMONY OF WILLIAM HENRY CURTIS)

that he found this little aperture thereafter and in so doing I referred to the map attached, or the sketch attached to the Chief Engineer's testimony. That is by way of a preliminary to this question that I want to ask you. What would you say was the process of contamination here? You have just said that fuel oil is heavier than cocoanut oil?

A. Yes.

Q. Now, will you explain what is the process of contamination, how the heavier oil gets up into the lighter oil?

A. Well, it is this, that after the stranding, that the oil, the cocoanut oil, was sufficiently light enough to force itself down through this aperture, filling up the double bottom, that making it full to the tank top. Therefore, as the ship rolled back and forth these two oils were mixed together by squirting back and forth up through the small aperture.

Q. That is, you think if the fuel oil tank was not quite full, if there was an empty space there—

A. Yes.

Q. A vacuum, let us say?

A. Yes.

Q. The cocoanut oil then being liquid would leak down through that little hole?

A. Yes.

Q. And fill up the fuel tank?

A. The fuel tank.

Q. That is, our principle of gravity and the principle of nature abhors a vacuum, is that right?

(TESTIMONY OF WILLIAM HENRY CURTIS)

A. That is right.

Q. Now, remember I am not a ship engineer, and if I do not understand this as I go along, I want you to correct me.

A. That is right.

Q. That is, it would fill up the tank?,

A. Fill up the tank.

Q. Now, supposing at the time this stranding occurs, supposing the fuel tank is almost full, what will happen then?

A. Well, it will fill up; it will press up that tank full, if the greater pressure is both forcing it down through and filling up the tank.

Q. In any case, you think unless that fuel oil tank is full, the motion of the ship will cause the oil to begin swinging back and forth between the two?

A. Swinging back and forth and fill it up. There is space enough, vacuum space, so that the oil will fill up. As the ship rolled it would be swinging back and forth and naturally it will force itself back and forth up through.

Q. I think I follow you on that. Captain Curtis, what is a sounding pipe, do you know? There has been testimony here and there in the depositions about sounding pipes. For instance, somebody testified as to taking findings or sampling the fuel oil through a sounding pipe. I wonder if you would make a little sketch for his Honor and show, for instance, take, say—take this deep tank, for instance, here.

A. Yes.

(TESTIMONY OF WILLIAM HENRY CURTIS)

Q. And the fuel tank below No. 3?

A. I think if I took a fore and aft view and would draw out a little one, his Honor could see it better.

Q. All right. Whichever way would be most clear.

A. Now, in all tanks, tanks that are concealed in a ship, or where liquids go into, they have pipes. Those pipes may be varying from 1 inch to 2 inches in diameter, but the majority of them are about an inch and a half in diameter. They run from the decks, sometimes between decks only, the majority of them run from the main deck down through. For instance, we will take that as the sounding pipe. This oil this is not close to the bottom. It may be two inches or more or less from the bottom, and that allows the oil to flow into this pipe when a certain level is in the tanks. Now, to find out, all these tanks are calibrated at certain marks, 1, 5 or 6 inches, whatever it may be. A sounding rod is marked off in inches and it corresponds with the depth of this tank. Now, for instance, if this tank is 45 inches, that sounding rod may be 48 inches to allow 3 inches above the tank top and they drop this down in—

Q. By the Court: The sounding rods may be 48 inches?

A. Yes.

Q. Where?

A. 48 inches long in one piece. The sounding rods vary in various ships, and forms. Some are links joined together about 6 inches apart. Others are solid. Steel rod or brass rod, whatever it is most convenient to get. In this case I think it was a solid steel bar marked off in inches. They use that to sound the bottoms with. In this particular case I think it is used only for sounding fuel oil. That is, by the Chief Engineer.

Q. By Miss Phillips: Let me see if I understand you. If a man wants to find out how much fuel oil is in that fuel oil tank, the man, the first officer, or whoever it was would drop this sounding rod down through this pipe into the fuel oil tank?

A. Yes.

Q. Drop it right down until it hits bottom?

A. Hits the shell of the ship.

Q. The shell of the ship. Would that be attached to a rope?

A. Yes.

Q. That would go down through the pipe?

A. They would have to have a rope attached to it in order to get it down there and pull it back.

Q. Then, after having dropped this so it hits the bottom of the tank, he pulls it up?

A. Yes.

Q. And then that bar, sounding bar, will show on it at what depth the fuel oil measured on it, is that right?

A. Yes. It will show on it the depth of oil in that tank.

Q. I see.

A. If it is full it will show 45 inches and different inches below that; it will show 1 inch less all the way down until it comes down to the bottom when it may be nothing at all.

(Testimony of William Henry Curtis)

Q. I see. I think that is quite clear. Now, Captain. I want you to explain to the Court again and let's see what is going to happen in this process of contamination which you have explained to us. Draw again a sketch of the deep tank and of the fuel tank.

Mr. Vermille: Pardon me, before you go to another one, you want to identify that one some way or other.

Miss Phillips: Yes, I am going to offer them both in evidence. I thought I would let him use this second sketch.

The Court: Better use this sketch that he has just drawn.

Miss Phillips: I think that is a good idea. There are so many things in the record to watch anyway.

Q. By Miss Phillips: Now, Captain, you said that this oil will measure on that sounding bar?

A. Yes.

Q. What the depth of the fuel oil is?

A. Yes.

Q. You have just described what you thought must have been the process of contamination, that is, that this little aperture or leak between the two tanks, the cocoanut oil tank, would leak down and fill the fuel oil tank, if it was not already full, that it would be full?

A. That it would be full.

Q. And then the oil would swish back—

The Court: Let me interrupt here. Show me just precisely where that aperture is.

A. That is on this?

(Testimony of William Henry Curtis)

The Court: On that diagram. Oh, on the one that you have used already?

Miss Phillips: Yes.

The Court: It is in the corner, as it were?

Miss Phillips: Yes.

The Court: The aperture produced an opening between the fuel tank and the deep tank?

Miss Phillips: Yes.

The Court: All right.

Q. By Miss Phillips: Now then, you think that the cocoanut oil would leak down and fill up that fuel tank?

A. Yes.

Q. Until it is full?

A. Yes.

Q. And then the oil would begin to sort of swish?

A. Swish back and forth.

Q. With the motion of the ship?

A. With the motion of the ship.

Q. The motion of the ship?

A. The motion of the ship. It would be rolling back and forth and squirting it up back and forth, as you say.

Q. So that is why the heavier oil goes up into the lighter oil?

A. The lighter oil, yes.

Q. Now, let me ask you this question: When this lower tank, fuel tank, is filled, will any oil come up in that sounding pipe?

A. Yes, the oil would be forced up and back up in this pipe to its own level. The pressure here being so much greater on the bottom, this should go right on through, so

(TESTIMONY OF WILLIAM HENRY CURTIS)

much pressure greater on the top than on the bottom would force it right on up to its own level.

Miss Phillips: Yes, that is clear to me. I may say, your Honor, in going over Chief Engineer Blinn's testimony, I am not sufficient of an engineer to be able to understand some of the terms that he used and that was why I was asking this witness to clarify a little further.

Q. By Miss Phillips: Captain Curtis, suppose that you have this process of contamination that you have described as being the one that must have occurred, your cocoanut oil leaking down into the fuel oil somewhat until this is full, whatever the depth was, and then the two beginning to swish?

A. Yes.

Q. Would it be true that the mixed fuel oil and cocoanut oil would come up into this sounding pipe too?

A. It would.

Q. It would?

A. It would. It would probably push, the fuel oil being in the sounding pipe already, would probably push this oil in, the fuel oil being on top. It would be somewhat of a semi-liquid form that would adhere or freeze to the top of the pipe. The fuel oil is already up in this pipe and as the cocoanut oil would come in on top, that would naturally freeze the fuel oil up above it and the fuel oil would be on top, even though it is the heavier oil.

Q. So the fuel oil would be forced through with the motion of the ship and this next, if I understand the witness correctly, would come up into the sounding pipe, is that correct?

(TESTIMONY OF WILLIAM HENRY CURTIS.)

A. That is correct.

Q. You said something in your earlier testimony that cocoanut oil solidified at a certain temperature?

A. Yes.

Q. Is that correct?

A. Yes, it is.

Q. Would it cause this sounding pipe, would that, having also cocoanut oil in it, tend to become mucky or soft?

A. Yes, it would be a kind of a mushy affair. The two oils mixing together and being cool around this pipe, it would adhere.

Q. It would come up and adhere?

A. It would come up and adhere to the pipe.

Miss Phillips: I might say, the reason I asked this witness, the Chief Engineer in his testimony said that at Kobe he found cocoanut oil up on this rope that he lowered down at a distance of 20 feet, and I was frankly at a loss to understand it. That is why I asked this witness the question and I think his explanation that the sounding pipe, any kind of a liquid seeking its own level would be forced up in here, mixing the cocoanut oil and the fuel oil, and as he said, the cocoanut oil solidifying in the pipe would cause cocoanut oil in there.

Q. By the Court: In other words, you conclude that the sounding pipe really was converted into a sounding pipe for the deep tank?

A. Yes, sir, for the deep tank.

Q. By reason of the aperture above?

A. No, no, not that.

(TESTIMONY OF WILLIAM HENRY CURTIS)

Q. No?

A. No, this pipe is here permanently all the time.

Q. I understand that, but instead of measuring merely the fuel content, it really measured the deep tank content?

A. Up in the pipe on the rope, yes.

Q. Yes.

A. Yes, it did.

Q. Because the opening was made there?

Mr. Vermille: And made one tank.

A. Made one tank, yes.

Q. By the Court: Made it all one tank?

A. Yes, sir.

Miss Phillips: May I offer this little sketch in evidence as exhibit No. 1?

The Clerk: Government's exhibit No. 1.

Miss Phillips: Yes.

Q. By Miss Phillips: Captain Curtis, you said a few moments ago that on arrival at Wilmington when you sounded the deep tanks, the fuel oil tanks, you found that they were full to the height of 3 feet?

A. Yes.

Q. 9 inches of empty space being there?

A. Yes.

Q. That is the total depth of those tanks, being 3 feet, 9 inches, and they were filled only to the degree. only to the depth of 9 inches—did your Honor want to adjourn or shall I finish the question?

The Court: Are you about to finish?

(TESTIMONY OF WILLIAM HENRY CURTIS)

Miss Phillips: Almost finished with my direct examination, yes, your Honor.

The Court: All right.

Q. By Miss Phillips: There is 9 inches of empty space. How do you explain the fact that if cocoanut oil was in fact leaking down into the fuel tank, how do you explain the fact that there is 9 inches empty space on arrival at Wilmington?

A. Well, that is possible to do, the congealing of the cocoanut oil after it got into cocoanut oil, after the tanks were full, up to the time of arrival in Kobe, they are all full, hard up—

Mr. Vermille: Just a minute. I think the witness is assuming something. That is not correct.

Miss Phillips: I am asking him, your Honor, to give an explanation as a ship master. You gave what must have been the proceses of contamination, the cocoanut oil leaking down and having a full fuel oil tank, one of the two oils mixed. Then a swishing between the two. Nevertheless, upon arrival at Wilmington the lower fuel oil tank has 9 inches of slack, he says. Now, I am asking the witness—

The Court: You want him to explain why there is any vacancy?

Miss Phillips: Yes.

The Court: Or any unoccupied space or space occupied only by air in the fuel tank?

Miss Phillips: In the fuel tank, yes.

The Court: Because the oil tank is above it and an aperture between it.

(TESTIMONY OF WILLIAM HENRY CURTIS)

Miss Phillips: He said yes. That is what I want to know. How can that be?

A. Well, that can be by the freezing or congealing of the cocoanut oil in the deep tank as the vessel laid in cold weather in Kobe, that was cold, the water was cold, that oil on the shell plating, that bottom would congeal and also the fuel oil at that time.

Q. By the Court: And congealing, would not flow through?

A. Would harden and would not flow in the cold atmosphere, which, as we find in Wilmington, several inches or feet, for that matter, of hard oil in the bilge and on the tank top.

Q. By Miss Phillips: Now, let me see if I understand you correctly. You say that 9 inches of empty space must have been because the cocoanut oil had congealed so as to plug up that hole?

A. Plug up that hole.

Q. Do I understand you rightly?

A. Keep it from flowing down into the double bottom and filling it up.

Q. Now then, would it not be true that cocoanut oil had not been filled up, plugged up, you would have had the oil flow down and fill up that empty space?

A. Yes, if it had not been hardened to prevent the soft oil from going down through, it would have filled up the double bottom the same as prior to arriving at Kobe.

Miss Phillips: I may say, your Honor, I am ready for the cross examination now.

(TESTIMONY OF WILLIAM HENRY CURTIS)

The Court: Very well. Let me ask a question here. What relation, or rather, where was the aperture with respect to the surface of the fuel oil, above it or below it?

A. The fuel oil was below.

Q. The aperture?

A. No, the aperture was between the fuel oil and the cocoanut oil.

Q. In other words, the aperture, then, was above the surface of the oil in the fuel oil tank?

A. It was. It was at that mark in that little cross. that is the division between the deep tank and the double bottom tank.

Q. If it happened to be below, then it might easily account for the presence of an air space in the top of the fuel oil tank, might it?

A. If it was below the cocoanut oil tank, it would have been outward; there would have been no cocoanut oil got into it. It would have been salt water.

Q. No, if the aperture communicating between the fuel oil tank and the cocoanut oil tank were below the surface of the oil in the fuel oil tank—

A. There would not have been any connection there at all, sir.

Q. What I am getting at, the air would have no chance to escape and therefore it would be compressed to some extent, would it?

A. It would.

Q. Wouldn't it?

A. Yes.

(Testimony of William Henry Curtis)

Miss Phillips: Your Honor, I don't think the witness understood your question, or something there. What he is saying is that the hole between the two is right up here at the turn. Now then, if you had had the hole between—

Mr. Vermille: Let's see what he said. Ask him to repeat it.

Miss Phillips: Yes, repeat it. Where is the hole, the little aperture, according to this sketch, between the fuel tank and the cocoanut oil tank?

A.   I will explain as to how it happened when the ship struck, your Honor. On the turn of the bilge here is where this shell bar or binding bar connects the top tank with the fuel tank. When she hit it made an imprint and it struck right on this angle bar and separated the margin plate from the angle bar, it might have been in the seam or it might have been in the rivet, made an opening there between the two, almost directly between the two, and on this bar because this angle bar here and this plate divide the two tanks, and this being open here, would allow the free motion of oil of both tanks.

The Court: Surely. Now, didn't you draw a sketch there?

Miss Phillips: Yes.

The Court: Let me have that.

Miss Phillips: Well now, the question which his Honor asked is—

The Court: Just wait a moment. Well, give me a blank piece of paper. This is the fuel oil tank?

A.   Yes, sir.

Q.   By the Court: Here is where the leak occurred?

A.   Yes, sir.

Q.   At the surface of the oil where, at this stage, oil leaking from the deep tank, would fill the fuel tank, but nevertheless, there would be no way for the air to escape?

A.   It would escape more or less up through the sounding pipe, but that sounding pipe—

Q.   Well, wait a moment.   If the mouth of the sounding pipe were below the surface of the oil, it could not escape, could it?

A.   Yes, the back pressure would press it up.   The back pressure; you see, this is opened down here.

Q.   Wait a moment.   Here is your sounding pipe?

A.   Yes.

Q.   That is the opening?

A.   That is the opening.

Q.   All right.

A.   Now, here is the cocoanut oil coming down through the bilge, the cocoanut oil coming down through here would press this up, also force it up this pipe, the back pressure would force it up.   As it come down, as it pressed up in here, it also had to go up in here as well. This being open space in here, it would press up.   So, if there was pressing enough here, this tank being hard pressed, if that pipe was a definite pipe, it would force it up.

Q.   You think that notwithstanding the mouth of the pipe is below the surface of the fuel oil, the pressure would compel the air to escape and go down?

(TESTIMONY OF WILLIAM HENRY CURTIS)

A. Not the air itself, no, sir.

Q. Not the air itself?

A. The air would be up in the pipe, the amount of air would be up in the pipe.

Q. No, no, but I am speaking of the quantity of air in this tank.

A. Yes.

Q. Would that get into the pipe and escape?

A. It would, yes.

Q. It would?

A. It would force itself up through, even if it come up in here, there was a vacuum here, there would be a bubble would go up wherever the least pressure is. The pressure of oil or the pressure of water, whatever it is, will go up where the least pressure would be.

Miss Phillips: Your Honor may remember, I think when your Honor reads the deposition you will find that there could not have been very much air in there anyway because they fill up leaving Manila, all the tanks are filled up, pressed up, then the engineer says they pump out a little, a few barrels, so as to relieve pressure.

The Court: I understand the testimony to be there is a 9 inch space of air there.

Miss Phillips: There is a 9 inch space. We did not say it was air.

The Court: You mean a vacuum?

Miss Phillips: Apparently it might be a vacuum. Say that the average oil tank is 3 feet 9 inches high, on arrival at Wilmington the level of the fuel oil tank is 9

(TESTIMONY OF WILLIAM HENRY CURTIS)

inches below the top. Now, that is not necessary that these 9 inches fill up with air. It could be vacuum. 9 inches vacuum.

The Court: All right.

Miss Phillips: Thank you, your Honor. I think these things help a great deal, your questions. May I offer that?

The Court: You offer the other sketch?

Miss Phillips: I do, your Honor.

The Court: If you think it is necessary to offer my own—

Miss Phillips: I don't know but what I will.

The Clerk: 1-B.

The Court: I prefer not.

Miss Phillips: Well, none of us prefer to have our sketches in. I think your Honor's is equal to the Captain's.

The Court: Recess until 2 o'clock.

(Whereupon, a recess was taken to 2 o'clock P.M.)

Los Angeles, California, Wednesday, May 3, 1933. 2 o'clock P.M.

Miss Phillips: Your Honor, I have another question or two that I would like to ask this witness.

The Court: Yes.

Miss Phillips: I am almost through with him.

(TESTIMONY OF WILLIAM HENRY CURTIS)

WILLIAM HENRY CURTIS,

resumed the stand for further direct examination, being previously duly sworn, testified as follows:

DIRECT EXAMINATION (Continued)

By Miss Phillips:

Q. Captain Curtis, I want you to assume that on October 4th the No. 3 fuel oil tank was full of fuel oil and cocoanut oil mixed, there having been a leakage down from this little aperature we have been talking about, a leakage from the cocoanut oil down into the fuel oil tank, and I want you to assume that on October 4th, prior to knowledge of the contamination of the cocoanut oil by the fuel oil, I want you to assume that oil was in fact pumped out of No. 3 fuel oil tanks and used in the operation of the ship. Now, I want you to also assume that on October 5th quite probably some more oil was pumped out and used in the ordinary way and that after that some time that day the contamination was discovered. Let us assume also that upon these events happening the Chief Engineer blanked off the pipe lines which ran into No. 3 fuel tank. Assume that he actually wired them so that no more oil could be used out of that tank. Would the pumping of oil on the 4th and the 5th, would that explain that vacuum of 9 inches which you found at Wilmington?

A. Yes.

Q. It would?

A. Yes.

Q. Would you say that on the occasion of the last pumping of that oil, of that No. 3 fuel tank, that the

(TESTIMONY OF WILLIAM HENRY CURTIS)

cocoanut oil in the upper tank must at that time have been congealed so as to plug up that little aperture?

A. Yes.

Q. Would you say, would that be the explanation of why no more cocoanut oil leaked down from the upper tank to fill up this empty space or vacuum in the lower tank?

A. Yes.

Miss Phillips: You may cross examine.

CROSS EXAMINATION

By Mr. Vermille:

Q. Captain, assuming that at Kobe now, the oil was in a liquid state, the cocoanut oil was in a liquid state at the time the contamination was found, that is on October 5th. Now, being in a liquid state, would it be possibble for the cocoanut oil to fall down into the deep tank containing fuel oil?

A. Yes.

Q. Is there any way that you can tell, Captain, when it might have been possible for the leak to have been stopped up with congealed hard cocoanut oil?

A. At any time?

Q. At any time?

A. No, no way that I can tell.

Q. Assuming, Captain, that the settling tanks are adjacent to the deep tank containing fuel oil, are those settling tanks warm at all times?

The Court: Are they what?

Miss Phillips: Warm.

(TESTIMONY OF WILLIAM HENRY CURTIS)

A. No, they are not warm excepting when the oil goes into it, goes into that temperature, they would stay warm until such time as they congealed when there is no steam on, and as a rule they don't keep steam on those tanks until four or five days of arriving in port.

Q. What would the temperature of the fuel oil in the settling tanks be when running the vessel?

A. Oh, probably 212 to 230 or 240 degrees.

Q. By Miss Phillips: Wait a minute. Is that Fahrenheit or Centigrade?

A. Fahrenheit.

Q. By Mr. Vermille: Now, the settling tanks, referring to the plan of the ship, will you point out to the Court where the settling tanks are?

The Court: I prefer to have that done over on the board.

Mr. Vermille: Oh, I see. I notice we have a blackboard now.

The Court: Where has our blackboard gone, Mr. Harris, do you know?

The Bailiff: It is in use in Judge McCormick's court.

A. These are the settling tanks right abaft the deep tanks.

Q. By Mr. Vermille: Now, the wall of the settling tank forms the wall of the deep tank?

A. In this ship there is a coffer dam around these. These tanks don't go all the way across the ship. After the ship was constructed, some time afterwards when they began to carry cocoanut oil, they put coffer dams around those tanks, to prevent any oil getting in to con-

(TESTIMONY OF WILLIAM HENRY CURTIS)

taminate the tanks. There is a false casing that goes around these tanks to prevent anything from the settling tanks to get in and contaminate any oil that might be in the deep tanks.

Q. By the Court: What are the settling tanks for?

A. The settling tanks are tanks that are used, for instance, they pump out of No. 1, 2, 4 or 6 sufficient fuel oil to last about a day. There are four. They pump into one. While this is settling, any sediment or oil, mostly water, they are using this one. After this one is used, they pump this one up and let it settle while they use this one to use in the boilers.

Q. Well, it is the fuel oil that does the settling?

A. It is the fuel oil that does the settling, yes. They draw the water off.

Q. Well, is all the oil put through the settling tank?

A. All the oil that is used in burning in the boilers goes through the settling tanks. The settling tanks are used for oil to burn in the boilers.

Q. By Miss Phillips: Now, will you point out to the Court where the boilers are in connection with that detail?

A. Well, there are three boilers in this ship. These are the boiler rooms here. They are situated three abreast. I think there are three in that ship. I am not positive about that. There are two and possibly three.

Q. Now, would there be quite a bit of heat or any heat generated from the boiler get into these tanks?

A. No, nothing to affect that. There is too much air space in there. All these boilers are lined with asbestos

(TESTIMONY OF WILLIAM HENRY CURTIS)

and very little heat would come out and go into the forward tanks to soften any oil that might be in there.

Q. How about the settling tanks?

A. Not that either to do any great harm.

Q. Where are the settling tanks?

A. These are the settling tanks. This is the side view looking up and down. This is the top view. These are the two tanks. This is where they come out. This is the termination here.

Q. Is that a part of it?

A. No, that is a small hatch and the hatches are on the side, as shown here.

Q. Can you point out where the two settling tanks are?

A. Yes, these are the settling tanks in here between these dotted lines. This is the bulkhead and this is the dotted line. This is the ribs of the settling tanks.

Q. This is not a bulkhead?

A. Why yes, it is a bulkhead of the settling tanks. The settling tanks comprise part of that bulkhead.

Miss Phillips: I suggest that the witness put his pencil, the actual point of the pencil on the two settling tanks.

A. Here are the settling tanks. This view is a side view looking up and down, and this is a view on the ends of it looking down on top of it. This is the fore part. This is the starboard. Here are the two. These small ones, hatches, on the side of them.

Q. How far would you say the settling tanks are away from the deep tanks?

(TESTIMONY OF WILLIAM HENRY CURTIS)

A. Well, they go into them, the settling tanks go into them with this coffer dam around it.

Q. The coffer dam, does that form a part of the settling tank, the outside of the settling tanks?

A. That forms a part of both tanks, the deep tanks and the settling tanks.

Q. That coffer dam is adjacent to and forms a part of the settling tanks and the deep tanks, does it?

A. Both. That coffer dam is empty at all times. There is nothing in there whatsoever. It is built purposely to keep away any fuel, leakages, or whatsoever, to get in from one tank to another.

Q. By the Court: What is it, solid?

A. It is solid, yes.

Q. Partition?

A. It is a solid partition, built of steel.

Q. Solid steel?

A. Solid steel of half an inch or five-eights or three-quarters—not three quarters.

Q. By Mr. Vermille: Then one side, Captain, of the coffer dam forms a side of the deep tank, is that correct?

A. Yes, supposed to, if it is built right.

Q. Then, how much space existed between the coffer dam and the settling tanks?

A. Well, that varies according to the size of the ships, anywhere from 8 inches to 24 inches.

Q. Could you tell by looking at this?

The Court: What fills that space?

(TESTIMONY OF WILLIAM HENRY CURTIS)

A.   Just air, the air in there. There is a manhole that goes down through it.

Q.   By Mr. Vermille: Are you talking about this ship, or just the custom of ships? Are you familiar with this ship?

A.   Oh, not any more with this ship than the other ships. They are all the 8800 type, practically all the same, all the Government ships.

Q.   Well, did the coffer dam form a part of the No. 3 deep tank?

A.   I assume it did. I am not positive. I did not go down in there.

Q.   Well, is it customary in the 8800 ship to have that done?

A.   After the ships were built. The original plans called for no coffer dam whatever. There was none here, just a straight bulk head across, but after they began carrying oil, they put a coffer dam around those settling tanks to prevent any oil, any contamination whatsoever.

Q.   By the Court: The purpose is to keep the fuel oil from leaking out and contaminating something?

A.   Yes, sir, contaminating any oil they might carry in the deep tanks.

Q.   By Mr. Vermille: Now, does the bottom of the deep tank form the top of the No. 3 double tank?

A.   It does.

Q.   Then in that instance the cocoanut oil, or whatever is carried in the deep tanks, is right next to the fuel oil?

(TESTIMONY OF WILLIAM HENRY CURTIS)

A. The fuel oil, with a half inch or three-quarters play between.

Q. Is it customary, Captain, to carry oil in those deep tanks, or do they carry water in them?

A. They carry oil in them. It is customary. It is customary for all ships to carry it.

Q. By the Court: As I understand you, these deep tanks are constructed for the purpose of carrying oil?

A. They are.

Q. Do you mean cocoanut oil?

A. Any oil. They are constructed to carry cocoanut oil, kerosene or gasoline, or anything they want to put in them. Of course, gasoline, they can't, that is prohibited, but any solid oils like fuel oil, *sold* oil, cocoanut oil of any kind.

Q. Getting back again to those settling tanks. You say the settling tanks carry what temperature?

A. Because they have oil designed to go into the boilers that may vary from 212 to 300 degrees.

Q. Then it is warm in the settling tanks?

A. It is warm in the settling tanks.

Q. Would it be possible for heat to be generated against the end of the coffer dam?

A. Not sufficient to go ahead and melt the oil.

Q. I am not talking about that. I am asking wouldn't it be possible for the heat to generate—

A. No, it would be warm in there but not hot.

Q. Well, would it be warm?

A. It would be warm in that space.

(TESTIMONY OF WILLIAM HENRY CURTIS)

Q. About what do you think the temperature would be?

A. Oh, I don't know. I never measured any temperature.

Q. But it would be warm in there?

A. Yes, it would be warm in there, surely.

Q. Then, one side of the deep tank would always be warm when the vessel is operated?

A. Yes.

Q. That is all. Now, you say it would be absolutely impossible to tell when this leak was stopped up with congealed cocoanut oil?

The Court: I regret to say,—the difficulty is mine and not yours;—I have difficulty in understanding you, Mr. Vermille. I will try again. Remain where you were.

Mr. Vermille: Well, I will get up closer if your Honor would prefer.

The Court: No, that is all right.

Q. By Mr. Vermille: Would it be possible, Captain, to ascertain when that leak was stopped up?

A. No.

Q. By the Court: You are referring to the leak—

Mr. Vermille: The leak between the deep tank and the double bottom tank containing fluid.

The Court: The aperture?

A. The aperture.

The Court: Yes. Well, as I understand the evidence. it was not stopped up when the vessel got into San Pedro or Wilmington?

Miss Phillips: What was that?

(TESTIMONY OF WILLIAM HENRY CURTIS)

The Court: The impression I have of the testimony so far is that the aperture or leak was not stopped up, not mended, when the vessel got to Wilmington?

Mr. Vermille: That is correct, the leak was never repaired until after the cargo was discharged.

Miss Phillips: Your Honor, you say stopped up in the sense of mending, but that is stopped up in the sense of being plugged—

The Court: Well, I mean—

Miss Phillips: Yes, repaired.

The Court: But if it was stopped up or plugged with caked oil at the time it got into Wilmington.

Q. By Mr. Vermille: Would that be stopped up with caked oil? The evidence shows that the oil at the time it arrived at Kobe was in a liquid state.

A. Positively no.

Q. Captain, are you familiar with the rules laid down by an association, such as Lloyd's American Bureau, regarding construction, maintenance and classification of vessels?

A. Somewhat, yes.

Q. What are the rules with regard to tank tops of tanks carrying oil with particular reference to whether they must be water-tight or oil-tight?

A. They are supposed to be oil-tight. Any tank to carry oil has to be oil-tight.

Q. Now, Captain, if a vessel sails from Kobe with a leak between her tanks unrepaired, is that in conformity with her rules?

(TESTIMONY OF WILLIAM HENRY CURTIS)

A. That is optional with the classification of surveyors.

Q. Now, Captain, apart from any rules, in your
opinion, is a vessel which sails from Kobe—

The Court: If what?

Q. By Mr. Vermille: Is a vessel which sails from
Kobe on a trans-Pacific voyage with a leak of unknown
dimensions in one of her tank tops, in an unseaworthy
condition—

Miss Phillips: Just a moment, your Honor. I think
this is not proper cross examination. I have not gone
into theoretical questions of seaworthiness with this witness. I have confined my examination to an examination
of the facts, the physical facts, with reference to a cargo
here in this port.

The Court: Read the question.

Miss Phillips: And his explanation of those physical
facts.

The Court: What?

Mr. Vermille: In her tank top, the leak existing between the bottom of the double bottom tank.

The Court: I know where you located the leak, of
course. I did not get the expression. I still don't get it.
You mean the top of the tank?

Mr. Vermille: That is what they call the tank top.

The Court: What is the question?

(Question read by Reporter.)

Miss Phillips: My objection to that was that that is
not proper cross examination.

The Court: I rather think that objection is good.

(TESTIMONY OF WILLIAM HENRY CURTIS)

Mr. Vermille: Well, your Honor, they have gone into the question on direct examination of a leak existing between the vessel's—

The Court: Yes.

Mr. Vermille: And they have gone into that pretty thoroughly showing exactly where the leak was. I think this witness drew a diagram.

The Court: Well, that is true.

Mr. Vermille: Now, the witness is qualified as a marine surveyor. They qualified him as a marine surveyor.

The Court: I think there is nothing in the witness' testimony, in the direct examination, relative to the seaworthiness of the vessel.

Miss Phillips: That is correct, your Honor. The testimony I have offered on that is contained in the depositions. I did not ask this witness any opinion.

The Court: Well, I think the objection is good. Sustained.

Q. By Mr. Vermille: Captain, upon the arrival of the vessel here at Wilmington, you were present when they discharged the cocoanut oil?

A. Yes.

Q. Was any part or portion of that cocoanut oil on arrival here in a liquid state?

A. Yes, it was, because it had been heated before it got here.

Q. Do you know?

A. By the log book, is all I know, and verbal conversation.

(TESTIMONY OF WILLIAM HENRY CURTIS)

Q. Oh, you have examined the log books, have you?

A. No, but I always get more or less information from the Chief Engineer when the vessel arrives.

Q. You discussed this matter with the Chief Enginer?

A. Not the particular damage, no, but the liquification of the oil, temperature of the oil, and so forth, when it comes in. I always get that on all ships, good and bad.

Q. Well then, upon the time of arrival here, part of it was in a liquid state?

A. It was.

Q. `How much would you say, approximately, was in a liquid state?

A. Oh, approximately 10 or 13 feet of hard oil.

Miss Phillips: What was that answer? I didn't get it.

A. Approximately 12 to 13 feet hard oil was found in the bottom.

Q. By Miss Phillips: Liquid 12 or 13 feet, and then you struck hard oil?

A. Struck hard oil, yes.

Q. By Mr. Vermille: Captain, when the vessel arrived here, was all the oil in the port tank contaminated?

A. To a certain extent, yes.

Q. It was all contaminated to a certain extent?

A. There might have been a little clear oil at the top, slightly there, but it was all more or less contaminated.

Q. And the further down you went in the tank the more contamination you found?

A. The more contamination was found.

(TESTIMONY OF WILLIAM HENRY CURTIS)

Q. Is that correct?

A. Yes, sir.

Q. Captain, assuming your vessel struck a severe storm after leaving Kobe and before arrival at San Francisco, would that tend to loosen any of the congealed cocoanut oil, if there had been congealed cocoanut oil in the leak existing between the double bottom and the deep tank?

A. No.

Q. A severe storm?

A. No.

Q. How hard would that oil get?

A. Well, that oil gets hard. It gets hard so that it cannot be pumped.

Q. With sufficient pressure could you force it up?

A. Well, you would have to have heavy pressure with the amount of hard oil there was, with that small pressure.

Q. There is nothing in the evidence to show how far that oil had become solid on the trip over from Kobe, or when it became solid?

A. Anything more than what was found here.

Q. Nothing more than what you found here?

A. Found here.

Q. If the oil had started to congeal, the cocoanut oil had started to congeal, it had not become solid yet, in the leak, it would not take as much pressure, much swishing around of this fuel oil to loosen it, would it?

A. If both were in a liquid form?

Miss Phillips: What was that answer?

(TESTIMONY OF WILLIAM HENRY CURTIS)

A.   If both were in a liquid form.

Q.   Did you make any distinction between liquid form and oil commencing to congeal, and hard oil?

A.   Yes, there is, I think. I think that oil that will pour is different than oil that is solid, that is, when you pick it up, it is lumps.

Q.   Now, if the cocoanut oil had not become solid next to this leak, would not there still be passing back and forth between this leak fuel oil and cocoanut oil?

A.   There would, if both were in liquid form, they would naturally surge back and forth.

Q.   Semi-liquid form, we will say, had not become solid?

A.   No, I don't think so.

Q.   Of course, your answer depends upon whether or not, or how hard the cocoanut oil was at the time, doesn't it?

A.   How hard the cocoanut oil was and how large the aperture was.

Q.   There is no evidence in this case as to the size of the aperture.

Miss Phillips: Just a moment. Counsel, the Chief Engineer testified quite in detail on that. I think the Court can draw a deduction as to the size of the aperture. It is not fair to say that there was no aperture at all.

Mr. Vermille: The exact—

Miss Phillips: The exact measurements are in evidence.

(TESTIMONY OF WILLIAM HENRY CURTIS).

The Court: Now, wait just one moment. I have an observation to make. I think that counsel had not finished his question. Am I right?

Mr. Vermille: I had, yes.

The Court: Had you finished?

Mr. Vermille: I had not.

The Court: No, he had not finished his question.

Miss Phillips: Oh, I beg your pardon.

The Court: Don't answer the question if there is to be an objection. Finish the question.

(Question read.)

Mr. Vermille: I will change that to "actual size."

The Court: Well, that seems to be an observation of counsel, so far. It is a preliminary. It is a part of the question, isn't it?

Mr. Vermille: That is it.

The Court: All right. Finish your question.

Q. By Mr. Vermille: If you did not know the size of the aperture it would be impossible to tell when that leak was sealed up, would it not?

A. Only from what statements that were given, that is all.

Q. You can answer that, I think, yes or no.

A. No.

Mr. Vermille: I think that is all.

Miss Phillips: I have just a few questions, your Honor.

(TESTIMONY OF WILLIAM HENRY CURTIS)

Q. This is the aft end of the deep tank right here?

A. Yes.

Q. And here are the settling tanks?

A. Yes.

Q. Is that correct?

A. Yes.

Q. You will agree with me, I have pointed out the correct lines on the chart, haven't I, of the blue-print?

A. That is correct?

Q. Now then, if the leak that was found is in the forward end of the deep tank, the forward corner between the deep tank and the fuel tank, is heat from the settling tank going to affect the hardening of oil around that forward leak?

Mr. Vermille: Just a minute. I don't think the witness is sufficiently qualified himself in reference to answering that question.

Miss Phillips: Your Honor, I asked him on direct examination—

(Question read.)

The Court: Well, yes, he can answer that question. He says he has a great deal of experience in the measuring of oil, and also so far as the condition of oil goes, I rather think. Answer the question.

A. No.

Q. By Miss Phillips: It will not?

A. It will not.

Q. Captain Curtis, referring now to the conditions you found on this chart, have you any memorandum in your hands as to how far down you struck the hard oil?

(TESTIMONY OF WILLIAM HENRY CURTIS)

A. Yes, approximately about 4 feet 6 inches each.

Q. Of hard oil?

A. Yes.

Q. That is what I wanted to see, if you had any memorandum of that?

A. About 4 feet 6 inches.

The Court: I understood the witness to say that there was 15 feet of hard oil, did I understand him?

Miss Phillips: 12 to 13.

The Court: What?

Miss Phillips: No, no, he said 12 to 13 of liquid oil and then I asked him—

The Court: How much hard oil?

Miss Phillips: How much hard oil? What did you say?

A. From 4 or 5 feet.

Q. By the Court: 4 to 5 feet of hard oil?

A. Yes.

The Court: Well, then, I misunderstood you. I understood you to say 15 feet once.

Miss Phillips: I think he was referring to the liquid oil. It was 12 to 13 feet.

A. There is a notation I made here at 6 A.M., "12 to 13 feet of hard oil, approximately 4 feet 6 inches deep, with tongues of oil adhering to ship's side."

Q. *Tons* of oil?

A. Tongues of oil adhering to ship's side, hard oil.

Q. Captain Curtis, counsel asked this question: He said that if the oil both in the fuel oil tank, the deep

(TESTIMONY OF WILLIAM HENRY CURTIS)

tank, the cocoanut oil tank, had remained liquid, it would then leak down into the lower tank, would it not?

A.   It would, yes.

Q.   And vice versa, if the oil around that leak became hard and plugged it up, then it would not leak down?

A.   No.

Q.   Is that correct?

A.   Yes.

Q.   Are we encountering here a phenomena like pouring hot oil down the kitchen sink?

A.   Absolutely.

Q.   Which, when it hardens, stops up the sink?

A.   Absolutely.

Miss Phillips: You may cross examine.

RECROSS EXAMINATION

By Mr. Vermille:

Q.   What was this 15 feet you referred to? Liquid oil or hard oil?

A.   About 12½ to 13 feet of liquid oil.

Q.   Well, do your notes show 15 feet or 13 feet of liquid oil. You said 15 feet. Were you looking at your notes?

A.   No, I did not say 15 feet. I said 13 feet.

Mr. Vermille: I misunderstood him.

Miss Phillips: Show him the notes. You are reading from notes.

The Court: The notes are not necessary, unless counsel wants them.

Miss Phillips: If counsel wants them, I meant.

(TESTIMONY OF WILLIAM HENRY CURTIS)

The Court: Any further cross examination?

Q. By Mr. Vermille: Do you know what the outage was of this deep tank?

A. The outage?

Q. Upon arrival?

A. Outage where; at the manhole or the four corners?

Q. Well, first, at the manhole?

A. Which one?

Q. The No. 3 deep tank port.

A. Yes, at the manhole it was 60⅜ inches.

Q. How much?

A. 60⅜ inches.

Q. Then you say the liquid oil would be around 14 feet?

A. Yes, sir.

Q. Then the hard oil about 4 feet 6 inches, is that correct?

A. Hard oil in the bottom about 4 feet 5 inches or 6 inches.

Q. Now, that condition existed at the time the vessel arrived here, is that correct?

A. Yes.

Mr. Vermille: That is all.

REDIRECT EXAMINATION

By Miss Phillips:

Q. Captain Curtis, counsel used the expression "outage"?

A. Yes.

(TESTIMONY OF WILLIAM HENRY CURTIS).

Q. Will you explain to the Court what is meant by that term, outage?

A. Well, that is the difference between the top of the oil and the top of the tank, which is the outage. That is what the tank holds minus the amount of oil there is in the tank.

Q. Am I correct in saying that when you speak about the outage of the tank you mean the number of inches of empty space?

A. Empty space at the top of the tank. That is the outage.

Miss Phillips: Is that clear to your Honor?

The Court: Yes.

Miss Phillips: It is atrocious English.

The Court: That is entirely clear.

Miss Phillips: I have a great time myself in figuring out that outage means the empty space. Have you anything further?

Mr. Vermille: No.

Miss Phillips: Excused.

The Court: Wait a moment. All the information you have of this case is what you discovered in performing your duties as a surveyor?

A. Yes, your Honor.

Q. By the Court: It is the business of a surveyor to examine the condition of the cargo, its quantity, defects, or contamination, as you call it? And all you can learn about it?

A. It is.

Q. I assume?

(TESTIMONY OF WILLIAM HENRY CURTIS)

A. Yes, sir.

Q. Among other things. You were employed by the —by whom here?

Miss Phillips: By the United States agents.

The Court: Wait a moment. We will let the witness answer.

Miss Phillips: I beg your pardon. The Court was looking at me. I thought you were addressing the question to me.

A. Employed by the agent acting as—

Q. By the Court: Yes, the agent of the ship?

A. The agent of the ship.

Q. In effect, by the United States?

A. By the United States.

Q. Shipping Board?

A. Yes, sir.

Q. Of course, that really is the defendant and the plaintiff, respectively. Now, this cargo was loaded, as I understand you, into two tanks?

A. Yes, sir.

Q. And they were some 20 feet deep, 20 feet high?

A. The depth of the tanks?

Q. Yes, let us have the depth of the tanks, total depth of the tanks, outage and all.

A. I have got the outage here. I am not positive, but I think I have the depth of the tank.

Miss Phillips: It is marked here on the map, your Honor.

Q. By the Court: What is the dimension given there?

(TESTIMONY OF WILLIAM HENRY CURTIS)

to go measuring the ship to know the dimensions of each of these two tanks.

A. Well, I never take those, your Honor.

Q. You never do?

A. No, sir; just take the outages of the oil.

Q. At any rate, they are both the same?

A. Practically both the same.

Q. Well, would you say they are 8 x 10 feet, expressed that way?

A. Oh, in that proportion they would be,—they would be about 20 x 20 feet.

Q. 20 x 20?

A. Yes.

Q. All right. That gives me a better idea. At any rate, they were sufficient—Resume the stand—They were sufficient to contain how many gallons of oil each? I think it was expressed in gallons, was it not?

A. Tons.

Q. Of cargo?

Mr. Vermille: 546. long tons was shipped. They were practically equal in each. The total amount of the shipment was 546.

A. The bill of lading expressed it in pounds.

Q. By the Court: In pounds?

A. Yes, sir.

Q. That was my impression.

Mr. Vermille: 1,223,583 pounds. That was the stipulation.

Q. 1 million—

A. 223,583 pounds.

(TESTIMONY OF WILLIAM HENRY CURTIS)

The Court: 1,223,583 pounds?

Mr. Vermille: Distributed equally in both tanks.

The Court: The ordinary *avoidupois* pounds, is it not?

A. Yes.

Q. The maritime business does not make any difference in them. Do you know how much oil weighs per pound or gallon or cubic foot, or what?

A. The various oils?

Q. I am speaking, of course, of this oil?

A. No.

Miss Phillips: Your Honor, may I say this: Some of the depositions cover that point.

The Court: Well, this is all preliminary.

Miss Phillips: Yes, your Honor.

The Court: All right. I merely wanted to get a more general view of the situation here.

Miss Phillips: Yes, your Honor.

The Court: There were two tanks. Well, apparently they were cubical tanks from the dimensions you have given me.

A. Yes, sir, they are.

Q. Cubical tanks?

A. Cubical tanks.

Q. Suppose this vessel were carrying as its freight petroleum, would that be all that it would carry, just enough to fill those two tanks?

A. If it was carrying for cargo—

Q. What?

A. Yes, sir, carrying for cargo.

Q. In other words, there was no other place in the vessel for cargo?

A. Oh, yes, they could use, if they wanted fuel oil, for instance, for which the tanks are used, that is, the double bottom tanks, and the after peak tanks, they could carry fuel oil in those tanks for cargo, which is done.

Q. Yes, the fuel oil tanks, which you have described in this case, however, were those for fuel for the ship?

A. Yes.

Q. Well, it would be the same for the fuel oil carrying ship, would it not?

A. Yes, sir.

Q. What they carried would not be available, or rather what they carried in those tanks they expect to use as fuel on the voyage?

A. In the double bottom boilers, not in the cargo tanks, of course.

Q. Well, naturally, of course. Otherwise there would not be any cargo; in other words, this is cargo space?

A. Cargo space.

Q. Supposing they were carrying flour, or lumber, or what not?

A. They can use it for that purpose too.

Q. That is about all the space in the ship available?

A. Oh no. They have 1, 2, 3 and 4 holds.

Q. Besides them?

A. Besides the deep tanks.

Q. But what we know as the tank space has the oil in the hold?

No......**7783**......

In the

United States
Circuit Court of Appeals

FOR THE NINTH CIRCUIT.

UNITED STATES OF AMERICA,
Appellant,

vs.

THE LOS ANGELES SOAP COM-
PANY, a Corporation, and WEST-
CHESTER FIRE INSURANCE COM-
PANY,

Appellees.

Apostles on Appeal

Appeal From the District Court of the United States,
Southern District of California,
Central Division

Independent-Review, Law Printers, 222 So. Spring St., Los Angeles. TU 1377

(TESTIMONY OF WILLIAM HENRY CURTIS)

Q. Deeper than the other holds?

A. No, they are not deeper than the other holds, but they are deep for a tank encased.

Q. Now, when you went down to see this vessel— by the way, what was the date that you went down and saw this vessel in Wilmington Harbor?

A. December 1st.

Q. December 1st?

A. December 1st.

Q. You found one of the tanks in perfectly good condition?

A. Yes, sir.

Q. No controversy over that?

A. No controversy whatsoever.

Q. In the other tank you found liquid oil down to a depth of about 13½ feet?

A. Yes, sir.

Q. Do I understand you to say that that was caked along the sides?

A. It was caked along the sides.

Q. To what depth along the sides?

A. Well, we did not take any depths of the thickness of the oil on the shell plate, on the sides.

Q. Well, you have some recollection?

A. Oh, that was probably 5 or 6 feet.

Q. 5 or 6 feet on each side?

A. On each side, yes. It tapered down, tapered down from the top as it came down to the turn of the bilge, down to the bottom.

Q. You mean the liquid?

(TESTIMONY OF WILLIAM HENRY CURTIS)

A.   The hard oil. I am speaking of the hard oil at present.

Q.   What was it that tapered?

A.   The hard oil as it melted in the ship it melted in the center.

Q.   No, I am not talking about its melting. As you went down, you went down and you found about 13 feet of hard oil?

A.   Yes.

Q.   And from the top down, as I understand you,— correct me if necessary,—there was about 4 or 5 feet of hard oil on the sides?

A.   4 or 5 feet on the bottom, about 4 feet 6 inches on the bottom of the tank.

Q.   Well, was there any hard oil on the sides?

A.   On the sides, yes, sir.

Q.   And how thick was it?

A.   About 6 feet; as the oil melts, it melts in the center.

Q.   Well now, I don't care whether this oil ever melts. I am asking you, when you went down and looked at it what you found?

A.   Well, I found hard oil on the bottom and the sides.

Q.   All right. Now, we are talking about the hard oil on the horizontal top of this tank, the surface of the oil.

A.   Yes.

Q.   That is clear. That for 13 feet down there it was liquid?

A. Yes.

Q. All right. Now, it was caked or hardened on the sides?

A. On the sides.

Q. I am trying to get the thickness of the hardened part of the oil on the side at the surface.

A. Well, that would vary from the top of the oil to the bottom.

Q. Well, I don't care. I am speaking of the top of the oil.

A. Well, maybe 2 inches; maybe 4 inches.

Q. And some little crust?

A. On the very top.

Q. It amounted to little or nothing?

A. Little or nothing.

Q. But it tapered down, did it?

A. Yes, sir.

Q. In other words, that got thicker as it went down?

A. Went to the bottom.

Q. And what would you say if you were in a position to give an estimate, what would you say the thickness was down at the depth of 13½ feet?

A. 13½ feet? What I have said before, that we had 4 feet 6 inches of hard oil on the top of the tank. On an angle from the center to the bilge it might have been 8, 10 or 12 feet.

Q. It was more or less of an inverted cone?

A. Inverted cone, yes.

Q. Of liquid oil?

A. Liquid oil.

(TESTIMONY OF WILLIAM HENRY CURTIS)

Q. I see. That was the condition that you found?

A. The condition I found.

Q. What, in your judgment, caused this oil to harden?

A. Well. it is an oil that congeals, anyway. When it is cold it congeals like a soap, hard.

Q. Well, you would think, then, that it all congeals together?

A. No, it won't congeal together because the cold atmosphere on the outside of the shell plate, the cold air, coagulates that and hardens it.

Q. Well, you think that the thickening or coagulation of the oil might have been due to temperature?

A. Yes.

Q. Did this fuel oil have anything to do with it?

A. It would if the fuel oil were cold. As a general rule, the fuel oil in those tanks is approximately the temperature of the water.

Q. Are what?

A. The temperature of the water.

Q. Well, I suppose the whole interior of the ship is all the same temperature except in this settling tank?

A. No, that varies too.

Q. Very well. You don't attribute the hardening, then, to the presence of the fuel oil in the cocoanut oil?

A. No.

The Court: All right. Well, did you make any analysis—well, that no doubt will appear in the evidence, the analysis of the oil?

Miss Phillips: Yes, your Honor. This gentleman is

(TESTIMONY OF WILLIAM HENRY CURTIS)

not a chemist and did not make an analysis, I am quite sure.

Q. By the Court: All right. Did you,—or rather, the oil, the fuel oil, was the ordinary crude petroleum, I suppose?

A. Well, it is not the crude petroleum. It is a fuel oil that is used a purpose for burning in boilers.

Q. Yes?

A. Where there is one extraction of gasoline, or something, run from the crude oil.

Q. Oh, this is not as it comes from the well?

A. It is not as it comes from the ground.

Q. It has had a run of gasoline from it?

A. Yes, gasoline, or some other substance.

Q. That would make it a little bit thicker?

A. It would thin it out.

Q. That would thin it out?

A. Thin it out.

Q. And in this tank where the oil was, and which is the lower tank and which is directly underneath the deep tank, there was some oil?

A. There was fuel oil.

Q. Fuel oil, yes. And you said a depth of about 3 feet?

A. About 3 feet.

Q. Then on top of that—how did you ascertain that?

A. By soundings.

Q. Yes, through this apparatus that you have described here?

A. Yes.

(Testimony of William Henry Curtis)

Q. All right. Did you,—or was the cocoanut oil removed while you were there?

A. It was.

Q. And was the fuel oil removed while you were there?

A. No fuel oil.

Q. Did you yourself personally see this leak or aperture that has been described here?

A. I did not.

Q. You did not?

A. No, sir.

Q. Well, did you examine, or did you try to examine. the boiler, or the tank, rather, to discover it?

A. There is too much crude oil and mixed oil in the bilge to get down at the aperture at the time that the oil was discharged at San Pedro.

Q. It was not a very nice place to be with clean clothes on, I suppose?

A. It is not at any time.

Q. Well then, you yourself have no personal knowledge of this leak?

A. No, sir.

Q. You simply reasoned that it was there because the oil was mixed?

A. The oil was mixed.

Q. Well then, maybe the leak was somewhere else other than the place where you think it was?

A. I don't think so. With the surveys and reports that had been tendered, show that this rupture was there at this point, and nowhere else.

(TESTIMONY OF WILLIAM HENRY CURTIS)

Q. I see; other engineers had examined it?

A. The engineers and the Bureau of Classification and surveyors, hold surveyors, and so forth.

Q. Well, but no one had examined the tank when it was empty up to that time, had they, Captain?

A. No, sir. No, not that part of the tank or that part of the ship.

Q. Well, because the tank, of course, was never empty?

A. Never empty, no.

Q. All right. A. Anything more than the indenture that they saw when she was on the dry dock at Kobe.

Q. When you speak of indenture you mean the inward—

A. The inward imprint, yes.

Q. The other tanks of oil, I assume, were unloaded in the usual way. How was this tank of oil unloaded?

A. Unloaded by pump. They have a pump there that they,—electric centrifugal pump that they put down into the oil, put a suction on the oil.

Q. That pumps the liquid oil out. Then how do they get the hard oil out?

A. Well, the hard oil, they have a small hose on this centrifugal pump that they force it down on the sides. Then with the steam heat on this, liquifies it and then they pump it out by the pump. Then after all is out by the pump, then they come down with scoops and shovels and scoop it up that way.

Q. This hard oil was more or less in the condition

(TESTIMONY OF WILLIAM HENRY CURTIS)

of bee's wax, or something of that kind, of the consistency of bee's wax?

A.   Well, not quite as hard as bee's wax; softer.

Q.   By the Court: What was the condition of the other tanks with respect to hardness or softness?

A.   Practically the same conditions as far as liquification and solidification of oil was concerned in the fore tank.

Q.   Practically the same?

A.   Practically the same, with the exception of the contamination.

Q.   You would conclude from that that the presence of fuel oil, as you have expressed the opinion, did not contribute to the hardening?

A.   No.

Q.   Well, did you discover anything about this tank that would indicate in any way to your mind that the presence of the oil was due to any other cause than this aperture that the engineers describe?

A.   No.

Q.   You are pretty sure that it could not have been?

A.   No other way.

Q.   Because every other part was sealed?

A.   Was sealed and tight.

Q.   Of course, you have to depend on the other engineers to know that because you yourself did not examine it?

A.   Well, we go around and examine, take in the majority of the ships, we go down into the tanks and examine the bulkheads, the longitudinal bulkheads, and the athwartship bulkhead, and the tank tops, and the deep tank bottoms. Then if possible we go down on the far side of the tank to see if there are any leaks in the rivets or seams. The same way in the engine room bulkheads.

Q. Well, you did do that in this case?

A. Yes.

Q. As soon as it was all cleaned up, then you got down on the bottom of the tanks?

A. I did not, no, sir.

Q. You did not?

A. I did not.

Q. Who did?

A. The machinists or the contractors who done the work.

Q. Well, you depend on them to report to you any—

A. No, no, sir, I did not. After the oil is all out and we see that the oil is all out of the tanks, they are cleaned out. That, as far as our job is concerned, is finished.

Q. Yes. I understand, but you expressed the opinion that there was no springing of a rivet, or anything of that sort?

A. That, yes.

Q. But on whom do you depend for that information?

A. Ourselves. We get down into the tank tops, go down into the tanks to see if there are any ruptures or leaks or holes.

(TESTIMONY OF WILLIAM HENRY CURTIS)

Q. That is what I thought. You did that in this case?

A. Yes.

Q. After the oil, however, was cleaned out?

A. After the oil was cleaned out.

Q. You did not get down into the bilge, however?

A. I did not, no, sir.

The Court: That is all, I think.

REDIRECT EXAMINATION

By Miss Phillips:

Q. I have just one other question. Captain Curtis, in your experience of surveying the shipments of cocoanut oil that come in from the Orient, what would you say as to their condition as to hardness on arrival at Wilmington?

A. Well, that varies. Now, it all depends. The majority of the ships get instructions for about 5 days before they arrive in port to turn steam onto the oil to liquify it so it can be pumped easily. Some come in here with temperature ranging from 100,—I have had it 160 down to 90 and down to 85, or 85 to 160.

Q. When that has been done, then the cocoanut oil is absolutely liquid?

A. Not always that. I have seen cocoanut oil come in 120 degrees, 135 degrees, and yet have solid oil at the skin of the ship.

Q. Where there has been no pumping, does it arrive in a solid condition or the liquid condition, I mean where there has been no heating prior to arrival?

(TESTIMONY OF WILLIAM HENRY CURTIS)

A. Where there has been no heating, it is in a solid condition on arrival.

Q. It may be solidified?

A. There may be a little soft oil right under the hatch sometimes where it has not had time to congeal entirely.

Q. Possibly towards the center?

A. Towards the center, yes.

Q. Now, there is another question I want to ask. When you speak about hardened cocoanut oil, I wish you would compare that with something we know. Is it as hard as lard?

A. Just about the same consistency as lard.

Q. I was going to compare it with something else, but if it is just about the same consistency as lard, we will let it go at that.

A. It is about the same consistency as lard.

Miss Phillips: Any other questions?

Mr. Vermille: Just one more question.

RECROSS EXAMINATION

By Mr. Vermille:

Q. Before the oil can be discharged from a vessel after it arrives here, it is necessary to heat it, is it not?

A. Yes, sir. That is, if they want to pump it. It can be shoveled off, if they want to take the time.

Q. Ever known them to do that?

A. No, I have not.

Q. Have you ever known of a vessel coming in here

(TESTIMONY OF WILLIAM HENRY CURTIS)

in all your experience with the deep tank full of hard cocoanut oil?

A.   Not entirely, no.

Q.   That is all.

A.   That is, I want to say,—countermand that; that is, be discharged here, no, but if it is to continue on to another port they have because they have not liquified it.

Mr. Vermille: That is all.

Miss Phillips: That is all, Captain.

MARTIN P. APPEL,

called as a witness on behalf of the Government, being first duly sworn, testified as follows:

Q.   By the Clerk: Your full name?

A.   Martin P. Appel.

The Court: Spell that again, please?

A.   A-p-p-e-l.

DIRECT EXAMINATION

By Miss Phillips:

Q.   Mr. Appel, what is your full name, please?

A.   Martin P. Appel.

Q.   And where do you live; where is your home?

A.   Richmond, California.

Q.   And what is your business, Mr. Appel?

A.   Marine engineer.

Q.   Marine engineer. What papers do you hold?

A.   I hold Chief Engineer for Steam and Chief Engineer for Diesel Engines.

(TESTIMONY OF MARTIN P. APPEL)

Q. You say you hold papers as Chief Engineer for Steam, for Steam Vessels. When did you get your papers as Chief Engineer for Steam Vessels?

A. 1925.

Q. 1925. And prior to that time had you received,— did you obtain papers on the lower grades of engineers?

A. Yes, ma'am.

Q. First and second assistant, and so on?

A. Yes, ma'am.

Q. Now, speak up so we can hear you. The Reporter has to get every word you say. You say you have papers for Chief Engineer on Diesel Engines?

A. Yes, ma'am.

Q. Diesel Engine vessels, is that?

A. Yes, ma'am.

Q. When did you get your license as Chief Engineer for Diesel Vessels?

A. 1928.

Q. In 1928?

A. Yes, ma'am.

Q. Where did you get your training for that?

A. In Kiev, Germany.

Q. Did you go back to Germany to study?

A. Yes, ma'am.

Q. Where did you study?

A. In the ship yard in Kiev.

Q. That was in 1928?

A. Yes, ma'am.

Q. Did you get a certificate from them?

A. I got a certificate for the time I studied there

(TESTIMONY OF MARTIN P. APPEL)

and I showed it to the inspector here and I got my license.

Q. And he gave you a license here?

A. Yes, ma'am.

Q. Were you ever a member of the crew of the West Cajoot?

A. Yes, ma'am.

Q. In what capacity?

A. Second assistant engineer.

Q. Now, what year was that?

A. 1928.

Q. 1928?

A. '27·

Q. 1927. Your voyage started where?

A. San Francisco.

Q. Where did you go from San Francisco?

A. San Pedro.

Q. And then from San Pedro?

A. To Melbourne and Australian ports.

Q. And then from the Australian ports?

A. To Ceylon and the Philippine Islands.

Q. To the Philippine Islands?

A. Yes, ma'am.

Q. Did you go to Manila?

A. Yes, ma'am.

Q. Then from Manila, where did you go from there?

A. We went from Manila to Hongkong.

Q. Then from Hongkong?

A. We went toward San Francisco and struck a reef on the Japanese coast.

(TESTIMONY OF MARTIN P. APPEL)

Q. Mr. Appel, what are your duties as a second assistant engineer?

A. To take care of the fire in the boilers, feed pumps and transfer pumps for the transferring of the oil.

Q. By Mr. Vermille: Did he say he was first assistant or second assistant?

Miss Phillips: Second asisstant, he said.

Mr. Vermille: I understood you to say first assistant.

Miss Phillips: I asked him if he had the papers for the intermediate grades, lower grades. He said he was second assistant.

(Answer read by the Reporter.)

Q. By Miss Phillips: For the transfer of oil from where?

A. From the different tanks.

Q. To what?

A. To the settlers.

Q. To the settling tanks? Tell me, just explain to the Court what those settling tanks are?

A. The settling tanks are two tanks located right in front of the fire room and we use one each time for fuel oil in the boiler, and the other one we use, we fill up and turn the oil out of it.

Q. Do you use the oil in the boilers from first one settling tank and then the other, see-saw back and forth?

A. Yes, ma'am.

Q. But on alternate days, is that it?

A. Ma'am?

Q. What I am getting at is this: While the oil is

(TESTIMONY OF MARTIN P. APPEL)

Q. By the way, what were your usual watches on board the ship?

A. From 12 to 4—that means the afternoon—and then from 12 midnight to 4 o'clock in the morning.

Q. To 4 in the morning. Mr. Appel, did you keep any record of what tanks you used from in filling the settling tanks?

A. Yes, ma'am.

Q. What kind of a record was it?

A. It is in the log book.

Q. It is in the log book?

A. Yes.

Q. Is that the book that is known as the rough engine log?

A. Yes, ma'am.

Q. Was it your practice to enter what you did?

A. Yes, ma'am.

Q. During your watch?

A. Yes, ma'am.

Q. And was it your practice to find the entry?

A. Yes, ma'am.

Miss Phillips: I will show this to counsel.

Q. By Miss Phillips: I am showing you now a book upon the face of which appears, "Reciprocating Engines, West Cajoot, San Francisco, Cal. Route Orient," and the dates, "8-10-27—12-8-27." I am now going to ask you to examine that book and tell me if you have ever seen it before? Have you?

A. Yes, ma'am.

Q. What is that book?

(Testimony of Martin P. Appel)

A.   That is the log book kept during the voyage.

Q.   Are the entries there, going through that book, marked "12 to 4 noon," and then "12 to 4 at night," the entry is signed "M. P. Appel," are those in your handwriting?

A.   Yes, ma'am.

Q.   Are those your signatures?

A.   Yes, ma'am.

Miss Phillips: Your Honor, if your Honor will look at the book you will see that it is quite smudged and dirty and rather hard to read. I have made a transcription of all those entries and I propose to have your Honor use a copy of that transcript, for the witness to use another copy, for counsel to have the log and the transcript. I think that would perhaps facilitate the questioning of the witness.

The Court: Well, this book is very neatly kept.

Miss Phillips: Well, the writing is small. I think he could use it. But we might move a little faster. It is kept in a very business-like way, I agree with your Honor.

The Court: Very well.

Q.   By Miss Phillips: Mr. Appel, I have shown you now this log. Have you examined the entries made by you in this log?

A.   Yes, ma'am.

Q.   When did you make them; when did you examine them?

A.   I examined them in San Francisco yesterday afternoon.

(TESTIMONY OF MARTIN P. APPEL)

Q. Just recently is that?

A. Yes, ma'am.

Q. And would you be able to remember all your entries in that book without referring to the log?

A. No.

Q. You would not?

A. No.

Q. You have forgotten the events?

A. Yes, ma'am.

Q. I have just shown you typewritten sheets marked at the top "Extracts from Rough Engine Log, West Cajoot," Have you ever seen those typewritten sheets before?

A. No, ma'am. Oh yes, yesterday afternoon.

Q. Day before yesterday, wasn't it?

A. Day before.

Q. I observe written over here—I have got it right here: "Compared this with original log and found to be correct."

A. Yes.

Q. Did you go right through these typewritten sheets and compare them with the original log?

A. Yes, ma'am.

Q. And they were correct, were they?

A. Yes, ma'am.

Q. I might say, your Honor, that the little red check on the margin here is not the witness' check. I did that to pick out who filled the settling tanks.

Q. By Miss Phillips: Now, Mr. Appel, the September 24th entry, that is,—I think the testimony, your

(TESTIMONY OF MARTIN P. APPEL.)

A. Yes, ma'am.

Q. On October 1st I observe you filled the settler from No. 2 port and starboard?

A. Yes, ma'am.

Q. On October 2nd, the 12 to 4, the noon watch, you filled it from No. 2 port and starboard?

A. Yes, ma'am.

Q. By the way, you say that you filled it during that watch. What was your practice; did you fill it at the beginning of the watch or the middle of the watch, or the end of the watch?

A. Right at the beginning of the watch.

Q. Right after you came upstairs from dinner?

A. Yes.

Q. Or rather, went downstairs from dinner?

A. After I went all over and see everything was in good running order; I started pumping.

Q. You started pumping. I notice on the entry 12 to 4 A.M., October 2nd, I notice there you have a number of little symbols that are copied in pencil. Do you know what those symbols mean?

A. Yes, ma'am.

Q. What do they mean?

A. That one went half ahead, another one went half astern, another went full astern.

Q. Mr. Appel, let me see if I understand your symbols here. A little triangle that way, does that mean slow ahead?

A. Slow ahead.

(TESTIMONY OF MARTIN P. APPEL)

Q. Which means?

A. That way there, the way you have got it there means full astern. In this case as a rule we always turn that upper line on the bottom. As a rule, that little line is on the bottom.

Q. Well, I think the symbols are sufficient explanation, your Honor, to be able to decipher them from the log book. I am going to offer the log book in evidence. This is just for the purpose of simplifying the examination.

Mr. Appel, I notice on your entry of October 3rd you appear to have filled the settler from No. 2 port and starboard?

A. Yes, ma'am.

Q. Again on the entry for October 4th, 12 to 4 P.M., on that day you appear to have filled the settler from No. 2 port and from No. 3 port and starboard?

A. Yes, ma'am.

Q. Now, is that from the No. 3 fuel tanks?

A. Yes, ma'am.

Q. That is?

A. Yes, ma'am.

Q. According to this log, that was the first occasion you used oil from the No. 3 fuel tanks?

A. Yes, ma'am.

Mr. Vermille: Just a minute. I object to that. I don't think the log shows that.

Miss Phillips: Well, the log is right there.

Mr. Vermille: What happened to the entry on Sep-

(TESTIMONY OF MARTIN P. APPEL)

tember 30th? Where did he fill any tanks on September 30th?

Miss Phillips: On September 30th; there seems to be no entry there on September 30th.

Mr. Vermille: No way of knowing where he filled the tanks from, then, on September 30th, is that correct?

Miss Phillips: Q. Just a moment. I notice on the log book for September 30th there does not appear,— this was prior to the collision,—there does not appear to have been any entry there as to where you filled the settling tanks from on that date. Do you notice?

A. Yes, ma'am.

Q. Do you think that you filled the settling tanks on that day?

Mr. Vermille: I object to that, if your Honor please. I don't think the witness is qualified to answer. This is 1927, and he has refreshed his memory from a log book and there is absolutely no entry in the log book on this.

The Court: There appears to be no filling of tanks on that day.

Miss Phillips: On that day.

The Court: She may ask why that was. You can answer any question as to why that was.

Miss Phillips: That is what I meant to convey, your Honor. Your Honor's form of the question is much better than mine.

Q. By Miss Phillips: Why is there no entry for the filling of the settling tank on September 30th?

A. The chances are there was an accident that we only used one boiler, or maybe it was two boilers, but

(TESTIMONY OF MARTIN P. APPEL)

we did not use much oil, enough oil, so it was not necessary to fill the settler.

Q. That may have been it?

A. Yes, ma'am; and there is a log right in here, it says, "Cut out center boilers, 3:45." That is a sign that maybe we slowed down, slowed down the ship.

Q. Is there any possibility that you might have used, transferred oil, that day, and forgot to put it in the log book?

A. No, not in this case.

Q. You don't think so?

A. No, ma'am.

Q. Well, people do sometimes forget things, don't they, the best of us?

The Court: That question is immaterial.

Miss Phillips: Yes, I think it is, your Honor.

Q. By Miss Phillips: However, the consumption of oil for that day, Mr. Appel, would indicate that you used quite a bit of oil. That appears on the lower page, doesn't it?

A. Yes, it is on the lower page what we have got on hand and what is used that day.

Q. Well, do you remember the approximate capacity of the settling tanks?

A. Yes, ma'am.

Q. About how much were they?

A. About 180, from 160 to 180.

Q. You don't remember exactly?

A. No, I don't.

Q. Somewhere between 160 and 180?

(TESTIMONY OF MARTIN P. APPEL)

A.   Yes, ma'am.

The Court: Barrels?

A.   Yes, sir.

Miss Phillips: Your Honor, the blueprint which we have tacked up here says that the settling tank capacity is 166 barrels.

The Court: That is, there are two settling tanks, are there?

Miss Phillips: Yes, your Honor.

The Court: Each 166 barrels?

Miss Phillips: Yes, your Honor.

The Court: Well, the witness explained that certain boilers were cut out on that day, and that would account for the fact that the settling tank was not filled. That is what you said?

A.   Yes, your Honor.

Q.   By the Court: However, you did use that day more than the capacity of one settling tank, didn't you?

A.   I want to see the revolutions. If we made the same revolutions, we should use the same amount of oil per mile. It says here one boiler is cut out, "center boiler cut out 3:45."

Q.   By Miss Phillips: Mr. Appel—

A.   Yes, ma'am.

Q.   —looking over that log do you now think that you did in fact fill the settling tank that day, or that you did not fill it; which do you think it is, looking over the log?

A.   I think I did not fill it.

Q.   You think you did not?

(TESTIMONY OF MARTIN P. APPEL)

A. No.

Q. You cannot be sure, can you?

A. No, I cannot.

Q. You cannot be sure. All right. Now then, Mr. Appel, I observe that between the date October 4th to November 1st there don't appear to be any entries in that log. Do you know why that was? I mean, there is no entry showing the day to day examination of fuel oil or the transfer of oil from the fuel tanks to the settling tanks between October 4th and November 1st. Do you know why this was?

A. We start work in the day-time as soon as we get on the dock. Whenever we work in the day-time we don't enter anything in the log that goes in the log book.

Q. By the Court: You were in dry dock?

A. Yes.

Q. And you don't make any entries in your log book?

A. No, sir.

Q. By Miss Phillips: She was then in the Port of Kobe, was she?

A. Yes, ma'am.

Q. And it was not customary to make these day to day entries while she was in port, is that right?

A. No, ma'am.

Q. Now then, in fact there is some consumption of oil going on while you are in Kobe aboard the ship?

A. Yes, ma'am.

Q. How is that?

A. We use winches and general auxiliaries, like ice machines and pumps, and we keep the boilers going.

(TESTIMONY OF MARTIN P. APPEL)

Maybe sometimes only one boiler. Sometimes we used two boilers. It all depends upon the cargo, and so on, what we use on deck.

Q. There is some little port use, then, that is, running the ice machine. Was your ship lighted with electric lights?

A. Yes, ma'am.

Q. Would you have to keep the batteries going?

A. Yes, ma'am.

Q. And that sort of thing. I see. Mr. Appel, I want you to look at the entries there on the voyage from November 1st sailing from Kobe homeward—and your Honor has compared that typewritten sheet there.

The Court: At this time we will take our recess.

Miss Phillips: Yes, your Honor.

(Short recess.)

(After recess.)

Q. By Miss Phillips: Mr. Appel, I think we were referring to the entries in your log from Kobe on towards Yokohama. I think I suggested—Does counsel want to have the original log and be following that with the copy?

Mr. Vermille: If it will help the witness any, he can keep it.

Q. By Miss Phillips: All right. I observe that on November 1st—you seem to have filled the settling tank from No. 5, No. 5 and 6 fuel tanks. That is correct, is it, November 1st?

A. Yes, ma'am.

Q. On November 1st it was from 5 and 6 tanks?

A. Yes, ma'am.

Q. And the same on the later watch on November 2nd. That is correct, isn't it?

A. Yes, ma'am.

Q. Now, on November 4th, I notice the entry, "Filled settler from No. 6 and from the after peak"?

A. Yes, ma'am.

Q. Did this vessel,—did this vessel carry fuel oil in her after peak tank?

A. Yes, ma'am.

Q. She did. Well now, what about the fore peak tank; what did she carry in the fore peak tank?

A. Water.

Q. Water. She carried water in the fore peak tank and fuel oil in the after peak?

A. Yes, ma'em.

Q. Was that true during the entire voyage?

A. During any voyage.

Q. During what?

A. I say, through all the previous voyages, too.

Q. Now then, I notice on November 5th you seem to have used it from 5 port and starboard tanks?

A. Yes, ma'am.

Q. On November 6th from the after peak, that is both the earlier watch, the noon watch and the midnight watch. And similarly, on the early watch on November 7th, you seem to have used it there from the after peak?

A. Yes, ma'am.

Q. On the midnight watch you seem to have used it there from 5 and 6?

(TESTIMONY OF MARTIN P. APPEL)

the noon watch, and then from the after peak from No. 6 on the midnight watch?

A. Yes, ma'am.

Q. And the same on November 9th, that is, both watches it seems to be there?

A. Yes, ma'am.

Q. On November 10th you seem to have taken from the after peak tank and from No. 5?

A. Yes, ma'am, 5 starboard.

Q. Yes, and then on the midnight watch you seem to have pumped from 6 and from the after peak?

A. Yes, ma'am.

Q. When you say "pumped from," just say from 6 without specifying whether it is port or starboard, which do you mean? Do you mean it is from both or from one?

A. I think 6 has a port and starboard in there.

Q. Oh, I see. Now, on November 11th, you seem to have pumped from the after peak and from No. 5 starboard. Then on the midnight watch that day you seem to have pumped from No. 6?

A. Yes, ma'am.

Q. Is that right?

A. Yes, ma'am.

Q. On the 11th, you seem to have pumped from the after peak No. 6, and in the midnight watch from the after peak and the starboard No. 5?

A. Yes, ma'am.

Q. By the way, I notice in your log two days, November 11th. Do you know why that is?

(TESTIMONY OF MARTIN P. APPEL)

A.   Ma'am?

Q.   Do you know why you have in your log two—
the date November 11th twice?

A.   Oh yes.

Q.   Two different denominations, both marked
November 11th. Do you know why that is?

A.   Well, that was a mistake.

Q.   Well, isn't there somewhere along the line that
you crossed what is called the date-line there?

A.   Oh, that might be the case.

Q.   The date-line?

A.   Yes.

Q.   Now then, on November 12th, you filled the
settler from No. 6, then again that night from the after
peak of No. 6, is that right?

A.   Yes, ma'am.

Q.   On November 13th from No. 1 and from the
after peak. Then the midnight watch from No. 5 port
and starboard?

A.   Yes, ma'am.

Q.   Your log shows that, does it?

A.   Yes, ma'am.

Q.   On November 14th, you seem to have used from
No. 5 fuel tank port and starboard, both the noon and
the midnight watch?

A.   Yes, ma'am.

Q.   And the same the next morning, the noon watch
of November 15th?

A.   Yes, ma'am.

Q.   The same on the 16th, both watches, and the same

(TESTIMONY OF MARTIN P. APPEL)

the noon watch on the 17th. On the 18th you seem to have filled from No. 5 port and starboard and from the after peak?

A. Yes, ma'am.

Q. That is in your letter, is it?

A. Yes, ma'am.

The Court: What is the materiality of this?

Miss Phillips: Your Honor, perhaps I should have stated. Some of the testimony, the depositions which opposing counsel, I believe, are offering in rebuttal, make the suggestion that the ship could have discharged the cocoanut oil into the after peak tank. Well, if the after peak tank was full of fuel oil, it would not be a very good place to put the cocoanut oil, and I am showing by this witness that that was the state.

Mr. Vermille: So that your Honor will understand—

The Court: Just a moment. Anticipatory of the suggestion that they might have saved the oil by taking it out and putting it into a tank that had—that was a fuel tank?

Miss Phillips: Yes, your Honor.

The Court: Well, of course, that would involve cleaning the tank.

Miss Phillips: It would involve emptying the after peak tank, doing away with the fuel oil there,—I don't know what,—and then cleaning it.

The Court: Well, are you proposing to offset that by showing the course of business, all this that was done?

Miss Phillips: I am showing that the fuel tank, the

(TESTIMONY OF MARTIN P. APPEL)

Q. By Miss Phillips: Was fuel oil pumped out of tank No. 3 any time during this voyage?

A. I don't know what you mean. You mean from the whole voyage, or do you mean from a particular place, from Hongkong to San Francisco, or from here to Hongkong?

Q. All right. Between Hongkong and Kobe was fuel oil pumped out of No. 3 at any time between leaving Hongkong and her time in Kobe?

A. Yes, ma'am.

Q. That is, in the entry of what date? Look at the bottom of page 4 of that memorandum.

Your Honor, may I direct the witness' attention?

The Court: Surely.

Q. By Miss Phillips: To the entry of "October 4th, 12 to 4 P.M. watch, filled settled from No. 2 port and from No. 3 port and starboard."?

A. Yes, ma'am.

Q. Yes. Now then, from the time you left, from November 1st, you notice through from November 1st right straight on to the homeward voyage, was fuel oil pumped out of No. 3?

A. No, ma'am.

Q. It was not. Tell me, have you any recollection of soundings being taken from No. 3 fuel tanks at Kobe?

A. I have a slight recollection, yes, ma'am.

Q. You have a slight recollection?

A. Yes, ma'am.

(TESTIMONY OF MARTIN P. APPEL)

Q. Do you think it was the day after you arrived in Kobe?

Q. By the Court: The day after or the day before?

A. I think it was the 5th of October.

By Miss Phillips:

Q. About the 5th of October?

A. Well, according to my log. No, I did not put that in my log at that time, but I know it was about the 5th of October.

Q. I see. But you haven't any very definite recollection about that?

A. No, ma'am.

Q. Mr. Appel, you have testified that there was a port use, use in port of fuel oil, some amount for running these various things on the ship, the ice machine, the electric lights, and so on. You did not enter in your log, though, where that oil was taken from, did you?

A. No, ma'am.

Q. Might you have taken some of the oil from No. 3 on October 5th, the day after this entry, after the 4th?

A. No, ma'am.

Q. Why not?

A. The chief gave orders to lock up the suction lines for No. 3 tanks, port and starboard.

Q. Was that after these soundings were taken?

A. Yes, ma'am.

Q. Do you remember what time of day that was?

A. No, I don't.

Q. He said to plug up the suction lines?

(TESTIMONY OF MARTIN P. APPEL)

Q. You left the West Cajoot at San Francisco, didn't you?

A. Yes, ma'am.

Q. What has been your employment since then?

A. I don't know it by heart, but I copied the names.

Q. Well now, just give us the names of some of the ships and some of the companies that you have been with.

A. I left the West Cajoot on November 23, 1927, and I joined the San Juan at San Francisco November 29th, in the year '27· And I was right here from March 4th, I was on there from November 29th to March 4th, '28· The ship was owned by the Los Angeles & San Francisco Navigation Company.

Q. Well now, don't go into too much detail on this. We don't want to spend too much of the Court's time. Then in the summer of 1928 you went to Germany and studied in the Krupp Works?

A. In the Krupp Works in Kiev.

Q. Now, coming back since then, can you just name some of the companies you have been with?

A. Yes, ma'am, every one of them.

Q. Some of the ships?

A. 14 of them.

Q. Don't take too much of the Court's time.

A. I went on the San Juan again as first assistant and I left there on August 2nd and went on the Coalingo temporarily for a sick man, then on the Eliah. I went chief of that for a month.

(TESTIMONY OF MARTIN P. APPEL)

CROSS EXAMINATION

By Mr. Vermille:

Q. You say you took soundings of the No. 3 double bottom tank. When did you take those soundings?

A. I am not positive there if it was the No. 3 double bottom or if it was the bilge. I could not tell you what it was. We took several soundings on port and starboard.

Q. All right. Have you got any record of what those soundings show?

A. No, I do not.

Q. You don't know whether the tank was full or empty?

A. I do not, no.

Q. What are the duties of taking soundings?

A. Well, the chief engineer was right there. He took it and I was sweating. I could not see nothing coming from below, and I did not pay no attention. I just give him the rod. He took the soundings.

Q. You are positive that no soundings were taken prior to arrival at Kobe, is that correct, No. 3 double bottom?

A. I don't know that. Maybe they have been taken by the chief engineer.

Q. I mean in your presence did you have anything to do with taking any soundings prior to the arrival of the vessel at Kobe?

A. No, sir.

Q. Then if the testimony shows that the chief engineer and you took soundings on September 30th of

(TESTIMONY OF MARTIN P. APPEL)

No. 3 double bottom tanks, which is correct? The chief is right, or you are right, which?

The Court: Did you say September 3rd?

Mr. Vermille: September 30th, prior to the accident.

The Court: Is there a question pending?

Mr. Vermille: There is a question pending.

A. Well, sir, I did not understand it.

Mr. Vermille: Will you read the question, please?

(The reporter thereupon read the question.)

A. I was not there present.

Q. If the chief said you were present at the time of soundings, would you say you were or were not?

A. I was not.

The Court: Is there a log book entry to that effect?

Mr. Vermille: The chief engineer's testimony, your Honor, in the deposition.

Miss Phillips: Your Honor, which we stipulated, which counsel offered and we welcomed the stipulation that the engineer was testifying at the time without the rough log and recognized that he might have been mistaken and might have been referring to the No. 2 double bottom.

Mr. Vermille: Nothing in connection with the soundings. There is nothing in the stipulation about soundings.

The Court: Well, the deposition will show that.

Miss Phillips: The deposition will show that. The witness said he does not remember.

(TESTIMONY OF MARTIN P. APPEL)

Mr. Vermille: No, the witness did not say he did not remember. He said he was positive.

Q. By Mr. Vermille: You left this vessel at San Francisco, did you not?

A. Yes, sir.

Q. You did not come down on the ship to San Pedro then?

A. No, sir.

Q. Or complete the voyage?

A. No, sir.

Q. Prior to sailing from Manila, which was the commencement of that voyage so far as this action is concerned, the Philippine Islands, did anyone leave your engine room force?

Miss Phillips: Your Honor—

A. Yes, sir.

Miss Phillips: Your Honor, just a moment. I object to this as not proper cross examination. I have not asked this witness any question about people leaving the engine room force at Manila.

The Court: Read the question, Mr. Reporter.

(Question read by the Reporter)

Miss Phillips: My objection to that was, it is not proper cross examination.

Mr. Vermille: Very well. I will withdraw it.

The Court: I think it related to the subject-matter, clearly. Objection overruled. The answer was no?

Miss Phillips: Counsel withdrew it after he answered. May I ask if counsel withdrew it or does not withdraw it?

(Testimony of Martin P. Appel)

Mr. Vermille: No, I do not withdraw it.

Miss Phillips: Your Honor overruled it, and may I have an exception? I just want to protect my record to know what to do, when counsel withdraws it and then changes it.

The Court: Exception to the ruling, you mean?

Miss Phillips: Yes, your Honor. Just a matter of form.

The Court: Give counsel an exception to the ruling of the Court. Is there a question pending?

Mr. Vermille: That question was answered, I think.

The Reporter: Yes.

Q.   By Mr. Vermille: Are you positive that no oil was used from the No. 3 double bottom tank until after the accident of stranding on the reef?

A.   According to the log, I am positive. I could not recollect it.

Q.   When did you make these entries in the log book with reference to time?

A.   At the end of the watch.   g

Q.   At the end of each watch you made the entries?

A.   Yes.

Q.   Then the entries that you made in here were made the same day, the same date?

A.   Yes, sir.

Q.   That you went on watch?

A.   Yes.

Q.   They were not made the day afterwards?

A.   No sir.

(Testimony of Martin P. Appel)

Q. Were any soundings taken of the No. 3 double botto immediately after the collision?

A. Sir?

Q. Were any soundings taken of the No. 3 double bottom immediately after the collision?

A. That is what I was just telling her. I don't know without we took—

Q. Did you take any soundings?

A. I did not, no, sir.

Q. Did you assist in the taking of any soundings?

A. Yes, sir. I have just got a slight recollection that I did on account of it being cold. I remember making the remark, "It is too cold for me; I am going down below."

Miss Phillips: The witness has obviously misunderstood the question. Will you read it?

(Question read by the Reporter.)

Q. By Mr. Vermille: Immediately after the stranding?

The Court: After the—

Mr. Vermille: The stranding of the vessel on the reef?

A. Immediately after the striking of the reef the first assistant and the chief went on all the tanks and took soundings, especially forward, on account of that is where we struck.

Q. By Mr. Vermille: Talking about No. 3 double bottom?

Miss Phillips: Just a moment.

A. No, not that I know of.

(TESTIMONY OF MARTIN P. APPEL)

mately what the amount for a 24 running hour day is, consumption of fuel oil?

A. Yes, it runs from 145 to about 180, according to the way we run and the way we are loaded.

Q. 145 to what?

A. '60 and sometimes '80·

Q. Do you remember of having any conversation with the chief engineer as to the using of fuel oil from the No. 3 double bottom?

A. No, sir.

Q. Does the chief ever instruct you not to use oil from the No. 3 double bottom at any time?

A. Yes, sir.

Q. When was that?

A. That was after they were sealed up on account I could not use it.

Q. When was that, do you remember?

A. No, I do not.

Q. After arrival in Kobe, or before?

A. After arrival in Kobe.

Q. Approximately how long after arrival in Kobe did you receive those instructions?

A. It was right after he stated that he found some oil—he did not tell me that, but when he called the mate that time. Then after that he told me to stop pumping from No. 3 and he told, I think, the first to plug up these suction lines.

Q. How long had you been in Kobe when he told you that?

A. About a day.

(TESTIMONY OF MARTIN P. APPEL)

Q. One day.

Q. By the Court: Just what did he tell you to do?

A. Not to take any more,—not to suck any more of the oil out of the No. 3 double bottom.

Q. By Mr. Vermille: Did he say why?

A. No, he did not tell me why.

Q. Did you assist in the taking of any samples of this cocoanut oil?

A. No.

Q. What is approximately the consumption of fuel oil while you were in port in running your ice machine and keeping steam on for the winches?

A. I don't know how much it was on this ship. As a rule—

Q. Did you ever keep a record of the consumption of fuel oil?

Miss Phillips: Wait a minute. You interrupted the witness. He was right in the middle of an answer.

Mr. Vermille: I thought he was all through. Pardon me.

A. Sometimes them settlers last for 3 or 4 days. That all depends on how much cargo they may have on the ship or how they use their deck winches. If they use all the deck winches, we might get long with one settler every 24 hours but I am not positive about on this ship at all. I haven't go no recollection of it, in fact.

Miss Phillips: Your Honor, it may shorten it up if I told counsel that the chief engineer's log, which I have proposed to offer in evidence—they were identified

(TESTIMONY OF MARTIN P. APPEL)

at the time his deposition was taken—shows the port consumption.

Mr. Vermille: I have never seen them.

Miss Phillips: I propose to offer them in evidence. Counsel can withdraw them and examine them at his leisure.

Mr. Vermille: That is all right. I did not know you had them.

Miss Phillips: Yes, I have them here.

Mr. Vermille: I had never seen them.

Miss Phillips: I think, counsel, at the time of the cross examination of the chief engineer the logs were there and he used them at that time.

Mr. Vermille: Yes, but I have never seen them.

Miss Phillips: Yes.

Mr. Vermille: Your Honor, I don't like to take up any more time than necessary, but I would like to know what companies this party has worked for after he left the West Cajoot.

The Court: Well, there has been no restriction suggested so far with the examination. Go after him. That is proper cross examination. Let me ask something I have in mind here.

Q. By the Court: Mr. Appel, you say that the chief engineer told you the day after you arrived in Kobe not to take any more oil out of No. 3?

A. Yes, your Honor.

Q. But on October 4th, filled settlers from No. 2 port and No. 3 port and starboard?

A. There was a mistake in the date. This was really

(TESTIMONY OF MARTIN P. APPEL)

after the sounding on deck on October 5th. That is the time that—

Q.   How was that, now?

A.   On October 5th when the chief engineer—

Q.   That was when he told you?

A.   Yes, sir.

Q.   Well, that is all right. Now, this No. 3—there were really two No. 3s?

A.   Yes, your Honor.

Q.   That is referred to as No. 1 and No. 2. And that was the same with all of the tanks, was it?

A.   Except the No. 6. There was no air-tight bulkhead.

The Court: All right. Proceed.

Q.   By Mr. Vermille: When did you leave the West Cajoot?

A.   November 23, 1927.

Q.   Were you discharged or did you leave voluntarily?

A.   I was discharged.

Q.   When did you next go to work?

A.   November 29th.

Q.   What vessel?

A.   The San Juan.

Q.   The San Juan?

A.   Yes, sir.

Q.   How long did you stay with that vessel?

A.   From November 29, '27, to March 4, '28·

Q.   When did you next go aboard a vessel?

A.   That was the year afterwards. I went to the

San Juan again in a different capacity on the 3rd of October, October 3, '28·

Q. When did you leave that vessel?

A. August 2, '29·

Q. What was the name of that vessel?

A. The San Juan.

Q. I thought you went on board the San Juan on the 29th of November, 1927, and left March 4, 1927. Then you went back again?

A. I went there twice.

Q. October?

A. And I think August.

Q. What other vessel? What next?

A. The Coalingo.

Q. All right.

A. August 3, '29· to September 13, '29· That was a temporary job also.

Q. A temporary job?

A. Yes.

Q.· All right. When next did you go aboard the vessel?

A. Next I went on the Unimack.

Q. All right. When did you go aboard the Unimack?

A. December 6, '29, to January 13, '30·

Q. All right. What other vessel did you go on after that?

A. The Lio.

Q. The Lio?

A. Yes, sir.

(TESTIMONY OF MARTIN P. APPEL)

Q. What was your capacity on these various ships that you said you worked on?

A. Oh, I worked in any capacity. I never looked out for anything particular.

Q. Referring to your memorandum there.

A. Yes, I have got it.

Q. On the San Juan, what were you there?

A. The first time I was third assistant.

Q. Third assistant?

A. The second time I was first assistant. The Coalinga I was first assistant. On the Unimack I was chief. On the Lio I was second, and on this one I was on an oiler.

Q. Wait a minute. The Wilmotor was next?

A. The Wilmotor. That was the one I was on. That was a motor ship.

Q. An oiler?

A. Yes. The Wilmington I was first. On the Saginaw I was second, and in the last two capacities I was junior engineer, two motor ships.

Q. Now, Mr. Appel, I wish you would explain in this log book November 11th—I show you a log book dated November 11th. Were those entries made on November 11th?

A. Well, this one here is—

Q. Directing your attention to what I am asking you—

A. This one here, yes.

Q. Is that November 11th?

A. According to what is written down there.

(TESTIMONY OF MARTIN P. APPEL)

Q. All right. Referring to the next entry on the log book on the next page, a complete day, what day was that an entry for, November 11th?

A. I don't know. I could not tell you that, on account I wrote down the 11th again and somebody put a 2 on top of it. Maybe I did; I don't know.

Q. Well, if you put a 2 on top of it and made it November 12th, where is the entry for November 13th?

A. If this is the 13th, there must be a mistake somewhere. I just explained that. We went past the Equator, then we have two days at that time. I remember those two. I did not put that 2 on top of there.

Q. In other words, then, it appears in this log book that you have two entries covering a complete day for the same day?

A. Yes.

Q. And different entries?

A. Yes.

Q. By Miss Phillips: May I ask counsel, to shorten up on this, does he remember that crossing from the east to the west there are in fact two days each time.

Mr. Vermille: I am just trying to have the witness explain that.

Miss Phillips: Oh, I see.

Mr. Vermille: I know you can explain that.

Miss Phillips: Well, I asked him that. I did not mean that. I thought you were trying to confuse the witness. I apologize.

Mr. Vermille: I wanted to find out what was in his

(TESTIMONY OF MARTIN P. APPEL)

mind when he put two entries down there for the same day or one for the next day.

The Court: Well, the witness apparently does not know. Is that correct?

A. Yes, your Honor.

Q. By the Court: Would crossing that line,—not crossing the line, but going from a point where day begins, have anything to do with it?

A. Yes, sir.

Q. You think that accounted for it? I would have to study considerably before—I mean, go over it before I could outline the process, but I could explain it, I suppose, after awhile. There is some time when you are coming from that Orient that you either lose a day or gain a day?

A. Yes, your Honor.

Q. You think that might account for this?

A. That might, yes.

Q. That might. Could you tell,—that is 180 degrees from Greenwich, isn't it?

A. Yes, your Honor.

Q. Could you tell whether you were in that neighborhood at that time?

A. No, I am not a navigator.

Q. No. Well, neither am I. I fail to see, really, the importance of that. What about that?

Mr. Vermille: Your Honor, when you read the chief engineer's deposition you will realize the importance of this examination.

Your Honor, at this time, I want to offer in evidence a United States Pilot Chart of the North Pacific Ocean. This is a hydrographic chart of the Navy, offered solely for the purpose of showing the Great Circle Route. The Master, in his testimony in the deposition which has been offered testified that he intended to take and did take the Great Circle Route. This map shows the Great Circle Route and shows averages of temperatures for the month of November. That will be the Government's exhibit next in order.

The Court: You don't mean November, 1927?

Miss Phillips: May I explain a little further on that?

The Court: What you mean is the general average?

Miss Phillips: The general average, yes, your Honor.

The Court: Kept by the Weather Bureau?

Miss Phillips: General average. I am going to offer this.

The Court: Very well. Any objection to it?

Mr. Vermille: No, no objection to show the average temperature.

Miss Phillips: Just the average.

Mr. Vermille: It does not show the temperature at this time?

Miss Phillips: I am now offering it — just simply averages for November on that route.

The Clerk: Government exhibit 3.

Miss Phillips: I also want to offer in evidence at this time certain log books which were identified upon depositions. What is called the smooth log of the West Cajoot, which was identified and used by the chief engi-

in New York City and Mr. Bacon was also a marine surveyor in New York City. Oh no. Mr. Charles V. Bacon is a consulting chemist, chemical engineer and surveyor of bulk holds.

The Court: You offered Mr. Bacon's deposition?

Mr. Vermille: Mr. Bacon's deposition.

The Court: Bacon is the chemist?

Mr. Vermille: Mr. Bacon is a consulting chemist, chemical engineer and surveyor of bulk holds.

The Court: And where is he located?

Mr. Vermille: New York City.

The Court: Is this in the way of expert testimony?

Mr. Vermille: Expert testimony. Thomas Lawrence Stanley is a consulting engineer and marine surveyor in New York City.

The Court: Those depositions were taken in New York City, I assume?

Mr. Vermille: Those depositions were taken in New York City. Call Captain Waters.

The Court: Are those all the depositions that you are going to have, Mr. Vermille?

Miss Phillips: Counsel is under promise to offer the depositions of two witnesses in San Francisco, because I wish to offer their cross examination in case he did not.

Mr. Vermille: I will offer them now. I haven't got the originals.

The Court: Well, you can offer them later when you find them.

Mr. Vermille: I will at this time offer the depositions of Joe Jory. He is the surveyor for the Board of

Marine Underwriters at San Francisco. I also offer deposition of W. E. Heppell. He is a marine surve in San Francisco representing the majority of steamship companies out of San Francisco.

EXTRACTS FROM
ROUGH ENGINE LOG "WEST CAJOOT"
MANILA toward HONGKONG

Sept. 24, 1927

    12-4 P.M.

        Hot well fresh
        Extra Feed 2½ Hr.
        Blew tubes of stbd boiler
        Water on deck 2 hrs. 15 min.
        Filled settler from No. 1 P & S
            M.P.Appel

    12-4 A.M.

        Hot well Fresh
        Filled settler from No.1 P & S
        Changed from high to low settler suction
        Extra feed 2½ Hrs.
            M.P.Appel

Sept. 25, 1927

    12-4 P.M.

        Hot well fresh
        Fire and Boat drill 1²⁰ O.K.
        Filled settler from No.1 P & S
        Extra Feed 3 hrs.
        Cut in feed heater 1 :30
            M.P.Appel

14-4 A.M.

> Hot well fresh
> Extra feed 1½ hr.
> Filled settler from No. 2 P & S
> > M.P.Appel

Sept. 26, 1927

12-4 P.M.

> Hot well fresh
> Extra Feed 2 hours
> Changed settled 3;50
> > M.P.Appel

12-4 A.M.

> Hot well fresh
> Filled settler from No. 2 P & S
> Std. by 2:25
> Stop 2:35
> > M.P.Appel

HONGKONG toward SAN FRANCISCO

Sept. 28, 1927

12-4 A.M.

> Hot well fresh
> Found feed heater cut
> Made and installed 2 blanks in place of
> bursted coil. Cut in Feed heater 3:30
> Extra feed 2½ hrs.
> Filled settler from 'No.2 P & S
> > M.P.Appel

Sept. 29, 1927

> 12-4 P.M.

>> Hot well fresh
>> Filled settler from No.2 P & S
>> Extra Feed 2½ hours.
>> Blew Tubes stbd. boiler

>>> M.P.Appell

> 12-4 A.M.

>> Advanced clock 3 min.
>> Run 237 Min.
>> Hot well fresh.
>> Extra feed 2 hours.
>> Cut out two low four inch tubes,
>> rolled in 2 new ones.

>>> M.P.Appell

Sept. 30, 1927

> 12-4 P.M.

>> Hot well fresh
>> Washed fire room tank tops
>> Extra feed 4 hours
>> Cut out center boiler 3:45
>> 1 Low four-inch tube bursted
>> 3 lbs. soda ash to boilers

>>> M.P.Appel

> 12-4 A.M.

>> Advanced clock 16 Min.
>> Run 224
>> Placed new 4-inch tube in center boiler
>> Cut center boiler in   3:00

Cut out Port Boiler   3:30
Extra feed 3½ hrs.
Hot well fresh
3 lbs. soda ash to boilers
     M.P.Appel

October 1, 1927

12-4 P.M.

Hot well fresh
Filled settler from No.2 P & S
3 lbs. soda ash to boilers
Extra feed 3 hours
Blew clean the three boiler uptakes
Replaced two cones in Port and Stb Boilers
     M.P.Appel

12-4 A.M.

Advanced clock 15 minutes
Run 225 Min.
Hot well fresh
Cut out two tubes of stb. boiler
Extra feed 3 hours.
     M.P.Appel

October 2d, 1927

12-4 P.M.

Replaced 5 4″ lower corroded tubes with
new ones in stbd. boiler
Cut in stbd boiler 2:45
Hot well fresh
Extra feed 3 hrs.
Filled Settler from No.2 P & S
     M.P.Appel

12-4 A.M.

Advanced clock 16 min.

Run 217 Minutes.

Hot well fresh

Filled settler from No.1 and No.2 P.

Extra feed 4 hrs.

3 lbs. soda ash to boiler

Full astern 12:59 stop 1"

(in pencil) I 1:14 D 1.19 4+ 2.06 4 1.21

M.P.Appel

October 3, 1927

12-4 P.M.

Ballast Pump, pumping from No.1
hold all watch

Extra feed 2 hrs.

Hot well fresh

Filled settler from No.2 P & Stbd.

Cut out feed heater 3:45

Coil bursted.

M.P.Appel

12-4 A.M.

Advanced clock 11 minutes.

Made and placed 2 blanks for
broken heater coil.

Cut in heater 3:15

Extra feed 2½ hrs.

Hot well fresh

Run 229 Min.

Ballast and fire pumps pumping
on No.1 hold and watch

M.P.Appel

October 4, 1927

  12-4 P.M.

      Filled settler from No.2 Port and
      No. 3 P & St.
      Hotwell fresh
      Extra feed 2½ hrs.
      Drained water from settlers all watch
      Steam on deck 1
          M.P.Appel

KOBE toward YOKOHOMA

Nov. 1, 1927

  12-4 A.M.

      Leaving Kobe Std By.12:23
      Meter 856890
      All clear 1:05
      Hot well fresh
      Extra feed 1 Hr.
      Bells account Hot L.P. crank
      (in pencil) L 1.38 4 1.43 4+ 1.46
      Filled settler from 5 & 6
          M.P.Appel

Nov. 2, 1927

  12-4 P.M.

      Hotwell fresh
      Extra feed 1½ hrs.
      Filled settlers from 5 and 6
      Water on deck 2.00-4.00
      Pumping water from No.3 stdb.overboard 2 hrs.
          M.P.Appel

12-4 A.M.

>   Order from bridge—make about 68 RPM 12:3
>   Hotwell fresh
>   Filled settlers from 5 P - S - 6
>   Extra feed 1 hr.
>
>   M.P.Appel

YOKOHOMA toward SAN FRANCISCO

Nov. 3, 1927

12-4 A.M.

>   Advanced clock 42 minutes
>   Run 198 Minutes
>   Hotwell fresh
>   Extra feed 1 hr.
>
>   M.P.Appel

Nov. 4, 1927 A.D.

12-4 P.M.

>   Hotwell fresh
>   Filled settler from No.6 & Aft peak
>   Extra feed 1½ hr.
>
>   M.P.Appel

12-4 A.M.

>   Advanced clock 13 min.
>   Run 227 Min.
>   Hot well fresh
>   Replacing broken main feed pump plunger
>   with spare. Also inserting spare piston,
>   piston and plunger rod.
>
>   M.P.Appel

November 5, 1927

12-4 P.M.

Hot well fresh
Extra feed 2 hrs.
Filled settlers from 5 P and S
6 and Aft Peak
Water on deck 1½ hrs.
M.P.Appel

12-4 A.M.

Advanced clock 20 minutes,
Run 220 Min.
Hot well fresh
M.P.Appel

November 6, 1927

12-4 P.M.

Hot well fresh
Filled settlers from aft peak
Extra feed 1½ hrs.
M.P.Appel

12-4 A.M.

Hot well fresh
Advanced clock 18 minutes
Run 222 minutes
Blew tubes of stbd boiler
Filled settler from aft peak
Extra feed 1½ hrs.
M.P.Appel

November 7, 1927

    12-4 P.M.

        Hot well fresh

        Filled settler from aft peak

        Extra Feed 1½ hrs.

        Engine racing in intervals all watch

                M.P.Appel

    12-8 A.M.

        Advanced clock 7 minutes,

        Run 233 Minutes

        Pumped No.1 and 2 holes P and S

        Hot well fresh

        Extra feed 1 hour

        Engine racing in intervals all watch

        Filled settler from 5 S and 6.

                M.P.Appel

November 8, 1927

    12-4 P.M.

        Hot well fresh

        Pumped No.1 and 2 holds

        Filled settler from aft peak

        Extra feed 1 hr.

        Cut out port boiler 12:20

        Engine racing in intervals all watch

                M.P.Appel

    12-4 A.M.

        Advanced clock 15 minutes

        Run 225 Minutes

        Pumped holds No.1 and 2

        Hot well fresh

Extra feed 1 hr
Filled settler from aft. peak and 6
Engine racing in intervals   all watch
M.P.Appel

November 9, 1927

12-4 P.M.

Hot well fresh
Extra feed 1 hr.
Filled settler from aft peak and 6
Engine racing in intervals all watch
Pumped holds 1 and 2
Boiler density
p 24.5   C 48   S 56 Grains
M.P.Appel

12-4 A.M.

Advanced clock 23 minutes
Run 217 minutes
1 and 2 holds   bilges dry
Engine racing in intervals   all watch
Filled settlers from Aft. Peak and 6
M.P.Appel

November 10, 1927

12-4 P.M.

Hot well fresh
Extra feed 1 hr.
Bilges of 1 and 2 holds pumped
Filled settler from aft peak and 5 S
M.P.Appel

Filled settler from aft peak and No.6
Extra feed 1½ hr.

M.P.Appel

12-4 A.M.

Condensate 3 grains,
Advanced clock 21 minutes,
Run 219 minutes
Engine racing and throttled all watch
Extra feed 1½ hr.
3 lbs soda ash for boiler
Filled settlers from aft peak and S 5

M.P.Appel

November 12, 1927

12-4 P.M.

Hot well fresh
Extra Feed 1½ hr.
Filled settler from No.6

M.P.Appel

12-4 A.M.

Advance clock 22 minutes
Run 218 minutes
Hot well fresh
Filled settler from aft peak and 6

M.P.Appel

November 13, 1927

12-4 P.M.

Hot well fresh
Boat and fire drill 1:00 O.K.
3 lbs soda ash to boilers

Filled settler from 1 and aft peak
Extra feed 1½ hr.

M.P.Appel

12-4 A.M.

Advanced clock 24 minutes
Run 216 minutes
Hot well fresh
Filled settler from No.5 P and S
3 lbs. soda ash to boilers

M.P.Appel

November 14, 1927

12-4 P.M.

Hot well fresh
Filled settler from No.5 P and S
Extra feed 1½ hr.
3 lbs soda ash to boilers

M.P.Appel

12-4 A.M.

Advanced clock 22 minutes
Run 218 minutes
Extra feed 1 hr
Filled settler from No.5 P and S
3 Lbs. soda ash to boilers

M.P.Appel

November 15, 1927

12-4 P.M.

Hot well fresh
Engine racing in intervals   all watch
Extra feed 1½ hr.

Filled settler from aft peak and No.5 P and S

3 lbs soda ash to boilers

M.P.Appel

12-4 A.M.

Advanced clock 14 minutes

Run 226 Minutes

Hot well fresh

Cut out stbd. boiler and gave same

one glass, bottom and surface.

Blow cut in 3:00

Engine racing and throttled all watch

M.P.Appel

November 16, 1927

12-4 P.M.

Hot well fresh

Extra feed 1½ hr.

Filled settler from aft peak and NO.5 P and S

3 lbs. soda ash to boilers

M.P.Appel

12-4 A.M.

Advanced clock 19 minutes

Run 221 minutes

Extra feed 1 hr.

Filled settler from aft peak and No.5 P and S

3 lbs. soda ash to boilers

Hotwell fresh

M.P.Appel

November 17, 1927

  12-4 P.M.

      Filled settler from aft peak and No. 5 P and S

      Hot well fresh

      Extra feed 1½ hr.

            M.P.Appel

  12-4 A.M.

      Advanced clock 22 minutes

      Run 218 minutes

      Hotwell fresh

      Extra feed 2 hrs.

            M.P.Appel

November 18, 1927

  12-4 P.M.

      Hotwell fresh

      Filled settler from No. 5 P and S and Aft Peak

      Extra feed 1½ hr.

      Stopped main feed pump 2:45 to replace

      broken steam valve chest pack   Pluner overhaul

      metallic piston rod packing

            M.P.Appel

  12-4 A.M.

      Advanced clock 17 minutes

      Run 223 Minutes

      Filled settler from aft peak and No.5 P and S

      Extra feed 2½ hr.

      Engine racing and throttled in

      intervals from 2-4

            M.P.Appel

November 19, 1927

    12-4 P.M.

        Filled settler from aft peak and No.5 P and S

        Hot well fresh

        Extra feed 1½ hr.

        Engine racing in intervals all watch

        3 lbs. soda ash to boilers.

                   M.P.Appel

    12-4 A.M.

        Advanced clock 20 minutes

        Run 220, minutes

        Filled settler from aft peak and 5 P and S

        Extra feed all watch

        Hot well fresh

        3 lbs. soda ash to boilers

        Gave P and C boiler 1 glass blow

               M.P.Appel

November 20, 1927

    12-4 P. M.

        Filled settler from No.5 P and S

        Hot well fresh

        Slowed engine 20 minutes to fasten set

        screw on pilot valve rod of main feed pump

        Extra feed 1½ hr.

        3 lbs. soda ash to boilers

              M.P.Appel

    12-4 A.M.

        Filled settler from 5 P and S

        Hot well fresh

Extra feed all watch
3 lbs. soda ash to boilers
Advanced clock 21 minutes
Run 219 Minutes.
Gave Stbd Boiler one glass blow
M.P.Appel

November 21, 1927

12-4 P.M.

Gave stbd. boiler 2 one glass blows
and P and C Boiler one glass blow
Extra feed all watch
Filled settler from No.5 P and S
Condensate 3 grains
M.P.Appel

12-4 A.M.

Advanced clock 26 minutes
Run 214 Minutes
Hotwell fresh
Extra feed 3 hrs.
M.P.Appel

November 22, 1927

12-4 P.M.

Gave each boiler 2 one-glass blows
Filled settler from No.5 P and S
Hot well fresh
Extra feed all watch
Steam on deck 1 hr. 20 min.
M.P.Appel

12-4 A.M.

> Filled settler from No.5 P
> Hotwell fresh
> Extra feed 2 hrs.
> Slowed engine to 60 R P M 1:30
> Slowed engine to 50 R P M 2:40
>
> > M.P.Appel
>
> > (NOTE ARRIVAL AT SAN FRANCISCO,
> > Pier 54 at 8:52 A.M.)
> > SAN FRANCISCO toward SAN PEDRO

December 1, 1927

> Arrival at San Pedro.
> No entries by Appel after San Francisco.

Endorsed: No. 3327 L A Soap v. U S A. 3663 U S A v. L A Soap. 3691 U S v. Westchester.

Gov Exhibit No. 2.

Filed 5/3 1933. R. S. Zimmerman, Clerk. By Cross Deputy Clerk.

––––––––

LEONARD ARTHUR WATERS,

called as a witness on behalf of the Los Angeles Soap Company and The Westchester Fire Insurance Company, being first duly sworn, testified as follows:

Q. By the Clerk: Your full name?

A. Leonard Arthur Waters.

Mr. Vermille: If your Honor please, if you will pardon me a minute. There is another witness here who

(TESTIMONY OF LEONARD ARTHUR WATERS)

was surveying a cargo down at San Pedro and I just understand that he would like to get away, and I would like to put him on ahead of the other witness, first.

The Court: Very well. You will retire for the moment, Mr. Waters.

Mr. Vermille: I will call Mr. Beedle.

WILLIAM F. BEEDLE,

called as a witness on behalf of the Los Angeles Soap Company and The Westchester Fire Insurance Company, being first duly sworn, testified as follows:

Q. By the Clerk: Your full name?

A. William F. Beedle.

The Clerk: How do you spell it?

A. B-e-e-d-l-e.

DIRECT EXAMINATION

Mr. Vermille: Q. Mr. Beedle, what is your business or occupation?

A. Chemist.

Q. How long have you been a chemist?

A. About 17 years.

Q. In connection with being a chemist, what has been your duties?

A. Well, that is a broad question.

Q. All right. What companies did you first work for as a chemist?

A. I was with Swift & Company, National Stockyards, about 7 years.

Q. What were your duties with Swift & Company?

(TESTIMONY OF WILLIAM F. BEEDLE)

A. I was assistant chief chemist about 4 of those 7 years and that was performing duties relative to analyzing oils and fats, fertilizers, and feeds.

The Court: For what purpose? Did you say what they were used for, the oils and fats?

A. Edible purposes.

The Court: Yes.

A. And inedible.

Q. By Mr. Vermille: What companies did you work for after that?

A. I worked at that time for Wilson & Company here in Los Angeles.

Q. When was that?

A. That was in 1923, about the time of September to the first of the year.

Q. What were your duties with Wilson & Company?

A. Well, I was supervising the manufacturing of byproducts and selling byproducts and was supposed to analyze byproducts. However, they had no laboratory and during that short period I did no analytical work.

Q. All right. Where next did you work?

A. I took charge of the Gooch Laboratories prior to the death of Mr. Gooch and at his death a Mr. Huffman and I bought the business from the widow and have since conducted it.

Q. What year was that?

A. 1924.

Q. You are still with the Gooch Laboratories?

A. Yes, sir.

(TESTIMONY OF WILLIAM F. BEEDLE)

Q. All right. What is your occupation in connection with the Gooch Laboratories?

A. The analysis—we specialize in vegetable oils, animal fats, fertilizers and feeds.

Q. Did you have anything to do with cocoanut oil?

A. Yes, sir.

Q. Did you make analysis of cocoanut oil for various companies?

A. Yes, sir.

Q. What companies?

A. Copra Oil & Meal Company, Los Angeles; Pacific Cottonseed Products Corporation, Los Angeles; Pacific Nut Oil Company, Los Angeles. That is a few I recall now.

Q. Did you ever do any work for the Vegetable Oil?

A. Oh yes, the Vegetable Oil Products Company, Wilmington. Well, they have a Los Angeles office, too.

Q. Are there any other oil companies here in Los Angeles outside of those you named, or in this vicinity?

A. Oh yes.

Q. The Los Angeles Soap Company, did you ever work for them?

A. Yes, sir.

Q. Globe Grain & Milling Company?

A. Yes, sir.

Q. You are familiar with the West Cajoot?

A. Yes, sir.

Q. Have you ever been on her?

A. Yes, sir.

(TESTIMONY OF WILLIAM F. BEEDLE)

Q. What has been your experience in connection with the discharge of cocoanut oil prior to going on board the West Cajoot, from vessels here at Wilmington?

A. We have represented Curtis & Tompkins in their survey work at the harbor.

Q. Who is Curtis & Tompkins?

A. They are chemists and engineers of San Francisco, and surveyors.

Q. Approximately how many surveys have you made of cocoanut oils on vessels?

A. Prior to the West Cajoot?

Q. Yes.

A. We had been doing that survey work about 2 years prior to that time. I would have to go through my file.

Q. You have been doing it ever since?

A. Yes, sir.

Q. You are familiar with the discharge of cocoanut oil from vessels?

A. Yes, sir.

Q. I show you a survey report marked "Curtis & Tompkins' exhibit No. 1," by Ernest E. Williams, U. S. Commissioner, which has been introduced into evidence. I ask you if you know anything about that survey report?

A. Yes, sir. I sent the original information to Curtis & Tompkins for this report and afterwards checked this report.

Q. Then you received this report back again and checked it?

(TESTIMONY OF WILLIAM F. BEEDLE)

A.   Yes, sir.

Q.   And found the same to be correct?

A.   Yes, sir.

Q.   That shows the true condition, does it, of the cocoanut oil that arrived on board the West Cajoot at Wilmington, taken December 1, 1927?

A.   Yes, sir.

Mr. Vermille: That is already offered in evidence, if your Honor please.

Q.   By the Court: You made the analysis?

A.   No, sir. Curtis & Tompkins of San Francisco made the analysis.

Q.   By Mr. Vermille: Did they make the analysis from the figures and statements and calculations that you sent to them?

A.   Yes, sir.

Q.   You received this report back from Curtis & Tompkins, did you?

A.   Yes, sir.

Q.   After you received the report, survey report, back from them, what did you do?

A.   O.k'd it.

Q.   You checked it with your original figures?

A.   Yes, sir.

Q.   Analyzed it and found it to be correct?

A.   Yes, sir.

Q.   By the Court: What is that firm?

A.   Curtis & Tompkins.

Q.   By Mr. Vermille: Mr. Beedle, I would like to

(TESTIMONY OF WILLIAM F. BEEDLE)

ask you a hypothetical question. Assuming that the Steamer West Cajoot on a voyage from Manila to Los Angeles by way of Hongkong and San Francisco was carrying fuel oil in her double bottom tanks and was also carrying a cargo of 1,223,583 pounds of cocoanut oil in her No. 3 port and starboard deep tanks, about half in each tank, which deep tanks were located immediately above the double bottom No. 3 tank. Assume also that on October 2nd, the vessel stranded while passing through the Van Diemen Straits in Japan. And that after she was floated from the stranding it was decided to make for Kobe, Japan, as a port of refuge. Assume further that after the stranding, the No. 1 hold and the No. 1 double bottom tank was sounded and it was discovered that sea water had entered said hold and tank. Assume further that after the arrival of the vessel in Kobe and on or about October 5th and before the vessel went into dry dock, it was discovered that there was a leak between the No. 3 double bottom tank and the port deep tank. Assume further that the vessel was put into the dry dock on October 8th. Assume further that either before or shortly after the vessel went into dry dock the cocoanut oil in the deep tanks was examined by taking samples from the different levels in the tanks and it was found that the oil in the starboard deep tank was uncontaminated, but that the oil in the port deep tank was contaminated by contact with fuel oil, this contamination, however, being confined to about the bottom 6 inches of said deep tank. And the upper layers of the tank being apparently clear and uncontaminated. In

(TESTIMONY OF WILLIAM F. BEEDLE)

view of these facts, what should have been done, in your opinion, in regard to the oil in the port deep tanks?

Miss Phillips: Just a moment; your Honor, may I make the objection that that question assumes as a fact that oil was found contaminated only in the bottom 6 inches. The evidence of the witnesses is to the contrary on that. It is assuming something in evidence which has not been testified to.

Mr. Vermille: If your Honor please, if there is any argument about that, I have here in front of me the survey made by and on behalf of the Government by Samuel Reid.

The Court: Well, as I understand it, in this matter of hypothetical questions, counsel is at liberty to ask a hypothetical question from his view of the evidence.

Miss Phillips: Very well, I will withdraw my objection.

Mr. Vermille: Objection withdrawn?

Miss Phillips: I withdraw my objection.

The Court: The accuracy of the question as found or may be found by the Court will go to the weight of the opinion.

Miss Phillips: I think your Honor is right. Yes, I think your Honor is right. I withdraw the objection.

Q. By Mr. Vermille: Did you follow me or would you like to have the Reporter read it?

A. No, I have that. In view of that fact, I would suggest that the oil be removed, the good oil be removed, and that damage be repaired.

(TESTIMONY OF WILLIAM F. BEEDLE.)

Q. Assume that the leak between the two tanks, that is, the double bottom tank and the deep tank, the double bottom fuel oil tank and the deep tank, containing the cocoanut oil, was discovered before dry docking the vessel, was it proper, in your opinion, to dry dock the vessel without making a complete examination of the cocoanut oil in the port deep tank?

Miss Phillips: Just a moment. I don't believe the witness has been qualified to answer that question.

Mr. Vermille: I withdraw that question.

Q. By Mr. Vermille: Assuming that a leak was discovered before the vessel went into dry dock, should there have been an examination of the oil made before the vessel went into dry dock?

A. Ask that question again, please.

Q. Assuming that the leak was discovered before the vessel went into the dry dock, should there have been an examination of the oil before the vessel went into dry dock? Assuming a leak, now, between the fuel—

A. That is, a leak in the double bottom?

Q. A leak in the double bottom?

A. If that were possible; if it were possible to examine that—

Q. No, the oil, I am talking about.

The Court: The cocoanut oil.

Q. By Mr. Vermille: The cocoanut oil. I will read the question again.

A. Read it, please.

Q. Assuming a leak was discovered between the deep tank containing cocoanut oil and the No. 3 double bottom

(TESTIMONY OF WILLIAM F. BEEDLE)

tank containing fuel oil before the vessel went into dry dock, should there have been an examination of the cocoanut oil before the vessel went into dry dock? Do you follow the question?

A.   I would like to know what kind of an examination you meant before I answer the question.

Q.   Any examination.

A.   Yes.

Q.   In your opinion, was it proper, knowing that some of the cocoanut oil in the bottom of the port deep tank was contaminated, to leave the oil in there when it was known the vessel had to go on dry dock and then proceed on a voyage to the United States?

A.   No.

Q.   Now, assume, Captain, that instead of the bottom 6 inches of the port deep tank being found contaminated, all of the cocoanut oil in the port deep tank was found to be somewhat contaminated, would it still be your opinion that the oil should have been removed?

A.   Yes, sir. That is, if it was fractionally contaminated.

Q.   Why.

A.   Because of salvage purposes.

Q.   Just explain to the Court, will you please, what you mean by salvage purposes?

A.   Well, even though the oil is contaminated, it still has a use or a salable value.

Q.   Would the contamination of that cocoanut oil be increased by continuing the voyage?

(TESTIMONY OF WILLIAM F. BEEDLE)

Miss Phillips: Just a moment. The witness has not qualified to answer that question, the navigation of a ship.

The Court: I think the question in a sense calls for a conclusion. The witness might describe the effect of its remaining in the condition that it was, I think, probably. Objection sustained.

Q. By Mr. Vermille: Could you describe or explain to the Court, if there be additional contamination, if the oil was not removed from the vessel, which was about to proceed on a voyage across the Pacific Ocean, which oil had been somewhat contaminated?

Miss Phillips: It seems to me counsel is asking the same question in a different form. If he wants the witness to describe what he considers the process of contamination and increase of contamination, I have no objection.

The Court: Well, the question in effect is whether the contamination was increased by the continuous voyage. The witness will answer the question.

Miss Phillips: Exception.

A. That depends on the state of the oil.

Q. By Mr. Vermille: Assuming the oil was in liquid state at the time the contamination was discovered?

A. It would have a tendency to diffuse, the contamination would have a tendency to diffuse through the oil with the rolling of the ship.

Q. Have you any samples of cocoanut oil with you?

A. Yes, sir.

Q. The samples contained in there?

(TESTIMONY OF WILLIAM F. BEEDLE)

A. Yes, sir.

Q. You stated, I think, that you made the survey of this oil. Was anybody present when you made this survey at Wilmington?

A. Yes, sir, Mr. Bennett, of the L. A. Soap Company.

Q. Who else?

A. Captain Curtis.

Q. Captain Curtis was present?

A. Part of the time at least.

Q. I have here a letter dated December 7, 1927, on the letter-head of Curtis & Tompkins, which is marked "Respondents for identification Bower No. 2." Mr. Bower was the chemist in Washington, D. C. I will offer that letter in evidence.

Miss Phillips: Well, may I have a look at that?

Mr. Vermille: Well, you have had it attached to the deposition.

Miss Phillips: Oh, well, that is already in evidence. Why offer it again?

Mr. Vermille: I thought it was for identification, that is all.

Miss Phillips: No, I think that is actually in evidence.

Mr. Vermille: All right. It is in evidence, then.

Q. By Mr. Vermille: I ask you to look at that letter and tell me whether or not you have made up samples in accordance with the various grades shown in this letter, grade No. 1, grade No. 2 and grade No. 3, of the cocoanut oil?

(TESTIMONY OF WILLIAM F. BEEDLE)

A. I have, yes.

Q. Will you produce the sample of the grade marked No. 1 of the cocoanut oil as it arrived here at Wilmington?

(Witness produces sample.)

Q. By Mr. Vermille: Now, where was that oil taken from?

A. This oil? That oil was—you mean the sample here?

Q. According to the report there, is that what you call grade No. 1?

A. That oil there has the same color as grade No. 1 had at the time it was discharged.

Q. In other words, this is not the original oil?

A. No, no.

Q. But you made up one to mate?

A. Made up one.

Q. Made up one to mate. Where was grade No. 1 oil taken from?

A. From the top.

Q. The top of the tank?

A. Yes, sir.

Q. Now, have you made up a sample of grade No. 2?

A. This is grade No. 2. (witness producing sample.)

Q. Now, where was that oil taken from?

A. From the lower level. These pumpings were principally starting from the top. Grade No. 1 was taken from the top.

Q. Then grade No. 2 was taken next?

A. Next.

(Testimony by William F. Beedle)

Q. Then grade No. 3?

A. It was taken down near the bottom.

Q. Just a minute. I show you another sample and ask you what that is?

A. This sample is a sample of crude cocoanut oil with the approximate color rating as that which was shipped.

Q. Is that the oil then approximately that was taken from the starboard tank of the vessel made up from the sample?

A. Yes.

Q. In other words, that was the color of the oil as it arrived in the starboard tank of the West Cajoot?

A. Approximate color.

Q. These other three samples are the various colors of the oil that was in the port tank starting with the top of the tank showing the lighter?

A. Yes, sir.

Q. And going down to the middle showing the darker and going down to the bottom showing the darkest?

A. Yes, sir.

Mr. Vermille: I would like to introduce those samples of oil in evidence.

Miss Phillips: No objection.

The Court: Well, now, are these samples of the identical oil?

Mr. Vermille: Samples made up from the analysis that was made at the time.

The Court: Samples made up by the witness?

Mr. Vermille: By this witness.

(TESTIMONY BY WILLIAM F. BEEDLE)

The Court: To agree in chemical content with the—

Mr. Vermille: And color.

The Court: With the actual samples that were analyzed, I suppose?

A. Yes.

The Court: He nodded his head. That was the only way he could talk.

A. Yes, sir, in color, your Honor.

Q. By the Court: Now, I am to understand that in your opinion if samples were taken and brought here from the depths that you have described, they would in your judgment resemble or closely resemble, or in fact exactly approximate the samples that you have?

A. Yes, sir.

The Court: All right.

Mr. Vermille: I might add this for your Honor's information: The Government has not introduced any samples of the cocoanut oil. As a matter of fact, all of the samples that were taken of the cocoanut oil and copra have been lost.

Miss Phillips: That is not correct.

Mr. Vermille: If not, I make a demand—

Miss Phillips: Just a moment. Counsel misstates part of the testimony that has been taken and part of the stipulation. The samples taken were shipped to Washington and were analyzed pursuant to a stipulation between counsel's correspondent in the east and the Government chemist back there analyzed it and testified on it. We have no samples other than the samples which went to Washington and were analyzed. I have searched the

(Testimony by William F. Beedle)

western continent for those samples and I find no others, but counsel saying there were no samples, we have never produced any, is contrary to the stipulation and to the testimony of a witness.

Mr. Vermille: There were two samples sent over here from Kobe. The deposition shows there were at least ten different samples taken from various levels of the vessel and I understand,—I may be wrong, but I understand from the testimony that the Government only received, or you only received, for analysis, and there was only analyzed two samples, one from the starboard and one from the port deep tank, is that correct?

Miss Phillips: That is correct. The rest were left on board the ship and we have not been able to find them.

Mr. Vermille: And they were not turned over here for analysis?

Miss Phillips: No, they were not. What I was objecting to, was that we haven't produced any. Well, we have produced them and they were stipulated to.

Mr. Vermille: Well, I meant in court.

Miss Phillips: All right.

The Court: These colors purport to represent the oil after its arrival in Wilmington?

Mr. Vermille: That is correct.

The Court: All right. Have any exemplars, if that is what they may be called, been made up to agree with those sent to Washington?

Mr. Vermille: Well, that is the trouble, if your Honor please. In Washington—I wish counsel would correct me if I am wrong—

(Testimony by William F. Beedle)

The Court: Well, I just want to know if they are?

Mr. Vermille: No. The analysis made by the Bureau of Standards in Washington was not complete.

Miss Phillips: Well now, I think, your Honor, he is making the argument now.

Mr. Vermille: I am just making this statement. They were not complete enough or sufficient enough from which anyone could make up samples.

The Court: That is your view at least.

Mr. Vermille: That is my view, and I think I can prove it.

The Court: All right.

Q. By Mr. Vermille: I now ask you, Mr. Beedle, to take a look at what purports to be the Bureau of Standards report marked "Respondents' exhibit Bower No. 1," and ask what that appears to be?

The Court: Are these samples to be placed in evidence? They are, I believe?

Miss Phillips: He has already offered them.

Mr. Vermille: The samples are in evidence, I believe.

The Court: You want one exhibit number?

Mr. Vermille: I think one exhibit number will cover them.

The Clerk: That will be Respondents' exhibit A.

Mr. Vermille: Do you call the Government respondent?

The Clerk: I have been calling the Government the libellant. There are three cases.

(TESTIMONY BY WILLIAM F. BEEDLE)

The Court: You were trying to accommodate this witness, I suppose?

Mr. Vermille: Well, I see now the cross examination will probably take it into tomorrow.

Miss Phillips: No, my cross examination will be very short.

Mr. Vermille: Well then, that will be perfectly all right if your Honor wants to adjourn.

The Court: You are going to keep him over, you mean?

Miss Phillips: My cross examination will be very short, your Honor, if your Honor wants to conclude with the witness.

The Court: We will take the recess at this time, then, gentlemen. It is after 5 o'clock. Recess until 10 o'clock tomorrow morning.

(Whereupon, a recess was taken to 10 o'clock A. M., Thursday, May 4, 1933.)

LOS ANGELES, CALIFORNIA, THURSDAY, MAY 4, 1933.
10 o'clock A. M.

———

The Court: Very well. Proceed.

Miss Phillips: If your Honor recollects, Mr. Beedle was on the stand at the close yesterday.

The Court: Did it not finish then?

Mr. Vermille: No, I had not finished with him.

The Court: Oh yes, this is the witness who was on the stand.

(TESTIMONY BY WILLIAM F. BEEDLE)

WILLIAM F. BEEDLE,

resumed the stand for further direct examination, being previously duly sworn, testified as follows:

DIRECT EXAMINATION (Continued)

By Mr. Vermille:

Q. Mr. Beedle, you have used the term, or the term has been used, "Lovibond color." I would like to have you explain to the Court what is meant by "Lovibond color."

A. "Lovibond color" is determined by using an instrument whereby you can read through a column of oil and match by standard glasses that red and yellow color in the oil of the column.

Q. By the Court: What do you call that; what term do you apply to it?

A. Lovibond.

Q. That is the name of a person, a discoverer?

A. It was conceived by a man in English by the name of Lovibond, and you use small glasses that are red to certain tints and are standardized to those tints; also yellow glasses of the same nature.

Q. Well, is that supposed to be a test?

A. Of the color.

Q. Merely the color?

A. Merely the color.

Q. But, of course, the color indicates certain things to a chemist, I suppose?

A. Yes, sir.

Q. Indicating chemical contents of the body of oil?

(TESTIMONY BY WILLIAM F. BEEDLE)

A.   No, not always. Most all vegetable oils have red and yellow color and sales ofttimes are made on a maximum color.

Q.   All right. Proceed.

Q.   By Mr. Vermille: Is the Lovibond color a standard term used by all chemists in testing various vegetable oils for color, is that the standard form established?

A.   It is for vegetable oil.

Q.   They all use that Lovibond color to test the color of the vegetable oil?

Q.   By the Court: You don't regard petroleum as a vegetable oil?

A.   No, sir.

Q.   By Mr. Vermille: Will you please explain to the Court what you do regard as vegetable oils?

A.   Oils expressed or extracted from the seeds of nuts or vegetables or herbs, plants, trees.

Q.   What are some of the standard vegetable oils here that the common term is used around that we all know?

A.   Cocoanut oil, sesame oil.

The Court: Don't overlook the castor oil. I guess that is a vegetable oil.

A.   Castor oil. Well, there is —— seed oil.

Q.   By Mr. Vermille: Linseed oil?

A.   Linseed, cottonseed oil.

Q.   As I remember, when you were on the stand last night or yesterday at the close of the session, you had before you a report of the Bureau of Standards which purports to be a report of the condition of a sample.

(Testimony by William F. Beedle)

not knowing where that sample, what part of the tank that sample came from of the vessel. I will show you now Curtis & Tompkins' report of an analysis made of the cocoanut oil on arrival here at Wilmington and ask you if it is possible to compare those two reports, that is, you as a chemist, with reference to the grade of the cocoanut oil, the color of the cocoanut oil—well, the color of the cocoanut oil?

A. You cannot compare the two reports as to color.

Q. Would it be possible, looking first at the report of the Bureau of Standards, then the report of Curtis & Tompkins, the report of Curtis & Tompkins dated December 7th and marked "Respondents for identification Bower No. 2," and the report of the Bureau of Standards marked "Respondents exhibit Bower No. 1," what do both analyses show with reference to the condition of the cocoanut oil? Is it possible to compare it?

The Court: Say with reference to what?

Mr. Vermille: Of the cocoanut oil.

The Court: To what of the cocoanut oil?

Mr. Vermille: The condition of the cocoanut oil at Kobe and the condition of the cocoanut oil on arrival at Wilmington?

The Court: Yes. Now, this is, as I understand it, as I recall it, the sample taken at Kobe?

Mr. Vermille: Sample taken at Kobe with the sample taken here.

The Court: The sample taken at Los Angeles?

Mr. Vermille: The sample taken at Los Angeles upon arrival of the vessel here.

(Testimony by William F. Beedle)

A. The report of the Bureau of Standards gives the color of the port tank as dark brownish amber.

Q. By the Court: You are speaking of the Kobe sample?

A. This is the Bureau of Standards, Respondents Exhibit Bower No. 1, report from the Bureau of Standards. The odor is cocoanut oil. The condition, "Clear with small amount of sediment." Saponification No. 255.3. On the starboard side the color is "dark straw, odor, cocoanut oil; condition, cloudy." The saponification No. 255.8. The contamination would not to much of a degree be indicated in the saponification number and, of course, as he reports color as dark brownish amber and dark straw, there is no way of knowing the amount of yellow or red that were in the samples.

Q. By the Court: You have nothing but the color?

A. Well, I would say that describing a color as dark brownish amber would not be very exact as to the actual color compared with Lovibond tintometer readings.

Q. By Mr. Vermille: I show you a sample marked "Lovibond 260 yellow, 44 red, 260 yellow, 44 red, 5 1/4," and ask you if that is a dark brownish color?

A. I beg your pardon. That is 5 1/4 inch column.

Q. Oh, 5 1/4 inch column, 260 yellow, 44 red. Is that a dark brownish color?

A. That is very difficult to say. If I may enlighten the Court with this, several years ago we went into the colors of fish oils as to pale, straw color, and in judging those colors, there was a wide range of yellow and red allowable before it was classed as the lower grade.

(TESTIMONY OF WILLIAM F. BEEDLE)

Q. By the Court: You conclude with reference to the fish oil that color was a difficult test to apply?

A. By stating whether it is straw or light.

Q. Yes. That would probably depend on the test or observation of the individual making the test. It might differ with different individuals.

A. The personal element entered into the—

Q. Yes.

A. —determination.

Q. By Mr. Vermille: Did that same situation exist with vegetable oil, I mean with cocoanut oil?

A. In reading cocoanut oils, you read very closely, using a Lovibond tintometer.

Q. Well then, what does it mean if somebody tells you it is a slight brownish amber? Does that mean anything to you?

Miss Phillips: Did you say slight brownish amber? I think you are mistaken.

Q. By Mr. Vermille: Beg your pardon. Dark brownish amber?

A. No, it does not.

Q. Would you call that a dark brownish amber?

Miss Phillips: Which exhibit are you pointing to?

Q. By Mr. Vermille: I am pointing to exhibit yellow 260, red 5—no, 1050 yellow, 260 red, 5 1/4.

A. Well, I would say that that has a greenish cast.

Q. Showing you again the sample 260 yellow, 44 red—

Miss Phillips: Which is the number of that? You

(TESTIMONY OF WILLIAM F. BEEDLE)

have offered them in evidence and it is just as easy to refer to the number.

The Clerk: They are all exhibit A, your Honor.

Mr. Vermille: I think we had better change them and mark them exhibits 1, 2, 3 and 4.

Miss Phillips: Yes.

Mr. Vermille: I think we will mark the crude cocoanut oil Lovibond color—

The Clerk: As A-1

Mr. Vermille: 35.2 red as exhibit A.

The Clerk: Exhibit A-1.

Mr. Vermille: We will mark the next one, the next one is 260 yellow, 44 red.

The Clerk: That will be A-2.

Mr. Vermille: The next one is 370 yellow, 68 red.

The Clerk: That will be A-3.

Mr. Vermille: The next one will be 1050 yellow, 260 red.

The Clerk: That will be A-4.

Miss Phillips: Now, the witness when he first was identifying these as having been made up according to certain specifications, he referred to a particular report. I think for the purpose of having it clear in the record he ought now to identify the various samples, 1, 2, 3 and 4, while he made them up.

The Court: Yes.

Miss Phillips: Otherwise, we are all mixed up in the record. Pardon me making the suggestion.

Mr. Vermille: I think that is a good suggestion. Thank you very much.

(TESTIMONY BY WILLIAM F. BEEDLE)

Miss Phillips: But we would all like to have it made perfectly clear.

Mr. Vermille: It will clarify the record.

Q. By Mr. Vermille: I show you exhibit A-1. I also show you purported analysis made by you in reference to the cocoanut oil on arrival at Wilmington on the West Cajoot, and ask you what that exhibit A-1 refers to?

A. This exhibit is not represented in this analysis.

Q. Well, what does that exhibit A-1 represent in accordance with the survey that was made and introduced in evidence as an exhibit which you have checked? That is an additional part of that letter of Curtis & Tompkins dated December 2nd.

A. This is an analyses or a color reading made on the oil from a sample drawn December 1, 1927, at the plant of the Vegetable Oil Products Company, Wilmington, from the starboard tank, SS. West Cajoot, and the color was found to be 30 yellow, 5.3 red. This standard was made up to be 30 yellow, 5.2 red, a tenth less.

The Court: Referring to A-1?

Q. By Mr. Vermille: What would be the difference in color between 30 yellow and 5.3 red—

Miss Phillips: What would be the difference in color between that,—I think that is so clear.

Mr. Vermille: I just wanted to bring it out so the Court will understand.

A. It would take an expert to distinguish the difference of a tenth in a Lovibond tintometer.

Q. By the Court: Well, this Lovibond test, is that

(TESTIMONY OF WILLIAM F. BEEDLE)

a mechanical device, that is, procured or done with a mechanical device?

A. It is done with the eye, your Honor.

Q. With the eye?

A. In a specified instrument with a certain amount of light reflected through the column.

The Court: I understand.

Q. By Mr. Vermille: Now, I show you exhibit A-2, and ask you what that represents?

A. That represents the grade as taken from the top portion of the port deep tank aboard the West Cajoot September 1, 1927.

Q. That was made upon the arrival of the vessel here at Wilmington, the West Cajoot?

A. Yes, sir.

Q. I show you exhibit A-3 and ask you what that represents?

A. This represents that part of the tank pumped after the first portion had been removed from the port deep tank of the West Cajoot December 1, 1927.

Q. Now, I show you exhibit A-4 and ask you what that represents?

A. This represents the last portion of the oil to be removed from the port deep tank aboard the West Cajoot December 1, 1927.

Q. By the Court: Now, let me see if I am clear on this. When the vessel got to—

Mr. Vermille: Wilmington?

Q. By the Court: —Wilmington, samples were taken of both tanks?

(TESTIMONY BY WILLIAM F. BEEDLE)

Mr. Vermille: This witness was present, your Honor.

The Court: What?

Mr. Vermille: This witness was present. He was the one that took the samples.

The Court: Yes, that is the situation. These samples were sent to the Bureau of Standards in Washington for analysis.

Mr. Vermille: No, your Honor.

The Court: They were sent then to this firm in San Francisco?

Mr. Vermille: Curtis & Tompkins.

The Court: What?

Mr. Vermille: Curtis & Tompkins of San Francisco.

The Court: Curtis & Tompkins in San Francisco for analysis. The samples are not now in existence, they are not available. The firm made an analysis and the 'report is what you hold in your hand, what you are reading from?

Mr. Vermille: That is correct, and which has been introduced in evidence.

The Court: Yes. Now then, these are not the identical samples analyzed, but they are a product made
                                                    and
up by you here in Los Angeles to correspond/ in your judgment it equalled the samples that were actually examined?

A. In color, yes.

Q. By the Court: Yes, in color, in color only. They equal in color, but the color is the only test that you can apply to the chemical contents. What I mean to say, the

(TESTIMONY BY WILLIAM F. BEEDLE)

color is the only test that you apply to the oil, is that correct?

A. No, your Honor. The analysis of Curtis & Tompkins also gives the free fatty acids, as oleic, moist, involved matter.

Q. The chemical contents, in other words?

A. Yes, these samples were made up from crude cocoanut oil that has recently been produced which may have a different free fatty acid content.

Q. Well, where is the chemical—here it is right here.

A. Yes.

Q. In making these up, did you make them up from the chemical percentage given there?

A. No, sir.

Q. Well, how did you make them up?

A. I took the crude cocoanut oil, read the Lovibond colors, and took fuel oil of approximately .96 gravity C., and denatured them to the extent of the colors, you see.

Q. Denatured which? Both the fuel oil and the other?

A. No, denatured the cocoanut oil with fuel oil to match the color.

Q. I see. Well, suppose that you had taken three—

A. Fatty acids—

Q. Fatty acids 3 per cent and moist and volatile matter in the regular proportions, then would you have a compound similar to those exhibits A-2 and so forth?

A. In color, yes.

(TESTIMONY BY WILLIAM F. BEEDLE)

Q. You would have?

A. Yes.

Q. However, that is not the way you did do it?

A. No, sir.

Q. You did it by following this color test that you have described, whatever the name is?

A. Lovibond.

The Court: All right. Go on.

Q. By Mr. Vermille: Now, if you had made an analysis of the sample with the various ingredients—if you had made samples containing the various items, as shown on the Curtis & Tompkins' report, namely, the free fatty acids, moisture involved in the mass, unsaponifiable matter—I will start over. If you had made up a sample from Curtis & Tompkins' report with the same proportion of free fatty acids, moist, volatile matter, insoluble impurities, total unsaponifiable matter, unsaponifiable matter in undamaged part of cargo, with the same color content on this report of Curtis & Tompkins, would the color of those samples be the same?

A. Yes, approximately the same.

Q. By the Court: Where do you get your 100 per cent?

A. There is no 100 per cent on there.

Q. Well, in giving the chemical contents of anything must not the sum of them all equal 100 per cent?

A. It is not usual,—in the analysis of fat it is not usually shown.

Q. What is the red? Do I understand that in this compound of grade 1 the percentage either by weight

(TESTIMONY OF WILLIAM F. BEEDLE)

or volume, or what ever it may be, of free fatty acids is
3.28 per cent out of 100 per cent?

A.   Yes, sir.

Q.   Well, what makes—you account for here something like 3 and a fraction per cent. What makes up the
100 per cent?

A.   The balance is the cocoanut oil.

Q.   I see.

A.   Nuts are composed of fatty acids and glycerine in
combination, or glycerides. In decomposition the fatty
acids split to a certain extent and form free fatty acids
and glycerine. And the free fatty acid content, as oleic
in this particular case, was 3.28 per cent.

Q.   What does "unsaponifiable" mean?

A.   Unsaponifiable is a matter that will not saponify
and make soap.

Q.   Oh, I see. That cannot be made into soap?

A.   Yes.

The Court: Very well.

Q.   By Mr. Vermille: Will you please look at the
two reports again, the report of Curtis & Tompkins and
the report made by the Bureau of Standards, and advise
whether or not the report of Curtis & Tompkins indicates any increase or decrease in contamination over
the analysis made by you at Wilmington for Curtis &
Tompkins?

A.   I would like to hear that question again.

(Question read by the Reporter.)

A.   Do you mean—

Q.   By Mr. Vermille: Is it possible to determine

(TESTIMONY OF WILLIAM F. BEEDLE)

whether there is any increase or decrease in contamination of the cocoanut oil from looking at those two reports?

The Court: Well, between what?

Q. By Mr. Vermille: Between the time one report was made and the sample taken at Kobe.

The Court: Oh yes.

Q. By Mr. Vermille: The Bureau of Standards report made a report of the sample taken at Kobe. Curtis & Tompkins made an analysis of the sample taken at Wilmington. Now, is it possible from looking at these two reports—

A. No.

Q. Do they indicate any increase or decrease in contaminination?

A. I could not tell.

Q. Well, why can you not tell?

A. The only figure as reported by the Bureau of Standards is that of saponification number and the report of Curtis & Tompkins does not report that determination.

Q. Does the report made by the Bureau of Standards indicate the extent of the contamination?

A. Not completely.

Q. Is that the reason why it is impossible to compare the two reports?

A. Yes, sir.

Q. Looking at the report of the Bureau of Standards and looking at exhibit A-2, exhibit A-3 and exhibit A-4, can you tell which exhibit that report might cover?

(TESTIMONY OF WILLIAM F. BEEDLE)

A. No, sir.

Q. Assuming that the entire port tank at Kobe was slightly contaminated, would the agitation of the vessel tend to increase that contamination?

Miss Phillips: Just a moment, your Honor; that question has been asked and answered. That was a part of the direct examination yesterday.

Mr. Vermille: I don't remember whether I asked that or not.

The Court: Someone has testified with respect to that. I don't remember whether it was this witness.

Q. By Mr. Vermille: Would the heating at Wilmington tend to increase the contamination?

A. Yes, sir.

Q. Is it necessary to heat cocoanut oil arriving from the Orient for discharge before you can discharge it?

A. Yes.

Q. Will you please explain to the Court the method used in discharging the cocoanut oil at Wilmington, as to how you discharged it?

A. You mean shore equipment and the gear use aboard ship?

Q. Just how you took the cocoanut oil out of the port deep tank?

A. The cocoanut oil was discharged by a centrifugal electric pump lowered as the oil level lowered.

Q. In other words, you discharged the oil from the top first?

A. Yes, sir.

Q. Why did you do that?

(TESTIMONY BY WILLIAM F. BEEDLE)

A. Well, that is the custom at this plant, I might say, first, and then in this particular case we would certainly find the contamination increased as you went down in depth.

Q. Now, before you discharged the cocoanut oil, did you take samples of it?

A. Yes, sir.

Q. And what did you determine from an examination of those samples as to the condition of the cocoanut oil in the port deep tank?

A. That it was contaminated fractionally, that is, the lighter one being on top.

Q. In other words, the contamination increased as you went down toward the bottom of the deep tank?

A. Yes, sir.

The Court: Which was the good tank, the port or the starboard?

Mr. Vermille: The starboard tank. The port tank was the tank that contained the contaminated oil. That is all.

CROSS EXAMINATION

By Miss Phillips:

Q. Mr. Beedle, there is a question I wanted to ask you that is not—I don't quite understand in my own mind. The Bureau of Standards' report gives a saponification number. I am referring now, your Honor, to the report which is attached to the deposition of the Witness Bower. It says the saponification number of the star-board tank was 255.3 and of the—no, the port side, 255.3, and the starboard side 255.8, and you said that the

Curtis & Tompkins' report did not give a saponification number. I will confess I don't know what is meant by a saponification number.

A. A saponification number is the parts of potassium hydroxide that will unite with the oil to form soap. In other words, that is reported in milligrams of potassium hydroxide per gram of fat used. Does that explain it?

Q. I think it begins to percolate.

A. We take a known strength lye solution and saponify a known amount of fat and farther on determine the amount of lye that was actually used in saponifying that known amount of fat, and that is reported as the number.

Q. I take it from what you said that that is an extremely accurate measure or method of determining the capacity of a given product to be turned into soap?

A. Yes, it is an accurate measure, but there are a number of influencing factors that might be other than fuel oil. Moisture may influence that saponification number.

Q. I see. Whereas, the Curtis & Tompkins' report specifies, for instance, in the three samples, it gives the unsaponifiable number of the three samples, .22 in the first, that is of the top sample, .24 of the second, .37 per cent of the bottom-most here. It does not give the saponification number, however. That was why you found it difficult to compare the two reports?

A. Yes.

Q. Because the two individual chemists were using different tests of saponification ability, is that correct?

(TESTIMONY OF WILLIAM F. BEEDLE)

A. Those samples were kept 90 days that I know of. That is our custom.

Q. They simply don't keep them after that?

A. No.

Q. I think, as a matter of fact, the man in Washington did the same thing. People don't keep stuff around indefinitely like that. Mr. Beedle, just a moment or two ago, you described the method of discharge, that is, by a pump, taking the top levels first, which have been made liquid, and then going down, at Wilmington?

A. Yes.

Q. You said that the actual heating of the oil at Wilmington in order to discharge it tended to increase the contamination?

A. Yes.

Q. Did I understand you correctly there?

A. Yes.

Q. And it is not necessary to heat oil in order to discharge it, is it?

A. Cocoanut oil, yes.

Miss Phillips: Cocoanut oil; yes. I will ask the Court's indulgence just a moment. I had some notes that I made.

The Court: We will have a 5 minute recess at this time.

Miss Phillips: Thank you, your Honor.

(Short recess.)

(After recess.)

Q. By Miss Phillips: Mr. Beedle, just before our short recess I had asked you the question whether the

(TESTIMONY BY WILLIAM F. BEEDLE)

heating of the oil in order to discharge it, which was necessary in order to discharge it, whether that would increase contamination, and you said you thought it would?

A. Yes.

Q. That is because you think that the practice of heating would stir it up?

A. Circulate the oil.

Q. Circulate it up. The samples that were taken from the—the last two samples were taken, were they not, after this heating had been going on and after the discharge?

A. I would have to refer to that.

Q. I wonder if you won't refer to your report on that, page 2 of your report. I think that gives the time of the taking of the samples.

Mr. Vermille: You mean this?

Q. By Miss Phillips: Yes. I notice your report says that the first sample seems to have been taken at 10:40 A. M., that is the top sample at that time. That the bottom sample was drawn that evening at 7:30 which represented the second pumping, and the last sample apparently was taken after it was pumped into a storage tank, the storage plant. I wonder if I understand that correctly?

A. Yes.

Q. That is on page 2. Correct me if I misunderstood it. I don't remember the time of taking the samples without reading your report. Can you tell us?

(TESTIMONY BY WILLIAM F. BEEDLE)

A. All right. The bottom sample was drawn at 7:30 P. M., which represented the second pumping from the port tank.

Q. That is, after the top had been pumped off, had been heating all through the day and had been pumping off, is that right?

A. The steam was applied, if you will look at this report, the steam was applied. Pumping began at the port tank at 11:06 A. M. and was delivered to storage tank No. 1 from the tank scale. Pumping stopped at 12:30 P. M., at which time all the melted oil had been taken off. About 4 feet 6 inches of hard oil remaining in the bottom.

Q. Now, I am trying to get the time of the taking of these last samples. That is what I am getting at. The first sample, apparently, was taken from the liquid oil at the time pumping started. Other witnesses show that that oil had been started by heating, I believe, from San Francisco on the way down so as to facilitate or hasten the discharge. That is, your top samples showed that. Now then your top sample is taken from the liquid oil on arrival; that is pumped off. And the second sample,— that is what I am trying to get at,—was taken when? The report there shows it.

A. 7:30 P. M.

Q. That is, after the heating, the pumping or the heating of this second level, is that right?

A. Yes, the heat was applied at 12:30 P. M.

Q. Then your second sample was taken after this heat had been applied; it had been liquified and con-

(TESTIMONY OF WILLIAM F. BEEDLE)

tamination increased, as you say, by the process of heating?

A.   Yes.

Q.   The last sample was taken when?

A.   There is no record of it here. It was taken at the tank scale.

Q.   That is after it is pumped out into the storage plant, isn't it?

A.   Yes.

Q.   Mr. Beedle, you just testified on direct examination that cocoanut oil seemed to be composed of acids, or did you say glycerine or glyceride?

A.   They are called glycerides, a combination of fatty acids and glycerine.

Q.   Tell me, is it true that cocoanut oil is very sensitive to contamination and odors and all that sort of thing? Is it a sensitive product to contamination?

A.   I would say in the crude state not more so than other vegetable oils.

Q.   Well then, I will extend my question. Are vegetable oils, generally speaking, sensitive to be contaminated by foreign substances?

A.   Do you mean by "foreign substances" fuel oil?

Q.   Well, I will explain what is in my mind. I observed that at Manila when they were preparing these tanks for the reception of this oil, the tanks were hosed out with salt water and scrubbed with copra meal, then washed out with   solution, and all that sort of thing, and the witnesses at San Francisco, Captain Heppell and Captain Jory, Captain Jory also testified

(Testimony by William F. Beedle)

that that was quite necessary, that you have got to have a very clean receptacle for cocoanut oil. Now, my question is, is that because cocoanut oil is sensitive to oils and foreign substances, generally?

A. Yes.

Q. It is. Using a very homely illustration, we have all had the experience of having in our refrigerator, I think, milk or cream or butter and then finding some morning that it has a clear taste to it, and then opening up our refrigerator and finding that accidentally we have put something in there that has a very strong odor, and the butter and the cream absorbed it. That is a very homely illustration. Is something of the same sort likely to happen with cocoanut oil?

A. Not so much with cocoanut oil.

Q. Not so much?

A. In other words, you could unstop the samples and I doubt very much if you could smell the fuel oil.

Q. But the actual—

A. The cocoanut oil odor would predominate.

Q. I wonder, can you tell me just how much fuel oil you put in, let us say—excuse me, your Honor—I am pointing now to sample A-2. Have you any idea how much fuel oil you actually put in A-2, A-3 and A-4 in order to get these various shades of darkness? Was it as much as a teaspoonful?

A. Oh no, no.

Q. It was not.

A. I did not make those samples up, though I checked the colors.

(TESTIMONY OF WILLIAM F. BEEDLE)

A. No.

Q. And that in the No. 2, which is the lighter of the three contaminated, you think that a drop could certainly have caused that?

The Court: No, he says a part of a drop.

Q. By Miss Phillips: A part of a drop. I am not trying to pin you too hard.

A. A part of a drop. Possibly a drop in this.

Q. Wait a minute. The second one, possibly a drop in this? The witness pointing to exemplar A-3. Mr. Beedle, we have been talking about the temperature, now then, at which cocoanut oil solidifies or becomes —well, solidifies is the word, or what is the other word we have been using for it? Congealed. Can you give us the temperature at which that is common?

A. Approximately 75 degrees.

Q. Approximately 75?

A. Fahrenheit.

Q. I believe a witness in San Francisco the other day said 72 to 75.

A. Yes, ma'am.

Q. Would you agree to that?

A. Yes, ma'am.

Q. Now, on direct examination yesterday afternoon you were asked the question whether if the contaminated oil was left in the No. 3 deep tank, whether the contamination would increase. Your answer, as I have it in my notes from yesterday afternoon, was, "yes, if the oil was in a liquid state, the rolling of the ship would diffuse it. Those are my notes that I have on that. Of

(TESTIMONY BY WILLIAM F. BEEDLE)

course, I take notes rather rapidly when the witness is testifying, but if that is a fair statement of your answer, would you explain it a little further? Is that about what you said?

A.   Yes.

Q.   All right, then. Can you elaborate a little bit on that?

A.   In a liquid state, the movement of the oil would be such that there would be a slight circulation in the rolling of the vessel. And in that way the fuel oil would be diffused through the tank.

Q.   Well now, let me use another very homely illustration. I don't mean that I always take things from a refrigerator to illustrate. But the illustration of making a salad dressing that most of us at one time or other have tried our hand at, you shake the vinegar and the oil in order to get an emulsion. Is that practically what is happening in the ship?

A.   The movement of the oil.

Q.   The movement of the oil itself in the ship causes the diffusion of the fuel oil up through into the cocoanut oil?

A.   Yes.

Q.   Is that about it?

A.   About it.

Q.   I want to refer to your report, page 2 of that report, and I want to see if you agree with the testimony of Captain Curtis on the stand yesterday afternoon. And, by the way, you were here in court when Captain Curtis was testifying, were you not?

(Testimony by William F. Beedle)

A. Yes.

Q. He said yesterday afternoon, testified, as I have it, that the oil at the time—I am not sure that he said at the time he started discharging or at the time of the ship's arrival, that the liquid oil was 12 to 13 feet deep. Do you agree with that?

A. Not exactly, because the depth of the tank is 20 feet 6 inches. To the top of the hatch the manhole plate was 2½ inches.

Q. Inches?

A. Inches.

Q. Yes.

A. And your outage was 5 feet ¾ of an inch. It was estimated—

Q. Well, all I am getting at now is, how much of this tank was liquid oil and how much was hard oil. Reading from your report page 2 about the 10th line from the top, I read: "Port side, 10:40 A.M., core sample to depth of 13 feet, beyond which it was hard oil."

A. Yes.

Q. Now, I take it from that that you thought the top 13 feet of that container or that tank contained liquid oil at the point at which you took the sample, about 13 feet. Do you agree?

A. That was 13 feet down from the tank top.

Q. From the tank top?

A. There is where the confusion is.

Q. From the tank top. Now, possibly Captain Curtis —that was not in my mind yesterday.

A. Yes.

(TESTIMONY BY WILLIAM F. BEEDLE)

Q. By the way, you took this,—you were there together measuring, were you not?

A. Yes.

Q. I think possibly I did not clear that up with Captain Curtis' testimony. Now then, how much hard oil was there below this liquid oil?

A. Approximately 4 feet 6 inches.

Q. Then your figure as to the amount of hard cocoanut oil agrees with his, does it?

A. Yes.

Q. Now, it is a fact, isn't it, that prior to arrival at Wilmington the chief engineer had heated the top levels of this tank in order to be able to start discharging, isn't it?

A. I don't know.

Q. Oh, you don't know. Isn't it a fact that your firm in San Francisco gave him instructions so to do?

A. Yes.

Q. I believe that all appears in the testimony of other witnesses. I won't go further on that. I observe that about the middle of your report you say that there was about 4 feet 6 inches hard oil to the bottom and that tongues of it were frozen to the skin of the ship and to the forward bulk head. I don't quite understand that. What do you mean that tongues of it were frozen to the skin of the ship and to the forward bulk head?

A. Thick walls of frozen cocoanut oil on the skin on the side of the vessel and on the forward bulk head.

Q. Well now, I wonder—I can always see a thing better when I have a picture of it or a sketch of it. I

(Testimony by William F. Beedle)

wonder if you can illustrate to me and to the Court, having a careful eye to those bottles, samples—let's move them over. How do you mean that, frozen to the sides?

A. This is the skin of a ship. There was cocoanut oil frozen to the sides.

Q. All right. Mark it "frozen." Now, Mark your level of hard oil as showing how your level of hard oil relates to that frozen to the side.

A. You want to remember I did not get down in this tank.

Q. I know, but you have something here on which you base that statement that it was frozen. We understand you are only giving us an approximate idea.

A. Yes.

Q. Let me see if I understand you. As we understand you, this is not drawn to scale. You have here the 4½ feet of hard oil. May I mark this "hard oil"?

A. Yes.

Q. And to the side of that,—this is on the skin, whereas in here, this is hard oil, while in here is the liquid oil?

A. Yes.

Q. And is that on both sides?

A. Well, we are taking this as a port tank.

Q. The port tank. The other side is the bulkhead?

A. We have an inverted bulkhead here.

Q. I understand you. And the fuel oil will be down here?

A. Yes.

(TESTIMONY OF WILLIAM F. BEEDLE)

Q.   The fuel oil tank.   I see.   So the situation is, then, that the oil melted in the center down to a degree, 4 feet and a half from the bottom, where you struck hard oil right across, but on the sides right on up there is oil still that did not stay melted?

A.   Yes, on the skin of the ship and on the forward bulkhead.

Q.   On the skin of the ship and on the forward bulkhead.   Have you any idea how far up this freezing on the sides stayed, or just approximately?   I don't mean to pin you down to exact inches here.

A.   Well, I would say it would be approximately the height of the level of the oil in the tank.

Q.   Somewhere near the level of the oil?

A.   Yes.

Q.   Well, that is near enough.   We won't try to proceed any further.   Just a moment.   I would like to have a little bit more explanation about how the heating and the discharge by a centrifugal pump might increase the contamination?

A.   The discharge by a centrifugal pump would not increase the contamination.

Q.   That is not the thing that stirs it up?

A.   No.

Q.   It is the heating that stirs it up?

A.   Heating.   Your heated oil rises and is replaced by cooler oil, thus causing a circulation.

Miss Phillips: I see.   I think that is very clear.   That is all.   Oh, your Honor, may I offer in evidence this

(Testimony by William F. Beedle).

sketch which the witness has as the next exhibit next in order?

The Clerk: No. 7.

Redirect Examination

By Mr. Vermille:

Q. Mr. Beedle, you say that you did not make up the samples. Did you test the samples after they were made up?

A. As to color, yes.

Q. Were the samples made up in your laboratory?

A. Yes, sir.

Q. Who were they made up by?

A. Mr. Huffman.

Miss Phillips: Your Honor, I have not made an objection on this.

Mr. Vermille: Well, that is in the record. That is all. I just wanted to clear it up.

Miss Phillips: Yes, I have not made any objection. I think this is all a matter of scientific work in the laboratory, and I would not demand that they bring the actual man who made them up. The witness said he checked them. That is all right.

Q. By Mr. Vermille: Now, Mr. Beedle, is it necessary to heat the cocoanut oil to discharge it if the cocoanut oil is in a liquid state?

A. No, if it is in a liquid state it is not necessary.

Q. I would just like to ask you one more question, and ask you to look at that report of the Bureau of

(TESTIMONY BY WILLIAM F. BEEDLE)

Standards again, and ask you if it is possible, looking at that report, to tell the extent of the contamination?

Miss Phillips: Just a moment, your Honor.

Mr. Vermille: I want to.

Miss Phillips: Wait a minute. The witness has testified on this in detail. This is not proper redirect examination. The questions were asked and answered anyway.

The Court: No. Nevertheless, he can answer the question. In a way it is an attempt to clarify some of the testimony heretofore given, I suppose.

Miss Phillips: Very well, your Honor. I withdraw my objection.

A. What is the question?

Mr. Vermille: Read the question.

(Question read by the Reporter.)

A. No.

The Court: Go on.

Mr. Vermille: That is all.

The Court: Is that all?

Miss Phillips: I have one more question—pardon me, your Honor. Did your Honor have a question too?

The Court: No, go on.

RECROSS EXAMINATION

By Miss Phillips:

Q. You just said on redirect examination, Mr. Beedle, that if cocoanut oil is in a liquid state it is not necessary to heat it. Referring to that little sketch you made for me 4 or 5 minutes ago, it is clear, isn't it, that the cocoa-

(Testimony by William F. Beedle)

nut oil congealed on the side of a ship, on the skin of a ship is the last to melt, isn't that right?

A.   I would not say that, knowing the construction of the steam coils in the tank.

Q.   How is that?   Tell me.

A.   They have the steam coils run up the side, up and down the side of the ship, also steam coils on the bottom.

Q.   Well, I don't understand.   After this had all melted in the center you say it was still frozen and hard on the side of the ship away up almost to the top level?

A.   Yes.

Q.   Well, how do you explain that?   I don't understand that.

The Court: Well, now, the witness and yourself have used the expression "sides of the ship."   You don't mean that this oil was congealed to the side of a ship, do you?

A.   Yes, sir, your Honor.

Q.   By the Court: Wasn't it congealed to the side of the tank?

A.   The side of the ship was part of the tank.

Q.   Oh, I didn't know that before.   This tank was not —it was built into the ship and the side of the ship served for the side of the tank?

A.   Yes, sir.

Q.   Well, but I understood the sides of this tank were vertical, is that correct?

A.   Yes, sir.

Q.   Well, the side of a ship is not vertical, is it?

(TESTIMONY OF WILLIAM F. BEEDLE)

A. Well, there may be a little concave appearance to it. Is that what you mean, your Honor?

Q. Well, certainly. I understand the side of a ship is concave from the inside and convex on the outside.

A. Yes.

Q. All right. Then the tank, the side of the tank, could not be vertical if the side of the tank was the side of the ship, it seems to me. Am I right? Or do you know?

A. In this ship, I don't know what convexture there is to that side.

Q. Well, probably I misunderstood the testimony yesterday. I wanted to get a clear idea of these tanks, and I got the idea that they were just what we understand as tanks, vertical sides, sides at right angles to each other. Now, they were a part of the ship, apparently, according to your idea?

A. Yes, sir.

Q. Maybe you didn't go down there; maybe you don't know?

A. I was down in the tank, your Honor.

Q. Yes. And the sides of the tank are vertical, are they, or were they—

A. Other than the slight convexture; this will show you.

Q. Well, they are vertical except that they are not vertical.

Miss Phillips: Well, it is a slight curve,—you mean it is a slight curve?

A. Yes, a slight curve.

(TESTIMONY BY WILLIAM F. BEEDLE)

Q. Then the side of a ship is vertical, if this is a correct delineation of it. Well, there is no matter about that. We will proceed.

Q. By Miss Phillips: These tanks are located almost in the center of the ship, are they not, Mr. Beedle?

A. Yes.

Q. Where the curve of the ship would be the least, isn't that true?

A. Yes.

The Court: Proceed.

Q. By Miss Phillips: Well now, going back to my question. You say that the coils—my question was, why was it that cocoanut oil remained congealed away up, frozen on the skin of the ship, whereas towards the center it was melted down to 4½ feet from the bottom? Why was that? Do you understand my question?

A. My explanation to that would be that the steam was not applied to the so-called bilge coil which run up the side of the ship or the skin of the ship.

Q. Then would this be your answer: The cocoanut oil on the skin of the ship being next immediately to the cold water outside would become hard and would stay there even though the center was melted until you applied heat to that skin of the ship?

A. Yes.

Q. Is that about right?

·A. Yes.

Q. Understand again now that I am dealing with terms that are out beyond my depth, so if I misstate your testimony I want you to correct me. Well now

(TESTIMONY OF WILLIAM F. BEEDLE)

then, I would take it that in the natural course of events the cocoanut oil against the skin of the ship, against the cold water, against the water on the outside, that in the natural course that would be the last to melt because it would naturally be the hardest, is that right?

A.   That all depends upon the amount of steam that is applied to the coil.

Q.   I said in the natural state of affairs. In the natural state of affairs without any heat at all?

The Court: Without any application of steam, you mean?

Q.   Miss Phillips: Yes. The cocoanut oil against the side of the ship is going to be the hardest because it is going to be nearest the water?

A.   That would depend upon your water temperature also.

Q.   I would say so too, but given cold water, that would be the hardest?

A.   Yes.

Q.   Or given cold air, that would be the hardest?

A.   Yes.

Q.   Also, in the natural course of events, that on the side would be the first to solidify, isn't it, in cold air, isn't that right?

A.   You see, the temperature of your tank would be almost the same.

Q.   Ah, but listen, I am talking about before you apply any heat with the cocoanut oil against the side of the ship without any heat applied to the ship at all,

(TESTIMONY BY WILLIAM F. BEEDLE)

would that have a tendency to become hardest if the air or the water on the outside was cold?

A. Yes.

Miss Phillips: It would? That is all.

REDIRECT EXAMINATION

By Mr. Vermille:

Q. I would like to have you explain, Mr. Beedle, explain to the Court if you know why the oil was not melted on the side of the ship. Did you use any special process?

The Court: Well, of what importance is that in this case?

Miss Phillips: Just to show, your Honor, that the heating was applied gradually on account of the contamination to save all the oil they could, from the top gradually as they went down the side, they just heated it gradually to save all the oil they could.

The Court: Well, of what importance is that?

Miss Phillips: Just to show that if the steam had been applied to the sides it would have all melted down. I don't know if your Honor understood that clearly, because the steam coils run up the sides of the tank. They were not used because, in the first place, it would have shot the contamination more through the tank than it otherwise would. They heated it gradually from the top down. Am I correct in that?

The Court: Now, wait a minute. You are conducting a conversation with the Court.

Mr. Vermille: All right.

(Testimony of William F. Beedle)

The Court: I am asking you of what importance to the merits of the case is the condition of the oil as to hardness or not at the time it arrived in this port? What is your theory of it?

Mr. Vermille: Well, at the time it arrived here, I would not say it made any difference.

The Court: What?

Mr. Vermille: At the time the oil arrived here all the contamination had been done.

The Court: Well, that is not what I asked you. I asked you of what importance to this case, in the determination of the case, is the condition of the oil with respect to hardness when it arrives at Wilmington?

Mr. Vermille: Because if the oil had not been hard you should have discharged it without heating. Is that what your Honor means?

The Court: Well, I am asking you. Don't ask me.

Mr. Vermille: It could have been discharged at Wilmington if the oil had been in a liquid state without heating.

The Court: All right. Assume that it could have been discharged, of what importance is that; what relevancy has that in the case, I am asking?

Mr. Vermille: Showing that it was in liquid form in Kobe, could have been discharged without heating. That heating the oil, in order to discharge it after it becomes hard, will force contamination to a certain extent through the whole tank.

The Court: Now, wait a moment.

(TESTIMONY BY WILLIAM F. BEEDLE)

Mr. Vermille: Is that what you mean? Is that what your Honor means?

The Court: Well, as you have your theory of the whole case. Now, I am asking you, the whole case is far from clear to me, I must say, but one of your ideas or theories is that it was incumbent upon the ship to remove the oil in Kobe?

A. That is correct.

Q. All right. I don't remember whether there is any evidence in the case to show what the condition of the oil in Kobe was.

Mr. Vermille: There is.

The Court: As to hardness.

Mr. Vermille: There is in the testimony; in the depositions.

The Court: All right. Then that is important.

Mr. Vermille: It is.

The Court: Of course, that is an element, a proper element in the case, as far as the question of the negligence of the ship goes. Now then, when it comes, however, to Los Angeles, to the harbor down here, why is it important to show the condition of the oil as to hardness there?

Mr. Vermille: To show the amount of heat that had to be applied and would circulate the contamination through the tank.

The Court: All right. Why is it important to show the amount of heat? What has that got to do to show the contamination?

Mr. Vermille: The heat will show the circulation of

(Testimony of William F. Beedle)

liquidfying does increase the dissemination or the contamination, as the term has been used, of the oil?

Mr. Vermille: That is it.

The Court: Now then, you present evidence as to the condition of the oil .

Mr. Vermille: That is it.

The Court: Will it be then for the Court to find out whether that was due, whether that was increased, aggravated, by the heating?

Mr. Vermille: To a certain extent, yes, your Honor.

The Court: To a certain extent. But, of course, obviously, the heating was necessary, and that was presumed to be within the contemplation of the parties?

Mr. Vermille: That is correct. The vessel was installed with heating appliances, steam heating, for the purpose of melting the oil so it could be discharged here.

The Court: So far as the actual escape of the fuel oil into the cocoanut oil is concerned, that was accomplished, completed, effected before the arrival here?

Mr. Vermille: No one knows.

The Court: No one knows?

Mr. Vermille: No one knows the size of the leak; no one knows where that leaked stopped.

The Court: You think it might have continued all the time?

Mr. Vermille: It might have. It is a possibility.

The Court: I suppose that it could be safely presumed that the escape of the oil, the fuel oil, into the cocoanut oil, stopped when the oil solidified, congealed, or what not?

Mr. Vermille: No one knows when that took place.

(TESTIMONY OF WILLIAM F. BEEDLE)

The Court: No, no, that is not the question that I am asking you. Now, you keep your eye precisely on what I am asking you, because you are quite familiar with all this case, but I can assure you that the Court is far from it.

Mr. Vermille: I see.

The Court: I say, can the Court assume that the process, the escape of the oil, fuel oil, I mean, from that lower tank into this cocoanut oil tank, cannot take place when the oil was in the condition described by the witness?

Mr. Vermille: That is correct.

The Court: That is, congealed?

Mr. Vermille: That is correct.

The Court: That is your theory?

Mr. Vermille: That is correct.

The Court: You think that would be correct?

Mr. Vermille: That is correct.

The Court: Well then, accepting that as a factor in showing the extent of the contamination, it seems to me that that testimony is unimportant except for that purpose.

Mr. Vermille: Except for the purpose to show it is necessary to heat it.

The Court: It is a little bit—

Mr. Vermille: Your Honor, I might be able to clarify the matter. The testimony shows in Kobe that at the time that they found the cocoanut oil was contaminated, the cocoanut oil at that time was in a liquid state, and it would not have been necessary to have heated the oil to discharge it.

The Court: That is the evidence—

(TESTIMONY OF WILLIAM F. BEEDLE)

Mr. Vermille: No, that is the evidence in the depositions taken in Kobe.

Miss Phillips: Your Honor, may at this time I make a little point to clarify this?

The Court: Yes.

Miss Phillips: Counsel's statement of that as a fact is his view of the evidence. I say that the evidence is clear and unmistakable that solidification and congealing had begun at Kobe, and furthermore, my two best witnesses on that are the two experts called in San Francisco, their testimony on it which yesterday I said if he did not offer the testimony in depositions, I wanted to.

The Court: Yes.

Miss Phillips: I am just talking about the view of the evidence here. We will brief all of this for your Honor.

The Court: But he makes the statement that when the ship got to Kobe the oil was in a liquid state. You make the statement that it began at Kobe.

Miss Phillips: That the solidification—

The Court: Let me call your attention to the fact that both statements may be correct.

Mr. Vermille: If your Honor please, the vessel was in Kobe for 28 days.

Miss Phillips: Your Honor, we can narrow down—

The Court: Now, wait a moment. Let me express my views, which are possibly not always clear to counsel. He takes the position that when the oil got to Kobe it was liquid. Very well. Apparently you did not coincide with that view because you stated that the solidification began

(TESTIMONY BY WILLIAM F. BEEDLE)

at Kobe. That leaves considerable space. The two situations are not necessarily opposite.

Miss Phillips: I had not finished my statement. It began at Kobe and the date of solidification is established quite clearly in the evidence.

The Court: That is very well. But the Court is expected, from the inference of counsel, to draw his,—that there was opportunity to remove the oil at Kobe, it being in a liquid state, without directly increasing the contamination.

Miss Phillips: Now—

The Court: Now, wait a moment.

Miss Phillips: I beg your pardon.

The Court: Yes, you must. Now, when you say the solidification began at Kobe, that is not contradictory in any sense or degree to the position taken by counsel, as I understand it. You don't say that began at Kobe. He says only that it arrived at Kobe in this state. Do you get my statement?

Miss Phillips: Perfectly, and I would like to answer it when you are ready to get my answer.

The Court: Well, I am ready now.

Miss Phillips: I didn't want to interrupt you again. And it is very rude upon the part of counsel to interrupt you. My contention is that solidification had begun on the 5th of October, the day they discovered this contamination, and that furthermore, the evidence shows it very clearly, and all the physical facts in the case prove that to be the fact.

(TESTIMONY OF WILLIAM F. BEEDLE)

The Court: Well, that is true, but the vessel got to Kobe on the 4th of October, didn't it?

Miss Phillips: The night of the 3rd.

The Court: The night of the 3rd. All right. Why couldn't they have gone immediately to work and removed it?

Miss Phillips: They discovered the contamination on the 5th, which—the 5th is the day that they made the discovery. My contention is that on the 5th solidification had begun.

The Court: Yes, but—

Miss Phillips: And the heating would have been necessary on that day to remove it.

The Court: I see. Well, of course, that will be cleared up by the evidence.

Miss Phillips: I think so, your Honor.

The Court: But whose duty was it to know the condition of the oil, assuming that it was liquid, when it got to Kobe; was there a duty imposed on the ship to know the condition of the oil and instantly to remove it?

Miss Phillips: Your Honor, this is all a matter we are going to have to argue out in the briefs. You see, there is the testimony of sixteen witnesses taken on that. I think we could right now begin opening up the depositions and answering some of these questions from the testimony of the witnesses. The only question is, does your Honor want it?

The Court: All right. Proceed. There is no further examination on either side?

(TESTIMONY OF WILLIAM F. BEEDLE)

Mr. Vermille: Just one more question, then, your Honor.

Q. By Mr. Vermille: If the oil had just commenced to congeal in Kobe, would it have been necessary to have heated it to discharge it? Just commenced to congeal?

A. No.

Mr. Vermille: That is all.

RECROSS EXAMINATION

By Miss Phillips:

Q. Mr. Beedle, to what temperature did your firm instruct the engineers to heat this oil in order to discharge it at Wilmington? What is the desired temperature for discharge?

A. Ordinary cargos, or this cargo?

Q. What is it?

A. Ordinary cargos or this contaminated cargo?

Q. Take both, give us both. What temperature, for instance, did you heat the starboard tank?

A. All right.

Q. Let me finish my question. To what temperature did you heat the starboard tank?

A. I will have to look at the report. The top temperature of the starboard tank was 96 degrees.

Q. And for heating the contaminated?

Mr. Vermille: Just a minute. For heating what?

Q. By Miss Phillips: The contaminated oil.

Mr. Vermille: What?

Miss Phillips: I am asking him about oil. That is all

(Testimony by William F. Beedle)

I am asking him about. I asked him what temperature did it heat the starboard tank. Now, I am asking the port.

A. The port top temperature was 84.

Q. 84?

A. Yes.

Q. Do you know what the temperature is to load it into the ship?

A. It is given on the survey report here.

Q. I might say, your Honor, it was stipulated that it was 88 to load it in.

A. The temperature was loaded in at 88.

Q. At 88. And you say it begins to congeal at somewhere between 72 and 75?

A. Yes.

Miss Phillips: That is all.

Mr. Vermille: That is all.

Q. By Miss Phillips: Were you ever in Kobe?

A. No, ma'am.

Miss Phillips: No.

The Court: Wait a moment, Mr. Beedle.

Q. By the Court: The analysis of the oil was made by the firm in San Francisco?

A. Yes.

Q. The samples being taken when the ship'ped arrived at Wilmington?

A. Yes.

Q. Does the analysis show the amount or quantity of fuel oil that had gone into the port tank?

A. Approximate of the grades that were sampled.

Q. Well, so far as the grades are concerned, the evi-

(TESTIMONY OF WILLIAM F. BEEDLE)

dence shows, and so far as the Court is advised, that the samples are a reproduction made by you of what you believe to be the actual oil at the various levels in the tank?

A.   Yes.

Q.   But I am asking about the quantity of fuel oil that it took to bring about that condition. Does your analysis show that?

A.   Yes.

Q.   All right. What is it?

Mr. Vermille: Have you the original entries, Mr. Beedle, from which this report was made?

The Court: Wait a minute.

A.   Curtis & Tompkins' report.

Q.   By Mr. Vermille: I thought that is what you had.

A.   No, it is not shown on there. Get that photostatic copy. (Referring to photostatic copy.) That fuel oil was shown by difference.

Q.   By the Court: Was shown by what?

A.   Difference, using the total unsaponifiable matter, including fuel oil and unsaponifiable matter in the oil of the undamaged tank.

Q.   Well, all right. Now, strike out the statement of the witness. Evidently the witness does not understand me, or else I am entirely incapable of making myself understood. You have here one tank on top of another, the port tank on top of the fuel oil tank?

A.   Yes.

Q.   The case is based upon the proposition that fuel oil escaped from the fuel oil tank, where it properly belonged,

(TESTIMONY BY WILLIAM F. BEEDLE)

into the cocoanut oil tank, where it did not belong. You understand that?

A. Yes.

Q. All right. The records which you have, do they show what quantity, gallonage, bottles, or what not, did escape?

A. No.

Q. It don't show that at all?

A. Percentage by difference; percentage by difference.

Q. Percentage by difference?

A. Yes.

Q. That falls upon the Court's ears meaningless. I don't know what it means.

A. Your Honor—

The Court: Never mind anything else. I want to try to make plain what I am inquiring about. You say that you cannot tell, and your records do not show, whether the quantity that got in there and produced all of this damage was one gallon, two gallons, one quart, one pint, one gill, or what not, is that correct?

A. Yes, sir.

Q. Well, wouldn't it be possible by making a chemical analysis of the cocoanut oil to know what amount of fuel oil went in there?

A. Yes, your Honor. There was approximately 3,000 pounds left in the bilges that was so badly contaminated and that was not analyzed at all.

Q. You mean 3,000 gallons of the mixture?

A. Pounds of the mixture.

(TESTIMONY BY WILLIAM F. BEEDLE)

Q.   3,000 pounds of the mixture?

A.   Yes.

Q.   And naturally you would think that that had a greater proportion of fuel oil than any other part—

A.   Yes.

Q.   So you don't know. Well, are you in any position to make an estimate?

A.   An approximate estimate from this analysis, or these analyses—there are three of the grades and we have the weight and the percentage of fuel oil by difference.

The Court: Well, read the question, Mr. Reporter.

(Question read by the Reporter.)

The Court: That calls for a yes or no answer.

Q.   By the Court: Can you by computation, I mean, taking those reports, and figuring them over, can you advise the Court as to how much oil in your judgment escaped from one tank into the other?

A.   No, because all the oil was not removed.

Q.   So, by reason of not having had a test of this bilge—

A.   Yes.

Q.   —you would not be able to. I can see how that could happen very readily. However, you had a test of certain sections in the tank?

A.   Yes.

Q.   Had you not? Well, couldn't you by figuring on those know what proportion of the whole mass at that particular level was fuel oil?

A.   By these analyses, yes.

(TESTIMONY OF WILLIAM F. BEEDLE)

Q. I wish you would do that. That would give the Court some kind of an idea, don't you see, as to how much fuel oil actually escaped. You will do that and have it ready this afternoon?

A. Yes.

Q. It will not be a very long process, I suppose, or very much figuring?

A. No.

Q. All right. Now, another question. Do you know whether or not the fuel oil tank showed the presence of cocoanut oil?

A. I do not.

Q. Do your reports indicate?

A. No, sir.

Q. I will ask counsel if that appears in the evidence anywhere, or will appear?

Mr. Vermille: The evidence, to a certain extent, shows that the cocoanut oil floated down through this leak into the fuel oil tank until the fuel oil tank was full and practically with one tank of the mixture with the fuel oil down at the bottom.

The Court: Yes.

Mr. Vermille: That the fuel oil tank was slack to a certain extent.

The Court: It was what?

Mr. Vermille: It was slack. There was an air space or a vacancy up at the top.

The Court: Yes.

Mr. Vermille: From the top of the fuel oil to the top of the fuel oil tank. That was slack. Well, I don't re-

(TESTIMONY OF WILLIAM F. BEEDLE)

member the approximate inches. Anyway, they always keep it slack, they fill it full and then they keep it slack. And when this leak occurred the cocoanut oil floated down into the fuel oil tank until the fuel oil tank was full and then started to come out into the cocoanut oil tank.

The Court: Well, you wouldn't say then, in your opinion, that the cocoanut oil did actually get down and intermingle with the fuel oil?

Mr. Vermille: That is correct.

The Court: I see no reason why it should not.

Mr. Vermille: That is correct.

Miss Phillips: The testimony of the chief engineer covered that point. He so testified.

Mr. Vermille: The chief engineer took soundings of the double bottom tanks.

The Court: Yes, but I did not understand there was any test that he made.

Mr. Vermille: The chief engineer took soundings of the fuel oil tank and from the soundings taken he found to exist certain quantities of—

The Court: On that rope?

Mr. Vermille: On that rope.

Miss Phillips: There is more testimony than that.

Mr. Vermille: There is no argument about that.

Miss Phillips: I am answering the question. First, your question is, is there any evidence covering the point that the fuel oil leaked down into the cocoanut oil tank?

The Court: Yes.

Miss Phillips: Yes, there is. Plenty of it; plenty of it.

(TESTIMONY BY WILLIAM F. BEEDLE)

The Court: Now, I suppose you cover the point in various depositions as to the value and actual damage done?

Mr. Vermille: The depositions show as near as possible at the time the survey was made there in Kobe the damage to the tank.

The Court: All right. Will the witness have that— give me that estimate at 2 o'clock? Recess this case until 2 o'clock.

(Whereupon, a recess was taken to 2 o'clock P.M.)

Los Angeles, California, Thursday, May 4, 1933.
2 o'clock P.M.

Mr. Vermille: If your Honor please, Mr. Beedle, in accordance with the understanding had between counsel and your Honor, made certain computations which your Honor wanted before he left, and I will read those into the record, and I will hand you what he made.

The Court: Yes. Let me see it. He finds a total of 457 pounds at the several points.

Mr. Vermille. That does not, however, include the oil that remained badly contaminated down in the bilge.

The Court: No. Well, that is what I wanted.

Mr. Vermille: Yes. I will read that.

Miss Phillips: I think counsel and I have stipulated that Mr. Beedle, if called, will so testify.

The Court: Just hand me that. I don't think you need to file it.

Miss Phillips: We thought it might be read into the record for the convenience of both sides.

(TESTIMONY BY WILLIAM F. BEEDLE)

The Court: Yes. Do that.

Mr. Vermille: If Mr. Beedle, the witness that was just on the stand, were present he would testify to the following facts: "Contaminated cocoanut oil, port deep tank SS. West Cajoot, 354,015 pounds cocoanut oil, grade 1, in storage tank 1, fuel oil by difference, .06 per cent equals 212 pounds of fuel oil. 167,500 pounds, grade 2, in storage tank No. 3, fuel oil by difference, .08 per cent, equals 134 pounds of fuel oil. 53,155 pounds grade No. 3 in storage tank 4, fuel oil by difference .21 per cent, equals 111 pounds of fuel oil. Approximate total pounds of fuel oil in above three grades of oil equals 457 pounds."

The Court: That 111 was in grade—

Mr. Vermille: 111 was in grade 3. That was only 533 pounds.

The Court: Grade 2, you say?

Mr. Vermille: No, grade 3.

The Court: 3.

Mr. Vermille: In 53,155 pounds of oil.

The Court: Yes.

Miss Phillips: Those percentages in storage No. 1, you say that is .06 per cent?

Mr. Vermille: Yes.

Miss Phillips: The next is—

Mr. Vermille: The next is .08 per cent, and the next is .21.

Miss Phillips: 100 per cent.

Mr. Vermille: Yes. "Impossible to estimate the fuel

(TESTIMONY OF WILLIAM F. BEEDLE)

oil remaining in cocoanut oil left in bilge because no analysis was made of this oil."

The Court: Any other witnesses?

· Mr. Vermille: Call Mr. Slater to the stand.

ELMER ORD SLATER,

called as a witness on behalf of the Los Angeles Soap Company and The Westchester Fire Insurance Company, being first duly sworn, testified as follows:

Q. By the Clerk: Your full name?

A. Elmer Ord Slater.

The Court: How do you spell it?

A. S-l-a-t-e-r.

DIRECT EXAMINATION

By Mr. Vermille:

Q. Mr. Slater, what is your business or occupation?

A. Chemical engineer.

Q. Who are you associated with?

A. I am the manager of Smith-Emory & Company.

Q. How long have you been a chemical engineer?

A. About 23 years.

Q. As a chemical engineer, have you had any occasion to analyze cocoanut oil?

A. Yes, sir.

Q. What has been your experience, Mr. Slater, along that line?

A. Well, we have handled numerous cargos of cocoanut oil coming into this port some years ago. There is none coming in now, but this was, oh, 4 or 5 or 6 years ago, and we get occasional samples now.

(TESTIMONY OF ELMER ORD SLATER)

Mr. Vermille: If your Honor will bear with me just a moment, I have lost and cannot find this photostatic copy of the Bureau of Standards.

The Court: Is this it?

Mr. Vermille: Thank you. I thought I had it.

Q. By Mr. Vermille: You also, do you, in your business, or occupation, have a great deal to do with all kinds of vegetable oils?

A. Yes, we do. We have both animal and vegetable oils.

Q. Mr. Slater, I show you what purports to be a report of the Bureau of Standards, marked "Respondents Exhibit Bower No. 1," and ask you to examine that report and advise the Court whether or not it is possible from looking at that report to estimate the extent of the contamination of the cocoanut oil?

The Court: The what of the contamination?

Mr. Vermille: The extent of the contamination.

The Court: Yes, the degree?

Mr. Vermille: The degree.

The Court: Or the extent.

Mr. Vermille: Of the contamination of the cocoanut oil.

A. It is not possible to determine with any degree of accuracy the extent of damage. The report is in too general terms. The only item that is specific is this saponification number, which is a rough index of what might be expected in the way of contamination.

Q. Is it possible to ascertain the color of the oil from that report?

(TESTIMONY OF ELMER ORD SLATER)

A. It gives a very general statement. It says, "Color, port side, dark brownish amber; starboard side, dark straw." There are very much more exact ways of determining color. These statements are so general that they might cover a large range of color.

Q. I will show you exhibit A-2 and ask you to look at that and I will show you exhibit A-3 and ask you to look at that, and I will show you exhibit A-4 and ask you to look at that. Then, if you will look at the Government's analysis made, or report. I will ask you if you can tell from looking at that report if that report identifies any one of those samples?

A. It would be impossible to say which one might be identified by this report, if any of them.

Q. Now, I show you a report of a letter dated December 7, 1932, respondent for identification Bower No. 2, and ask you to examine that report. From examining that report, is it possible to determine the extent of the damage or contamination to cocoanut oil?

Miss Phillips: Counsel, I did not hear your last words there.

Q. By Mr. Vermille: Is it possible from examining that report to determine the extent of the damage to the cocoanut oil?

A. This report shows the percentage of fuel oil in three different samples, and also shows the color of the same three samples. The extent of the damage would be determined principally by the color, so that one could get a very good estimate of the extent of the damage from this report.

(TESTIMONY OF ELMER ORD SLATER)

The Court: What report are you now referring to? What exhibit?

Mr. Vermille: Exhibit Respondents for identification Bower No. 2. That is attached to the deposition of Mr. Bower taken in Washington, D. C.

Miss Phillips: That is the report, the chemical report of Curtis & Tompkins.

Q. By Mr. Vermille: Now, Mr. Slater, I will ask you again to look at these reports,—both of these reports, the report of the Bureau of Standards and the report of Curtis & Tompkins, and ask you if it is possible to make a comparison between those two reports as to the extent of the damage to the cocoanut oil?

A. It is not possible to make a good comparison of the extent of the damage by the use of these two reports.

Q. Why is that?

A. Because the report of the United States Bureau of Standards is given in too general terms.

Q. I will ask you to examine both Curtis & Tompkins' report and the report of the Bureau of Standards again and ask you if the report of Curtis & Tompkins shows either a degree or an increase of contamination over the report made by the Bureau of Standards?

A. It is impossible for me to tell from these two reports, again, for the reason that the United States Bureau of Standards' report is so indefinite that I cannot draw an accurate estimate of the amount of damage it represents.

(TESTIMONY OF ELMER ORD SLATER)

Q. Now, Mr. Slater, I will ask you to listen to this long hypothetical question. By the way, are you familiar with the Steamer West Cajoot? Do you know the type of that vessel?

A. I know the type of the vessel, yes. I don't know the vessel itself.

Q. What type is she?

A. She is, as I understand, the tanker type, at least it has tanks for carrying oil.

Q. Have you ever had anything to do with surveys of oil coming off of vessels bound from the Orient?

A. Yes.

Q. I will ask you to assume that the Steamer West Cajoot on a voyage from Manila to Los Angeles by the way of Hongkong and San Francisco, was carrying fuel oil in her double bottom tanks and was also carrying a cargo of about one million, two hundred twenty-three thousand, five hundred eighty-three pounds of cocoanut oil in her No. 3 port and starboard deep tanks, about half in each tank, which deep tanks were located immediately above the No. 3 double bottom. Also assume that on October 2, 1927, the vessel stranded while passing through the Van Dieman Straits in Japan, and that after she was floated from the stranding, it was decided to make for Kobe, Japan, as a port of refuge. Assume further that after the stranding, the No. 1 and the No. 2 double bottom tanks were sounded, and it was discovered that sea water had entered said oil and tank. Assume that after the arrival of the vessel in Kobe and on or about October 5, 1927, and before the vessel went

(TESTIMONY OF ELMER ORD SLATER)

into dry dock, it was discovered that there was a leak
between the No. 3 double bottom tank and the port deep
tank. Assume further that the vessel was put into the
dry dock on October 8, 1927. Assume further that either
before or after the vessel went into the dry dock the
cocoanut oil in the deep tanks was examined by taking
samples from the different levels in the tanks. And it
was found that the cocoanut oil in the starboard deep
tank was uncontaminated, but that the oil in the port
deep tank was contaminated by contact with fuel oil,
this contamination, however, being confined to about the
bottom 6 inches of said deep tank, and the upper layers
of the tank being apparently clear and uncontaminated.
In view of these facts, what should have been done, in
your opinion, in regard to the oil in the port deep tanks?

A. I think it should have been salvaged as soon as
possible.

Q. Just explain, will you please, what you mean by
salvaged?

A. Why, I think it should have been removed from
that tank, beginning at the top and pumping the oil down,
watching it as the pumping proceeded, segregating it so
that if possible you would keep oil that had not been contaminated in one lot, oil slightly contaminated in another,
and oil more grossly contaminated would either be left in
the tank or taken out—possibly taken out, so that there
would be no further contamination.

Q. Why, in your opinion, should it have been taken
out immediately upon discovering the contamination?

A. For the reason that when oil is held in storage, that

is, when cocoanut oil is held in storage and it is still liquid, and fuel oil has gotten into it, the fuel oil is missible with the cocoanut oil.

The Court: Is what?

A.   It is missible, that is, it will mix readily with it. I mean by that, it differentiates between getting water into the oil, which would stay on the bottom and not have a tendency to work up into the oil. There are several factors that would tend to make the fuel oil work up into the cargo of the cocoanut oil so long as it is liquid. One of those is by diffusion, what we speak of as diffusion. That means that when you have two missible oils together, they have a tendency to mix and equalize, even though they may be of different specific gravity. Also, any motion the vessel might have would tend to move the oil in this tank and mechanically mix the two oils together. There may be other reasons why the oils would mix. One I have in mind is that cocoanut oil freezes, if it is allowed to become cold, and in that process it is possible that it would cause the fuel oil to disseminate more rapidly into that portion which was not frozen, the frozen portion starting at the bottom and sides of the tank holding it.

Q.   Could you compare an analogy of that freezing with anything we are all familiar with?

A.   Yes, the freezing of ice. When ice is frozen the water is put in a can and the pure ice freezes on the bottom and sides of the can and the impurities segregate into the unfrozen portion of the water. There is another reason, too: If that oil were allowed to solidify, it would be necessary to heat it before it could be removed, and of necessity the heating process would also tend to disseminate the fuel oil through the cocoanut oil and thus further contaminate it, so that if it could be removed while still in a liquid state, it could be removed in a purer condition than it could after it had once frozen or congealed and then been reheated in order to melt it.

Q.   Assuming now, Mr. *Salter,* that all of the oil, cocoanut oil, in the port deep tank was more or less contaminated by fuel oil, would you still consider it necessary to remove the cocoanut oil?

A.   Well, there are two considerations there, one would be that under certain conditions you might lose some of your cocoanut oil if the hole would allow cocoanut oil to get into the tank. Unless a pressure was maintained on that particular area, the cocoanut oil might get out of the tank and be lost and it is a valuable oil. Furthermore, the oil might become more generally contaminated than it was at the time of the contamination when it was only contaminated, say, more at the bottom and less at the top, as I understand the situation. I guess I did not really answer your question, though.

Q.   No.

A.   With those considerations, I would still consider it advisable to take the oil out of the tank.

Q.   Can oil in a liquid state be discharged from a vessel without heating?

A.   It can.

Q.   Can oil in a semi-liquid state, but not frozen, be discharged from a vessel without heating?

(TESTIMONY OF ELMER ORD SLATER)

A. It can, yes.

Mr. Vermille: That is all.

CROSS EXAMINATION

By Miss Phillips

Q. Just a question or two, Mr. Slater. Have you ever been in Kobe?

A. I never have, no.

Q. So when you say it was advisable immediately to remove the oil, "immediately" indicates you think they should begin at once. Does that mean to pump it over into the water on the side of the ship, or where?

A. Well, I said to salvage it, and of course, that would imply pumping it into some other tank either on board ship or on a shore tank.

Q. Then, your theory that it should have been pumped out, you condition that upon the obtaining of proper receptacles in which to put it, of course?

A. That is natural.

Q. Naturally. In making a comparison of the reports of the two chemists in this case, are you saying, Mr. Slater, that the results of these examinations, say, for instance, the result of Curtis & Thompkins', that that is very exact when they specify so much, so much, so much percentage of this, that and the other? You have examined the report. You mean that that is a very exact and accurate result?

A. I have examined the report, and I know their ability to do that work and I should judge from that that it is quite exact, yes.

(TESTIMONY OF ELMER ORD SLATER)

Q. The reason why I asked you that question, Mr. Slater—understand, I am not a chemist—is that at the bottom of a page of this exhibit, I have here,—I see somewhere a note on one part of it, "Results only relative and very approximate."

A. That refers to the reference to the different colors.

Q. To the different colors?

A. They took the colors in a 1 inch standard, I notice, in a 1 inch cell, and in order to get that into the 5 inch cell or a 5¼ inch cell, they had made the calculation. I did not look exactly, but they probably had multiplied it by 5¼ times and they say "approximate" because if you have that type color and are trying to examine it, you might not get exactly the same figure you would by your calculation.

Q. Then, according to this report, then, their color tests, they would indicate on their face that they are relative and very approximate?

A. I understand that only refers to the figures after the 5¼ inch cell, but the figures after the 1 inch cell are accurate.

Q. I see. I think that is self-explanatory, your Honor, when you read the report. I won't spend any further time on that. I think I have just one more question. Well, I think I have two more.

You say that oil in a liquid state can be discharged without heating. Have you ever done so?

A. Yes, that is, I have never been present when it was done. You see, we certify to the quantity and quality of

(TESTIMONY OF ELMER ORD SLATER)

oil. We don't actually do the pumping ourselves. I have been present and generally supervised the work.

Q. Will you tell me the circumstances under which you were present when they were discharging oil in the liquid state which had not been heated?

A. Are you talking about cocoanut oil?

Q. Oh yes, we are talking about cocoanut oil here. Did your answer refer to other oils besides cocoanut oil when you said oil could be discharged in a liquid state?

A. It refers to any oil.

Q. Now, I am confining my question to cocoanut oil. Do you mean that cocoanut oil in the liquid state can be discharged without heating?

A. That is true, yes.

Q. Have you ever seen cocoanut oil discharged?

A. I have never seen cocoanut oil discharged that way, no.

Q. Similarly, you said oils, semi-liquid or not entirely frozen, that is, where the freezing was beginning but not complete. Were you referring there to cocoanut oil, or some other oil?

A. That would be cocoanut oil.

Q. Have you ever personally done it?

A. I have not personally, no, but I have had supervision of a number of men that have been present and had charge of such work.

Q. Well now, tell us a little bit more about that, that is, the discharging of oil in a semi-liquid state, that is where it has been in a mushy state, I take it you mean?

A. That is right.

Q.   But not yet hard?

A.   That is right.

Q.   How is that discharged?

A.   It is pumped by a centrifugal pump and so long as that oil is fluid enough to flow, a suction pump, such as a centrifugal pump will force it into the pump—

Q.   Even then you are assuming that the oil is fluid or liquid?

A.   Oh, yes, it must be fluid enough to be sucked up into the pump.

Q.   I see. We have spoken several times about this centrifugal pump. Is that an apparatus in use here in Wilmington?

A.   Yes.

Q.   Do you know if that is in general use, or is that a special apparatus you have there?

A.   No, it is in general use.

Q.   In general use. Just a moment. When you are using a centrifugal pump to mix up and actually pump out the contents of the container, does the action of the pump itself tend to mix it, mix the oil? Does putting this pressure and sucking up into the pump?

A.   I think I will have to explain that this way, that it does not tend to mix the oil in the vessel itself, because it sucks the oil up, and only that portion to which the pipe actually has contact is being moved. Now, there may be a little oil right around the opening to that pipe that is being mixed due to the currents that are introduced in that oil, but when the oil is pumped up into or sucked up into the pump, then in the pump itself that small portion of

(TESTIMONY OF ELMER ORD SLATER)

the oil that is in the pump at any one time is pretty fairly mxed up at that stage of the pumping.

Q. Yes. And that would be a fairly continuous process as long as the pumping goes on?

A. It is, yes.

Miss Phillips: Thank you. That is all.

Mr. Vermille: That is all. Call Mr. Bennett to the stand.

HARVEY C. BENNETT,

called as a witness on behalf of the Los Angeles Soap Company and The Westchester Fire Insurance Company, being first duly sworn, testified as follows:

Q. By the Clerk: Your full name?

A. Harvey C. Bennett, B-e-n-n-e-t-t.

DIRECT EXAMINATION

By Mr. Vermille:

Q. Mr. Bennett, what is your business or occupation?

A. I am chief chemist for the Los Angeles Soap Company.

Q. You say you are a chemist?

A. Yes, sir.

Q. Will you please describe briefly your experience as a chemist?

A. Well, I hold the degree of Bachelor of Science and Chemical Engineering. I have been the chief chemist for the Los Angeles Soap Company since 1914, handling and supervising the testing and the disposition of all fatty materials coming into the place.

(TESTIMONY OF HARVEY C. BENNETT)

Q.   What had been your experience before going with
the Los Angeles Soap Company?

A.   I had had various experiences. I spent one summer
with the Armour Soap Works in Chicago. Otherwise not
pertaining to oils, in general.

Q.   Have you had a great deal to do or anything to do
with cocoanut oil?

A.   There has been under my jurisdiction for quite a
number of years the handling and the testing and disposition of same.

Q.   And the analyzing of it?

A.   And the analyzing, yes, sir.

Q.   Are you familiar with the vessel West Cajoot?

A.   Yes, sir.

Q.   Were you down aboard the vessel on December 1st,
when she arrived at Wilmington?

A.   Yes, sir.

Q.   Did you have occasion to observe the cocoanut oil
in the tanks of the vessel?

A.   Yes.

Q.   I will ask you what you observed when you arrived at Wilmington and looked into the tanks of the
vessel containing cocoanut oil? It was contained, as I
understand it, in No. 3 deep tanks.

A.   On the starboard tank it was apparently uncontaminated and the port tank was contaminated with, apparently with fuel oil.

Q.   Were you present at the time of discharging the
cocoanut oil?

A.   Yes, I was.

(TESTIMONY OF HARVEY C. BENNETT)

Q. Will you please describe to the Court the extent of the contamination of the port deep tank as you discharged the oil? By the way, how was that oil discharged?

A. By pumping with a centrifugal pump through a suction hose—

Q. Did you discharge the oil from the top and go down?

A. Yes, the pump was suspended and lowered as required. They started unloading from the top and tried to segregate the less contaminated material from the more badly contaminated.

Q. And as you got down deeper into the tank, what did you find?

A. I found that large quantities were solid on the sides and bottom and they discharged the liquid portion and then discontinued pumping until they heated what remained in there before continuing with the pumping on that particular tank.

Q. The contamination, then, increased as you would go down lower in the tank, is that it?

A. Yes, it became more general.

Q. I wish you would listen, Mr. Bennett, carefully to this long hypothetical question.

Miss Phillips: Your Honor, to shorten the matter, I think counsel—

Mr. Vermille: Will you stipulate he will testify—

Miss Phillips: No; wait a minute. I think counsel can shorten it and ask him if he heard the question he put to the previous witness.

(TESTIMONY OF HARVEY C. BENNETT)

Mr. Vermille: I don't know whether he was here.

Q. By Mr. Vermille: Were you here when I propounded the question to the previous witness?

A. Yes.

Q. You were?

Miss Phillips: Well, counsel ought to be permitted to handle it in his own way, but whatever way you want to suits me. Go ahead any way you want to.

Mr. Vermille: I don't think we can shorten it in the record.

Miss Phillips: Well, go ahead in your own way. I was trying to help you and I think I have not helped you.

Q. By Mr. Vermille: I ask you, Mr. Bennett, to assume that the vessel West Cajoot was on a voyage from Manila to Los Angeles by way of Hongkong and San Francisco, was carrying fuel oil in her double bottom tanks, and was also carrying a cargo of 1,223,583 pounds of cocoanut oil in her No. 3 port and starboard deep tanks, about half in each tank, each of the deep tanks were located immediately above the No. 3 double bottom. Assume, also, that on October 2nd the vessel stranded while passing through the Van Dieman Straits in Japan, and that after she was floated from the stranding it was decided to make for Kobe, Japan, as a port of refuge. Assume further that after the arrival of the vessel in Kobe on or about October 5, 1927, and before the vessel went into the dry dock, or shortly after the vessel went into the dry dock, the cocoanut oil in the deep tanks was examined by taking samples from the different levels in the tanks and it was found that the oil

(TESTIMONY OF HARVEY C. BENNETT)

in the starboard deep tank was uncontaminated, but that the oil in the port deep tank was contaminated by contact with fuel oil, this contamination, however, being confined to about the bottom 6 inches of said deep tank; and the upper layers of the tank being apparently clear and uncontaminated. In view of these facts, what should have been done, in your opinion, in regard to the oil in the port deep tank?

A. I think it should have been salvaged by pumping to other tanks or possibly into drums, if no tanks were available, down to the point where they struck the contaminated oil which could then have been segregated.

Q. Assuming the oil at that time was in a liquid state, would the oil have to be heated to discharge it?

A. No, sir.

Q. Assume further, Mr. Bennett, that instead of the bottom 6 inches of the port deep tank being found contaminated, all of the oil in the port deep tank was found to be slightly contaminated. Would it still be your opinion that the oil should be removed?

A. It depends upon the degree of contamination, in my estimation. I should think that a slight contamination, it would be advisable to remove it before it contaminated further, for the reason that a very slight contamination might be possibly corrected by chemical treatment.

Q. I show you reports of the Bureau of Standards marked "Respondent's Exhibit Bower No. 2." I will ask you to examine that report. After examining that report

(TESTIMONY OF HARVEY C. BENNETT)

can you ascertain the extent of contamination of the cocoanut oil?

A.   Only in a very general way.

Q.   I ask you to look at exhibit A-2, exhibit A-3 and exhibit A-4 and I will ask you again to look at that report.   Can you tell from looking at that report which one of those exhibits that report might refer to?

A.   No, you certainly could not.

Q.   You could not?

A.   Could not, no, sir.

Q.   Now, I show you a report marked "Respondent's for identification, Bower's No. 2."   I ask you to examine that report.

A.   I have examined it.

Q.   Now, is it possible in looking at that report to determine which is exhibit No. A-1, exhibit A-2 and exhibit A-3.

A.   Yes, it is very possible.   The color is given here in definite amounts so that they could be picked out by eye without further testing.

Q.   I ask you to again look at exhibit A-2, 3 and 4, and ask you which exhibit contains the most fuel oil?

A.   This one would contain the most fuel oil.

Q.   Referring to exhibit A-4.   The witness referred to exhibit A-4 as containing the most cocoanut oil.

A.   Fuel oil.

Q.   Fuel oil.

A.   This one contains the intermediate amount.

Q.   Witness referring to exhibit A-3 as containing the intermediate amount of fuel oil.

(TESTIMONY OF HARVEY C. BENNETT)

A. This one contains the least.

Q. Witness referring to exhibit A-2 as containing the least amount of fuel oil.

Now, I will ask you, Mr. Bennett, to again look at the report marked "Respondent's exhibit Bower No. 1," and the report—that is, of the Bureau of Standards, and the report of Curtis & Tompkins, marked "Respondent's for identification Bower No. 2," and ask you to compare the extent of the contamination of cocoanut oil from those two reports.

A. It is impossible to compare them. They don't speak the same language. The Bureau of Standards' report is very indefinite, whereas the Curtis & Tompkins' report is quite definite.

Q. I ask you again to look at those reports and state whether Curtis & Tompkins' report indicates any increase in contamination, or analysis made by Curtis & Tompkins' report?

Miss Phillips: I object to that on the ground it has been asked and answered. Counsel just asked the witness that question and he answered it. Now he is asking it again. Isn't once enough?

Mr. Vermille: It is not the same question.

The Court: Let him answer it again.

A. Will you repeat the question?

(Question read by the Reporter.)

A. You refer to the Curtis & Tompkins' report first?

Q. By Mr. Vermille: Over the Bureau of Standards' report?

A. It is impossible to compare them.

(TESTIMONY OF HARVEY C. BENNETT)

Q. Will you please explain to the Court why it is impossible to compare the two reports and why it is impossible to determine the contamination existing in the samples that were taken in accordance with the Bureau of Standards' report?

A. The only indication of contamination in the Bureau of Standards' report is the reference to the color. It is like saying the day is hot. It does not give any measure. You say it is a hot day but you don't give any temperature. Whereas, as an illustration of this Curtis & Tompkins' report, you have a definite measure there if you can get some indication what it means.

Q. Mr. Bennett, when cocoanut oil solidifies, what do you have to do to discharge it?

A. It must be heated, liquified.

Q. Would the heating process tend to further increase contamination if the oil had been contaminated with fuel oil?

A. If there is variation of the contamination in one part of the tank, the heating certainly would increase the diffusion of the fuel oil and increase the general contamination.

Q. Assuming that the vessel West Cajoot, while at Kobe, Japan, contained contaminated oil, slightly contaminated oil, in her port tank with fuel oil, the contamination being with fuel oil, would that contamination throughout the tank be increased by the vessel's voyage to the United States?

A. Yes, in my opinion it would.

Mr. Vermille: That is all.

(TESTIMONY OF HARVEY C. BENNETT)

CROSS-EXAMINATION

By Miss Phillips:

Q. Have you ever been in Kobe, Mr. Bennett?

A. No, I have not.

Q. Then, when you suggested that you thought the oil should be removed to the tank, removed from the tank, removed where?

A. To another tank, or possibly drums. Drums are a common commodity.

Q. You are assuming, then, that there were proper, fit receptacles to put it in, are you?

A. That is the assumption, yes.

Q. Your answer is based on that assumption?

A. Yes.

Q. You spoke about the use of a centrifugal pump and then through a suction hose that is used in pumping the cocoanut oil out here in Wilmington. You pumped it out into your own lighters or storage cars, or what?

A. It is pumped directly from the ship's tanks, I mean from the centrifugal pump through pipes to a receiving tank on land, this receiving tank discharging then into a scale tank where the weight of the oil is ascertained before pumping to the storage tank.

Q. I see. You use a centrifugal pump down into the tank. Then do you have a hose that comes out attached to the pump, that goes over the side of the ship?

A. Yes, that's it.

Q. What length hose is required for that?

A. Well, it depends on how far away the boat is

(TESTIMONY OF HARVEY C. BENNETT)

from the rigid connection of pipe on the dock. Ordinarily it is about 100 feet, possibly.

Q.   About 100 feet of hose is necessary?

A.   Yes.

Q.   And if there were no rigid pipe there the hose might have to be even longer than that, is that it?

A.   Yes, that would be the case, if there is no pipe, but the pipe is a part of the installation.

Q.   You have a special pipe installation there that assists you in pumping?

A.   Yes.

Q.   Tell me, is this hose that is used, is that a special hose for the use of cocoanut oil?

A.   Yes.

Q.   If that hose was used for other oils, the cocoanut oil going through it would be contaminated, would it not?

A.   No, it would not, because it is customary to clean that hose very thoroughly by steam before it is ever used again.

Q.   I see what you mean. You can use the same hose for several different kinds?

A.   Yes.

Q.   Of vegetable oils?

A.   Yes, sir.

Q.   And each time after you use it you specially cleanse it in order to make it fit for the next kind of oil, is that it?

A.   Yes.

(Testimony of Harvey C. Bennett)

Q. By the way, who provides that, is that your own hose?

A. No, that is provided by the stevedoring company who does the unloading.

Q. I see. In comparing those two chemists' reports, when you said that you could not compare them, did you refer primarily to the color, or did you refer to their statement as to saponifiable matter?

A. Well, I took that into consideration, as well as the color, but the saponification value is no measure in that particular case of contamination. It shows practically no contamination there, as a matter of fact.

Q. As a matter of fact, both reports have an accurate or scientific report as to the saponification—

A. Saponification?

Q. —ability—I am coining a new word, I am afraid —of the oil, do they not?

A. No, they don't. The Bureau of Standards' report gives the saponification number or the amount that might be saponified, whereas the Curtis & Tompkins' gives just the opposite, the unsaponifiable, which is the measure of the contamination.

Q. Well, a witness testifying this morning,—I think it was Mr. Beedle,—said that both tests are scientific tests of the capacity of the oil to be turned into soap. Do you disagree with him, or have I misunderstood one or the other of you?

A. Why, by the Curtis & Tompkins' reports, I see no reference as to the percentage that might be saponifiable except indirectly by difference. If you add the unsaponi-

(TESTIMONY OF HARVEY C. BENNETT)

fiable and subtract that from 100, the balance is saponifiable.

Q. That is what I meant, the Curtis & Tompkins' report show a very small amount unsaponifiable?

A. Yes.

Q. Meaning the rest can be turned into soap?

A. Yes.

Q. Whereas, the Bureau report a very large amount of saponifiable matter and does not report the amount of unsaponifiable matter, is that right?

A. Yes.

Q. That is, the two reports together, you are looking at the reverse sides of the coin, is that about right?

A. Yes.

Miss Phillips: That is all.

REDIRECT EXAMINATION

By Mr. Vermille:

Q. Just one more question. The last question was, in looking at two reports you were merely looking at the reverse side of the coin. I will ask you again to look at the reports of the Bureau of Standards and ask you if it is possible from that report to determine the extent of the contamination?

A. No, it is not.

RECROSS EXAMINATION

By Miss Phillips:

Q. In speaking about the reverse sides of the coin, I was there referring to saponifiable matter. I was not referring to the color. You so understood me, didn't you?

(TESTIMONY OF HARVEY C. BENNETT)

A.   Yes, I understood you.

Miss Phillips: Yes. That is all.

Q.   By the Court: Wait a moment. I want a little information, Mr. *Slater*. How is that oil made, exclusively from the cocoanut?

A.   Yes, sir.

Q.   Crushed, I suppose?

A.   The meats of the cocoanut are first dried, either over a smoky flame, or in the sun, and then subjected to pressure and heat, thereby removing the oil.

Q.   With a fibrous outside on it still?

A.   No, they take off the husk and the shell and then just the meat is the raw material.

Q.   Well, do they have mills or packing houses, or what not, over in that country to handle them?

A.   Yes, the business of crushing copra is a separate business.

Q.   Well, just what is copra?

A.   Copra is the term applied to the dried cocoanut meats from which cocoanut oil is made.

Q.   Well, naturally, I suppose the oil that they produce that way might have different colors originally and be perfectly pure oil, might it not?

A.   Yes, sir.

Q.   Frequently it is, no doubt?

A.   Sure.

Q.   Either due to the character of the fruit itself or to the process of manufacture?

A.   Yes.

(TESTIMONY OF HARVEY C. BENNETT)

Q. There is nothing in this record to show, except the sample taken from the tank that was not contaminated, just what the original color was, is that not true?

A. Only by a surveyor's report at the time of rolling.

Q. Yes. You assumed that both tanks were of uniform color, I suppose, at that time?

A. Well, it might be assumed, although it is unnecessary because there is always a chemist's report—

Q. Oh, there is?

A.—accompanies the loading.

Q. I see. That will describe the color as well as other things?

A. Yes, a measure that a chemist can understand.

Q. Yes. Now, you conclude that in that exhibit—is it A-1?

Mr. Vermille: A-1 is the uncontaminated one.

Q. Yes, that that contains no fuel oil?

Mr. Vermille: Yes.

Q. You conclude that No. 2 contains a slight amount or some fuel oil?

A. Yes.

Q. You heard Mr. Beedle say that that contained a fraction of a drop. I don't know whether he referred to the quantity in that bottle or not. He did, I believe, did he?

A. I did not hear that testimony.

Q. Well—

A. Though I have duplicated that color myself and find that that is quite the case, it is a very small amount.

(TESTIMONY OF HARVEY C. BENNETT)

Q. A very small amount will give color to a much larger mass?

A. Yes.

Q. And that is true of the exhibit A-3, there is a very small quantity in that, also?

A. Yes.

Q. And a greater quantity, I think you testified to that, in exhibit A-4. You don't depend. however, cn the color to know or inform you as to what quantity of fuel oil is in the mass, do you?

A. No. We determine the unsaponifiable matter, that is the matter which will not make soap, which will not saponify.

Q. Well, just what about the unsaponifiable matter?

A. Well, there is naturally present in oil unsaponifiable matter and then the increase over the natural amount represents what might be contamination.

Q. Yes, the contaminating element of material?

A. Yes.

Q. How do you go about to ascertain that?

A. Well, the oil is first saponified with a caustic potash to form a soap. Then the principal, the soap, is dissolved with other solvents, alcohol, leaving the unsaponifiable matter, which in this case is simply fuel oil, and then that is put in solution and evaporated down, weighed. It is quite a lengthy process. It takes several days to do it.

Q. That is—

A. Unsaponifiable.

Q. Say, for instance, you take your sample, one of

(TESTIMONY OF HARVEY C. BENNETT)

those bottles, and you would first find out how much
of it would go into soap?

A.   Well no, we first form a soap. Then by doing
that we are able to separate from the soap.

Q.   You first what?

A.   Form a soap by saponifying it.

Q.   Yes. You make a soap out of that?

A.   Yes.

Q.   You do that by what method?

A.   By the adidtion of caustic potash in alcohol solution. The unsaponifiable matter stays with it and may
be extracted then by proper solvents. That is the way
we separate it from the saponifiable matter.

Q.   In other words, that is the chemical test?

A.   The chemical test.

Q.   You get a certain amount of unsaponifiable matter in the purest oil?

A.   Yes.

Q.   Now, you were down at the wharf when this oil
—at least after it came in?

A.   Yes, when it arrived.

Q.   And you conducted the examination itself?

A.   Yes.

Q.   Are you from San Francisco?

A.   No, I am from Los Angeles.

Q.   You represent this—

A.   Los Angeles Soap Company.

Q.   Oh!

A.   In line of my duty, I have met all cargos of bulk
shipments of oil. That is a part of my duties.

(TESTIMONY OF HARVEY C. BENNETT)

Q. Well, when you got down there you found a certain part of this tank liquid oil?

A. Yes.

Q. That you removed in the usual way by pumping?

A. Yes.

Q. Suction pumping. And then had there been heat applied to the tank before that?

A. I believe there was heat applied previous to arrival by heating it with coils near the top, that is, special coils that were added to drop into the tank. I could not swear to that positively. I don't recall.

Q. You did not find any in there?

A. No, I don't recall that I did, no.

Q. Yes, I see. That is a custom, according to the testimony here, I believe, as the vessel approaches where it is going to deliver the cargo, they do heat the oil?

A. They heat the oil with the ship coils. That is the usual practice. I thought in this particular case you referred to the liquid portion or the contaminated.

Q. No.

A. I believe that was heated, as I recall it, by special coils.

Q. Well, that to your knowledge—whether or not that oil had been heated before its arrival would be from what you heard from others?

A. Yes.

Q. You did not see any evidence of it yourself. You took out what you could of that and then you had it heated?

A. Yes.

(TESTIMONY OF HARVEY C. BENNETT)

Q. And that enabled you to take out all except what was in the bilge, is that correct?

A. Yes.

Q. Well, how do you account for the fact that the contaminated element varied with the depth of the tank, as it seems to be the case?

A. Well, after removing the better portion of it, as soon as you apply the heat to the bottom coils, you start a natural circulation and any contaminated material in the bottom would be mixed in by the natural circulation in the oil.

Q. Well, do you think that there was more contaminated material at the bottom than at the top?

A. Yes.

Q. What leads you to that conclusion?

A. From the serious contamination which was evident in the bilge.

Q. From what?

A. From the very deep contamination that was in the bilge. It was very much more contaminated there.

Q. Well, there were samples taken after the arrival of the vessel in Los Angeles at different depths, were there not?

A. As far as we could go in the liquid portion.

Q. Oh, only in the liquid portion?

A. Then you struck the hard oil, you see.

Q. Yes. And there was no test or sample taken of the hard oil on the bottom?

A. Well, it is impossible to.

Q. Why was it impossible?

(Testimony of Harvey C. Bennett)

A. Well, it is solid. You can't get at it without liquifying it.

Q. Well, you have an apparatus that would go down and take a chip out of it, wouldn't you?

A. It might be possible. It would have been very difficult.

Q. Something like a dropping tube?

A. Not through a solid material. I don't believe it would be very practical.

Q. Now, you conclude from the Government report that you could not tell,—I should say from the report of the Bureau of Standards,—do I understand that from that report you are not able to know just what quantity of contaminated material or what degree of contamination existed in the oil?

A. That is correct. You cannot determine to what degree it is contaminated by their report.

Q. Then, as I understand you, in a general way, that is because they had referred to it by colors?

A. Well, the reference to color is indefinite. They merely state, "Dark brownish amber." Well, that might be anything—

Q. Yes, I appreciate that, but that is the reason why the report to you is unintelligible, is it not?

A. Yes.

Q. The sole reason?

A. They refer to the saponification number there which shows a very small difference, and that indicates possibly some contamination and possibly not. There is

(Testimony of Harvey C. Bennett)

a slight variation in determining the saponification number. You might have that experimental error.

Q.   Because I notice the saponification number is 255.8 and 255.3, describing respectively the starboard tank, which was good, and the port tank, which was the injured one?

A.   Yes.

Q.   A very small difference there?

A.   A very small difference. If you had that information alone you would judge there was no contamination at all.

Q.   I read from exhibit No. 1: "The saponification number indicates that there is only very slight contamination with fuel oil, which is confirmed by further examination. There might, however, be present a very small quantity of fuel oil sufficient to change the color of the cocoanut oil, but which could not be determined by the regular methods of analysis." Well, do I understand from that that the Bureau of Standards says there is only a slight contamination with fuel oil? That is what they say, isn't it?

A.   That is true.

Q.   Of course, we don't know how much "slight contamination" is?

A.   What might be slight in one case might be gross in another. Slight with fuel oil, as you see, is possibly a drop in the bottle, but it makes it unsuitable for edible or soap use.

Q.   Well, that was the case here, the whole mass of

(TESTIMONY OF HARVEY C. BENNETT)

the tank of oil was rendered unfit or unsuitable for use, is that correct?

A. For use in a light colored soap for which it was intended.

Q. Yes. I suppose that is covered, of course, to some extent in other parts of the deposition.

Miss Phillips: I think not, your Honor. There has nothing been taken on that point.

The Court: Where is your damage, then?

Mr. Vermille: Well, we were going to stipulate.

The Court: Oh, I see.

Mr. Vermille: To a reference on admiralty matters as to the amount of damage. The only thing for your Honor to decide would be the liability.

The Court: Oh, I see.

Mr. Vermille: Counsel and I were going to stipulate as to the amount of damage.

Miss Phillips: Yes, we thought we would shorten it up that way.

The Court: I have no objection to it.

Mr. Vermille: Are you through with this witness?

Miss Phillips: All through.

RECROSS EXAMINATION

By Miss Phillips:

Q. You said that this contamination rendered the cocoanut oil suitable for edible purposes or a light colored soap?

A. Yes.

Q. It was suitable, however, for a darker soap, or could be purified so as to be usable?

(TESTIMONY OF HARVEY C. BENNETT)

A. Well, it possibly could be put into a very low grade soap.

Q. What I am getting at, though, it is not a total loss, it was used?

A. Oh, it was used. We could use it ourselves.

Miss Phillips: The extent of damage would be a matter of reference which can be stipulated. We won't take up the time of the Court on that. That is all.

Mr. Vermille: That is all. I will now call Captain Waters.

The Court: Recess at this time for about 5 minutes.

(Short recess.)

(After recess.)

Mr. Vermille: I would like to call Captain Waters.

LEONARD ARTHUR WATERS,

recalled as a witness on behalf of the Los Angeles Soap Company and The Westchester Fire Insurance Company, being previously duly sworn, testified as follows:

DIRECT EXAMINATION (Continued)

By the Clerk: You were sworn yesterday?

A. Waters, yes.

By Mr. Vermille:

Q. Captain Waters, what is your business or occupation?

A. At the present time, transportation of edible oils.

Q. Have you ever been a marine surveyor?

A. Yes.

Q. What has been the extent of your marine surveying?

(TESTIMONY OF LEONARD ARTHUR WATERS)

A. 7 years.

Q. What did you do before that?

A. Shipmaster.

Q. What papers do you hold?

A. Unlimited American Steam, Steam and Diesel, Ocean, any Tonnage; Unlimited British, the same; Unlimited Canadian, the same; Unlimited Colonial, the same; American, British and Canadian.

Q. Before you were shipmaster, what were you?

A. Chief officer.

Q. By the Court: What?

A. Chief officer.

Q. By Mr. Vermille: You mean by chief officer, first mate?

A. Yes.

Q. Have you operated or had anything to do with vessels similar to the type of the West Cajoot?

A. I was in command of several Shipping Board vessels operated by agents.

Q. Are you familiar with the Vessel West Cajoot?

A. Yes, I surveyed it several times.

Q. Familiar with her construction throughout?

A. Yes.

Q. Have you ever been in charge of a vessel carrying vegetable oils?

A. Yes.

Q. Are you familiar with the Port of Kobe?

A. Yes, I have been there a number of times.

Q. When was the last time you were there?

A. 1928.

(Testimony of Leonard Arthur Waters)

Q. Captain, I will ask you to listen to this question: Assuming that the Steamer West Cajoot on a voyage from Manila to Los Angeles, by way of Hongkong and San Francisco, is carrying fuel oil in her double bottom tanks, is also carrying a cargo of 1,223,583 pounds of cocoanut oil in her No. 3 port and starboard deep tanks, about half in each tank, which deep tanks were located immediately above the No. 3 double bottom. Assume also that on October 2nd the vessel stranded while passing through the Van Diemen Straits in Japan, and that after she was floated from the stranding, it was decided to make for Kobe, Japan, as a port of refuge. Assume further that after the stranding the No. 1 and the No. 2 double bottom tanks were sounded and it was discovered that sea water had entered said hold and tank. Assume also that tests were made to determine whether there was any water in No. 2 and No. 3 holds, and it was found that there was none, but later, by subsequent soundings, a leak was discovered in the No. 2 hold, but not in the No. 3, and that no soundings were made in the No. 3 double bottom.

In view of the above facts, what is your opinion as to whether the No. 3 double bottom tank should have been sounded or not after the vessel had floated from the reef?

A. May I answer that question at length? Immediately the vessel was stranded and was taken off, soundings should have been conducted at least every half hour in every sounding tank of the ship, starting from the fore peak tank to the double bottoms, to the after peak tank to the bilges, and the double bottoms, also the peak tank, every half hour.

(TESTIMONY OF LEONARD ARTHUR WATERS)

Q. By Mr. Vermille: Why is that, Captain?

A. To see if the ship was making water, as a precaution. It should be entered in the chief officer's log book and the chief engineer's log book.

Q. Would that be true if no leak was discovered in the No. 3 hold?

A. Absolutely.

Q. Now, Captain, I will ask you to assume the same facts which I related, but assume further that after the vessel arrived at Kobe on or about October 5, 1927, and before the vessel went into dry dock, it was discovered that there was a leak between the No. 3 double bottom tank and the port deep tank. Assume further that the vessel was put into the dry dock on October 8, 1927. Assume further that either before or shortly after the vessel went into the dry dock, the cocoanut oil in the deep tanks was examined by taking samples from the different levels in the tanks and it was found that the oil in the starboard deep tank was uncontaminated, but that the oil in the port deep tank was contaminated by contact with fuel oil, this contamination, however, being confined to about the bottom 6 inches of such deep tank and the upper layers of the tank being apparently clear and uncontaminated. In view of these facts, what should have been done, in your opinion, in regard to the oil in the port deep tanks?

A. Again I ask you, may I answer that question at length? Was the ship already under survey or was the personnel—

The Court: I don't hear, Captain. I am unable to hear distinctly what you are saying.

(TESTIMONY OF LEONARD ARTHUR WATERS)

Mr. Vermille: Will you please read it again, Mr. Reporter?

The Court: No, he says he is going to answer it in detail.

A.   I want to ask a question before I answer your question. Was the ship surveyed immediately on arrival?

Q.   By Mr. Vermille: I am just asking you to assume the facts that I have related, and I am wondering if the Reporter would be kind enough to repeat the question.

A.   I understand the question.

Q.   You understand the question?

A.   Yes. I asked, was the ship surveyed on arrival or not?

Q.   She was.

A.   Yes, the oil should have been removed.

Q.   Assume further, Captain, that the leak between the two tanks was discovered before dry docking the vessel. Was it proper, in your opinion, to dry dock the vessel without having a complete examination of the cocoanut oil in the port deep tank?

A.   The vessel should be dry docked to determine the extent of the damage and to repair the vessel, if necessary, and the cocoanut oil could have been discharged to determine the leak or the extent of the leak between the double bottom and the tank.

Q.   I don't think you understood my question, Captain. Would you be kind enough to repeat that, Mr. Reporter?

(The preceding question was thereupon read by the Reporter.)

A.   It was proper to dry dock the vessel.

(TESTIMONY OF LEONARD ARTHUR WATERS)

Q. By Miss Phillips: I did not understand you.

A. It was proper to dry dock it.

Q. By Miss Phillips: It was proper?

A. Yes.

Q. By Mr. Vermille: Did you understand the question, Captain?

A. May I answer that, after removing the oil—

The Court: The question, as I understand it is this: Assuming that the leak had been discovered, was it proper to dry dock the vessel before removing the cocoanut oil?

Mr. Vermille: That is the question.

A. Remove the oil first and then dry dock the vessel.

Q. By Mr. Vermille: Now, that is the question. Now, in your opinion, was it proper, knowing that some of the oil in the bottom of the port deep tank was contaminated, to leave the oil in there when it was known the vessel had to go on dry dock, and then proceed on her voyage to the United States?

A. I would remove the oil in any case.

Q. Assume, Captain, that instead of the bottom 6 inches of the port deep tank being found contaminated, all of the oil in said tank was contaminated, would it still be your opinion that the oil should have been removed?

A. Absolutely.

Q. Would the contamination be apt to be increased by continuing the voyage without discharging the cocoanut oil?

A. I should say yes.

Q. In your opinion, Captain, was the West Cajoot with

(TESTIMONY OF LEONARD ARTHUR WATERS)

a leak between the port deep tank and the No. 3 double bottom tank, in a fit condition to go to sea from Kobe?

A.   From where?

Q.   From Kobe to the United States?

A.   I answer it no.

Q.   The Port of San Francisco?

A.   No.

Q.   Now, you are familiar, Captain, with the rules laid down by the association, such as Lloyd's American Bureau, the Bureau of Records, regarding the construction, maintenance and classification of vessels?

A.   Generally, yes.

Q.   What are the rules with regard to tank tops of tanks carrying oil, with particular reference to whether they must be water or oil tight?

A.   Both.

Q.   You mean by both, what?

A.   Oil tight and water tight, put them under hydrostatic pressure to determine that.

Q.   Now, would a vessel sail from Kobe with a leak between her tankers unrepaired? Is that in conformity with the rules?

A.   No, sir.

Q.   Now, apart from any rules, Captain, in your opinion, would a vessel that sailed from Kobe on a trans-Pacific voyage down to San Francisco and thence to the Port of Los Angeles, with a leak of unknown dimension in one of her tank tops, be in a seaworthy condition?

A.   That would be very poor judgment.

Q.   Is the vessel in a seaworthy condition?

(Testimony of Leonard Arthur Waters)

A. No, sir.

·Q. How would the cocoanut oil ordinarily be re-moved from a vessel?

A. With a portable pump, a centrifugal pump, or a steam driven pump with hose especially adapted for that purpose.

Q. Well, Captain, in what kind of receptacles could that oil be removed?

Miss Phillips: Just a moment. I don't believe counsel—

Q. By Mr. Vermille: (Continuing)—into what kind of receptacle?

Miss Phillips: Just a minute. Is counsel confining his question to removal of the oil at Wilmington or Kobe or at Manila?

Mr. Vermille: I have not arrived at Wilmington yet. I am talking about Kobe.

Miss Phillips: That is why I wanted to make sure, because I want to make my objection. I don't believe he has qualified the witness to answer as to the receptacles available in 1927 at Kobe.

The Court: That was not the question.

Mr. Vermille: That was not the question.

The Court: Read the question.

Mr. Vermille: Could have been removed at Kobe?

The Court: In what kind of a receptacle could it have been removed at Kobe?

Mr. Vermille: At Kobe.

Miss Phillips: That is why I am making the objection. He has not yet qualified the witness to answer.

(TESTIMONY OF LEONARD ARTHUR WATERS)

The ship, you see, was at Kobe in 1927. He is asking in what kind of receptacle could that oil have been removed in October, 1927, at Kobe, the first week in October, when she arrived. He has not yet qualified the witness to answer that question.

The Court: Yes, I believe so.

Q. By Mr. Vermille: Pardon me. Did your Honor rule on it? How many times have you been in Kobe?

A. About twelve times.

Q. Are you familiar with the facilities in Kobe?

A. In a general way, yes; I have loaded and discharged cargos there several times.

Q. What size port is Kobe?

A. It is one of the largest ports in the Orient. The largest port in the Orient.

Q. The largest port in the Orient?

A. Also, it is adjacent to the largest manufacturing center in Japan, within a distance of 20 miles.

Q. What center is that?

A. Osaki.

Q. What is the principal business at Osaki?

A. General manufacturing.

Q. Do they have various kinds of oils, fish oils?

A. Soya bean oil, grape seed oil, sesame oil.

Q. That is all vegetable oil, is it?

A. Yes, sir.

Q. Now, what facilities were there at Kobe that you know of for discharging cocoanut oil?

A. I took the vessel to Kobe and sold to Japanese interests to be carrying vegetable oils.

(TESTIMONY OF LEONARD ARTHUR WATERS)

Miss Phillips: May I ask the witness to specify dates?

A. Yes, 1913.

Q. By Mr. Vermille: When were you in Kobe after that?

A. I was in Kobe in '16·

Q. When were you in Kobe after that?

A. I don't remember; I don't recollect the exact date.

The Court: What?

A. I don't recollect the date. I was in the Standard Oil service, making voyages several times a year.

Q. By Mr. Vermille: When was the first time you were there?

A. The first time in Kobe?

Q. Yes.

A. 1910.

Q. And when was the last time you were in Kobe?

A. Last time in 1928.

Mr. Vermille: Your Honor, I think the witness is qualified to answer the question.

The Court: Yes, I think so.

Miss Phillips: Your Honor, for the sake of the record, may I have my exception?

The Court: Yes.

Miss Phillips: May I renew my objection?

The Court: Yes.

Miss Phillips: I take it from counsel's question, he is asking this witness to say whether or not at the time when the ship, the West Cajoot, arrived in Kobe on the night of the 3rd of October, on October 5th, between

(TESTIMONY OF LEONARD ARTHUR WATERS)

October 5th and 8th, when she went into dry dock, whether or not facilities were available which were proper and fit for her to discharge the cocoanut oil into and which she could have then and there have obtained. My objection is the witness has not been shown to be qualified to answer that question.

Mr. Vermille: If your Honor please, that is not the question. If the Reporter will read the question, I think counsel has elaborated considerably on the question I asked.

The Court: Well, the objection is good specifically, but the witness has stated what his knowledge of the Port of Kobe is and I rather think the Court could take judicial knowledge that a port of that size is supposed to have facilities necessary for the care of the business. I think he could properly express an opinion as to what facilities the port afforded for this work. He does not know that there were a certain number of empty tanks on the walls, or anything of that sort, naturally. But this port, I would assume, would have sufficient facilities for its ordinary business.

Miss Phillips: He is qualified to describe the port generally, your Honor; if that is counsel's question for him to describe it generally, I would have no objection. But I took it he is asking him a very specific question here. Perhaps I misunderstood him. Now, if he wants him to describe it generally—

Mr. Vermille: You misunderstood the question. If the Reporter will read away back—

Miss Phillips: Well, don't waste time reading away

(Testimony of Leonard Arthur Waters)

back—ask the question again, if that is what you want, a general description of the Port of Kobe.

Q. By Mr. Vermille: My question was, as I remember, into what kind of receptacles could the cocoanut oil be removed at a port like Kobe?

A. Into standard equipment that is there from year to year, continuously there, such as tank cars, oil tanks, lighters, and drums, and also trans-shipment to another vessel, or failing all that, trans-shipment to other similar tanks in the ship to be cleaned out for the purpose. This equipment which I have described, such as tank cars, oil tanks, and so forth, has been there for a number of years, to my knowledge.

Q. That is all on that.

A. And not changed from day to day.

The Court: Anything further?

Q. By Mr. Vermille: Yes. Captain, there has been testimony in this case that it would not have been practicable from a business standpoint to transfer the oil to another large vessel. Would there have been any such impracticability?

A. None whatever.

Q. How would you transfer the cocoanut oil to another vessel?

A. Put two ships alongside and use a portable pump, pump from the tank of one ship into the other.

Q. Would there have been any difficulty in doing that?

A. None whatever. Move the ship under the direction of a pilot and a tug.

(TESTIMONY OF LEONARD ARTHUR WATERS)

Q. Would the cost of transferring oil in that way to another vessel have been great?

A. No, sir.

Q. There has also been testimony in this case, Captain, that ordinary oil lighters would not have been suitable for discharging cocoanut oil into. I will also ask you that assuming such lighters had carried oil before, would there have been any difficulty in cleaning out such lighters?

A. None whatsoever.

Q. Will you please state to the Court how the lighters would have been cleaned out for the reception of cocoanut oil?

A. There are various methods of cleaning them. I have cleaned a number of tanks personally. I have supervised the cleaning of tanks, and I have also been in the tanks and helped to clean them out, and in the particular case, taking cocoanut oil, the usual practice is to steam the tank down for a number of hours, to cut the oil off the sides of the tanks, wash down with heavy hose and hot water, and a lye or a caustic is used. After that it is pumped out and washed down, dried. Sometimes it is washed out with fresh water and then they take cocoanut meal, wipe the tank down with cocoanut meal, and sometimes they use the oil itself to wipe the tank out. Then this is done under survey and when the surveyor approves the tank fit to take the oil, it is taken aboard and taken into the tank.

Q. Would there have been any difficulty in transferring the cocoanut oil to tank cars?

(TESTIMONY OF LEONARD ARTHUR WATERS)

Miss Phillips: Your Honor, it is understood that my objection goes along to all of this?

The Court: Yes.

Miss Phillips: I don't want to waste the Court's time with too many objections, but I still renew the objection that the witness has not been shown to be qualified to testify to actual conditions there at that time.

The Court: Overruled.

Miss Phillips: Exception.

Q. By Mr. Vermille: Did you understand the question?

A. What is the question?

Q. Would it have been difficult to clean the tank cars for the reception of cocoanut oil?

A. No more than any other tanks.

The Court: No more than what?

A. Than any other tanks.

Q. By the Court: Than any other tanks?

A. Yes.

Q. I don't understand you.

A. You clean the tank out the same way.

Q. Did you say obtain or clean?

Mr. Vermille: Clean.

A. Clean.

The Court: Oh, clean. Is that the method used after a container of cocoanut oil is emptied, always? I mean is it cleaned in the way you have described?

A. Generally, sir.

Q. Generally, not always?

A. It depends on what they have taken into the tank.

(TESTIMONY OF LEONARD ARTHUR WATERS)

If they are taking cocoanut oil back again, if it is used,—
if it has just been used for cocoanut oil,—it is cleaned
out, steamed out, wiped out, and then the cocoanut oil
back again, but if another tank is used, then they go
through the same procedure that I have described.

Q.   Then what?

A.   They use the same procedure that I have described
before.

Q.   Yes.

Q.   By Mr. Vermille: Captain, there has been some
testimony in this case that there were some large tanks
of the Rising Sun Petroleum Company near Kobe which
had been used for the purpose of storing gasoline and
kerosene. The testimony is that these tanks could not
have been cleaned perfectly to put the cocoanut oil in
them. What is your opinion in that regard?

A.   I think they could have been cleaned.

Q.   Would there have been any difficulty in cleaning
them?

A.   No more than cleaning any other tank.

Q.   There has also been testimony in this case, Captain, that the best plan was to leave the oil where it was
because there would not be material for the contamination on the remaining legs of the voyage. What do you
have to say in that regard?

A.   I believe there would be more contamination.

Q.   Assuming, Captain, that only approximately the
bottom 6 inches of the port tank was found to be contaminated, in your opinion could the upper layers of the

oil have been removed from the tank without further material contamination?

A. The oil on top could have been taken out without stirring up the oil below.

Q. Assuming, Captain, that between October 6, 1927, before the vessel went on the dry dock, that after she arrived at Kobe, and October 12th, after the vessel went on dry dock, that the amount of oil in the port deep tank increased 4 inches and that in the starboard tank decreased 4½ inches, what would that indicate to you?

A. Indicate the oil had access from one tank to the other tank.

Q. Would you say how?

A. Well, if a ship is lying afloat with a list, the outage may be measured differently than when a ship is brought on even keel, or a ship on a dry dock may lay, if she has been on a floating dry dock, she may lay with her stern a little lower than her bow. If she is on a perfectly even keel at both times at sea and some time on the dry dock, and then there was a difference in the oil, that would mean there was a leak between the two tanks, probably through the longitudinal bulkhead.

Q. You mean, between the two tanks?

A. Port and starboard tanks.

Q. Oh, port and starboard tanks?

A. There is a longitudinal bulkhead between the two tanks. It may be occasioned by the vessel having a list while lying afloat.

Q. What effect would that have on your answers with

(TESTIMONY OF LEONARD ARTHUR WATERS)

reference to the desirability of removing cocoanut oil from the port deep tank?

Miss Phillips: That is objected to as indefinite. I cannot make out for the life of me what effect that would have. The witness just testified to several alternatives.

The Court: Reframe the question.

Q. By Mr. Vermille: All right. Assuming a vessel at Kobe, in the harbor of Kobe, while in the harbor of Kobe, before the vessel went on dry dock, that the amount of oil in the port deep tank increased 4 inches—

The Court: In what tank?

Q. By Mr. Vermille: (Continuing)—increased in the port deep tank.

The Court: The port deep tank is the tank?

Mr. Vermille: Port deep.

The Court: Deep tank, yes; that is the one that had the oil in it, contaminated oil. Did you say it increased what?

Q. By Mr. Vermille: 4½ inches; and that the oil in the starboard deep tank decreased 4 inches, the amount of oil in the port deep tank increased 4 inches, and the oil in the starboard tank decreased 4½ inches; what would that indicate to you?

A. It would indicate that the oil found its own level through some access through the bulkhead.

Q. Would that indicate a leak in the bulkhead?

A. Yes, I would assume that it would. There is no other way that it could.

Q. Now, I will repeat the other question. Would that

(TESTIMONY OF LEONARD ARTHUR WATERS)

have any effect, in your answer to the question, to the desirability of removing the cocoanut oil?

A.   I would remove the oil from the port deep tank for two reasons, one, to determine—the only way of determining the extent of the leak, and the other to save the oil, if possible, from further contamination.

Q.   Captain, there is a blueprint of the vessel on the blackboard. I will ask you to step down and examine the blueprint.

(The witness thereupon left the witness-stand and examined the blueprint on the blackboard.)

Q.   Can you point out to the Court, please, the vessel's fore and after peak tanks?

A.   Fore and after peak tanks?

Q.   Fore and after peak tanks, yes?

A.   That is the fore peak tank; (indicating) that is the after peak tank (indicating).

Q.   Will you explain to the Court the capacity of the various tanks that you have just pointed out?

A.   They are on a scale.

Q.   Will you advise the Court as to what capacity those tanks are?

A.   4 foot tanks, 108½ tons, and after peak tank, 241.7.

Q.   By the Court: Are those tons, did you say?

A.   Yes, sir.

Q.   Or barrels?

A.   Tons. It is figured out 66.7 barrels to the ton.

Q.   How many?

A.   6.7 barrels to the ton.

(TESTIMONY OF LEONARD ARTHUR WATERS)

Q. Do you know how much you say a gallon of cocoanut oil will weigh?

A. Approximately 8½ pounds.

Q. 8½ pounds.

Q. By Mr. Vermille: Will you look at that blueprint again and look at the scale, and I will ask you if you can state, approximately, Captain, how much cocoanut oil there would be in the bottom 6 inches of the port deep tank?

A. 6 inches?

Q. The port deep tank, 6 inches, the bottom 6 inches?

A. 7 or 8 tons.

Q. Now, I will ask you to explain again, would the fore peak tank and the after peak tank be of sufficient capacity to have held—

A. May I make a calculation? You say 6 inches?

Q. 6 inches.

A. 6 inches, and not 6 feet?

Q. 6 inches.

A. Well, that is not more than a couple of tons. One side of a deep tank?

Q. The port deep tank, the bottom 6 inches of the port deep tank?

A. That is 6 inches from the top of the double bottom?

Q. Of the double bottom?

A. It would be about 2 tons.

Q. Including the bilges?

A. Oh, the bilges? It would run more.

Q. It would run more. How much, then, approximately?

(TESTIMONY OF LEONARD ARTHUR WATERS)

A. 4 tons, 2 tons to a side. That would bring it up to about 5 tons altogether.

Q. Approximately 5 tons?

A. Yes. If I would give it a little more consideration, I could figure it out.

Q. Now, Captain, I will ask you to examine the blueprint of the vessel again and advise the Court whether or not the forward peak tank and the after peak tank was of sufficient capacity to have held the remaining oil of the No. 1 or the No. 3 port deep tank?

A. Two tanks would hold one side of the deep tank, the port deep tank, around.

Q. By the Court: By two tanks, what are you meaning?

A. The fore peak tank, sir, and the after peak tank. This tank here.

Q. What are you getting at?

Mr. Vermille: The storage of the cocoanut oil if no facilities were available to store it in the vessel itself.

A. The fore peak tank and the after peak tank are about the same capacity as the port deep tank, approximately 350 tons.

The Court. Oh, they were full of fuel oil?

Q. By Mr. Vermille: The Court asked the question that they were full of fuel oil. Would there have been any difficulty in removing the fuel oil from the after peak tank and the fore peak tank and making those tanks suitable for the storage of cocoanut oil?

A. That would depend on the amount of space elsewhere in the ship to transfer the oil to. If any of the

(Testimony of Leonard Arthur Waters)

double bottom tanks were empty, you could run the oil from the peak tanks into the double bottom.

Q.   Assuming, Captain, that the vessel went out to sea after arriving in Kobe, but before going on the drydock she went out to sea and emptied her bilges. Now, would it have been possible at that time to have emptied the fuel oil from the fore and after peak tanks?

A.   Yes, if they had the space in the bottom, certainly, remove it any time, laying at the time at sea or anywhere.

Q.   We are talking about the space in the—I am talking about emptying the fore and after peak tanks of fuel oil. Any difficulty at all in doing that?

A.   None whatever.

Q.   By the Court: Well, that would mean putting it out on the sea?

A.   Dumping it overboard?

Q.   By Mr. Vermille: Yes.

A.   Not necessarily. Not if you wanted to save it.

Q.   Where could that have been put if they were in port?

A.   Fill the settling tank first and then run into the other tanks; part in one tank and part in another. I assume that the ship would have space enough at that particular time after leaving Manila.

Q.   I was just going to ask you, assuming the vessel on a voyage from Manila to Hongkong and then to Kobe did not take on any fuel oil during that trip, would certain tanks in the vessel be empty of fuel oil, or would fuel oil have been consumed from any parts or tanks of the vessel?

(Testimony of Leonard Arthur Waters)

A. Well, it is optional with the master and chief engineer as to where the oil should be used from. Now, if a vessel goes to sea and she has oil in her double bottoms and her peak tanks,—what I mean by the peak tanks is this fore and this after peak tank, they always use that first before touching the double bottoms. That is on account of ballasting the ship. It is always taken from the fore peak tank first because a vessel is always better with her stern being down a little more than the bow. It makes better speed. So it is always the better practice to remove the oil from the fore peak tank first and from there go to the after peak tank, and drain the after peak tank, unless the ship is very light in the water. If the ship is very light in the water, they will keep the peak tank until the very last. They on the double bottom, they start on the No. 1 tank and they go back to No. 5 and No. 6. They alternate. Now, on the passage from Manila to Hongkong and Kobe, approximately 3 steaming days to Hongkong. In about a week's steaming time she would use, let us say,—this is an 8800 ton ship.

Q. And you surveyed that ship, Captain?

A. Yes, twice.

Q. And you are familiar with it?

A. Yes.

Q. Do you know how much fuel oil she would use, just approximately?

A. A little over a thousand barrels of oil from Manila to Hongkong to Kobe.

Q. Approximately?

A. Approximately.

(TESTIMONY OF LEONARD ARTHUR WATERS)

Mr. Vermille: If your Honor please, I don't like to interrupt, but I have here an expert chemist that has to get back.

The Court: What is that?

Mr. Vermille: I have here an expert chemist. I just notice that he came in, and if it would be agreeable to your Honor and agreeable to counsel, I would like to call him.

The Court: No, let's finish with this witness. I prefer that you finish with this witness. I don't suppose his cross examination will be very long.

Mr. Vermille: Very well. All right, Captain, will you please take the stand again?

Q. By the Court: The thousand barrels that you mention, how would that compare with the capacity of the port deep tank?

A. The thousand barrels? Will you excuse me a minute? It would be about half the capacity.

Q. About half the capacity?

A. Approximately.

The Court: Of the port deep tank. Yes, that is what it is. Proceed.

Q. By Mr. Vermille: Now, Captain, I don't know whether I asked you this question or not, but would there have been any difficulty in cleaning out the after peak tank if the fore peak tank contained fuel oil, for the reception of cocoanut oil?

A. No, no more than it would have been a dirty job. There would be no trouble to clean it.

Q. In other words, then, in your opinion, they could

have used the after peak tank of that vessel for the storage of cocoanut oil?

A. Provided the tank was sound, yes.

Q. How was that?

A. Provided the tank was sound and certified.

Q. Assuming that the after peak tank was sound, the after peak tank was in sound condition?

A. It was in sound condition?

Q. Could it have been used for the cocoanut oil?

A. It would; in an emergency. It is not the general practice.

Miss Phillips: I wish the witness would speak up. He sinks his voice and it is almost impossible to get it. Was his statement there that it was not the general practice to carry cocoanut oil in the peak tanks? I did not get that. Was it?

The Court: The failure to speak distinctly is the characteristic of ladies on the witness-stand. Seldom of able-bodied men. It has appeared in this case, however, to a considerable extent. The witness becomes absorbed in his tesitmony and neglects to speak up. Read the answer, Mr. Reporter.

(Answer read by the Reporter.)

A. It is not the general practice to carry cargo in peak tanks, but the tanks are perfectly sound and cargo can be carried in them in an emergency.

Q. By Mr. Vermille: And cargo can always be stored in them?

A. Yes, sir.

Q. Now, assuming, Captain, that there were no

(Testimony of Leonard Arthur Waters)

facilities whatsoever in Kobe for the transfer of this cocoanut oil. What would you have done with this cocoanut oil?

Miss Phillips: That is not for the witness to speculate. Your Honor, he was not there. Asking him what he would have done if he was there and he would have known the conditions. I don't believe his answer would assist the Court at all.

Mr. Vermille: Read the question.

(Question read by the Reporter.)

The Court: Answer the question. You mean, according to the practice?

Mr. Vermille: Yes.

The Court: Or seamanship requirements?

Mr. Vermille: That's it.

A. Transfer the oil to other tanks in the ship, or failing that, I would have tried to sell it.

Q. By the Court: Does the master have authority to do that? He does, I suppose, under certain circumstances.

A. Under survey with the advice of the surveyor. I have done it before.

Q. By Mr. Vermille: Now, assume, Captain, that as the result of the stranding in this case there was damage to the fore peak tank in that there were three floor plates with their frame angles slightly buckled and the tank was flooded; what would you say about the availability of the fore peak tank for the transferring of the cocoanut oil under those circumstances?

(TESTIMONY OF LEONARD ARTHUR WATERS)

A. You could not transfer it until the tank had been repaired.

Q. To your mind, approximately how long would it have taken to have repaired that dent?

Miss Phillips: Just a moment. That certainly—the witness is not qualified to answer that.

The Court: I don't think so.

Miss Phillips: And certainly has not shown any experience with repairs at Kobe.

A. I certainly have.

Miss Phillips: You may, but you have not qualified him.

A. I certainly have.

Mr. Vermille: I will qualify him.

Q. By Mr. Vermille: Captain, what has been your experience with a vessel of the size of the West Cajoot?

A. I supervised the building of a vessel like the West Cajoot, and I supervised the repairing of many of these vessels.

Q. Where was the West Cajoot built, if you know?

A. The West Cajoot was built in the Los Angeles Ship Yard.

The Court: Leave off all of that. It would first be necessary to remove the oil before the repairs could be made.

Mr. Vermille: Your Honor, I did not understand the question. The question was this: If the fore peak tank had been damaged to a certain extent—

The Court: Had been damaged?

Q. By Mr. Vermille: Had been damaged by the stranding what would have had to have been done to

(TESTIMONY OF LEONARD ARTHUR WATERS)

that fore peak tank to have made it available for the storage of cocoanut oil?

The Court: If I understand it right, you say if the fore peak had been damaged by the accident?

Mr. Vermille: That is it. This is the fore peak.

The Court: Well, is that in the evidence?

Mr. Vermille: That is in the evidence, if the Court please.

The Court: All right. Tell us all about it. What would have been necessary?

A. Put the ship on dry dock, repair the damaged plates, and put the ship back into her condition as the specifications of the American Bureau call for under survey.

Q. By Mr. Vermille: Then, if that was done, would the tank have been available for the storage of cocoanut oil?

A. Absolutely. It would have had to be.

The Court: Anything further?

Q. By Mr. Vermille: Approximately how long would that have taken to repair that damage?

A. Three days.

Q. Captain, this cocoanut oil was stored in the No. 3 double bottom hold. It appears that the settling tanks were just abaft the deep tanks. It further appears that there was some sort of a coffer dam in between the settling tanks and the after part of No. 3 hold. Would the coffer dam have generated any heat, or the settling tanks have generated any heat at all into the No. 3 port deep tank?

(TESTIMONY OF LEONARD ARTHUR WATERS)

A. It would have the same effect if you light a gas heater in the room. You warm the air in the room by lighting a gas heater and the air in the coffer dam would have become the same temperature as the plate and which also in the length of time would have heated the side of the deep tank wall.

Q. Have you ever been down in the vessel, Captain, which has settling tanks, or were you captain of a vessel similar to this?

A. Yes, sir.

Q. What did you find the conditions down there?

Miss Phillips: Just a moment, your Honor. I think he is going away around. He is asking now for him to describe the conditions he found in another vessel. I object to that as incompetent in this case. If he wants to ask him about this particular ship, the location of these settling tanks, that coffer dam and these deep tanks, I have no objection; but for him to go on and describe another ship, I think that is incompetent in this case.

Mr. Vermille: If your Honor please, these ships are all sister ships. They are built on scale. I would like to have the Captain explain. They are all alike.

Miss Phillips: Well, here is a blueprint. Let him sit down and talk to this.

A. I can describe this ship the same.

The Court: It calls for his knowledge of conditions on this particular ship by reason of your knowledge of other ships. That is the question, isn't it?

A. Yes, sir.

Mr. Vermille: Of the same construction.

(TESTIMONY OF LEONARD ARTHUR WATERS)

A.   Yes, sir. They are all built alike.

The Court: Objection sustained.

Q.   By Mr. Vermille: Have you ever been down on this ship making a survey?

A.   Yes, sir, twice.

The Court: I am not following you at all, Mr. Vermille.   Please explain what you are directing this evidence to.   Now, I understand there is a coffer dam, of course, different from my idea of a coffer dam, but it is a coffer dam.

Mr. Vermille: That is what they call it.

The Court: And it is a steel—

Mr. Vermille: Bulkhead.

The Court: Plate.

Mr. Vermille: A coffer dam, your Honor, is a space between two bulkheads.

A.   In oil tankers it is used to separate the cargo or oil cargo from the fuel of the ship.   In this particular instance, I understand that this ship had one built into it before she started to carry cocoanut oil .

Q.   By Mr. Vermille: Well, what you call a coffer dam is a space?

A.   An empty space.

Q.   Rather than a partition?

A.   Yes, sir, between two partitions.

The Court: All right.   Now then, what difference does it make in the case whether it carried heat to the tank or not?

Mr. Vermille: To keep the cocoanut oil in a liquid state longer than it otherwise would.   If the cocoanut

(TESTIMONY OF LEONARD ARTHUR WATERS)

oil had been stirred up here in the fore peak tank forward of No. 1 hold, it would have solidified much quicker than it would in No. 3 bottom.

The Court: Well, if it had solidified, what difference does that make, I mean in copra?

Mr. Vermille: If it had?

The Court: Yes, if it had solidified or had not solidified, what importance is it?

Mr. Vermille: Why, on the discharge of the cocoanut oil if it had been solidified they would have had to heat it.

The Court: Well, suppose so. It was not solidified, however, when it got to Kobe. That, I take it, is admitted in the case?

Mr. Vermille: I don't know whether counsel disputes me there or not.

Miss Phillips: Well, your Honor, there is a lot of testimony.

The Court: I am not asking for any discussion at all. I am merely asking whether it is or is not admitted. Now, that is my understanding from the questioning heretofore, I think that that is rather remote.

Mr. Vermille: Very well, your Honor. I will try and speed it up. And I will pass that.

Q. By Mr. Vermille: Now, Captain, assuming that the oil, the cocoanut oil, was liquid when the vessel was at Kobe upon arrival and upon discovery of the contamination, the first discovery of the contamination, what effect would that have had upon your opinion as to the advisabilitiy of removing the oil to prevent further contamination?

(Testimony of Leonard Arthur Waters)

A. As I said before, I would have the oil removed from the tank.

Q. It could have been removed—

A. Unless I was overruled by the agent of the ship, which was very often done on those particular ships.

Q. What is this?

Miss Phillips: Just a moment. I object to that, your Honor, and ask that that be stricken from the record. The witness is assuming something here that he does not know a thing in the world about.

The Court: No. This is maritime practice, I understand. The ship has an agent in the port?

A. Yes, sir.

The Court: He said, and I think that is proper, that his advice would have been and his action, to remove the oil unless that was countermanded by the agent of the owner of the oil, I suppose; the agent of the ship, anyhow.

Miss Phillips: I don't object to that, but his aside, "as was frequently done in these particular ships," I object to that and ask that it be stricken from the record.

A. It has happened to me in many ships.

The Court: Just a moment. No, motion denied.

Miss Phillips: Exception.

Q. By Mr. Vermille: Finish with your statement.

A. In many cases of this type the master's opinion is overruled by the agent on the matter of expense. In other words, the judgment of the master that oil should be removed after some accident, there is very often a difference of opinion. I have had several cases of it in

(TESTIMONY OF LEONARD ARTHUR WATERS)

these particular 8800 ton ships. My judgment has been overruled as a question of expense by the agent on shore. It has been done in pilotage, it has been done in cargo, and in various other matters.

The Court: Well, no matter about that. Your opinion, briefly, is that proper practice would have required the removal of the oil, but that had the custom or the person in charge ordered that, it might have been counter-manded by the ship's agent?

A. That is what I mean, sir.

The Court: All right. That is all.

Q. By Mr. Vermille: Now, Captain, if this oil had not been in a liquid state, would you have removed it?

A. If it had not been in a liquid state?

Q. Yes.

By the Court: You say could it have been removed?

Q. By Mr. Vermille: Could it have been removed, or would you have removed it?

A. I would have removed it and determined the amount òf damage to the vessel before proceeding on a trans-Pacific voyage in the winter time unless my judg-men was again overruled by my owners. In a case like that, I would apply to my owners for permission to do so.

Q. I don't remember whether I have asked this ques-tion or not, but just one more question. Would a vessel, or the West Cajoot, be in a seaworthy condition if she left Kobe bound for San Francisco with a leak of un-known dimensions, or any leak existing between the port deep tank and the double bottom tank No. 3?

(TESTIMONY OF LEONARD ARTHUR WATERS)

Miss Phillips: That has been asked and answered.

Mr. Vermille: I don't remember whether I asked it.

A. No, she would not be in a seaworthy condition.

Mr. Vermille: That is all.

Miss Phillips: Is that your last question?

Mr. Vermille: I am trying to hurry.

CROSS EXAMINATION

By Miss Phillips:

Q. Captain, I noticed when you were first asked a question of opinion, the first hypothetical question was put to you about assuming certain facts, and so on. Before you would answer that you said, "I want to know whether she was surveyed on arrival." Do you remember your answer to that?

A. Yes.

Q. Why did you ask that question?

A. Because in any case of damage immediately upon arrival in port you call for a survey either by Lloyd or the American Bureau of Shipping, if it is an American ship, or if neither one of them is available, then you call for a survey by the most competent people in the port.

Q. And that is the first thing to be done before anything else is done, is that right?

A. Absolutely.

Q. Put divers to work and find out what the damage is before anything is done, is that right?

A. Whatever the surveyors decide upon.

Q. And the reason for that is there are competent men there on the ground and it is important for them

(TESTIMONY OF LEONARD ARTHUR WATERS)

to see and make up their mind as quickly as possible, is that right?

A. The master is governed by the survey which is made. He can have any opinion which he likes himself, but a survey should be called in the interest of the owners of the ship, in the interest of the owners of the cargo, and in the interest of the insurance.

Q. To get disinterested people who will exercise their best judgment on the ground, on the spot, as quickly and as efficiently as possible, now is that it?

A. That is it.

Q. That is the idea. Now, you said, the substance of your testimony is, I think, that finding a leak between the port deep tank and the fuel oil tank, you would have removed that oil before she went on dry dock in any situation. Isn't that about the size of it?

A. Yes, ma'am.

Q. That is, whether the oil was liquid, or whether it was hard, or whether it was contaminated throughout, or whether it was contaminated in part, you would have removed it, is that it?

A. Yes, I would have removed the oil to determine the extent of the damage.

Q. I see. Now, you have suggested a number of things that could have been done. One was that you could pump the cocoanut oil from the tank—from the deep tank to the fore peak and to the after peak tank. Now, you are asked to assume and you were told that in fact the fore peak tank was damaged in the collision. Your answer was that could not be used until the ship

(TESTIMONY OF LEONARD ARTHUR WATERS)

was dry docked and that was repaired, which would
amount to 3 days. Is it your idea then that before using
the fore peak and the after peak tank you would put the
ship in dry dock, repair the fore peak tank, and then get
the after peak tank ready, is that your idea?

A.   Get the after peak tank ready while I was repairing the fore peak tank.

Q.   I see.

A.   To save time.

Q.   And in the event the after peak tank was regularly used for fuel oil, you would do something with that
fuel oil, would you?

A.   I would put it in the double bottoms.

Q.   You would put it in the double bottoms. Now, is
it your idea that you would after pumping that cocoanut
oil into the after peak tank and the fore peak tank, that
you would go out to sea with it in those tanks, carry it
clear back to San Francisco in those tanks?

A.   No, in that particular case the tank would be repaired, the port deep tank would be repaired, and they
could put it back there or get a surveyor's report allowing you to proceed to San Francisco with that oil where
you have it.

Q.   You mean with the oil in the fore peak tank?

A.   Yes, if you had already removed the oil and put
it in the fore peak tank and the after peak tank, then if
the surveyor passed the ship as being seaworthy, there
would be no necessity of putting it back in the port deep
tanks.

Q.   In other words, if the surveyor said it was proper

(TESTIMONY OF LEONARD ARTHUR WATERS)

for you to carry that oil from Kobe home in the fore peak tank and the after peak tank, you would do so, is that right?

A. Yes. Of course, you confer with the surveyor. The surveyor does not have the absolute power because he gives you his opinion.

Q. Yes. But I am assuming, now, that the surveyor is a fellow who is competent, efficient and disinterested, acting for the interest of all concerned. Now, that is what you assumed at the start and that is what I am assuming.

A. Absolutely.

Q. Ordinarily, the fore peak tank is used for fresh water, isn't it?

A. Yes.

Q. And you get water on ship?

A. Yes.

Q. You have got to have water. The testimony in this particular ship is that the fore peak tank was used for fuel oil, so what you are asked is if those two tanks were used for the cocoanut oil with the permission of the surveyor you would have to put the water and the fuel oil somewhere else, is that about the size of it?

A. Yes.

Q. It is true, isn't it, that a vessel leaving Kobe for the trans-Pacific voyage in the winter-time has got to have an ample allowance both of water and of fuel, hasn't she?

A. Absolutely.

(TESTIMONY OF LEONARD ARTHUR WATERS)

Q. Absolutely. She dare not risk storms or delayed voyages, or mishaps where she runs short of either, isn't that correct?

A. Correct.

Q. She must have not only an ample allowance, but she must have a margin besides, mustn't she?

A. Yes, that is determined on the daily consumption and the factor—it is what is called the safety factor. If you want that, I can give it to you for every thousand miles. If the distance between Yokohama and San Francisco is 4,000 miles, then the safety factor is considered 4 days extra fuel above the normal consumption, of the ship.

Q. But even so, a cautious shipmaster does not even run short on a safety factor, does he?

A. No, that is very often determined, though, by what you can get. Sometimes the owners have different opinions.

Q. I see. Captain Waters, from what you have said, I take it that a shipmaster must consult and have a good deal of respect for the opinion of the surveyors at the port of refuge to which he has applied, is that correct?

A. Yes. A good deal depends, of course, who the surveyors are. If the surveyors are the American Bureau or Lloyd's surveyors, they carry a great deal of weight. If the surveyors are just picked, say, two shipmasters from another ship, or some minor official, well, you generally arrive at some opinion between the three or four of you, some common opinion.

Q. But when it is the shore surveyor, men who are in

the business of classifying ships, make a profession of it, certifying all kinds of ships, he should have a good deal of respect for their judgment, is that right?

A. They give you a report, what they call a seaworthy certificate. When a ship sails from port, that is signed by the surveyor and that relieves you as to the safety factor of a ship going to sea.

Q. When a man gets such a certificate from the surveyor of the port, that really gives him a comfortable feeling as to the safety of the ship, is that it?

The Court: Your answer, sir?

Miss Phillips: His answer was nodding.

A. I beg your pardon. Yes.

Q. By Miss Phillips: Captain Waters, in testifying as to facilities available at Kobe, in the first week of October, or during the month of October, 1927, you are not having in mind any idea that you were actually there at the time, are you? You were not there?

A. Not on that particular date, no.

Q. You did not, when you were there, make inquiries of various—you were not there to make inquiries of various concerns, were you?

A. No, I was there for discharging a little cargo.

Q. You were not. You never had particular occasion to rent lighters, tank cars, and the like, for using as receptacles during the period of repairs, did you?

A. Only for the cargo that we were scheduled to unload.

Q. That is, only during the discharging and unloading, is that right?

(TESTIMONY OF LEONARD ARTHUR WATERS)

A. Except through making inquiries through agents, which I have done in the last few days. I have made inquiries through agents who are loading in Kobe as to the possibilities of unloading cocoanut oil.

Q. Well, if you are relying for your testimony on them, I would like to show you official correspondence with the American Consul at Kobe as to that, if your testimony as to what is available is based upon reports that friends told you, will you permit me to show you the official correspondence I have had with the American Consul there as to what is there?

A. No, I am basing my testimony only on what I found while I was there.

Q. Will you tell me now if you are not basing it on any conversation you have had with other people in the last few days as to what was available at Kobe?

A. I have been there a number of times and I am going exactly on what I saw when I was in Kobe.

Q. All right. If there is going to be hearsay correspondence, I will give you that, too.

The Court: You stated something about some development in the last few days, if I understood you right.

A. I am interested in a company that will be transporting considerable oil and will be doing a considerable business with Japan in the matter of fish oil, and I have had occasion before this came up,—in fact I have been north to survey a ship for the carrying of oil and to make sales in Japan for the oil.

Q. By the Court: Well, I understand, but the Court's understanding of what you have testified to is from

(TESTIMONY OF LEONARD ARTHUR WATERS)

your knowledge and observation gained during up to, say, 1928?

A. Yes, sir.

Q. That is correct, is it?

A. Yes, sir.

Q. Well, what did this what you have learned in the last few days have to do with it, anything?

A. Oh, just I misinterpreted what you asked as to the facilities at Kobe in a general way at the present time.

Q. By Miss Phillips: No, I was confining my questions to October, 1927, your knowledge of conditions, that is, whether you were there, whether you made any investigation yourself as to what you could rent or lease, as to what could be rented or leased during the indefinite period of repair which confronted this ship, and have you any basis at all for stating whether facilities were or were not in fact available during that month?

A. 1928 was the last time I was in Kobe to discharge cargo, 1100 tons of cargo.

Q. What kind of cargo?

A. General cargo, oils in drums; principally oils in drums.

Q. How long were you in port?

A. Three days.

Q. Three days. And did you take on cargo?

A. Some.

Q. So that was the last occasion on which you were there?

A. Yes.

(TESTIMONY OF LEONARD ARTHUR WATERS)

Q. What was the last occasion before that 1928 occasion?

A. '16·

Q. And 1916?

A. An oil tanker.

Q. Captain, in discussing the various possibilities when counsel asked you to assume that oil as a practical matter could not be transferred, he asked you then what you would try to do, and I think your answer was that you would have tried to sell it, was that it?

A. Yes—

Q. Yes?

A. With the advice of the agent. We would confer.

Q. And you also said with the advice of the surveyor? You are just nodding now.

A. I would not take it upon myself to sell the ship cargo without consulting the agent or the agent for the owners, or the owners direct by wire, or the parties themselves that owned the cargo.

Q. And there again the surveyors at the port come in?

A. The surveyors.

Q. Because, as a matter of fact, prices of cocoanut oil at Kobe that near Manila might be very much lower than they would be in this country?

A. Possibly.

Q. And you might let the people in for a big loss. mightn't you?

A. Possibly.

Q. By selling it?

A. Possibly.

(TESTIMONY OF LEONARD ARTHUR WATERS)

Q. Have you ever had occasion to repair your ship in a port of refuge?

A. Yes.

Q. How long a time were you laid up for repairs?

A. Take in *Shanghi,* one of the steamers—

Q. How long were you laid up?

A. We were laid up for 6 weeks.

Q. 6 weeks. Could you tell at the beginning of that delay, that lay-up, how long you were going to be laid up?

A. No. I will describe briefly to you, if I may.

Q. Oh no, I don't want to go into detail. I am just asking you the question. Could you tell at the beginning how long you were going to be there?

A. Yes, because when estimates are called for repairs and a survey is made and an estimate is called for repairs and a job is generally given out on bids to different ship yards. They bid on the job, and the usual custom, like any other contract, the low bidder generally gets the job. And in the bid specifies the number of days that it will take them to repair the ship. Outside of that, they pay demurrage.

Q. Usually, then, after the ship's repairs are completed, they have to be tested and pass inspection and surveyed and the rest of it?

A. Repaired, under survey,—under survey.

Q. I think that is all, your Honor. Just a moment. By the way, you said you did not know what the Rising Sun tanks could be used. Whereabout are the Rising Sun tanks to which you referred?

A. A little outside of Kobe.

(TESTIMONY OF LEONARD ARTHUR WATERS)

Q.   Outside of Kobe. How far out?

A.   Just a few miles. I don't remember the exact distance. You can see the tanks in the distance. You see, the inflammable oils have to be kept outside of the exact port limits. In other words, that is, outside of the breakwater, and so forth.

Q.   That is a few miles outside of Kobe, isn't it?

A.   Yes.

Q.   Are those big tanks like those great big gasoline tanks we are familian with around the oil fields here on the tank farms?

A.   Well, they vary in size for the type of oil that they contain.

Q.   They are very large tanks, are they not?

A.   Some are large and some are moderate size.

Q.   Are they used for oil, for gasoline, and other fuel oils to be piped to them for shipside?

A.   Yes, the oil is brought over in oil tanks, fuel oil, Diesel oil, gasolines and lubricating oils.

Q.   Then my question is, are they actually run through an oil pipe from the lighters, and so on, over?

A.   Yes.

The Court: Just a moment. There is no suggestion here that the cocoanut oil should have been put into those.

Miss Phillips: Yes, your Honor, that is what counsel asked him on direct examination.

The Court: Oh, it was?

Miss Phillips: If they could not have cleaned those tremendous tanks and then piped that cocoanut oil into those tanks.

(TESTIMONY OF LEONARD ARTHUR WATERS)

A. He did not say by the pipes.

Q. By Miss Phillips: He did not say by the pipes, but I am asking you, aren't there pipe? You could not use the ordinary gasoline pipes?

A. No, if those tanks could have been used for cocoanut oil, they would have had to block off the pipe and transfer with hose.

Q. And you don't know how far that is and what length hose was available, do you?

A. I am not sure.

Q. That is all.

REDIRECT EXAMINATION

By Mr. Vermille:

Q. Captain, did you ever hear of the vessel Achilles?

A. One of the Blue Funnel Liners.

Q. Is that the name of the steamship?

A. Alfred Holt & Company, Liverpool.

Q. Do you know the vessel?

A. I have seen it several times.

Q. If that vessel had been in Kobe during the time that the West Cajoot was there, could the oil have been transferred from that vessel?

Miss Phillips: Just a moment. That is asking the witness to assume that the vessel was there; second, that she had empty tanks that may have been used; third, that the empty tanks were available.

Mr. Vermille: I am asking him to assume that.

The Court: Well, in the first place, the question is not

redirect. Now, you have taken this witness over the road here quite a little. The objection is sustained.

Mr. Vermille:　Very well.

The Court:　Is that all?

Miss Phillips:　That is all.

Mr. Vermille:　That is all.

A.　May I state one thing before I leave the stand? I refer to vessels of this type. These small freighters, the captain in many instances is not allowed the same discretion as with a larger ship, as running a line steamer, and in all particular matters of cargo you have to consult—I did not make that reference in a derogatory way to the owners, or anybody else, but in the way of his agents appointed at these different ports.

Mr. Vermille:　Call Mr. Huffman to the stand, please. It won't take more than a couple of minutes with him. He is the other expert, your Honor.

REUBEN G. HUFFMAN,

called as a witness on behalf of the Los Angeles Soap Company and The Westchester Fire Insurance Company, being first duly sworn, testified as follows:

Q.　By the Clerk:　Your full name?

A.　Reuben G. Huffman.

Q.　How do you spell your first name?

A.　R-e-u-b-e-n.

And　And your last one?

A.　H-u-f-f-m-a-n.

(TESTIMONY OF REUBEN G. HUFFMAN)

(DIRECT EXAMINATION

By Mr. Vermille:

Q. Mr. Huffman, what is your business or occupation?

A. Chemist.

Q. Will you, please state briefly your experience as a chemist?

A. The number of years, you mean?

Q. The number of years and what you analyze, and what your principal business has been, and how long you have been engaged in that business?

A. I have been engaged since leaving school in 1914. The first two years in general work and explosives and chemical work at the Mare Island Navy Yard. During the war as a war-time chemist in the war-time service. After the war for six years 'with the Globe Cotton Oil Mill, analyzing and working in the plant on the cottonseed oil and various oils handled by the company, and for the past 7 or 8 years as part owner of the George W. Gooch Laboratories, analyzing miscellaneous material.

Q. Are you what they call—I forgot to ask the other witnesses—are you what they call a graduate chemist?

A. Yes, sir, I hold a Master of Arts in Chemistry at the University of Nebraska.

Q. Mr. Huffman, I will ask you to examine what purports to be a report of the Bureau of Survey, the Bureau of Standards, Respondent's Exhibit Bower No. 1. I will ask you to examine that report. You have examined that report, have you?

A. Yes, sir.

(Testimony of Reuben G. Huffman)

Q. Is it possible from your examination of that report to determine the extent of the contamination of the fuel oil with cocoanut oil?

A. No, this report is rather indefinite as far as contamination goes.

Q. I show you Respondent's for identification Bower No. 2, which is a letter of Curtis & Tompkins, and ask you if you can tell from an examination of that report, if you can tell the extent of the contamination of the cocoanut oil?

A. Yes, these figures are definite in that respect.

Q. Mr. Huffman, I will call your attention to exhibit A-2, exhibit A-3 and exhibit A-4, and ask you to examine those various exhibits. (Witness examining exhibits.)

Q. I will ask you now to refer to the report of the Bureau of Standards, and see if it would be possible for you to ascertain in that report whether or not the samples that they had for examination was A-1 or A-2, A-3 or A-4? Could you differentiate between the three of them from that report?

A. The only thing you could possibly tell would be from the dark brownish amber color; you might say this lightest colored one, you might call dark brownish amber. Now, that sample depends on what your idea of dark brownish amber is. We never use indefinite terms on colors of oil.

Q. Now, I will ask you again to examine those reports and ask you if both analyses in those reports indicate the same thing?

A. Well, they might, and again, they might not. On

(TESTIMONY OF REUBEN G. HUFFMAN)

the Bureau of Standards report you have a difference between a dark straw color and a dark brownish amber, which might be due to fuel oil. You have a difference there in the saponification value of 255.8 to 255.3, which might be due to fuel oil, but again, it might be due to most any other kind of contamination, water, moisture, meal, or anything like that.

Q. I ask you to look down at the bottom of the report and see what that says about it.

A. Well, the conclusion there, the saponification number indicates that there is only a very slight contamination of fuel oil. I would not say exactly that. I would say he would be correct in saying the saponification number indicates that there was /some slight contamination. It might indicate that, and again it might not. We find that cocoanut oils will vary in their saponification value. That is not a definitely fixed value. That is, it is fixed within certain ranges, but not within the range of .5 of one point. There might, however, be present a very small quantity of fuel oil, sufficient to change the color of the cocoanut oil, but which cannot be determined by regular methods of analysis.

Q. Can that be determined?

A. That can be determined, perhaps not exactly to a hundredth of a per cent, but at least approximately close.

Q. I ask you again to look at those reports and state whether or not the Curtis & Tompkins' report indicates any increase in contamination over the Bureau of Standards' reports?

A. Well, the reports are not in the same language. It

(TESTIMONY OF REUBEN G. HUFFMAN)

would be pretty hard to render an expression that way, because they did not determine the same thing.

Q. In other words, the report of the Bureau of Standards, it is impossible from the report of the Bureau of Standards to determine the contamination of fuel oil, is that correct?

A. Well, I would say that, yes, that the report is not definite, sufficiently definite to determine the amount of contamination.

Mr. Vermille: That is all. I just shortened it.

Miss Phillips: I have just a question or two. Pardon me, are you through? I beg your pardon. I thought you were through.

Mr. Vermille: Go ahead.

CROSS EXAMINATION BY MISS PHILLIPS

Q. Mr. Huffman, when did you first see these two reports?

A. I saw these reports about Monday, I believe it was.

Q. Monday. This is Thursday. It was three days ago?

A. Yes.

Q. You did not actually make a test according to the report? You simply examined the two reports?

A. I simply examined the reports, yes.

Q. Let me ask you this question: If you had the Curtis' report before you and you had a sample of oil before you, and you tested the oil, could you then with that sample before you and with the Curtis' report before you, look at the two and say, "Well, I believe they are about the same"?

(TESTIMONY OF REUBEN G. HUFFMAN)

A. If I had a sample of oil and an analysis from Curtis & Thompkins, I could, yes.

Q. You could?

A. Yes.

Q. Even if you did not put it in the report, you could mentally make the comparison?

A. Well, I would have to examine the oil.

Q. Oh yes.

A. I can't tell just from looking at those samples that the Curtis & Tompkins' report means nothing at all.

Q. I understand you. I did not mean to even suggest that. I mean having the Curtis & Tompkins' report, having the sample, and proceeding to analyze that sample?

A. Yes, ma'am.

Q. You could say that the sample before 'you was substantially the same as the Curtis' report, couldn't you?

A. I could.

Q. Even though you did not put all that in your written report?

A. I would not need to check up everything. In fact, just from the color and knowing from whence the color was derived, I could know that it was very similar to the report reported in the report of Curtis & Tompkins.

Miss Phillips: That is all.

REDIRECT EXAMINATION

By Mr. Vermille:

Q. Just one more question. Would it be possible to make up samples of the cocoanut oil according to the report of the Bureau of Standards?

A. No, it would not.

(TESTIMONY OF REUBEN G. HUFFMAN)

Miss Phillips: That is all.

Mr. Vermille: That is all.

Miss Phillips: Your Honor, both sides have closed the case, now. I would like to have, your Honor,—for the sake of the record, I would like to have the record show a motion for a judgment for the United States, the libelant in Case No. 3663, for a contribution in general average from the respondent, and I ask a reference to ascertain the amount of general average due.

May I say at this time, your Honor, that in taking the depositions I started to prove the items of general average in the general average report so as to be able to compute this in court. Counsel on the other side at the time stopped me and said, "You are piling up the record on this; this is proper for a reference." That is why this evidence on the amount of general average item is not in evidence, but to follow the admiralty practice, that if your Honor decides the principle of liability, then to order a reference to ascertain the damages. Counsel is in the same position with reference to the damage to the cocoanut oil, to ask a reference to ascertain the damages.

Mr. Vermille: If liability is established here—

Miss Phillips: I haven't finished my motion.

Mr. Vermille: Pardon me. I thought you were all through.

Miss Phillips: Just on that question, the amount of damage. Then I also want to move in Case No. 3691, the same motion, motion for judgment in favor of the United States for a contribution in general average, the amount to be determined upon a reference. In case No. 3327, I move for judgment in favor of the United States on the following points: The first point, that the United States was made a party to this action after the Statute of Limitations had run against the United States, and that the Statute fails to confer jurisdiction to give judgment against the United States for that reason. The second point, I move for judgment in favor of the United States on the ground that the evidence fails to show that there was negligence on the part of the agents and officers of the ship in the care and custody of the cargo; on the further ground, the damage was clearly caused by the stranding of the ship and was not caused by the enforced delay at Kobe, and on the ground that no contribution in general average was due from the United States to the cargo owner.

Now, if counsel wants to make his motions, we can both have them in the record.

Mr. Vermille: I understand, your Honor, that this matter is going to be submitted on briefs, and that those things would be taken up in briefs, but if counsel makes the motions, of course, I would make a similar motion that in the event of no liability on the vessel for the damage, we be allowed a general average contribution for the damage to our cargo.

The Court: The motions will be submitted—

Miss Phillips: What is the pleasure of the Court upon briefs?

The Court: Wait a moment. You make your motion for judgment, and so forth, which calls for a determination at this time. It will be sufficient for your record to take a denial of the motions and an exception; will it not?

Miss Phillips: I think we can submit all the motions to your Honor.

The Court: Very well, then. The matter will be taken under submission. Let that be the order with respect to the motions made by counsel for the Government. Very well. Do you have any motions to make, sir.?

Mr. Vermille: Well, my motion is that this matter either be referred to a referee to ascertain the amount of damage or counsel for both sides will get together.

The Court: Will what?

Mr. Vermille: Will get together and agree among themselves and stipulate as to the extent of the damage.

The Court: Yes. That is a formality that comes after judgment.

Miss Phillips: Yes, your Honor.

The Court: Well now, then—

Mr. Vermille: One other motion probably that should be made at this time. I understand that your Honor is going to submit the matter on briefs and it is absolutely impossible to pass on these motions without having all the evidence before you in the way of the depositions that have been introduced, but I would like to make this motion in the event—that in any event the libelant, the Los Angeles Soap Company, should be allowed a general average contribution for the damage to its cargo. Of course, all these matters will be taken up in the briefs.

The Court: Very well, then. All motions stand submitted. * * *

(Endorsed): Filed May 27 1933 R. S. Zimmerman, Clerk. By Theodore Hocke, Deputy Clerk.

IN THE DISTRICT COURT OF THE UNITED STATES IN AND FOR THE SOUTHERN DISTRICT OF CALIFORNIA, CENTRAL DIVISION.

THE LOS ANGELES SOAP COMPANY, a corporation,	))	
Libelant,	)	No. 3327-C
vs.		IN
UNITED STATES SHIPPING BOARD, MERCHANT FLEET CORPORATION,	))	ADMIRALTY.
Respondent.	)	

THE UNITED STATES,		
Libelant,	)	
vs.	)	No. 3663-C
THE LOS ANGELES SOAP COMPANY,	)	
Respondent,	)	

THE UNITED STATES,		
Libelant,	)	
vs.	⟨	No. 3691-C
WESTCHESTER FIRE INSURANCE COMPANY,		
Respondent.	)	

Tuesday, April 8th, 1930.

_____

DEPOSITION OF ARCHIE CUTHBERT WATSON

ARCHIE CUTHBERT WATSON,
called for the respondent, sworn:

DIRECT EXAMINATION

Miss Phillips: Q. Will you please give your full name? A. Archie Cuthbert Watson.

(TESTIMONY OF ARCHIE CUTHBERT WATSON)

Q. Where do you live, Mr. Watson?

A. Livermore.

Q. What is your occupation?

A. I am located on a farm; I presume I would be a farmer.

Q. How long have you been living at Livermore?

A. A year last month.

Q. What was your occupation previous to that time?

A. Steamship business.

Q. How long had you been in the steamship business?

A. Since 1906.

Q. Whereabouts?

A. I worked for the Pacific Coast Steamship Company, American Hawaiian, the Pacific Steamship Company, Admiral Line, Struthers & Barry and Swayne & Hoyt.

Q. Whereabouts were you employed in October of 1927?

A. I was in Japan.

Q. Whereabouts in Japan?

A. Kobe.

Q. Did you have any connection with the United States Shipping Board at that time?

A. In the capacity of an agent for one of the operators.

Q. At what city?

A. Kobe.

Q. Which operator?

A. Swayne & Hoyt, Incorporated.

Q. How long were you stationed at Kobe?

(TESTIMONY OF ARCHIE CUTHBERT WATSON)

A. From January, 1921 until September, 1928.

Q. Were you in Kobe in October, 1927?

A. Yes ma'am.

Q. Do you know the Shipping Board vessel West Cajoot?

A. Yes.

Q. When did you first know that vessel?

A. The year I am unable to recall, but I handled it a number of times during my period there.

Q. By whom was the West Cajoot operated?

A. Swayne & Hoyt.

Q. Now directing your attention to October 2, 1927, do you recall any unusual circumstance occurring about that date, or about the first of October, 1927?

A. Yes ma'am.

Q. Just state what it was.

A. I received a wireless from the Master of the SS West Cajoot stating that he was in trouble, that he had run aground in—I have forgotten the name of the port— in Japanese waters.

Mr. Derby: By the way, I understand, Miss Phillips, that under the stipulation all objections except as to the form of the question are reserved?

Miss Phillips: Yes, that is satisfactory.

Q. Just make it quite brief; I am bringing you up to the matter of what you did when the West Cajoot arrived in Kobe, if she did arrive in Kobe. You do not need to go into unnecessary detail. You received a wireless from the Captain of the West Cajoot that he was in trouble?

(TESTIMONY OF ARCHIE CUTHBERT WATSON)

A. Yes.

Q. Did the West Cajoot arrive in Kobe thereafter?

A. He arrived on the 3rd of October, if I remember.

Q. In the morning or afternoon or evening?

A. It was in the evening, around about 7 o'clock.

Q. Do you know whether she arrived on her own power?

A. Yes ma'am, she did.

Q. Did she come to the dock or was she out in the stream?

A. She anchored out in the bay to a buoy.

Q. Did you go on board?

A. Yes ma'am.

Q. What day did you go on board, if you remember?

A. Immediately upon the arrival of the vessel in port.

Q. Did anybody accompany you?

A. The Port Superintendent of the United States Shipping Board, the general agent.

Q. Please give the name, Mr. Watson.

A. Mr. Ralph Johnson, superintending engineer, the general agent for the Shipping Board Mr. Thornton, a surveyor whom I had appointed by the name of Captain S. Reid, and Mr. Suzuki who represented the stevedores.

Q. You mean he was a stevedore or master stevedore, something of that sort?

A. He was the stevedore who had been doing our stevedoring before.

Q. Now when you boarded the West Cajoot what was done. Just go ahead and describe in your own language, Mr. Watson, what was done, that is confining yourself of course to your personal knowledge, or what you did, or what was done in your presence.

A. We went aboard and proceeded into the Captain's room where a conference was held by the Shipping Board representative, the surveyor and members of the crew, the chief engineer, chief officer and of course the Captain; we discussed the entire phase from the period of stranding until arrival in Kobe, discussing ways and means of handling the damage to the ship as well as the cargo. After the discussion it was decided that a portion or all of the cargo in No. 1 hold would be discharged, lightered ashore and re-conditioned.

Q. Were the hatches opened at that time or was any examination made of the ship?

A. Hatch No. 1 was opened, the cover was off.

Q. Do you recall whether there was water in the hatch?

A. It showed an indication of dampness.

Q. Do you recall at this time whether the ship appeared to be down by the head or was she on an even keel?

A. She was down by the head.

Q. Was a survey made, Mr. Watson, of the ship and of the damage to the ship so far as that could be done?

A. Not at that time; on account of the darkness, of course, and the condition no one would have been able to make a survey of that vessel until she was actually in the dry dock, other than of course a diver's examination.

(TESTIMONY OF ARCHIE CUTHBERT WATSON)

Q. This was at night that this first conference was held?

A. In the evening.

Q. The evening of arrival?

A. Yes.

Q. You spoke of an examination by divers. Was an examination by divers made?

A. The following day after the arrival the diver made an examination of the bottom of the vessel.

Q. Did the West Cajoot go into dry dock?

A. Yes ma'am.

Q. What dry dock?

A. Mitsubishi.

Q. Where is that dry dock?

A. It is located in Kobe.

Q. Prior to the vessel going into dry dock do you know if any cargo was discharged?

A. There was considerable cargo discharged from No. 1 hold and hatch.

Q. What cargo was this, what kind of cargo?

A. Copra in bulk and in bags.

Q. Was all of the cargo discharged from No. 1 hold or was only a portion of it; how was that?

A. All of the cargo was discharged from No. 1 hold and a portion was discharged from the tween decks.

Q. You mean the tween decks of No. 1?

A. Of No. 1.

Q. What cargo was taken from No. 1 tween decks?

A. Copra.

Q. Was any cargo left in the tween decks?

(TESTIMONY OF ARCHIE CUTHBERT WATSON)

A.   There was some cargo left in tween decks.

Q.   Was there any cargo discharged from any other hold?

A.   There were some fire crackers in cases discharged from No. 2 hatch.

Q.   Why was that?

A.   On account of the harbor regulations, the officials considered fire crackers hazardous things and therefore would not permit the vessel to dry dock with those stowed on board.

Q.   Mr. Watson, do you know whether any oil of any kind was discharged from the ship before she went into dry dock?

A.   There was the residue which had leaked into the No. 1 hold of the ship.

Q.   What kind of oil was that?

A.   That was crude oil which had leaked in from the double bottom of the ship.

Q.   Was any fuel oil discharged from the ship?

A.   There was no fuel oil other than that which I have just mentioned.

Q.   How long did it take to discharge the ship's cargo that you have described?

A.   They started to work on the morning of the 4th of October and she was completely discharged on the evening of the 7th of October.

Q.   When did she go to dry dock?

A.   The following morning.

Q.   In that interval between October 7th and October 8th did the ship do anything?

(Testimony of Archie Cuthbert Watson)

A.   On the evening of October 7th the vessel proceeded to sea for the purpose of discharging the fuel oil which had leaked into the double bottom—fuel oil together with salt water—

Q.   (Interrupting) Which had leaked into the double bottom?

A.   Which had leaked into the hold.

Mr. Derby: Q.   Do you not mean leaked from the double bottom?

A.   From the double bottom, yes.

Miss Phillips: Whereabouts did she go to discharge this?

A.   Of course I am unable to definitely state that but she steamed all night long at sea; I presume she passed outside of the three mile limit.

Q.   Why was it that the vessel had to proceed out to sea to discharge this accumulated fuel oil, etc.?

A.   It was for the purpose of getting rid of the mess, cleaning the vessel out, making her ready for repairs.

Q.   Was it possible to discharge that there in the harbor?

A.   Under the circumstances it was not.

Q.   Why not?

A.   We were unable to secure sufficient barges to discharge this residue into.

Q.   Had you made efforts to get barges?

A.   Yes ma'am.

Q.   Was there any additional hazard in the ship being sent out to sea for that purpose?

A.   Well, personally I felt there was, in that the ves-

(TESTIMONY OF ARCHIE CUTHBERT WATSON)

sel was unseaworthy, considered un-seaworthy, due to the damage of the vessel.

Q. Could the vessel discharge the fuel oil right in the harbor over the side?

A. No ma'am; on account of the harbor regulations they would not permit her to do it.

Q. Mr. Watson, do you recall whether there was any cocoanut oil on board the ship?

A. Yes ma'am.

Q. Was there?

A. There was.

Q. How do you know?

A. I saw the manifest, I also saw samples of cocoanut oil taken from the deep tank.

Q. Whereabouts was the oil stowed?

A. In the deep tank.

Q. Whereabouts are the deep tanks?

A. They were amidships.

Q. How many of them are there?

A. Two, port and starboard.

Q. Was any examination made of the cocoanut oil?

A. I do not understand that.

Q. You said that you saw samples taken of the cocoanut oil.

A. There was an examination made from the samples, they were sent to a chemist who analyzed them.

Q. When were these samples taken?

A. I believe it was the following day after the arrival of the vessel.

Q. From which tank?

(TESTIMONY OF ARCHIE CUTHBERT WATSON)

A.   Both the starboard and port tanks.

Q.   Can you describe the containers—

Mr. Derby: The starboard and port tanks were the number 3 deep tanks, were they not?

A.   The only knowledge I have is what they were called, the deep tanks, the starboard and port tanks.

Q.   Those were the only two deep tanks?

A.   That had cocoanut oil in.

Miss Phillips: Q. Mr. Watson, can you describe the appearance of the samples that were taken. In the first place what sort of containers were they placed in?

A.   They were placed in glass bottles, and their color was you might say yellowish—I would hardly know how to explain it—it looked something like possibly olive oil.

Q.   About what size containers were they. Can you compare them with any object that would give us an idea of the size?

A.   I would say they were about four or five inches long and possibly, I might say, about the same size as the receiver on the telephone in diameter.

Q.   You mean the top or the bottom?

A.   Where you have your hand.

Q.   That is the body of the receiver itself. I would say that is possibly one and a half inches in diameter, would you not, Mr. Derby?

Mr. Derby: I guess so.

Miss Phillips: Were they marked?

A.   They were marked.

Q.   How?

A.   By labels, and they bore starboard and port—it

(TESTIMONY OF ARCHIE CUTHBERT WATSON)

might have been "S" and "P", I am not positive as to that, but they were identified and known to us as port and starboard side samples, taken from the tanks.

Q. They were marked as to which tank they came from?

A. Yes.

Q. Do you remember whether there was any initial or any sort of mark upon them or any name on them?

A. I think the surveyor put his initials or name on; I am not positive as to that.

Q. Are you familiar with the appearance of cocoanut oil in normal condition, Mr. Watson?

A. Well, I know in a measure what it should be, but I could be fooled very easily by giving expression as to the color of it.

Q. You do not pretend to be a cocoanut oil expert, then?

A. No ma'am.

Q. Now when the samples were taken and the bottles marked, do you remember whether the oil was in liquid or in a solidified condition?

A. The oil was in a liquid form.

Q. Do you recall observing the condition of the samples thereafter?

A. Some time after the oil was placed in the containers, the contents solidified, and I noticed a change in color; that is one container was perfectly clear while the other one was darker.

Q. What was the appearance of the container; where

you said the oil seemed to be clear, can you compare that with any object that would be familiar to us?

A.   Well, I could say lard, for instance.

Q.   What was the appearance of the solidified oil in the container that was darker, how would you compare that?

A.   It looked similar to what might have been lard before it was a darker, or yellowish or brownish color.

Q.   Was the difference between the two samples perceptible or noticeable or was it slight; what was your judgment?

A.   It was quite noticeable.

Q.   Do you recall which of the containers showed this dark appearance? Was it port or starboard?

A.   I believe it was from the port.

Q.   Mr. Watson, was the cocoanut oil discharged from the ship before she entered dry dock?

A.   No ma'am.

Q.   Did you consider the advisability or possibility of discharging the cocoanut oil before the ship went into dry dock?

A.   Yes ma'am.

Q.   When?

A.   The time when we boarded the vessel and several times afterwards, after first boarding the vessel.

Q.   Why did you give attention and consideration to the discharging of the cocoanut oil?

A.   Primarily the reason was believing that the vessel was damaged to the extent that it would be necessary to discharge it for the purpose of making repairs, and

(TESTIMONY OF ARCHIE CUTHBERT WATSON)

further than that it would aid in lightening the vessel before dry docking.

Q. Now did you make any effort directed toward a discharge of the cocoanut oil prior to entering dry dock? Did you do anything directed to that purpose?

A. I attempted to secure empty lighters or barges to be used for the purpose of holding the cocoanut oil.

Q. What firm or firms in Kobe did you make inquiry from?

A. Standard Oil, Rising Sun and Kowasaki Dockyard Co.

Q. To your knowledge were there at that time any companies in Kobe engaged in shipping or transshipping of cocoanut oil?

A. Not of cocoanut oil, to my knoweldge.

Q. Were there any companies in the shipping or transshipping of any kind of oil?

A. There are barges for the purpose of shipping fish oil.

Q. Any other kind of oil?

A. Oil companies have barges for the purpose of conveying crude oil from their property to vessels.

Q. Which of these companies had barges for use in the conveying of crude oil?

A. The Rising Sun and the Standard Oil.

Q. And which companies had barges used in the conveying of fish oil?

A. Nutsui.

Q. Were there any other companies having lighters

(Testimony of Archie Cuthbert Watson)

or tank barges suitable for the holding of oil other than you have mentioned?

A.   I am not positive about that but I do believe there were possibly one or two little concerns which perhaps owned one or two barges, lighters.

Q.   You made inquiry, you say, from those companies. What did you find the situation to be as to the rental or the possibility of rental of barges for holding of the cocoanut oil?

A.   We were unable to procure any at all.

Q.   How did that happen? Why was that?

A.   The barges are so limited in number or tonnage that they are generally needed by the concerns owning them to handle their own business. Then too there was a question of being held up for the period that the vessel might be making her repairs.

Q.   Was it known at that time how long or how extensive a time the repairs would take?

A.   It was generally known but I do not believe it was a definite matter at the time.

Q.   That is, I take it you mean that it was known that it might last a considerable period but just how long was not definitely known?

A.   No ma'am?

Q.   Mr. Watson, were there any facilities in Kobe at that time for storing cocoanut oil?

A.   No ma'am.

Q.   How is that?

A.   There were not.

Q.   Now who made the repairs to the vessel?

(TESTIMONY OF ARCHIE CUTHBERT WATSON)

A.   The Mitsubishi Drydock Company.

Q.   The Mitsubishi Drydock Company?

A.   Yes.

Q.   Where was this drydock company located?

A.   In Kobe.

Q.   Were repairs made under contract?

A.   Yes.

Q.   State how this contract was obtained?

A.   The Port Superintendent of the Shipping Board, Mr. Johnson, sent out tenders.

Q.   Do you know this of your own knowledge?

A.   Yes ma'am.

Q.   Go ahead.

A.   I believe in all there was five sent out, that is to the best of my recollection.

Q.   To whom were the tenders sent?

A.   That I do not remember, the names.

Q.   What kind of concerns?

A.   They were all reliable concerns.

Q.   But I mean were they street car companies or what?

A.   Shipbuilding yards and repair work.

Q.   That is tenders were sent out and these concerns invited to make a bid: Is that what you mean?

A.   Yes ma'am.

Q.   Who put in the lowest bid?   ·

A.   The lowest bid, I do not believe, was given the contract because it was a question of number of repair days that entered into it. As I recall the Mitsubishi

(TESTIMONY OF ARCHIE CUTHBERT WATSON)

Company gave the vessel the quickest dispatch, and also it was a reasonable price.

Q. In your judgment the Mitsubishi bid the best under the circumstances that could be expected?

A. Yes.

Q. How long was the vessel in drydock?

A. She came out at the end of the month, which I believe was the 28th of October.

Q. When did she sail?

A. The first of November.

Q. Were you on the vessel during the month, Mr. Watson?

A. Yes ma'am.

Q. What was the occasion of your going to the vessel?

A. I usually went every day just for the purpose of watching the work progress, to see how they were getting along. I went personally a number of times and other times our surveyor was with me.

Q. Was that any part of your duty in your capacity as port agent for the company?

A. I considered it such.

Q. That is the general work of seeing that the repairs and work was properly done? Is that correct?

A. I went aboard for my own satisfaction, for the protection of the vessel, as I considered it part of my duty to know what was going on.

Q. Did you have anything to do with paying the bills for the West Cajoot while she was in the port of Kobe?

A. Yes.

Q. Just state what you had to do with that.

A. The bills were all made out by the vendors and sent to me, they were checked, the extensions, the prices, and finally approved by me for payment; they were then sent to the United States Shipping Board for approval, after which they were returned to me and we made out checks and paid them from the fund furnished by the United States Shipping Board.

Q. This process that was gone through before a bill was actually paid, was that in line with your duties at the port?

A. That was in line with my duties; also it was the instructions issued by the United States Shipping Board.

Q. Now, Mr. Watson, I have a file of bills here which I would like to get before you one by one and have you examine and testify to. I may say, Mr. Derby, that for a convenience in this portion of the deposition and in following the case, I am going to take now the average adjustment prepared for the West Cajoot by Marsh & McLennan, average adjustors, at San Francisco, California, beginning with page 34 of the adjustment. Of course more than one witness will be called later to prove these items of the average adjustment. At this time, however, I want to identify the bills which were put in the average adjustment, and I am following the order in which the bills appear upon the average adjustment beginning at page 34, insofar as this witness has the knowledge of the circumstances under which the expenses and disbursements were incurred and paid.

(TESTIMONY OF ARCHIE CUTHBERT WATSON)

Mr. Derby: I understand from the stipulation under which the deposition is taken that all objections are reserved both as to the admissibility of the bills themselves and also as to whether they constitute proper charges in the general average, and that being the understanding I shall follow the bills to be identified and put in as speedily as possibly without interposing lengthy objections at this time.

Miss Phillips: That is correct.   I am quite willing to stipulate that objections may be reserved to the admissibility of the bills as proper items in the general average adjustment; however if you have objections to the form of the question I will appreciate it if you will make the objections.

Q.   Mr. Watson, the first bill which I will question you on is the bill *d* marked S. Hitani in the sum of 74.50 yen ,which we will have marked as Exhibit No. 1 for identification; this appears to be a bill for pilotage. What is your information with respect to this bill and the services which it represents?

A.   That was the pilot who brought the vessel from sea to her anchorage.

Q.   How was this bill computed, do you know?

A.   By the tariff which is published by the Pilot Association in Kobe.

Q.   Was this bill accurately made out?

A.   Yes.

Q.   I mean correctly computed?

A.   Yes.

(TESTIMONY OF ARCHIE CUTHBERT WATSON)

Mr. Derby: I submit that the witness is not able to answer a question like that of his own knowledge.

Miss Phillips: I think if you will look at the bill you will see that it is computed from tonnage and draft according to the rate. The witness has just said that the computation was according to a tariff and the bill itself shows the draft and tonnage of the vessel.

Q. Was pilotage required at the port of Kobe, Mr. Watson?

A. It is not compulsory, but it is generally understood you always use a pilot.

Q. It is customary in that port, is it?

A. Yes.

Q. Did you approve of this bill for payment?

A. Yes ma'am.

Q. Is that your signature appearing on it?

A. Yes.

Q. Was the bill actually paid?

A. The bill was paid.

Q. 'Did you consider it a reasonable bill?

A. Yes ma'am.

Q. The second bill is one of T. Tsuji in the sum of 179.80 yen, which we will mark No. 2 for identification; that appears to be a pilotage bill for October 7th and 8th, 1927. Do you know under what circumstances this bill was incurred?

A. That was the bill of the pilot for service rendered in taking the vessel to sea and returning during the time the fuel oil was pumped from the No. 1 hold—the fuel oil and salt water from No. 1 hold.

(TESTIMONY OF ARCHIE CUTHBERT WATSON)

Q. That is that matter to which you have already testified?

A. Yes.

Q. Prior to the vessel going into drydock she went out to sea?

A. Yes.

Mr. Derby: Q. In order to make this clear, which double bottom was the oil pumped out of?

A. It was pumped from No. 1 hold.

Q. No. 1 hold only?

A. Yes; the bilges were probably cleared out throughout the ship.

Q. But oil was not pumped from any other hold except the No. 1 hold?

A. It was the oil which leaked through and caused the damage.

Miss Phillips: Q. That is the matter to which you have already testified on the previous direct examination?

A. Yes.

Q. This bill, as I understand it, is the bill for pilotage which was incurred when the vessel went out in the way you have described?

A. Yes.

Q. Was this bill actually paid?

A. Yes ma'am.

Q. Did you consider it a reasonable bill?

A. Yes.

Q. The next bill which we will mark No. 3 for identification is a bill in the sum of 2,013.88 yen, dated October 31, 1927, which appears to be a bill for dis-

(TESTIMONY OF ARCHIE CUTHBERT WATSON)

charging copra and fire crackers. What have you to say of this bill?

A.   That was for services rendered in discharging copra and fire crackers and re-loading them.

Q.   This appears to be a bill of Kawanishi Soko Kabushiki Kaisha. What does that concern, do you know?

A.   That was the stevedoring concern.

Q.   Was this the regular stevedoring concern to which you have referred a few moments ago as customarily doing the stevedoring for the vessel?

A.   Yes.

Q.   Who arranged to employ this firm?

A.   I did.

Q.   Was this bill actually paid?

A.   Yes ma'am.

Q.   Were the services referred to in this bill actually rendered?

A.   Yes.

Q.   ˏDid you consider the bill a proper one?

A.   I did.

Q.   Is this your signature appearing on the bill ap-proving it for payment?

A.   Yes.

Q.   The next bill is the bill of Young & Co., appearing on page 36 of the average adjustment, which we will mark No. 4 for identification; this appears to be a bill in the sum of 201.88 yen for tallying. Do you know the circumstances under which that bill was incurred?

A.   That was incurred by the checkers who checked

(TESTIMONY OF ARCHIE CUTHBERT WATSON)

the cargo out of the ship and checked it back into the ship.

Q.   Is that your signature on the bill approving it for payment?

A.   Yes.

Q.   Was the bill actually paid?

A.   The bill was paid.

Q.   Who arranged for this firm to be employed?

A.   I did.

Q.   Did you consider this a reasonable bill?

A.   Yes ma'am.

Q.   Was it a proper expense in your opinion?

A.   Proper expense, yes.

Q.   The next bill is a bill entitled Young & Co., in the sum of 237 yen, which we will mark No. 5 for identification; this appears to be a bill for checkers employed in assorting, drying and re-conditioning damaged copra, from October 8th to October 24th. Will you state the circumstances under which this expense was incurred?

A.   That was to cover the expense of employing checkers, tally clerks during the period of assorting, drying and re-conditioning while on shore.

Q.   Is it correct that the copra referred to in this bill was the copra which was removed from No. 1 hold?

A.   Yes ma'am.

Q.   And during the period after the vessel arrived and during the period of her repair?

A.   Yes ma'am.

Q.   Who employed this firm?

A.   I did.

(Testimony of Archie Cuthbert Watson)

Q. Was the bill actually paid?

A. Yes ma'am.

Q. Is that your signature on it approving it for payment?

A. Yes.

Q. In your judgment was the bill a reasonable one?

A. Yes, the bill was a reasonable one.

Q. Were the services actually rendered?

A. Yes.

Q. The next bill is a bill of Kawanishi Soko Kabushiki Kaisha in the sum of 321.75 yen, which we will mark No. 6 for identification; this appears to be a charge upon fire crackers. Will you state the circumstances under which this expense was incurred, if you can.

A. That was for the employment of lighters to hold the fire crackers which we discharged from No. 2 hold. They were stored in these lighters during the time the vessel was under repair, after which they were re-loaded into the ship.

Q. Who employed this firm?

A. I did.

Q. Do you know whether the services were actually rendered?

A. Yes.

Q. Is that your signature approving this bill for payment?

A. Yes.

Q. Was the bill actually paid?

A. The bill was paid.

Mr. Derby: Q. What is the item for demurrage in

that bill? What does that mean? Why is there a lighter charge and also a demurrage charge?

A. As I recall it—I cannot definitely say but my recollection is there was a shortage of lighters during the period, and we held them for a longer period than we should have.

Q. But demurrage was charged for the whole 21 days that the lighters were employed.

Miss Phillips: Q. Examine the bill, Mr. Watson. On the face of the bill it says lighterage, 45 tons at 4.00 yen per lighter capacity, amounting to 180 yen. How are lighters usually employed in that port, Mr. Watson, if you know?

A. Well, usually we had nothing to do with the lighter charges at all; the consignees always pay the loading charges; and as far as the owners of the vessel are concerned we had nothing to do with it. But under these circumstances we had to charter these lighters for the purpose of handling that copra. That is in accordance with the public tariff too.

Q. Was it possible to store the fire crackers ashore?

A. No, that was impossible.

Q. Why?

A. The harbor regulations would not permit it.

Q. I observe the bill says "Demurrage 21 days, anchored outside the harbor limits", and a charge of so much per ton per day?

A. They were anchored outside of the harbor limits —what the port officials considered a dangerous anchorage for the purpose of coal oil, gasoline, powder, etc.

(TESTIMONY OF ARCHIE CUTHBERT WATSON)

Q. Was there any other lighterage bill rendered for the fire crackers other than this one?

A. No.

Q. Was this bill actually paid, Mr. Watson?

A. Yes ma'am.

Q. Did you at the time consider that a reasonable bill?

A. I did.

Q. The next bill is entitled Kawanishi Soko Kabushiki Kaisha in the sum of 5,683.24 yen, which we will mark No. 7 for identification. What is this bill, Mr. Watson, if you know?

A. That is for coolie hire handling copra.

Q. What was done with the copra?

A. That was during the period it was being reconditioned or dried on shore.

Q. Just state what was done, what arrangement you made in that connection, Mr. Watson.

A. First of all we tried to get storage space where we could spread this copra out on the ground or on the floor to dry, and finally we were able to get something like 200 cubos of ground where this copra was unbagged and laid out on old sacks and things to dry.

Q. Why was it necessary to lay it out to dry?

A. Because the bags were saturated with oil and salt water.

Q. Do you know whether copra has any tendency to heat or spoil if it is water-soaked?

A. Yes, it has; it heats to quite a degree.

Q. Was this expense necessary to save the copra?

(Testimony of Archie Cuthbert Watson)

A. Yes.

Q. Was the bill actually paid?

A. The bill was paid.

Q. Is this your signature approving it for payment?

A. Yes.

Q. The next bill is for the same concern, Kawanishi Soko Kabushiki Kaisha in the sum of 8,495.20 yen, which we will mark No. 8 for identification. What is this bill, Mr. Watson?

A. That was for lighter hire, holding and storing the copra in bulk during the period the vessel was on the dry dock, you might say it was used as warehouse space.

Q. What arrangements did you make for the renting of these lighters?

A. That was verbal and then later confirmed by letter as to the price.

Q. Did you make any effort to solicit bids upon this feature of the work?

A. I did.

Q. From what source, do you remember?

A. I believe it was Nicholas & Lyons—there were others solicited, but I did not consider them because of their standing in the community.

Q. Nicholas & Lyons and Kawanishi were the two firms from whom you solicited bids?

A. Yes.

Q. Which had the lower bid?

A. Kawanishi.

(TESTIMONY OF ARCHIE CUTHBERT WATSON)

Q. The bid put in by Kawanishi, did that represent the bill as paid?

A. That bill originally was considerable more but after the work had been performed and the bill presented I took the matter up, asking for a reduction, which they granted me and presented me a new bill.

Q. Is that customary in Japan to beat down even a bid?

A. Yes.

Q. Was this bill actually paid?

A. Yes.

Q. Did you consider it a reasonable bill?

A. Yes ma'am.

Q. The next bill is a bill from Kawanishi in the sum of 244 yen, which appears to be for launch service, the launch service being set forth in the bill, which we will mark No. 9 for identification. Mr. Watson, will you tell me the circumstances under which this bill was incurred?

A. That launch was used for the purpose of conveying the Captain, chief engineer from the ship to shore on ship's business, and the Shipping Board officials, our surveyors and myself.

Q. I observe that the bill is for various occasions, on the 11th, 13th, 14th, 17th, 20th, 27th and 28th of October. Whereabouts did this launch operate?

A. It took those whom I have just mentioned from the shore over to the drydock, back and forth.

Q. Why was that necessary?

A. It was the cheapest and quickest means of getting to the ship.

(Testimony of Archie Cuthbert Watson)

Q. I observe the bill also covers launch service from October 3 to 7, and also October 29 to 31.

A. The 3rd to the 7th was during the period the vessel was discharging, or upon the arrival of the vessel and for complete discharge.

Q. Did you say that the vessel left the drydock on the 28th of October?

A. At the end of October; it was the 28th or 29th, I am not just positive.

Q. Mr. Watson, was this bill actually paid?

A. Yes ma'am.

Q. Is this your signature on it approving it for payment?

A. Yes.

Q. Mr. Watson, the next bill appears to be a bill of Sakiyama Shoten in the sum of 283.35 yen for ventilators used in restoring the bags of copra. Will you extend the circumstances under which this expense was incurred, Mr. Watson.

A. That covered the purchase price of ventilators which we used on board the vessel during the period of restoring the copra.

Q. Why was that necessary, or was it necessary?

A. It was necessary in order to get proper ventilation into the copra.

Q. Do you know whether this copra had completely dried out?

A. It was not entirely dry, but it was as nearly dry as it was possible to have it under the circumstances..

Q. Was the bill actually paid?

A. Yes.

Q. Is that your signature approving it for payment?

A. Yes.

Q. Do you recall what sort of weather conditions·
obtained during the month that the vessel was in Kobe?

A. The weather was very much against us, in that
there was considerable rain during that period.

Q. Did that hamper the drying of the copra at all?

A. Considerably.

Q. Did that have anything to do with the buying of
these extra ventilators in the restoring?

A. No, they would have been purchased under ordinary circumstances anyway.

Q. The next bill appears to be a bill of one Oliver
Evans & Co., in the sum of 88 yen for cold storage
charges on assorted meats, coolie hire and packing mats.
Under that circumstance was this expense incurred?

A. These meats were taken ashore from the ship.
At the time of the drydocking the vessel was not in
operation to run the refrigerators, and therefore it was
necessary to take the meats up to keep it from spoiling.

Q. Was the bill actually paid?

A. Yes ma'am.

Q. Did you consider it reasonable?

A. Yes ma'am.

Q. I will mark that Oliver Evans & Company bill
No. 11 for identification. Now the next bill is Union
Insurance Society of Canton in the sum of 1,010.20 yen
which appears to be a premium for insurance policies.
Will you state the circumstances under which that bill

(TESTIMONY OF ARCHIE CUTHBERT WATSON)

was incurred, which we will mark No. 12 for identification.

A. That was in connection with insurance on the cargo which we had discharged from the ship.

Q. That was the insurance covering the copra and the fire crackers, is that right?

A. That is correct.

Q. While it was out of the ship?

A. Yes ma'am.

Q. Did you have anything to do with procuring this incurance?

A. Yes, I made the arrangements for it.

Q. Was the premium in order?

A. It was very good.

Q. Did you actually pay it?

A. Yes.

Q. The next bill is the bill of Mitsubishi Zozen Kaisha, Ltd., in the sum of 53,994.09 yen which we will mark for identification No. 13. What is this bill, Mr. Watson?

A. That covers the total expense in the matter of the repairs to the vessel?

Q. Is this bill for the repairs made by the Drydock Company?

A. Yes.

Q. This was obtained by a bid as you have previously described?

A. Yes.

Q. Mr. Watson, you are not an engineer, are you?

A. No ma'am.

Q. What Shipping Board representative at Kobe would have the best knowledge about that bill and the repairs that were actually made?

A. Mr. Johnson, the superintending engineer.

Q. The next bill is the bill of the Kobe Works, Mitsubishi Zozen Kaisha in the sum of 1,240.16 yen, which we will mark No. 14 for identification; will you examine this bill, Mr. Watson, and tell us what it is?

A. As I remember it that was damage done to the winch at the time and the ballast pump at the time she stranded, and I think that was brought on after the refloating.

Q. I observe that of the total bill of 1,240.16 yen, there were a general average charge only in the sum of 393.16 yen, with a note that general average is charged only with items 8 and 9; the chief engineer, I presume, would have more knowledge of this item than you would?

A. Mr. Johnson really is the man that went over this, and although I discussed it with him at the time I pro rated that.

Q. You mean you pro rated the amount here?

A. Yes.

Q. Was the bill actually paid?

A. Yes.

Q. And is this your signature approving it for payment?

A. Yes.

Q. The next bill is a bill which we will mark No. 15 for identification of the Higashide Engine & Iron Works,

(TESTIMONY OF ARCHIE CUTHBERT WATSON)

in the sum of 120 yen, and is for renewing two lengths
of steam pipe of windlass, etc. Do you know the circumstances under which that bill was incurred?

A. I believe that was the same thing, during the
period of refloating, they damaged these pipes running
to the winch when they raised the anchors.

Q. Is this your signature approving it for payment?

A. Yes.

Q. Did you consider it a necessary and reasonable
expense?

A. Yes ma'am.

Q. And the next item is that of the Garlock Packing
in the sum of $10 which we will mark No. 16 for identi-
fication. Do you know the circumstances under which
that bill was incurred?

A. That was used, I think, for repacking of the
ballast pump.

Q. The next bill Higashide Engine & Iron Works
in the sum of $18 which we will mark 17 for identifica-
tion, do you know what that was?

A. That is in connection with the same damage on
the winch.

Q. The next is a bill of Higashide Engine & Iron
works in the sum of 65 yen which we will mark No. 18
for identification. This appears to be a supply of packing, bolts and nuts and valve grinding compound. Do you
know the circumstances under which that expense was
incurred?

A. My recollection is that that damage was incurred
at the time of the refloating of the vessel.

(TESTIMONY OF ARCHIE CUTHBERT WATSON)

Q. Is that your signature approving it for payment?

A. Yes ma'am.

Q. Was that bill actually paid?

A. The bill was paid.

Q. The next appears to be the bill of Captain V. D. Trant in the sum of 107. 53 yen which we will mark No. 19 for identification. What is that?

A. Might I say that gentleman's name is Trout. That was the sum paid Captain Trout for being present and conducting the Board of Inquiry after the accident.

Q. What was the purpose of the Board of Inquiry?

A. Getting the facts while they were fresh in the minds of the crew.

Q. As to the circumstances under which the grounding occurred?

A. Yes.

Mr. Derby: Is that a proper *gerenal* average charge?

Miss Phillips: I don't know. Possibly that item is subject to objection. I have not gone carefully into the law upon that subject.

Q. The next is the bill of H. Nobu, which appears to be a bill for laundry in the sum of 92.10, which we will mark No. 20 for identification. What is that, do you know? A. That was for laundry used during the period the vessel was in Kobe, I believe.

Q. Did you approve it for payment? A. Yes ma'am.

Q. The next are two bills by S. Reid, each in the sum of 400 yen which we will mark 21 and 22 for identification. What were those bills, Mr. Watson? A. One of those bills was, or rather both of those were for making

(TESTIMONY OF ARCHIE CUTHBERT WATSON)

a survey and inspection of the vessel and issuing a report; one was for the salvage association and the other one for the account of the Shipping Board vessel itself.

Q. Just what services did Captain Reid render? A. Mr. Reid made the general survey of the vessel and made recommendations as to the repairs to be made, and he saw that they were conducted along the lines of his recommendation, and finally certified that they had been carried out to his satisfaction.

Mr. Derby: Have you those reports, Miss Phillips?

Miss Phillips. I think I have. I think I have a copy of them.

Mr. Derby: I would like to see them.

Miss Phillips: Now?

Mr. Derby: Yes.

Miss Phillips: Q. Did he make any survey on the cargo as well. A. Yes.

Q. Did this include that survey of cargo? A. That included that as well.

Q. Did you approve these two bills for payment? A. Yes ma'am.

Q. Is this your signature approving them for payment?

A. Yes ma'am.

Q. Were they paid? A. Yes.

Q. Did you consider Mr. Reid's services necessary? A. Yes.

Q. Did you consider his charge a reasonable charge? A. Yes.

Q. And the next is a bill of the Imperial Japanese

(TESTIMONY OF ARCHIE CUTHBERT WATSON)

Marine Corporation in the sum of 390 yen, which we will mark 23 for identification. What was that bill for? A. That was for surveying the damage to the vessel both before repairs were started and after completion, and for issuance of the sea worthiness certificate to permit the vessel to proceed home.

Q. What is the Imperial Japanese Marine Corporation?

A. The Imperial Japanese Marine Corporation represents the American Lloyds—that is the name.

Q. A bureau of registry, is it? A. That is it, the American Bureau.

Q. Just what was the service rendered by this corporation? A. Their surveyor boarded the vessel and made his recommendation as to the necessary repairs and watched the repairs during their progress to see that they were carried out to his entire satisfaction and upon the completion of the repairs he made final inspection and issued the sea worthy certificate.

Mr. Derby: I would like to see that survey also.

Miss Phillips: I am not sure that I have that.

Q. Mr. Watson, the next bill is the sum of 74.97 yen, made out to A. C. Watson, agent, which appears to be a bill for cables. Can you state what this bill is? A. That is for reimbursing myself of money expended in sending cables.

Q. Sent where? A. To the United States Salvage Association.

Q. That is to New York? A. To New York.

Q. Reporting and asking for instructions? A. Yes.

(Testimony of Archie Cuthbert Watson)

Q. We will mark this 24 for identification. There appears to be two bills; we will mark the second one 25 for identification; it is in the sum of 254.06 yen. Was that of the same general character? A. That was reimbursement to myself for moneys expended in sending cables.

Mr. Derby. Q. Are these yellow copies of cables attached to that large bill in the sum of 254.06 yen the cables covered by that bill? A. These yellow sheets are all copies of the cables sent and the bill is a recap of all of them.

Mr. Derby: I wish to state at this point, that having examined the cables attached to No. 25, it is perfectly obvious that a great many of these are clearly not proper general average charges.

Miss Phillips: That can be taken up, I suppose, and issue made on that. I am not sure what issues are made by the answers, Mr. Derby.

Q. Mr. Watson, the next bill appears to be one of J. Kametaka which we will mark No. 26 for identification; this appears to be a bill for pilotage incurred on November 1. What is that? A. That was for service rendered by the pilot in taking the vessel to sea after she had been completely repaired and cargo reloaded.

Q. The vessel sailed on November 1, I believe you said some time ago? A. Yes.

Q. Was the bill actually paid? A. The bill was paid.

Q. Is this your signature approving it on the reverse side? A. Yes.

Q. The next bill is in the sum of 537.63 yen to your-

(TESTIMONY OF ARCHIE CUTHBERT WATSON)

self as agent, which we will mark 27 for identification. Will you state what that bill is? A. That was for services rendered the vessel and all concerned due to the grounding of the vessel, and acting in the capacity of agent.

Q. This was service rendered in connection with the discharge, repair and reloading of the cargo? A. Yes.

Q. The services you have described in your testimony today? A. Yes.

Q. What was your arrangement for compensation, Mr. Watson? A. I worked entirely on a commission basis.

Q. You did not receive any salary at all? A. I received no salary.

Q. Your service then was for each ship as she came in, is that what the service amounted to? A. I operated my own business, paid all my own expenses and collected a commission for every job I did.

Q. The next is also to yourself as agent in the sum of 236.76 yen, which we will mark No. 28 for identification. What is that? A. That covers a flat agency fee allowed by the Shipping Board for the handling of any vessel in distress or coming into port in distress.

Q. Does that cover other or different services than the previous bill you have testified to, No. 27? A. No. 27 is special services which is considered by the Shipping Board aside from the regular agency duties.

Q. What is covered in the agency duties? A. The arrangement under which I worked was when a vessel would come in I charge a two and a half per cent com-

(TESTIMONY OF ARCHIE CUTHBERT WATSON)

mission on the gross of the manifest or the figures
shown in the manifest; inasmuch as this vessel had no
cargo for discharge in Japan I would be unable to collect
any fees on the gross, therefore the Shipping Board
made a flat charge of $100 for that particular service.

Q.   I observe postage and petties charges also?   A.
They allow $10 for petties, etc.

Q.   That converted into yen makes the sum of 236.56
yen?   A.   Yes ma'am.

Q.   Was that bill actually paid, Mr. Watson   A.   Yes
ma'am.

Q.   That was computed at the rate of exchange on
October 31?   A.   The day the bill was paid.

Q.   The bill is dated October 31.   A.   No, I am
wrong in that.   The exchange was taken as of the date
of the arrival of the vessel.

Q.   As of the date of the arrival of the vessel?   A.
Yes ma'am.

Q.   The next bill in the average adjustment appears
to be one in the sum of 256.45 yen, payable to yourself
for various disbursements, such as tonnage dues, fresh
water, launch hire, night work permits, telegrams and the
like, which we will mark No. 29 for identification.   Just
state what that is.   A.   That was paid and disbursed
from my own pocket for the account of the vessel, for
the convenience of the vessel, for which I reimbursed
myself.

Q.   The item of tonnage dues, what is that?   A.   That
is a standard rate according to the tariff, that every

(TESTIMONY OF ARCHIE CUTHBERT WATSON)

vessel entering a Japanese port pays the Japanese government.

Q. Fresh water, what was that? A. That was necessary for boilers and drinking water.

Q. There seems to be a charge for launch hire of one day of 15 yen. Do you recall what that was for? A. That was for the purpose of conveying the Captain, Chief Engineer, Shipping Board officials, surveyor and myself aboard the vessel.

Mr. Derby: I notice that all of the other disbursements so far have been at Kobe. I notice that bill of disbursement is at Yokohoma. Are you going into that?

Miss Phillips: Yes, I am going to take that up in just a minute.

Q. Mr. Watson, did the vessel put into Yokohoma after leaving Kobe? A. Yes.

Q. This bill appears to be rendered at Yokohoma on November 5. Why did she go to Yokohoma, if you remember. A. To secure bunker fuel.

Q. Why was that? Why didn't she take them at Kobe? A. They were unavailable at Kobe.

Q. Put into Yokohoma for that purpose? A. Yes.

Q. Did she? A. Yes.

Q. What is the fact on that? A. That is what she went for, to secure bunkers.

Q. Do you know of your own knowledge that bunkers were not available at Kobe. A. The arrangement was this, the Shipping Board had a contract with the Standard Oil to furnish bunkers to all their vessels at

Yokohoma at a given price; that is the reason she went in there, to fulfill her contract and secure bunkers.

Q. Was there any advantage in that? A. Well, I don't know as there was any advantage. It was the Shipping Board instructions.

Q. I notice that the average adjustment says that the current price of fuel oil was $2.58 per barrel, but that the contract let with the Standard Oil was $1.65 per barrel. Have you any knowledge of the terms of the contract? A. No, only in a general way.

Mr. Derby: Q. Do you mean to seriously say that no bunkers were available at Kobe? A. No, I did not say that. It might have been possible to have secured Bunkers at Kobe, but the Shipping Board instructions were for the vessel to proceed to Yokohoma and secure bunkers.

Mr. Derby: I must have misunderstood you.

Miss Phillips: I think I did too, Mr. Watson. Have you any recollection or any knowledge upon the point whether or not there was a difference in the contract or market rate and the contract rate, which would make it to the advantage of the vessel to go to Yokohoma? A. Yes ma'am.

Q. What is your information upon that? A. That it was much cheaper than I could buy or it could be purchased on the local market.

Q. But just how much cheaper, you do not recall at this time? A. No.

Mr. Derby: Q. Did you go to Yokohoma with the vessel? A. No. I had my own office in Yokohoma.

(TESTIMONY OF ARCHIE CUTHBERT WATSON)

Miss Phillips: Q. .Then your testimony as to disbursements there, what was your means of information.? A. My agent in Yokohoma sent these bills to me and I pay them.

Q. You pay them? A. Yes.

Q. The next bill in the sum of 129.04 yen is to. A. C. Watson, on November 2—this appears to be an agency fee for bunkering at Yokohoma. We will mark this 30 for identification. Will you state the circumstances of that bill? A. That was a flat agency fee for bunkering allowed by the Shipping Board, $50, plus $10 for petty expenditures.

Q. Making a total agency fee of $60? A. $60.

Q. In return for what services rendered? A. Making arrangements for the bunkering, entering and clearing the vessel, and taking care of whatever ship's business is necessary.

Q. Was that bill actually paid you? A. Yes ma'am.'

Q. Mr. Watson, the next bill in the average adjustment is allowance for wages and provisions, which we will mark No. 31 for identification, in the average adjustment and the papers upon that, appearing in the bill, will mark 31-A, 31-B and 31-C. This appears to be a computation of the salary roll of the ship, the total salary roll and it is computed for the period of 28 days both for salary and for provisions. First, did you make the computation as to the wages? A. No ma'am.

Q. You did not? A. No.

Q. That was made out by somebody else? A. This

(TESTIMONY OF ARCHIE CUTHBERT WATSON)

was made out by the head of the department on the vessel.

Q. Now the computation for provisions, 38 men for 28 days at the rate of 75 cents per man per day, $798, do you know that was computed, or did you have anything to do with computing that? A. No, I have no knowledge of that.

Q. I observe in the list of bills which I passed a few moments ago without marking, being a bill to one Oliver Evans & Co., for provisions and supplies, which you approved for payment. Do you recall now whether or not the vessel took on any supplies at Kobe? A. Yes, it did.

Q. Did you approve this bill for payment? A. Yes ma'am.

Q. I may say this bill is not incorporated in the record as such but the computation is at the rate of 75 cents per day for 38 men. Then apportionment of that wage bill and the provision bill for the period the vessel was in the port of Kobe was not made by you? A. No.

Q. The next bill which we will mark 32 for identification is an apportionment of fuel and stores used, which amount to $1,384.17. This appears to be a computation of fuel oil, lubricating oil, grease and the like which is made by the chief engineer of the vessel. Did you have anything to do with this, Mr. Watson? A. I had nothing to do with it.

Miss Phillips: We will mark this 32 for further identification, 32-a, 32-b, 32-c and the like. That is all.

(By consent a recess was here taken until 1:45 P.M.)

(Testimony of Archie Cuthbert Watson)

Afternoon Session, 1:45 P. M.

Archie Cuthbert Watson,

recalled:

Cross Examination

Mr. Derby: Q. Mr. Watson, referring to exhibit 29, with regard to expense at Yokohoma, I understand that I was incorrect in assuming that you said no bunkers were available at Kobe? A. Well, if I said that, that was not my intention, because I made no inquiry regarding the bunkers.

Q. I notice in a note to this exhibit 29 in the general average adjustment that it says there that "The current price of fuel oil at Kobe was $2.58 per barrel, whereas you could get it at $1.65 per barrel at Yokohoma under the United States Shipping Board contract. Now that difference in price I presume was the reason you bunkered at Yokohoma instead of Kobe? A. Well, I do not recall that that was discussed at all. I think that we were instructed to dispatch the ship to Yokohoma for bunkers.

Q. Who gave you those instructions? A. The shipping Board.

Q. What man on the Shipping Board? A. I think that it was the general agent Mr. Thornton.

Q. You unquestionably could have got the bunkers in Kobe if you had wanted to, could you not? A. I do not think I made any inquiry.

Q. You made no inquiry? A. I do not remember of having. As a matter of fact I doubt very much if we could have gotten them there anyway.

(TESTIMONY OF ARCHIE CUTHBERT WATSON)

Q. This ship stranded in Van Dieman Straits, did she not? A. Yes.

Q. Was it contemplated when the vessel started from Manila and Hong Kong that she was going to go to Japan at all? A. Not to my knowledge.

Q. Do you know how she happened to be going through Van Dieman Straits? A. I could not tell you.

Q. Now you first received news of this stranding, as I understand it, on October 2, 1927, the day the stranding took place. She got into Kobe on the night of October 3? A. Yes.

Q. Practically as soon as she got there, you with these other gentlemen that you have mentioned, went right on board the vessel? A. Yes.

Q. I believe the first of those gentlemen that you mentioned was Ralph Johnson, the superintending engineer of the Shipping Board? A. Yes.

Q. Was he the head engineer of the Shipping Board for Kobe? A. For Japan, yes.

Q. For the whole of Japan? A. Yes.

Q. How about this general agent Mr. Thornton? A. His title was general agent for Japan; I think that he had jurisdiction over the port superintendent.

Q. He was then the general representative of the Shipping Board in Japan? A. Yes.

Q. And Mr. Johnson would have been under him? A. Yes.

Q. I presume that you kept these two men thoroughly advised of everything that took place from the time the vessel arrived in Kobe until she left Kobe? A. I can

(TESTIMONY OF ARCHIE CUTHBERT WATSON)

say that there was scarcely anything down that there was not a conference about at which Mr. Thornton and Mr. Johnson, the surveyor and of course I was usually present.

Q. And of course putting the boat on the dry dock with the cargo of cocoanut oil still on board was done with their entire approval? A. Yes.

Q. I understood you to say on direct examination that you considered the practicability of discharging the cocoanut oil at the time you first boarded the vessel? A It was talked about discharging, if necessary.

Q. Did you know at that time that the cocoanut oil was contaminated? A. No.

Q. When did you discover that it was contaminated? A. Samples were taken the following day after the arrival, and it was several days before we discovered that it was actually contaminated, after having taken the samples.

Q. You say it was several days? A. Yes.

Q. Before you discovered that it was contaminated? A. Yes.

Q. I notice in this average adjustment on page 7 the following entry purporting to be taken from the Master's extended protest: "On October 5th stevedores continued to discharge cargoes from No. 1 hold to lighters. At 1 P. M. it was discovered that there was a leak from the port deep tank to the No. 3 double bottom". The port deep tank was where the cocoanut oil was stowed, was it not? A. Yes.

Q. And the No. 3 double bottom was one of the tanks

(Testimony of Archie Cuthbert Watson)

where the fuel oil was stowed? A. That I could not actually tell you, but there is no question about it.

Q. You certainly knew then at that time on October 5, at 1 P.M. that there was a leak between those two tanks, did you not? A. I don't know as I did.

Q. Would not the master undoubtedly have told you what he discovered? A. It sounds reasonable to assume that.

Q. How soon did you get the chemist's report after you turned the samples over to him? A. We never did have a chemist's report on it.

Q. I thought you said you did. A. I said we were having it analyzed. As a matter of fact we wanted a chemist's report but there was no one, or we considered there was no one qualified to give us an analysis.

Q. That is there were no chemists in Kobe who could give you an analysis? A. That is the supposition; we had druggists there who did that sort of work but there was no one there in that business of cocoanut oil.

Q. Wasn't there any chemist in Japan who could have given you that information? A. I presume we could have gotten it by sending it possibly to one of the colleges or to Osaka.

Q. Osaka is right close to Kobe, is it not? A. Yes.

Q. Did it occur to you to do that? A. No.

Q. If you could not get any chemist's report how did you discover that this cocoanut oil was contaminated by contact with fuel oil? A. Well, I never did actually learn whether it was fuel oil or what foreign matter it

(TESTIMONY OF ARCHIE CUTHBERT WATSON)

was. After the cocoanut liquid had solidified into a solid mass then the discoloration was quite apparent.

Q. Did you not suspect long before that time that the cocoanut oil had been damaged by fuel oil? A. Yes sir.

Q. When did you first have that suspicion? A. I think it was the following day after the vessel arrived.

Q. What led you to that suspicion? A. You could hardly conceive that vessel could have the damage she did and not do any damage to the tank holding the cocoanut oil.

Q. Then you would have assumed that there would be a leak from the deep tank into the double bottom tank? A. I felt that way, yes.

Q. I call your attention, Mr. Watson, to a telegram attached to exhibit No. 25, which is one of the bills for cable charges, a cable by you to Swayne & Hoyt under date of October 14, saying among other things "SS West Cajoot—contamination cocoanut oil in bulk—deep tank samples—mailed SS Maru". Is that the first time you advised Swayne & Hoyt of the contamination? A. By cable.

Q. Did you advise them in any other way? A. By letter.

Q. Did you advise Mr. Johnson and Mr. Thornton of the contamination as soon as you discovered it? A. Yes.

Q. Now I understood you to say—I may be wrong in this but I understood you to say on direct examination that you believed that it was necessary to discharge the cocoanut oil from the deep tank, is that correct? A. No, I think you must have misunderstood me, or if you did

(TESTIMONY OF ARCHIE CUTHBERT WATSON)

not, certainly it was not my intention to say that I did
consider it necessary. The thought was if it did become
necessary we wanted to be prepared to discharge whatever was necessary so as to make the repairs.

Q. At the time you discovered it was contaminated did
you not consider that it was necessary to discharge it if
possible? A. We would like to have, yes.

Q. Would you not without question have discharged
it if you had had the facilities for so doing? A. Only in
the case, Mr. Derby, if that vessel was unable to proceed
to her home part without making repairs.

Q. Will you answer that question? In this case you
had to be repaired in Japan? A. That is true.

Q. Would you not have discharged the cocoanut oil—
and didn't you consider it necessary to discharge the
cocoanut oil under circumstances if you possibly could
have done so? A. At that time it was talked over, as soon
as we discovered the contamination.

Q. As soon as you discovered what? A. As soon as
we actually knew that there was a leak in that tank, we
considered that the cocoanut oil, if damaged had been
damaged already and could not be saved under any circumstances.

Q. Didn't you know, Mr. Watson, that there would
inevitably be further damage of the sound cocoanut oil
that was left with the fuel oil in the double bottom tanks?
A. Well, I know so very little about cocoanut oil, I certainly made plenty of inquiries during this particular time
and I was told that if cocoanut oil came in contact with
any foreign matter it was ruined right then and there;

(TESTIMONY OF ARCHIE CUTHBERT WATSON)

and I was told it was like a blotter or a sponge, and any foreign matter, if mixed into it, it actually deteriorated the cocoanut oil to the extent that it was, that you would be unable to salvage it.

Q. But did you seriously think, Mr. Watson, that all of the damage to this cocoanut oil had already been done between the time of the stranding and the time of this vessel's arrival in Kobe? A. No, I did not.

Q. Didn't you know that that damage was going to continue to go on as long as the two different classes of oils were left in the two tanks adjoining each other? A. I did.

Miss Phillips: I believe I will object to that as not proper cross examination. This witness has said he was not an expert on cocoanut oils. He has testified on direct examination as to inquiry and efforts made for discharging oil if it could be done at Kobe but he has not testified to being an expert on oils. I move to strike out the answer. I was making the objection at the time that the witness was answering. Mr. Watson, you want to be careful and not answer when counsel is making an objection.

Mr. Derby: Q. If you did not consider it necessary to discharge the cocoanut oil why did you make these efforts that you have testified to to discharge it? A. I do not just understand.

Q. You say that you applied to these various oil companies for barges to discharge the cocoanut oil into? A. Yes.

Q. Why did you do that? A. The purpose of making

inquiries was to have them on hand or available should it become necessary to discharge the cocoanut oil.

Q. I see. It was done for the purpose of having the barges available if you decided to discharge the cocoanut oil? A. Yes.

Q. If there had been barges available would you or would you not have discharged the cocoanut oil into the barges? A. I do not believe I could answer that for this reason, that it would have been entirely up to all concerned, that would be the Shipping Board's representative, the Master of the vessel, and surveyor; in all probability there would have been a discussion and it would have been decided right then and there.

Q. After you discovered that the oil was contaminated was not the matter further discussed? A. It was discussd continuously, but when we made inquiries or I made inquiries, I did not make them with the idea that the oil had been contaminated.

Q. I see; that was before you had discovered that the oil had been contaminated? A. Yes.

Q. After you had discovered that the oil had been contaminated did you make any further inquiries? A. No, because I had gone the limit prior to that discovery.

Q. Now I understand that these inquiries were made at the Standard Oil Company, the Rising Sun Petroleum Company, and the Mitsubishi Oil Company, is that correct? A. Not the Mitsubishi Oil Company; the Kowasaki Dockyard Co.; I appealed to their influence with outside interests; where I would be unable to secure

(Testimony of Archie Cuthbert Watson)

tonnage, I felt that the drydock people might be able to use pressure in some way.

Q. But all of those efforts were made before you discovered that the cocoanut oil had become contaminated? A. Yes.

Q. No efforts were made afterwards? A. No.

Q. No further efforts were made afterwards? A. No.

Q. The Rising Sun Petroleum Company I presume is a branch of the Shell Company? A. I don't just know what their affiliations are.

Q. They had offices in Kobe, did they not? A. The Rising Sun, yes.

Q. And they had their fleets of lighters in Kobe? A. They had some lighters.

Q. They had at least five lighters, had they not? A. I could not tell you that.

Q. What was the nature of your efforts made with that Company. Did you write them any letters? A. No. I went to the lighter department and made my inquiries there.

Q. Were the inquiries made of the clerk in charge of the lighter department? A. I don't recall now who the gentleman was.

Q. What was the nature of the lighter department— just a sort of desk in the office of the Rising Sun Petroleum Company? A. I don't know how to say it.

Q. Was it a man behind the counter? A. Behind a desk, yes.

Miss Phillips: Let me interrupt, because perhaps it will save a little time. Mr. Watson, you should state in

(TESTIMONY OF ARCHIE CUTHBERT WATSON)

respect to Mr. Derby's question quite fully what you did
in that connection. Will you please state just what you
did? A. I went to the Rising Sun and asked them, the
gentleman in charge of the lighter department about it—
I told him my troubles, what I wanted—I told him the
trouble that the ship was in and possibly we would like
to charter lighters.

Mr. Derby: Q. Was he an Englishman or a Japanese? A. It was a foreigner.

Q. Was he young or old?

Miss Phillips: That is objected to as immaterial.

Mr. Derby: Go ahead and answer the question. A. I
should say a middle aged man. I don't recall.

Mr. Phillips: That is objected to as immaterial, what
his age or the color of the man's eyes or what the color
of his hair was.

Mr. Derby: Q. He told you that no lighters were
available, did he? A. I do not recall the exact conversation, but I was told that we could not have lighters
from that concern. I was not told in that language at
all, but they did not have anything that they could
charter to us.

Q. Did you go to anyone else in the company besides
him? A. No.

Q. You did not inquire of any of the officials of the
company? A. I believe this gentleman was considered
to be an officer.

Q. You did not inquire of any other officer of the
company then? A. No.

Q. Now what was the extent of your inquiry at the

(TESTIMONY OF ARCHIE CUTHBERT WATSON)

Standard Oil Company. In the first place, I will ask you where the Standard Oil Company was located? A. The Osaka Building.

Q. Did you go to Osaka to see them? A. No.

Q. How did you handle the matter with them? A. The Osaka Building in Kobe is where the office at that time was located.

Q. Who did you make inquiries of there. A. Mr. Jordan.

Q. Who is Mr. Jordan? A. He is the man in charge.

Q. In charge of what? A. Oh, I think, the marine department, I am not positive as to that.

Q. The marine department of the Standard Oil Company in Kobe? A. In Kobe, yes.

Q. The principal offices of the company however were in Osaka, was it not? A. No, they were at Kobe.

Q. Did you make inquiries of anyone else besides this man who had charge of the marine department? A. No. That is the Standard oil you mean?

Q. Yes. Who did you inquire of in the Mitsubishi Company? A. In the Kowasaki Company, I appealed through our stevedores, who Kawanishi Soko Kabushiki Kaisha, and they appealed to Kowasaki.

Q. You don't know anything about what they did, do you? What did you ask them to do?

Miss Phillips: Just a minute. I think the witness was about to start to say something and you interrupted him.

Mr. Derby: All right, it seems to me obviously it would be hearsay, but if Miss Phillips wants him to go ahead let him go ahead. Complete your answer.

(TESTIMONY OF ARCHIE CUTHBERT WATSON)

A. The Kawanishi Soko Kabashiki Kaisha were affiliated with Kowasaki, and Mr. Suzuki of Kawanishi seemed to be a go-between of the foreigners there and Japanese, and so far as I was concerned, if I really was in trouble in any way, shape or form, that I thought the Japanese could be reached, I went to Mr. Suzuki, and in this particular case I asked Mr. Suzuki.

Q. You went direct to Mr. Suzuki then yourself? A. Yes; Mr. Suzuki is connected with Kawanishi Soko Kabushiki Kaisha, and the answer came back that there were no available lighters.

Q. He was the head of the stevedoring gang that was unloading the ship? A. Yes.

Q. Was he the only person you talked to in connection with the Kowasaki Company? A. Yes.

Q. And these inquiries were all made, as I understand it, before you didcovered that the oil had been contaminated? A. Before we actually knew it.

Q. And the inquiry was simply whether you could have lighters if you subsequently needed them? A. That was the inquiry.

Q. And those were the only efforts you made to secure lighters? A. I might say, in my testimony this morning I omitted to include Mitsui Company. I went personally to the manager of the Mitsui Company—I have forgotten the department, the export department—the man who was in charge of those barges and made inquiries of him. They had lighters but nothing that they could assist us with.

Q. You mean lighters for the carriage of oil? A. Yes.

(TESTIMONY OF ARCHIE CUTHBERT WATSON)

Q. Who did you see in Mitsui & Company? A. I just saw the manager of the export department.

Q. Of the export department? A. Yes.

Q. And that also was before you discovered that the oil had been contaminated? A. Yes.

Q. And after you discovered that the oil had been contaminated you made no further efforts to secure lighters? A. I made no further efforts.

Q. I understand from your direct examination that one of the objections to the furnishing of the lighters was that they did not know how long it would take to repair the vessel and therefore did not know how long you might want to retain those lighters into which you pumped the cocoanut oil. That was one of the objections? A. That is correct, we could not tell.

Q. Don't you think if they had known you were only going to use the lighters for a very short time you might have secured one or more of those lighters?

Miss Phillips: I think that is assuming something not in evidence.

Mr. Derby: I am asking the witness.

Miss Phillips: Furthermore I think you had better define to him what you mean by a very short time. The vessel did not leave Kobe until November 1 according to the testimony in the case.

Mr. Derby: Read the question to him.

(Last question read by reporter.)

A. Do you want me to answer?

Q. Yes. A. We did not actually know how long we could use the lighters.

(Testimony of Archie Cuthbert Watson)

Q. No, but suppose you had been able to promise them that you would only need them for say two or three or four or five days, don't you then think you could have secured one or more of these lighters, if you could have given them that promise? A. I do not believe so.

Q. You don't know, though? A. I don't know, no.

Q. You made no effort to get a lighter for such a short period? A. I did not mention any time at all.

Q. Now has not the Rising Sun Petroleum Company oil tanks? A. Yes.

Q. Situated in Kobe for the purpose of storing oil? A. They have oil tanks, yes.

Q. Did you make any inquiries as to whether any of those oil tanks would be available for holding this cocoanut oil? A. I made no inquiries, no.

Q. Did I understand you incorrectly in believing that you testified on direct examination that there were no facilities for storing cocoanut oil on shore? A. I do not believe there are any, I am not positive.

Q. Hasn't the Rising Sun Petroleum Company got numerous tanks on shore for the storage of oil? A. Of crude oil, but I do not think that it would be possible to handle cocoanut oil.

Q. Couldn't the tanks be steamed out and cleaned for the purpose of holding cocoanut oil in those tanks, if the tanks were available? A. It might be possible; I could not say as to that.

Q. You don't know whether the tanks were full or empty at the time? A. No.

(TESTIMONY OF ARCHIE CUTHBERT WATSON)

Q. If they had been empty and could have been put in a condition to safely hold cocoanut oil it would have been a very simple matter for a lighter to have taken the oil to these tanks and put it into these tanks until the vessel was ready to take into port again? A. I made no inquiry regarding tanks at all for storage ashore.

Q. There are plenty of tank cars in Japan, are there not. A. I am not positive about that either.

Q. Don't you know that Japan is full of tank cars that are suitable for the storage of oil? A. No, I do not. I do not recall. I do not recall—I do not believe I ever saw a rail tank in Japan.

Q. Now, Mr. Watson, if tanks cars had been available for storing this cocoanut oil would it not have been a very simple thing while this vessel was on the dry dock to have run these tank cars down to the drydock and then pumped the oil into the tank cars? A. I cannot answer that because I do not know.

Q. You don't know? A. No.

Q. Arent there facilities at the Mitsubishi Drydock for running cars right close to the ship? A. I do not think so.

Q. You do not think so? A. No sir.

Q. Then it is different from most of the drydocks that I know about. A. Indeed it is.

Q. Is not the Mitsumishi drydock a very efficient plant? A. Yes.

Q. You made no inquiries as to whether any tank cars could be used? A. No.

(TESTIMONY OF ARCHIE CUTHBERT WATSON)

Q. Did you give any consideration when you found that you could not get these regular oil lighters to getting ordinary steel cargo lighters? A. Not for the discharge of the cocoanut oil, no.

Miss Phillips: I do not believe I understand the question. Let the question be read to him again.

(Last question read by reporter.)

Miss Phillips: Do you mean by that tank lighters?

Mr. Derby: No, I mean regular steel lighters fit for the carriage of general cargo. A. I gave that no consideration.

Q. Why not, Mr. Watson? A. Well, it never occurred to me, nor was it suggested by anyone else.

Q. Had you ever heard of using ordinary steel lighters fit for the carriage of general cargo for the storage of oil after being supplied with portable heating coils? A. No.

Q. Can you conceive of any objection to that course of procedure? A. I do not know enough about cocoanut oil to state.

Q. Was it not your duty at that time to find out all that you could possibly find out about cocoanut oil? A. I tried to.

Q. But you gave no consideration to hiring ordinary steel lighters for general cargo and putting portable coils in them? A. No.

Miss Phillips: Just what do you mean by portable coils?

Mr. Derby: Portable coils are coils that can be put in practically any lighter or vessel in case regular oil tanks are not available for carrying of oil; and I under-

(TESTIMONY OF ARCHIE CUTHBERT WATSON)

stand that such portable coils are carried by practically every efficient drydock company in the United States and presumably in Japan.

Miss Phillips: I think perhaps you are assuming there; certainly you will have to make some proof of it; but what I meant to ask you was do you mean by portable coils coils especially built or constructed or adapted for use in the shipping of cocoanut oil?

Mr. Derby: Coils adapted for the shipment of oil; not necessaryily cocoanut oil, but for any kind of oil, including cocoanut oil.

Miss Phillips: You mean vegetable oil or fuel oil, kerosene and the like?

Mr. Derby: I mean practically all kind of oil; all that is necessary is to thoroughly clean out the lighters, put in the portable coils and pump the oil in.

Miss Phillips: I move to strike out the last answer. I do not believe Mr. Derby is shown to be qualified nor sworn as a witness in the case. My question as to portable coils was because I was not sure that your question was clear to the witness, and I wanted him to understand clearly what you were getting at.

Mr. Derby: Q. Do you know whether there were any portable heating coils available in the Kobe? A. No.

Q. The United States Shipping Board, Mr. Watson, is in effect an agency of the United States Government, is it not? A. As far as I know it is.

Q. Do you know whether the boats of the Japanese Navy, such as battleships, cruisers, submarine boats and

(TESTIMONY OF ARCHIE CUTHBERT WATSON)

torpedo boats burn fuel oil? A. I do not know positively; I understand some of them do.

Q. They have numerous barges to supply these vessels with oil, do they not? A. I am not sure, but I believe they do, though.

Q. Did you make any inquiry on behalf of the Shipping Board of the Japanese Navy yard in Kobe whether they could furnish you with any barges? A. No.

Q. How far away from Kobe is Yokohoma? A. If I remember it, it is in the neighborhood of 360 miles.

Q. An ordinary 10 knot boat could run that distance in about 36 hours, could it not? A. I believe out vessels average it in about 36 hours.

Q. How do the general facilities at Yokohoma compare with the facilities at Kobe? A. Not as good.

Q. Not as good? A. No.

Q. Is there not more shipping done, more of a shipping business done in Yokohoma than in Kobe? A. Do you mean generally speaking that there are more vessels?

Q. Generally speaking. A. That is the first and last port of call in Japan for practically all of the trans-Pacific vessels.

Q. Is it not considered a more important port, considered as a port, than Kobe? A. Not so far as facilities are concerned.

Q. Did you make any inquiry as to whether you could secure any oil lighters in Yokohoma? A. No.

Q. Why not? A. It never occurred to me because I did not think it was practical, I suppose.

(TESTIMONY OF ARCHIE CUTHBERT WATSON)

Q. There are plenty of fast tugs in Yokohoma, are there not, which could have towed down oil lighters from Yokohoma to Kobe?

Miss Phillips: That is something that the witness has stated contra-wise. He said the facilities at Yokohoma were not as good as at Kobe.

Mr. Derby: I am now asking him about a special facility in the way of tugboat.

Miss Phillips: But your question assumes that there were more lighters at Yokohoma than at Kobe.

Mr. Derby: I did not assume that there were more lighters at Yokohoma than Kobe. I assume that there were lighters at Yokohoma and they might have been available if they had been applied for; and I am assuming also that there were tugs, and I am asking the witness if there were not plenty of fast tugs at Yokohoma which could have towed such lighters down to Kobe? A. I do not believe it would have been possible to have gotten a tow boat to tow it from Yokohoma to Kobe.

Q. Why not? A. First of all there is nothing there but a salvage seagoing tow boat; to my knowledge there is no tow boat at Yokohoma aside from possibly one ship yard, or maybe two, that have an ocean-going license for a tow boat.

Q. How about these tugs that bring in the big steamships to the dock at Yokohoma? A. I do not believe you could find one at all that could go outside; the customs owns the tow boats.

Q. That will be a matter on which proof can be secured very easily. When you say, to your knowledge

(TESTIMONY OF ARCHIE CUTHBERT WATSON)

there was not, you mean that you know that there were not such tugs there? A. I don't know for an actual fact.

Q. But you gave no thought to getting lighters from Yokohoma? A. No.

Q. I understand that in taking these samples you found that the oil was still in liquid form?

Miss Phillips: At what time, Mr. Derby?

Mr. Derby: Q. At the time these samples were drawn?

A. They were in liquid form, yes.

Q. And the presumption would therefore be that the cargo of cocoanut oil had at that time not had time to solidify? A. Yes.

Q. And I also got it from your direct examination that one of the samples was taken from one tank and another sample from the other tank; that is one sample was taken from the port tank and one sample from the starboard tank? A. Yes.

Miss Phillips: I do not believe the witness confined himself to one sample.

Mr. Derby: I am not trying to assume that either.

A. There were samples taken from both tanks.

Q. I also understood you to sau afterwards that the contaminated part was all in the port tank and that there was no contaminated oil in the starboard tank? A. Not that I know anything about.

A. I mean didn't you say that the sample which was discovered was marked as coming from the Port tank? A. I believe I did.

(Testimony of Archie Cuthbert Watson)

Q. And that the sample which was clear came from the starboard tank? A. Yes.

Q. Did they hold about an equal amount, these two tanks? A. I think they did, but I do not believe there was an equal amount of oil in each tank.

Q. Which had the most? A. I don't remember that.

Q. That would indicate, would it not, that the leak was in the port tank and not in the starboard tank? A. I don't know how these tanks were loaded, or know the tonnage in each tank. That is something I could not say.

Q. That is not an answer to my question, Mr. Watson.

A. Perhaps I misunderstood you. I understood you to mean because one tank showed more oil than the other.

Q. No, did not the samples indicate that there was contaminated oil in the port tank and no contaminated oil in the starboard tank?

A. That is correct.

Q. And in that case if you had unloaded any of the oil in order to discover and repair the leak you would only have had to unload the oil from the port tank and not from the starboard tank?

A. Well, that too is a question that would have to be decided by all concerned. I am not qualified to answer technically, but I would assume that the amount of oil out of one tank would not put the vessel on an even keel. It would take the tonnage off of one side and therefore I believe there would be a list—it would make the vessel list.

(TESTIMONY OF ARCHIE CUTHBERT WATSON)

Q. Yes, but you could have filled up that port tank again with something else, could you not? A. Well I might conclude, you believe that in order to repair the vessel the idea was to pump the oil out of that tank?

Q. Yes. A. But if you put something back into that tank she would list.

Q. The list would not actually have affected the vessel while she was lying at the dock or while she was in the dry dock, would it? A. It would not, but as I say I am not qualified to answer. If my opinion counts for anything she would be unable to drydock I believe without an even keel or as nearly an even keel as you could possibly get.

Q. Aren't there lots of other ways in which she could have been brought on an even keel?

Miss Phillips: The witness has stated several times, Mr. Derby, he was not qualified to answer that.

Mr. Derby: Read the question.

(Last question read by the reporter.)

Miss Phillips: I object to the question as calling for an expert opinion on the part of the witness on which the witness has said very frankly he did not feel qualified.

A. Do you want me to answer?

Mr. Derby: Yes.

Miss Phillips: I really do not think it is quite fair.

Mr. Derby: I think it is perfectly fair.

Miss Phillips: This witness has not claimed to be an expert shipbuilder or ship repairer and you are really calling on him now to express an opinion that calls for very expert technical knowledge.

Mr. Derby: Well, let us see what he says.

A. I believe there are many ways.

Q. At the time the vessel arrived at Kobe how much fuel oil was in this No. 3 double bottom tank? A. I don't know.

Q. Did you not investigate that? A. No, that Mr. Johnson did, the superintending engineer, but I did not.

Q. Did you give any consideration to pumping out the fuel oil from No. 3 double bottom tank? A. No.

Q. Did Mr. Johnson or Mr. Thornton give any consideration to that subject? A. I could not tell you that, I don't know; that would be something out of my jurisdiction entirely, anything having to do with the mechanical end of the vessel, as agent.

Q. Then as I gather you really had nothing to do with the decision whether the cocoanut oil was to come out of this vessel or not? A. Yes, I did.

Q. Who had the final say on that subject? A. As I said before there would be a conference of all concerned, and whatever was decided was to the best advantage of all concerned would have been worked out.

Q. Now did you and Mr. Johnson or Mr. Thornton discuss at all getting the fuel oil out of the No. 3 double bottom tank? A. I don't remember that particular tank at all.

Q. That was the one that was below the deep tank containing the cocoanut oil. A. Personally that never came to me at all.

Q. Do you know whether or not any fuel oil had

(TESTIMONY OF ARCHIE CUTHBERT WATSON)

been used out of the No. 3 double bottom tank prior to the arrival of the vessel in Kobe? A. No, I do not.

Q. Will you state once more, Mr. *Johnson,* so that I may be perfectly clear on the point, what your reason was for not making any further effort to secure lighters after you discovered that the cocoanut oil was contaminated by contact with fuel oil? A. It was felt that the cargo had already been damaged and we could not salvage any of it by making further inquiry.

Q. In other words you felt that the damage had been done and there could be no further damage? A. Not exactly that, but I felt there was damage and possibly there was to be a salvage, but we could not help it any by discharging it.

Q. I do not understand you, Mr. Watson. A. I did not see where we could have helped that cargo any by dischagring it into a barge or lighter; that would not have saved it, that is what I mean.

Q. You do not think any further damage took place then after the vessel arrived at Kobe? A. Do you mean additional damage?

Q. Yes. A. I do not think so.

Q. You think that all of the oil had been contaminated that was going to be contaminated? A. I believe that is true.

Q. Did you discuss that question with Mr. Johnson and Mr. Thornton? A. It was discussed, yes.

Q. I will have to ask you again, Mr. Watson, exactly what your purpose was in inquiring as to the availability of the lighters to receive the cocoanut oil.

(TESTIMONY OF ARCHIE CUTHBERT WATSON)

Miss Phillips: That question has been asked and answered several times.

Mr. Derby: Yes, but I will have to ask it again.

A. Well, prior to the arrival of the vessel we knew that she was considerably damaged, and we did not know what the circumstances were going to be until of course she would drydock, and that was the purpose of making inquiries for the lighters so as to know, if this double bottom had to be repaired, that we could discharge that oil into lighters and make the proper repairs.

Q. Let me ask you again, if you could have got these lighters to have discharged that cocoanut oil, would you have discharged it or would you not? A. I don't know what the outcome would have been without a conference of all concerned. If it had been deemed advisable, which was my opinion at that time, if it developed repairs on the bottom, we would have had to discharge it. That was actually the idea.

Q. What do you mean by repairs on the bottom, Mr. Watson? A. If the ship's bottom was damaged by striking the rocks.

Q. But you would not have considered discharging it as I understand you in order to remedy the leak which had developed between the double bottom tank and the deep tank? A. If that leak was sufficient to warrant a repair out there, if it would have been necessary to repair it, the oil would have had to come out even though it had been dumped into the bay in order to make the repairs.

Q. What did you know about the extent of that leak?

(TESTIMONY OF ARCHIE CUTHBERT WATSON)

A.   I did not know anything.

Q.   How did you know then whether it was big enough to require repairs or not?

Miss Phillips: What time are you referring? Are you referring to the time prior to the survey or subsequent?

Mr. Derby: I am following up the answer of the witness to my recent questions.

Miss Phillips: I think I will object to your question on the ground it is not specific enough.

Mr. Derby: That is clearly in line with the previous question.

Miss Phillips: I object to the question as being indefinite.

Mr. Derby: I will try to clear it up a little. You said that if the leak between the two tanks had been extensive enough to require repairs that you would undoubtedly havd discharged the cocoanut oil from the deep tank in order to make those repairs. Now how did you know, at any time we will say, when the vessel was in Kobe, how extensive that leak was? A. We did not know at all.

Q.   Then how did you know whether it was necessary or not to discharge the cocoanut oil? A. We did not know. Even to this day I could not tell you the extent of the damage in that tank.

Q.   You cannot say now, Mr. Watson, whether if lighters would have been available you would have used them or not? A. No.

(TESTIMONY OF ARCHIE CUTHBERT WATSON)

Q. You don't know what you would have done in that respect? A. No.

Q. Then at the time you inquired for the lighters from all of these companies you really did not know whether you would have any use for them or not? A. That is a fact.

Q. When did you leave Kobe, Mr. Watson? A. In September, 1928.

Q. You do not know anything at all then about what happened to this vessel after she arrived in San Francisco? A. No.

Q. I have not been able to discover from your examination, Mr. Watson, exactly who was in charge of this situation in Kobe, as to whether it was you or Mr. Thornton or Mr. Johnson? A. Well, Mr. Thornton was actually the direct representative of the Shipping Board, and as owners representative he actually was the boss.

Q. And you had practically daily conferences with him? A. Every day, yes.

Q. And also with Mr. Johnson? A. Yes.

Q. And therefore he was as much responsible as you were for putting the steamer on the drydock with her cargo on board? A. He was more responsible because he was qualified or considered to be qualified to know what he was doing.

Q. And the decision not to pump out this cocoanut oil was his decision just as much as it was yours? A. And the Captain also was included in there and the surveyor.

(Testimony of Archie Cuthbert Watson)

Q. The fact that the cocoanut oil had not yet solidified would have made it very much easier to pump it out, would it not, than if it had solidified? A. I do not think there is any question about that, it would have been quicker.

Q. It would not have taken so long to heat it? A. No.

Q. In regard to these samples do I understand that some of these samples were for your use in Kobe and some were for Swayne & Hoyt in San Francisco and were forwarded to them? A. There were samples forwarded to Swayne & Hoyt at San Francisco; there was samples put aboard the vessel; one set I believe was given to the Chief Engineer and one to the Captain, and the surveyor retained a set.

Q. Did I understand you to say that no *on* in Kobe or elsewhere in Japan analyzed these samples? A. Not officially, no.

Q. Who did it unofficially? A. There was a friend of the surveyor's that did it.

Q. Did he make any report? A. There was never a report, no.

Q. What did he tell you? A. Well, the surveyor reported to me that there was a contamination.

Q. Did you know anything about where the heat coils were in the deep tank in which this cocoanut oil was stowed? A. No.

Q. There is one subject that I forgot to ask you about: Were there any other Shipping Board vessels in

(TESTIMONY OF ARCHIE CUTHBERT WATSON)

Kobe at the time the West Cajoot got there? A. I do not recall.

Q. There were Shipping Board vessels coming in and going out of Kobe all the time, were there not? A. Yes.

Q. Vessels like the West Cajoot? A. Well, the same type.

Q. Did you give any consideration to transferring this shipment of cocoanut oil from the West Cajoot to any other Shipping Board vessel? A. No.

Q. Why not? A. Well, I do not believe that—I do not know what to say, only to say that there are no homebound vessels calling there or there were not at that time. There may have been one occasionally that would go to North Japan, but I do not think there was anything home bound that would have a deep tank available.

Q. Did you make any inquiries as to that situation at the time? A. No, I did not.

Q. You don't really know whether there was a vessel available or not? A. No.

Q. The West Cajoot arrived in Kobe on the evening of October 3rd? A. Yes.

Q. And went in drydock on the 8th? A. Yes.

Q. How long did she stay in the drydock? A. She came off I believe on the 28th of October.

Q. On the 28th of October? A. Yes.

Q. And departed for Yokohoma on November 1st? A. Yes.

Q. She was there in Kobe almost a month? A. From the 3rd of October to the 1st of November.

(TESTIMONY OF ARCHIE CUTHBERT WATSON)

Q. During that time the cocoanut oil remained on board of her? A. Yes.

Q. I understood you to say on your direct examination that you considered the question of the advisability of discharging the cocoanut oil not only on the first night you boarded the vessel but several times afterwards. What did you mean by several times afterwards? A. That the vessel was discharging her cargo from the 3rd to the night of the 7th and we were aboared the vessel every day, and I think that subject was brought up from time to time.

Q. Was it ever brought up again after she went on the dry dock? A. I do not think it was.

Q. I will ask the reporter to read to the witness the question and answer on direct examination: "Q.—Did you consider the advisability or possibility of discharging the cocoanut oil before the ship went into drydock? A.— Yes." Did you at that time believe that it would be necessary to discharge the cocoanut oil? A.—I did not know at that time. Q.—When did you discover that it would not be necessary? A. To discharge the cocoanut oil?

Q. To discharge the cocoanut oil. A. We actually did not discover that until the divers had made their examination, and even the soundings from the deep tank after that did not display any apparent intake of water or oil or increase in the sounding of the tank.

Q. Now you have brought up a new subject, Mr. Watson. You say that soundings were taken. Of what tank? A. Of the deep tank.

(TESTIMONY OF ARCHIE CUTHBERT WATSON)

Q. Did you also take soundings of No. 3 double bottom tank? A. I don't know about that.

Q. Well, if there was no cocoanut oil from the deep tank going into .the double bottom tank at that time or any fuel oil coming from the double bottom tank into the deep tank, how do you explain why there was any contamination at all?

Miss Phillips: I believe that is assuming a knowledge of this witness. A knowledge of the witness, Mr. Derby, that he has not said he had. He has not said he took soundings of or that he knows what the soundings were.

Mr. Derby: He must have known what the soundings were to reach the decision which he said he reached on account of the soundings.

Miss Phillips: Do you know what the soundings were, Mr. Watson? A. No ma'am.

Mr. Derby: Q. What did the soundings have to do with your position? A. Will you please read that question to me again.

(Question read by the reporter.)

Miss Phillips: I object to the question as being speculative, triple barreled and assuming something that has not been proved and which the witness had not testified to.

Mr. Derby: That question has been read to you three times and I would like you to answer it.

A. Well, my judgment, in answering that question, would lead me to say that if the ship's hull was punctured, a hole in the bottom of the ship where naturally salt water would come in, in addition to the fuel oil, and if it dod come in it would naturally raise the volume of the contents of the deep tank.

Q.   That is still not an answer to my question, Mr. Watson. How do you explain in view of the soundings which were taken how there was any contamination of the cocoanut oil?

Miss Phillips: I renew the objection that I made.

A.   I can only say this, that I am not a technical man or ship's hull man. All I can say is what my opinion and observation would tell me; if there was foreign matter in that deep tank it had to come in from the outside somewhere; if the ship's bottom was punctured, salt water would naturally come in together with the oil.

Q.   But the double bottom tank was not fractured, was it?   A.   I think it was, I don't know.

Q.   Do you think there was leakage into the ship from the bottom of the No. 3 double bottom tank?   A.   Well, I believe this, there must have been a strain somewhere.

Q.   Were any repairs made to the bottom of the No. 3 double bottom tank at Kobe?   A.   I don't know, but I do not recall anything.

Q.   If it was leaking you certainly would have made some repairs, would you not?   A.   If it was deemed necessary that would have been done.

Q.   The conclusion therefore is that the No. 3 double bottom tank was not leaking when the vessel was at Kebe?   A.   I sat there in the capacity of agent and the Shipping Board had an expert, and we appointed a surveyor and used him for the purpose of making a decision as to whether or not repairs were necessary; and my position was that I could only be guided entirely by their knowledge and ability, and regardless of what I might have to say, it would not hold good in making any repairs.

Q. Who was this surveyor that you referred to? A. The American Bureau surveyor Teikoku Kaiji Kyoki, the surveyor appointed for the ship Mr. Reid, and Mr. Johnson.

Q. I do not see a word in these reports that you refer to about the contamination of the cocoanut oil. A. I do not believe that it would have anything in there; the American Bureau would not, because it is more interested in repairs.

Q. But if there was a leak between the two tanks it would have to be repaired? A. It would be repaired, yes, but out there, I don't know as to whether or not it would have been.

Q. Did you consult with these surveyors that you mentioned about the contamination of the cocoanut oil? A. The American Bureau man would have nothing to do with that.

Q. Did you consult with the others there about it? A. He was consulted, yes.

Q. I see that it is practically useless for me to pursue this subject much further, but I will ask you when you reached the decision that it was not necessary to discharge the cocoanut oil.

Miss Phillips: Mr. Derby, I think you have repeated your question in a great many different ways, and I think you are leaving out a good many facts of the witness'

(TESTIMONY OF ARCHIE CUTHBERT WATSON)

testimony in that question. I believe I will object to further questioning along this line.

Mr. Derby: Very well. I am trying under great difficulty to bring out the facts in regard to this case and any additional facts that you wish to bring out in redirect examination you are fully at liberty to do.

Miss Phillips: I think part of your difficulty has been that on cross examination you have been covering a good many matters not covered on direct examination and upon which the government plans to call expert witnesses who are qualified; I think that has been part of your difficulty, that you have been trying to get from this witness so many matters which properly Mr. Reid and Mr. Thornton and Mr. Johnson are qualified to testify to and will testify to.

Mr. Derby: I think all my questions on cross examination have been clearly responsive to the questions on direct examination.

Miss Phillips: I do not believe so. I think I have been very liberal in letting you run along this way, but I preferred not to make many objections to the examination; but I believe that my objections would have been sustained by the Court as being many respects not proper cross examination.

Mr. Derby: I will put that last question to the witness and I think I will let it go at that.

A. I do not think that decision was ever reached. When I learned that there could be no barges or lighters secured there was nothing further done about it.

(TESTIMONY OF ARCHIE CUTHBERT WATSON)

Q. Now, Mr. Watson, referring to another cable attached to exhibit 25, which is a cable apparently sent by you to Swayne & Hoyt at Manila, which cable reads as translated as follows: "November 7, 1927. No. 737-San Francisco, No. 717—Post office authorities—Inform us samples—forwarded by Mayebashi Maru due to arrive—your port November 2nd—contamination—very probably caused by—leakage liquid fuel—from the double bottom". I will ask you, how you reached the conclusion that the contamination was probably caused by the leakage of the liquid fuel oil from the double bottom. A. That was probably an assumption. I say in the telegram "Very probably caused by leakage liquid fuel from the double bottom."

Q. Why did you send that telegram to Swayne & Hoyt at that time? A. I believe that I am replying to a cable that they sent me asking for that information.

Miss Phillips: The cable says on its face it was in reply to a cable sent by Swayne & Hoyt from San Francisco.

A. Yes, because I am referring to their number of cable.

Mr. Derby: Q. Were any additional efforts to secure lighters made by Mr. Thornton or Mr. Johnson in addition to the efforts made by you or were you the man to whom was turned over the job of making those efforts? A. I do not believe that they made any efforts at all. I believe that it was entirely up to me, as I remember it.

Mr. Derby: That is all.

(TESTIMONY OF ARCHIE CUTHBERT WATSON)

REDIRECT EXAMINATION

Miss Phillips: Q. Mr. Watson, was there at that time a market for cocoanut oil in Kobe? A. I do not remember making any inquiries as to that at all.

Q. What I mean is was Kobe a place where there was any considerable amount of dealing in cocoanut oil, to your knowledge? A. No ma'am.

Q. Is your answer no to my question? A. They did not deal in cocoanut oil to any extent to my knowledge.

Q. Mr. Watson, on cross examination I observed that several times Mr. Derby asked you a question about the discovery of the contamination of the oil and I believe on each occasion you used the language that you knew for certain that the oil was contaminated on or about a certain time. Just what did you mean when you said you knew for certain?

Mr. Derby: I object to the question as leading and suggestive and not in my opinion correctly quoting the testimony of the witness given on cross examination.

Miss Phillips: Q. I will not take the time to go back and have that read; I have it here in my notes. "I first larned of the contamination when the oil evidenced a change of color." You mean by that when the oil solidified as you have already testified. A. Yes.

Q. I believe that on cross examination Mr. Derby said to a radio or cablegram of about October 14th and you said that was your first radio but you thought that you advised them by letter also. A. I think that was under date of October 14th.

(TESTIMONY OF ARCHIE CUTHBERT WATSON)

Q. Yes, I believe it was under date of October 14th. You also made some reference, or a little more extended reference on cross examination as to an analysis of some kind made by some friend of the surveyor, Mr. Reid. Do you recall now at this time who that person was? A. I could not tell you.

Q. Mr. Watson, I am going to show you what appears to be a letter under date of October 14 to the San Francisco office—I do not believe it refers to this in any way.

Mr. Derby: I would like to see it.

Miss Phillips: Q. Mr. Watson, referring to the question you just testified to, that upon the solidification of the samples the difference in color indicated to you that there must have been a contamination, and that in your testimony you said a friend of the surveyor, Captain Reid, analyzed it, do you recall now whether or not that was a chemist or an employee of any one of the oil companies? A. He was I believe one of the engineers of one of the oil companies.

Q. Which one? A. I think it was the Vacuum Oil, I am not positive. It was one of the oil concerns.

Q. You stated, I believe, on cross examination that you never did get an official written analysis or report. Did you get any kind of report? A. There was just simply a memorandum given to the surveyor, unsigned— that was I believe on account of the individual making the analysis not being in a position to do it officially.

Q. In this letter here, written on the same date as the telegram, omitting the first few paragraphs reads, referring to the damage to the copra: "We find the bagged stuff has deteriorated much more than the bulk. This no doubt is due to its stowage in the ship, where it seemed to be in the way of fuel oil which leaked in through the double bottoms. Some of the bulk is also badly saturated with oil, but to a much lesser degree.

"We are doing our best to segregate the oil damage from the sea water damage, so when it is re-shipped, it will come out at yours on one batch.

"Another very severe damage came to light yesterday. Samples of the cocoanut oil in bulk were taken from the deep tanks. The samples taken from the starboard tank indicates that the oil is apparently in good condition, but the samples taken from the port tank evidence a contamination. We are having the samples analyzed and as soon as we get the results we will cable you.

"We are also sending you samples by the SS Siberia Maru which sails from Yokohamo tomorrow. The shipment of oil came aboard at Manila, and is consigned to 'Order of the First National Bank of Los Angeles, notify Los Angeles Soap Co., Los Angeles.'

"In all, there is about 546 tons, split up in both tanks, so in the port tank there must be between 250 and 275 tons."

The analysis to which you refer in this letter, was that the informal analysis to which you have testified? A. Yes.

Q. Was there any other? A. No ma'am.

Q. Now the cable which Mr. Derby referred to on cross examination, says "Samples forwarded by Mayebashi Maru due to arrive your port November 2". Would that have been the sample referred to in this letter? A. I think so.

Q. You think so. That would be your best estimate now?

A. I remember something about that; I made inquiry—in my letter here I referred to the Siberia Maru, and I mailed then, I think, addressed them care or via the Siberia Maru, and without the cable referred to here, I believe that I went to the postoffice and they told me it did not go via the Siberia Maru.

Q. Mr. Watson, on cross examination you testified in some degree as to the oil tanks which the Rising Sun Company had at Kobe. What kind of tanks were they? A. I think they were fuel oil tanks.

Q. Do you know where they were? Where were they located in Kobe? A. In a general way I know.

Q. Whereabouts were they located in Kobe? A. Their station is right off or near the quarantine station.

Q. Where is that? A. I should say four or five miles from Kobe proper.

Q. Is the quarantine station in the outer harbor? I am not familiar with the harbor of Kobe. A. The quarantine station is located at the entrance of the port of Kobe, off the breakwater, and is about in the neighborhood of four or five miles from the city of Kobe.

Q. How many tanks are there there, do you know? A. I could not tell you. There are quite a number of big storage tanks.

Q. Was it customary at that time for oil burning

steamers to take on bunkers at this place, or do you know? A. I have not any idea of the number that are bunkered, but I believe there are some bunkered in Kobe.

Q. You mean at Kobe or at this place at the quarantine station? My question is really directed to where the tanks were.

A. No, I don't believe they would be bunkered out there where the tanks are located.

Q. What are those tanks used for? A. I think they are storage tanks used for fuel oil. I believe that is what they are used for.

Q. Fuel oil is used by vessels, is it not? A. Yes.

Q. Do I understand then that the vessels which want to take on fuel oil at Kobe take on bunkers further in, inside of the port and not at this outside position at the quarantine station?

A. I have never actually bunkered any vessels in the Rising Sun station and therefore do not know, but I do believe that they bunker partly outside of the breakwater or just inside of the harbor limits, but not at the tank storage grounds.

Q. Do you know anything about the size of these tanks?

A. I have not the least idea of the capacity. They are as large as the ones that are over in Richmond, great big ones, but I have not any idea of the number or their capacity.

Q. Mr. Watson, some inquiry was made on cross examination as to a navy yard in Kobe. There is a navy yard at Kobe, isn't there? A. There is not.

(TESTIMONY OF ARCHIE CUTHBERT WATSON)

Q. There is not? A. No.

Q. Was there at that time? A. No ma'am.

Q. Does the Japanese Navy keep any considerable portion of the navy at Kobe? A. I do not think they have any.

Q. Then the question on cross examination as to whether it would have been possible for you to borrow barges or lighters of some sort from the Japanese navy, do you think that that would have been a possible course to take? A. I do not think it would have been possible under any circumstances.

Q. Mr. Watson, what is the Mitsui Company to which you referred on cross examination? A. They are large exporters and importers.

Q. Do they operate ships? A. They have some of their own vessels.

Q. Did they at that time have vessels of their own? A. I think so.

Q. In the cargo or in the passenger trade or on both? A. They had cargo vessels. I do not believe they own any passenger vessels.

Q. You did include the Mitsui Company on direct examination but you amplified that on cross examination. Do you recall whether the Mitsui Company had any barges or lighters in Kobe at that time? A. They had some lighters. They were lighters that had been used and were being used for the carriage of fish oil.

Q. Do you recall how many of them there were and their capacity? A. No, I have no idea of the number.

(Testimony of Archie Cuthbert Watson)

Q. Just what was said between yourself and this representative of the Mitsui Company with regard to whether or not you could charter lighters? A. He told me that there was nothing available at the time, that they were in use.

Q. What sort of business did the Mitsui Company have?

A. They are exporters and importers.

Q. What use did they have for lighters? A. As far as I know their lighters are used entirely for the transportation of the fish oil from the shore to the vessel on which it is loaded in the port of Kobe.

Q. Mr. Watson, did the Shipping Board vessels ordinarily touch at Kobe on the homeward bound voyage? A. No ma'am.

Q. They touch there on the outward voyage? A. You mean Swayne & Hoyt?

Q. Yes.

Mr. Derby: Why confine it to Swayne & Hoyt?

Miss Phillips: The witness knows more about Swayne & Hoyt.

A. Swayne & Hoyt vessels did not call there as a port of call homeward bound. The Columbia Pacific vessels did occasionally call home bound.

Q. Where did the Columbia Pacific vessels operate? A. They almost parallel the same route as Swayne & Hoyt did.

Q. Where were they home bound? A. Their home port was Portland.

(TESTIMONY OF ARCHIE CUTHBERT WATSON)

Q. When you speak of Swayne & Hoyt's vessels do you mean Shipping Board vessels under the management of Swayne & Hoyt· or do you mean vessels individually owned by Swayne & Hoyt? A. Vessels owned by the Shipping Board and operated by Swayne & Hoyt.

Q. Then in your testimony today when you have referred to Swayne & Hoyt vessels, did you mean by that the Shipping Board vessels under the management of Swayne & Hoyt? A. I meant, I did not know whether there were any other Shipping Board vessels.

Q. What I wanted to get clear was your terminology; Swayne & Hoyt as ship owners might own vessels privately and might operate vessels for the Board. I wanted to make sure what you meant in your examination. Now did Swayne & Hoyt at that time operate vessels of their own in and out of Kobe? A. No.

Q. Now referring to other Shipping Board vessels, what other lines, what other companies or what other firms were Shipping Board agents in Kobe other than yourself as representative of Swayne & Hoyt's vessels? A. Robert Dollar Company and the Columbia Pacific Shipping Company.

Q. Do you recall now where the Robert Dollar line operated between? A. Some of their vessels operated from Seattle, that is the vessels that the Robert Dollar Company were agents for operate from Seattle operate from Seattle and some from the Atlantic Coast, both of which occasionally called at Kobe homeward bound.

Q. Your testimony as I understand on cross examination was that you did not recall now whether there

was any other Shipping Board vessels in Kobe at the
time to which transfer might have been made, is that
correct? A. That is correct.

Miss Phillips: I think that is all.

Recross Examination

Mr. Derby: Q. In this letter of October 14th to the
San Francisco office of Swayne & Hoyt, I call your
attention to the following paragraph which has already
been read to you by Miss Phillips: "Another very serious damage came to light yesterday. Samples of the
cocoanut oil in bulk were taken from the deep tanks.
The samples taken from the starboard tank indicate that
the oil is apparently in good condition, but the samples
taken from the port tank evidence a contamination. We
are having these samples analyzed and as soon as we
get the result we will cable you." Refreshing your memory from that letter which is signed by you, Mr. Watson, that would indicate that until October 13 you did
not know that there was any contamination of the cocoanut oil, would it not? A. Yes.

Q. Is that the fact? A. Well, I knew it several
days before because it had been in the hands of—I suspected it but I actually did not know it until I wrote
that letter.

Q. Referring again to the Master's extended protest
and the entry under October 5, reading as follows: "At
1 P. M. it was discovered that there was a leak from
the port deep tank to the No. 3 double bottom"; I will
ask you whether you did not at least suspect that there

was contamination of the cocoanut oil at that time? A. I suspected there was, yes.

Q. I was apparently mistaken, Mr. Watson, in assuming that there was a navy yard at Kobe. I presume that there are almost always some Japanese warships or government vessels in Kobe?

A. Very seldom, only perhaps on some special occasion.

Q. You do not think there would be any government barges in Kobe? A. I do not believe there would be any found there.

Q. If that is a mistake my point in that regard will not be good; I am not yet willing to admit that it is not good. What time was it you saw Mitsui & Company, I mean about what date was it? A. I think it was the day following the arrival of the vessel.

Q. The day after the arrival of the vessel? A. Yes.

Q. Was that the same day that you made your inquiry of the other companies? A. Yes.

Q. Were they all made on the same day? A. As I remember it, yes.

Q. I understood you to say no further inquiries were made later? A. No.

Q. I also understood from your redirect examination, that your testimony that Shipping Board vessels did not generally touch at Kobe when they were home bound was confined to the vessels operated by Swayne & Hoyt? A. Swayne & Hoyt vessels did not ordinarily.

Q. Your testimony in that regard was confined to the vessels which were operated by Swayne & Hoyt?

(TESTIMONY OF ARCHIE CUTHBERT WATSON)

A. Yes, but it was not my intentions—there were and there are, I believe, still yet some of the vessels operated by other concerns that call there occasionally home bound.

Q. But you did not investigate whether there were any vessels there at the time the West Cajoot was at Kobe? A. No.

Mr. Derby: Now, Miss Phillips, I refer to an informal demand on you which I think was not made a part of the record for the production of the deck and engine room logs of the West Cajoot for the purpose of facilitating my cross examination of this witness and your reply to me was that you did not have them at this time. I make no point of the fact that the logs were not produced on this occasion, but I demand that they be made available to counsel for the respondent Los Angeles Soap Company before any further testimony or depositions are taken in this case.

Miss Phillips: I think as to that, the Shipping Board is going to have to take depositions in several different places at different times, so that the logs, if they were to be shipped back and forth from the Orient to Washington the case would drag out interminably. The logs were not forwarded to me and I did not make any particular effort to get them for this deposition because I knew the witness was not an officer of the ship. I do plan to have them however, for the taking of the testimony of the Chief Engineer whom I expect to be in San Francisco month after next, and also when the Captain's testimony is taken, because it will be very

(TESTIMONY OF ARCHIE CUTHBERT WATSON)

necessary for both sides to have them at that time, and I would assume that the logs would be necessary primarily in examining the officers of the ship rather than a shore representative who would not have first hand knowledge of any of the entries.

Mr. Derby: I suggest to meet Miss Phillips' suggestion in regard to the logs having to be in different places at the same time that photostatic copies be made of the material portions of the logs.

Miss Phillips: Yes, that can be done.

Mr. Derby: I think that is all.

Miss Phillips: That is all.

(Endorsed): Filed Aug. 30 1930.

[TITLE OF COURT AND CAUSE]

IN ADMIRALITY.

No. 3327-C

No. 3663-C

No. 3691-C

FRIDAY, DECEMBER 19, 1930.

DEPOSITION OF PAUL FRAZIER BLINN.

BE IT REMEMBERED, that on Friday, December 19, 1930, pursuant to stipulation of counsel, at Room 415 Postoffice Building, in the City and County of San Francisco, State of California, personally appeared before me, ERNEST E. WILLIAMS, United States Commissioner for the Northern District of California, authorized to take

acknowledgments of bail and affidavits, et cetera, PAUL
FRAZIER BLINN, a witness called on behalf of the United
States.

S. H. DERBY, ESQ., of Messrs. Derby, Sharp, Quimby
& Tweedt, appeared as proctor for the Los Angeles Soap
Company, and MISS ESTHER B. PHILLIPS, appeared as
proctore for The United States, and the said witness,
having been by me first duly cautioned and sworn to
testify the truth, the whole truth and nothing but the
truth, in the causes aforesaid, did thereupon depose and
say as is hereinafter set forth.

It is hereby stipulated and agreed by and between the
Proctors for the respective parties that the deposition
of the above named witness may be taken in shorthand
by EDWIN J. SEKINS,

It is further stipulated that the deposition, when written up, may be read in evidence by either party on the
trial of the causes; that all questions as to the notice of
the time and place of taking the same are waived, and
that all objections as to the form of the questions are
waived unless objected to at the time of taking said
deposition, and that all objections as to the materiality,
relevancy and competency of the testimony are reserved
to all parties.

It is further stipulated that the reading over of the
testimony to the witness and the signing thereof are
hereby expressly waived.

(TESTIMONY OF PAUL FRAZIER BLINN)

PAUL FRAZIER BLINN,
called as a witness for The United States, having been
duly sworn as hereinbefore stated, testified as follows:

DIRECT EXAMINATION.

Miss Phillips: Q. What is your business, Mr. Blinn?
A. Marine engineer.

Q. How long have you been a marine engineer?
A. About twelve years.

Q. Have you any license? A. Chief engineer's
license.

Q. How long have you held a chief engineer's
license?

A. Let me see,—four years.

Q. Four years? A. Four years in November.

Q. What preparation for the work of a chief engineer did you have prior to going to sea, if any? A.
Motion picture camera man, and an automobile mechanic.

Q. Did you have any experience or training in machine shop work? A. Yes.

Q. How much experience in machine shop work?

A. I served my apprenticeship for three years in
railroad shops.

Q. Will you name what vessels, if any, of which you
have been chief engineer? A. My first engineer's position was on the WEST CAJOOT.

Q. Have you ever been chief engineer on any other
vessels?

A. The WEST IVAN which was later renamed the
GOLDEN WEST, and the GOLDEN COAST, and the GOLDEN
BEAR, which was formerly the WEST CAJOOT.

(TESTIMONY OF PAUL FRAZIER BLINN)

Q. Are you on any vessel now? A. Yes, I am chief engineer on the GOLDEN BEAR.

Q. Which was formerly the WEST CAJOOT? A. Yes.

Q. Were you chief engineer on the WEST CAJOOT during her voyage when she stranded in 1927? A. Yes.

Q. Were there deep tanks on the WEST CAJOOT? A. Yes.

Q. Where were the deep tanks? A. The deep tanks are built amidship fore to the fire room.

Q. Did the deep tanks have anything in them at the time of her stranding? A. Cocoanut oil.

Q. Do you know where the cocoanut oil was taken aboard?

A. The cocoanut oil was taken aboard in Manila.

Q. Do you know whether these tanks carried any cargo in the voyage prior to her arrival at Manila? A. No.

Q. I don't mean just the immediate port, but I mean do you know what was the last cargo carried in these deep tanks?

A. There was no cargo. There was fuel oil.

Q. Oh, fuel oil. And where was that discharged?

A. The fuel oil was consumed by the ship.

Q. Were the deep tanks empty on arrival at Manila?

A. No, they were not empty; they were filled with water.

Q. Now, Mr. Blinn, can you state approximately the capacity of the deep tanks of the WEST CAJOOT?

A. The deep tanks, in barrels, carried 4,121 barrels of fuel oil.

(TESTIMONY OF PAUL FRAZIER BLINN)

Q. Do you mean each tank, or several tanks together?

A. No, the two tanks.

Q. Two tanks. A. Each carried half of that.

Q. Each tank carried about one-half? A. Yes.

Q. Did you have anything to do with the loading of the cocoanut oil in Manila? A. Yes. I inspected the tanks on cleaning them, to see that the tanks were perfectly clean.

Q. Were you on duty while the tanks were being cleaned?

A. Yes.

Q. Can you describe, just briefly, how, or what method was used in cleansing the cocoanut oil tanks?

A. First the tanks are filled with water so that we can test the bulkheads around the tanks, in the fireroom and the cargo holds and on the sides of the ship. If there is no leakage, the water is pumped out and a crew of Filipinos are put into the tanks, and they wash it down with a solution of soda of some kind, and then later it is wiped down with cocoanut meal.

Mr. Derby: Just a second. I am getting a little behind.

Miss Phillips: I might say, Mr. Derby, I think the depositions on file at Los Angeles, of the two surveyors in the Orient, describes this in much more detail. I had intended to cover it with this witness rather briefly.

Mr. Derby: Have those been returned? I don't think so.

Miss Phillips: My impression is they have been, but

(TESTIMONY OF PAUL FRAZIER BLINN)

perhaps I am wrong in that. I was asking this witness questions mostly because it is corroborative.

Q. Mr. Blinn, were there any surveyors acting with you or at the same time that you acted, in the cleansing of these tanks?

A. Yes. The ship was really in charge of Mr. Harris of the American Bureau of Shipping.

Q. Can you tell me whether any test was made to ascertain whether the deep tanks were perfectly tight?

A. Yes.

Q. Just what was that test? A. Well, the test that I described on the outer leakage. And then after the tanks are cleaned, there is a test made on the double bottoms, from the fuel oil tanks, by putting a head on the double bottom fuel oil tanks to see whether there is any leakage from the bottom of the tank.

Q. Now, was such a test used on this occasion?

A. Yes.

Q. What was found? A. The tanks were found to be tight.

Q. Did you find any leaky rivets? A. Nothing more than what we call a weep around a rivet here and there, which were caulked.

Q. Then after this cleansing and testing that you have described, as I understand it, the cocoanut oil was then loaded?

A. Put into the tank, yes.

Q. Mr. Blinn, are there any fuel oil tanks below the deep oil tanks? A. Yes, the number three double bottom tanks are below the deep tanks.

(TESTIMONY OF PAUL FRAZIER BLINN)

Q. Can you tell me about the capacity of the fuel oil tanks below the deep tanks, that is, the number three fuel oil tank?

A. Yes. There are—I have them in my pocket.

Q. Have you a memorandum upon that capacity?

A. Yes.

Q. Where did you get the memorandum? A. From the scale on the ship.

Q. Is that from the blueprints? A. That is from the blueprints.

Mr. Derby: Where are the blueprints?

Miss Phillips: Mr. Derby, I may say in this I am very much embarrassed. I telegraphed on December 10th for the blueprints and got a reply the same date that they were being mailed. I certainly expected them yesterday at the latest. I have made two inquiries at the post office this morning, and they simply are not here. Whether or not they have been delayed by the Christmas mail, I don't know. If they come in in the course of the day, you can have them. If they do not come in before this deposition is completed, I will send them to your office and let you examine them at your leisure. And if there are points covered in this deposition which the blueprints would contradict as to measurements or capacities or anything of that sort, I will stipulate that the blueprints are correct,—I mean would show whatever facts you would want to prove.

Mr. Derby: I want to say it is very embarrassing not to have the blueprints here. I have had letters in this case from New York dated as late as December

(TESTIMONY OF PAUL FRAZIER BLINN)

13th, and there is no reason, in my opinion, why the blueprints should not have got here in time for this deposition.

Miss Phillips: I think you are absolutely right. I think it is inexcusable on the part of the office in Washington to which I telegraphed for the blueprints, and I can't understand why they are not here. There is no excuse possible for such a delay or negligence.

Q. Now, Mr. Blinn, what would you say is the capacity of the number three fuel oil tank? A. 750 barrels; 375 barrels in each tank.

Q. I was going to ask you that. Are there two fuel oil tanks beneath the deep tanks? A. Yes.

Q. And their total capacity you say, is 750 barrels? A. Yes.

Q. Do you know about what their measurement in depth is?

A. Three feet, nine inches.

Q. At what point? A. That is in the deepest part of the ship,—the keel.

Q. Have you ever taken such a measurement yourself?

A. Yes.

Q. Now, Mr. Blinn, did the vessel take on fuel oil at Manila?

A. Yes.

Q. Was that in your charge,—a part of your duty to have fuel oil loaded? A. Yes, it is my duty.

Q. Do you know what quantity you took on at

(TESTIMONY OF PAUL FRAZIER BLINN)

Manila? Did you make any record of it at the time? A. Yes. There was a record made of it.

Q. Where? What sort of a record? A. It is entered in the log book.

Q. Did you also give a receipt to the company?

A. I signed a receipt for the oil company for the delivery.

Q. Mr. Blinn, I hand you here two books entitled, "Reciprocating Engines, Division of Operations, U. S. Shipping Board Emergency Fleet Corporation, Engineer's Log Book, S. S. WEST CAJOOT," and ask you if you can identify those log books?

A. Yes. The log books are in my handwriting.

Q. They are in your handwriting. Is that a day to day record of the operations in the engine room? A. Yes.

Q. Do you recall at this date what quantity of fuel oil you took on board the WEST CAJOOT? A. Yes. This amount is recorded in the log book.

Q. You would not have any independent recollection of the precise quantity, would you? A. No, it has been too far back.

Q. Was the record you made at that time correct so far as you could make it? A. Yes.

Q. How much does the log book show you took on?

A. 5760 barrels.

Q. Was fuel oil stowed in the fuel tanks number three, beneath the double bottom tank? A. Yes.

Q. Do you recall whether or not the number three tanks were filled to their capacity, approximately. A. Yes, they were filled to capacity in Manila, and a head was put on the tanks for a test.

Q. I see. Prior to the loading of the cocoanut oil?

A. Yes.

Q. Mr. Blinn, is a record kept in the engine room of the day to day consumption of fuel oil? A. Yes.

Q. Can you tell me just how that record is kept?

A. By a fuel oil meter and by sounding the settling tanks each day at noon.

Q. What are the settling tanks? A. The settling tanks are tanks built forward of—around—in the deep tanks, to pump the oil we burn, in case of water or settlage of sediment in water, so that we can separate it from the oil to burn it,—which hold approximately 160 barrels apiece.

Q. That is, the settling tanks? A. Yes.

Q. How many settling tanks are there? A. Two.

Q. Go ahead and just explain the way you used fuel oil in the engine room. What is your method of operation?

A. First the oil is pumped from the double bottoms into the settling tanks, and it is pumped from the settling tanks through a heating process in to the boilers, under a pressure of about seventy pounds. Each day at noon those settling tanks are changed over, unless the fuel consumption is beyond the capacity of the settling tank.

Q. What do you mean when you say you change it over at noon?

A. Changed from one tank to another.

Q. Then do I understand that you use up the full

(TESTIMONY OF PAUL FRAZIER BLINN)

content of one settling tank, and then when you finish that you change over to the next settling tank? A. Yes. Correct.

Q. On an average, what was the quantity of the oil used on the WEST CAJOOT for twenty-four hours running day?

A. From 160 to 165 barrels.

Q. That was your average, under average conditions?

A. Yes.

Q. Now, how did you measure the quantiy of oil used?

A. By a steel scale that is measured off in inches, which we drop into the tanks,—where the fuel oil leaves a mark; and we read the scale on the rod and compare that with the blueprints of the tanks on the ship.

Q. You mentioned an oil meter. What is that?

A. The oil meter is built onto the oil line to measure the oil that goes through it, to measure the capacity in gallons,—the same as a water meter.

Q. What is the purpose of measuring your oil by meter and also taking soundings? A. Well, that is to give us as near a correct consumption reading as we can get.

Q. What is your part in this measurement of oil, Mr. Blinn,—or what was your part in the measurement of oil?

A. Well, I am the one that makes the usual measurement by meter and soundings and have it written in the log book.

(Testimony of Paul Frazier Blinn)

Q. That is, you compute what is the actual barrel consumption during the preceding twenty-four hours?

A. Yes.

Q. Taking it from the meter and the soundings?

A. Yes.

Q. Is that correct? A. Correct.

Q. Mr. Blinn, on what day did the West Cajoot sail from Manila, do you recall, or need you refer to your log?

Mr. Derby: Do you mean from Manila, or for Manila?

Miss Phillips: Q. From Manila?

A. Well, I would have to refer to the log for that date.

Q. Very well, use your log then to refresh your recollection.

A. That would be September 23rd.

Q. About what time of day? A. My log book, at twelve o'clock noon on September 23rd, shows that my running time was two hours and fifty-two minutes.

Q. That would indicate, then, that you left shortly after nine o'clock that morning; is that right?

A. I see no record here of that.

Q. Well, somewhere along about nine o'clock; is that right? A. About nine o'clock.

Q. What was your next port, Mr. Blinn?

A. Hongkong.

Q. And what day did you arrive in Hongkong?

A. I will have to refer to the log book.

(TESTIMONY OF PAUL FRAZIER BLINN)

Q. Very well, do so. A. We arrived at Hongkong September 26th.

Q. At what time? A. About two o'clock.

Q. In the morning, or afternoon, or at night?

A. In the afternoon.

Q. Two-thirty-five, two-thirty, two o'clock?

Mr. Derby: About two o'clock, he said.

A. Two o'clock. That would be in the morning.

Miss Phillips: Q. Two a. m. Mr. Blinn, what quantity of fuel oil was consumed between the two ports, that is, between Manila and Hongkong? A. Well, I can figure that from the log book, Miss Phillips.

Q. You would not remember now what the quantity was? A. No, I would not.

Q. By the way, Mr. Blinn, in making these entries, was it your purpose to enter the facts truly and correctly?

A. Absolutely.

Q. And do you believe your log to be a true and correct record of the voyage? A. Yes.

Q. Please refer, then, to your log, to find the consumption of fuel oil between the two ports? A. It would be 470 barrels.

Q. 470 barrels. Now, that is from what day to what day,—what hour? A. From the day that we sailed from Manila until the arrival at Hongkong.

Q. Is that after you passed immigration and pratique? Is it just arriving at the gate of the port? A. That is arriving into the harbor.

(TESTIMONY OF PAUL FRAZIER BLINN)

Q. That is arriving into the harbor? A. Into the harbor; at anchorage.

Q. Mr. Blinn, did you at that time keep any record of which tanks you were using the fuel oil from? A. As a matter of form and a matter of safety, the oil is first taken from the—

Q. Just a moment. I think you misunderstood my question. I said, did you keep a record in your log, or in any other book, of the tanks from which you used fuel oil? A. No. There is no place in the book to keep a record of that, so we didn't enter it.

Q. You did not customarily do so, then, on that vessel?

A. No.

Q. By the way, in your experience as an engineer, is that customary on ships? A. Some of the chiefs keep a record and some do not; mostly do not.

Q. Then you have no written record showing from which tank you drew fuel oil during the run from Manila to Hongkong, is that right? A. That is right.

Q. Do you recall, and do you know, from what fuel oil tanks you did use the oil during this voyage from Manila to Hongkong?

Q. Which tank did you draw the oil from?

A. The number three double bottoms.

Q. Why was that, Mr. Blinn? A. As a matter of safety, valuable cargo that was stowed on top of the fuel oil tanks.

Q. Are you positive of that? A. I am positive of that.

(TESTIMONY OF PAUL FRAZIER BLINN)

Q. How long were you in Hongkong? A. I will have to refer to the log.

Q. Very well. Wherever you are uncertain about dates or times, Mr. Blinn, say so, and refer to your log.

A. We sailed September 27th.

Q. About what time? A. That would be about— that would be somewhere around seven o'clock.

Q. Seven a. m. or seven p. m.? A. Seven p. m.

Q. What was your next port intended to be?

A. San Francisco.

Q. Now, Mr. Blinn, will you just state your consumption of fuel oil from the day you left Hongkong up to October 1st,—noon of October 1st? A. I can figure that consumption from my log book, Miss Phillips.

Q. Very well, do so, please. A. You want that from Manila until—

Q. No, I said from Hongkong. A. From Hongkong.

Q. You have already given it from Manila to Hongkong.

A. To what date did you want that, Miss Phillips?

Q. Noon of October 1st. A. It would be 712 barrels of oil.

Q. Does that include any port consumption of oil while you were in the harbor of Hongkong? A. No. That is from the time we left the pilot station at Hongkong until noon, October 1st.

Q. Did you use any fuel oil while you were in Hongkong?

A. Yes.

(TESTIMONY OF PAUL FRAZIER BLINN)

Q. About how much? A. About an average of forty barrels a day.

Q. You are just giving that on an average now, without looking it up? A. Yes. I can look that up in the log book and tell you.

Q. Well, suppose you do so, as long as you have the log there? A. I have made a mistake in my figures in that 712 barrels, Miss Phillips.

Q. Just correct it, then. A. I took that at arrival at Hongkong. The port consumption would be 54 barrels.

Q. At Hongkong? A. At Hongkong.

Q. What were the corrected figures you would give from the time of leaving Hongkong until noon of October 1st?

A. 658 barrels.

Q. Mr. Blinn, do you know from which tank you were drawing fuel oil during the voyage from Hongkong outward, up until noon of October 1st? A. Yes. Number three double bottoms.

Q. Did you at any time, in or around that date, take any soundings yourself? A. I was standing by with the second assistant engineer to check the soundings of the fuel oil tanks.

Q. The number three tanks you mean? A. The number three tanks.

Q. And at the time those soundings were taken, what did the soundings show? A. Three inches.

Q. Three inches of fuel oil? A. Three inches of fuel oil.

(TESTIMONY OF PAUL FRAZIER BLINN)

Q. Do you recall the date on which those soundings were taken, Mr. Blinn? A. My recollection is the day before we struck the reef.

Q. Well then, assuming that you struck the reef at midnight, October 1st, would that be during October 1st, or during September 30th? A. That would be about September 30th.

Q. That you recall taking soundings? A. Yes.

Q. Mr. Blinn, when you get down to having three inches of fuel oil left in a fuel oil tank, in your opinion, is it possible to pump out all of the remainder there? A. Some tanks you can pump down to about one inch; others to two or three inches.

Q. On this occasion did you continue to use from number three tanks? A. My orders were given to use the fuel from the number one tanks.

Q. And that was after or before this sounding was taken? A. That was after the sounding was taken.

Q. Now, directing your attention to the evening of October 1st, do you remember about what time you retired? A. About nine-thirty.

Q. Do you remember what the weather conditions were when you retired? A. Yes. It was rather misty, rain, and the wind was blowing quite hard.

Q. Did the vessel strand during the night of October 1st? A. Yes.

Q. Will you just tell us what you felt and saw, of the stranding? A. Well, I was about half asleep, and I felt the vessel begin to shake and bump, and I jumped out of bed and rushed below, without putting any clothes on, to give the engineers on watch orders to stand by and have their pumps ready.

Q. Did you make any record at or about the time, of the orders that you gave? A. I believe there is a record made in the log book.

Q. Did you make any written report to the captain or to the Shipping Board authorities at Kobe, which contained your statement of what you saw and did at the time? A. Yes.

Q. Is your recollection now perfectly clear on everything that you did that night, or do you find it necessary to supplement your recollection by referring to the log or to any other record you may have made at or about that time? A. To get a correct statement I may have to refer to my records.

Q. Suppose you go on and tell us, Mr. Blinn, just what you recall of having done that night, and then afterwards we can refer to any record you may have made, to see if you have left out anything pertinent? A. Well, I went below to the engineroom and gave the engineer orders not to let anyone leave the engineroom, and to get all pumps ready in case of leakage. I then went back to my room to put on my clothes, and went to the captain's room for further orders. I found the captain in the chart room checking his position. In the meantime the ship had orders from the bridge to go full speed astern. I asked the mate for soundings of the cargo holds to find out which hold was leaking so that I could put the pumps onto it. I found that number one hold was taking water. I went below and ordered the

(Testimony of Paul Frazier Blinn)

engineers to put the pumps on number one hold. Soundings were taken in number two hold and at first did not appear to be taking water. Later the soundings showed that number two hold was leaking, too, and the pumps were also put on number two hold.

Q. Were any soundings taken of number three double bottoms, or any tests made there? 'A. There were no soundings taken in number three, but a test was made by fuel oil pumps to find out whether there was any water in it or not, which is very hard to determine whether there is water, by soundings, on account of the fuel oil on the sounding rods.

Q. What did that test on your fuel oil tank show?
A. No water.

Q. Mr. Blinn, I am showing you an abstract here, of a paper entitled "Abstract of Engineer's Log Book of the S. S. West Cajoot, October 1st, 1927." Is that your signature on it?

A. Yes.

Q. Does that give in minutes and half minutes, the various maneuvers which the engines were making during this period you have described? A. Yes. That is taken from the bell book.

Q. I believe I will ask you to read this into the record, Mr. Blinn.

Mr. Derby: Well, I don't see anything very material in the paper, but I certainly object to the witness reading any paper like that into the record. He can refresh his recollection from the paper, but he can't read the paper into the record.

(TESTIMONY OF PAUL FRAZIER BLINN)

Miss Phillips: Q. Mr. Blinn, do you recall at this time the precise operations of the engineroom from minute to minute, or from hour to hour, during that night, giving exact times for different maneuvers? A. No. That I couldn't refresh my recollection. It is too far back.

Miss Phillips: All the authorities indicate, Mr. Derby, under that circumstance we can offer this, at least, in evidence. You may put in your objection.

Mr. Derby: Well, all objections are reserved, so there is no necessity for making any objection.

Miss Phillips: Q. Mr. Blinn, is that your signature upon this transcript of the record?

A. Yes, that is my signature.

Q. Is that a correct statement? A. That is a correct statement.

Q. Was it intended to be correct at the time?

A. At the time, yes.

Q. Now, at this time, reading this, do you believe this to be a correct statement? A. Yes.

Q. But independently you would not remember the exact things done in the engineroom, and the particular times?

A. No, I couldn't remember that.

Miss Phillips: I will offer this in evidence, as exhibit number one to this deposition.

Mr. Derby: I understand that all objections to the competency, relevancy, and materiality, of the testimony are reserved on this deposition, and therefore refrain

(TESTIMONY OF PAUL FRAZIER BLINN)

from encumbering the record with objections at this time.

(Thereupon the document was marked "Government's Exhibit No. 1, Deposition of P. F. Blinn, and attached to the original deposition.)

Miss Phillips: Q. Mr. Blinn, will you go on now and describe just what was done, and what the ship did, during the next two days? A. Well, as soon as the ship was clear of the reef we proceeded to sea, and made our destination as Kobe, the nearest drydock and shipyard, which was about—I don't remember how long it did take us from the time we struck until we got in, but the log will give that time.

Q. What steps were taken to keep the ship going during that period? A. Well, the main engine was going, and we were traveling as fast as the engine would shove us through the water without damaging the ship, which was approximately full speed,—standard speed. And the pumps were being continually kept on the holds to keep the water out of the ship. And we finally found that number one hold was leaking faster than we could pump it out, and when number two hold started to leak I told them to let number one hold fill up and put the pumps on number two hold to keep that dry and in order to save the cargo and save the vessel from sinking.

Q. Before you got to Kobe the pumps were abandoned on number one and you concentrated on number two? A. Yes.

Q. Before we leave the scene of the stranding, Mr. Blinn, you spoke about going up to the chart house a few moments after the collision. Do you recall observing what the weather conditions were at that time? A. Yes. It was a misty rain, and the wind was blowing quite hard.

Q. Could you see any reef? A. No. I looked over the side with my flashlight to see if I could see a reef, but all I could observe was breakers. There was nothing visible to show signs of land or anything.

Q. You saw some breakers breaking as though there were something underneath? A. Yes.

Q. Did you see any pinnacles or any promontories or anything of that sort? A. No. The only thing I saw last was a light, just before I turned in to my bed, indicating that there was an island which the skipper was using to observe his position from.

Q. When was that, that you observed this light? You mean after the stranding or prior? A. No, that was prior to the stranding.

Q. You mean before you went to bed, around nine or nine-thirty, is that it? A. Yes.

Q. Now, Mr. Blinn, what time did the ship get into Kobe? A. My recollection is, about dusk in the evening; and the time I don't quite remember.

Q. Of what day? A. I would have to refer to the log for that.

Q. Well, go ahead, refer to the log, and tell us if you can what was the quantity of fuel oil consumed up to the evening of your arrival in Kobe? A. That would be October 3rd.

(TESTIMONY OF PAUL FRAZIER BLINN)

Q. About what time did you get in? A. I don't see the record in here of the time of arrival, but I should judge it was about seven o'clock.

Q. Can you tell me what was the consumption of fuel oil between noon of October 1st, and noon of October 2nd?

A. Yes. I can give you that from the log book.

Q. What was it? A. From what day, Miss Phillips?

Q. Noon of October 1st, to noon of October 2nd.

A. It would be 322 barrels.

Q. Between noon of October 1st and noon of October 2nd? A. No, not between noon of October 1st and October 2nd. That was my arrival.

Q. That is good enough. That is up to the time of your arrival in Kobe that evening? A. Yes.

Q. That is the question I first asked you, anyway. Now, Mr. Blinn, on arrival in Kobe, what steps were taken looking towards the repair of the ship? A. The diver was called out to go below and locate the leak.

Q. What steps did you consider the most urgent? A. To send the diver below to find the leak and plug it.

Q. And when was this done? A. That was done, if my recollection is right, immediately on arrival in Kobe, or the following morning.

Q. And this was done immediately? A. Yes.

Q. Did you yourself consider at that time whether or not the cocoanut oil should be discharged from the deep tanks?

A. No, I never gave that a thought.

(TESTIMONY OF PAUL FRAZIER BLINN)

Q. Did you at any time discover that there was a leak between the double bottom fuel tanks and either of the number three deep tanks? A. Yes.

Q. How did you discover it, and when did you discover it? A. By soundings in the number three double bottoms.

Q. Will you just go on and tell me now when that happened, and how it came about? A. I asked my second assistant what tank he was taking fuel from to burn. He said "Number three." I said, "How can you take oil from your number three when they are empty?" He said, "They are not empty"—that they were full, to my surprise, which I later took a sounding and found the fuel oil was up in the sounding pipe and approximately level with the cocoanut oil in the deep tanks.

Q. What day did this incident happen, Mr. Blinn?

A. If I remember right, Miss Phillips, that was the day after arrival in Kobe.

Q. Did you make any entry of it in the log?

A. Yes. There is an entry of it in the log.

Q. Just look at your log now to get the date, to be sure of it. What day was it, Mr. Blinn? A. October 5th.

Q. Now, you say you took a sounding when the second assistant, or which ever one it was, told you this. When did you take the sounding? A. That was the day of October 5th.

Q. Did you go down yourself? A. I was right there, because the sounding pipes are right near the engine room.

Q. Now, explain that a little more in detail. The

sounding pipe which you then sounded goes down into the fuel oil tanks?

A. It goes down to the fuel oil tanks from the top of what we call the bridge deck of the ship.

Q. Does that sounding pipe have any connection with the deep tank?

A. No, that sounding pipe goes through what is known as the cofferdam which separates the settling tanks from the deep tanks.

Q. When you take that sounding, how is the level shown? How do you see the level? You said the level of the sounding pipe was on a level with the cocoanut oil in the deep tanks. Explain that. I don't understand that.

A. Well, the sounding rod will show the depth of oil when you put it in there, and if it goes above the sounding rod it will be on the rope. The depth of the sounding pipe in this particular case is about thirty-five or thirty-six feet. And when I pulled the rope—or, the second assistant pulled the rope up, and I saw fuel oil on the rope, approximately twenty feet, I knew that something was wrong.

Q. Did you examine the rope,—look at it yourself?

A. I examined the oil with my finger, and took some of the oil off the sounding rod and smelled it, and discovered there was cocoanut oil with the fuel.

Q. Now, what, if anything, did this sounding indicate to you?

A. That there was a leak in the port tank,—from the deep tank to the fuel tank.

Q. Is this sounding you just described,—was that of the port fuel oil tank? A. That was the port fuel oil tank.

(TESTIMONY OF PAUL FRAZIER BLINN)

Q. Did you make any of the starboard fuel oil tank number three?

A. Yes. There was a sounding immediately made of number three starboard.

Q. What did that show? A. It showed that there was—the tank had approximately, if I recollect right, three inches of oil,—which I have no record of.

Q. Now, were you present at any time when any samples were taken?

A. Yes. I took the samples myself.

Q. When? A. I will have to refer to the log, if I have a record of that.

Mr. Derby: Where was the sample taken from?

Miss Phillips: Just a moment. He said he took it himself.

Mr. Derby: Yes, I know, but where from?

Miss Phillips: Well, let me ask. I can't ask all the questions at once, you know.

Mr. Derby: All right, Miss Phillips.

Miss Phillips: Q. Mr. Blinn, you said you took the samples yourself. Now, I want you to state how you took the samples and approximately when you took them, and what you did with them?

A. Now, I got a bottle and I tied a weight to the bottom of it and I put a screw eye and a cork so that I could fasten a string to it, and I had a string around the neck of the bottle also, and lowered the bottle into the tank as near the bottom as I could possibly get it, and pulled the cork out allowing the bottle to fill with cocoanut oil at that level. Then I withdrew it from the tank and put it into a

(TESTIMONY OF PAUL FRAZIER BLINN)

container; which I repeated several times, and obtained about, approximately, a gallon all told, from the tanks all told, for samples.

Q. Were they taken at different levels, these samples you have spoken of? A. Yes, they were taken at different levels: The bottom, center, and the top of the tank.

Q. What is your recollection as to the number of times you took samples? Was there more than one occasion on which you took samples?

A. Yes. I was asked for samples on two different occasions, as well as I remember, which I took from the tank.

Q. Now, when was this? When were these occasions that you took the samples. A. I will have to look this up and see if there is a record of that, Miss Phillips, which I don't very well remember of making a record of.

Q. What is your testimony, now, Mr. Blinn, as to when, and the occasions on which you took samples?

A. I find that October 12th I have taken samples from port and starboard tanks.

Q. Where was the ship at that time? A. In drydock in Kobe.

Q. Now, do you recall whether or not you took any samples from the number three deep tanks before October 12th?

A. I can't say positively whether I took samples, but I think I took samples the following day on discovery that there was fuel oil in the cocoanut oil.

Q. Is that your best recollection now, that you did take samples at that time? A. Yes.

(TESTIMONY OF PAUL FRAZIER BLINN)

Q. What did you do with the samples that you took?

A. I kept one sample aboard the ship and the rest I sent to the agent in Kobe.

Q. Do you remember who the agent was? A. Mr. Watson.

Q. Have you any samples, now, of the cocoanut oil, which was drawn at that time, Mr. Blinn? A. No.

Q. Have you made a search on the ship for it?

A. Yes, I have looked on the ship to see whether they are there.

Q. Have you any very good place on the ship for keeping samples of this sort for any great length of time?

A. No. No safe place.

Q. Now, you said the ship was in drydock on October 12th when the log shows you took the samples. Were you living on board the vessel while she was in dry dock? A. Yes.

Q. Do you recall what drydock it was? A. It was Mitsubishi.

Q. Is that in Kobe? A. That is in Kobe.

Q. Mr. Blinn, did you have anything to do with the work of repair?

A. Well, as an overseer on the job.

Q. Well, what were your duties, or what did you do in fact, during the repair of the ship? A. Well, to watch and see that everything was correctly done.

Q. What day did the vessel go into drydock, Mr. Blinn?

A. I will have to refer to the log. We entered drydock October 8th, 8:46 a. m.

(TESTIMONY OF PAUL FRAZIER BLINN)

Q. Previous to entering drydock had the vessel discharged any fuel oil? A. We pumped fuel oil out of number one and number two double bottom, into the Bay—into the sea.

Q. Did you have to go out of the harbor to do that?

A. Yes. We went approximately eight or ten miles out at sea to dump that out, to keep from polluting the water in the harbor.

Q. Then came back and the ship went into drydock the next moring, is that correct? A. Yes, that is correct.

Q. Mr. Blinn, before I forget it, I would like to ask you something: Will cocoanut oil burn as fuel oil for a ship of this kind?

A. Yes.

Q. Now, going on with the drydock proceedings, Mr. Blinn, did you yourself go around and about the ship while she was under repair?

A. Yes. I was continually watching the repairs on the bottom of the ship.

Q. Did you see any blueprint at the time showing the repairs which had to be made there at Kobe? A. Yes. I had a blueprint in my charge.

Q. You did? Is this it, Mr. Blinn, this document I am showing you?

A. Yes, that is it.

Q. Will you examine this blueprint which I am showing you, Mr. Blinn, and tell me if that appears to be the blueprint or like the blueprint which you lhad in your charge?

(TESTIMONY OF PAUL FRAZIER BLINN)

A.   Yes, that is a copy of the blueprint which I had aboard the ship.

Q.   Were the repairs made at Kobe as indicated upon that blueprint?

A.   The repairs made at Kobe were the damaged part of number one hold.

Q.   What was done on number two? A. There was a patch put over the leak on number two, to permit us to come home in safety.

Q.   Was anything done on number three? A. No, there was nothing done on number three, because number three didn't appear to have any leakage, on the outside, and there was only one or two dents in the plates.

Q.   Now, while the vessel was in drydock, as I understand it, she is blocked up so that it is possible to go all around her, and under her, to see exactly what is being done; is that correct?

A.   Yes. The ship is approximately three or three and a half feet off the bottom of the drydock so you can walk under it.

Q.   Then, Mr. Blinn, while the ship was under repair, did you have occasion to climb around and look at it and see what was going on?

A.   Yes. Every day I was down below watching the repair work.

Q.   Now, referring to the number three tanks, was there anything observable or to be seen from the outside of that tank?

A.   Yes. There was several plates that were dented, that is, shoved in, where she had struck something.

(TESTIMONY OF PAUL FRAZIER BLINN)

Q. But not broken? A. Not broken.

Q. Does this blueprint show the dents on the number three fuel tank? A. Yes. This damage here (indicating), covers plate numbered D-8.

Q. That is, the damage on number three where it was bent in, is D-8? A. Yes.

Q. Will you mark it out here on the margin?

A. Yes.

Q. Just mark it in your own handwriting, if you will.

A. Yes (Marking on blueprint).

Q. "This is the damaged plate in #3 double bottom." That is number three double bottom on the port side?

A. Yes.

Q. Suppose you put that down, "On port side."

(Witness marks on blueprint.)

Q. Mr. Blinn, I observe here upon this blue print the words, "boiler room." Is that correct? A. No, that is not correct. That should be "number three hold."

Q. That would indicate—The map itself would indicate that is an error in transcription? A. Yes.

Q. That couldn't possibly be a boiler room?

A. That couldn't possibly be.

Q. Suppose you correct this, then, to make this read right, "Number Three Hold."

(Witness marks on blueprint.)

Q. Now, as I understand it, all that showed on number three was some dents, but no breaks? A. No breaks.

Q. And no repairs were done at Kobe? A. No.

Miss Phillips: I am going to offer this as exhibit next in order, which will be number two.

(TESTIMONY OF PAUL FRAZIER BLINN)

Mr. Derby: All objections reserved as heretofore.

(Thereupon the document was marked "Exhibit Number 2, Deposition of P. F. BLinn," and is appended to the original deposition.)

Miss Phillips: Q. Now, Mr. Blinn, were the repairs made as shown upon that blueprint, there at Kobe, and as indicated on the blueprint? A. Yes.

Q. Are there any railroad lines into the drydock where the ship was repaired? A. The only railroads I have recollection of were just the railways for the shipyards own use for shipping their material around the yard.

Q. Shipping supplies? A. Supplies and heavy stuff. Just a small tramway, you might say.

Q. You don't recall any outside lines which came into the drydock?

A. No, I don't recall any outside lines.

Q. By the way, Mr. Blinn, you have had some experience on ships carrying cocoanut oil, haven't you, prior to this voyage?

A. Yes.

Q. It is a fact, isn't it, that cocoanut oil has to be a liquid when it is stored on board? A. Yes.

Q. Do you know whether after a time, given the proper weather conditions, cocoanut oil congeals,—solidifies?

A. Yes. Cocoanut oil will congeal in cool weather.

Q. Do you recall what the weather conditions were between Hongkong and Kobe? A. The temperature, I didn't take any notice of, but we kept a temperature log in

(TESTIMONY OF PAUL FRAZIER BLINN)

the log book of the sea water, which is approximately the same as the atmosphere.

Q. At this day, do you remember whether it was especially cold or especially warm? Have you any recollection on it at all?

A. No. It was getting cooler as we got further north.

Q. Now, what about the weather in Kobe? How was it on your arrival there? A. Well, I would say it was just a moderate climate, about the same as we have here in California.

Q. Moderate fall weather for that time of the year?
A. Yes.

Q. Now, on the occasion when you took samples from the deep tanks, do you recall whether there was any indication that the cocoanut oil had become solidified or hardened?

A. When the first samples were taken, they were not, but on taking the second samples I noticed that the cocoanut oil was beginning to congeal.

Q. The second samples being those taken in dry dock?
A. Yes.

Q. When did the ship come off drydock, Mr. Blinn?

A. I will have to refer to the log book, Miss Phillips.

Q. Very well, go ahead. A. October 28th, my log book shows we were afloat from drydock at 10:53 a. m.

Q. And when did you leave Kobe? A. We had a departure November 1st, 1:05.

Q. Where did you go from Kobe? A. To Yokohoma.

Q. Did you take any fuel oil on between leaving Kobe

(TESTIMONY OF PAUL FRAZIER BLINN)

and arrival at the Pacific Coast? A. Yes, I took fuel oil on at Yokohoma.

Q. How much did you take on there? A. I will have to refer to the log book for that amount. 1984 barrels of fuel.

Q. Were taken on at Yokohoma? A. Yes.

Q. Mr. Blinn, you spoke of having to go out of the port of Kobe to discharge fuel oil from number one and number two fuel tanks. Do you know approximately the quantity you lost in this way?

A. I can give an approximate amount, taken from my log.

Q. Well, just give us the approximate amount. Perhaps we can look that up during the noon hour and save a lot of time on this.

Mr. Derby: Yes.

A. Yes, I will have to figure that out.

Miss Phillips: Would it be convenient, for you, Mr. Derby, to resume at two o'clock?

Mr. Derby: Yes.

Miss Phillips: I think he can figure that out more easily during the noon hour. Two o'clock, then Mr. Reporter.

(Thereupon a recess was taken until two o'clock, p. m., Friday, December 19, 1930.)

FRIDAY, DECEMBER 19, 1930—2 o'clock p. m.

(The taking of the deposition was continued at this time, as per adjournment, the same parties being present as previously mentioned.)

(TESTIMONY OF PAUL FRAZIER BLINN)

Miss Phillips: Will you give me the last few questions and answers?

(The reporter thereupon read as directed.)

Miss Phillips: Q. Mr. Blinn, did you look over your log to get your estimate of how much you lost there?

A. Yes. I think there was 1405 barrels.

Q. 1405 barrels? A. Yes.

Q. Now, let us go back, Mr. Blinn, and get our totals of fuel oil. I don't believe we have been given the total figures at any time. Leaving Manila, how much fuel oil did you have on board the ship? A. We will have to refer to the log.

Q. Yes, you will have to refer to your log in giving these figures. A. Leaving Manila we had 6696 barrels of fuel. No, wait a minute. There is a correction. 6626 barrels.

Q. That is leaving Manila? A. Leaving Manila.

Q. Now, on arrival at the Kobe docks, what is your record as to the amount on board at that time? A. I will have to refer to the log again. Arriving in Kobe, that is to the dock, 5187 barrels.

Q. Now, what date was that you went outside the harbor to pump out the number one and number two fuel oil tanks?

A. I will have to refer to the log to get that. We went to sea October 7th at 4:45 p. m.

Q. And came back the same evening? A. We came back October 8th. I finished pumping the tanks at 4:30 a. m., arrived at drydock at 7:09 a. m., October 8th.

(TESTIMONY OF PAUL FRAZIER BLINN)

Q.   Now, while you were in port was there any consumption of fuel oil on board the ship, other than this voyage out beyond the harbor to dump the fuel oil from numbers one and two?

A.   Yes. The usual consumption on running a ship's electric light and refrigeration plant, and keeping heat for cooking purposes, and so on.

Q.   Did that continue while the ship was in drydock?

A.   No. The ship was shut down for several days.

Q.   Did it continue for any part of the time the ship was in drydock?

A.   Yes. I think there should be a record here of the amount of days we were shut down. We shut down the plant October 11th at 3:30 p. m. Now, I have here: Boosted steam three times during the night. In shutting down the boilers we have to keep the steam up, and every once in a while light a fire under them to keep that steam from going down altogether.

Q.   As I understand it then for a part of the time you were in drydock, the whole plant was shut down entirely?

A.   Yes.

Q.   But during the remainder of the time there was some daily consumption of oil on account of these various uses which you have spoken of? A. Yes.

Q.   Now, Mr. Blinn, what does your log show was the quantity of fuel oil on board the ship when you left Kobe?

A.   Leaving Kobe there was 3270 barrels of fuel oil.

Q.   Will you give me your day to day consumption of fuel oil from October 3rd, through October 31st? A. I can give you that from the log book.

(TESTIMONY OF PAUL FRAZIER BLINN)

Mr. Derby: Can't he give the total instead of for each day?

Miss Phillips: I don't believe he has added up the total.

Q. You may give me the total of consumption, if you can?

A. I can give you the total of consumption

Q. All right. Then give me the total consumption from October 3rd. Your last figure was, on arrival at the dock, 5187. Now, give us the day to day consumption, not including any fuel oil that you dumped out at sea. Do I make myself clear?

Mr. Derby: October 3rd to October 31st?

Miss Phillips: Yes.

A. From the time the ship arrived at the dock until we sailed?

Miss Phillips: Q. That is it exactly.

A. That would be 1980 barrels.

Q. Now, does that figure include the 405 barrels which you dumped?

A. 1405. Yes, that includes that.

Q. I want to make myself clear. In giving that total there did you go through the log adding up your day to day consumption, or did you simply take the totals as shown by the books?

A. I have taken the total as shown by the books.

Q. Now, supposing you go through, from October 3rd, until the day you sailed, and just add the total of actual consumption during that period. You will simply have to go through each page.

(TESTIMONY OF PAUL FRAZIER BLINN)

Mr. Derby: I thought he had just done that.

Miss Phillips: He took that from the totals. I asked him to make an actual check over the books themselves, adding up the day to day consumption.

A. The total there is 542 barrels consumption from the time of arrival of the ship at the dock up to the time of her sailing. I have made a mistake in my figures, the first ones I figured my total from.

Q. Now, let us have your totals again, Mr. Blinn?

A. The total I said before, that should be 1917 minus the 1405; it should be 512 barrels consumed in port.

Q. Your consumption in port, however, was something under 550 barrels?

A. Yes.

Q. Now, what was the total amount you had on board leaving Kobe?

Mr. Derby: He has already testified to that.

Miss Phillips: Q. Well, let us have it now. Leaving Kobe, what was it. A. 3270 barrels.

Q. I believe you have already testified you went to Yokohoma and that you there took on a certain quantity of oil?

A. Yes.

Q. How long were you in the port of Yokohoma?

A. About three hours.

Q. Have you any record there of port consumption at Yokohoma?

A. Yes. My consumption in Yokohoma was approximately twenty barrels.

Q. Leaving Yokohoma, what was the amount?

(TESTIMONY OF PAUL FRAZIER BLINN)

A. 4954 barrels.

Q. Mr. Blinn, at any time after leaving Manila, was fuel oil pumped into number three double bottom tanks?

A. No.

Q. Did you at any time prior to arrival in San Francisco, make a check up by means of soundings or meters, or whatever way there was of making a check up, of the quantity of fuel oil on board the ship? A. Yes. I checked that quite frequently at sea.

Q. Leaving Yokohoma did you make any check up at that time? A. Yes.

Q. Why? A. To determine the correct amount of fuel I had on the ship for safety in making the voyage.

Q. Is the record put in the book, upon the quantity of oil, correct, so far as you can make it correct? A. No. It is hard—We always figure—It is hard to get within a hundred barrels of fuel, more or less, on the ship. If we are within that we figure we are all right, and we never make any corrections on the log at all.

Q. Allowing for that variation, do you consider this record of consumption, and the amount of board, is correct?

A. Is correct.

Q. Mr. Blinn, after the tanks are filled, is there any practice of pumping off any of the fuel oil tanks? Is there such a practice as that? A. Yes, we do. As a rule, we get the tanks full of oil, we press these tanks up so that we know they are full, and the first procedure at sea is to take the head off each one of these tanks, pump a certain amount of oil out of each tank, so there

(Testimony of Paul Frazier Blinn)

wont be any direct pressure on the tank, to keep the tank from overflowing from expansion of heat.

Q. Was this done after the filling of the tanks on this voyage? A. Yes.

Q. Does that in part account for the fact you allow a variation of a hundred barrels either way? A. Yes.

Q. How much fuel oil did the ship have on board upon arrival at San Francisco, Mr. Blinn? A. I will have to refer to the log. 1096 barrels.

Q. Did you take on any oil at San Francisco?

A. Yes. We received oil in San Francisco.

Q. How much? A. I will have to look to my log. Just a minute. I thought there was a record here of that. Oh! I received 1094 barrels.

Q. You say you received 1094 barrels? A. Yes.

Q. Do you want to make any correction as to how much was on board the ship on arrival at San Francisco? A. Well, this should be a correct figure arriving at San Francisco, 1096 barrels arriving.

Q. What day did you arrive? A. We arrived November 22nd.

Q. And what day did you take on fuel oil? A. November 28th.

Q. After you took on the 1094 barrels, how many did you have on board at that time? A. When we finished receiving, I had 1924. barrels.

Q. And during the previous six days had you been discharging or otherwise engaged here in the port of San Francisco?

(TESTIMONY OF PAUL FRAZIER BLINN)

A. Yes. We were discharging cargo, and there was a daily consumption of fuel while in port.

Q. Mr. Blinn, do you remember, just in a general way, what sort of a voyage you had from Yokohoma to San Francisco?

A. If I recollect, it was rather a rough passage; what we would call a moderate sea.

Q. Do you remember whether your daily consumption of fuel oil was in excess of the usual average which you have previously referred to, or how was it? Just what is your recollection of that? A. Well, of course by increasing the speed of the ship it will consume more oil than our average running; and we did rather push the ship along, speed the ship up, which gave us a fuel oil consumption of around 165 barrels a day.

Q. Have you looked over your figures there to see how your average consumption was during the voyage? A. No, I have not.

Q. Just run over the pages now,—leaving Yokohoma, —and give us a few of the totals as you run along, just to see how your average consumption was running.

Mr. Derby: Just a second. If you want me to, Miss Phillips, I will stipulate the witness will testify to the figures shown by the log.

Miss Phillips: All right. To shorten it up, then, the witness would testify that on November 4th—

Mr. Derby: Why not put in the log itself for that purpose?

Miss Phillips: Yes. I have planned to identify this and offer it.

(TESTIMONY OF PAUL FRAZIER BLINN)

Mr. Derby: That would save a great deal of time on this very minor subject.

Miss Phillips: Well, I think as long as we have started this we might as well complete it. Consumption for November 4th, 164; November 5th, 190; November 6th, 180; November 7th, 149; November 8th, 150; November 9th, 165; November 10th, 187; November 11th, 185; November 12th, 180; November 13th, 180; November 14th, 180; November 15th, 170; and so on.

Mr. Derby: I would like to know, if you care to state, Miss Phillips, what the purpose of making proof of these amounts is?

Miss Phillips: Why, I think that it is just as well to have a deposition as complete on all possible features as you can have it. If there is a charge in this case that any large amount of fuel oil got into the cocoanut oil, it seems to me that the amount of fuel oil that was actually consumed by the ship in navigation is pertinent.

Q. Mr. Blinn, did you take on fuel oil any place between Yokohoma and San Francisco?

A. No.

Q. You did not. Whereabouts was the cocoanut oil discharged? A. The cocoanut oil was discharged at San Pedro, The Vegetable Oil Company's dock.

Q. Was there any particular method used in discharging the cocoanut oil, as far as you know? A. Yes. I received instructions from the insurance company to heat the oil in the port tank from the top, and leave the solidified oil, approximately a foot of solidified oil on the bottom of the tank; and keep the port tank below the level of the starboard tank.

Q. Do you know what the purpose was to keep the level of the port tank below the level of the starboard tank?

A. Well, in *arming* this oil into liquid, in case of a leakage between the division plates, the good oil would leak into the bad instead of the bad oil leaking into the good oil and contaminating that too.

Q. And this would be avoided by keeping the level of the port tank below that of the starboard; is that right?

A. Yes.

Q. Did you follow this method of discharging?

A. We followed the method as closely as possible, and found that it worked very well.

Q. At what point did you stop, do you remember, in the discharging of the oil? What point did you find the solidified oil in the course of discharging it? A. We pumped approximately half the oil from the port tank and I then transferred the pump to the starboard tank and pumped oil from there, still keeping the level above the port tank. That is to keep the ship from taking a list on account of the weight.

Q. You see-sawed, then, between the two tanks,— alternating? A. Yes. And when we got to the bottom of the port tank, we found there was approximately a foot and a half of solidified oil on the bottom.

Q. In the port tank? A. Yes, in the port tank.

Q. You are not pretending to give us exact measurements here, are you, Mr. Blinn? A. No. I remember

(TESTIMONY OF PAUL FRAZIER BLINN)

those figures, because they said it was approximately a foot and a half. It worked very well.

Q. You are just describing the method of discharge?

A. Yes.

Q. Where was the ship finally repaired?

A. At Moores Dry Dock, San Francisco.

Q. Was any of the repair work done at Kobe taken out at San Francisco? A. Yes.

Q. What? A. There was one plate on the port bow that had been welded and replaced, and was condemned by the American Bureau of Shipping, and a new plate installed. And the construction of the ship made it necessary that some of the plates in number one hold be taken out so they could remove the old plate after the cargo was discharged from number two hold, to get to them, on account of the overhang.

Q. Other than that, was there any other work taken out that you recall? A. No.

Q. Was the amount taken out at the Moores Dry Dock of the Kobe work, a substantial amount? A. No.

Q. Or would you say it was inconsequential, considering the amount of the work? I don't know what you would consider substantial, Mr. Blinn. I didn't mean to lead you on this. A. No, I wouldn't say it was substantial, because the plate we didn't figure was seaworthy. Any plate that had been damaged and welded would be overruled by the American Bureau of Shipping, and condemned.

Q. I see. Did you ever get down into the port deep

(TESTIMONY OF PAUL FRAZIER BLINN)

tank, yourself? A. Yes, I went down into the port deep tank.

Q. When? A. After the discharge of cocoanut oil, to try to locate the leak.

Q. Did you find it? A. I discovered what I thought was a leak, when I found that the T-bar into which the margin plate is riveted was ruptured where riveted on to the double bottom.

Mr. Derby: Wait just a moment. Will you read that to me?

(The answer was read by the reporter.)

Miss Phillips: Q. Mr. Blinn, did you, in the course of the last few weeks, prepare a sketch so as to explain to me just what happened in this connection?

A. Yes.

Q. Is this it (Exhibiting to the witness)?

A. Yes.

Q. Where did you get this drawing that you have marked up in this way? A. I took that from an engineer's magazine.

Q. This drawing, then, does not pretend to represent the WEST CAJOOT herself? A. No.

Q. You took it because it represented the conditions substantially, without being drawn to scale, or anything of that sort; is that correct? A. Yes.

Q. Now, I wish you would explain just where you found this leak?

A. On the port side of the ship where I have drawn this line representing the margin plate—

(TESTIMONY OF PAUL FRAZIER BLINN)

Q. You have marked now,—you have written the word "Margin plate" with an arrow pointing. Now, just what is that margin plate?

A. The margin plate is the side of the tank where built up into the hold of the ship, representing the double bottom,—the inner bottom of the ship.

Q. And the tanks containing the cocoanut oil you have marked "Port Deep Tank," and "Starboard Deep Tank," have you?

A. Yes.

Q. You have marked "Tank top" the covering to the fuel oil tanks, is that right? A. That is right.

Q. Can you mark on this little sketch the precise place where the leak was, and I will ask you to mark it in a red pencil.

A. (Marking on sketch) On the top sketch I will mark approximately where the damage was, showing the outside of the hull. That damage where the plate is shoved up right where the margin plate is riveted on to the bilge on the side of the ship.

Q. Now, in that lower sketch, point out the place where the leak was?

A. On the lower sketch, where the margin plate is riveted to the bottom of the ship (marking).

Q. I wish you would explain a little bit more, now, how that place was made? A. You mean how the tank is built?

Q. Yes. You said you examined it in Kobe, and you saw a dent there, but no leak? A. There was no leak showing on the outside of the hull, but showing a dent in

(TESTIMONY OF PAUL FRAZIER BLINN)

the plate. But I couldn't identify the exact spot inside; I wasn't sure whether it was the margin plate that was ruptured, or whether it was ruptured or not, until after I got inside.

Q. Now, will you just go ahead and explain what happened there?

A. Why, the T-bar that I spoke of is a bar in the shape of a T which is riveted along the bottom of the ship.

Mr. Derby: Q. Is that called the bounding bar?

A. The bounding bar. And the margin plate is riveted to that and then to the top of the tank which separates the fuel oil tank from the deep tank.

Miss Phillips: Q. What effect would the dent you saw have upon the margin plate and the T-bar?

A. Well, that would raise that T-bar from the bottom sufficient enough to cause a leak from one tank into the other.

Q. Did you find any other leak between the two tanks, other than this? A. No.

Q. Did you find any leaky rivets? A. No.

Q. Did you find any fractures? A. No fractures.

Q. Mr. Blinn, I have a few bills here that I want you to identify, that were used in preparation of the General Average Adjustment, and I believe you have knowledge of. The bill marked number—

Mr. Derby: I think if you would care to show me all the bills it might save time.

Miss Phillips: Well, it is the bill I have marked in red pencil, number fourteen in the General Average Adjustment, which is for the cost of repairing a feed pipe.

(TESTIMONY OF PAUL FRAZIER BLINN)

Q. Have you any recollection of a feed pipe being broken during the voyage? A. Yes, the feed pipe to the boilers,—from the feed pump to the boilers, was broken shortly after we had the collision.

Q. When did you first observe the break?

A. I don't quite recollect, but I think the pipe started to leak the day after the collision.

Q. Would the effort of the ship to back off the reef be instrumental in causing such a break or leakage? A. Yes, because the pipe goes through the bulkhead of the ship, and the twisting and straining of the ship would be sufficient to break that pipe.

Mr. Derby: Let me call your attention, Miss Phillips, to the fact that the renewing of this feed pipe is not charged against us in the General Average Adjustment.

Miss Phillips: It is not?

Mr. Derby: No.

Miss Phillips: Very well, then.

Mr. Derby: You see, there are only certain items charged against us.

Miss Phillips: Yes, I see. Thank you very much.

Q. Now, was it a part of your duties, Mr. Blinn, to approve and certify for payment certain engine room stores and supplies?

A. I didn't quite get that?

Q. Was it a part of your duty to approve for payment engine room stores supplied and actually used? A. Yes. I have to approve all bills.

Q. I wish you would look at this bill of Higishide Engine & Iron Works, Limited, which I have marked

(TESTIMONY OF PAUL FRAZIER BLINN)

number eighteen on the Adjustment, apparently for sixty-five Yen. Can you tell me what those supplies were? A. Yes. Those supplies are the packing, steam packing, that is necessary to have on the ship in renewing work while the ship is in port.

Q. Is that your signature there upon the bill?

A. Yes.

Q. Okaying it for payment? A. Yes.

Q. Were those supplies actually used in port?

A. They were actually used in port.

Q. The next bill I would like to call to your attention is the bill which I have marked in the Average Adjustment, thirty-one. As head of the engine room department, did you know at that time what was the pay roll of the engine room department?

A. No, I couldn't say, because I never keep check of that. The purser takes care of that.

Q. That is part of his duties? A. Yes.

Q. Do you enter in the engine room log the names of the different members of the crew, and their pay roll? A. Yes.

Q. Does that appear in this log book (indicating)?

Mr. Derby: Well, as long as this witness has no personal knowledge of it, I don't think it matters whether it appears in that log or not.

Miss Phillips: He has entered it in his log.

Mr. Derby: Well, that would not enable him to testify to it.

Miss Phillips: Now, let me see, I think perhaps he does know more about it.

(TESTIMONY OF PAUL FRAZIER BLINN)

Q. Mr. Blinn, did you know who was on board your ship at the time, in your own department? A. Yes.

Q. Did you know what their duties were, whether an oiler on water-tender, or what they were? A. Yes. That is part of my job.

Q. Part of your job? A. Yes.

Q. Did you have anything to do with approving their time slips for work, overtime work, or anything of that sort?

A. Yes, I have to approve all that.

Q. That was part of your job? A. Yes.

Q. Now, did you at any time make a record of how much the men were paid, how much they were signed on for, the rate at which they were signed on? A. Yes, I make that record in the log book.

Q. Is this it (indicating)? A. That is it, yes.

Miss Phillips: He may not have paid them, but he knows their rate of pay.

Q. Now, comparing that with this pay roll appearing here upon your log book, Mr. Blinn, this bill that I have marked 31-B, does the pay roll appearing on this bill of the engine department agree with the pay roll appearing in that log? Glance at it and see.

A. No. The last two figures here show a difference,— the wipers.

Q. The wipers? A. Yes. I show $52.50, and their's show $57.50.

Q. Excepting for that one item, the wipers, you say were signed on $52.50 and they appear in this bill as $57.50?

(TESTIMONY OF PAUL FRAZIER BLINN)

A. Yes.

Q. Other than that, is this a correct statement of the pay roll?

A. Yes.

Q. Did you keep your crew with you during this voyage?

A. No. There was some of them that were discharged in Australia and some in Sydney—I mean some in Manila. Of course, the crew changes as we go along.

Q. There at Kobe was the engineroom crew kept with the ship?

A. Yes, they were kept aboard the ship.

Q. Yes. They may not have been the same men you started out with. I think I have one more bill. Referring now to the allowances for fuel and stores, marked thirty-two in the Average Adjustment, I believe you have already given the consumption of fuel oil during the voyage, at different points. A. Yes.

Q. Does the vessel use lubricating oil, Mr. Blinn?

A. Yes.

Q. What sort of oil is that? What is it for?

A. The lubricating oil is to lubricate the working parts of the machinery.

Q. Was that used during the time the vessel was laid up in Kobe?

A. Yes. Every day.

Q. Both to Kobe and while it was at Kobe as well?

A. Yes.

Q. About how much a day does that run?

(TESTIMONY OF PAUL FRAZIER BLINN)

A. I can refer to the log and give you the figures on that.

Q. Well, let me see, then. Just in round figures, can you give an idea what it averages a day? A. Yes. It generally runs about a gallon a day.

Q. About a gallon a day. I notice the General Average Adjustment claims twenty-eight gallons, which would seem fairly near. Now, there is one more bill; it is the one which I have marked thirty-six in the Average Adjustment, a bill of forty-eight—Oh, that isn't charged, you say?

Mr. Derby: No.

Miss Phillips: That is all right, then. That is all.

Q. By the way, Mr. Blinn, in whose employ are you at the present time? A. The O. & O.,—the Oceanic & Oriental Steamship & Navigation Company.

Q. That is a subsidiary of the Matson Navigation Company?

A. Yes.

Q. When did you leave the employment of the Shipping Board, approximately? A. I left them, I think it was, in 1928.

Q. 1928. And in giving the various vessels of which you had been at one time or another chief engineer, I did not ask you as to the earlier positions you held prior to becoming a chief engineer. Did you work up from the lower positions, assistant engineer up to chief engineer? A. Yes.

Miss Phillips: That is all. You may cross-examine.

(Testimony of Paul Frazier Blinn)

Cross-Examination.

Mr. Derby: Q. Mr. Blinn, this voyage on the West Cajoot was your first experience as a chief engineer, was it not?

A. Yes.

Q. And where did you join the vessel?

A. I joined the vessel in San Francisco.

Q. San Francisco. And you made the voyage out and back?

A. Yes.

Q. Now, I understood you to say that in Manila Mr. Harris had charge of cleaning out the deep tanks?

A. Yes.

Q. Did you have anything to do with cleaning them out at all, personally? A. As far as cleaning the tanks themselves, I had no authority; it was just as a matter of an inspector, to be sure that the tanks were perfectly clean. I had no authority over the cleaning gang at all.

Q. You did nothing personally with regard to the cleaning at all?

A. No; just inspection.

Q. And how much of an inspection was that?

A. Well, Mr. Harris and myself—on arriving in port the tanks were filled with salt water—and the two of us went below into the fireroom to examine the bulkheads there, and into number two hold and examined the bulkhead and the tank tops, and after the water was pumped out then we put a head on the oil tanks in number three to get the pressure of oil against the tank top in number three which was the bottom of the deep tanks.

(TESTIMONY OF PAUL FRAZIER BLINN)

Q.   Were you there when that was done?

A.   Yes, I was there when that was done.

Q.   Did you say that was before the cocoanut oil was put in?

A.   That was before the cocoanut oil was put in.

Q.   And you say the tanks were cleaned out with salt water?

A.   No. We put salt water into them to use it for ballast, and then the water was pumped out, and then the tanks were washed down with salt water to get the superfluous oil out, and then it was cleaned with a soda solution,—I don't know what it is they use,—and then later it was wiped down with cocoanut meal to clean up all the excess oil that is about the tank.

Q.   But the man in charge of that job was Mr. Harris?

A.   Yes.

Q.   He would know much more about it than you would, wouldn't he?

A.   No. As a matter of fact I think I saw every movement that was made in the tank at the time the cleaning was going on; I was there more than he was.

Q.   Now, when you put this head of water on I understood you found a few weeping rivets?   A.   Yes. You will find that in most all the tanks.

Q.   Did you say those were caulked up?

A.   They were caulked.

Q.   Did you observe them caulked up yourself?

A.   Yes. It was after they were caulked there was another test put on the tanks.

(TESTIMONY OF PAUL FRAZIER BLINN)

Q. After that was the cocoanut oil loaded into the tanks?

A. Yes.

Q. And after the cocoanut oil was loaded in the tanks, was any head put on the fuel oil below? A. No, the head was taken off the tank before the cocoanut oil was put in.

Q. Then there was no pressure exerted, as I understand it, on the fuel oil tanks at Manila, after the cocoanut oil was loaded? A. No, no pressure at all.

Q. At that time were the number three double bottom tanks full of fuel oil? A. Yes, they were full of fuel oil at the time.

Q. Had the head been taken off before the cocoanut oil was put in? A. Yes, right after the test was found satisfactory, the head was immediately taken off the tanks.

Q. From Manila, I understand, you proceeded to Hongkong?. A. Yes.

Q. And from Hongkong you meant to go directly to San Francisco? A. Yes.

Q. And if you had not stranded on this reef you would have gone straight on to San Francisco without stopping at Kobe or Yokohoma or anywhere else? A. Yes.

Q. Now, this stranding took place on the night of October 1st? A. Yes.

Q. I think you said that you did not sound the number three double bottom tanks, is that correct. A. The night of the stranding?

(TESTIMONY OF PAUL FRAZIER BLINN)

Q. Yes. A. No, not that night I didn't sound them. I sounded them the day before.

Q. The day before the stranding? A. Yes.

Q. Why didn't you sound the number three double bottom tanks the night of the stranding? A. Well, it doesn't do much good to sound those. As a matter of fact I never gave it a thought at the time, because most of the damage seemed to be the forward end of the ship. And to sound for water it would be impossible,—I wont say impossible, but very hard to tell whether there is any water in a fuel oil tank when there is oil in it; and the only way you can determine that is by pumping on the tank to see whether there is any water.

Q. I thought you testified the oil in the number three double bottom tank had got down to about three inches at that time? A. Yes.

Q. Wouldn't it have been a simple matter to sound, under those circumstances? A. It would. I may have sounded the tanks at the time, but I don't remember it, because we made a sounding in all the double bottoms, but I didn't specify whether I sounded at that time on those tanks.

Q. Didn't you testify to some kind of a test on the fuel oil tanks, on your direct examination,—I mean on the number three double bottom fuel oil tanks? A. Yes.

Q. What was the nature of that test? A. That was to find out whether there was any water in them or not.

Q. When was that test made? A. That test was made as shortly after stranding as we could get to it.

Q. What was the nature of the test?

(Testimony of Paul Frazier Blinn)

A. It was to find out whether there was any leaks in the double bottoms.

Q. I mean, how did you make that test?

A. By putting the pump on it and pumping it into the settling tanks and at the same time a small drain line, to look for water; if there is water in the tanks the pump will pick it up first.

Q. Is that as accurate a method as sounding the double bottom tank itself? A. No, it is not as accurate. It is just merely a matter of form to determine whether there is any water in there or not.

Q. When, after the stranding, did you first sound the number three double bottom? A. That I don't remember.

Q. Did you sound it at all before you got to Kobe?

A. I don't remember whether we sounded that or not.

Q. But you went on the assumption that there was no damage to the number three double bottom tank? A. Yes.

Q. At that time you had no suspicion of this indentation in the shell plating—

Miss Phillips: May I have that question, Mr. Derby's question, read back to me there?

(Last question read by the reporter.)

Miss Phillips: No, the question before that.

(The previous question was read by the reporter.)

Mr. Derby: Q. —which you marked on the blueprint which was introduced in evidence this morning?

A. No. I didn't think there was any damage done that far back.

(TESTIMONY OF PAUL FRAZIER BLINN)

Q. If you had thought there had been any damage to the number three double bottom tanks, you would have undoubtedly sounded the tanks, would you not? A. Oh, yes, I would.

Q. Now, is it your recollection that you did not sound the number three double bottom tanks until after you got to Kobe? A. I wouldn't say that, because it has been so long ago. Just as I do in my present job, we would sound the tank probably every day for a while, and then go along for a week and not sound it.

Q. You wouldn't let it go along for a week after a stranding of this kind, would you? A. No.

Q. If you had sounded the number three double bottom tanks before you got to Kobe, you would have inevitably have discovered the leakage of cocoanut oil into the number three double bottom tank, would you not? A. I may have.

Q. And the leakage of cocoanut oil into the number three double bottom tank, as I understand it, was not discovered by you until October 5th, which was two days after you arrived in Kobe? A. Yes.

Q. How did you happen to sound it at that time?

A. I asked my second assistant where he was pumping his oil from, to burn in the ship, and he told me, "Number three." I says, "No, there's no oil in number three: how can you pump oil from number three?" He said, "Yes, the port tank is full."

Q. Hadn't you already instructed him to discontinue pumping from number three. A. Yes.

Q. How did he happen to be pumping from number

(TESTIMONY OF PAUL FRAZIER BLINN)

three if you had instructed him not to? A. Well, he found there was oil in there. I always told the engineers to drag and get all the oil out of the tank they can,— after they are empty there is a certain amount that will run down. And this particular man I had, he was a man that wasn't of sound mind, and a man that couldn't remember anything.

Q. What was his name? A. Martin Appel.

Q. Was he the man that you had to promote to the job of assistant engineer because of one of the engineer's leaving you at Manila? A. No. No, I wouldn't promote him, because he was not a responsible man for the position.

Q. What was his position on the ship? A. Second assistant engineer.

Q. Did you know he was of unsound mind when you departed from Manila? A. Yes.

Q. And you think that was why he didn't obey your orders? A. Yes.

Q. Do you know when he began pumping oil from the number three tank after you had instructed him to discontinue?

A. Why, he filled one settling tank.

Q. How many barrels does a settling tank hold?

A. Full, 160.

Q. 160. And this was after the stranding, was it not?

A. Yes.

Q. Now, Captain, all through your examination you have given the amount of oil, fuel oil, consumed by the

(TESTIMONY OF PAUL FRAZIER BLINN)

ship during the different periods of the voyage. I understand from your direct examination that that is the total consumption from all the tanks, is that correct? A. That is correct.

Q. And you did not keep any record of the fuel oil pumped from each particular tank? A. No. There is no particular record, only when the tank is empty, that is all; that is a check of itself.

Q. Did I understand you to say that it is not customary to keep a record of fuel oil that is used from each particular tank? A. Well, we keep that as a total; as we go along and pump from one tank, why, we watch by the soundings, and add the rest of the tanks to that, giving us a complete total of all the oil.

Mr. Derby: Will you read that question and answer, again?

(Question and answer read by the reporter.)

Mr. Derby: Q. That is not an answer to my question, Chief. I want to know whether I understood you to testify on direct examination that it is not customary to record the amount of oil taken from each tank? A. No.

Q. Do you still pursue that custom? A. No. Our logs now are arranged so that our tanks are numbered, and we take a certain amount of oil that each tank has each day, and log it,—the depth of it.

Q. And the logs furnished you by the Shipping Board were not arranged for that purpose? A. No.

Q. You could, however, have put it down somewhere ·

in that log, if you had wished to, couldn't you? A. Yes, it could be put down.

Q. Since you left the Shipping Board have you been constantly keeping records of the amount taken from each particular tank? A. Yes.

Q. What was done with this cocoanut oil that leaked down into the number three double bottom tank? A. That was eventually burned.

Q. When was it burned? A. It was burned after the cocoanut oil had been discharged and the ship repaired.

Q. Do I understand you to mean, from the time you left Kobe until the final discharge at San Pedro, that no oil was used from the number three double bottom tanks? A. None whatever, not from the time we discovered the oil leaking in there.

Q. But you knew on October 5th, 1927, at Kobe, that there was a considerable amount of cocoanut oil in that number three double bottom tank? A. Yes.

Q. How did you make the sounding from which you determined that? A. Through the sounding pipe from the deck,—through the sounding rod.

Q. Did this cocoanut oil come right up to the top of the sounding pipe? A. No, it didn't come to the top. The cocoanut oil was approximately the same level in the sounding pipe as the—on a level with the cocoanut oil in the deep tank.

Q. Did you pump any oil out of the number three double bottom tank in Kobe? A. No. That was just when the second told me that he had pumped the settling

(TESTIMONY OF PAUL FRAZIER BLINN)

tank from the number three double bottom; that was the only time there was any oil pumped from it.

Q. What was the condition of that tank when you left Kobe,—of the number three double bottom tank? Was it full? A. It was full.

Q. Did you put a head on that tank at any time while you were in Kobe? A. No.

Q. Are you sure of that, Mr. Blinn? A. I am positive of that, because there was already a head on that tank when we discovered there was cocoanut oil in it.

Q. Are you perfectly sure you were not instructed by Mr. Watson at Kobe to put a head on the number three double bottom tank in order to prevent any further leakage of cocoanut oil into the number three double bottom? A. No. I don't think he told me to put a head on it. I was told to keep the head on that tank as it was.

Q. Oh, to keep it as it was? A. To keep it as it was.

Q. Now, as I understand it, the first entry in your log about the examination of any samples is on October 12th, 1927. Is that correct? A. October 12th?

Q. Look at your log and see. A. I think that was the second sample. I took samples twice, and I think that was the second sample that was taken, on October 12th.

Q. But is that the first sampling that appears in the log? A. That is the first sampling that appears in the log. I forgot to enter the other one.

Q. And you think the previous sampling was taken on October 6th? A. October 6th.

Q. The day after you discovered that cocoanut oil was   .

(TESTIMONY OF PAUL FRAZIER BLINN)

leaking into the number three double bottom? A. Yes, it was October 6th.

Q. And you made that sampling yourself? A. Yes. I took those myself.

Q. And that was done by means of a bottle and a screw eye and a cork, as you have described on your direct examination?

A. Yes.

Q. And I understand you to say that you took several samples from different levels of the tank? A. Yes.

Mr. Derby: We call for the production of those samples in due course.

Q. Did all of the samples show contamination of the cocoanut oil by fuel oil, or only the sample taken from the bottom of the tank?

A. No, they all—The oil seemed to be about the same color all the way through, from the bottom to the top of the tank.

Q. How do you explain fuel oil getting into the number three deep tank? I can understand it leaking down, but how do you explain—I can understand the cocoanut oil leaking down into the fuel oil, but how can you explain the fuel oil getting up into the cocoanut oil? A. That is in the—the motion of the ship does that, the rolling of the ship. The oil would naturally slush to one side, and going back it creates a vacuum and a pressure. It rolls to one side and it will create a vacuum on that side and create a pressure, and therefore circulate this oil through these leaks.

(TESTIMONY OF PAUL FRAZIER BLINN)

Q. Wasn't the hole you found between the two tanks a very small one?

A. It wasn't necessarily a hole; it was just where the beams had been raised up from the tank.

Q. It was a very small leak, wasn't it?

A. A very small leak, yes.

Q. Do you seriously think the motion of the ship could have forced the fuel oil up through that little aperture?

A. Oh, absolutely it could.

Q. You didn't test those samples yourself at all, did you?

A. The only way I made a test of one of the samples, I made a sample soap from it, just as a matter of curiosity on my own part. I didn't give it to anyone for anything at all, I just simply told one of the chemists in San Francisco that I had made a sample soap from it, and he had some, and it was practically the same kind that I had made.

Q. Did that enable you to discover at what parts or different levels this contamination existed? A. No.

Q. On what do you base your statement that the contamination was the same in all the samples? A. Well, I am taking mine from the color of the oil, by three different bottles, and just comparing colors. They looked the same. I don't know whether that would be more or less—But the color looked the same to me by sight.

Q. Who was present when you made these samplings?

A. I don't just remember. The mate was there.

Q. Do you know Mr. Reed, the surveyor in Kobe?

A. Yes.

Q. Was he present when the samplings were taken?

(TESTIMONY OF PAUL FRAZIER·BLINN)

A. I think Mr. Reed was there; I am not positive, but I *a* most sure he was there.

Q. If Mr. Reed were to testify that the samplings only showed contamination in the bottom six inches of the number three deep tank, would you disagree with him on that?

Miss Phillips: Just a moment. I think that is assuming something. I don't believe there was any such testimony as that.

Mr. Derby: I don't know whether there is or not. I know that is one of the questions that was asked Mr. Reed on cross-examination.

Miss Phillips: That is quite correct. I withdraw any objection to that. Let Mr. Blinn answer it as best he can.

A. Well, I would come out and say just what I said, that the oil looked the same color; the oil looked the same to me from the three samples.

Mr. Derby: Q. These three samples were taken at different levels?

A. Different levels.

Q. At the time you took these samples, how full was the number three deep tank, the port deep tank? A. Well, that was up in the sounding pipe the same level with the oil in the deep tank.

Q. No, I mean how full was the deep tank?

A. Oh, how full was the deep tank?

Q. Yes. A. I don't remember what the soundings were, but they were, I should judge, about three feet from the top.

(TESTIMONY OF PAUL FRAZIER BLINN)

Q. About three feet from the top. How deep is that tank?

A. The tank is twenty feet, ten inches.

Q. There was only then a shortage of three feet there?

A. Well, they never fill those tanks full of cocoanut oil on account of expansion; they always leave about a three foot space in those tanks when they put cocoanut oil in them.

Q. If they always leave a three foot space there, how do you explain there still being a three foot space after a lot of this cocoanut oil has seeped down into the double bottom tank?

A. Well, I don't know just what the soundings were on those tanks when the oil was put in. The mate had those soundings, and I am just giving approximate figures, not accurate. But there couldn't be the same amount of oil in there after it leaked down as there was when they filled it; there was bound to be a shortage there.

Q. But as far as you know the tank was full up to about three feet of the top? A. Yes. I know after the leak the port tank was below the level of the starboard tank, and Mr. Johnson and I thought it was a good idea it was so, because the bad oil wouldn't leak into the good oil.

Q. How full was the starboard tank?

Miss Phillips: Just a minute, Mr. Blinn. If you did not take any of these soundings yourself, and don't actually know, you should say so.

Mr. Derby: Well, he said on direct examination that he himself took these soundings.

(TESTIMONY OF PAUL FRAZIER BLINN)

Miss Phillips: Not in the deep tank.

Mr. Derby: Oh, yes.

Miss Phillips: Oh, no.

Mr. Derby: I think so.

Miss Phillips: No. I think the sounding was in the fuel tank.

A. The sounding was in the fuel tank, yes. I didn't sound the deep tanks.

(Discussion off the record.)

Mr. Derby: Q. You examined—even though you may not have taken soundings, you examined both the port deep tank and the starboard deep tank, did you not?

A. Yes.

Q. Now, how full was the starboard deep tank?

A. Well, I don't remember, just as a memory off-handed, without making any soundings. As I say, we always filled those tanks to within two or three feet of the top. But I noticed the mate, he took the soundings on the tank, and I forget now just what the figures were, but the port tank was lower than the level of the starboard tank. But I don't know what those soundings were, because I didn't take them.

Q. Then the starboard tank must have been within one or two feet of the top, if the port tank was three feet?

Miss Phillips: Just a moment. I think Mr. Blinn has made it very clear, Mr. Derby, that he didn't take any of these soundings, and that anything he says on this is a guess. You have the ship's log here that will show exact measurements of the outages on this, if you wish to know—

Mr. Derby: I am not concerned with the outages of

(TESTIMONY OF PAUL FRAZIER BLINN)

fuel oil. There hasn't been any testimony as to the outages of cocoanut oil.

Miss Phillips: Well, I am saying now, that if, as he says, the mate took soundings of the cocoanut oil tank, as I understood Mr. Blinn to say, there may be records in the ship's log on that, and you can get exact figures if you want them.

Mr. Derby: Are you going to call the mate as a witness, Miss Phillips?

Miss Phillips: I have the captain.

Mr. Derby: Q. Have you since that time had occasion to take samples of oil from the tanks?

A. No, not since then.

Q. Are you familiar with the device for taking samples known as "oil thief"? A. Yes.

Q. Isn't that a much more efficient way to take samples than the bottle and cork method? A. Well, yes, it is. We had none at the time.

Q. Well, couldn't you have got one in Kobe?

A. Well, I didn't even try. I figured I could take one with a bottle just as well as I could with a "thief".

Q. Isn't |the bottle and cork and string method considered an antiquated method nowadays? A. Oh, yes. I don't know whether—

Q. Don't you know—

Miss Phillips: Wait a minute. He was saying something.

A. I don't remember whether Mr. Watson tried to get one. He asked me if there was some way of getting a sample from the tank, and I mentioned I had no .

(TESTIMONY OF PAUL FRAZIER BLINN)

"thief," but I could get a sample with a bottle. And he said, "Go ahead and take that." I remember that now.

Mr. Derby: Q.   Do you think you may have asked Mr. Watson to get you a "thief" if he could?

A.   No, I don't think I asked him at the time to get me one.

Q.   There are plenty of chemists in Kobe, are there not, from whom you could have gotten a "thief" if you tried?

A.   Yes.

Miss Phillips: Now, that is assuming something, Mr. Derby, that is not quite fair. This witness has answered your question fairly.

Mr. Derby: I think it is fair.

Miss Phillips: You don't know whether, in the first place, there are cocoanut shipments coming into Kobe. Certainly this witness hasn't testified there were.

Mr. Derby: Lots of cocoanut oil shipments come into Kobe.

Miss Phillips: Well, I would like to see you prove that. I would like to have you show that Kobe is a port of importation and exportation of cocoanut oil; I should be very much interested if you prove any such thing as that.

Mr. Derby: I do know this, and that is that there is a market for cocoanut oil in the port of Kobe.

Miss Phillips: Well, we will see. Go ahead.

Mr. Derby: Q.   Now, why was it, Mr. Blinn, that you used the oil from the number three double bottom tanks before using the oil from the number one? A. Well,

(TESTIMONY OF PAUL FRAZIER BLINN)

that is always customary in carrying cargo of oil in the deep tanks, so that there won't be any danger of a rupture and the fuel getting into the cocoanut oil.

Q. The purpose of using the oil from the number three deep tanks was to avoid the possibility of a rupture between the two tanks?

A. Yes.

Q. You don't anticipate any such rupture, do you?

A. Oh, no.

Q. Now, are you perfectly positive that oil was used from the number three double bottom tanks before you went on the reef?

A. I am positive of that.

Q. Do you know that of your own knowledge?

A. I know that of my own knowledge, because I was there to see the soundings. I checked the soundings on the fuel oil tanks myself to make sure of it. The second assistant, as a rule, makes the soundings, but ever so often I go around myself and check them. And the number three tanks which were handy right near my room, I was watching him and saw the sounding myself.

Q. Are there any records anywhere which would tell us whether any fuel oil was taken out of the number three double bottom tanks?

A. No. No, we never as a rule make a habit of logging that; that is, we didn't at that time. We do now.

Q. Do you have what is known—Did you have at that time what is known as a port log? A. No. We keep our port log in our regular steaming log. The port log was done away with.

(TESTIMONY OF PAUL FRAZIER BLINN)

Q. Wouldn't there be any log kept in the port of San Francisco showing the amount of oil in the different tanks at the time the ship arrived here? A. No.

Q. Are you positive of that? A. Positive of that.

Q. What happened to these samples, Mr. Blinn? You turned them over to Mr. Watson? A. I turned them over to Mr. Watson. I kept some of the samples on board the ship in my room until we arrived in San Francisco, and I don't remember whether I gave those to the Shipping Board or whether I threw them away.

Q. I see. How many samples did you give to Mr. Watson?

A. I gave him samples two different times, and I don't remember just how many bottles, how many sample bottles I gave him.

Q. Well, give us your best guess as to the number you gave him?

A. Well, that would be hard. I don't remember whether they were small sample bottles or large ones, now.

Q. I don't care anything about the size of the bottles. I want to know how many bottles you gave him?

A. Oh, I should judge he had about ten bottles.

Q. About ten bottles. That would presumably be five on each of the two occasions you made the samples? A. Yes.

Q. Taken from different levels? A. Yes.

Mr. Derby: We call for the production of all of those samples in due course.

Miss Phillips: Before we leave this subject, may I

(TESTIMONY OF PAUL FRAZIER BLINN)

ask Mr. Blinn if he took samples from the starboard tank at the same time as the port tank?

A.   Yes, there were samples taken from the starboard tank, too.

Q.   Do the ten bottles include samples from the starboard tank?

A.   Yes. Now, that is just approximate. There may have been more. There was, I should say, a gallon, approximately, of cocoanut oil taken from each tank.

Mr. Derby: Q. Yes. And put in small containers?

A.   And put in small containers, yes.

Q.   How large was this bottle that you used to take the samples?

A.   That was about a quart bottle.

Q.   And from approximately how many different levels were those samples taken? A. Three different levels.

Q.   Would that be the bottom, the middle, and the top?

A.   The bottom, middle, and top.

Q.   And you took at least those three samples from the port tank on both occasions when you did the sampling, didn't you?

A.   Yes.

Q.   Were those all turned over to Mr. Watson?

A.   Not all of them. There was a few small bottles kept aboard the ship. The mate had some, and I had some.

Q.   But you gave Mr. Watson samplings from all the different levels?

(TESTIMONY OF PAUL FRAZIER BLINN)

A. Yes, I gave Mr. Watson samplings from all three different levels, because the containers were marked before we put the oil into them, and put the samples into the containers marked that level.

Q. Well, an anlaysis of those containers would unquestionably show, would it not, whether the cocoanut oil was contaminated by fuel oil in each one of those samples? A. Yes.

Q. I believe you testified on direct examination, and I want you to correct me if I state your testimony incorrectly, that you never gave a thought to the question of discharging the cocoanut oil?

A. No.

Q. Were you ever consulted about that by anyone?

A. No.

Q. Did you have any consultations whatever with Mr. Thornton? You knew Mr. Thornton, didn't you, of the Shipping Board?

A. Yes.

Q. You knew Mr. Johnson of the Shipping Board?

A. Yes.

Q. And you knew Mr. Reed, the surveyor? A. Yes.

Q. And you knew Mr. Watson? A. Yes.

Q. Did you have any consultations with any of those gentlemen in regard to the discharging of the cocoanut oil at Kobe?

A. No.

Q. Did you have any conversations with any of those gentlemen as to the discharging of the oil in the number three double bottom tanks at Kobe? A. No.

(TESTIMONY OF PAUL FRAZIER BLINN)

Q. I suppose you have no idea about how much it would have cost to do that? A. No. I have never paid any attention to that, because that is more or less up to the captain. And I presume that is the reason they never said anything to me. They probably spoke to the captain about discharging that oil. If there was any questions asked about it at all, he would be the one they would take it up with. They wouldn't notify me until they were ready to discharge it.

Q. And were any of the four gentlemen I have named present when you took the samples from the port deep tanks?

A. I think Mr. Reed was the only one; I am not sure whether he was present or not, but I think he was there at the time.

Q. Well, if he was present, he would know what the sample showed just as well as you would, would he not? A. Yes.

Q. I want to read you the following from the engineer's log, on September 21st, at Manila: "M. J. Peralta, Junior, First Assistant Engineer, paid off to transfer to S. S. CRISSFIELD as chief engineer. W. Parke refused to be raised to second assistant engineer. All engine gang threatened to walk off ship if M. P. Appel was raised to first assistant. Unable to get engineers on shore. Under these conditions I was forced to raise J. L. Mone, water tender, to first assistant engineer, Mr. Mone having in his possession discharges to certify that he has held a chief engineer's position on foreign ships."

Are those entries correct? A. Correct.

(TESTIMONY OF PAUL FRAZIER BLINN)

Q. Who were the vessel's agents at Manila?

A. Swayne & Hoyt.

Q. Did you report to them this trouble with Mr. Appel?

A. Yes.

Q. Did you tell them he was of unsound mind?

A. Yes.

Q. What did they have to say to that? A. Well, they didn't say anything,—to get along with him until we got back to 'Frisco.

Q. I notice the statement there that there were no engineers available in Manila. A. No.

Q. What do you know about that? A. We tried to get them. As a matter of fact I went aboard the President Cleveland and tried to get engineers from her.

Q. Is that the extent of your efforts to get another engineer?

A. No. I think the Shipping Board tried to locate some.

Q. Anything else? A. A Mr. Sawyer came down and said it was impossible, there were no engineers ashore, and I would have to get back the best I could without one.

Q. This is Mr. Sawyer of the Shipping Board?

A. Yes.

Q. And that was the extent of your inquiries?

A. Yes.

Q. Did you get rid of Mr. Appel as soon as you arrived in San Francisco? A. Yes. Just the minute we paid off I got rid of him.

(TESTIMONY OF PAUL FRAZIER BLINN)

Q. Why was no attempt made to discharge the cocoanut oil in the number three double bottom at Los Angeles?

A. Well, they said it wasn't any good, they didn't want it.

Q. Who said that? A. The Vegetable Oil people. I asked the man in charge if he wanted that oil, that there was cocoanut oil in that double bottom, and I asked him if he wanted it. And he said, no, it wasn't any good.

Q. Do you know whether any test of it was made there?

A. I don't remember. I think we put a sounding rod down in the tank and got some of it, and he just took it with his fingers and said, no, he didn't want it. That is as far as I can recollect.

Q. That was after it had been mingled with the fuel oil in the bottom of the tank all the way from Kobe? A. Yes.

Q. I think you testified that there were no railways, outside railways, running into the Mitsubishi Drydock?

A. Yes.

Q. Isn't your testimony that you didn't observe any? Do you know of your own knowledge whether there were any?

A. I couldn't say positively there were or were not. I didn't see any in the yard itself, outside of just the shipyard's.

Q. You weren't looking for any? A. I wasn't looking for any.

Q. You never gave any thought to the necessity of discharging this cocoanut oil? A. No.

(TESTIMONY OF PAUL FRAZIER BLINN)

Q. Have you been in Kobe often? A. That was my first visit there.

Q. That was your first visit. I suppose you don't know, then, whether there were railways running down to any of the other docks or not? A. No, I don't know.

Q. In your direct examination I understood you to testify that you received instructions from "the insurance company" in regard to heating the oil in the port tank. Now, what did you mean by your reference to "the insurance company"?

Miss Phillips: That was here at San Francisco, you mean, after he got to the coast?

Mr. Derby: Yes.

A. Yes. Well, they were the people that surveyed the oil here, the damage of it, after we arrived, and they were trying to—didn't want to damage the oil any more than they could, taking it out.

Q. Exactly. But what I·mean is, what did you mean by your reference 'to the insurance company? A. Well. they were the ones that I got the letter from. I don't remember who they were. But the people in the office, the shipping office, said it was the insurance company.

Q. Wasn't the letter in fact, a letter from Curtis & Tompkins, Chemists, of San Francisco, addressed to Swayne & Hoyt, the vessel's agents? A. Come to think of it, 1 think it was Curtis & Tompkins.

Q. I show you what purports to be a copy of a letter from Curtis & Tompkins, to Swayne & Hoyt, Incorporated, dated November 26, 1927, and ask you whether that is not the letter you refer to?

(TESTIMONY OF PAUL FRAZIER BLINN)

Miss Phillips: Yes, I am familiar with this letter.

Mr. Derby: I would say, for Miss Phillips' information, that that letter, as I understand it, is a part of the claim papers that were submitted with our claim in this case.

Miss Phillips: I don't know whether that was or not.

Mr. Derby: Well, I think it was. I don't know either. But I am informed it was.

Miss Phillips: I don't think it makes any material difference whether it was or was not. I think the point is, did Mr. Blinn get such a letter of instructions, and did he follow it as best he could. That is the point.

Mr. Derby: Q. Is that the letter, Mr. Blinn?

A. That is the letter, yes.

Mr. Derby: I don't like to part with this copy, and if there is no objection, Miss Phillips, I will have the stenographer copy this into the record and return it to me.

Miss Phillips: Yes, that will be all right. That is, you are offering this as containing the instructions as to the discharge, not any other proof or any other statement contained in this letter?

Mr. Derby: I offer that in evidence as a copy, authenticated by the witness, of the letter sent by Curtis & Tompkins to Swayne & Hoyt, Incorporated, the vessel's agents, giving their advice as to how the cargo should be discharged.

Miss Phillips: I have no objection to this going into evidence, excepting in this respect,—I haven't reread this letter lately, and I don't know whether or not this letter states Curtis & Tompkins' understanding of the facts. I

Lightning Source UK Ltd.
Milton Keynes UK
UKHW020351221118
332685UK00012B/2089/P